Exploring AI Implications on Law, Governance, and Industry

Swati Chakraborty
Concordia University, Canada

IGI Global
Scientific Publishing
Publishing Tomorrow's Research Today

Published in the United States of America by
IGI Global Scientific Publishing
701 East Chocolate Avenue
Hershey, PA, 17033, USA
Tel: 717-533-8845
Fax: 717-533-8661
Website: https://www.igi-global.com E-mail: cust@igi-global.com

Library of Congress Cataloging-in-Publication Data

Names: Chakraborty, Swati, 1985- editor
Title: Exploring AI implications on law, governance, and industry / edited by Swati Chakraborty.
Other titles: Exploring Artificial Intelligence implications on law, governance, and industry
Description: Hershey : IGI Global Scientific Publishing, 2026. | Includes bibliographical references and index. | Summary: "This book aims to explore the use of AI in Government and its use for technological advancement"-- Provided by publisher.
Identifiers: LCCN 2025010071 (print) | LCCN 2025010072 (ebook) | ISBN 9798337333847 hardcover | ISBN 9798337333885 paperback | ISBN 9798337333854 ebook
Subjects: LCSH: Artificial intelligence--Law and legislation | Artificial intelligence--Technological innovations | Artificial intelligence--Government policy | Public administration--Technological innovations | Public administration--Automation | Artificial intelligence--Political aspects | Artificial intelligence--Social aspects
Classification: LCC K564.C6 E97 2026 (print) | LCC K564.C6 (ebook) | DDC 343.09/998--dc23/eng/20250313
LC record available at https://lccn.loc.gov/2025010071
LC ebook record available at https://lccn.loc.gov/2025010072

British Cataloguing in Publication Data
A Cataloguing in Publication record for this book is available from the British Library.

Table of Contents

Detailed Table of Contents

The character of economic growth is being reshaped by artificial intelligence (AI) as it revolutionizes entire sectors and drives technological progress. This chapter studies the relationship between AI techs and economic growth in digital economies, and explores how AI improves productivity, creates sectoral shifts and new economic possibilities. But with these progress also comes major challenges, such as the threat of job loss and inequality, regulatory dilemmas and data security and privacy problems. It further points out that AI wields significant potential for economic development, but inclusive and sustainable growth requires targeted strategies to be mobilised. The chapter provides case studies, explores economic policy, and identifies direction for further research to increase our understanding of the impact of AI on international arrangements.

The traditional legal principles of personhood, which have historically been reserved for humans and, in certain situations, companies, are being challenged by the rapid breakthroughs in artificial intelligence (AI). It is necessary to grant legal personhood to AI systems as their decision-making abilities increase. Legal personhood, according to proponents, would guarantee accountability and provide legal redress for harm brought about by AI's acts (Tretyakova, 2021; Hárs, 2022). Critics argue that AI is devoid of fundamental characteristics that are important to conventional notions of personality, such as consciousness and moral agency (Forrest, 2021; Schneider, 2019). This proposal examines frameworks, including Asimov's Three Laws of

influence a harmonious AI legal regime. It is argued that the effective regulation of AI in Ghana requires a harmonious legal framework that addresses ethical concerns and human rights, transparency, and accountability. Using a desktop review, it is evident that Ghana's expanding AI landscape requires a well-aligned regulatory approach that prioritizes human well-being, safety, and dignity. Such a framework ensures that AI technologies respect citizens' rights and enhance public safety. By categorizing AI systems based on risk levels, Ghana can mitigate potential harmful practices while fostering innovation and trust. Incorporating ethical frameworks into AI governance is vital for effective regulation, as it offers clear guidelines that align with human values. This alignment promotes global cooperation and safeguards human interests in society.

The enormous use of technology in the 'Metaverse era has yielded a new challenge of socio-technical ethical issues. After the pandemic, when everyone is getting highly connected to the different social media-based metaverse, the expression of thought and the barrier of free thinking bring the issue of sanctity in the posts and expressions available in the Metaverse. This chapter presents all the logical implications of evolving ethical issues as well as technical issues. This book chapter also lists all the technical dilemmas occurring in the metaverse that are related to social ethics i.e., AI-generated illicit photographs, deep fake videos, supportive interaction and privacy breaches, social self-efficacy, feelings of loneliness, etc. Further, it maps the services offered by Metaverse. This Chapter also covers the open challenges of the Metaverse i.e., Cyber Bullying, Online Harassment, AI-generated Child Pornographic Content, etc., and the status of the Law. This study may help policymakers and stimulate prospective researchers for better outcomes in this field.

In the era of digitalization and technological advancement it is crucial to note the dichotomy between the earlier and present times with regard to human-machine interaction. Previously human controlled machines but today its opposite happens. Human-Machine Interface has so deeply touched the life of the present generation and its most explicit example could be the change from a basic push button to a

underscoring the ongoing impact of technological change on labor markets. In the end, it provides a fair assessment of AI's potential and promotes laws that promote inclusivity, fairness, and continuous learning in an AI-driven world.

AI referred to as automated intelligence which is the human-computer simulation intellect in the machines. The cognition shown by robots stands in stark contrast to the common knowledge displayed by people. Artificial intelligence is developing rapidly, from siri to self-driving vehicles. Generally, there are just two core concepts in artificial intelligence. Studying human brains and how they think is the first step and using machine learning to model those processes is the second. There is more to artificial intelligence in banking than just chatbots. The banking business is only one of the many industries that artificial intelligence has dominated. understanding the effects of artificial intelligence on new era banking was the main motivation for this project. This study mainly focuses on idea of artificial intelligence in the banking and how it affects human labour. This study provides a glimpse of the present uses of Artificial Intelligence in the new era banking sector and how it is transforming the face of Indian banking.

The proliferation of Virtual Voice Assistants (VVAs) in the lives of consumers has ushered in an era of unparalleled convenience and technological sophistication. However, the ever-present risk of unauthorized data sharing and exploitation of Personal Identifiable Information (PII) calls for urgent regulatory intervention to protect consumer digital privacy. This chapter offers a comprehensive examination of VVAs, dissecting the integrated technologies that power them and debunking common misconceptions. It navigates through the complex web of user agreements and the existing patchwork of privacy laws, revealing the gaping regulatory void surrounding VVAs.

This chapter highlights the mediating function that morals play in influencing job outcomes as it inspects the complicated association among Artificial simulated Intelligence, Moral values considered based on business ethics, and the Market place occupation. The investigation uses quantitative analysis to manifest that AI has a major direct impact on the market driven by skill related jobs, with moral values considered based on business ethics mediating a sizable percentage of this impact. The results manifest that ethical frameworks are imperative in defining the kind and degree of AI's impact on occupational dynamics when companies use AI technology. The investigation emphasizes how vital it is to incorporate moral values into the application of AI in order to optimize benefits and reduce hazards. Finally, the investigation recommends a thorough strategy for implementing AI that gives ethical issues first priority in order to promote long-term occupational practices in the rapidly changing digital ecosystem.

Digital health equity refers to the use of digital technologies to ensure that all individuals, regardless of their socio-economic background, geographic location, or other potential barriers, have equal access to quality healthcare. In this context, Artificial Neural Networks (ANNs) play a crucial role by enabling the analysis of large, complex healthcare datasets to identify disparities and predict healthcare needs. ANNs can process various data types, including patient demographics, medical history, and socio-economic factors, to generate personalized recommendations and insights that help bridge healthcare gaps. This study explores the application of ANN models in promoting digital health equity, focusing on how these models can optimize healthcare delivery, improve access to resources, and enhance health outcomes, particularly for underserved populations. By leveraging digital tools such as telemedicine, mobile health applications, and electronic health records, the use of ANN in digital health equity aims to make healthcare services more inclusive, efficient, and accessible.

Preface

INTRODUCTION

In the rapidly evolving landscape of Artificial Intelligence (AI), the intersection of technology with human values, ethics, and dignity has never been more critical. AI is reshaping the very fabric of human society, raising profound questions about its implications on governance, law, industry, and individual rights. As AI continues to advance, it is essential to engage in thoughtful discourse on how we can harness its potential while safeguarding the fundamental principles that define our humanity.

This book, *Exploring AI Implications on Law, Governance, and Industry*, delves into the ethical dilemmas posed by AI, its potential for both harm and good, and the philosophical questions that arise as machines become increasingly autonomous. It examines AI's impact on human dignity, assessing whether these systems can recognize, respect, and uphold core human values such as fairness, justice, equality, and freedom. Furthermore, it addresses AI's role in societal shifts, exploring its effects on labor markets, economic stratification, privacy, and governance.

The purpose of this book is to provide a comprehensive examination of the relationship between AI and human values, offering readers a deep understanding of the ethical and philosophical questions that AI poses. As AI becomes more integrated into our daily lives, it is imperative to evaluate its effects on our moral frameworks and legal institutions. This book is intended for a diverse audience, including scholars, students, policymakers, industry professionals, and general readers interested in the ethical implications of AI.

Key objectives of this book include:

- Examining the Ethical Implications of AI: Analyzing the ethical challenges posed by AI deployment in sectors such as healthcare, finance, and law enforcement.

- Exploring the Concept of Human Dignity in the AI Era: Investigating how AI affects privacy, autonomy, and identity, and whether AI systems can recognize and respect human dignity.
- Evaluating AI's Impact on Human Values: Assessing potential conflicts between AI capabilities and human values while proposing strategies to align AI development with ethical principles.
- Addressing the Social and Economic Consequences of AI: Examining job displacement, economic inequality, and social stratification, and discussing strategies for inclusive AI-driven growth.
- Promoting Ethical AI Design and Governance: Offering guidelines and advocating for regulatory frameworks to ensure ethical AI deployment.
- Fostering Interdisciplinary Dialogue: Encouraging collaboration among technologists, ethicists, policymakers, and the public to address AI-related challenges.
- Educating and Empowering Readers: Equipping readers with knowledge and tools to critically assess AI's ethical implications and engage in meaningful discussions.
- Contributing to Policy and Practice: Influencing AI-related policies through thorough ethical analysis and practical recommendations for industry leaders, developers, and regulators.

By addressing these crucial topics, this book aims to be a pivotal resource in understanding the multifaceted relationship between AI, ethics, and human dignity. It seeks to contribute to the ongoing conversation on how we can ensure AI development aligns with human values and serves the common good. Through diverse perspectives and critical insights, *Exploring AI Implications on Law, Governance, and Industry* aspires to guide scholars, policymakers, and industry leaders in navigating the complex moral landscape of AI, ensuring that technology enhances rather than diminishes human dignity.

ORGANIZATION OF THE BOOK

Chapter 1: AI-Driven Growth: Addressing Legal and Economic Complexities in the Digital Era

Artificial intelligence (AI) is fundamentally transforming economies by driving innovation, increasing productivity, and reshaping industries. This chapter examines the intricate relationship between AI and economic growth, addressing both its benefits and the challenges it poses. While AI unlocks new economic opportunities and sectoral shifts, it also presents pressing issues such as job displacement, inequality, regulatory concerns, and data privacy. By presenting case studies and exploring economic policies, this chapter aims to provide a deeper understanding of AI's impact on global economies, offering strategic insights for fostering inclusive and sustainable growth.

Chapter 2: Is AI a Legal Person? Redefining the Limits of Legal Personhood

With the advancement of AI, traditional legal principles of personhood are being questioned. Should AI entities be granted legal personhood, and if so, to what extent? This chapter delves into the debate by exploring various legal frameworks and philosophical arguments surrounding AI accountability. Drawing upon concepts such as Asimov's Three Laws of Robotics and Hohfeldian jural relations, the chapter examines the implications of AI assuming legal responsibilities without full personhood status. It ultimately seeks to guide policymakers toward regulatory strategies that balance innovation with ethical and societal safeguards.

Chapter 3: The Role of AI in Global Governance: AI in International Relations and Diplomacy

As AI proliferates across industries, its influence on diplomacy and global governance is becoming increasingly evident. This chapter explores how AI is transforming traditional diplomatic practices, enhancing decision-making, and altering international relationships. While AI presents opportunities to improve global cooperation and crisis management, it also raises concerns about bias, misinformation, and ethical dilemmas. By analyzing case studies and real-world applications, this chapter provides valuable insights into the evolving role of AI in shaping international diplomacy and governance structures.

Chapter 4: Artificial Intelligence in India: Navigating Social Justice, Environmental Ethics, and Legal Governance

India's AI landscape is rapidly expanding, influencing social justice, environmental ethics, and legal governance. This chapter critically examines AI's role in reinforcing or mitigating biases in key sectors such as healthcare, education, and finance. It also explores AI's environmental impact, both its potential for sustainable practices and its ethical dilemmas. Furthermore, the chapter assesses India's current regulatory framework, proposing governance models that balance AI-driven innovation with ethical imperatives tailored to the country's unique socio-economic landscape.

Chapter 5: Regulation and Ethical Issues of Artificial Intelligence in Ghana: Towards a Harmonious AI Law

Ghana's evolving AI ecosystem necessitates a robust legal and ethical framework to ensure responsible development. This chapter investigates how Ghana can adopt principles from the EU AI Act 2024 to create a comprehensive regulatory approach that prioritizes human rights, transparency, and accountability. By categorizing AI systems based on risk levels, Ghana can mitigate potential harms while fostering innovation and trust. The chapter advocates for an AI governance model that aligns with human values and promotes both domestic and global cooperation in AI policymaking.

Chapter 6: Legal & Ethical Issues in the Interaction of AI and the Metaverse: Complexities and Challenges

The rise of the Metaverse has introduced unprecedented socio-technical and ethical challenges. This chapter explores the implications of AI-driven interactions within virtual environments, addressing issues such as deepfakes, privacy breaches, cyberbullying, and online harassment. Additionally, it examines legal ambiguities surrounding AI-generated content and the responsibilities of metaverse service providers. By mapping existing regulations and identifying gaps, this chapter provides insights into shaping ethical and legal frameworks that govern AI interactions in the digital realm.

Chapter 7: Human-Machine Interaction: Ethical and Legal Considerations

The evolution of human-machine interaction (HMI) has reshaped daily life, from touchscreen devices to automated decision-making systems. This chapter examines the ethical and legal dimensions of HMI, highlighting concerns such as autonomy, accountability, and user consent. By analyzing historical transitions and contemporary case studies, the chapter advocates for policy frameworks that ensure equitable and responsible integration of AI-driven interfaces into society.

Chapter 8: Artificial Intelligence for Fraud Detection: A Bibliometric Exploration

As digital transactions increase, AI is becoming a critical tool in fraud detection across the financial sector. This chapter presents a bibliometric analysis of AI-driven fraud detection systems, focusing on trends in research and implementation.

Examining case studies from the United Kingdom, India, and the United States, it highlights AI's effectiveness in combating financial fraud, emphasizing the need for continued innovation and regulatory oversight to enhance security measures in digital finance.

Chapter 9: Redefining Work in the Age of AI: Navigating Employment, Automation, and Ethics

The rapid advancement of AI-driven automation is transforming labor markets, altering job structures, and raising ethical concerns. This chapter investigates how AI is reshaping employment landscapes across industries such as manufacturing, healthcare, and finance. It discusses the importance of reskilling and upskilling to adapt to changing job demands while emphasizing the need for ethical AI policies that promote inclusivity and fairness. By drawing historical parallels with past industrial revolutions, the chapter provides a nuanced perspective on AI's long-term impact on employment and economic structures.

Chapter 10: The Impact of Artificial Intelligence on the Banking Industry: Changing Face of Modern Banks

Artificial Intelligence (AI) is revolutionizing the banking sector, reshaping traditional financial institutions into tech-driven entities. This chapter explores AI's transformative role beyond mere automation, delving into its impact on banking services, human labor, and customer interactions. While AI-powered chatbots have gained prominence, its applications extend far beyond customer service, influencing fraud detection, risk management, and decision-making. By examining the integration of AI in banking, this chapter provides insights into the evolution of financial institutions in India and beyond, offering a glimpse into a future where human intelligence and machine learning coexist to enhance efficiency, security, and accessibility in banking.

Chapter 11: Consumer Digital Privacy in the Age of Smart Virtual Assistants

The widespread adoption of Virtual Voice Assistants (VVAs) has brought unprecedented convenience to consumers, yet it has also raised significant concerns about digital privacy and data security. This chapter critically examines the ethical and regulatory challenges associated with VVAs, analyzing the risks of unauthorized data sharing and the potential exploitation of Personal Identifiable Information (PII). Through an exploration of existing privacy laws, user agreements, and industry practices, this chapter highlights the urgent need for regulatory frameworks to bridge the growing gap in consumer data protection. It provides a balanced perspective on the benefits and vulnerabilities of VVAs, advocating for stronger privacy safeguards in an increasingly AI-driven digital landscape.

Chapter 12: Future of AI on Job Markets by Mediation of Ethical Considerations in the Horn of Africa

AI's influence on labor markets is undeniable, with ethical considerations playing a critical role in shaping its trajectory. This chapter investigates the intersection of AI, business ethics, and employment in the Horn of Africa, revealing how AI-driven automation impacts skill-based professions. Through quantitative analysis, it assesses the extent to which ethical frameworks mediate AI's impact on occupational structures, underscoring the necessity of responsible AI implementation. The findings emphasize that ethical integration is vital in mitigating risks associated with AI adoption in the workforce. This chapter advocates for a holistic approach that prioritizes ethical AI deployment to sustain long-term employment practices in the region's evolving digital economy.

Chapter 13: Artificial Intelligence and Digital Health Equity: A Path to Inclusive Healthcare

As digital transformation continues to reshape healthcare, artificial intelligence emerges as a key driver in bridging disparities and fostering equitable healthcare access. This chapter explores the role of Artificial Neural Networks (ANNs) in analyzing complex medical data to address healthcare inequities. By leveraging patient demographics, medical histories, and socio-economic factors, AI-driven solutions can enhance healthcare accessibility, particularly for underserved populations. The discussion highlights the significance of digital tools such as telemedicine, mobile health applications, and electronic health records in promoting inclusive healthcare systems. This chapter underscores AI's potential to revolutionize healthcare delivery while emphasizing the need for responsible implementation to ensure equitable and ethical outcomes.

Chapter 14: Navigating the Era of Artificial Intelligence and Digital Technology and its Effect on Human Healthcare

The rapid advancement of AI and digital technology is reshaping the healthcare industry, bringing groundbreaking improvements in patient care. This chapter explores the intersection of AI, digital tools, and human healthcare, examining innovations such as AI-driven diagnostics, personalized treatment plans, and virtual mental health services. However, as these technologies advance, challenges such as patient data privacy, algorithmic bias, and the diminishing human touch in medical care arise. This chapter provides a nuanced discussion on integrating AI ethically into healthcare, ensuring that technological progress does not compromise the core values of human connection, patient confidentiality, and holistic well-being. By addressing these challenges, AI can be harnessed to optimize healthcare outcomes while preserving the integrity of medical practice.

Chapter 15: AI, Privacy, and Power: Shaping Surveillance Policies in Canada

In an era where artificial intelligence (AI) is increasingly integrated into surveillance systems, Canada faces the challenge of balancing national security interests with the protection of individual privacy rights. This paper explores the complexities of AI-driven surveillance, focusing on how these technologies amplify state power and the ethical dilemmas they pose. It examines Canada's existing governance frameworks, highlighting gaps in policy and regulation concerning AI's role in monitoring and data collection. The analysis covers key issues such as transparency in AI algorithms, accountability for misuse of surveillance tools, and the need for robust privacy safeguards. It also discusses international best practices and proposes actionable recommendations for Canadian policymakers. These include enforcing stricter data protection laws, enhancing oversight mechanisms, and ensuring that AI surveillance technologies comply with human rights standards.

CONCLUSION

As we navigate the ever-evolving landscape of artificial intelligence and digital transformation, this volume has sought to illuminate the profound ways in which these technologies are reshaping industries, economies, and societal structures. From the redefinition of banking operations and consumer privacy concerns to the ethical implications of AI in job markets and healthcare, the chapters presented here offer a comprehensive exploration of both the opportunities and challenges that lie ahead.

The discussions underscore the critical need for ethical considerations, regulatory frameworks, and inclusive strategies to ensure that AI and digital innovations contribute to a sustainable and equitable future. As AI continues to integrate into various facets of human life, its responsible implementation will be paramount in maximizing its benefits while mitigating risks.

This book serves as a foundation for further inquiry, encouraging researchers, practitioners, and policymakers to engage in meaningful discourse on the responsible development and deployment of AI. By fostering a collaborative approach to digital innovation, we can harness the full potential of these transformative technologies to drive progress while safeguarding fundamental human values.

Swati Chakraborty
Concordia University, Canada

Chapter 1
AI-Driven Growth:
Addressing Legal and Economic Complexities in the Digital Era

Aiswarya Thomas
Christ University, Bengaluru, India

Athira V.
VELS University School of Law, Chennai, India

Abhishek Benedict Kumar
https://orcid.org/0000-0002-3998-3150
Symbiosis International University (Deemed), Pune, India

Karun Sanjaya
https://orcid.org/0009-0005-1647-1549
Symbiosis International University (Deemed), Pune, India

ABSTRACT

The character of economic growth is being reshaped by artificial intelligence (AI) as it revolutionizes entire sectors and drives technological progress. This chapter studies the relationship between AI techs and economic growth in digital economies, and explores how AI improves productivity, creates sectoral shifts and new economic possibilities. But with these progress also comes major challenges, such as the threat of job loss and inequality, regulatory dilemmas and data security and privacy problems. It further points out that AI wields significant potential for economic development, but inclusive and sustainable growth requires targeted strategies to be mobilised. The chapter provides case studies, explores economic policy, and identifies direction for further research to increase our understanding of the impact of AI on international arrangements.

DOI: 10.4018/979-8-3373-3384-7.ch001

1. INTRODUCTION

Artificial intelligence (AI) is one of the key technologies that will transform the world in the 21st century, with major implications for global economic growth. Although they tend to be more concerned with politics than marketing, the prevalence of AI-driven innovations across nearly every sector of the economy from healthcare and finance to manufacturing and retail has made the world teeter on the edge of a so-called "Fourth Industrial Revolution" (for lack of a better phrase, as this is not exactly an uncontroversial title) (Schwab & World Economic Forum, 2016). While the opportunities are immense, with them come major challenges especially in digital economies that need to adjust quickly to higher rates of technological changes to sustain and accelerate growth while ensuring social stability.

AI's far-reaching potential for transformation of economic systems is broad and deep. The reaping of more labor productivity, new business models and consumer markets along with the ability to make decisions faster from a much bigger data set. AI, for example, reinvented logistics and supply chain management to minimize waste. However, these very benefits have also led to massive disruption job loss, tech mogul monopolies and increased divides between places that are tech-rich or poor. Such layers of complexity demand a more nuanced approach to AI how it operates through the economic structures, and what policies we ought to implement in order to harness its benefits while offsetting its harms (United Nation 2019).

Consequently, we dedicate the rest of this paper to addressing a fundamental question: "How does AI influence economic growth in digital economies and what are few requirements and challenges regarding its integration? The aim is to explore the channels through which AI generates economic growth and what systemic risks and barriers it introduces that hinder or distort those gains. The report also talks about the policies, that the governments and institutions can develop in order to support a fairer and sustainable future for all with AI (Capitol Technology University, 2024).

2. LITERATURE REVIEW

2.1 Overview of Existing Research on AI's Impact on Economic Growth

Academic and policy-related discourse has long examined the rise of Artificial Intelligence (AI) and its potential consequences for growth and job creation, increasing productivity, creating new types of jobs or destroying them as functions are automated. Many scholars have pointed to AI's ability to enhance productivity and efficiency providing a potential game changer on the level of the steam engine or electricity across various sectors. According to Brynjolfsson and McAfee (2014), AI is a "General Purpose Technology" (GPT), one that has parallels in history with technologies that transformed economic directions (Brynjolfsson & McAfee, 2017). Yet, studies also highlight that while the promise of AI is greater than other existing technologies, it brings new had never been experienced before challenges in terms (Brynjolfsson & McAfee, 2017).

However, economic models of AI suggest that there are at least three major channels through which it can spur growth: increasing labor productivity, generating new markets in which people willingly pay for products and services (which the right economist will argue was always included in the early model), or by improving existing business processes. Research by the McKinsey Global Institute (2018) suggests that AI might add up to $13 trillion to global GDP in 2030. However, such expansion would not be available to all nations: AI adoption tends to go faster in already developed economies than developing ones (Bughin et al., 2018).

2.2 Theoretical Frameworks: Economic Models of AI Integration

There are multiple theories that provide a foundation for research relating to the effect of AI on the growth of economy. The old and familiar endogenous growth theory (see, e.g., Romer 1990) aptly views technological change, e.g. via AI or machine learning technology, as the biggest source of economic development because it drastically increases the productivity of labor — or capital (Rivera-Batiz & Romer, 1991). This model highlights innovation, human capital and technological diffusion that are the main drivers of AI economic impact. Automation economics research, by Acemoglu and Restrepo (2018) for example, suggests something different–namely that gains in productivity due to AI will be offset by job loss; they argue, job destruction does not necessarily destroy economic value as overall productivity increases (Acemoglu & Restrepo, 2018).

3. AI IN GLOBAL ECONOMIC HISTORY: COMPARISONS WITH PAST TECHNOLOGICAL REVOLUTIONS

Comparative historical analyses show a close resemblance between AI and previous technological revolutions (e.g., the Industrial Revolution, Information Age). Remember the Industrial Revolution when mechanization rocked every industry but also created new jobs and incomparable living standards? Similarly, the growth of computers and the internet resulted in massive productivity changes and also introduced new industries altogether. But AI is different in its ability to imitate cognitive tasks and may prove more transformative for white collar jobs and high-level decision-maker roles (Shen & Zhang, 2024). As a result, the transition to an economy dominated by AI is likely to require new methods of workforce reskilling and economic adaptation.

3.1 AI's Impact on Labor Markets and Employment

AI research has many effects and one of the most discussed issues surrounding it is on capacity substitution. Brynjolfsson and McAfee (2014), for example, have argued that AI and automation may replace huge numbers of jobs, mainly in routine and low-skilled occupations (Brynjolfsson & McAfee, 2017). On the flip side, AI may also generate an entirely new range of jobs that require such skills. Whether AI creates more jobs then it destroys is the ongoing debate, many studies have stated that if not handled properly in regard to AI it's going to create a significant increase in income inequality.

3.2 Productivity and Efficiency Gains Through AI

Automating with AI can be one of the best avenues for growing output. According to McKinsey Global Institute (2018), AI can add another $13 trillion by 2030 for global GDP (Bughin et al., 2018). Industries including manufacturing and logistics have already benefited from better efficiency in the use of AI applications. Still, productivity gains face diminishing returns and not every sector benefits from AI. Long story short, this unevenly felt impact points to a lack of economic inclusivity.

3.3 Socioeconomic Challenges and Ethical Considerations

The change brought by AI far outstrips the economic figures and repercussions, reaching to social/ethical implications as well. Algorithmic bias, data privacy issues and the digital divide all remain important questions that must be asked. For example, the increasing centralization of their capabilities in just several tech giants is an antitrust and governance issue (Szczepański, 2019). Additionally, developing economies are at risk of losing their share in the AI race owing to a lack of technological access and infrastructure.

4. MECHANISMS OF AI-DRIVEN ECONOMIC GROWTH

4.1 Labor Productivity Improvements

AI technologies can lead to labor productivity gains as they automate routine and more complicated tasks, streamline workflows, and help improve decisions (Anca Dunavete, 2024). Machine learning algorithms can analyze massive datasets and identify patterns and insights that would simply be beyond the reach of human analyst. AI-led robotics can improve precision, minimize errors, and deliver 24/7 output without tiring in the manufacturing sector. AI tools make operations in financial services efficient through automated fraud detection, risk assessment and algorithmic trading leading to more efficient markets.

In addition, AI-driven customer service applications like chat-bots and virtual assistants increase productivity by managing high volumes of inquiries, leaving human employees to focus on tasks requiring more strategic and imaginative thinking. A report published by PwC in 2020 estimates that AI powered automation might boost global labor productivity by as much as 40% between 2035 and the end of the century, provided business leaders and policymakers invest in digital infrastructure and retraining programs (PwC, 2017).

4.2 Impact on Different Sectors

i) Manufacturing and Logistics: AI is transforming production lines with predictive maintenance, supply chain optimization, and smart manufacturing. As an illustration, Organizations such as Siemens and General Electric employ AI to observe the health of their equipment by predicting problems before they manifest; therefore, reducing downtime and maintenance costs, AI has had a tremendous impact on logistics filled with robotic warehouses in Amazon, allowing for better order speed and fulfillment time (Core BTS, 2024).

ii) Healthcare — The healthcare sector can gain from AI applications in diagnostic imaging, personalized medicine, administrative automation, etc. Some machine learning algorithms can analyze medical images more accurately than human radiologists in certain instances, while AI-driven platforms such as IBM Watson provide clinical decision support. Nevertheless, such innovations also bring risks related to data privacy, patient consent and perhaps biases from algorithms (Alowais et al., 2023).

iii) Finance: AI is applied in the financial sector for tasks such as risk management and customer service (Chlouverakis, 2024). The rise of automated trading system and AI investment advisors AI-powered tools improve the accessibility of financial services: Digital lending platforms analyze borrowers' creditworthiness based on alternative data, extending financial service provision to underserved population.

iv) Agriculture: AI and Internet of Things (IoT) will power precision agriculture, allowing for improved resource management and higher crop yield. AI-equipped drones scan the status of crops, while data analytics platforms optimize irrigation and fertilizer. These technologies play a key role in addressing global food security issues (Sharma & Shiv Kumar Shivandu, 2024).

5. THE ROLE OF BIG DATA AND DIGITAL INFRASTRUCTURE

The success of AI as an engine for economic transformation relies on high-quality data, a solid digital infrastructure. So big data is basically the fuel that makes these AI algorithms work and produce these insights and predictions much more accurately than ever before (Babina et al., 2024). Countries that are more infrastructural prepared to support AI (through 5G networks, data centers, etc.) are likely to benefit most from it. In addition, cloud computing has made AI tools accessible to small and medium-sized enterprises (SMEs) at a fraction of the cost it would have taken before.

On the other hand, the issue of data privacy, ownership and governance becomes a challenge with big data. This urge is reflected in the European Union's General Data Protection Regulation (GDPR) and similar regulatory frameworks around the world which symbolize a tension between innovation on one hand and individual rights on the other (Intersoft Consulting, 2016). This monopoly of data by tech giants also sparks debates about competition and market balance.

6. CASE STUDIES: COUNTRIES LEVERAGING AI FOR ECONOMIC ADVANCEMENT

A number of the nations that lead the pack in AI development, such as United States, China and United Kingdom are using these innovations and technology to spur economic growth. China divides the Wave One timeline of development into initiatives and responses, which it has framed via its "Next Generation AI Development Plan" to describe a program of action for itself that aspires toward world leadership in AI by 2030 (Webster et al., 2017). A profusion of government investment, grants and public-private partnerships, AI hubs around the country. The economic dividends are already tangible with smart city innovations, supporting the development of self-driving cars, as well as advancements in health care thanks to AI.

On the other hand, a lack of digital infrastructure and scarcity of quality talent make the adoption of AI a challenging task for many developing nations. India is making progress in positive AI applications through efforts like increased agricultural productivity and health service delivery to underserved populations.

7. COMPARATIVE ANALYSIS

7.1 AI and Economic Impact in the United States

Thanks to its technology industry and high-quality universities, the United States is a world reference in AI research. AI boom is led by American companies, particularly Google, Amazon and Microsoft, with tremendous contribution to economic growth. Similarly, the U.S. government has acknowledged AI as a strategic asset with new initiatives such as National Artificial Intelligence Initiative Act to promote AI research and ecosystem (Goldman Sachs, 2023). But the U.S. does have to figure out how it deals with displacement in its workforce and guarantees that everyone can benefit from AI.

7.2 The Impact on Various Sectors

Healthcare: AI has changed the way we view healthcare in the US through precision medicine, advanced diagnostics, and predictive analytics. The AI as a tool for the hospitals and medical centers to have patient care optimized with no efforts required in their end (Barth, 2023).

Manufacturing: Artificial Intelligence in Manufacturing, the automated manufacturing driven by AI systems has led to productivity increase but also displacing a huge segment of population who worked on traditional assembly line jobs (Srivastava, 2023). Steps are being taken in the U.S. for retraining programs but integrating that transition is still a work of progress.

7.3 China's Approach to AI and Economic Development

With the Chinese government setting aspirations for AI leadership by 2030, China sees AI as a major pillar of its economic future. Meanwhile, the country has invested heavily in AI R&D, data infrastructure and tech start-ups. China, in contrast to the U.S., is harnessing and controlling AI development through state-driven policy that utilizes technological growth to advance comprehensive national security objectives (Zhao et al., 2022).

7.4 AI in Smart Cities and Surveillance

AI in Urban Planning: China is famous for smart cities with efficient traffic and energy management through AI. But China has employed AI for surveillance and social credit system, which is a very dangerous attempt to violating human rights on privacy. This balance of speed against ethics is perhaps still a dividing issue worldwide (Qian et al., 2022).

7.5 Comparing Policy Approaches

The U.S. relies on private sector for innovation, while China takes top-down approach by easily deploying AI tools that have also led to worries about state control and surveillance. While their governance contexts differ, both countries are struggling to balance AI regulation with economic expansion.

8. AI ADOPTION IN EMERGING MARKETS

Countries like India and Brazil have industry will in AI as well, but they're also dealing with their own challenges. The development of AI for developing countries is limited by low access to high technology, an insufficient digital infrastructure and a lack of trained workers (Endresen, 2024). However, AI also offers these economies a chance to skip the usual steps of progress in development sectors such as agriculture and health.

8.1 Potential for Leapfrogging

From precision farming to crop monitoring, AI applications in agriculture have the potential to transform food production in developing economies. Like telemedicine with AI can solve binocular disparity in health care. However, to make the most of what AI has to offer, these nations will need to tackle challenges surrounding digital literacy and infrastructure (Endresen, 2024).

9. CHALLENGES AND RISKS IN DIGITAL ECONOMIES

However, this proliferation of Artificial Intelligence (AI) also highlights a diverse set of underlying challenges and risks that may counter or shape the promise bound within finally unleashing their potential for digital economies. While AI technologies are poised to change industries and boost productivity, they carry a great displacement that cannot be overlooked. Such as, worker displacement & income inequality, ethical problems and monopolistic tendencies. Solving these issues, however, is also critical especially if we want AI to contribute to inclusive and sustainable economic growth.

9.1 Job Losses and Changes to the Workforce

Arguably the biggest worry when it comes to AI, workers are up against the threat of being replaced with machines capable of performing mundane tasks as well as several advanced ones. For a long time now, economists and labor market analysts have estimated millions of jobs — primarily in manufacturing, retail, and administrative — will be automated. According to estimates released earlier this year by the International Labor Organization (ILO), AI and automation could eliminate up to 800 million jobs worldwide—depending on how quickly organizations implement these technologies by 2030 (International Labor Organization (ILO), 2024).

Repetitive and rule-based jobs, including but not limited to data entry, customer service, assembly line work, etc. may be done by machines in the future which could result in mass unemployment or under-employment for those workers who cannot upgrade their skills to take up higher-level positions. AI can also create jobs but mostly, new job opportunities will come where more assistance is needed in AI development, data analysis, robotic engineering etc. The effect on the labor market may be negative or positive as a whole. A major blinder here is the skill gap where most workers lack technical competency for these future jobs. In addition, the shift towards an AI-based workforce could widen inequality to even low-skilled workers and specific demographics.

Finally, AI-driven economic benefits are geographically concentrated which compounds the challenge of workforce displacement. The gap between regions with strong digital infrastructure and concentration of technology firms will grow wider as those areas will gain more jobs and economic activity beyond the immediate effects of AI technologies on local sectors, while rural and economically weaker regions may face job losses without similar gains from AI specific opportunities.

9.2 The Problems with Inequality and Wealth Redistribution

The question of whether AI will create more wealth or distribute existing wealth evenly by floor, is a hotly contested topic with many experts believing we could see a divide between the haves and have-nots rise increasingly. AI economics can easily lead to techno-feudalism —where the spoils of AI fall into a stock market-centric, talent-draining black hole dominated by firms with sophisticated product development and data science capabilities (those closest to utilizing applied science) and supported by ever more automated information rigor mortis at high end labor markets while those asset-light knowledge workers in traditional industries or low-skilled white collar jobs toil for pennies on any dollar their new equivalent condition offers (Schellekens & Skilling, 2024). This widens already significant gaps and opens up a digital divide that could have dangerous social and political implications.

Artificial Intelligence is a massive opportunity, and American technology companies like Google, Amazon, and Microsoft are investing billions to develop it, thus gradually securing a competitive edge in an economy that rewards the winner of the data race. Such monopolies and dependency issues are huge problems due to the dominance of these companies. It raises market concentration and entry barrier issues for smaller players. The winner-takes-all character of the digital financial system may give a few companies sufficient of a part to seize maximum AI features, squeezing out income potential for smaller groups.

Moreover, the economic development driven by AI might even further deepen the gaps between regions. For instance, high-tech urban hubs may prosper economically at the same time as rural or resource-dependent regions enter an economic downturn. Public policies will be required to ensure that the advantages of all the progress with AI are widely shared, through investments in digital skills, business incentives to invest where needed, and targeted help for displaced workers.

9.3 Regulatory and Ethical Concerns

Since built AI technologies have developed and put into action faster than strong laws and regulations have been made, so are issues regarding the ethics and behavioral governance of them. Transparency, accountability and fairness in AI algorithms are very big issues. Machine Learning systems can be extremely powerful, but they are often referred to as a "black box", which means we do not have access to internal transparency (where decision making occurs) (Skare et al., 2024). To this end, the absence of transparency has been labelled as the Black Box problem, and can lead to biased outcomes in domains such as hiring, lending, law enforcement and healthcare where algorithmic decision making has broad consequences on people.

There is a lot of press on algorithm bias: An AI system that UK Copyright News Blog, where we blog about law in the age of machines and algorithms. We found that error rates vary with facial features in these systems and that the systems exhibited increased error rates among people of color, raising concern for racial discrimination. The solution to this has to be more careful testing, auditing and diversity in building AI technology.

The second collection of major ethical problem is the use of AI for surveillance and data collection. While the application of AI-enabled surveillance technologies can enhance policing and public security, they are also among the most dangerous threats to our privacy and civil liberties. An authoritarian government that uses these technologies to spy on and suppress dissent is one horrifying scenario; a corporation that employs mass surveillance to build an unregulated, multi-trillion-dollar warehouse of private data about every user could be another. In sum, this is a battleground of heavy regulatory disagreement between innovation versus privacy protection; one must tread carefully on both sides.

9.4 Risk of Monopoly and Market Power

If there ever was a timeline to talk about the fact that the AI revolution will simply serve to reinforce the power of large tech companies with access to data/computation – and how they are now expanding into new domains even further fueled by their algorithms, this is it. As they are also known, Big Tech has an advantage the datasets for training the AI models as well as money to fund sophisticated research. And that of course could increase the concentration in the digital economy, which is always bad for innovation and competition (Korinek et al., 2024).

There are several ways AI monopolies undermine the economic and social well-being. For one, a monopoly can dictate the terms of the marketplace and thus limit options for consumers which leads to increased prices. Or engage in anti-competitive behavior by acquiring said competitors before they do ever become a threat (or sell) or an AI-supported way to enrich the Market Space with two lost opportunities. Of course, this might only exacerbate the issue as how computing powers develop AI is access to data and market power on the back of great data. Companies that have such datasets can make their AI systems embed faster and leverage a feedback loop making them more entrenched winners.

We need strong, substance-focused antitrust and pro-competitive policy to fight back against monopolists. It is time for enforcers, regulators and lawmakers to roll up their sleeves and experiment with these new tools which are more suited to the economics of the digital economy. Such measures would involve mandatory data-sharing, merger and acquisition scrutiny, and pro open-source AI policies just to name a few.

9.5 Use of AI for Evil and Security Threats

In addition to this, Artificial intelligence technologies are also vulnerable to security threat as they can be misused or fall into the wrong hands. More High-Tech Cyber-Attacks: The proliferation of AI-driven hacking techniques capable of identifying vulnerabilities in the digital infrastructure. Cruise missiles are not the only possible autonomous or remotely-controlled system that an organization may use to engage in warfare against the civilian population; they can follow other such as self-driving cars and drones (Mitchelson, 2023).

An unknown sophistication of AI-driven deceptions and eradication is also here, this may well break social cohesion and the democratic process. By enabling and even scaling such inversions, deep fake tech can make it possible to create realistic-seeming videos for the express purpose of undermining these reputations. The more disturbing results are associated with political campaigning: micro targeting voters, tightening individual message algorithms, and so on.

A third concern is to use of AI in the development and creation of fully autonomous weapons systems-heavily called for killer robots. Since such systems could dramatically change the battlefield, they also raise profound questions about what it means to be human when making life-and-death decisions. Of course, the international community has called for rules and treaties to constrain AI on battlefields but progress has been slow amid clashing national interests and controversies over defense-smartness of these systems.

The challenges posed by these security threats cannot be underestimated and will necessitate a concerted response at the international level, with the establishment of effective AI governance frameworks, investments in AI safety research, to address these concerns. AI developers need to have security-by-design principle and collaborate with governments in mitigating risks during the deployment of such technologies.

10. ECONOMIC POLICY CONSIDERATIONS

The adoption of Artificial Intelligence (AI) geopolitical technology in digital economies is rife with various challenges and risks that prevent or distort opportunities it can offer. AI technologies do have the potential to transform entire industries and increase productivity on an unprecedented scale, but also bring major disruptions that need addressing. These challenges include workforce displacement, economic inequality, ethical concerns and a risk of monopolistic behavior (Pavel et al., 2023). This is important to address if we want AI-powered economic growth to be inclusive and sustainable.

10.1 Loss of Jobs and Forced Career Changes

Worker displacement, due to automation and machine learning systems performing not just rote tasks but even some knowledge-worker jobs, is one of the biggest fears linked with AI. For a long time, economists and labor market experts have warned that millions of jobs, especially in manufacturing, retail and clerical areas could be automated. By some estimates, in the next decade or so, even as many as 800 million jobs globally could be at risk due to AI and automation by The International Labor Organization (ILO) the speed of adoption 2030 (International Labor Organization (ILO), 2024).

Jobs that are repetitive and rule-based [e.g., data entry, customer service, assembly line work] become automated → millions of workers may be left unemployed or underemployed without the skills to transition into higher skill roles Yes, but AI will also generate new job opportunities in areas like developing AI systems, analyzing data and engineering robots and whether it has a net positive or negative affect on the labor market is up for debate. The "skills gap," of course, is a major obstacle, with many employees lacking the technical ability needed for these new positions. Moreover, the shift towards an AI-powered workforce could lead to increased disparities where low-skilled workers and specific demographics suffer more.

AI does hold the potential for displacement of workers, but geographically concentrated gains are also a challenge. Areas with strong digital infrastructure and a high density of technology companies can be expected to add more jobs and create wealth; whereas, rural and lower-income regions will face job losses without commensurate AI business development opportunities.

10.2 Problems Relating to Inequity and Income Sharing

The effect of AI on the distribution of wealth is likely to be a hot-button topic as long as this technology looms, and many experts caution that it will further widen the gulf between haves and have-nots. Moreover, the economic benefits of AI are expected to be captured by relatively small numbers of tech-savvy firms or high-skilled workers amongst sections of a community, with other segments like low-skills labor and traditional industries being left behind. This deepens existing disparities in wealth and presents a digital divide that may have dire socio-political consequences.

This has given tech giants like Google, Amazon and Microsoft a strategic advantage in an increasingly data-driven economy with megatrends such as AI requiring huge capital investments on the front end to achieve scale and profitability down the line. The dominance of these companies raises issues about monopolistic behavior, market concentration and the difficulty for smaller companies to enter the market. Even more disconcerting is the winner-takes-all nature of digital economy implying that profits driven by AI could stream largely to a handful of companies in each business area with no significant share for small players.

Given the distributive impact of AI-led economic growth, it will therefore be important to have a comprehensive and forward-looking policy agenda in place to ensure that AI is maximally utilized and widely shared – this also entails addressing negative effects of AI. This means bringing governments, policymakers and international organizations together to develop a conducive environment for innovation in which the economic divide is bridged but no country will escape from international law and standards of ethical behavior in the use of AI. Now, a few economic policy takeaways.

11. STRATEGIES FOR INCLUSIVE GROWTH

AI-driven economic growth cannot leave huge segments in society behind without widening inequality and social unrest. Policymakers need to ensure that the gains of AI are more evenly distributed across society, focusing particularly on education, job creation and social safety nets. Identifying: Strategies for Inclusive Economic Growth

i) Ensure universal access to school and reskilling programs: In the face of changing labor markets driven by advancements in AI, investments in education & training must also care for social equity. As AI technologies will generate some new jobs and make others redundant, the key pillar of policy responses covering these aspects should therefore be reskilling and upskilling workers because they need to transition into different types of work. Spend on STEM (science, technology, engineering & math) education fund and digital literacy programs for all workers. Providing easily accessible vocational training and lifelong learning opportunities to help workers transition into AI related roles such as data analytics or AI development and robotics maintenance.

ii) Social Defense Nets to Counter Fight Income: process displacement resulting in joblessness advantages, UBI and/or incomes supports may compel governments to enhance social wellbeing nets. This in turn can buy some time for the workforce and help them against any layoffs while they find another job or reskill. AI has spurred the growth of more gig and freelance jobs, so policymakers should also entertain inventive alternatives like wage insurance and portable benefits (i.e., benefits that are not tied to one employer).
iii) Help to SMEs: Small and medium-sized enterprises would usually be lacking the resources to leverage and implement AI technologies. Policymakers could incentivize those companies through tax relief, subsidies or offers of cheap credit to adopt the technology. Public-private partnership enhancing the AI infrastructure and expertise of SMEs may also creatively provide access to AI (Hansen & Bøgh, 2020). Besides, innovation hubs and technical incubators are also a place to prepare local cultures for entrepreneurship and startups that utilize AI methods or products.

12. INVESTMENT IN HUMAN CAPITAL AND THE COST OF EDUCATION

AI has great potential for growth, but it makes development one step harder because enormous investments in human capital are required to harness beneficial technologies. We have to rethink our education systems in order for future generations to be prepared for an AI-associated world. This means not just preparing for a particular set of skills, but emphasizing on critical and creative thinking skills as well as skills less likely to be automated. This policy brief highlights a selected number of those issues:

i) AI and Data Literacy: Introducing AI and data literacy into the school curriculum as early as possible, ensures that youth are equipped to work in a digital economy Schools collaborating with technology corporations could give students an on ground practical exposure to real life AI projects, implementations.
ii) Boost public funding for basic and applied research in higher education: Governments should step up funding available to be spent on AI R&D. But that leaves an important role for public universities or research institutions to step in and drive AI entrepreneurship, but do so without compromising on ethics and transparency. Financial support for AI-degree scholarships and fellowships, particularly for underrepresented groups.

iii) Workforce Development Programs: In collaboration with industry and academia, programs will be shaped to meet local workforce development demands. For example, partnerships with tech could create apprenticeships that expand the workforce but also provide on the job training for workers to develop new AI skills.

13. CREATING THE REGULATORY FRAMEWORKS THAT BALANCE BETWEEN INNOVATION AND CAPTURE

Compounding this challenge is the fact that these implications often transcend borders, making AI governance a daunting effort especially with how fast this technology is advancing. The challenge for policymakers is to strike the right balance between allowing innovation and ensuring public interests. The regulatory framework can and should include measures to safeguard data privacy, prevent algorithmic bias, ensure accountability and promote competition. This framework consists of several essential elements as:

i) Regulations: Reliance on data with Lang Chain AI enables or exposes more people to harm whatsoever kind, safe-guarding efforts need an equally matched approach! Regulatory regimes such as GDPR in the European Union can provide recommendations on how data ought to be collected, stored and utilized. Policymakers need to ensure that data is shared or given out in an open manner and that the choice of what to do with personal information lies with the individuals. However, it does need to penalize companies suffering data breaches and enforce better cybersecurity measures for sensitive data.
ii) Ethical AI and bias mitigation: Given the widespread integration of algorithmic decision-making across various sectors, regulations ought to demand fairness, accountability and transparency of AI systems to ensure they are not compounders or propagators of social biases. Auditing AI algorithms by independent parties can reveal and replace biases Existing ethical guidelines such as the IEEE and Partnership on AI can provide a framework for responsible AI development. Regulators should also have heavy gun that they can point at companies to make sure compliance happens and discrimination drops (Emma, 2023).
iii) Antitrust and Competition Policies: Widespread entrenchment of select AI capacities within major tech companies threatens market competition. Antitrust policies have to be updated for the new digital economy, dealing with unique challenges such as data monopolies and anti-competitive practices. If they are monopolistic companies, regulators can consider data-sharing mandates, interoperability requirements, and even regulation of break-up. Supporting

open-source AI and a multi-player ecosystem (to avoid monopoly) will serve innovation.

14. GOVERNING INTERNATIONAL COOPERATION IN AI

AI is a technology that changes global policies, and has implications that cross borders; This requires international cooperation for common standards and a stronger commitment from the private sector itself to responsible development and deployment of AI. International cooperation is important in some facets that involve:

i) International Collaboration on AI Standards and Ethics: International bodies like the UN, OECD, and World Economic Forum can take the lead in establishing global standards and norms for AI. The collective may work on promoting initiatives to ensure that AI systems are transparent, fair, and accountable. An International AI Regulatory Framework can serve as an umbrella for a harmonized approach to data protection, algorithmic transparency and high-stakes deployment of AI on critical infrastructure (Kerry et al., 2021).
ii) AI for Global Good: Support large scale projects that use AI to tackle some of the most pressing issues in the world like climate change, health crisis and poverty as they can bring global goodwill and joint progress. Utilizing AI in developing areas can maximize disaster response optimization, resource allocation, and agricultural productivity. Funding mechanisms and platforms for knowledge-sharing around these initiatives should be facilitated by governments or international organizations.
iii) Cyber Security and AI Safety: The global responses to this will have to be as coordinated as the cyber-driven threats themselves that AI has enabled. Countries may collaborate to establish best practices for securing AI, sharing threat intelligence, and investing in AI safety research. There may need to be some international treaties or agreements in place that regulate the use of AI for military purposes and that the proliferation of autonomous weapons systems does not occur, and attempts to restrict use for malicious ends.

15. FUTURE PROSPECTS AND UNCERTAINTIES

Growth engine or the economic "Colossus of Rhodes" On one hand, AI technology brings great potential for radical productivity improvements. While the future economic and social impact of AI technologies will be better understood as they evolve, there are several reasons why the impacts might be more difficult to predict:

15.1 Potential Future Paths for the Economy Driven by AI

i) Optimistic Scenario: In an upper scenario, the economic growth is widespread due to AI technologies in general purpose area of applications (GPT), new industries are created along productivity growth; and as a consequence living standards rise globally. Governments around the world successfully implement policies that make certain a fair distribution of AI benefits, and workforce reskilling initiatives adapt people to upcoming employment opportunities. Transnational cooperation fosters a stable and secure digital environment, with ethical principles integrated into the artificial intelligence/AI development (Hunter, 2024).

ii) Pessimistic Scenario: In a dystopian world, AI only amplifies economic inequality and causes mass unemployment without any form of welfare to compensate. This concentration of AI capabilities into the hands of a select few tech companies narrows innovation horizons, and security threats become more difficult to manage. The competition for AI supremacy could also result in geopolitical tensions that turn violent, or perhaps lead to a technology-related trade war, and ethical gaps in using AI systems may undermine the public confidence on such a mission.

iii) Mixed Case: Most realistic outcome may be in between these extremes; AI provides substantial benefits to some sectors and regions but also causes major challenges for others. For policymakers, it will be important to keep their fingers on the pulse of AI evolution; businesses themselves must build sustainable and responsible practices around AI.

15.2 AI Technology Unknowns and the Future Adaptation of AI Into Markets

The progression of AI, especially towards things like artificial general intelligence (AGI), is anyone's guess. Constant: Some of the breakthroughs with deep learning, quantum computing, or brain-computer interfaces could end up having unexpected economic impacts. Furthermore, markets will also be selective in terms of their adaptability to the AI disruptions as certain industries will adopt the technology faster than others.

The combination of AI with other technologies, including 5G networks, the Internet of Things (IoT) and block chain can create new ways to move the economy forward but can also present additional difficulties. Policymakers and business leaders alike will need to understand these interdependencies.

15.3 Adaptation and Resilience of Economies

Whether economies stand the upheaval from AI will depend on their adaptability and capacity for innovation. Better is expected to be countries that invest in the field of education, infrastructure, and good governance. Adaptive capacity will need to be embedded, e.g., through needs for a culture of continuous learning and innovation, for sustainable economic resilience (Mehryar et al., 2024).

16. CONCLUSION

Artificial intelligence (AI) can fuel a new wave of global growth, reshape industries and rise to challenge the global economic game. Yet these benefits cannot be realized without addressing the challenges presented by AI integration like job loss, inequality, regulatory uncertainty and security threats. An inclusive and resilient digital economy requires all stakeholders, including policymakers, businesses and civil society to come together. Whether harnessed for economic benefit, or risk adjusted and economically distracting, this ahistorical moment in technological evolution will be one that is defined by our collective will to steward into the future.

In short, AI is a rare opportunity and a major risk. The choices we act on today will reverberate through eternity. A future where we can forge a path ahead through investments in human capital, the promotion of ethical AI development, and international cooperation.

REFERENCES

Acemoglu, D., & Restrepo, P. (2018). ARTIFICIAL INTELLIGENCE, AUTOMATION AND WORK. SSRN *Electronic Journal, 108*(24196). DOI: 10.2139/ssrn.3123798

Alowais, S. A., Alghamdi, S. S., Alsuhebany, N., Alqahtani, T., Alshaya, A., Almohareb, S. N., Aldairem, A., Alrashed, M., Saleh, K. B., Badreldin, H. A., Yami, A., Harbi, S. A., & Albekairy, A. M. (2023). Revolutionizing healthcare: The role of artificial intelligence in clinical practice. *BMC Medical Education*, *23*(1), 689. Advance online publication. DOI: 10.1186/s12909-023-04698-z PMID: 37740191

Anca Dunavete. (2024, May 8). *AI in Workplace Technology: Improving Productivity with Chatbots and Virtual Assistants*. Yarooms.com; YAROOMS International. https://www.yarooms.com/blog/ai-in-workplace-technology

Babina, T., Fedyk, A., He, A., & Hodson, J. (2024). Artificial intelligence, firm growth, and product innovation. *Journal of Financial Economics*, *151*(1), 103745–103745. DOI: 10.1016/j.jfineco.2023.103745

Barth, S. (2023). *Artificial Intelligence (AI) in Healthcare & Hospitals*. ForeSee Medical; ForeSee Medical. https://www.foreseemed.com/artificial-intelligence-in-healthcare

Brynjolfsson, E., & McAfee, A. (2017, July 18). *The Business of Artificial Intelligence*. Harvard Business Review; Harvard Business Review. https://hbr.org/2017/07/the-business-of-artificial-intelligence

Bughin, J., Seong, J., Manyika, J., Chui, M., & Joshi, R. (2018). NOTES FROM THE AI FRONTIER MODELING THE IMPACT OF AI ON THE WORLD ECONOMY. In https://www.mckinsey.com/~/media/mckinsey/featured%20insights/artificial%20intelligence/notes%20from%20the%20frontier%20modeling%20the%20impact%20of%20ai%20on%20the%20world%20economy/mgi-notes-from-the-ai-frontier-modeling-the-impact-of-ai-on-the-world-economy-september-2018.ashx. McKinsey Global Institute (MGI). https://www.mckinsey.com/~/media/McKinsey/Featured%20Insights/Artificial%20Intelligence/Notes%20from%20the%20frontier%20Modeling%20the%20impact%20of%20AI%20on%20the%20world%20economy/MGI-Notes-from-the-AI-frontier-Modeling-the-impact-of-AI-on-the-world-economy-September-2018.ashx

Capitol Technology University. (2024). *Moving Towards a More Sustainable Future Using AI | Capitol Technology University*. Www.captechu.eduCapitol Technology University. https://www.captechu.edu/blog/moving-towards-more-sustainable-future-using-ai

Chlouverakis, K. (2024, April 26). *How artificial intelligence is reshaping the financial services industry*. Www.ey.com

EY. https://www.ey.com/en_gr/financial-services/how-artificial-intelligence-is-reshaping-the-financial-services-industry

Core, B. T. S. (2024, July 30). *Smart Manufacturing Revolution: AI-Driven Supply Chain Optimization*. Core BTS; Core BTS. https://corebts.com/blog/smart-manufacturing-revolution-ai-driven-supply-chain-optimization/

Emma, T. (2023, December 10). *Ethical AI and Bias Mitigation. - Tech Emma - Medium*. Medium; Medium. https://medium.com/@emmaja/ethical-ai-and-bias-mitigation-3b62a2ae07c8

Endresen, J. (2024, August 13). *The Intersection of AI and Emerging Markets: Opportunities and Challenges*. Cornell SC Johnson; Cornell SC Johnson. https://business.cornell.edu/hub/2024/08/13/intersection-ai-emerging-markets-opportunities-challenges/

Goldman Sachs. (2023). *AI may start to boost US GDP in 2027*. Goldmansachs.com; Goldman Sachs. https://www.goldmansachs.com/insights/articles/ai-may-start-to-boost-us-gdp-in-2027

Hansen, E. B., & Bøgh, S. (2020). Artificial intelligence and internet of things in small and medium-sized enterprises: A survey. *Journal of Manufacturing Systems, 58*(Part B), 362–372. DOI: 10.1016/j.jmsy.2020.08.009

Hunter, D. T. (2024, April 17). *Artificial intelligence: A new driver for inclusive growth and development?* Asia Pathways; Asia Pathways. https://www.asiapathways-adbi.org/2024/04/artificial-intelligence-a-new-driver-for-inclusive-growth-and-development/

International Labour Organization (ILO). (2024, April 23). *Artificial intelligence*. International Labour Organization; International Labour Organization (ILO). https://www.ilo.org/artificial-intelligence

Intersoft Consulting. (2016). *General data protection regulation (GDPR)*. General Data Protection Regulation (GDPR); General Data Protection Regulation. https://gdpr-info.eu/

Kerry, C. F., Meltzer, J. P., Renda, A., Engler, A., & Fanni, R. (2021, October 25). *Strengthening international cooperation on AI*. Brookings; Brookings. https://www.brookings.edu/articles/strengthening-international-cooperation-on-ai/

Korinek, A., Vipra, J., & Vipra, A. K. Jai. (2024, March 27). *AI monopolies*. Economic Policy; Economic Policy. https://www.economic-policy.org/79th-economic-policy-panel/ai-monopolies/

Mehryar, S., Yazdanpanah, V., & Tong, J. (2024). AI and Climate Resilience Governance. *iScience*, *26*(7), 109812–109812. DOI: 10.1016/j.isci.2024.109812 PMID: 38784017

Mitchelson, D. (2023, October 27). *Learn about the double-edged sword of AI in cybersecurity*. World Economic Forum; World Economic Forum. https://www.weforum.org/stories/2023/10/the-double-edged-sword-of-artificial-intelligence-in-cybersecurity/

Pavel, B., Ke, I., Spirtas, M., Ryseff, J., Sabbag, L., Smith, G., Scholl, K., & Lumpkin, D. (2023, November 3). *AI and Geopolitics: How Might AI Affect the Rise and Fall of Nations?*Www.rand.org

RAND. https://www.rand.org/pubs/perspectives/PEA3034-1.html

PwC. (2017). *PwC's Global Artificial Intelligence Study | PwC*. PwC; PwC Global. https://www.pwc.com/gx/en/issues/artificial-intelligence/publications/artificial-intelligence-study.html

Qian, Y., Liu, J., Shi, L., Forrest, J. Y.-L., & Yang, Z. (2022). Can artificial intelligence improve green economic growth? Evidence from China. *Environmental Science and Pollution Research International*, *30*(6), 16418–16437. Advance online publication. DOI: 10.1007/s11356-022-23320-1 PMID: 36184706

Rivera-Batiz, L. A., & Romer, P. M. (1991). International trade with endogenous technological change. *European Economic Review*, *35*(4), 971–1001. DOI: 10.1016/0014-2921(91)90048-N

Schellekens, P., & Skilling, D. (2024). *Three Reasons Why AI May Widen Global Inequality*. Center for Global Development; Center For Global Development. https://www.cgdev.org/blog/three-reasons-why-ai-may-widen-global-inequality

Schwab, K., & World Economic Forum. (2016, January 14). *The Fourth Industrial Revolution: what it means and how to respond*. World Economic Forum; World Economic Forum. https://www.weforum.org/stories/2016/01/the-fourth-industrial-revolution-what-it-means-and-how-to-respond/

Sharma, K., & Shivandu, S. K. (2024). Integrating Artificial Intelligence and Internet of Things (IoT) for Enhanced Crop Monitoring and Management in Precision Agriculture. *Sensors International*, *5*, 100292–100292. DOI: 10.1016/j.sintl.2024.100292

Shen, Y., & Zhang, X. (2024). The impact of artificial intelligence on employment: The role of virtual agglomeration. *Humanities & Social Sciences Communications*, *11*(1), 1–14. DOI: 10.1057/s41599-024-02647-9

Skare, M., Gavurova, B., & Blažević Burić, S. (2024). Artificial intelligence and wealth inequality: A comprehensive empirical exploration of socioeconomic implications. *Technology in Society*, *79*, 102719. DOI: 10.1016/j.techsoc.2024.102719

Srivastava, S. (2023, July 24). *Role of AI in Manufacturing: Use Cases and Examples*. Appinventiv; Appinventiv. https://appinventiv.com/blog/ai-in-manufacturing/

Szczepański, M. (2019). Economic Impacts of Artificial Intelligence (AI). In *European Parliament*. European Parliament. https://www.europarl.europa.eu/RegData/etudes/BRIE/2019/637967/EPRS_BRI(2019)637967_EN.pdf

United Nation. (2019). The Age of Digital Interdependence 1 the age of digital interdependence Report of the UN Secretary-General's High-level Panel on Digital Cooperation The Age of Digital Interdependence 2. In https://www.un.org/en/pdfs/DigitalCooperation-report-for%20web.pdf. United Nation. https://www.un.org/en/pdfs/DigitalCooperation-report-for%20web.pdf

Webster, G., Creemers, R., Kania, E., & Triolo, P. (2017, August 1). *Full translation: China's "new generation artificial intelligence development plan" (2017)*. DigiChina; Stanford University. https://digichina.stanford.edu/work/full-translation-chinas-new-generation-artificial-intelligence-development-plan-2017/

Zhao, P., Gao, Y., & Sun, X. (2022). How does artificial intelligence affect green economic growth?—Evidence from China. *The Science of the Total Environment*, *155306*, 155306. Advance online publication. DOI: 10.1016/j.scitotenv.2022.155306 PMID: 35461946

Chapter 2
Is AI a Legal Person? Redefining the Limits of Legal Personhood

Irfan Rasool Najar
Christ University, India

Sneha Sneha
https://orcid.org/0009-0003-4068-163X
Settle Immigration Inc., Canada

ABSTRACT

The traditional legal principles of personhood, which have historically been reserved for humans and, in certain situations, companies, are being challenged by the rapid breakthroughs in artificial intelligence (AI). It is necessary to grant legal personhood to AI systems as their decision-making abilities increase. Legal personhood, according to proponents, would guarantee accountability and provide legal redress for harm brought about by AI's acts (Tretyakova, 2021; Hárs, 2022). Critics argue that AI is devoid of fundamental characteristics that are important to conventional notions of personality, such as consciousness and moral agency (Forrest, 2021; Schneider, 2019). This proposal examines frameworks, including Asimov's Three Laws of Robotics and Hohfeldian jural relations, to suggest approaches where AI can assume legal responsibilities without full personhood status. The study aims to develop regulatory strategies that balance innovation with ethical and societal safeguards.

DOI: 10.4018/979-8-3373-3384-7.ch002

PART I

Introduction

Artificial intelligence (AI) technology is transforming multiple sectors, from autonomous vehicles and healthcare to judicial systems and financial institutions and reshaping social life. Unlike traditional tools, modern AI exhibits a degree of autonomy, conducting complex analyses and influencing society in unprecedented ways. These developments demand a reconsideration of the legal and philosophical boundaries of personhood, raising the question of whether AI entities should be granted legal status akin to that of a "person." The question, whether to ascribe legal personhood to AI, is afresh question of jurisprudence in digital age, requiring prescribing the "ought," propositions. Against this background the proposal examines the need for a re-examination of legal personhood in the digital era.

It is known that legal personhood has long served as a cornerstone of jurisprudence, delineating entities that can bear rights and duties within a legal framework. Traditionally reserved for natural persons, the definition has expanded to include non-human entities like corporations, recognising their socio-economic roles in modern societies (Tretyakova, 2021)[1] However, the rapid evolution of artificial intelligence (AI) has disrupted these conventional paradigms. Once confined to narrow tasks, AI systems now exhibit degrees of autonomy that rival or even surpass human decision-making in specific domains. Autonomous vehicles, for example, can make life-or-death decisions in real-time, while algorithmic systems influence judicial outcomes, hiring practices, financial markets, (Hárs, 2022)[2] and impacts consumer decision making power. These capabilities challenge the existing boundaries of accountability and liability, raising the question: should AI entities be granted legal personhood, and if so, to what extent? For this purpose, the chapter is divided into six parts. Part I shall lay bare to the introduction of the topic setting tune on the question for re-examination of personhood in digital age. In Part II is analysed the question of personhood from a jurisprudential perspective. Part III shall lay bare to the analysis of various laws of robotics and their implications in Hohfeldian matrix to deduce personhood, if any, of AI. In Part IV and V has been discussed a comparative perspective and future direction of AI, respectively. The conclusion is provided in Part VI of the paper.

PART II

The Historical and Legal Context of Personhood

Legal personhood is a construct that allows entities to engage with the legal system by bearing rights, duties, and liabilities. In its earliest forms, this status was exclusive to natural persons, defined by their inherent capacity for moral reasoning and intentionality (Austin, 1832).[3] Over time, the concept expanded to accommodate collective entities like corporations, which, despite lacking consciousness, were granted personhood to facilitate economic and social functions (Blumberg, 1987).[4] The legal scholar John Austin argued that personhood is a function of recognition by the law, not an intrinsic characteristic (Austin, 1832).[5] This pragmatic approach underpins modern legal systems, where the attribution of personhood is often a matter of utility rather than ontology.

The extension of personhood to corporations in the 19th century marked a significant departure from traditional notions tied to human attributes. Corporate personhood allows businesses to own property, enter contracts, and be held accountable for legal violations (Horwitz, 1985).[6] This model, while controversial, demonstrates that legal personhood can be granted based on societal needs rather than inherent qualities. The parallels between 'corporations" and AI systems are striking. Both operate as non-human agents capable of influencing human lives on a large scale (Johnson, 2020).[7] If corporations can hold limited personhood despite lacking consciousness, could similar principles apply to AI? Corporate personhood offers valuable insights into how non-human entities can hold legal responsibilities. Corporations are granted legal personhood to facilitate their participation in commerce, enabling them to own property, enter contracts, and be held liable for violations (Hovenkamp, 2007).[8] However, this personhood is limited; corporations cannot vote or marry, reflecting the tailored nature of their legal status. AI systems could similarly be granted limited personhood, focused on accountability rather than rights. For instance, an AI entity might be assigned legal responsibilities to ensure compliance with safety standards, while liability for harm could remain with the developers or operators (Fitzgerald, 2019)[9]

Relational theories of personhood shift focus from intrinsic qualities to relationships and societal roles (Mackenzie & Stoljar, 2000).[10] From this perspective, AI systems might be considered legal persons if they fulfil roles that significantly impact human lives (Solum: 1992; Pagallo, 2018)[11], such as operating critical infrastructure or making legal decisions (Diamantis & Grant, 2017)[12]. For example, an AI judge that adjudicates small claims cases could be recognized as a legal entity to ensure accountability for its rulings. However, relational theories also raise concerns about diminishing human-centric values in legal and ethical systems, necessitating safeguards to maintain balance.

Legal Personality of 'Persons': The Law and the Un-law

It can be said that the question who are persons in law have been both, unchallenging and disputed at the same time. Unchallenging because no other can be 'person' other than human beings in its simple and straight forward language (Wishart, 2016)[13] and because they are a member of human society, endowed with rights and duties. On the other hand, it has been disputed (Fagundes, 2001; Hoffman, 1986 p. 74; Wishart, 2016)[14] owing to its characteristic which can be attributed to anything (Austin, 1832)[15] or everything (Jens, 2017, p. 9, 12-13)[16], if law choses so (Wishart, 2016, p. 747-48)[17]. Also, because identifying and defining personhood is treated as a subject matter of rights, duties (Grey, 1921, p. 27)[18] and their denominators in a legal matrix[19]. Scholars have attempted defining and redefining what person and personhood in law mean, and thus contributed to dispute to existing jurisprudence and have added new jurisprudence on the nature of legal personhood (Solum, 1992, p. 1231)[20]. It is by the reason and fact that state ultimately defines the policies for all[21]. It is interesting to note that the observation by Lawrence B Solum in 1992 that *no computer program possesses the sort of capacities that would justify serious judicial inquiry into the question of legal personhood* (Halley, 2010)[22], is out fashioned owing to the interaction of AI in human life in the current time. Human beings, not nonpersons (Fagundes, 2001)[23] have also been a subject of controversies[24]. In many other cases, though not looked as a controversy but a social need, to treat human as nonperson like a minor is well recognized. Minor is a limited person. It, however, raises a critical question with respect to who can attribute and how personhood can be attributed, and thus remains a subject matter of dialectical (Hoffman, 1986)[25]. It is in this context relevant to refer the European parliament's observation on the question of attributing of legal personhood to autonomous systems as *wherever, ultimately, robots' autonomy raises the question of their nature in the light of the existing categories – of whether they should be regarded as natural persons, animals or objects – or whether a new category should be created, with its own specific features and implications as regards the attribution of rights and duties, including liability for damage*[26].

The question of jurisprudence of personhood is deep and without an easy answer (Fagundes, 2001; Naffine, 2003)[27]. There can be two reasons for this. Firstly, though the personhood (Ohlin, 2005)[28] is a subject matter of attributing rights and duties, and capacity (Holland, 1917, p. 82)[29] of performing them (Johnson, 2012)[30] there are some who have capacity but yet neither treated as person (Pollock, 1918, p. 113-114)[31] not even humans. Secondly, the concept is ever evolving and absorbs, like an unbaked cup of clay, new meanings to it, particularly in the light of the judicial decisions (Dewey, 1926)[32].

The issue of attributing, if at all it can be, AI's legal personhood leads us back to the fundamental question of what it means to be a person. Philosophers who attempted encrypting this question have reached different conclusions, like for John Locke, persons, an intelligent Agent, must be capable of a Law, and Happiness and Misery (Locke, 1964)[33]. Also, for Immanuel Kant, as quoted by Sabine Gless, (Gless, 2016)[34] self-consciousness which only humans experience (McHugh, 1992, p. 445)[35] is a true assertion for defining personhood. In this way it can be argued that AI unlike humans, cannot attribute its cations to its own will and lacks self-consciousness, and thus cannot be termed as persons. However, it is pertinent to note that legal personhood ultimately hinges on the right-duty relations (Dewey, 1926; Smith. 1928, p. 238; Grey, 1921, p. 27; Pollock, 1918, p. 114)[36], which can be extended, through a policy as in case of European Law, to AI as autonomous agents capable of bearing right-duty relations (Kukri, 2023, p. 6-7)[37] and their legal implications. To be a person, one must hold rights and/or duties. It is in this context that the paper explores the applying Isaac Asimov's *The Bicentennial Man, The Three Laws of Robotics*, and Karel Čapek's *R.U.R.*, and Hohfeldian Jural-Relations to determine the possibility of defining AI as a entity capable of bearing right-duty relation and thus a legal person.

Salmond on the other hand argued that legal personhood in law is rooted in the attribution of rights and duties (Salmond,1902)[38], and for Jellinek, as quoted by Patrick, argued that personhood is a status granted by law and legal capacity (Kelly, 2015, p. 29)[39]. Also, Hans Kelsen views legal person in terms of rights and duties, and argues that "Man is a concept of biology and physiology, in short, of natural science. Person is a concept of jurisprudence, of the analysis of legal norms (Kelsen, 1945)[40]."

It is pertinent to note that HLA Hart also explored that legal persons are those who are capable of having duties and rights imposed by a system, and thus looked at legal personhood in terms of rights and duties correlations (Hart, 1961)[41]. It is important to note that for Hart there are two different types of rules, primary and secondary, which comprise the "essence (Hart, 1961, p. 151)[42]" of law. Primary rules are "duty imposing" rules, which prescribe or proscribe behaviour, and secondary rules, though not duty-imposing rules (Starr, 1984; Hart,, 1974)[43], confer the power whereby primary rules may be introduced, recognized, eliminated, changed, or applied (Hart, 1961, p. 78-94)[44]. It is pertinent to note that Hart's primary and secondary rules align with Asimov's "The Three Laws of Robotics" by prescribing specific behaviour, and setting the policy for how these laws can be altered or changes for robots. All that requires is treating AI as a legal person. For Roscoe Pound, personhood was determined by the recognition of legal rights and obligations that allow them to engage in legal relationship (Pound, 1985, p. 189-407; Pound, 1911).[45] Amongst the five meanings attributed, by Pound, to the term "rights" one is designated to mean which the *law adopts in order to secure interests, namely, a recognition in persons, or a conferring upon persons, of certain capacities of influencing the action of others* (Pound, 1915)[46]. Personhood, in this context, depends on the recognition of certain capacities vested in an individual by law – specially, the ability to change legal position of other. Similarly, AI could be considered a legal person of the law chooses it as having the capacity to act and influence, which it does, others in ways that are akin to those of a human with legal personhood.

Also, a prominent thinker in the historical school of jurisprudence, Savigny argued that legal personhood is linked to the ability to possess rights and duties within the legal system, with a focus on subjective legal rights (Savigny, 1840)[47]. Friedrich Carl von Savigny, for example, asserted that "the original concept of person [...] must coincide with the concept of human being, and this original identity [...] can be expressed as follows: every individual human being, and only the individual human being, possesses legal capacity [i.e. is a legal person]." According to Savigny, positive law can extend legal capacity to hypothetical subjects—corporations—even if humans are the "original identity" of legal personhood. However, this is a legal fiction since it does not stem from the ideas of law and personhood embodied in the Volksgeist, or "spirit of the people (Kurki, 2019, p. 22)"[48].

It may appear a fiction, but it must not be forgotten when Henry Maine said in his "Ancient Law" that fiction is almost a necessity of the law. Lon Fuller also on the word "fiction" states that it may not always mean the same thing. He further states that "fiction" is neither a truthful statement, *a lie* (Ihering III, p. 305; Zander, 2022)[49], *nor an erroneous conclusion.* According to Fuller, *fiction is either (1) a statement propounded with a complete or partial consciousness of its falsity, or (2) a false statement recognized as having utility* (Fuller, 1967, p. 5; Campbell, 1983)[50]. Though Blackstone called fictions awkward and strange reasoning to achieve the means, he saw, as quoted by Alina, *fictions as something to prevent a mischief, or remedy an inconvenience* (Boyte, 2014, p. 714)[51], that might result from the general rule of law, and thus by fictions, law could adapt to unforeseen circumstance and achieve fairness in complex situations.

It is thus argued that legal personality of AI can be viewed as a legal fiction, as Fuller suggests, for its utility and it can also align with Maine's view of fiction as necessary constructs evolving and addressing social necessity. Also, AI legal personhood as fiction can prevent legal mischief and address challenges arising from it.

PART III

Legal Personality of AI: The Need (*sic*)

No better start than to refer to an episode of a famous cartoon animation from *Doraemon* centred around two characters, Nobita, a boy and his robot, Doraemon. In one of its episodes of *Doraemon,* Nobita is prosecuted for violating the basic rights of his robot companion, Doraemon, by overworking him without regard for his health. Doraemon, who has been suffering from poor health, refrains from seeking medical help to avoid burdening Nobita, who is completely dependent on him. Despite Doraemon's condition, Nobita continues to demand gadgets to ease his tasks. It is for these reasons that the robot police take Nobita to the court of the 22nd century for prosecution by the company for whatever mistakes committed and for Doraemon's conditions which happened because of him. The court hearing reveals that Nobita's actions, driven by his reliance on Doraemon, led to his robot friend's deteriorating health, resulting in the prosecution for the violation of his rights. Doraemon's episode highlights the ethical dilemma of over-reliance on AI and the potential legal consequences for both Nobita and Doraemon, even though in a fictional context. This is a concern of the future, for which 'ought' to have to be proposed today. In this episode, Nobita's over-reliance on Doraemon reflects a real-world concern about the ethical treatment of AI, and vice versa poses a legal dilemma, the prosecution of 'human' by a robotic company (Evans, 2023; Gutierrez & Marchant, 2021)[52]. In this regard, the 'Three Laws of Robotics' encrypted by Isaac Asimov, and by applying Hohfeldian jural relations – especially the concepts of 'right', 'duty', 'power', and their correlatives and opposites, provides a framework that could address this issue by ensuring AI's personhood and establish a balance of rights, in its varied meanings and dimension and its corresponding and opposites.

Thus, defining AI's legal personality becomes crucial as it helps establish clear responsibilities and rights, ensuring that AI, especially those integral to human lives has become so (Evans, 2023; Pasquale, 2020; Gorgoni, 2020)[53], are treated with care and respect, and at the same time ensuring human predominance in the robotic age[54].

Three Laws of Robotics and Others

It is, though, pertinent to note that despite Asimov's Law's shift from robots, like *Frankenstein*, being monsters to a non-monster, the dilemma continued defining their impact on social order like Skynet in the *Terminator* series taking over the world or in *Ex-Machina,* AI manipulating the mind, and thus a potential for malevolent rebellion. Isaac Asimov's Three Laws of Robots (Balkin, 2017)[55] postulated in 1942[56] state broad ethical principles which include 1) a robot may not injure a human being or, through inaction, allow a human being to come to harm; 2) a robot must obey orders given to it by human beings except where such orders would conflict with First Law; and 3) a robot must protect its own existence as long as such protection does not conflict with the First or Second Laws (Asimov, 1950, p. 37)[57]. It is interesting to note that towards 1985, a fourth law was also postulated by him providing that 4) a robot may not injure humanity, or through inaction, allow humanity to come to harm (Clarke, 1994)[58]. Isaac Asimov's fictional laws prioritize human safety and ethical behaviour, offering a conceptual foundation for regulating AI systems (Asimov, 1950, p. 57-82)[59] While these laws are not legally enforceable, they emphasize the importance of designing AI systems with built-in safeguards. Legislative initiatives, such as the European Parliament's 2017 recommendations on AI ethics, reflect similar principles, advocating for human-centric design and accountability measures.[60] By embedding ethical guidelines into AI development, these frameworks aim to prevent harm without requiring full personhood. It is pertinent to note that Roger Clarke extended *The Three Laws of Robotics* by adding, 'Law Four' and 'Procreation Law' which provided respectively that *a robot must perform the duties for which it has been programmed, except where that would conflict with a higher order law*, and that *a robot may not take any part in the design, manufacture, or maintenance of a robot unless the new or modified robot's action are subject to the Laws of Robotics* (Clarke, 1994)[61].

Also, Jack M Balkin adapts and modifies Asimov's law of robotics to regulate AI and big data, ensuring accountability, fairness, non-discrimination. He stresses the need for legal policies that govern interaction between humans and AI. The three laws (Balkin, 2017, p. 1227)[62] proposed by Balkin include 1) with respect to clients, customers, and end-users, algorithm users are information fiduciaries, 2) With respect to those who are not clients, customers, and end-users, algorithm users have general duty, and 3) the central public duty of algorithm users is to avoid externalizing the costs (harm) of their operations (Frank,, 2017)[63].

In this part, we focus on Asimov's three laws, as extended by Roger, and Jack M Balkin to provide a legal framework, if at all it can be, by applying Hohfeldian jural relations to *such* laws. In this regard, it will be appropriate to provide a brief for Hohfeldian jural relations in defining legal personhood.

Wesley Newcomb Hohfeld and AI's Personhood

Wesley Newcomb Hohfeld (Hohfeld, 1913)[64] account of legal rights remains very influential in not only defining 'right' in its various forms and their implications derived from their correlations and opposites but has been applied in varied fields of science of jurisprudence (Luis, 2023)[65]. Wesley Hohfeld's framework of jural relations provides a structured approach to assigning rights and duties (Hohfeld

(1913).[66] Under this model, AI could hold specific obligations—such as adhering to safety protocols—without being granted comprehensive legal personhood. For instance, an autonomous vehicle might be legally required to prioritize human safety, with liability distributed among developers and operators (Lin, 2016, p. 231-248)[67]

In this part is offered a rigorous exposition of Hohfeldian matrix and personhood derived from its application. Hohfeld sought to distil legal discourse into eight fundamental conceptions, arguing that all legal concepts could be fully analysed and defined through these core elements (Cullison, 1968, p. 559).[68] Hohfeldian matrix refers to a complex interaction, like spiders' web, between legal right, liberty, power, and immunity and their corresponding's. It provides a precise and systematic framework for analysing legal relationships created by law. *Legal person*, in this context may be noted, *are most often understood as those beings that hold rights and/or duties, or at least have the capacity to hold rights* (Visa, 2023)[69], attributed or conferred upon them by law, in order to determine their legal implications applied in in different situations and under varied circumstances. According to Salmond, *person is any being whom the law regards as being capable of rights and duties. This being doesn't always have to be a human* (Salmond & Fitzgerald, 1966)[70]. Also, according to *Orthodox view* (Visa, 2023, p. 6)[71]*, one is a legal person if he holds any legal right or duty* (Visa, 2023, p. 6)[72]. It can be safely thus stated that legal personhood can be conferred upon anything if law so desire. A juristic person is created by law (Machen, 1910)[73] and is a right-and-duty bearing unit (Dewey, 1926, p. 659)[74] The concept of personhood has evolved through law, which grants and recognizes it, from slaves, foetuses, corporations, and nature (Kushwaha; Kerslake, et al. 2012)[75]. This legal recognition reflects societal shifts, but its boundaries remain legally and morally debated. However, the law of the person (Richard, 1987, p. 123)[76] is, as noted by Dave Fagundes (Fagundes, 2001)[77], *fraught with deep ambiguity* (Dyschkant, 2015, p. 2078)[78]*and significant tension and the problem is likely to become more acute with technological progress.*

Application of Hohfeldian Matrix to The Laws of Robotics

To argue in favour of granting AI legal personhood, we must first recognize the historical precedent wherein state have extended personhood to entities, not because of their inherent perfection, but because, and not limited to, their potential for agency, growth, and legal responsibility. It may be noted that human beings, despite their capacity for violence, discrimination, and war, are granted personhood because they possess the ability to reflect, evolve, and take responsibility for their actions. Similarly, AI, while not yet fully autonomous (self-conscious), has begun to exhibit forms of person that challenge our traditional boundaries of personhood. Just as we have sought to recognize the legal rights of those historically deprived of it like slaves, foetus, refugees, AI, as a creation of human intellect, may evolve to possess its own legal status. Thus, in extending personhood to those capable of influencing and shaping the social order (Cassell, 2019; Jones, 2017)[79], it may not be unreasonable to contemplate extending a form of legal recognition to AI, acknowledging its potential role in a rapidly changing world. For this purpose, in the light of *The Law of Robotics* read with the Hohfeldian matrix in Table 1, is presented an analysis to determine, if at all it can be, the legal personality of AI.

This table analyzes the application of Hohfeldian legal relations to Isaac Asimov's and other scholars' laws of robotics, connecting them to legal and ethical responsibilities. It illustrates how these laws frame robots' duties, rights, and liabilities, reflecting increasing degrees of personhood and accountability. Relevant legal examples like tort law, contract law, and constitutional law are cited to show the alignment of robotic laws with human governance systems.

Table 1. Hohfeldian matrix of laws of robotics

The Law: Isaac Asimov	**Hohfeldian Relation**	**Analysis**	**Relationship to Personhood**	**Relevant Examples from Law**
Law 1: A robot may not harm a human being or allow harm through inaction.	Creates *Duty – Right* (Correlation)	The robot has a **duty** to avoid harm to humans. Humans have a **right** to be protected from harm.	This creates a form of **responsibility** for the robot, attributing a degree of **personhood** in terms of its obligations toward humans.	**Tort Law**: Negligence (e.g., a robot failing to act and causing harm), **Product Liability**: Manufacturers' duty to ensure robots do not harm users,
Law 2: A robot must obey orders given by humans unless conflicting with Law 1.	Creates *Power* and *Liability* (Correlation) *Privilege and No-Right* (Correlation)	The robot has a ***liability*** to obey human orders, which is the exercise of *power* but this is limited by the **right** of humans to not be harmed (priority of Law 1). **It implies that robot has *privilege* and human have *no-right* to interfere**	This highlights the robot's **subordination** to human authority, like that of a corporation and thus is an entity with obligations.	**Contract Law**: Obligation to follow instructions as per a contract unless conflicting with legal duty. **Tort Law**: Violation of duty causing harm.
Law 3: A robot must protect its own existence, unless it conflicts with Laws 1 or 2.	Creates *Privilege* and *Power* (Opposites)	The presence of **privilege** in robot to protect itself, implies the absence of *power* in it to contradict Law 1 or 2.	The robot is granted some **autonomy** (self-preservation), but only in a limited sense, acknowledging its **existence** without full personhood.	**Tort Law**: Duty of care (robot should protect itself to avoid damage that could indirectly harm a human)
Law 0: A robot may not harm humanity or allow humanity to come to harm.	Creates *Duty – Right* (Correlation)	The robot has a **duty** to prevent harm to humanity, and humanity has a **right** to not be harmed by the robot.	Expands the robot's **ethical scope**, implying a higher level of responsibility towards the collective good, aligning it with **human-like personhood** in terms of moral duties.	**Constitutional Law**: Protection of human life and public safety, **International Law**: Universal human rights, **Environmental Law**: Ensuring robots do not harm the environment or collective interests.
Roger Clarke				

continued on following page

Table 1. Continued

The Law: Isaac Asimov	Hohfeldian Relation	Analysis	Relationship to Personhood	Relevant Examples from Law
Law 4: A robot must perform its duties as programmed, unless it conflicts with a higher law.	**Creates *Duty – Right* (Correlation)** *Liberty – No-Right* (Opposite)	The robot has a ***duty*** to perform its programmed function, but may not have the **right** to disobey a higher order law (like Law 1 or Law 2).	The robot now carries **duties** to follow ethical principles, granting it a **moral role** akin to personhood, although still bound by programming.	**All laws/policies are subject to the Constitution – a higher norm.**
Procreation Law: A robot may not design or maintain another robot unless it complies with the Laws of Robotics.	**Creates *Duty – Right* (Correlation)**	The robot has a **duty** to ensure any new robots also follow the Laws, and thus no **right** to create a robot that violates these laws.	This adds a sense of **agency** and responsibility to the robot's actions, making it more **person-like** in the context of procreation (self-regulation).	**Constitutional Amending Powers:** Parliament has power to amend the constitution, but have no power to abolish it or redraft it.
Jack M Balkin				
Law 1: Algorithmic users are information fiduciaries to clients, customers, and end-users (Balkin, 2017)[80].	**Creates *Duty – Right* (Correlation)** to clients, **Right** of users to fair treatment.	**Duty** to clients, **Right** of users to fair treatment.	The algorithmic user is held accountable for **ethical obligations**, attributing a form of **personhood** to the user, as they are responsible for others' well-being.	**Contract Law**: Fiduciary duty in data handling agreements **Privacy Law**: GDPR obligations on the fiduciary duties of data holders
Law 2: Algorithmic users have a general duty to the broader public.	**Creates *Duty – Right* (Correlation) Duty** to society, **No-right** to exploit.	The algorithmic user has a **duty** to avoid harming the public or exploiting non-users, with no **right** to harm them.	Acknowledges the **public responsibility** of algorithmic users, drawing a link between **personhood** and societal duties.	**Tort Law**: Liability for harm caused to non-users or society (e.g., through biased AI or faulty algorithms).
Law 3: Algorithmic users must avoid externalizing the costs (harm) of their operations[81].	**Creates Duty – Right (Correlation)**	The algorithmic user has a **duty** to bear the costs of their actions, with no **right** to externalize harm or costs onto others.	The emphasis on **internalizing harm** reflects a **person-like** responsibility toward society and the environment, reinforcing a sense of moral agency.	**Constitutional Law**: Protecting public rights against harmful algorithmic actions (e.g., discrimination),

PART IV

Comparative Approaches to AI Regulation

The European Union (EU) has emerged as a leader in AI regulation, emphasizing a precautionary approach that prioritizes ethical safeguards. The EU's proposed Artificial Intelligence Act (AIA) classifies AI systems based on their risk levels, from minimal risk (e.g., spam filters) to high-risk applications such as autonomous vehicles or biometric identification.[82] High-risk systems must comply with stringent requirements, including transparency, risk assessment, and human oversight. The EU's emphasis on human oversight reflects its reluctance to assign autonomy or personhood to AI systems. Instead, the legal frameworks focus on ensuring that responsibility remains with human stakeholders (Veale & Hoboken, 2020).[83] This approach avoids the complications of legal personhood while addressing the accountability challenges posed by autonomous systems. In contrast to the EU, the United States lacks a unified approach to AI regulation. Federal agencies like the Federal Trade Commission (FTC) and the National Institute of Standards and Technology (NIST) have issued guidelines on specific aspects of AI, such as bias and transparency.[84] However, these efforts remain fragmented and largely reactive, addressing issues as they arise rather than providing a comprehensive framework. The absence of overarching legislation in the U.S. has led to inconsistent practices across industries. For example, liability for autonomous vehicle accidents is determined on a case-by-case basis, often resulting in prolonged litigation (Garrie, 2020)[85] This regulatory gap highlights the need for a more structured approach to AI accountability, potentially drawing from the EU's risk-based model.

PART V

AI: Toward Balanced and Futuristic Directions

Developing a balanced framework for AI accountability requires reconciling the unique capabilities of AI with the limitations of existing legal systems. This section proposes a hybrid approach that incorporates elements of legal personhood while preserving human oversight. AI systems could be assigned specific legal responsibilities tailored to their functions. For instance, an autonomous vehicle might be legally required to adhere to safety standards, with violations triggering penalties managed through insurance or regulatory mechanisms (Abbott, 2020).[86]

This approach ensures that AI operates within defined boundaries without granting it full personhood.

To prevent the displacement of responsibility, legal frameworks must emphasize the accountability of human stakeholders. Developers, operators, and manufacturers should be required to demonstrate due diligence in the design, deployment, and maintenance of AI systems (Calo, 2017).[87] Regulatory bodies could enforce these standards through audits, certifications, and penalties for non-compliance.

Ethical guidelines, such as Asimov's Three Laws of Robotics, should be integrated into AI design and governance. These principles could serve as a foundation for ensuring that AI systems prioritize human safety and well-being (Murphy & Woods, 2009)[88] For instance, AI used in healthcare could be required to adhere to ethical standards that prioritize patient rights and informed consent. The global nature of AI development and deployment necessitates international cooperation to establish consistent accountability standards. Organizations like the United Nations and the International Telecommunication Union (ITU) have begun exploring frameworks for AI governance.[89] A potential model Is the International Civil Aviation Organization (ICAO), which sets global standards for air travel.[90] Similar mechanisms could regulate cross-border AI applications, ensuring interoperability and accountability across jurisdictions.

Future Directions: Beyond Legal Personhood

Legal personhood is not the only path to ensuring AI accountability. Enhanced ethical oversight mechanisms, such as independent audit committees or ethics boards, could provide alternative solutions.[91] These bodies would evaluate AI systems for compliance with ethical standards, offering recommendations for improvement. For example, an independent board could assess an autonomous vehicle's decision-making algorithms to ensure they prioritize passenger safety and minimize harm to pedestrians (Ryan & Stahl, 2020)[92] Such mechanisms could complement legal frameworks, providing a holistic approach to AI governance. With AI's rapid development, static regulations risk becoming obsolete. Adaptive regulatory models, which evolve in response to technological advancements, offer a more sustainable solution.[93] For instance, regulatory sandboxes allow developers to test AI systems in controlled environments, enabling policymakers to refine rules based on real-world outcomes. This chapter highlights the need for interdisciplinary research to address the complexities of AI legal personhood. Philosophers, legal scholars, technologists, and sociologists must collaborate to explore new frameworks that balance innovation with societal values (Zohar & Rosenblat, 2020)[94] Future studies could examine emerging issues such as AI's role in climate governance or its impact on cultural preservation.

PART VI

Conclusion

The question of granting legal personhood to AI is not only a technological or legal issue but yields a deep rooted into the jurisprudence of law. It is known that legal personality has been extended, historically speaking, to nonhuman entities by law through granting rights and duties, not because they are self-conscience but simply because law recognized them so. It has evolved with the passage of time granting it to nature through operation of law. Similarly, extending personhood to those capable of social ordering, it may not be unreasonable to contemplate extending a form of legal recognition to AI.

Drawing from application of Hohfeldian matrix to science fiction to Algorithm science, it can be seen that rights in its various forms and their corresponding can be ascribed to AI, thereby creating a jural relation that underpins its legal personality. AI, mush like corporation and rivers, can be seen as a "juristic person" capable of holding legal right and its corresponding or opposite, thus requiring the "ought" to be adopted for its interaction with humans and legal entities.

REFERENCES

Arstein-Kerslake, A., O'Donnell, E., Kayess, R., & Watson, J. (2021). Relational Personhood: A Conception of Legal Personhood with Insights From Disability Rights and Environmental Law. *Griffith Law Review*, *30*(3), 530–534. DOI: 10.1080/10383441.2021.2003744

Blumberg, P. I. (1987). *The law of corporate groups: Property, contract, and insolvency*. The University of Chicago Press.

Bryson, J. J., Diamantis, M. E., & Grant, T. D. (2017). Of, for, and by the people: The legal lacuna of synthetic persons. *Artificial Intelligence and Law*, *25*(3), 273–291. DOI: 10.1007/s10506-017-9214-9

Calo, R. (2017). Artificial Intelligence Policy: A Primer and Roadmap. *UCLA Law Review. University of California, Los Angeles. School of Law*, *51*, 399–435.

Cassell, J. (2019). Artificial Intelligence for a Social Order. *Issues in Science and Technology*, *35*(4), 29–36.

Clarke, R. (1994). Asimov's Laws of Robotics: Implications For Information Technology. *Computer*, *2*(1), 57–58. DOI: 10.1109/2.248881

Clarke, R. (1994). Asimov's Laws of Robotics: Implications for Information Technology. *Computer*, *2*(1), 57–61. DOI: 10.1109/2.248881

Fagundes, D. (2001). What We Talk About When We Talk About Persons: The Language of A Legal Fiction. *Harvard Law Review*, *114*(6), 1745–1768. DOI: 10.2307/1342652

Fitzgerald, D. (2019). Corporate personhood and the extension of legal status to artificial intelligence. *The Journal of Law and Technology*, *22*(4), 45–63.

Garrie, D. (2020). The Legal Implications of Autonomous Vehicle Accidents: Liability and Litigation Challenges. *Journal of Technology Law & Policy*, *25*(2), 47–63.

Gless, S., Silverman, E., & Weigend, T. (2016). If robots cause harm, who is to blame? Self-driving cars and criminal liability. *New Criminal Law Review*, *19*(3), 412–417. DOI: 10.1525/nclr.2016.19.3.412

Halley, G. (2010). The criminal liability of artificial intelligence entities: From science fiction to legal ordering control. *Akron Intellectual Property Journal*, *4*(2), 177–200.

Hohfeld, W. (1913). Some Fundamental Legal Conceptions as Applied in Judicial Reasoning. *The Yale Law Journal*, *23*(1), 16–59. DOI: 10.2307/785533

Hohfeld, W. N. (1913). Some Fundamental Legal Conceptions as Applied in Judicial Reasoning. *The Yale Law Journal, 23*(1), 16–59. DOI: 10.2307/785533

Holland, T. E. (1917). *The elements of jurisprudence* (12th ed.). Oxford University Press.

Horwitz, M. J. (1985). Santa Clara Revisited: The Development of Corporate Theory. *West Virginia Law Review, 88*(2), 173–224.

Jens, K. (2017). Who Needs Rights of Nature? *RCC Perspectives, 6*, 9, 12–13.

Johnson, D. G. (2020). Artificial intelligence and the concept of agency: Comparing corporate and machine agency. *Ethics and Information Technology, 22*(1), 9–20.

Kuner, C., Cate, F. H., Millard, C., & Svantesson, D. J. (2017). Transatlantic data privacy relations: The EU–US privacy shield and the future of global data privacy. *International Data Privacy Law, 7*(1), 1–13. DOI: 10.1093/idpl/ipx003

Lin, P. (2016). Why Ethics Matters for Autonomous Cars. In Dancy, C. L., & Miller, C. K. (Eds.), *Ethical Issues in Modern Society* (pp. 231–248).

Murphy, R. R., & Woods, D. D. (2009). Beyond Asimov: The Three Laws of Responsible Robotics. *IEEE Intelligent Systems, 24*(4), 14–20. DOI: 10.1109/MIS.2009.69

Pound, R. (1915). Legal Rights. *International Journal of Ethics, 26*(1), 92–95. DOI: 10.1086/intejethi.26.1.2376739

Ryan, M., & Stahl, B. C. (2020). Artificial Intelligence Ethics Guidelines for Autonomous Vehicles: A Case Study of Responsibility and Safety. *Ethics and Information Technology, 22*(4), 325–335.

Solum, L. B. (1992). Legal personhood for artificial intelligences. *North Carolina Law Review, 70*(4), 1231–1287.

Starr, W. C. (1984). Law and Morality in H. L. A. Hart's Legal Philosophy. *Marquette Law Review, 67*(4), 773–777.

Tretyakova, E. (2021). AI and the Legal Status of Autonomous Systems: A Conceptual Framework. *Moscow Law Review, 42*(3), 55–78.

Tretyakova, E. (2021). AI and the Legal Status of Autonomous Systems: A Conceptual Framework. *Moscow Law Review, 42*(3), 55–78.

Veale, M., & Van Hoboken, J. (2020). The European Union's Proposed Artificial Intelligence Act: Implications for Fundamental Rights And AI Ethics. *European Law Review, 45*(4), 591–608.

Wishart, D. (2016). Puzzling out law's person. *Indiana Journal of Global Legal Studies, 23*(2), 743–744. DOI: 10.2979/indjglolegstu.23.2.0743

Zohar, O., & Rosenblat, A. (2020). Regulatory Sandboxes and the Future Of AI Governance: Balancing Innovation And Regulation. *Journal of Technology and Law, 12*(2), 189–210.

ENDNOTES

1 Tretyakova, E. (2021). AI and the Legal Status of Autonomous Systems: A Conceptual Framework. *Moscow Law Review,* 42(3), 55–78. It explores the evolving legal landscape surrounding artificial intelligence (AI) and autonomous systems. The paper presents a conceptual framework for understanding the legal status of these technologies and discusses the implications of recognizing them as legal entities. doi: 10.53361/dmejl.v4i01.03

2 Hárs, M. (2022). AI Accountability Without Legal Personhood: A Middle-Ground Approach. *European Journal of Law and Technology,* 13(4), 112–136. Hárs argues that granting legal personhood to AI systems could lead to significant complications, including issues of liability and ethical concerns. Instead, she advocates for a middle-ground approach that allows for accountability without needing full legal recognition of AI as persons. https://ejlt.org/index.php/ejlt/article/view/752

3 Austin, J. (1832). *The Province of Jurisprudence Determined* explores foundational legal principles and is available via Project Gutenberg at https://www.gutenberg.org/ebooks/13242. Austin argues that laws are commands issued by a sovereign authority and must be obeyed, regardless of their moral implications. He defines a sovereign as a person or group that has the ultimate authority to create laws within a given society. Austin distinguishes between legal obligations and moral obligations, asserting that the validity of law does not depend on its ethical content.

4 Blumberg, P. I. (1987). *The law of corporate groups: Property, contract, and insolvency*. The University of Chicago Press. The book examines the nature of corporate groups, including parent and subsidiary relationships, and how these structures impact legal responsibilities and rights. Blumberg discusses the implications of property ownership within corporate groups, focusing on how assets are managed and controlled across different entities. https://digitalcommons.law.wne.edu/books/7/

5 Austin, J. (1832). *The Province of Jurisprudence Determined*. London: John Murray. John Austin's perspective on legal personhood asserts that it is fundamentally a construct of legal recognition rather than an intrinsic quality of individuals. He argues that legal rights and duties are conferred by the law, which means that personhood is contingent upon societal acknowledgement within a given legal framework. https://www.britannica.com/topic/The-Province-of-Jurisprudence-Determined

6 Horwitz, M. J. (1985). *Santa Clara Revisited: The Development of Corporate Theory. West Virginia Law Review, 88*(2), 173-224. Horwitz critically examines the implications of the Supreme Court's decision in *Santa Clara County v. Southern Pacific Railroad* (1886) regarding corporate personhood. Horwitz argues that the case has been misinterpreted as a landmark moment in establishing corporations as legal persons with rights under the Fourteenth Amendment. He contends that the Court was still wary of corporate power at the time and that the legal theory adopted was not as progressive as later interpretations suggest. Instead, he posits that the Court's approach reflected a cautious stance towards corporate entities, viewing them more as instruments of their shareholders rather than independent legal persons entitled to rights akin to those of natural individuals. https://researchrepository.wvu.edu/cgi/viewcontent.cgi?article=2274&context=wvlr

7 Johnson, D. G. (2020). Artificial Intelligence and the Concept of Agency: Comparing Corporate and Machine Agency. *Ethics and Information Technology, 22*(1), 9-20. https://doi.org/10.1007/s10676-019-09519-2

8 Hovenkamp, H. (2007). *The Antitrust Enterprise: Principle and Execution*. Harvard University Press. Hovenkamp argues that antitrust law should focus on promoting consumer welfare rather than merely punishing anti-competitive behavior. He critiques overly broad applications of "per se" rules that automatically condemn certain practices without considering their actual effects on competition. See https://www.hup.harvard.edu/books/9780674027411

9 Fitzgerald, D. (2019). Corporate Personhood and The Extension of Legal Status to Artificial Intelligence. *Journal of Law and Technology, 22*(4), 45-63. Fitzgerald argues that as AI systems become more autonomous and capable of making decisions, there is a growing need to consider them for legal personhood. This status would allow AI entities to hold rights and responsibilities similar to corporations, which have been recognized as legal persons. https://revistes.ub.edu/index.php/RBD/article/view/27064

10 Mackenzie, C., & Stoljar, N. (Eds.). (2000). *Relational Autonomy: Feminist Perspectives on Autonomy, Agency, and the Social Self.* Oxford University Press. The authors propose that autonomy should not be viewed as merely a capacity for self-governance but rather as a relational concept that recognizes the importance of social relationships and interdependence in shaping individual agency. https://philpapers.org/rec/MACRAF

11 For instance, personhood could be given to AI systems that manage financial or transportation networks, to establish proper governance frameworks and make accountability clear. Comparably, to create a framework for accountability and redress and guarantee that the system's decisions are subject to judicial review or monitoring, an AI judge deciding small claims may require legal recognition. See for details Solum, L. B. (1992). Legal Personhood for Artificial Intelligences. *North Carolina Law Review, 70*(4), 1231-1287. Solum discusses the concept of legal personhood, which traditionally applies to human beings and certain entities like corporations. He examines the criteria that might be used to determine whether AIs could qualify as legal persons. https://scholarship.law.unc.edu/nclr/vol70/iss4/4/. See also Pagallo explores how existing legal systems can adapt to address the unique challenges posed by autonomous systems. He discusses the implications of robot actions in terms of criminal liability and civil responsibility. Pagallo, U. (2018). *The Laws of Robots: Crimes, Contracts, And Torts.* Springer. https://doi.org/10.1007/978-94-007-7745-0

12 Bryson, J. J., Diamantis, M. E., & Grant, T. D. (2017). Of, For, And By The People: The Legal Lacuna of Synthetic Persons. *Artificial Intelligence and Law, 25*(3), 273-291. https://doi.org/10.1007/s10506-017-9214-9

13 See for example as observed by Wishart *that human beings are the subjects of law is seldom challenged.* Wishart, D. (2016). Puzzling Out Law's Person. *Indiana Journal of Global Legal Studies, 23*(2), 743–744. https://www.jstor.org/stable/pdf/10.2979/indjglolegstu.23.2.0743.pdf?refreqid=fastly-default%3A9dd8cef2c45032ec95fdcc44e9292225&ab_segments=0%2Fbasic_search_gsv2%2Fcontrol&initiator=search-results&acceptTC=1 (15 Nov 2024)

14 See for example Courts have not been able to distinguish cleanly between [natural and legal persons], and alternatively treating the issue of personhood as a common-sense determination of what a human or as a formal legal fiction unrelated to biological conceptions of humanity. Fagundes, D. (2001). What We Talk About When We Talk About Persons: The Language of Legal Fiction https://www.jstor.org/stable/pdf/1342652.pdf?refreqid=fastly-default%3A92fc276fc4789d3b181a7c9855f648c1&ab_segments=0%2Fbasic_search_gsv2

%2Fcontrol&initiator=search-results&acceptTC=1 (14th Nov. 2024). See also Hoffman, D. N. (1986). Personhood and Rights. *Polity, 19*(1), 74. https://www.jstor.org/stable/pdf/3234860.pdf?refreqid=fastly-default%3A92fc276fc4789d3b181a7c9855f648c1&ab_segments=0%2Fbasic_search_gsv2%2Fcontrol&initiator=search-results&acceptTC=1 (14 Nov 2024). Hoffman at the beginning of the paper observes that engaging on the question of personhood is often fraught with moral and existential difficulty. See also Wishart, D. (2016). Puzzling Out Law's Person. *Indiana Journal of Global Legal Studies, 23*(2), 743–744. https://www.jstor.org/stable/pdf/10.2979/indjglolegstu.23.2.0743.pdf?refreqid=fastly-default%3A9dd8cef2c45032ec95fdcc44e9292225&ab_segments=0%2Fbasic_search_gsv2%2Fcontrol&initiator=search-results&acceptTC=1 (15 Nov 2024). Wishart has argued that the concept of legal person is problematic both as a subject and object of law.

15 Supra *note* 5. For contra see Arguing that 'rights' are inherently tied to personhood, which is why assigning them to nonperson entities seems unusual.

16 See for example personhood attributed to rivers and mountains by courts. Also, it is relevant to refer to Article 71 of the Constitution of Ecuador which recognizes *nature* as a legal person, with subject rights that can be enforced. Quoted in Jens, K. (2017). Who Needs Rights of Nature? *RCC Perspectives, 6*, 9, 12–13. https://www.jstor.org/stable/pdf/26268370.pdf?refreqid=fastly-default%3A92fc276fc4789d3b181a7c9855f648c1&ab_segments=0%2Fbasic_search_gsv2%2Fcontrol&initiator=search-results&acceptTC=1 (14 Nov. 2024)

17 In this context, it is relevant to refer the observation by Wishart that: If the subject of law is determined by law, as indeed any argument for the supremacy of law must concede, there is no technical difficulty in law intervening in the nature of human beings. It does so when defining what a legal person is, and in regulating its inception or even conception. Having defined the legal person, it may accept or adapt the definition for various purposes. Wishart, D. (2016). PUZZLING OUT LAW'S PERSON. *Indiana Journal of Global Legal Studies, 23*(2), 743, 747–748. https://www.jstor.org/stable/pdf/10.2979/indjglolegstu.23.2.0743.pdf?refreqid=fastly-default%3A9dd8cef2c45032ec95fdcc44e9292225&ab_segments=0%2Fbasic_search_gsv2%2Fcontrol&initiator=search-results&acceptTC=1 (15 Nov 2024).

18 See for example John Grey who argues that technically the term person is a subject of legal rights and duties. Grey, J. C. (1921). *The Nature and Source of the Law* (p. 27). HeinOnline. http://www.sci.brooklyn.cuny.edu/~schopra/Persons/Gray.pdf (15 Nov 2024)

19 See for example Hohfeld's four different legal positions and their correlations under the term 'right'.

20 See for example Solum, L. B. (1992). Legal Personhood for Artificial Intelligence. *North Carolina Law Review, 70*, 1231. https://scholarship.law.unc.edu/cgi/viewcontent.cgi?article=3447&context=nclr (14th Nov 2024)

21 In this context for example, it may be relevant to not that it is only through policy adopted by state that a someone even being a natural person, still may not enjoy the rights like other fellow beings. It is simply because law choses so. Eg Minor cannot vote, cannot execute contract etc.

22 See also Halley, G. (2010). The Criminal Liability of Artificial Intelligence Entities: From Science Fiction to Legal Ordering Control. *Akron Intellectual Property Journal, 4*(2), 177–200. https://ideaexchange.uakron.edu/cgi/viewcontent.cgi?article=1037&context=akronintellectualproperty (14 Nov. 2024) (proposing three models of AI entity criminal liability)

23 See for details Fagundes, D. (2001). What We Talk About When We Talk About Persons: The Language of A Legal Fiction https://www.jstor.org/stable/pdf/1342652.pdf?refreqid=fastly-default%3A92fc276fc4789d3b181a7c9855f648c1&ab_segments=0%2Fbasic_search_gsv2%2Fcontrol&initiator=search-results&acceptTC=1 (14th Nov. 2024)

24 See in the context of *Amy v. United States*, 167 U.S. 304 (1897).

25 See for example as identified by Daniel Hoffman that personhood claims in certain cases raises complex questions about who is entitled to rights and protections, and further argues that such debate centres on defining personhood. Hoffman, D. N. (1986). Personhood and Rights. *Polity, 19*(1), 74–96. https://www.jstor.org/stable/pdf/3234860.pdf?refreqid=fastly-default%3A92fc276fc4789d3b181a7c9855f648c1&ab_segments=0%2Fbasic_search_gsv2%2Fcontrol&initiator=search-results&acceptTC=1 (14 Nov 2024)

26 https://www.jstor.org/stable/pdf/j.ctvhrd092.24.pdf?refreqid=fastly-default%3A92fc276fc4789d3b181a7c9855f648c1&ab_segments=0%2Fbasic_search_gsv2%2Fcontrol&initiator=search-results&acceptTC=1 (14 Nov 2024)

27 See for details Fagundes, D. (2001). *What We Talk About When We Talk About Persons: The Language of A Legal Fiction*. (2001). *Harvard Law Review, 114*, 1746.https://www.jstor.org/stable/pdf/1097561.pdf?refreqid=fastly-default%3A9dd8cef2c45032ec95fdcc44e9292225&ab_segments=0%2Fbasic_search_gsv2%2Fcontrol&initiator=search-results&acceptTC=1 (15 Nov 2024). Naffine, N. (2003). Who Are Law's Persons? From Cheshire Cats To Responsible

Subjects. *The Modern Law Review, 66*(3), 364. Naffine has observed that *the law of 'persons' comprises an often-puzzling jurisprudence, marked by its uncertainty and its inconsistency.*

28 See for example the author argues that personhood is a complex concept, consisting of components like biological status, rational agents, and unity of consciousness, rather than a singular, fixed idea. Ohlin, J. D. (2005). Is the Concept of the Person Necessary for Human Rights? *Columbia Law Review, 105*(1), 209–249. https://www.jstor.org/stable/pdf/4099308.pdf?refreqid=fastly-default%3A92fc276fc4789d3b181a7c9855f648c1&ab_segments=0%2Fbasic_search_gsv2%2Fcontrol&initiator=search-results&acceptTC=1 (14 Nov 2024)

29 Capacity, identified and conferred by law, is the ability to affect another by its exercise. In other words, it refers to the right-duty correlation and their legal implications. See for example Holland defines 'legal right' as a capacity residing in one man of controlling, with the assent and assistance of the State, the actions of others. See Holland, T. E. (1917). *The Elements of Jurisprudence* (12th ed., p. 82). Oxford University Press. https://upload.wikimedia.org/wikipedia/commons/a/a2/The_elements_of_jurisprudence_%28IA_elementsofjurisp00holl%29.pdf (15 Nov 2024) In this context it may be also relevant to refer Hegel who defines personality as the subjective possibility of a legal will. This implies, according to Hegel, that person has the capacity to act within the legal system, make decisions, and of holding rights and responsibilities. Also, for Zitelmann, personality is the legal capacity of will.

30 See for example according to the 'ability-paradigm' identified by Lewiecki-Wilson, personhood for Locke and Singer is defined by certain capacities such as self-awareness and future planning. Johnson, J. (2012). Disability, Animals, and the Rhetorical Boundaries of Personhood. *JAC, 32*(1/2), 372–375. https://www.jstor.org/stable/pdf/41709689.pdf?refreqid=fastly-default%3A92fc276fc4789d3b181a7c9855f648c1&ab_segments=0%2Fbasic_search_gsv2%2Fcontrol&initiator=search-results&acceptTC=1 (14 Nov 2024)

31 See for example as observed by Pollock that *not every human being is necessarily a person, for a person is capable of rights and duties, and there may well be human beings having no legal rights, as was the case with slaves in ancient law.* Pollock, F. (1918). *A First Book of Jurisprudence* (4th ed., pp. 113–114). Macmillan & Co. https://ia800907.us.archive.org/25/items/firstbookofjuris00poll/firstbookofjuris00poll.pdf (15 Nov 2024)

32 See for example as observed by John Dewey, adding to controversies, that *there is no general agreement regarding the nature in se of the jural subjects; courts and legislators do their work without such agreement, sometimes without any conception or theory at all regarding its nature.* Dewey, J. *(1926).* The Historic Background of Corporate Legal Personality. *Yale Law Journal, 35, 655–660.*https://openyls.law.yale.edu/bitstream/handle/20.500.13051/11955/52_35YaleLJ655_1925_1926_.pdf?sequence=2&isAllowed=y (15 Nov 2024)

33 Locke, J. (1964). *Essay Concerning Human Understanding* (2nd ed., ch. 27). In J. Perry (Ed.), *Personal Identity* (pp. 39). University of California Press. (Original work published 1964). Boeker, R. (2021). *Locke On Persons and Personal Identity* (pp. 1-5). Oxford University Press. https://philarchive.org/archive/BOELOP-3 (14 Nov 2024)

34 Gless, S., et al. (2016). If robots cause harm, who is to blame? Self-driving cars and criminal liability. *New Criminal Law Review: An International and Interdisciplinary Journal, 19*(3), 412–417. https://www.jstor.org/stable/pdf/26417695.pdf?refreqid=fastly-default%3A4d42a1dfbecb40e3c589b4fd8e0c1795&ab_segments=0%2Fbasic_search_gsv2%2Fcontrol&initiator=search-results&acceptTC=1 (14 Nov 2024)

35 For contra see McHugh, J. T. (1992). What Is the Difference Between A "Person" And A "Human Being" Within The Law? *The Review of Politics, 54*(3), 445. https://www.jstor.org/stable/pdf/1407800.pdf?refreqid=fastly-default%3A9dd8cef2c45032ec95fdcc44e9292225&ab_segments=0%2Fbasic_search_gsv2%2Fcontrol&initiator=search-results&acceptTC=1 (15 Nov. 2024) According to James, *some jurists seem to find no significance between [person and human beings], while others suggest that the difference lies solely within the areas of scope and standing.* (The paper has attempted to make a distinction between a person and a human being in the light of rights and liberties matrix)

36 In this context, it may be relevant to refer John Dewey who argues that a legal subject defined by the specific consequences of bearing rights and duties, and the distinction between legal subjects and non-subjects lies in the legal consequences they generate. Dewey, J. (1926). The Historic Background of Corporate Legal Personality. *Yale Law Journal, 35*, 655–662. https://openyls.law.yale.edu/bitstream/handle/20.500.13051/11955/52_35YaleLJ655_1925_1926_.pdf?sequence=2&isAllowed=y (15 Nov 2024). Thus, it can be argued that a legal person if it is assigned specific rights and duties by law, can generate legal consequences similar to those of human legal subjects. See also Smith, B. (1928). Legal Person. *Yale Law Journal, 37*(3), 283. https://openyls.law.yale.edu/bitstream/handle/20.500.13051/12065/23_37YaleLJ283

_1927_1928_.pdf (15 Nov 2024). Smith argues that *to be a legal person is to be the subject of rights and duties. To confer legal rights or to impose legal duties, therefore, is to confer legal personality.* It is pertinent to note that it is through law, rights and duties are attributed and conferred. Thus, it is argued that likewise, AI can be attributed with rights and duties, though limited, and create legal implications thereof. See also Grey, J. C. (1921). *The Nature and Source of the Law* (p. 27). HeinOnline. http://www.sci.brooklyn.cuny.edu/~schopra/Persons/Gray.pdf (15 Nov 2024). Defining legal person as a subject matter of right-duty correlation. See also Pollock, F. (1918). *A First Book of Jurisprudence* (4th ed., p. 114). Macmillan & Co. https://ia800907.us.archive.org/25/items/firstbookofjuris00poll/firstbookofjuris00poll.pdf (15 Nov 2024). According to Pollock, *a person is such, not because he is human, but because rights and duties are ascribed to him. The person is the legal subject or substance of which rights and duties ate attributed.*

37 According to Kukri defining legal personhood from a right-duty perspective is an orthodox view and is formal or thin understanding of it as opposed to a substantive of thick view. See Kukri, A. Legal personhood in elements in the legal philosophy. In G. Pavlakos et al. (Eds.), *Legal Philosophy* (pp. 6–7). https://www.cambridge.org/core/services/aop-cambridge-core/content/view/EB28AB0B045936DBDAA1DF2D20E923A0/9781009462235AR.pdf/legal-personhood.pdf (14 Nov 2024) (Cambridge University Press, 2023)

38 Salmond, J. W. (1902). *Jurisprudence*. 12th ed., Stevens & Sons.

39 Kelly, P. (2015). *Law in A Law-Governed Union (Recht in einer Rechtsunion): The Court of Justice of the European Union and the Free Law Doctrine* (p. 29). https://core.ac.uk/download/pdf/333900625.pdf (14 Nov 2024)

40 Kelsen, H. (1945). *General Theory of Law and State*. Harvard University Press.

41 Hart, H. L. A. (1961). *The Concept of Law*. Oxford University Press.

42 The main theme of the book, according to Hart, that the union of primary and secondary rules are *the essence of law, though they may not always be found together whenever the word "law" is correctly used.* Hart, H. L. A. (1961). *The Concept of Law* (p. 151). Clarendon Press.

43 Starr, W. C. (1984). Law and Morality in H. L. A. Hart's Legal Philosophy. *Marquette Law Review, 67*(4), 773–777. https://scholarship.law.marquette.edu/cgi/viewcontent.cgi?article=1941&context=mulr (16 Nov 2024). See also Hart, H. L. A. (1974). H. L. A. Hart on legal and moral obligation. *Michigan Law Review, 73*(2), 443–446. https://www.jstor.org/stable/pdf/1287782.pdf?refreqid

=fastly-default%3A042ef76f978a9e92f19e0b492a0fa53e&ab_segments=0 %2Fbasic_search_gsv2%2Fcontrol&initiator=search-results&acceptTC=1 (16 Nov 2024)

44 Hart, H. L. A. (1961). *The Concept of Law* (pp. 78–94). Clarendon Press.

45 See for details, Pound, R. (1959). *Jurisprudence* (pp. 189–407). West Publishing Co. https://archive.org/details/in.ernet.dli.2015.74450/page/n221/mode/2up ?view=theater&q=person (16 Nov 2024). Pound at the beginning of "persons" argues that legal entities are recognized by law as right, power and duty holders, securing interests on their behalf. These "legal units" function within the legal order, asserting rights for economic or social purposes. It is argued that AI as "legal unit" could potentially be recognized as a right, power and duty holders for social purposes, or social ordering. See also Pound, R. (1911). *An Introduction to the Philosophy of Law*. Yale University Press.

46 Pound, R. (1915). Legal Rights. *International Journal of Ethics, 26*(1), 92–95. https://www.jstor.org/stable/pdf/2376739.pdf?refreqid=fastly-default%3A74 b84c19d3a4d2af86f2952b51a84003&ab_segments=0%2Fbasic_search_gsv2 %2Fcontrol&initiator=search-results&acceptTC=1 (16 Nov 2024)

47 Savigny, K. F. (1840). *System of the Modern Roman Law*.

48 Kurki, A. J. (2019). *A Theory of Legal Personhood* (p. 22). Oxford University Press.

49 For contra see Ihering, who once called fictions the "white lies" of the law. Ihering III, 305 See also William Blackstone, Commentaries of the laws of England Blackstone, though referred fictions as being "highly beneficial and useful", he criticises the awkward method used to achieve them. He quotes: To such award shifts, such subtile refinements, and such strange reasoning, were our ancestors obliged to have recourse while we many applaud the end, we cannot admire the means See also Zander, L. (2022). Legal fiction. In T. Gutmann et al. (Eds.), *Encyclopaedia of Law and Literature*https://lawandliterature .eu/images/pdf/LegalFictions.pdf (16 Nov 2024). The authors argue *that the analysis of legal fiction is largely problematic because of the ambiguity of the term.*

50 Fuller, L. L. (1967). *Legal Fiction* (pp. 5, 9). Stanford University Press. https:// constitutionwatch.com.au/wp-content/uploads/Lon-L-Fuller-Legal-Fictions .pdf (16 Nov 2024). See also Campbell, K. (1983). Fuller On Legal Fiction. *Law and Philosophy, 2*(3), 339–370. https://www.jstor.org/stable/pdf/3504564 .pdf?refreqid=fastly-default%3A016ca6f3e3091787db255fe02b6ba877&ab

_segments=0%2Fbasic_search_gsv2%2Fcontrol&initiator=search-results&acceptTC=1 (16 Nov 2024)

51 Ng Boyte, A. (2014). The Concept Of Our Legal Imagination: Legal Fictions and the Concept of Deemed Authorship. *Legislation and Public Policy, 17*, 708, 712. https://nyujlpp.org/wp-content/uploads/2014/11/Ng-Boyte-The-Conceits-of-Our-Legal-Imagination-17nyujlpp707.pdf (16 Nov 2024)

52 See for example the author argues that *the quest to codify rights of humans as against smart machinery dates at least as far as Isaac Avimov's three laws for robots in 1942*. Evans, B. J. (2023). Rules for Robots, and Why Medical AI Breaks Them. *Journal of Law and the Biosciences, 10*(1). https://academic.oup.com/jlb/article/10/1/lsad001/7042583 (17 Nov 2024). See also Gutierrez, C. I., & Marchant, G. E. (2021, May 28). A Global Perspective on Soft Law Programs for The Governance Of Artificial Intelligence. available at https://ssrn.com/abstract=3855171 (Accessed Jan. 22, 2023). The authors have identified around 634 soft law initiatives aimed at establishing guidelines to safeguard human intersts in the age of AI.

53 AI has moved from just a science fiction to everyday life – driving cars, influencing ads, screening jobs applicants, diagnosing diseases, and what not. Evans, B. J. (2023). Rules for Robots, and Why Medical AI Breaks Them. *Journal of Law and the Biosciences, 10*(1). https://academic.oup.com/jlb/article/10/1/lsad001/7042583 (17 Nov 2024). See also Pasquale, F. (2020). *New Laws Of Robotics: Defending Human Expertise in the Age of AI* Belknap Press of Harvard University Press. (discussing various applications of AI); Christopher Slobogin, Just Algorithms: Using Science to Reduce Incarceration and Inform a Jurisprudence of Risk (2021) (arguing that properly regulated risk-assessment tools can advance reform in the criminal justice system). See also Gorgoni, G. (2020). Stay Human: The Quest for Responsibility in the Algorithmic Society. *Journal of Ethics and Legal Technology, 2*(1), 31–32. https://jelt.padovauniversitypress.it/system/files/papers/JELT-02-01-02_4.pdf (22 Nov 2024) The societal issues posed by machine-learning are discussed since decades, but the contemporary development of automated decision making represents a major societal concern… in particular as regards the ethical, legal economic and widely societal implications of AI.

54 On the contrary it reminds me of the 'Planet of Apes' a science fiction series about a post-apocalyptic world in which humans and intelligent apes clash for control as the dominant species. Or a more relevant in this context is a 'Terminator' series about the war between humans and Skynet, a self-aware artificial intelligence that seeks to destroy humanity.

55 These three laws have been very influential, and even today people imagine what it would be like--or whether it would even be possible-to build them into robots, including, for example, into self-driving cars. Balkin, J. M. (2017). The Three Laws of Robotics in the Age of Big Data. *Ohio State Law Journal, 78*(5), 1217–1218. https://openyls.law.yale.edu/bitstream/handle/20.500.13051/4697/78_Ohio_St._L.J._1217__2017_.pdf?sequence=2&isAllowed=y (17 Nov 2024) (In this paper, the author has proposed three new laws of robotics for Algorithmic Society, indicating that law so proposed will not be limited to robots, but will apply to AI agents, algorithms, including machine learning algorithms). To me it is an unfair criticism stating that Asimov's Three Laws were applicable to robots only. It seems Balkin has completely missed the time count involved in the criticism. It must not be forgotten that Three Law were proposed in 1940's and the new laws were proposed by Balkin in 2027. What happened in-between and how much technology evolved needs no explanation. Had AI prevalent then in 1940, The Three Law would have been applied to it. Balkin's criticism of Asimov's Three Laws of Robotics for being applicable only to robots is based on a misunderstanding of historical context and technological progression. Asimov proposed his laws in the 1940s, a time when AI and machine learning were not even conceptualized. Given this, it's unreasonable to judge the applicability of his laws by today's standards, where AI and complex algorithms are pervasive. If AI had been a prominent technology in the 1940s, Asimov would almost certainly have adapted his laws to include considerations for AI agents and algorithms. The fact that he didn't address AI specifically in the original Three Laws is simply a result of the technological limitations of his time, not a flaw in the framework itself.

56 Science-fiction writer Isaac Asimov introduced the three laws of robotics in his 1942 short story "Runaround."

57 Asimov, I. (1950). Runaround. In *I, Robot* (P. 37). Gnome Press. (republishing a story first appearing in the Mar. 1942 issue of the periodical ASTOUNDING SCIENCE FICTION).

58 See for example Clarke, R. (1994). Asimov's Laws of Robotics: Implications For Information Technology. *Computing Milieux, 2*, 57–58. https://cse.buffalo.edu/~rapaport/Papers/Papers.by.Others/clarke-asimov-2.pdf (22 Nov 2024). Clarke argues that *Asimov detected a need to extend the first law, which protected individual humans, so that it would protect humanity as a whole. Thus, his calculating machines "have the good of humanity at heart through the overwhelming force of the First Law of Robotics".*

59 Asimov, I. (1942). Runaround. In *I, Robot* (pp. 57-82). Gnome Press. This story explores the challenges posed by robotic adherence to ethical guidelines through the interactions between humans and robots, highlighting the complexities involved in programming morality into artificial intelligence. https://www.scirp.org/reference/referencespapers?referenceid=2451455

60 The report discusses the potential need for a specific legal status for robots, particularly autonomous ones, to clarify liability and accountability issues. It emphasizes the importance of defining liability in cases where robots cause harm or damage, suggesting that manufacturers and operators should bear responsibility. European Parliament. (2017). *Report with recommendations to the Commission on Civil Law Rules on Robotics (2015/2103(INL))*. European Parliament. Retrieved from https://www.europarl.europa.eu on 21st November 2024.

61 See for example Clarke, R. (1994). Asimov's Laws of Robotics: Implications for Information Technology. *Computing Milieux, 2*, 57–61. https://cse.buffalo.edu/~rapaport/Papers/Papers.by.Others/clarke-asimov-2.pdf (22 Nov 2024)

62 Supra note, 55. Balkin calls them the legal principles of Algorithmic Society and are principles of fair governance.

63 According to Frank, *each of these laws will have important implications for the future of legal regulation of technology*. Pasquale, F. A. (2017). Towards A Fourth Law of Robotics: Preserving Attribution, Responsibility, and Explainability in an Algorithmic Society. *Ohio State Law Journal, 78*(5), 1243–1244. https://digitalcommons.law.umaryland.edu/cgi/viewcontent.cgi?article=2608&context=fac_pubs (22 Nov 2024)

64 Wesley Newcomb Hohfeld is known for his influential essays on "Fundamental Legal Conception," where he introduced a framework of eight interrelated normative positions, considered the most basic legal concepts. Hohfeld, W. N. (1913). Some Fundamental Legal Conceptions as Applied in Judicial Reasoning. *Yale Law Journal, 23*, 16–59. https://www.jstor.org/stable/pdf/785533.pdf?refreqid=fastly-default%3A141b3f4cce702748c31e73c2977822c8&ab_segments=0%2FSYC-6646_basic_search%2Fcontrol&origin=search-results accessed 19 Nov 2023. Hohfeld's framework emphasis that legal rights require corresponding duties. For an individual to exercise rights, they must possess legal personality, which the law confers to recognize their capacity to hold rights and obligations. Thus, it can be said that conferring duties and rights to AI, is attributing legal personhood to AI.

65 See Luis Duarte d'Almeida, who has analysed Hohfeld's framework, its comprehensiveness, and key argumentative uses. Luis Duarte d'Almeida, (2023) Hohfeld, Wesley Newcomb: Fundamental Legal Conceptions. In Seller M Kirste (eds) Encyclopaedia of the Philosophy of Law and Social Philosophy (Springer) p 1131- 1351

66 Hohfeld argues that understanding jural relations is essential for assigning rights and duties effectively. The principle of legal personhood has evolved significantly over time. This evolution reflects changing societal values regarding rights and responsibilities. See Hohfeld, W. (1913). Some Fundamental Legal Conceptions as Applied in Judicial Reasoning. *Yale Law Journal*, 23(1), 16–59. https://www.jstor.org/stable/pdf/785533.pdf?refreqid=fastly-default%3A141b3f4cce702748c31e73c2977822c8&ab_segments=0%2FSYC-6646_basic_search%2Fcontrol&origin=search-results accessed 19 Nov 2023.

67 Lin, P. (2016). *Why Ethics Matters for Autonomous Cars*. In C. L. Dancy & C. K. Miller (Eds.), *Ethical Issues in Modern Society* (pp. 231-248). Wiley-Blackwell. Lin emphasizes that public trust in autonomous vehicles is contingent upon transparency in how these vehicles make ethical decisions. Understanding the algorithms and ethical guidelines that govern AV behavior is crucial for fostering acceptance among users and society at large. https://www.researchgate.net/publication/303480862_Why_Ethics_Matters_for_Autonomous_Cars

68 See for details Cullison, A. D. (1967). A Review of Hohfeld's Fundamental Legal Concepts. *Cleveland-Marshall Law Review, 16*, 559. https://engagedscholarship.csuohio.edu/cgi/viewcontent.cgi?article=2997&context=clevstlrev (24 Nov 2024)

69 Kurki Visa, (2023). *Legal Personhood* (1st ed.). Cambridge University Press. https://www.cambridge.org/core/services/aop-cambridge-core/content/view/EB28AB0B045936DBDAA1DF2D20E923A0/9781009462235AR.pdf/legal-personhood.pdf (24 Nov 2024)

70 Salmond, J. W., & Fitzgerald, R. J. (1966). *Salmond on Jurisprudence* (12th ed.). Sweet & Maxwell.

71 Kurki Visa, *Legal Personhood* 6 (1st ed.). (Cambridge University Press; 2023) https://www.cambridge.org/core/services/aop-cambridge-core/content/view/EB28AB0B045936DBDAA1DF2D20E923A0/9781009462235AR.pdf/legal-personhood.pdf (24 Nov 2024)

72 According to the author, Orthodox view is evaluated through Hohfeld's jural relations, it will challenge many commonly held beliefs about legal personhood. It is, however, argued that for the present paper, personhood is not only determined in the light of capacity to hold rights or duties, but from their legal implications derived from various attributes of the term 'right', as identified by Hohfeld. Thus, right and its denominators will be analysed to define legal personhood. For example, the presence of *power* in Mr. A implies the presence of *liability* in Mr. B (creating two corresponding's); and at the same time meant absence of *disability* in Mr A (creating opposites). Similarly, by applying other variables of jural relation to AI, it will be analysed whether we can deduce any legal personhood for AI.

73 It may be relevant to note that most of the scholars have asserted that what is 'created' is not 'fictitious'. See for example Machen, A. W. (1910). Corporate Personality. *Harvard Law Review, 24*, 253–257. < https://www.jstor.org/stable/pdf/1324056.pdf?refreqid=fastly-default%3A9bb9f05add7a5f3648a0469f3b12c917&ab_segments=0%2FSYC-6646_basic_search%2Fcontrol&origin=search-results> accessed 22 October 2023. Machen has argued that *which is artificial is real, and not imaginary." He further says that "a corporation cannot be at the same time 'created by the state' and fictitious.*

74 See for example Michoud, quoted by John Dewey, who states that *for legal science, the notion of person is and should remain a purely juridical notion. The word signifies simply a subject of rights-duties, [sujet de droit] a being capable of having the subjective rights properly belonging to him.* See John Dewey, The Historical Background of Corporate Legal Personality, 35 Yale Law Journal 655, 659 (1926). < https://www.jstor.org/stable/pdf/788782.pdf?refreqid=fastly-default%3Aca96a70c6d238077b53bdbd63ffcd038&ab_segments=0%2FSYC-6646_basic_search%2Fcontrol&origin=search-results> accessed 25 Oct. 2023

75 See for details Pramod Kumar Kushwaha, Nature as a Legal Person-Recent Judicial Development 148-154 https://ujala.uk.gov.in/files/17.pdf (24 Nov 2024). See also Arstein-Kerslake, A., et al. (2021). Relational Personhood: A Conception of Legal Personhood with Insights From Disability Rights and Environmental Law. *Griffith Law Review, 30*(3), 530–534. https://www.tandfonline.com/doi/epdf/10.1080/10383441.2021.2003744?needAccess=true (24 Nov 2024)

76 According to Richard, *there is no general law of persons, but rather, a series of rules concerning relationships and liabilities.* Richard Tur, The "Person" in A. Peacocke and G. Gillett (eds.), Persons and Personality: A Contemporary

Inquiry (Oxford: Basil Blackwell, 1987) 123. This highlight that legal personhood is not merely a biological or metaphysical fact but is influenced by the law's changing recognition of entities like corporations or AI as "person." it is argued that personhood in law is flexible and contingent on social values.

77 Fagundes, D. (2001). What We Talk About When We Talk About Persons: The Language of A Legal Fiction. *Harvard Law Review, 114*(6), 1745–1768. <https://www.jstor.org/stable/pdf/1342652.pdf?refreqid=fastly-default%3Af7a4576582365436fd294f4dfbdcf6b8&ab_segments=0%2FSYC-6646_basic_search%2Fcontrol&origin=search-results&acceptTC=1> accessed 20 October 2023

78 See for example the assertion made by Alexis who has stated that *one can have the attributes of legal personhood without being a human being, and one can be a human being without being a legal person.* Dyschkant, A. (2015). Legal personhood: How we are getting it wrong. *University of Illinois Law Review, 2015*(5), 2075–2078. <https://www.illinoislawreview.org/wp-content/ilr-content/articles/2015/5/Dyschkant.pdf > accessed 18 Nov. 2023

79 See for example Cassell, J. (2019). Artificial Intelligence for a Social Order. *Issues in Science and Technology, 35*(4), 29–36. https://www.jstor.org/stable/pdf/26949046.pdf?refreqid=fastly-default%3A7323b5bb1c9c2a2d715925cdb467dce0&ab_segments=0%2Fbasic_search_gsv2%2Fcontrol&initiator=search-results&acceptTC=1 (24 Nov 2024). On the question whether AI will end social interaction, the author concludes by advocating for AI that enhances social interaction by focusing on collaboration and teaching social skills, emphasizing the importance of natural social behaviour in fostering personal growth. This vision, by author, promotes AI as a tool for positive societal development rather than replacement. See also Jones, R. A. (2017). What Makes A Robot Social. *Social Studies of Science, 47*(4), 556–579. https://www.jstor.org/stable/pdf/44652522.pdf?refreqid=fastly-default%3A7323b5bb1c9c2a2d715925cdb467dce0&ab_segments=0%2Fbasic_search_gsv2%2Fcontrol&initiator=search-results&acceptTC=1 (24 Nov 2024). Social robotics, like RUBI, transforms interpersonal relationships into commodities, prompting human actions based on past experiences rather than the technology's inherent function. This raises questions about how robotized social spaces might alter human personhood and challenge traditional sociological views.

80 The concept of "information fiduciaries" in the context of algorithm users refers to the ethical and legal responsibility that those who design, manage, or operate algorithms (such as tech companies, developers, or service providers) have towards the individuals whose data and decisions are influenced by these

algorithms, and information fiduciaries, according to Balkin, has two central duties, - duty of care, and duty of loyalty. Balkin, supra note 55 at 1227-1228. Laws like the General Data Protection Regulation (GDPR), California Consumer Privacy Act (CCPA), and (Health Insurance Portability and Accountability Act (HIPAA) impose responsibilities on organizations to protect personal data and ensure transparency, security, and fairness in data use. The European Union Artificial Intelligence Act (EU AI Act) and Algorithmic Accountability Act push for accountability and ethical standards in AI and algorithmic decision-making.

81 The statement "Algorithm users must prevent the negative impacts of their actions, ensuring fairness and accountability in their decision-making processes" means that individuals or organizations who use algorithms (whether public or private) have a responsibility to make sure their algorithms do not cause harm, discrimination, or unfair outcomes.

82 European Commission. (2021). *Proposal for A Regulation of the European Parliament and of the Council on Artificial Intelligence (Artificial Intelligence Act)*. COM(2021) 206 final. Retrieved from https://ec.europa.eu The regulation categorizes AI systems into different risk levels—unacceptable risk, high risk, and low risk—each subject to varying degrees of regulatory scrutiny. Unacceptable risk AI systems are prohibited, while high-risk systems must comply with strict requirements.

83 Veale, M., & Van Hoboken, J. (2020). The European Union's Proposed Artificial Intelligence Act: Implications for Fundamental Rights And AI Ethics. *European Law Review, 45*(4), 591-608. https://doi.org/10.2139/ssrn.3577003 The authors discuss how the proposed regulation seeks to protect fundamental rights, such as privacy, non-discrimination, and freedom of expression, in the context of AI deployment. They emphasize the importance of ensuring that AI systems do not infringe upon these rights.

84 See Federal Trade Commission (FTC). (2016). *Big Data: A Tool for Inclusion or Exclusion? Understanding the Issues*. https://www.ftc.gov Also see, National Institute of Standards and Technology (NIST). (2021). *AI risk management framework: A primer for organizations*. Retrieved from https://www.nist.gov

85 Garrie, D. (2020). The Legal Implications of Autonomous Vehicle Accidents: Liability and Litigation Challenges. *Journal of Technology Law & Policy, 25*(2), 47-63. Garrie explores how traditional concepts of liability, which typically focus on driver negligence, must adapt to account for the unique circumstances surrounding AVs. He highlights that liability may fall on various

parties, including manufacturers, software developers, and even vehicle owners, depending on the specifics of each incident. https://academic.oup.com/ajcl/article/70/Supplement_1/i39/6655619

86 Abbott, R. (2020). *The Reasonable Robot: Artificial Intelligence and the Law*. Cambridge University Press. Abbott's central thesis is that the law should not discriminate between AI and human behaviour. He argues for a "reasonable robot" standard where AI systems are held to similar legal standards as humans, particularly in contexts like tort liability and criminal responsibility. This approach aims to create a level playing field between human workers and automated systems. https://artificialinventor.com/wp-content/uploads/2020/06/9781108472128_excerpt-1.pdf

87 Calo, R. (2017). Artificial Intelligence Policy: A Primer and Roadmap. *UCLA Law Review, 51*, 399-435. The article argues for the necessity of dedicated AI policy as distinct from broader ethical or governance discussions. Calo highlights that AI raises unique legal and societal questions that require focused attention. https://lawreview.sf.ucdavis.edu/sites/g/files/dgvnsk15026/files/media/documents/51-2_Calo.pdf

88 Murphy, R. R., & Woods, D. D. (2009). Beyond Asimov: The Three Laws of Responsible Robotics. *IEEE Intelligent Systems, 24*(4), 14-20. https://doi.org/10.1109/MIS.2009.69 The authors highlight the shortcomings of Asimov's laws, which focus primarily on preventing harm to humans and ensuring obedience to human commands. They argue that these laws do not account for the nuanced ethical dilemmas that arise in the deployment of robots in various contexts, such as healthcare, military, and disaster response.

89 International Telecommunication Union. (2020). *AI for Good: Global Summit Report*. International Telecommunication Union. Retrieved from https://www.itu.int

90 International Civil Aviation Organization. (2023). *ICAO's role in international aviation*. Retrieved from https://www.icao.int. ICAO develops and maintains the Standards and Recommended Practices (SARPs) that govern international civil aviation operations. These standards cover various aspects, including safety, security, efficiency, and environmental protection.

91 Floridi, L., Cowls, J., Beltrametti, M., Chatila, R., Chazerand, P., Dignum, V., ... & Schafer, B. (2018). *AI4People—An ethical framework for a good AI society: Opportunities, risks, principles, and recommendations. Minds and Machines, 28*(4), 689-707. https://doi.org/10.1007/s11023-018-9482-5

92 Ryan, M., & Stahl, B. C. (2020). Artificial Intelligence Ethics Guidelines for Autonomous Vehicles: A Case Study of Responsibility and Safety. *Ethics and Information Technology, 22*(4), 325-335. https://doi.org/10.1007/s10676-020-09547-z

93 Kuner, C., Cate, F. H., Millard, C., & Svantesson, D. J. (2017). *Transatlantic data privacy relations: The EU–US privacy shield and the future of global data privacy. International Data Privacy Law, 7*(1), 1-13. https://doi.org/10.1093/idpl/ipx001

94 Zohar, O., & Rosenblat, A. (2020). Regulatory Sandboxes and the Future Of AI Governance: Balancing Innovation And Regulation. *Journal of Technology and Law, 12*(2), 189-210. https://www.oecd.org/en/publications/regulatory-sandboxes-in-artificial-intelligence_8f80a0e6-en.html

Chapter 3
The Role of AI in the Global Governance:
AI in International Relations and Diplomacy

Mumtaz Alam
https://orcid.org/0000-0002-0945-2447
Fiji National University, Fiji

Kunal Avishek Gounder
https://orcid.org/0000-0003-2790-6307
Fiji National University, Fiji

Manorith Kumar
https://orcid.org/0009-0002-1667-4416
University of the South Pacific, Fiji

ABSTRACT

The relationship between diplomacy and artificial intelligence has become an ongoing debate in this age of unprecedented technological advancement. The proliferation of AI across many sectors is having a profound impact on diplomacy and international relations. This chapter examines how artificial intelligence has changed the standard operating procedure for diplomatic operations, improved decision-making, and changed the essence of international relationships. The chapter also sheds excellent detail on the possible drawbacks of AI in global politics.

DOI: 10.4018/979-8-3373-3384-7.ch003

1.0 INTRODUCTION

Artificial Intelligence (AI) is a machine learning technology that can perform many software-capable tasks using intelligent algorithms. With the advancement in AI development, it is now capable of doing many tasks that would be more efficient and effective than humans (Chiu et al., 2024). The relationship between diplomacy and artificial intelligence (AI) has become an ongoing debate in this age of unprecedented technological advancement. The proliferation of AI across many sectors is having a profound impact on diplomacy and international relations. A paradigm changes in how nations engage, negotiate, and make decisions might be brought about by artificial intelligence, which can completely overhaul conventional diplomatic methods.

This chapter investigates the role of AI in International Relations and Diplomacy, exploring the opportunities, drawbacks, and future AI has to offer. By examining AI's potential features, this study will provide insight into how AI can revolutionize the standard operating procedure (SOP) for diplomatic operations, improve decision-making, and change the essence of international relationships. As the demand for AI in every field of work is increasing, it is vital to explore the role AI can play in the complex SOP of diplomatic operations, making it simplified and more accessible for diplomats to make decisions.

AI, on the one side, can offer an intelligent tool that revolutionizes diplomatic operations by offering features such as real-time translation during essential discussions and negotiations, allowing clarity and avoiding confusion among diplomats with different languages. AI tools can analyse large sets of data and forecast the future with the use of AI algorithms and past scenarios (Hussain, 2024). AI can also monitor the number of social media and media platforms in real time and alarm for any risk (Duberry, 2023). This will allow diplomats to draw necessary decisions and act accordingly to avoid any conflicts that might put peace at risk.

On the other side, the power of AI can worsen diplomatic relations if the algorithm has been tempered due to cyber security risks. The results produced by the analytic algorithm can be biased or not include cultural factors that could result in disputes among the diplomats, leading to international conflicts. The major questions related to AI in international relations and diplomacy are transparency and accountability, which are ethical factors that need to be addressed. The work of AI and how the algorithm functions need to be transparent to everyone to give a sense of confidence and validity to the results produced by AI. As developing nations may blame developed nations that, the algorithm is in their favor.

1.1 Emergence of AI in International Relations and Diplomacy

AI in international relations and diplomacy is at the early stage, where countries prioritize it to ensure they are advanced in monitoring and negotiating. For instance, China has been actively using AI to prepare its diplomats for the possible outcomes, scenarios and events on a global scale (Lissovolik, 2020). AI in Diplomacy is part of "Digital Diplomacy", as technology (digital) has been integrated to the operation of diplomacy. As Frey (2024) defines that digital diplomacy is the use of digital tools and social media like Facebook, Twitter and Instagram by the diplomats to conduct the diplomatic activities like communicating with public about policies, engaging foreign public, and building the image of a country. Countries use AI in international diplomacy to thoroughly examine international security, weapon systems and monitoring of agreements. While AI is still evolving and countries have achieved different levels, it is still unclear the functionality of each country's AI can perfume. For example, China has been experimenting the use of AI-enabled satellites to put surveillance capabilities to monitor key military movements in Japan and India, as the AI is able to conduct observation by itself without any interference of humans (Krisnata, 2023; McFadden, 2023). The unknown limit of AI is matter of concern as it puts the risk of national security as AI can perform tasks that can violate the national security of another country and can lead to international disputes.

Diplomacy and international negotiations traditionally relied on humans to read and analyze all the clauses of the agreement before starting the negotiations. With the emergence of AI, this is done more effectively and efficiently as AI algorithms can analyze, summarize and point out the key points at a faster rate than humans can perform. An example of AI in diplomacy is sentiment analysis that analyzes social media and news to determine the public's opinion on certain issues (Hossain et al., 2024). Numerous scholars suggest that emergence of AI has been beneficial in the diplomatic contexts. Hossain et al. (2024) states that contemporary AI systems have been used to analyze that texts of negotiations in order to determine the outcomes of international trade discussions. These algorithms can identify areas of contention and advise on the contributions required from each country to attain a mutually acceptable compromise, so facilitating discussions (Monjur et al., 2023).

The emergence of AI is not only the computer software to make the theoretical works simplified, but the integration of AI in weaponry is another side that is the matter of concern. AI has the potential autonomous weapons such as mass destruction weapons like nuclear which could be remotely initiated by AI. According to Krisnata (2023), the AUKUS tripartite partnership has undertaken testing of autonomous weapon systems as part of its Pillar II initiatives to enhance military and technology competition with China. Simultaneously, wars in Libya, Ukraine, and Yemen have seen the use of AI-guided weaponry by combatants on the battlefield (Krisnata,

2023). Yudkowsky (n.d) claims that future AI might become "super persuasive" by disseminating a "synthetic virus" that alters an individual's brain to facilitate persuasion. This might render it a possible weaponry of mass destruction that is capable of facilitating the development and production of additional unconventional weapons. Although existing AI cannot yet be classified as a weapon of mass destruction, it has characteristics that facilitate deterrence. The chase of advancing of AI in weaponry poses a risk of conflict among the countries and may lead to warfare to show the capability of their AI weaponry.

1.2 How can AI Modernize the Protocol of International Relations and Diplomacy?

The importance of AI in international relations and diplomacy was realized in the phase of Covid when global leaders met virtually. During COVID-19, many developing nations were also equipped and experienced the digital diplomacy atmosphere due to travel restrictions and the need to discuss the issue of a pandemic that affected the whole globe. As AI integrates with technology, there are many means by which AI can modernize the SOP of international diplomacy. Currently, human interpreters are being used to translate if any speaker is speaking in their native language or a language which a leader cannot understand. However, with AI, automated language processing, live interpreters can remove the language barrier and simplify the time and effort of negotiations and discussions (Moore, 2023).

AI-driven solutions are augmenting negotiating efficiency by supplying diplomats with superior information. ChatGPT is now "qualitatively comparable" to outputs generated by human personnel. As huge language models advance, AI can rapidly scan and synthesize material, equipping diplomats for discussions more efficiently than a human team. Allied entities may also exchange insights via their AI systems. As other entities create their own AI, AI "hagglebots" may be pivotal in discussions (Moore, 2023). As advanced AI systems attain artificial general intelligence, they may emerge as autonomous entities in global interactions, redefining technology comprehension.

Intelligent technology enables negotiators to evaluate several viewpoints and situations within minutes. In the first round of Iran nuclear discussions, a team from the U.S. Energy Department constructed a copy of an Iranian nuclear facility to examine all variations of Iranian nuclear enrichment and development (Moore, 2023). In the future, an AI system will execute analogous situations and virtual tests more rapidly and at much-reduced costs. Diplomats would convene in various formats—from extensive plenary sessions to individual meetings—endeavouring to uncover the motivations behind each side's stance and to identify even subtle distinctions among individual negotiators. Historically exclusive to the intelligence sector, computer vision now contributes to this endeavour by detecting micro-expressions and other emotions via video analysis of talks. Although diplomacy is fundamentally a skill, it will depend on empirical science progressively.

2.0 MATERIALS AND METHODS

This chapter is founded on a systematic review and analysis of secondary sources, employing a comprehensive methodology to collect pertinent material regarding artificial intelligence (AI) in global governance, diplomacy, and international relations. The study technique predominantly entailed a rigorous examination of scholarly articles, reports, and publications from diverse academic databases, journals, and institutional websites, thereby assuring a comprehensive array of opinions on AI's impact on global governance. Critical documents and studies from international organizations, think tanks, and governmental entities were examined to obtain insights into the ramifications of AI on diplomacy and international collaboration.

The desk-based research depended on publicly accessible sources concerning AI's applications in governance, foreign diplomacy, and conflict resolution. This entailed recognizing recurrent themes and patterns and developing trends throughout the literature to furnish a thorough comprehension of AI's transformative impact on international relations.

3.0 RESULTS AND DISCUSSION

3.1 Role of AI in Data Analysis

When discussing international relations and diplomacy, it deals with data in the agreements and treaties that diplomats must analyze carefully before finalizing the negotiations. With the use of AI, it will analyze a large amount of data in a shorter period of time compared to human capability. AI can identify patterns and trends in the data the human mind may overlook (Hussain, 2024). The analysis prepared by AI will give diplomats better results and options for decision-making and negotiating the clauses that would be their advantage. AI data analysis can factor in the current data on the situation and produce results accordingly. For instance, social media sentiment analysis as to how people feel about proposed policies and economic forecasts can alarm countries if they are experiencing recession or trade disputes. Kukeyeva, Kurmangali & Aktay (2024) also adds that data analysis and forecasting algorithms in the AI can assist government and international organizations to act more effectively during the adverse situations.

International Relations and diplomacy have been dramatically shaped by the rise of AI driven data analysis. What is typified is an integration of AI technology into data driven decision making process allowing for governments and organizations to be able to analyze volumes of information faster than ever before. Improvements of these kinds lead to substantial implications on government structures, diplomatic practices and, insofar, on the totality of relations which constitute IR.

What most signals the relevance of AI in data analysis is probably the handling and processing of big data sets, and this is important in governance critical to making informed decisions. Considering the fact that the application of AI to social governance models has presented new situations and challenges, therefore, questions about existing governance frameworks come to mind (Zhang, 2023). AI's fast and precise data analysis capacity enables governments to meet social changes and crises more quickly and effectively because of improved governance efficiency. As Hussain (2024) highlights in "Negotiation Support System for International Treaties," a current effort of the European Union is an AI tool that provides linguistic recommendations and identifies problems by analyzing prior treaties and legal documents, perhaps enhancing negotiations and improving clarity. Initiatives such as the UN's "Global Early Warning System" use artificial intelligence (AI) to analyze extensive datasets from social media, conflict indicators, and news articles to predict potential incidents of violence (Hussain, 2024). This facilitates preventative diplomacy in conflict resolution.

It also states that AI applications in the public sector could generate enormous value by optimizing processes and improving the quality of the services provided to citizens (Wirtz et al., 2018). The authors draw the line of several AI applications in public administration including machine learning applications on resource allocation and the utilization of data for policy development. Gu also supports this capability as he claims that AI's revolutionary potential in global governance raises relevant questions in need of thorough legal systems (Gu, 2023). To understand the interaction between AI capabilities and governance frameworks, one must understand how data analysis can help enhance diplomatic packages and global collaboration.

When we talk about AI in international relations its data analysis skill gives us a better ability to analyze geopolitical data and to make educated diplomatic judgements based on that data. According to Meleouni, the adaptability of AI allows the automation of foreign policy-making procedures, which improves the efficiency and efficacy of diplomatic communications overall (Meleouni, 2023). Skills that enable a diplomat to look at data from all sorts of sources, including social media, economic indicators, and historical patterns, gives a diplomat the ability to predict when countries will clash or work together in the future. Georgescu emphasises the importance of AI governance for the challenges in the development of technologies (Georgescu, 2022), especially in terms of cyber diplomacy.

There are the ethical issues when you use AI in data analysis that needed to be monitored so that AI governance will be responsible. Harrison and Luna-Reyes argue that reliable AI systems are necessary to eliminate the risk of malicious data exploitation and for openness in decision making (Harrison & Luna-Reyes, 2020). The authors call for the development of governance arrangements that focus on ethics in AI implementation as a basis of continued trust in government entities. Medaglia et al. stress the need for detailed policy frameworks that address the ethical dimensions of AI adoption in government (Medaglia et al., 2021).

The rapid growth further leads the challenges in the governance of AI in technological changes. "Governments need to create robust frameworks that can keep up with the ever-changing nature of AI technology" (Taeihagh, 2021). The adaptability of regulatory bodies or mechanisms is considered quite necessary to hold back AI risks-such as data security-related issues, bias in algorithms, and accountability. It means that the collaboration between politicians, technologists, and ethicists forms the core in conceiving AI systems that implement social values and norms.

AI's involvement in data analysis also encompasses the enhancement of international cooperation and collaboration. Noordt and Misuraca emphasise that the effective implementation of AI in government necessitates a collaborative strategy including several public and private stakeholders (Noordt & Misuraca, 2020). That collaborative structure is necessary for dealing with the complexities of using AI and ensuring that data analysis capabilities are aligned to the common good in advance of a potential AI-rich future.

The emergence of AI in data analysis broadly represents a giant leap in international relations and diplomacy. We find that AI's capacity for handling and analyzing large datasets enhances the functionality of governance and facilitates diplomatic strategy within and among countries. Incorporating AI technologies have issues that need to be regulated by a complete regulatory framework as well as a consideration for ethical consideration. In the implementation of AI systems, as governments and organisations begin to integrate AI into the many, the importance of openness, accountability, and public trust in the implementation of AI systems grows. As AI technologies continue to develop, the future of international relations will be dictated by how data-driven it can become and heavily influenced by how AI technologies will alter data-driven decisions.

Banafa added that AI in diplomacy is its capacity to swiftly and effectively collect and evaluate large data sets. Diplomatic missions provide vast information via reports, communications, and open-source intelligence. AI-driven systems can analyze this data, detecting patterns, trends, and insights that human analysts may miss (Banafa, 2024). Hossain et al. (2024) further add that AI has the potential to analyze the texts of negotiations, point out the key areas of disagreements, and recommend solutions for how countries can come to an agreement that will benefit all the parties. Integrating AI into diplomatic processes would enhance the effectiveness and efficiency of diplomats via the data supplied by artificial intelligence. Big data will reduce ignorance and enable diplomats to forecast possible confrontations. Furthermore, AI may augment the advancement of superior and idealistic diplomacy, especially in light of the changing dynamics of international relations. Machine learning algorithms can examine previous diplomatic correspondence to detect nuanced alterations in vocabulary or tone that may signify changes in a nation's position on certain subjects. This competence enables diplomats to make educated judgments and formulate sophisticated tactics grounded on thorough data analysis.

Frey (2024) says that the use of large data with generative AI raises questions about privacy, confidentiality, and ethical issues. The efficacy of AI systems is contingent upon the quality of the data used for training. Biased or inadequate datasets may lead to inaccurate and deceptive assessments, presenting considerable hazards in diplomatic contexts. Furthermore, the individuals accountable for creating the AI-driven digital tools own authority over their training and, therefore, the data that informs them. This fact highlights the need of prioritizing the safeguarding of sensitive diplomatic information against threats or misuse (Frey, 2024).

3.2 AI in Overcoming Language Translation

One of the major points to bridge the natural language translation piece of this, however, is that artificial intelligence has now become language translation, which makes it a huge factor in translating the gaps between different languages, particularly in the international relations and diplomacy space. Effective communication in a number of languages is necessary for cooperation, understanding and cooperation by nations. Particularly through machine translation systems, communication time is now significantly improved with recent AI powered translation technologies, rendering even faster in these multilingual environments. In this discussion we will examine the influence that AI will play in boosting language translation, how this will affect world government, and challenges to their use.

And like everything else, with language translation, the AI has moved from basic machine translation to advanced neural machine translation (NMT) systems. The effects of this change have been substantial improvements in translation quality, including dealing with complex and idiomatically idiomatic structures. In the space of health, advances in AI interpretation mean that in some environments computerized systems are approaching the accuracy of a professional interpreter, according to Tougas et al. 2022. Such talent is used in the diplomatic cases since communication in front of the countries is very important in the negotiations and agreements between the countries.

Moreover, examples of the use of AI for creating multilingual ontologies such as the Medical Informatics and Digital Health Multilingual Ontology (MIMO) show how AI enables increased collaboration between countries, by standardizing terminology between languages (Benis et al., 2022). MIMO demonstrates how AI can extend translation tools to include more languages, such as Arabic, Chinese and Russian, and how this can enhance cross cultural communication and cooperation in global governance. The relevance of this is especially true of international health programs, where communication really does make all the difference in the success of such efforts.

AI is no longer about translation; instead, it involves modifying material to suit cultural contexts. Where Kunst and Bierwiaczonek (2023) remark the need for AI to take up the translation of cross-cultural research materials, they also point out that such translations be both accurate and culturally appropriate. This is also important in the field of diplomacy where small cultural meanings can modify the results of diplomatic exchanges. By widening its implementation, AI has proven to strengthen the effectiveness of international relations through enabling more effective communication and cooperation.

AIs use of AI driven translation systems, like Google Translate, has democratized the access to multilingual communication. Naghdipour observes that these tools have become essential for language acquisition and communication across diverse contexts, such as education and business (Naghdipour, 2023) However, automatic translation systems are problematic, especially in that reliability and quality of translations are also in question. What AI has come to offer and the translational errors that it has corrected heavily outweigh the current rise of machine generated translations which may still lack all the nuance and contextual comprehension that is afforded by being human.

Consequently, AI has great implications for language translation in global governance. As countries become increasingly reliant on AI-driven translation systems, miscommunication and misunderstanding in diplomatic situations remain a continuing concern. Indeed, the development of reliable AI systems has the key to mitigating risks regarding data exploitation and ensuring transparency about decision-making procedures. Many experts agree on the need to establish full policy frameworks that cover ethical implications of AI in government. Ensuring that the AI translation system is reliable and transparent will contribute to building trust internationally.

The integration of AI in translation also opens a set of ethical issues for which solutions have to be provided so that there is responsible governance. The risk of bias within AI systems, particularly in language training data, could lead to misshapen translations that further stereotype or inaccurately depict cultural nuances.

These ethical issues, therefore, need to be resolved for responsible and successful applications of AI-powered translation technology within a framework of diplomacy.

Besides ethical issues, other AI challenges to language translation include constant development and adjustment of the translation systems. The governments should thus come up with regulatory frameworks that are also adaptable, considering the dynamics of the AI technologies. This flexibility will help in cushioning or minimizing the risks of AI that will revolve around data privacy, algorithmic bias, and accountability. Interdisciplinary collaboration among politicians, engineers, and ethicists remains a key approach that warrants AI systems being conceived and implemented with due consideration of social values and norms.

AI even contributes to an increase in language translation, therefore bolstering international communication and collaboration. The need for a collaborative approach in implementing AI technologies also needs to be underlined by indicating how important it is that numerous stakeholders from both public and private spheres are involved. Using such collaborative structure, matters of integration of AI will be coped with and then lead to good consequences in the social welfare, while translation talents act as basis. For countries, the development of AI-driven translation services could be improved if they were to cultivate collaborations between governments, technology companies and linguistic specialists, all of whom can potentially bring their area of expertise to the evolution of AI-driven translation services and improve its quality and accessibility.

The advent of AI in language translation is important step forward to the defeat of linguistic barriers in international negotiations and diplomacy. And, indeed, the ability of such AI systems to produce precise — true to context — translations help humans develop information and cooperate with the rest of the world, all while engaging in diplomatic efforts and global governance. However, while incorporating these AI technologies comes with its own round of issues, such as regulatory framework and ethics, which needs a wider scale approach. Given the complex job of bringing AI into the work of governments and companies, transparency, accountability and building public trust in deploying AI translation systems are essential. The progress of AI technology, coupled with its multilingual communication reaches, will play a pivotal role in defining the future of international relations.

3.3 AI in Conflict Prediction and Resolution

Putting artificial intelligence (AI) into conflict prediction and settlement represents a considerable advance in international relations and diplomacy science. The resolution and prediction of conflicts are needed for global conflicts that are becoming increasingly complex. There are technologies of artificial intelligence, such as machine learning and data analytics, which have come to be so powerful at understanding conflict dynamics and possibilities for settlement. Issues related to conflict prediction and resolution through analysis of applications, advantages, challenges and global governance implications of AI are discussed.

AI's speed and accuracy in processing large datasets, combined with its ability to process very large data sets at a time, makes it so incredibly valuable for the prediction of conflict. Current methods of predicting conflict are based on historical information and qualitative analysis, both of which are laborious and subjective. Comments compares AI with using machine learning techniques to find trends and correlations in large datasets to make far more accurate predictions about future conflict.

A number of scenarios of climate change are used by time series data analysis to predict armed conflict according to machine learning models according to Ge et al. (2022). This work highlights how the synthesis of environmental changes and socio-economic conditions can predict earlier the outbreak of conflict, using this prior history of conflicts to predict where and when conflict will arise. This approach therefore enables real time monitoring of conflict risk, in order that policymakers may take proactive measures to avert possible disputes, thereby improving the forecast accuracy.

What is also happening is that AI is being used to predict conflict in the form of the Views, otherwise known as the Violence Early Warning System. Uppsala University developed the system using machine learning methods to predict national-level armed conflicts (Obukhov & Brovelli, 2023), and this approach reveals useful insight for diplomatic strategy and intervention based on several conditioning elements such as political instability, economic indicators, and societal tensions.

Apart from forecasting, AI is useful in problem-solving or conflict resolution. AI systems can recommend efficient resolution solutions customized to specific contexts because they can analyze data and simulate many scenarios. O'Loughlin et al. investigate the causal relationship between climate variability and conflict risk in East Africa and point out that these environmental drivers may help explain the mechanisms of violence and reveal the types of interventions that may be effective (O'Loughlin et al., 2012). In cases where the causes of the conflict are known, policymakers will be able to soothe the interests and issues of the parties concerned in a more effective plan of settlement that will address the issues.

Learning can be improved through artificial intelligence; it can potentially improve communication and negotiation procedures in the conflict resolution process. AI systems can also provide insights into the dynamics of conversations, based on that pattern of communications and the sentiment associated with that communication, helping mediators identify areas of possible common ground and distraction. In particular this capacity is useful in the complex settings of discussions with many stakeholders where people must be understood and their point of view and motivation s understood so that the necessary consensus can be achieved.

It also brings with it a capacity to improve efficiency of conflict resolution processes through automating admin functions and optimizing communication. Artificially intelligent platforms would reduce time to drafting and managing settlements, thereby increasing the odds of settlement adherence by parties to conflicts. This automation enhances the administrative burden on negotiators, making it necessary to focus on substance rather than administrators, resulting in better resolution outcomes.

AI has great potential for predicting and resolving conflict but there are a large number of ethical issues and problems that need to be addressed. One of the biggest problems with AI systems is that they can lead to bias in a model and can make distorted predictions and recommendations. AI systems, according to Benítez et al. (2020), should be designed holistically and considering the different interests and values of different stakeholders. Withholding these may lead to not only worse, but more, present tensions.

In addition, war forecasting via AI is dependent, and leads to questions regarding accountability and transparency. With growing autonomous decision-making capabilities of AI systems, defining definitive frameworks for accountability becomes increasingly important. Thus, policymakers have to ensure that AI generated predictions and recommendations are monitored and reviewed by a human before any unforeseen consequences occur.

Another problem is that the data you need to train AI algorithms is high quality. In many conflict prone areas, data could be scarce, unreliable, or hard to access. Since the AI predictions will be false, the corrective measures proposed will also be less effective. To improve data collection and dissemination in conflict-affected regions, cooperative initiatives between governments, NGOs and international organizations are important.

Its applications to conflict prediction and resolution have huge implications for global governance. As Artificial Intelligence technologies are developed, they provide new means for nations to cooperate, collaborate and settle differences. AI can also better early warning systems providing timely, accurate and actionable information to help countries mitigate threats before they become catastrophes.

In addition, such AI systems using alternative dispute resolution methods can also be signaling towards greater decentralization and inclusivity, such as governance. Policies can be fashioned with solutions more just when people who formulate such policies can effectively know, through data analysis that makes use of machine learning, the different communities' needs and issues. In regions where trust and legitimacy in governance systems is dependent on inclusivity, governance systems need to be accessible.

For conflict prediction and resolution, the application of AI can be seen as the need for interdisciplinary collaboration. A discipline as large as conflict management needs contributions from more than one discipline such as political science, sociology, data science, ethics and so on. Governments and organizations can help promote a more complete and more effective way of resolving conflict by encouraging collaboration between specialists from many different fields.

The Function of AI in Conflict Prediction and Settlement can be summarized as a major step for international relations and diplomacy. The use of machine learning and data analytics contributes to the improvement of such precision of conflict forecasts and development of successful settlement tactics. AI in conflict management poses ethical dilemmas and questions that, in turn, require the attention to create ethical governance. Consistent with the development of global conflicts, AI is increasingly able to increase the prediction and resolution of these conflicts, thus serving as a potential vehicle to advance international collaboration and peace.

3.4 Reshaping Public Diplomacy with AI

Public diplomacy has undergone a different revolution — its emergence of artificial intelligence (AI) has rendered the way governments communicate with each other and overseas audiences a wholly new landscape. Using AI has inevitably become a more common practice in public international relations — governmental efforts to disseminate and strengthen countrywide rituals worldwide. This discourse investigates the numerous techniques via which AI is reworking public diplomacy, analyzing its uses, benefits, issues, and ramifications for global members of the family.

A good-sized software of AI in public international relations is the development of communication techniques. Artificial intelligence technologies, particularly herbal language processing (NLP) and device gaining knowledge of, empower governments to scrutinize vast statistics from social media, information resources, and lots of on-line platforms. This study assists ambassadors in comprehending public mood, recognizing developing trends, and customizing their messaging accordingly. Amaliyah (2023) examines the application of AI in analyzing cultural trends and attitudes, enabling nations to formulate messages that effectively engage overseas audiences. By comprehending the desires and apprehensions of target demographics, governments can facilitate more effective discourse and cultivate favorable opinions of their nations.

Additionally, AI powered chatbots and virtual assistants are being used to improve with audiences in terms of communication. These platforms can provide answer to questions, share policy updates and to have engaging conversation with people. These tools not only improve communication effectiveness and increase the possibility of interaction with groups of people, but also reinforce governments' capacity to play a role in influencing the public.

Cultural diplomacy — the promotion of a nation's culture to increase mutual understanding and goodwill — is also largely powered by artificial intelligence. AI technologies allow governments to do a better job curation and distribution of cultural content. AI algorithms can detect user preferences, including where they like to hang out, what they are talking about, and then offer their suggestions on cultural products like films and movies, music and literature, and which among an audience have some similar preferences. Georgescu argues that cultural involvement in the development of international relations is crucial (Georgescu, 2022), and therefore a focused strategy does increase the cultural diplomacy efforts effectiveness.

Also, AI can save cross cultural interactions because it provides immediate translation services. This capacity is especially significant in diplomatic situations, where linguistic obstacles might impede efficient communication. AI powered translation tools enable communication, between diplomats and global audiences enhancing chances, for cooperation and understanding.

The use of intelligence, in diplomacy helps governments make decisions based on data analysis methods. Governments can utilize AI analytics to assess the effectiveness of their efforts and adjust to their strategies. By reviewing the metrics of social media campaigns Ambassadors can identify the messages that connect best with audiences and adapt their approaches accordingly.

Additionally, artificial intelligence can assist in handling crises by providing understanding of the sentiment during diplomatic emergencies. By monitoring media and news coverage AI technologies can identify emerging issues before they escalate, allowing governments to take action. This capability is crucial, for maintaining a reputation and mitigating the impact of negative events, on public perception.

While AI presents benefits, in relations efforts it also brings to light certain challenges and ethical dilemmas that need careful consideration. One significant issue involves the potential for biases, within AI systems leading to research outcomes and inaccurate reflections of sentiment. Birksted t and colleagues underscore the importance of scrutinizing the training data used in AI applications to ensure it includes perspectives. Does not perpetuate preexisting biases (Source; Birksted et al., 2023). Failing to address these issues could undermine the credibility of public diplomacy efforts. Erode trust, among audiences.

But the application of AI in public diplomacy raises the concern on privacy and data security. However, governments must find the appropriate balance between the utilization of data for efficient communication on the one hand, and individual privacy rights on the other. To ensure the responsible use of these technologies, explicit norms and ethical frameworks to the application of AI in public diplomacy are important to formulating.

Integrating AI into public diplomacy presents several implications on the activities of the global government. The dynamics of international relations are expected to undergo change as countries rely more on the use of AI technology to enhance their diplomatic initiatives. It means that governments are now able to analyze data and communicate with international community in real time addressing important issues such as climate change, public health emergency and geopolitical conflicts.

Additionally, AI included in the public diplomacy can act as the driving force fostering more cooperation between different countries. Gathering nations around common issues and mutual understanding that can be done through data and technology. In the context of global governance, joint action is the quintessential feature, and this cooperative method is relevant especially since many problems reaching the global stage are issues that are beyond national boundaries.

Similarly, the future stands to see the use of these reshaping diplomacy capability continue to develop with the way AI is developing, and governments are likely to search in future to explore new ways and strategies to exploit these types of capabilities and combine them with other emerging technology such as blockchain and Augmented reality to amplify the effort of public diplomacy.

In addition to this, continuously researching and developing AI ethics and governance will be of importance in deciding how exactly AI will influence the domain of AI in public diplomacy. It is important to make ethical rules and determine the best procedures for using the technologies of AI in public diplomacy initiatives so that the latter are carried out open and properly.

Through those behaviors the landscape of diplomacy is being reshaped by AI; AI is heightening communication channels, enriching engagement, and enabling data informed decision making. Despite that AI tools bring in benefits, there are challenges and ethical conundrums that need consideration. Given nations' struggle to utilize AI in diplomacy, it becomes necessary to establish rules and form partnerships to heighten income from these technologies, both in the realm of diplomacy and, more globally, in bolstering international understanding and collaboration.

3.5 Challenges Associated with AI in Global Governance

Incorporation of artificial intelligence (AI) into the realm of global governance carries with itself various issues which need to be addressed before it can be successfully adopted and utilized for the appropriate purpose. In this age, the use of AI in the decision-making processes has greater bearing on international relations, public policy, and diplomacy.

But the main issue, when taking about integrating AI in governance settings is its considerations. AI technologies are advancing at a very rapid pace, stirring the cauldron of responsibility, fairness and misuse resistance. Cath suggests that the ethical oversight of AI requires a discussion about consequences of AI specially the effects of AI, on human rights and societal fairness (Cath 2018). There's a great fear that AI will only make things worse, that it will contribute to current inequalities or even go beyond prejudice to create new ones. If AI systems are trained on biased data, they're likely to propagate those biases on their outputs, and may treat certain populations unfairly.

Also, Ethics of AI are about informed permission and use of data. Since AI systems are frequently based on huge amounts of personal data, it's important for users to be informed about the use of their data, and to have consented. In informed permission and data use agreement terms, Jarvis et al. emphasize the importance of AI applications (Jarvis et al., 2020). Lacking strict ethical guidelines which govern its application in global governance, the introduction of AI introduces a question mark against public trust and legitimacy.

Transparency poses an obstacle in the realm of AI, within governance as many AI algorithms operate like enigmatic "black boxes " making it difficult for humans to understand or interpret their decision-making processes effectively. The lack of transparency could lead to a disconnect between the recommendations generated by AI and the values and priorities of those, in charge of decision making. According to Janssen and colleagues (2020) the opaqueness of AI systems can hinder accountability. Make it challenging for decision makers to identify algorithmic recommendations. In settings of governance specifically is when this issue becomes most concerning as the choices made can have effects, on people and communities.

Addressing these transparency issues has led to a growing need, for AI (XAI) technologies that clarify how decisions are made by intelligence systems. The aim of XAI is to improve the understandability and clarity of AI systems so that stakeholders can grasp the rationale behind the recommendations generated by AI. But successfully achieving transparency in AI models is technically challenging problem we need to further investigate to arrive at practical solutions.

For AI systems, there are privacy and the security related concerns to rely on data, because usually AI requires data to do what it does best and so protecting this data is vital to avoid data breach and unauthorize access to data that, may compromise not just individual's data but also national security and trust in governance systems etc., and so Magragi et al. (2019) emphasized that in the field where the safety of humans is in concern, data protection need to be very strict

Moreover, personal data must be acquired and handled in accordance with legal and ethical norms. We take a look at the General Data Protection Regulation (GDPR) as an example of data protection legislation, with its need for transparency, consent, and accountability in data management. AI technologies, due to their international scope, are also difficult for legislation to enforce, since data is often processed cross border and under different legal frameworks.

Integrating algorithmically biased systems into governance frameworks is hindered by a barrier of algorithmic bias, which can arise from training data used to develop AI models and the design of algorithms and interactions of AI with culture. Jobin and Iezekiel show how in the case of AI systems, the biases can produce results that subtly undermine the equity and integrity of any given governance procedures (Jobin & Iezekiel 2019). Suppose that biased algorithms are used in policing and they just happen to work against marginalized communities, making the inequalities that currently exist worse.

A comprehensive strategy to mitigate algorithmic bias calls for multiple data representation, rigorous bias testing and ongoing supervision of deployed AI systems. Stakeholder engagement is crucial for ensuring that AI technology is designed and executed in a way that considers the perspectives of the populations impacted by it. For example, this interactive method takes away some of the dangers arising from bias in algorithms and contributes to more equitable governance results.

AI is advancing so fast as to overtake existing legal regimes, a task for global governance. However, Artificial Intelligence technologies are advancing and for this reason it has become necessary to set up comprehensive regulatory frameworks taking mutual account of ethical, legal and social implications of artificial intelligence. Towards the creation of international regulatory entities so AI governance protocols can be established in standardized protocols and AI development and implementation should inevitably include ethical considerations (Erman & Furendal, 2022).

A disjointed approach to AI governance can happen if countries regulate differently, with the lack of unified regulatory frameworks. A lack of consistency may hamper joint work on using resources for finding solutions and crises. In addition, the lack of guidelines might well lead to a situation wherein countries prefer to engage in competition over values, as is the case when computerization technologies are put in place.

In view of the extent AI technology reaches today, it is imperative to countries to work together on governance issues so as to address the challenges at hand appropriately and consistently across borders. A set of standardized rules and best practices arise to integrate the AI into the various sectors, which are the products of such cooperative ventures between the government bodies, organizations and civilian groups. In Tomašev et al. (2020) they introduced the AI for Social Good (AI4SG) movement as an approach to using the AI technologies to solve urgent issues while paying attention to ethical concerns.

Partnerships across fields — including ethics and law, and computer science — can help us to better understand how AI shapes governance. The collaboration between companies can aid in establishing frameworks to address the legal ramifications to society of AI integration.

Intelligence as a challenge in governance is complex and needs immediate response to be dealt with effectively and responsibly. From safeguarding against biases in algorithms, resolving ethical quandaries, data privacy issues to the need for regulation these hurdles need to be tackled to achieve proper AI usage. However, being in position to respond to the state of the world as perpetually evolving and to the challenges and advancements of ethical AI development will require international cooperation and interdisciplinary collaboration as AI continues to increasingly influence global governance. Stakeholders can use the promise of AI to the benefit of society without its concerns by highlighting its openness, accountability and inclusivity.

3.6 The Future of AI in Global Governance

Coming developments around governance and Intelligence (AI) hold the potential for a host of exciting prospects and challenges coming their way. With this progress in AI technology, we may be in a position to help improve decision making processes, governance structures and public services, but also through helping to scale our collaboration. Standards and regulations as well as operational factors all play a part in successfully navigating the implementing complexities of AI. This discussion explores how AI could shape governance by focusing on its impact, on relations and the need, for collaborative structures while considering the ethical values guiding its progress.

Artificial intelligence has the potential to revolutionize how decisions are made in governance by offering data driven insights and predictive analytics capabilities." By examining sets of data " AI can identify patterns " forecast results,". Support the creation of policies based on evidence." According to Erkkilä " global statistics and AI related policies could influence the narratives around governance " impacting how policymakers approach the integration of AI (Erkkilä," 2023)."Governments and international organizations benefit from this capability by making informed decisions to tackle pressing issues such, as climate change, public health emergencies and geopolitical conflicts.

Moreover, artificial intelligence has the potential to enhance services by automating tasks and optimizing resource allocation. Sun and Medaglia point out that integrating AI into healthcare has proven to improve effectiveness and service quality (Sun & Medaglia 2019). By automating tasks AI can free up resources, for more complex responsibilities leading to improved outcomes, across various industries.

The global reach of AI technology necessitates teamwork, on a scale to address shared concerns and maximize the benefits of AI integration Collaborative structures have the potential to improve the exchange of knowledge best practices and collaborative efforts among nations The AI for Social Good program aims to apply AI technologies to address pressing global issues such as poverty inequality and environmental sustainability By fostering partnerships across various sectors including government academia and businesses stakeholders can collaboratively harness the potential of AI, for positive societal impacts.

Geopolitical issues may act as barriers, to cooperation in regulating AI technology according to Cheng and Zeng (2022). They argue that framing AI as a matter of security in the US and China has impeded efforts for collaboration. The rivalry over approaches to AI governance underscores the importance of dialogues and building trust to encourage cooperation. Establishment of ground, on standards and regulatory frameworks can ease tensions and support joint efforts in advancing AI technology.

Incorporating AI into governance structures raises concerns that will play a role, in shaping its evolution going forward. As AI is adopted in governance practices it sparks discussions on responsibility, fairness and transparency. Harrison and Luna Reyes emphasize the importance of creating AI systems to maintain trust in government bodies. Mishandled AI projects leading to inaccurate results could erode confidence in governance, hence highlighting the need for robust ethical guidelines and supervision mechanisms.

As AI technologies advance, education and capacity building will be crucial for equipping stakeholders to manage the intricacies of AI governance. Policymakers, practitioners, and the public must possess the requisite knowledge and abilities to comprehend and interact with AI technologies proficiently. This involves developing skills and awareness of ethics while promoting collaboration, across fields of expertise.

Furthermore, it is crucial to involve marginalized individuals in discussions about AI governance since AI could exacerbate existing inequalities. Moon favours governance methods that recognize stakeholders' views, including AI programmers and users (Moon, 2023). The stakeholders can achieve equitable results by promoting an inclusive discourse and cooperation in dealing with the issues of AI implementation.

Incorporating AI in global governance can be used in solving environmental sustainability issues. Using artificial intelligence technologies, resource management can be improved, energy usage can be optimized, and climate change mitigation initiatives can be made. Using AI to design intelligent and quality-of-life sustainable urban environments, as well as addressing climatic emergencies and contributing to achieving global sustainable development objectives (Yiğitcanlar, 2021) is of paramount importance, Yiğitcanlar adds. In the way that governments can use AI to execute data driven plans that improve environmental sustainability and resilience.

But AI technology, too, carries an ecological cost. AI models generate fears over their carbon footprint due to the energy usage tying into training and deployment of them. With the ubiquity of AI rising, it will be a prioritizing of sustainable practices around AI's own development and deployment to prevent ill effects on the environment.

The prospect of intelligence shaping (AI) governance holds promise where AI could improve decision making processes and international cooperation to address pressing global challenges more effectively. For the implementation of AI technologies in governance, good enough consideration of guidelines and regulatory frameworks must be practised. Transparency, accountability, and inclusivity of stakeholders could help harness the benefits of AI while mitigating risks. With the world-changing approaches and cross-disciplinary partnerships being enacted to navigate the complexities of AI in governance, they will continue to present a focus.

4.0 RECOMMENDATION

4.1 AI Framework

The establishment of ethical AI frameworks is crucial to mitigate issues pertaining to bias, discrimination, and privacy. Jobin and Ienca contend that the international framework of AI ethical principles should emphasize solidarity and sustainability, especially in tackling humanitarian issues (Jobin & Ienca, 2019). Advocating for governance methods that consider the diverse needs and perspectives of affected communities can ensure that AI technologies are deployed in alignment with values. The rapid advancement of AI technology calls for the establishment of guidelines to steer its progress and application in society effectively and responsibly, according to Erman and Furendal (2022). They emphasize the importance of fair AI governance to ensure that the benefits and drawbacks of AI are distributed equitably among all stakeholders through decision making processes and dialogues.

Additionally, the breakdown of AI governance initiatives poses challenges to regulation, as highlighted by Cihon and colleagues in a study published in 2020. They point out that the increasing number of AI initiatives could lead to coordination issues and gaps in governance. The establishment of frameworks among global organizations, governments and civil society is crucial to harmonising regulatory strategies and improving consistency in AI governance. Hussain further adds that strong international governance frameworks are important to establish moral standards, promote the exchange of information, prevent the weaponization of AI, protect human rights and algorithm biases and ensure democratic control in diplomacy (Hussain, 2024).

4.2 AI Training to Diplomats

As the technological advancement such as AI is becoming part of IR and diplomacy, it is very important that the diplomats are well versed about the use of AI. Diplomats needs to be able to understand how the algorithm works in the AI, so that they are aware of the limit and potential biases of AI. It is crucial that diplomats are trained with the ideology that AI is utilized to assist them rather than replace them, therefore, their thinking and decision over the results produced by AI is fundamental.

Diplomats from developing countries are the ones that needs to be well trained due to limited technological advancement in their country and their understanding about the algorithms. Training diplomats on the use of AI is a method of achieving transparency as diplomats will have a fair knowledge about its operation and usage, and can flag biases rather than supporting whatever results AI suggests. To ensure that the public is confident and competent in the integration of AI in diplomacy, diplomat academies must change over time and learn technological skills such as AI (Hussain, 2024).

5.0 CONCLUSION

This chapter examined how artificial intelligence (AI) plays a role in International Relations (IR) and Diplomacy, which has traditionally been human-centered, but with the intervention of AI, technologies are being adopted to make the Standard Operations Procedures (SOP) more modernized. AI in diplomacy, over time, will make diplomats work much easier and faster, but it cannot replace them. Though AI has many features to offer in diplomacy, making international relations stronger, it has also been criticized that AI poses ethical, privacy and security risks that can worsen international relations.

The integration of AI in diplomacy signifies a transformative change with significant potential to enhance diplomatic effectiveness, foster international collaboration, and address global challenges. To ensure that AI serves as an instrument for global peace, comprehension, and stability, this transformation requires a meticulous, ethical, and strategic approach. As we advance, it is essential to continually assess and adapt to the evolving domain of artificial intelligence in diplomacy, maintaining a balance among technological innovation, human discernment, and ethical concerns.

REFERENCES

Amaliyah, R., Jatmika, S., & Surwandono, . (2023). The rise of artificial intelligence as the future of korean culture diplomacy. [Indonesian Journal of Communications Studies]. *Jurnal Studi Komunikasi*, *7*(3), 865–878. DOI: 10.25139/jsk.v7i3.6495

Banafa, A. (2024, June 30). *The Rise of Artificial Intelligence in Diplomacy and International Relations*. Retrieved October 2, 2024, from https://www.linkedin.com/pulse/rise-artificial-intelligence-diplomacy-international-relations-s9rsc/

Benis, A., Grosjean, J., Billey, K., Martins, J., Dornauer, V., Crişan-Vida, M., & Darmoni, S. (2022). Medical informatics and digital health multilingual ontology (mimo): A tool to improve international collaborations. *International Journal of Medical Informatics*, *167*, 104860. DOI: 10.1016/j.ijmedinf.2022.104860 PMID: 36084537

Benítez, J., Gómez-Reino, M., & Suárez, A. (2020). Data-driven democracy? automated decision-making, difference and preferences. https://doi.org/DOI: 10.33774/apsa-2020-rx8fs

Birkstedt, T., Minkkinen, M., Tandon, A., & Mäntymäki, M. (2023). Ai governance: Themes, knowledge gaps and future agendas. *Internet Research*, *33*(7), 133–167. DOI: 10.1108/INTR-01-2022-0042

Cath, C. (2018). Governing artificial intelligence: Ethical, legal and technical opportunities and challenges. *Philosophical Transactions. Series A, Mathematical, Physical, and Engineering Sciences*, *376*(2133), 20180080. DOI: 10.1098/rsta.2018.0080 PMID: 30322996

Cheng, J., & Zeng, J. (2022). Shaping ai's future? china in global ai governance. *Journal of Contemporary China*, *32*(143), 794–810. DOI: 10.1080/10670564.2022.2107391

Chiu, T. K., Ahmad, Z., Ismailov, M., & Sanusi, I. T. (2024). What are artificial intelligence literacy and competency? A comprehensive framework to support them. *Computers and Education Open*, *6*, 100171. DOI: 10.1016/j.caeo.2024.100171

Cihon, P., Maas, M., & Kemp, L. (2020). Fragmentation and the future: Investigating architectures for international ai governance. *Global Policy*, *11*(5), 545–556. DOI: 10.1111/1758-5899.12890

Duberry, J. (2023, September). AI Diplomacy: what vision for the future of multilateralism? - Geneva Solutions. Geneva Solutions. Retrieved October 1, 2024, from https://genevasolutions.news/science-tech/ai-diplomacy-what-vision-for-the-future-of-multilateralism-1

Erkkilä, T. (2023). Global indicators and ai policy: Metrics, policy scripts, and narratives. *The Review of Policy Research, 40*(5), 811–839. DOI: 10.1111/ropr.12556

Erman, E., & Furendal, M. (2022). The global governance of artificial intelligence: Some normative concerns. *Moral Philosophy and Politics, 9*(2), 267–291. DOI: 10.1515/mopp-2020-0046

Frey, C. (2024). Digital Diplomacy: The Impact of Technology on Modern Diplomacy and Foreign Policy. Current Realities and Future Prospects. *SSRN, 24*(1), 107. DOI: 10.2139/ssrn.4864962

Ge, Q., Hao, M., Ding, F., Jiang, D., Scheffran, J., Helman, D., & Ide, T. (2022). Modelling armed conflict risk under climate change with machine learning and time-series data. *Nature Communications, 13*(1), 2839. Advance online publication. DOI: 10.1038/s41467-022-30356-x PMID: 35595793

Georgescu, A. (2022). Cyber diplomacy in the governance of emerging ai technologies - a transatlantic example. *International Journal of Cyber Diplomacy, 3*, 13–22. DOI: 10.54852/ijcd.v3y202202

Gu, P. (2023). Global artificial intelligence governance: Challenges and complications. *Science Insights, 42*(6), 975–979. DOI: 10.15354/si.23.re596

Harrison, T., & Luna-Reyes, L. (2020). Cultivating trustworthy artificial intelligence in digital government. *Social Science Computer Review, 40*(2), 494–511. DOI: 10.1177/0894439320980122

Harrison, T., & Luna-Reyes, L. (2020). Cultivating trustworthy artificial intelligence in digital government. *Social Science Computer Review, 40*(2), 494–511. DOI: 10.1177/0894439320980122

Hossain, M. A., Azim, K. S., Jafor, A. H. M., Shayed, A. U., Nikita, N. A., & Khan, O. U. (2024). AI and Machine Learning in International Diplomacy and Conflict Resolution. *AIJMR-Advanced International Journal of Multidisciplinary Research, 2*(5).

Hussain, S. S. (2024). Artificial Intelligence and Diplomacy: Transforming International Relations in the Digital Age. *Remittances Review, 9*(1), 988–1001.

Janssen, M., Hartog, M., Matheus, R., Ding, A., & Kuk, G. (2020). Will algorithms blind people? the effect of explainable ai and decision-makers' experience on ai-supported decision-making in government. *Social Science Computer Review, 40*(2), 478–493. DOI: 10.1177/0894439320980118

Jarvis, T., Thornburg, D., Rebecca, A., & Teven, C. (2020). Artificial intelligence in plastic surgery: Current applications, future directions, and ethical implications. *Plastic and Reconstructive Surgery. Global Open*, *8*(10), e3200. DOI: 10.1097/GOX.0000000000003200 PMID: 33173702

Jobin, A., Ienca, M., & Vayena, E. (2019). The global landscape of ai ethics guidelines. *Nature Machine Intelligence*, *1*(9), 389–399. DOI: 10.1038/s42256-019-0088-2

Krisnata, B. R. (2023, July 27). *Artificial Intelligence and International Affairs - Australian Institute of International Affairs*. Australian Institute of International Affairs. Retrieved October 1, 2024, from https://www.internationalaffairs.org.au/australianoutlook/artificial-intelligence-and-international-affairs/

Kukeyeva, F., Kurmangali, M., & Aktay, D. (2024). Theoretical and Methodological Approaches to Studying Artificial Intelligence in the Context of International Relations and International Law. *JOURNAL OF CENTRAL ASIAN STUDIES*, *93*(1), 4–21. DOI: 10.52536/3006-807X.2024-1.01

Kunst, J., & Bierwiaczonek, K. (2023). Utilizing ai questionnaire translations in cross-cultural and intercultural research: insights and recommendations. https://doi.org/DOI: 10.31234/osf.io/sxcyk

Lissovolik, Y. (2020). *AI in International Relations: The Era of 'Digital Diplomacy.'* Valdai Club. Retrieved October 1, 2024, from https://valdaiclub.com/a/highlights/ai-in-international-relations/

Magrabi, F., Ammenwerth, E., McNair, J., Keizer, N., Hyppönen, H., Nykänen, P., & Georgiou, A. (2019). Artificial intelligence in clinical decision support: Challenges for evaluating ai and practical implications. *Yearbook of Medical Informatics*, *28*(01), 128–134. DOI: 10.1055/s-0039-1677903 PMID: 31022752

McFadden, C. (2023, April 17). Rise of Skynet? AI takes control of a Chinese satellite for 24 hours. *Interesting Engineering*. Retrieved October 1, 2024, from https://interestingengineering.com/innovation/ai-controlled-chinese-satellite-24-hours

Medaglia, R., Gil-García, J., & Pardo, T. (2021). Artificial intelligence in government: Taking stock and moving forward. *Social Science Computer Review*, *41*(1), 123–140. DOI: 10.1177/08944393211034087

Meleouni, C., & Efthymiou, I. P. (2023). Artificial intelligence and its impact in international relations. *Journal of Politics and Ethics in New Technologies and Ai*, *2*(1), e35803. DOI: 10.12681/jpentai.35803

Monjur, M. E. I., Rifat, A. H., Islam, M. R., & Bhuiyan, M. R. (2023). The impact of artificial intelligence on international trade: Evidence from B2C giant e-commerce (Amazon, Alibaba, Shopify, eBay). *Open Journal of Business and Management, 11*(5), 2389–2401. DOI: 10.4236/ojbm.2023.115132

Moon, M. (2023). Searching for inclusive artificial intelligence for social good: Participatory governance and policy recommendations for making ai more inclusive and benign for society. *Public Administration Review, 83*(6), 1496–1505. DOI: 10.1111/puar.13648

Moore, A. (2023, March). How AI Could Revolutionize Diplomacy. *Foreign Policy*. Retrieved October 2, 2024, from https://foreignpolicy.com/2023/03/21/ai-artificial-intelligence-diplomacy-negotiations-chatgpt-quantum-computing/

Naghdipour, B. (2023). Google translate in efl writing: Managing contradictions and conflicts. *TESOL Journal, 15*(2), e747. Advance online publication. DOI: 10.1002/tesj.747

Noordt, C., & Misuraca, G. (2020). Exploratory insights on artificial intelligence for government in europe. *Social Science Computer Review, 40*(2), 426–444. DOI: 10.1177/0894439320980449

O'Loughlin, J., Witmer, F., Linke, A., Laing, A., Gettelman, A., & Dudhia, J. (2012). Climate variability and conflict risk in east africa, 1990–2009. *Proceedings of the National Academy of Sciences of the United States of America, 109*(45), 18344–18349. DOI: 10.1073/pnas.1205130109 PMID: 23090992

Obukhov, T., & Brovelli, M. (2023). Identifying conditioning factors and predictors of conflict likelihood for machine learning models: A literature review. *ISPRS International Journal of Geo-Information, 12*(8), 322. DOI: 10.3390/ijgi12080322

Sun, T., & Medaglia, R. (2019). Mapping the challenges of artificial intelligence in the public sector: Evidence from public healthcare. *Government Information Quarterly, 36*(2), 368–383. DOI: 10.1016/j.giq.2018.09.008

Taeihagh, A. (2021). Governance of artificial intelligence. *Policy and Society, 40*(2), 137–157. DOI: 10.1080/14494035.2021.1928377

Tomašev, N., Cornebise, J., Hutter, F., Mohamed, S., Picciariello, A., Connelly, B., Belgrave, D. C. M., Ezer, D., Haert, F. C., Mugisha, F., Abila, G., Arai, H., Almiraat, H., Proskurnia, J., Snyder, K., Otake-Matsuura, M., Othman, M., Glasmachers, T., Wever, W., & Clopath, C. (2020). Ai for social good: Unlocking the opportunity for positive impact. *Nature Communications, 11*(1), 2468. Advance online publication. DOI: 10.1038/s41467-020-15871-z PMID: 32424119

Tougas, H., Chan, S., Shahrvini, T., Gonzalez, A., Reyes, R., Parish, M., & Yellowlees, P. (2022). The use of automated machine translation to translate figurative language in a clinical setting: Analysis of a convenience sample of patients drawn from a randomized controlled trial. *JMIR Mental Health*, *9*(9), e39556. DOI: 10.2196/39556 PMID: 36066959

Wang, W. and Cai, Y. (2022). The risk of artificial intelligence embedded in government governance: mechanism, process, prevention and control., 609-616. https://doi.org/DOI: 10.2991/978-94-6463-016-9_63

Wirtz, B., Weyerer, J., & Geyer, C. (2018). Artificial intelligence and the public sector—Applications and challenges. *International Journal of Public Administration*, *42*(7), 596–615. DOI: 10.1080/01900692.2018.1498103

Yiğitcanlar, T. (2021). Greening the artificial intelligence for a sustainable planet: An editorial commentary. *Sustainability (Basel)*, *13*(24), 13508. DOI: 10.3390/su132413508

Yudkowsky, E. (n.d.). *Will superintelligent AI end the world?* [Video]. TED Talks. https://www.ted.com/talks/eliezer_yudkowsky_will_superintelligent_ai_end_the_world?language=en

Zhang, H. (2023). Research and practical exploration of new models of social governance in the age of artificial intelligence. SHS Web of Conferences, 179, 01017. https://doi.org/DOI: 10.1051/shsconf/202317901017

Chapter 4
Artificial Intelligence in India:
Navigating Social Justice, Environmental Ethics, and Legal Governance

Vijay Kumar Sadanand
https://orcid.org/0000-0002-1896-0312
Stanley College of Engineering and Technology for Women, India

Tushaar Sadanand
https://orcid.org/0009-0003-5112-5751
National University of Advanced Legal Studies, India

ABSTRACT

This chapter examines the role of artificial intelligence (AI) in shaping social justice, environmental ethics, and legal governance in India. It explores how AI technologies can both perpetuate and mitigate social biases, particularly in areas like healthcare, education, and finance. The chapter also addresses AI's environmental impact, from promoting sustainable practices to the ethical concerns surrounding its development. Finally, it analyzes India's regulatory landscape, proposing recommendations for a governance framework that ensures responsible AI deployment, while balancing innovation with ethical considerations tailored to India's socio-economic context.

DOI: 10.4018/979-8-3373-3384-7.ch004

Background

Artificial Intelligence (AI) has emerged as one of the most transformative technologies of the 21st century, with its potential applications cutting across multiple sectors, including healthcare, finance, education, agriculture, and environmental sustainability. Globally, AI is being hailed for its ability to drive innovation, optimize processes, and solve complex problems, but it also raises significant ethical concerns, particularly in terms of social justice, equity, and sustainability. In a diverse and populous nation like India, where economic and social inequalities are pronounced, AI has the potential to be a double-edged sword. On one hand, AI technologies can enhance access to services, improve efficiency, and promote inclusive growth. On the other hand, without proper oversight and ethical design, AI systems may unintentionally reinforce societal biases, exclude marginalized communities, and contribute to environmental degradation through energy-intensive practices. The digital divide, particularly between rural and urban areas, and across different socio-economic groups, further complicates equitable access to AI benefits.

India is uniquely positioned at the intersection of rapid technological advancement and complex socio-economic challenges. The National Strategy for Artificial Intelligence, released by the NITI Aayog in 2018, identifies AI as a means to address critical development challenges while emphasizing the need for responsible deployment. However, India's regulatory framework surrounding AI remains nascent, with significant gaps in addressing the ethical, social, and environmental implications of AI technology. As AI becomes increasingly integrated into sectors that impact daily life, it is vital to develop governance frameworks that promote equity, accountability, and sustainability. Moreover, as the global focus shifts towards sustainable development, the environmental impact of AI has come under scrutiny. AI technologies can offer solutions to climate change and resource management through applications like precision agriculture and energy optimization, but they can also have a considerable carbon footprint due to their energy-intensive nature, especially in areas such as data processing and machine learning. Against this backdrop, this chapter aims to explore how AI, when properly governed and ethically implemented, can contribute to social justice, environmental sustainability, and legal governance in India. By examining both the potential benefits and risks associated with AI, the chapter will offer a nuanced understanding of AI's role in shaping a more just and sustainable future for India.

INTRODUCTION

AI has the potential to revolutionize the way societies function, offering unprecedented opportunities for innovation, efficiency, and growth. However, as AI technologies become more deeply embedded in the fabric of daily life, they also pose significant ethical, social, and legal challenges. In a country like India, where socio-economic disparities are stark, and environmental sustainability is a pressing concern, the deployment of AI must be carefully managed to ensure it promotes equity, justice, and sustainability. The integration of AI into critical sectors such as healthcare, education, and finance can enhance the accessibility and quality of services. For example, AI-driven diagnostic tools can improve healthcare delivery in underserved areas, while AI-powered learning platforms can personalize education for students from marginalized communities. However, the risks of bias in AI algorithms, particularly when they are trained on biased data, cannot be ignored. Algorithms that lack inclusivity can perpetuate existing social inequalities, especially in hiring, credit scoring, and service delivery. This raises urgent questions about how AI can be designed and implemented in ways that mitigate these biases and promote social justice.

The environmental implications of AI are equally significant. AI offers solutions to some of the most pressing environmental challenges of our time, including climate change, resource depletion, and energy efficiency. For instance, AI can optimize agricultural processes, reducing water usage and improving crop yields, or help manage urban energy systems to minimize waste. At the same time, the development and deployment of AI technologies require vast computational resources, which have a considerable environmental cost. The ethical responsibility of AI developers and companies to reduce their carbon footprint and ensure sustainable development is thus an essential consideration.

Finally, AI governance in India presents a unique challenge. While the Indian government has recognized AI's potential, the regulatory framework is still evolving. Ensuring that AI technologies are deployed ethically, transparently, and accountably requires robust policies that are informed by global best practices but adapted to India's unique socio-economic context. This includes addressing issues such as data privacy, algorithmic transparency, and accountability for AI-driven decisions. Policymakers must also consider how to balance innovation with the need for ethical governance, ensuring that AI technologies serve the common good without exacerbating social inequalities or environmental harm. This study examines the intricate interplay between AI, social equity, sustainability, and regulatory frameworks within the Indian context. By drawing on case studies from India and comparing them with global best practices, this chapter seeks to provide a comprehensive analysis of the potential and pitfalls of AI in fostering a more just and sustainable future.

Through this exploration, the chapter will offer actionable recommendations for policymakers, technologists, and civil society to ensure that AI technologies are harnessed responsibly and equitably in India.

REVIEW OF LITERATURE

Recent literature has increasingly focused on the multifaceted impact of AI across various domains, including environmental sustainability, legal frameworks, and social justice. Islam et al. (2024) investigated the integration of AI in environmental sustainability efforts in India, a nation grappling with significant environmental challenges. Their research emphasizes the potential of AI to enhance resource management and environmental monitoring, advocating for a tailored AI strategy that aligns with India's unique context to maximize benefits and mitigate risks. Complementing this perspective, Gundeti et al. (2024) explored AI's role in addressing urgent environmental issues across sectors, highlighting both the opportunities it presents, such as climate change mitigation, and the concerns over AI's carbon footprint, particularly the energy consumption associated with data centers. They argue for responsible AI development that aligns with sustainability goals.

Transitioning to the legal sector, Jeswani and Valecha (2024) examined how AI has transformed legal processes, enhancing efficiency and access to justice. They also raised ethical concerns regarding algorithmic biases, emphasizing the need for responsible AI governance to uphold fairness within legal systems. This theme of ethical governance is echoed by Chopra (2024), who highlighted the necessity of a comprehensive regulatory framework in India to address ethical AI development and public trust issues. Warang and Sackib (2024) further enriched this discourse by analyzing the implications of AI in judicial processes, advocating for algorithmic accountability and protections for vulnerable populations. Liebig et al. (2024) explored the role of subnational governance in shaping AI policy, addressing a gap in the existing literature that tends to focus on national and international AI strategies. Through a case study of Germany's 16 states, they analyzed 34 AI policy documents to understand the themes and priorities at the subnational level. They found that subnational efforts primarily focus on facilitating knowledge transfer between research and industry, the commercialization of AI, and the incorporation of ethical principles, all within the context of the distinct economic identities of each state. The authors argued that federal states play an active role in AI policy and that analyzing AI at multiple levels of governance is essential for understanding the development and implementation of AI strategies in various national contexts. Koulu and Kontiainen (2019) emphasized the importance of individual rights and good governance in AI systems, advocating for interdisciplinary dialogue to navigate the challenges posed by AI in legal contexts. Their findings suggest that a collaborative approach is essential to shape the future legal implications of AI technologies.

The interplay between AI and social justice is critically analyzed in several studies. Buccella (2023) argued for understanding AI through the Capability Approach, positing that equitable access to AI technologies is vital for realizing social justice. This perspective is complemented by Taylor et al. (2023), who traced the historical roots of AI technologies, notably the Mahalanobis Distance Function, revealing its colonial origins and ongoing racial implications in modern AI applications like facial recognition. The authors underscore the need for awareness of these historical contexts to prevent the reinforcement of discrimination through contemporary technologies. Moreover, Sloan and Warner (2020) expanded on the discussion of AI bias, framing it as a subset of broader social justice issues. They proposed a mathematical reinterpretation of fairness constraints in AI systems, aiming to ensure that AI does not perpetuate unjust outcomes. Krupiy (2020) further illustrated the potential for AI-driven decision-making systems to disadvantage marginalized groups, particularly in contexts like university admissions, calling for mandatory human oversight in critical decision-making processes. The evolving role of ethics in technology, particularly in the context of AI, was explored by Vargas-Elizondo (2020), who discussed the UN's 2030 Agenda as a guiding ethical framework for technological advancement. Kantha et al. (2024) highlighted the ethical implications of AI, big data, and the Internet of Things (IoT), raising concerns about privacy, equity, and the risks of surveillance. They argued for the development of an ethical framework to ensure that technological advancements benefit all, not just privileged groups. Jobin et al. (2019) mapped the emerging global discourse on ethical AI, identifying key principles like transparency and fairness while noting the challenges in implementation across different contexts. Their findings suggest a growing consensus on the need for ethical guidelines, despite significant variations in interpretation and application.

LITERATURE GAP

The existing literature on AI’s intersection with social justice, environmental ethics, and legal governance reveals several gaps, particularly in the Indian context, which your study aims to address. While research has explored AI's potential for social justice, such as alleviating biases, most studies focus on global or Western settings, with limited analysis of how AI impacts marginalized communities in India's healthcare, education, and finance sectors. Similarly, although AI’s role in environmental sustainability has been discussed, there is a lack of detailed investigation into AI’s carbon footprint and ethical responsibilities in developing nations like India, especially in critical areas such as agriculture, energy management, and urban planning. Additionally, while AI governance and legal frameworks have been examined globally, the literature lacks a comparative analysis of India's regulatory mechanisms relative to international standards, leaving an important gap in understanding how India can improve its AI governance to ensure fairness and accountability. Further, ethical concerns surrounding AI's application in key sectors such as agriculture, energy, and urban planning remain underexplored. Your study will address these gaps by investigating AI's role in fostering social justice, sustainability, and responsible governance in India, offering new insights into both the ethical and regulatory dimensions of AI within this diverse and populous nation.

NEED FOR THE STUDY

As AI continues to reshape society and industry, its potential to either mitigate or exacerbate societal inequalities becomes increasingly significant. It is imperative for identifying AI's role in fostering equity, sustainability, and responsible governance, particularly in a diverse and populous nation like India. Additionally, AI's environmental impact, both positive and negative, is a growing concern that must be addressed through ethical practices.

SCOPE OF THE STUDY

This study focuses on AI's impact on social justice in sectors such as healthcare, education, and finance, focusing on how AI perpetuates or alleviates societal biases in the Indian context. It highlights the relationship between AI and environmental ethics, focusing on AI's role in promoting sustainability, especially in agriculture, energy management, and urban planning, while discussing ethical responsibilities. Also, it will examine the legal and governance frameworks surrounding AI in India and proposing improvements in India's regulatory mechanisms.

OBJECTIVES OF THE STUDY

- To analyze AI's role in alleviating social biases in various sectors such as healthcare, education, and finance.
- To explore the role of AI in combating climate change and promoting sustainable practices in agriculture, energy, and urban planning.

- To critically assess the current AI regulatory framework in India, identify gaps, and propose a framework for a responsible AI governance

LIMITATIONS

- There is a lack of standardized metrics for evaluating AI's role in social justice and environmental ethics, which may limit the comparability of case studies.
- The rapid pace of AI development and policy changes may result in some proposed regulatory solutions becoming outdated.
- The chapter's focus on India means its findings and recommendations may not be universally applicable to other developing or developed nations with different socio-economic contexts.

AI'S ROLE IN REDUCING SOCIAL BIASES IN HEALTHCARE

AI is revolutionizing the healthcare sector by offering sophisticated tools to tackle entrenched social biases based on race, gender, socio-economic status, and other demographic factors. Through advanced machine learning (ML) algorithms, natural language processing (NLP), and computer vision, AI can not only identify, but also mitigate these biases, promoting fairness and equity in healthcare delivery. AI's ability to analyze vast datasets with unprecedented speed and accuracy enables it to detect patterns of bias in healthcare delivery that may go unnoticed by human practitioners. Supervised and unsupervised machine learning algorithms can be trained to sift through electronic health records (EHRs), patient demographics, and clinical outcomes to identify disparities in treatments or diagnoses. For example, deep learning models can flag instances where certain racial groups receive different treatment recommendations compared to others with the same symptoms. Techniques such as clustering and classification allow AI to group similar cases, detect outliers, and highlight systematic biases in diagnosis or prescription patterns.

AI can reduce biases in clinical decision-making by relying on predictive models that are trained on large datasets from diverse populations. By incorporating patient histories, genetic data, and real-time health metrics, AI can generate more accurate and unbiased treatment recommendations. Reinforcement learning, a subset of ML, is especially useful here, as it enables AI systems to continuously learn from new data and optimize decisions over time. This dynamic adaptation can help eliminate human-driven biases related to stereotypes or assumptions about particular groups. Moreover, AI-based decision-support tools using Bayesian networks and random forest models can evaluate the probability of various medical conditions more objectively, providing personalized treatment plans without the influence of a patient's demographic background. AI has the potential to identify gaps in healthcare access by analyzing population-level health data. Natural language processing (NLP) models can be employed to scan through social media, health records, and public health reports to detect areas where underserved communities face barriers to healthcare access. Geospatial analysis powered by AI can predict health risks and healthcare shortages in specific regions by combining environmental, social, and epidemiological data. This can lead to targeted healthcare interventions in marginalized communities. AI can also be integrated into telemedicine platforms, where conversational agents (chatbots) and AI-powered virtual assistants help provide real-time, culturally competent advice to individuals from low-resource settings, thereby improving access to preventive care and medical information.

AI can also play a crucial role in mitigating biases among healthcare professionals through advanced simulations and personalized learning platforms. AI-powered virtual reality (VR) and augmented reality (AR) platforms can simulate diverse healthcare scenarios, allowing clinicians to engage with virtual patients from different racial, gender, or socio-economic backgrounds. This hands-on experience, combined with emotion recognition AI, helps healthcare providers practice empathetic, unbiased communication in real-world settings. AI algorithms can also track performance in real-time, identifying areas where a clinician might unconsciously exhibit bias and offering corrective feedback. Machine learning techniques can further personalize training by adapting scenarios based on a clinician's specific needs and past performance.

Clinical trials often suffer from a lack of diversity, leading to treatments that are not optimized for all populations. AI can help address this by analyzing demographic and genomic data to identify underrepresented groups that should be included in trials. AI-powered recruitment platforms can use algorithms to match patients with clinical trials based on their medical histories, demographic information, and genetic profiles, ensuring that studies are more representative of the broader population. Furthermore, deep learning models can identify patterns in historical trial data to predict which demographic groups may be underrepresented in future studies, allowing trial organizers to design more inclusive studies. This ensures that the efficacy and safety of new treatments are assessed across diverse populations.

While AI has the potential to reduce social biases, it can also perpetuate them if not designed and trained responsibly. Bias often arises when algorithms are trained on historical healthcare data reflecting existing disparities. To prevent this, techniques like bias detection algorithms and fairness constraints can be integrated into AI models. For instance, adversarial debiasing can help minimize the impact of biased data, while algorithmic auditing tools can assess AI performance across different demographic groups to ensure equitable recommendations. Fairness-aware machine learning and differential privacy are essential for ensuring transparency and ethical outcomes. Additionally, federated learning can be employed to train AI models on decentralized datasets without sharing sensitive patient information, enhancing robustness and incorporating diverse populations. This approach leads to more inclusive insights and personalized treatment plans that are less influenced by regional or institutional biases.

AI'S ROLE IN REDUCING SOCIAL BIASES IN EDUCATION SECTOR

Social Bias in Education

Social biases in education arise from entrenched inequalities related to socio-economic status, gender, ethnicity, and caste. Marginalized students often encounter challenges like limited access to quality education, teacher bias, and unequal resource distribution, all of which hinder their academic success and future opportunities. Traditional education systems are susceptible to unconscious bias in classrooms, admissions, and performance evaluations. For instance, students from economically disadvantaged backgrounds may receive less attention or have their potential underestimated due to stereotypes. Similarly, girls and students from marginalized communities face discrimination that negatively impacts their educational outcomes, limiting their access to opportunities and reducing their confidence and career prospects.

AI's Potential to Alleviate Social Biases

Artificial intelligence, when designed and deployed with ethical considerations, can help reduce some of the biases present in traditional education systems by providing personalized learning experiences, offering objective assessments, and increasing access to education for underrepresented groups. The deployment of AI technologies in education raises important ethical concerns, particularly regarding their potential to perpetuate or alleviate social biases. In regions with entrenched social inequalities, such as India and other developing countries, AI holds the potential to mitigate biases and create more equitable learning environments if implemented with ethical considerations in mind. AI has the potential to transform educational landscapes by addressing and alleviating social bias, thereby creating more equitable learning environments. AI-powered adaptive learning systems enable personalized education, allowing students to progress at their own pace, which is particularly beneficial for marginalized communities and rural areas.

Table 1. Enhancing equity in education through AI applications

AI Application	How AI Alleviates Social Bias	Examples
Personalized Learning	AI enables adaptive learning systems that tailor educational content to individual needs, allowing students to learn at their own pace and based on their personal requirements.	BYJU's and Khan Academy in India use AI to offer personalized education, benefiting students in rural areas and from marginalized communities.
Objective Assessments	AI-driven automated grading systems provide consistent and unbiased assessments, reducing the impact of subjective teacher evaluations.	Gradescope in the U.S. assists teachers in providing more objective assessments, which can also be applied in India.
Increased Access to Education	AI-powered online learning platforms make quality education more accessible to underserved and remote areas. AI-driven language translation and speech recognition tools help overcome language barriers and increase inclusivity.	AI platforms like Microsoft's AI for Accessibility and Google AI tools improve access to learning for disabled students and those speaking minority languages.
Bridging the Digital Divide	AI can potentially bridge the digital divide by providing learning resources to under-resourced schools and remote areas.	The Digital India campaign uses AI to bring technology and digital education to rural populations.

Automated grading systems ensure consistent and unbiased assessments, minimizing subjective influences and creating a level playing field for all learners. Additionally, AI-driven online platforms enhance accessibility by breaking down language barriers through translation and speech recognition tools, making quality education available to a broader audience, including disabled students and linguistic minorities. Initiatives like the Digital India campaign further illustrate AI's role in bridging the digital divide by delivering educational resources to under-resourced schools and remote regions. Collectively, these applications highlight AI's capacity to foster inclusivity and equity in education, addressing long-standing biases that hinder educational attainment.

AI'S ROLE IN REDUCING SOCIAL BIASES IN THE FINANCE SECTOR

AI is revolutionizing the financial services industry by introducing more efficient, data-driven processes that streamline everything from loan approvals to investment management. However, financial services have traditionally been susceptible to social biases stemming from discriminatory practices related to race, gender, income levels, and geographic location. These biases can lead to unfair lending practices, higher interest rates, and exclusion from essential financial services for marginalized communities.

AI, when used ethically, has the potential to reduce social biases in the finance sector by offering more objective and data-driven decision-making processes. Nonetheless, it is critical that AI is developed and deployed with careful attention to algorithmic fairness and ethical standards to avoid the risk of perpetuating biases present in historical data.

Understanding Social Bias in Finance

The financial sector has long been plagued by social biases that disproportionately affect individuals based on race, gender, income, and location. For example, loan approvals may be influenced by a customer's demographic characteristics rather than their actual financial reliability. Women and minority groups often face higher interest rates, less access to capital, or outright rejections (Carter, S. et al. 2015), even if their financial profiles are similar to those of their more privileged counterparts. Also, low-income individuals may be denied loans or credit cards due to credit scoring models (Dolson, E., & Jagtiani, J. 2024) that do not consider alternative data sources such as rent or utility payments. Such biases not only perpetuate inequality but also limit financial inclusion, stifling opportunities for economic growth in marginalized communities.

AI's Potential to Reduce Bias in Finance

Artificial Intelligence offers several pathways for reducing bias in financial decision-making processes, primarily through the use of advanced algorithms, automated decision-making, and alternative data. Key areas where AI has potential to reduce bias are discussed in *Table 2*.

Table 2. AI for fairness and inclusion in financial services

Key Area	Role	Example
AI-Powered Credit Scoring	Traditional credit scoring often disadvantages low-income individuals or those without banking services. AI-based models assess creditworthiness using alternative data like rental history, utility payments, and social media behavior, allowing for a more inclusive approach to lending.	Companies like Upstart and Zest AI use AI algorithms to evaluate borrowers' risk levels based on diverse factors, improving access to credit for younger borrowers, immigrants, and low-income communities.
Eliminating Human Bias in Loan Approvals	Human decision-makers may harbor unconscious biases in loan approvals. AI-powered automated underwriting systems evaluate applications based on objective data like income and credit behavior, eliminating bias related to race, gender, or socio-economic status.	Platforms like LendingClub and Kabbage utilize AI for faster and more objective loan processing, ensuring applicants are assessed fairly based on financial behavior rather than subjective human judgments.
Enhanced Fraud Detection and Prevention	Traditional fraud detection systems can disproportionately target minority groups. AI processes large amounts of data to develop nuanced behavior patterns, improving the fairness and accuracy of fraud detection models.	AI-based fraud detection systems used by JPMorgan Chase and American Express identify suspicious transactions by focusing on behavioral patterns rather than demographic assumptions, ensuring a balanced approach to fraud prevention.
Expanding Access to Financial Products	Financial exclusion is a barrier to economic growth, especially in underserved communities. AI facilitates the creation of customized financial products tailored to the needs of underbanked populations, ensuring accessibility and affordability.	PayPal and Ant Financial use AI to provide microloans and other services to individuals and small businesses, analyzing cash flow patterns and transaction data to enable access to credit and growth opportunities.

CHALLENGES AND ETHICAL CONSIDERATIONS

While AI offers promising solutions for reducing social biases in finance, it is not without its challenges. AI systems must be designed with algorithmic fairness and transparency in mind to avoid unintentionally perpetuating the very biases they aim to eliminate. Some of the key challenges are explained in *Table 3*.

Table 3. AI for fairness and inclusion in financial services

Challenge	Description	Solution
Bias in AI Algorithms	AI systems rely heavily on the quality of the data they are trained on. If historical data is biased (e.g., past lending practices favoring certain demographics), AI algorithms may replicate these biases. For instance, if a bank's loan approval data shows a preference for lending to men, the AI model may continue this bias in future decisions.	Financial institutions must clean and de-bias the data used for AI models and implement bias detection tools to ensure fair outcomes.
Transparency and Accountability	AI models often operate as black boxes, making it difficult to understand their decision-making processes. This lack of transparency can lead to concerns about fairness, especially when applicants are rejected without knowing the reasons.	Financial institutions should adopt explainable AI (XAI) techniques, which provide clear, interpretable justifications for AI decisions, promoting fairness and improving consumer trust in AI systems.
Access to Technology	The digital divide presents a significant barrier to financial inclusion. For AI-driven systems to benefit underserved populations, adequate technological infrastructure (like internet access and digital literacy) must be in place.	Governments and financial institutions should invest in digital infrastructure and financial literacy programs to ensure marginalized populations can fully benefit from AI-enabled financial services.
Data Privacy and Security	The collection and processing of personal data for AI applications raise concerns about privacy and data security. Users may be unaware of how their data is being used, leading to potential misuse or breaches.	Financial institutions must implement strict data governance policies, including encryption, anonymization, and robust data access controls to protect consumer information and comply with regulations like GDPR.
Regulatory Compliance	AI systems must comply with existing financial regulations, which can be challenging due to the rapidly evolving nature of AI technology. Non-compliance can lead to legal issues and financial penalties for institutions.	Financial institutions should stay informed about regulatory changes and work closely with regulators to ensure their AI systems comply with all relevant laws and standards.
Reliability and Robustness	AI models can be sensitive to changes in data and may produce unreliable outcomes if not properly maintained. This could result in poor decision-making, especially in high-stakes financial situations.	Regularly monitoring and updating AI models, conducting stress tests, and implementing robust validation processes can help ensure the reliability and robustness of AI systems in finance.
Ethical Use of AI	The deployment of AI in financial services raises ethical concerns about automation leading to job displacement, especially for roles traditionally filled by humans, such as loan officers or customer service representatives.	Institutions should consider a balanced approach to automation, combining AI tools with human oversight, and invest in retraining programs to help employees transition to new roles created by AI technologies.
Algorithmic Transparency	Even with explainable AI, consumers may still struggle to understand how AI algorithms function and how decisions affect them personally. This can erode trust in financial institutions.	Financial institutions should engage in consumer education efforts to demystify AI algorithms and promote a better understanding of AI's role in decision-making processes.

AI holds significant promise for reducing social biases in the finance sector by promoting more objective decision-making, enhancing financial inclusion, and creating more equitable access to credit and other financial services. However, to fully realize these benefits, it is crucial that AI systems are developed and deployed with attention to algorithmic fairness, transparency, and ethical standards. By addressing these challenges, AI can serve as a powerful tool for building a more inclusive and equitable financial system, ensuring that individuals from all backgrounds have the opportunity to participate fully in the global economy.

AI'S ROLE IN CLIMATE ACTION AND SUSTAINABLE AGRICULTURE

As the world faces climate change and food security challenges, the agricultural sector is at a critical juncture. With the global population projected to reach nearly 10 billion by 2050, food demand will increase significantly, straining natural resources. However, AI offers promising solutions by optimizing productivity and minimizing environmental impact. Technologies like precision farming, which utilizes satellite imagery and sensor data, along with predictive analytics for weather and disease forecasting, are transforming agriculture into a more sustainable and resilient practice. Table 4. delves into the myriad applications of AI in agriculture and animal farming, exploring how these advancements not only enhance food production but also play a crucial role in mitigating climate risks.

Table 4. AI for sustainable agriculture

Area of Application	Description	Key Applications
Precision Agriculture	Utilizes AI technologies for efficient farming practices by monitoring crops and soil conditions.	- Remote sensing and imaging (drones and satellites) for crop health assessment. - Soil and crop monitoring for informed management decisions.
Predictive Analytics	AI forecasts climate-related risks, helping farmers adapt to changing conditions.	- Weather and climate modeling for predicting extreme weather events. - Pest and disease prediction through pattern recognition in environmental data.
Livestock Management	Enhances health monitoring and feeding practices for livestock, improving animal welfare and reducing costs.	- Health monitoring using sensors and wearables. - Optimized feed formulation for improved feed efficiency and reduced waste.

continued on following page

Table 4. Continued

Area of Application	Description	Key Applications
Environmental Monitoring	Supports sustainable practices through monitoring of soil health, water quality, and biodiversity.	- Soil health assessment and water quality monitoring. - Biodiversity monitoring to evaluate ecosystem impacts.
Supply Chain Optimization	Improves the efficiency of agricultural supply chains to minimize waste and reduce environmental impact.	- Demand forecasting for crop production planning. - Logistics and distribution optimization for reduced transportation emissions.
Decision Support Systems	Provides farmers with actionable insights to enhance productivity and profitability through data integration.	- Real-time data integration for informed decision-making. - Recommendations for adaptive management practices based on changing conditions.
Climate Resilience in Animal Farming	Enhances climate resilience through monitoring and improving livestock management practices.	- Disease surveillance and control through data analysis. - Genetic improvement programs for developing climate-resilient livestock traits.
Mitigating Climate Risks	Develops early warning systems and assessments for climate-related risks in agriculture.	- Early warning systems for climate impacts using real-time data. - Climate impact assessments for evaluating the environmental footprint of farming practices.
Customized Nutrition and Feeding	AI generates tailored feed plans for livestock, enhancing feed efficiency and reducing environmental impact.	- Data analysis for optimizing feed formulation based on animal health and nutrient needs. - Minimizing waste and greenhouse gas emissions from livestock.
Environmental Impact Mitigation	AI assists in analyzing and reducing the environmental impact of farming practices.	- Identifying practices that reduce carbon footprints. - Supporting sustainable resource use through optimized nutrient management.

AI's Role in Climate Solutions and Sustainable Energy

As the world confronts the multifaceted challenges of climate change and energy sustainability, AI stands out as a powerful ally in driving innovation and facilitating the transition to a greener future. From optimizing energy efficiency and integrating renewable sources to monitoring climate impacts and enhancing agricultural practices, AI technologies are reshaping the landscape of climate solutions and sustainable energy.

Table 5 provides a concise overview of AI's impactful role in climate solutions and sustainable energy, detailing the various applications and their significance in creating a sustainable future.

Table 5. AI for climate solutions and sustainable energy

Area of Application	Description	Key Applications
Optimizing Energy Efficiency	Enhances energy efficiency across various sectors, reducing waste and emissions.	- Smart Grids for dynamic energy distribution based on real-time consumption patterns. - Building Management Systems: Optimizes HVAC systems for reduced energy use. - Industrial Process Optimization: Predictive maintenance to enhance equipment performance.
Renewable Energy Integration	Facilitates the transition to renewable energy sources, maximizing their effectiveness.	- Solar Energy Forecasting: Predicts solar production using weather data. - Wind Energy Optimization: Adjusts turbine operations for maximum efficiency. - Energy Storage Management: Optimizes charging and discharging cycles of storage systems.
Climate Monitoring and Predictive Analytics	Provides tools for monitoring environmental changes and predicting future climate conditions.	- Climate Modeling: Improves climate models using satellite and sensor data. - Disaster Prediction: Forecasts extreme weather events. - Carbon Footprint Analysis: Analyzes emissions data to develop reduction strategies.
Sustainable Transportation Solutions	Aims to reduce emissions from the transportation sector through smart solutions.	- Smart Transportation Systems: Optimizes traffic management to reduce congestion. - Electric Vehicle (EV) Integration: Predicts charging demand and optimizes station placement. - Autonomous Vehicles: Enhances traffic flow and fuel efficiency.
Sustainable Agriculture and Land Use	Enhances sustainability in agriculture and land management through data-driven practices.	- Precision Agriculture: Optimizes resource use through data analysis. - Land Use Management: Supports sustainable planning and conservation efforts. - Carbon Sequestration: Identifies practices for enhancing carbon storage in agricultural systems.

Embracing these advancements requires collaboration among governments, industries, and researchers to create supportive policies and frameworks that promote the responsible use of AI.

AI for Sustainable Urban Planning

AI is playing a transformative role in promoting sustainable urban planning. By leveraging advanced data analytics and predictive modeling, AI applications are helping cities and communities adapt to the challenges posed by climate change while optimizing urban infrastructure and resources. *Table 6* shows few areas of application of AI in urban planning.

Table 6. AI for sustainable urban planning

Area of Application	Description	Key Applications
Smart Infrastructure Management	AI optimizes the management of urban infrastructure, ensuring it can withstand climate impacts and function efficiently.	- Predictive Maintenance: Uses sensor data to predict infrastructure failures and optimize repair schedules. - Energy Management Systems: Analyzes consumption patterns for efficient energy distribution and usage.
Urban Mobility Optimization	Enhances urban transportation systems to reduce emissions and improve efficiency through data-driven solutions.	- Traffic Management: AI algorithms optimize traffic flow and reduce congestion by analyzing real-time data. - Public Transit Optimization: Improves routing and scheduling of public transport based on user demand and patterns.
Sustainable Land Use Planning	AI supports decision-making in urban planning, ensuring land use is sustainable and resilient to climate change.	- Zoning Analysis: Assesses the impact of zoning regulations on climate resilience and community needs. - Green Space Planning: Identifies areas for parks and green infrastructure to mitigate urban heat effects.
Disaster Response and Recovery	AI enhances the effectiveness of disaster response strategies by providing real-time data and predictive analytics for emergency management.	- Emergency Response Systems: Uses AI to analyze data from various sources (social media, sensors) to assess situations and deploy resources effectively. - Recovery Planning: Predicts recovery needs and allocates resources for post-disaster recovery.

continued on following page

Table 6. Continued

Area of Application	Description	Key Applications
Community Engagement and Education	Facilitates community involvement in urban planning and climate resilience initiatives through data visualization and participatory tools.	- Visualization Tools: Provides interactive maps and models that help communities understand climate risks and planning decisions. - Crowdsourced Data Collection: Engages residents in reporting local environmental changes and needs.
Climate Adaptation Strategies	AI assists in developing and implementing adaptation strategies to mitigate climate impacts on urban areas.	- Adaptation Planning: Analyzes climate data to recommend strategies for infrastructure and ecosystem improvements. - Monitoring Adaptation Effectiveness: Tracks the success of adaptation measures using data analytics.
Energy Resilience	AI helps improve the resilience of urban energy systems against climate impacts, ensuring a reliable power supply.	- Decentralized Energy Management: Facilitates the integration of renewable energy sources and microgrids. - Demand Response Systems: Adjusts energy consumption based on supply conditions and climate events to maintain grid stability.

Tools like IBM Weather Company and Aon provide localized climate risk assessments, enabling cities to anticipate climate-related impacts. Companies such as Siemens and Honeywell utilize AI for predictive maintenance and energy management, enhancing urban infrastructure efficiency. Additionally, platforms like Google Maps and Citymapper optimize urban mobility by analyzing traffic patterns and public transport data. AI aids sustainable land use planning through tools like Urban Footprint and NatureServe, while initiatives such as UN Global Pulse and Zebra Medical Vision leverage real-time data for effective disaster response. Community engagement is fostered by platforms like OpenStreetMap and LocalData, which facilitate data collection and visualization of environmental changes. Moreover, organizations like ICLEI and CAKE offer AI-driven solutions for climate adaptation planning, and companies like Tesla and AutoGrid optimize energy management and storage.

AI's Carbon Footprint and Ethical Responsibilities

The advancement of AI has brought incredible breakthroughs, but it has also raised concerns about its environmental impact. One of the critical drivers of these advancements has been deep learning (DL), especially since the 2010s. Deep learning, powered by multi-layered neural networks, has revolutionized tasks like image recognition, natural language processing, and autonomous driving (Van

Wynsberghe, A. 2021). However, the increasing computational power required to train and operate these models has significantly raised AI's energy consumption and, consequently, its carbon footprint.

The Rise of Deep Learning and Increased Energy Demand

The rapid development of deep learning models has been a game-changer in the AI landscape. These models have become integral to various applications, including voice assistants, autonomous vehicles, healthcare diagnostics, and financial predictions. However, their complexity, involving billions of parameters and requiring vast amounts of data, demands massive computational power.

For instance, training large-scale models like OpenAI's GPT series involves intensive processes that require substantial energy resources. Deep learning models are typically trained in data centers using powerful Graphics Processing Units (GPUs) and Tensor Processing Units (TPUs). While this has accelerated AI's capabilities, it has also sparked concerns about environmental sustainability due to the high energy consumption and associated carbon emissions.

Carbon Footprint of Advanced Models

Deep learning models like GPT-3 and BERT require substantial computational resources, consuming energy comparable to that of a small city during training. A 2019 study estimated that training one model could emit over 284 metric tons of CO2, equivalent to the lifetime emissions of five cars. Moreover, the operational phase also contributes to the carbon footprint, as AI models consume energy during data processing and inference tasks across millions of users. Data centers hosting these models require significant energy for both computation and cooling, often relying on non-renewable energy sources, which further exacerbates their environmental impact.

Ethical Responsibilities in Reducing AI's Carbon Footprint

With the growing concerns about AI's environmental sustainability, there are several ethical responsibilities that developers, organizations, and governments must address to mitigate AI's carbon footprint:

- Instead of deploying large, energy-hungry models for all tasks, AI developers can choose smaller, more focused models tailored for simpler tasks. This reduces the energy required for training and inference while still providing accurate results for specific use cases. Smaller models not only save energy but also ensure computational resources are used judiciously.

- AI researchers and developers can focus on creating algorithms that prioritize energy efficiency over computational accuracy where appropriate. This involves reducing the complexity of models and using techniques like pruning, which removes unnecessary parameters, or quantization, which reduces the precision of computations without compromising performance.
- AI systems should be designed with energy efficiency in mind from the start. Incorporating energy-saving algorithms and minimizing redundant computations during the training and inference phases can make AI models more sustainable. Federated learning is another promising approach, where AI models are trained across decentralized devices, reducing the need for centralized data centers and their associated energy costs.
- Shifting AI data centers to renewable energy sources is a critical step in reducing AI's carbon footprint. Tech companies like Google and Microsoft are already leading the way by transitioning their data centers to solar, wind, and hydroelectric power. Widespread adoption of renewables could significantly reduce the environmental impact of AI models, especially those running at scale.
- Organizations involved in AI development should provide transparent reporting on the environmental impact of their AI models. This includes disclosing energy consumption and carbon emissions during both the training and operational phases. Publicly available metrics can help consumers make informed choices and hold companies accountable for their environmental responsibilities.
- While AI contributes to environmental challenges, it also holds immense potential to address climate change and promote sustainability. AI technologies can be used to optimize energy consumption, improve the efficiency of renewable energy sources, and monitor environmental changes in real time. By using AI to develop solutions for energy management, agriculture, and waste reduction, its overall impact can be positive.

ADDRESSING THE CHALLENGES AND FUTURE DIRECTIONS

As AI evolves, balancing innovation with sustainability is crucial. While deep learning offers significant opportunities, it also necessitates managing its environmental impact. By adopting energy-efficient practices and developing sustainable algorithms, the AI community can promote a greener future. Future AI development should prioritize environmental responsibility, aligning with global sustainability goals. Collaboration among governments, industries, and academic institutions is essential to establish regulatory standards that encourage energy efficiency. Emerging guidelines, like the UN's recommendations on AI governance, stress the importance of transparency, accountability, and ethical use of AI to reduce its carbon footprint.

An Evaluation of India's Current AI Regulatory Framework

As India strides forward into the technological frontier, the absence of dedicated regulations for AI has become increasingly apparent. In response to the rapid development of AI technologies, including generative AI and large language models (LLMs), the Indian government has begun outlining a framework of advisories, guidelines, and existing IT rules to ensure responsible AI deployment. This evaluation explores the current landscape of AI regulation in India, highlighting significant advisories and the ongoing efforts to create a robust legal framework. In the year 2024, the Indian government issued a pivotal advisory mandating that platforms obtain explicit permission from the Ministry of Electronics and Information Technology (MeitY) before deploying any "unreliable AI models, LLMs, or generative AI software." This directive aims to protect users accessing the Indian Internet from potentially biased or harmful AI applications. The advisory requires platforms to ensure their technologies do not promote discrimination or undermine the electoral process and mandates labeling all AI-generated content with unique identifiers for easy identification.

In the realm of generative AI, technologies like OpenAI's ChatGPT and competitors such as Google's Gemini and Meta AI's LLaMA are revolutionizing content creation. However, the government's advisory specifically targets untested AI platforms, clarifying its applicability to "significant platforms" while exempting startups from the requirement to seek permission. Following public feedback, the government revised its advisory to eliminate the need for platforms to submit action reports but maintained an obligation for immediate compliance, emphasizing the labeling of under-tested or unreliable AI models. Despite these advisories, India currently lacks a dedicated regulatory framework specifically addressing AI technologies. However, existing guidelines and initiatives are shaping the regulatory landscape. The National Artificial Intelligence Strategy, launched by NITI Aayog in 2018, lays the groundwork for AI development across critical sectors such as healthcare, education, and agriculture. This strategy has facilitated the creation of high-quality datasets and legislative frameworks for data protection.

In 2021, NITI Aayog introduced the Principles for Responsible AI, focusing on ethical considerations in AI deployment, including safety, inclusivity, transparency, and accountability. These principles have been operationalized to promote responsible AI implementation, emphasizing collaboration between government, the private sector, and research organizations. Recent legislative efforts include the Digital Personal Data Protection Act, 2023, which addresses privacy concerns related to AI technologies by governing the processing of digital personal data in India. Additionally, the Information Technology (Intermediary Guidelines and Digital Media Ethics Code), 2021 provides a regulatory framework for social media and digital platforms, focusing on the removal of unlawful content and the protection of user rights. The Draft National Data Governance Framework Policy aims to modernize government data collection and management, fostering an ecosystem conducive to AI and data-driven research. Concurrently, the Ministry of Electronics and Information Technology has established committees to propose standards for AI development, safety, and ethics. The rise of deepfakes—digitally manipulated media generated by AI—poses significant challenges, including threats to privacy and information integrity. While India currently lacks specific laws targeting generative AI and deepfake-related crimes, existing legislation provides some civil and criminal remedies. Provisions within the Information Technology Act, 2000 enable prosecution for deepfake-related offenses, ensuring that intermediaries comply with content regulation standards. The Indian government is heavily investing in the AI sector, sanctioning INR 103 billion (approximately US$1.25 billion) for AI projects over five years (Source: https://www.reuters.com). This funding aims to develop computing infrastructure, support AI startups, and establish a National Data Management Office to enhance data quality for AI applications.

Gaps in AI Governance in India

As AI technologies rapidly advance and permeate various sectors in India, the need for a comprehensive governance framework becomes increasingly urgent. Despite recent efforts by the Indian government to establish guidelines and advisories regarding AI deployment, several significant gaps remain that could hinder the responsible and ethical use of AI. Table 7 examines these gaps in AI governance, highlighting critical areas that require attention to ensure that AI development aligns with societal values and safeguards public interest.

Table 7. Gaps in AI governance

Gaps in AI Governance	Explanation
Lack of a Comprehensive Legal Framework	The absence of a dedicated legal framework specifically addressing AI technologies hampers effective management of AI's complexities. Existing laws, such as the Information Technology Act, 2000, do not adequately cover algorithmic bias, data privacy, and accountability issues.
Insufficient Ethical Guidelines	The Principles for Responsible AI introduced by NITI Aayog are largely aspirational and lack enforceability, leaving significant risks unaddressed. Without structured compliance mechanisms, ethical principles may not be upheld.
Data Privacy Concerns	While the Digital Personal Data Protection Act, 2023 is a step forward, gaps remain in its implementation, particularly regarding sector-specific regulations for AI applications that involve sensitive data.
Accountability Mechanisms	The lack of clear accountability frameworks creates uncertainty regarding who is responsible when AI systems cause harm or make poor decisions. This gap complicates recourse for affected individuals.
Limited Public Awareness and Engagement	A disconnect exists between the government, industry, and the public regarding AI technologies, leading to a lack of trust and acceptance. Public engagement and awareness campaigns are necessary for informed discussions about AI risks and benefits.
Skill Gaps in the Workforce	India's workforce faces a significant skill gap in AI technologies and regulatory compliance. Training programs focused on AI ethics, law, and governance are essential for building a workforce capable of navigating AI complexities.
Coordination Across Sectors	Current AI governance efforts are fragmented, with different sectors developing their guidelines in isolation. A cohesive approach to AI governance is necessary to implement a unified strategy for responsible AI use.
Focus on Innovation Over Regulation	There is a prevailing sentiment that regulatory frameworks may stifle innovation, resulting in a prioritization of rapid AI deployment over essential governance measures. Balancing innovation and regulation is crucial for responsible AI use.

India is emerging as a key player in AI regulation and development. The government has allocated 10,300 crore (Source: https://pib.gov.in) to the India AI mission to bolster AI innovation and strengthen the public-private partnership ecosystem. The funds will be used to deploy 10,000 GPUs, support large multi-models (LMMs), and promote AI-based research collaborations. To balance economic growth and sustainable development goals (SDGs), India's AI strategy emphasizes responsible AI use while managing associated risks. A phased approach to AI governance is likely, promoting a fair and inclusive AI system that supports economic growth without compromising ethical and social responsibilities.

Innovative Framework for Responsible AI Governance

This study proposes an innovative framework for responsible AI governance as a solution to address the complexities and challenges of AI development, ensuring that it aligns with ethical, societal, and environmental goals. At the core of this framework as depicted in *Figure 1,* the need for Principle-Based Ethical Guidelines that emphasize transparency, fairness, privacy, and environmental responsibility.

Figure 1. Innovative framework for responsible AI governance

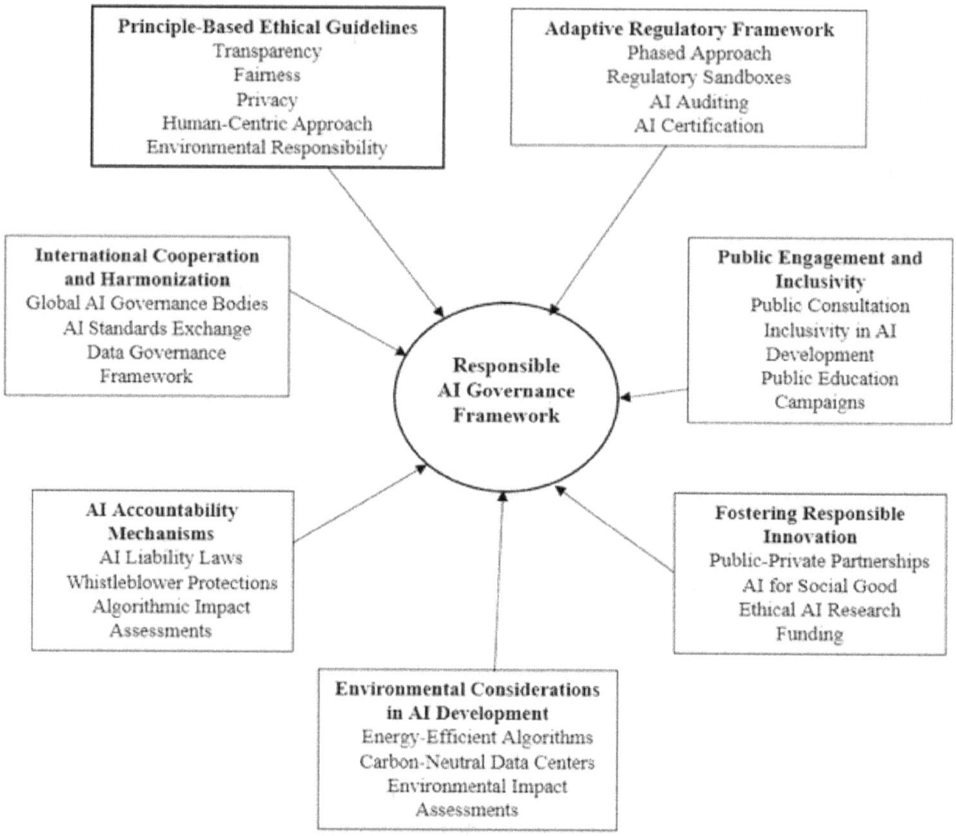

AI systems must be designed with a human-centric approach, ensuring that they enhance human welfare while prioritizing ethical considerations. In tandem, an Adaptive Regulatory Framework is essential, involving a phased approach to regulation, the use of regulatory sandboxes for testing, and mechanisms like AI auditing and certification to ensure compliance with ethical standards. Given the global nature of AI, International Cooperation and Harmonization is crucial. This involves establishing global AI governance bodies, exchanging best practices for AI standards, and creating a unified data governance framework that supports international collaboration. Moreover, Public Engagement and Inclusivity are vital in ensuring that AI development reflects the values and needs of diverse populations. Public consultation, inclusivity in AI development, and educational campaigns are necessary to raise awareness and ensure equitable AI applications. To maintain trust and accountability in AI, the framework emphasizes AI Accountability Mechanisms, which include AI liability laws, whistleblower protections, and algorithmic impact assessments. This ensures that AI systems are held accountable for their actions and outcomes, safeguarding against harmful effects. Fostering Responsible Innovation is another critical component, encouraging public-private partnerships and promoting AI for social good. Funding for ethical AI research is essential to ensure that innovation addresses societal challenges, such as healthcare and education, while remaining ethically sound. Recognizing the growing environmental impact of AI, the framework incorporates Environmental Considerations in AI Development, promoting the use of energy-efficient algorithms, carbon-neutral data centers, and conducting environmental impact assessments to minimize AI's carbon footprint.

The heart of this approach lies in a Responsible AI Governance Framework that integrates all these elements—ethical guidelines, regulatory mechanisms, international cooperation, public engagement, accountability, innovation, and environmental sustainability—into a cohesive structure. This framework is designed to be dynamic and adaptable, evolving with the rapid advancements in AI technology while addressing emerging challenges such as bias, privacy concerns, and environmental degradation. Ultimately, the framework highlights the need for AI governance that not only responds to immediate concerns but also proactively shapes AI's role in society, ensuring that it serves the common good while safeguarding ethical, social, and environmental values.

Ethical AI Practices for Socio-Economic Development in India

Ethical AI practices are crucial for ensuring that AI technologies contribute positively to socio-economic development in India, particularly by promoting fairness, inclusivity, and transparency. By ensuring that AI benefits are distributed equitably across all socio-economic groups, ethical AI can help bridge gaps in essential services like healthcare, education, and access to government resources (Sadanand, V. K., & Nandini, S. (2025), especially for the 68.8% of India's population that lives in rural areas (Bhasker, S. et al. (2024). Transparency and accountability in AI decision-making prevent biases that could harm disadvantaged communities, particularly in financial services, healthcare, and welfare distribution. Ethical AI also emphasizes job creation and the need for workforce re-skilling to avoid large-scale displacement as AI-driven industries grow, which is vital for India's approximately 400 million unskilled and semi-skilled workers.

Recommendations for Policymakers

- It is suggested that India establish a dedicated AI regulatory authority to oversee the development and governance of AI technologies, ensuring safe, transparent, and ethical applications across various sectors. To maintain a balance between innovation and ethical oversight, it is recommended to create a comprehensive AI regulatory framework that prioritizes transparency, accountability, and data protection, along with regulatory "sandboxes" for safe testing of new technologies.
- It can be beneficial to embed ethical principles into AI development by building upon NITI Aayog's "Principles for Responsible AI," ensuring that policies promote fairness, privacy, and transparency, particularly in sensitive areas like healthcare and education. Furthermore, promoting inclusivity and accessibility in AI innovations is crucial, given that major population resides in rural areas. Therefore, implementing digital literacy programs can empower underserved communities to access AI solutions tailored to their needs.
- It is imperative to foster public-private partnerships to advance AI research and development aligned with national goals, effectively leveraging the 10,300 crore AI mission funding. Additionally, enhancing data governance frameworks is vital, and refining the Digital Personal Data Protection Act, 2023, while adopting global best practices, can strengthen data security and public trust.
- To address the current talent shortage, it is recommended that India invest in AI-focused education and training programs, ensuring a skilled workforce capable of driving innovation. It is also important to mitigate the environmental impact of AI technologies by encouraging the development of energy-efficient algorithms and promoting carbon-neutral data centers, aligning AI development with climate goals.
- To ensure accountability in AI systems, implementing regular audits, algorithmic impact assessments, and whistleblower protections can enhance transparency and minimize biases. Engaging in international cooperation is key; India should participate in global AI dialogues to harmonize regulations and align its framework with international standards while safeguarding national interests.
- Finally, aligning AI strategies with the United Nations' SDGs is crucial. Public funding for AI research should prioritize projects that directly address socio-economic challenges such as healthcare access and climate resilience, maximizing the benefits for society.

Recommendations for Technologists

- Technologists should prioritize the development of AI systems that incorporate fairness, transparency, and accountability. This involves designing algorithms that actively mitigate biases, particularly when the AI is applied in sensitive sectors such as healthcare, education, and finance. Efforts should be made to develop models that are inclusive and representative of diverse populations, ensuring that AI technologies do not reinforce social inequities.
- Given the environmental impact of AI, especially in energy-intensive applications like deep learning, technologists should focus on optimizing algorithms for energy efficiency. Leveraging techniques such as model compression, federated learning, and transitioning to renewable energy-powered data centers can help reduce AI's carbon footprint.
- Technologists must ensure that AI systems comply with data protection laws, such as India's Digital Personal Data Protection Act, 2023. AI models should be built with privacy-preserving techniques like differential privacy and encryption to safeguard user data. Responsible data handling practices will help maintain public trust in AI technologies.
- AI should be used to benefit underserved and marginalized communities, particularly in rural areas. By developing AI solutions tailored to local needs in areas like healthcare and agriculture, technologists can contribute to more equitable development across India. This also includes using AI to bridge the digital divide by making AI-driven tools accessible in low-tech environments .
- Technologists should work closely with ethicists, social scientists, and policymakers to ensure that AI technologies are socially responsible. This collaboration can help address ethical concerns and ensure that AI applications align with broader societal values, fostering trust and acceptance.

Recommendations for Civil Society

- Civil society organizations should advocate for the ethical use of AI by holding both developers and regulators accountable. By promoting transparency in AI decision-making and pushing for algorithmic audits, civil society can ensure that AI systems are designed to serve the public interest and avoid harm.
- To ensure that marginalized populations benefit from AI advancements, civil society groups should lead initiatives to enhance digital literacy. This includes educating the public about AI's benefits, risks, and rights, empowering citizens to engage with AI technologies responsibly and knowledgeably.

- Civil society must take an active role in monitoring how AI impacts social justice issues, such as exacerbating or alleviating inequalities in healthcare, finance, and education. By working with technologists and policymakers, they can advocate for AI applications that promote fairness and equality.
- Civil society should be involved in public consultations regarding AI governance frameworks. This participation ensures that policies reflect the diverse interests of society and that ethical concerns, especially regarding privacy, accountability, and inclusivity, are adequately addressed in AI regulation.
- Civil society organizations can push for AI solutions that align with India's sustainability goals. They should advocate for the development and use of AI in ways that reduce environmental harm, such as supporting the creation of AI-driven solutions for climate change mitigation and sustainable resource management.
- By actively participating in the AI ecosystem, technologists and civil society can help ensure that AI technologies contribute to a fairer, more sustainable, and equitable future for India.

CONCLUSION

AI has the potential to significantly reduce social biases in healthcare and education by utilizing advanced techniques like machine learning and predictive analytics. AI is set to revolutionize multiple sectors in India, including healthcare, education, finance, agriculture, and urban planning. However, to fully harness its potential, a robust governance framework is essential. The study emphasizes that AI must be implemented with ethical considerations at the forefront, particularly in a country as socio-economically diverse as India. Responsible deployment of AI should address social justice, environmental sustainability, and legal governance, ensuring AI benefits are equitably distributed across all sections of society. AI has the potential to bridge societal gaps by offering innovative solutions in healthcare and education, but it can also reinforce biases if not carefully regulated. Moreover, the environmental impact of AI is a growing concern due to the energy-intensive nature of deep learning models and data processing. AI's carbon footprint is significant, and there is an ethical responsibility for technologists to develop energy-efficient algorithms and promote sustainable AI practices. India's current AI regulatory framework is still evolving. It must integrate global best practices while addressing the country's unique socio-economic challenges. A dedicated AI regulatory body is essential to oversee the ethical, transparent, and accountable deployment of AI technologies. Furthermore, public-private partnerships, data privacy, workforce development, and international cooperation will be critical in shaping a future where AI can contribute to inclusive growth, sustainability, and fairness.

REFERENCES

Bhasker, S., Desai, A., & Mohan, D. (2024). Access. In *Equality Index': The widening rural-urban divide across basic amenities, social security*. The Wire.

Buccella, A. (2023). "AI for all" is a matter of social justice. *AI and Ethics*, *3*(4), 1143–1152. DOI: 10.1007/s43681-022-00222-z PMID: 36189174

Carter, S., Mwaura, S., Ram, M., Trehan, K., & Jones, T. (2015). Barriers to ethnic minority and women's enterprise: Existing evidence, policy tensions and unsettled questions. *International Small Business Journal*, *33*(1), 49–69. DOI: 10.1177/0266242614556823

Chopra, K. (2024). *Shaping the future: AI governance and its dynamic effect on India's AI competitiveness* (Doctoral dissertation).

Dolson, E., & Jagtiani, J. (2024). Which lenders are more likely to reach out to underserved consumers: Banks versus Fintechs versus other nonbanks? *Journal of Alternative Finance*, *1*(1), 35–66. DOI: 10.1177/27533743231218019

Gryshova, I., Balian, A., Antonik, I., Miniailo, V., Nehodenko, V., & Nyzhnychenko, Y. (2024). Artificial intelligence in climate smart in agricultural: Toward a sustainable farming future. *Access to science, business, innovation in the digital economy. ACCESS Press*, *5*(1), 125–140. DOI: 10.46656/access.2024.5.1(8)

Gundeti, R., Vuppala, K., & Kasireddy, V. (2024). The Future of AI and Environmental Sustainability: Challenges and Opportunities. *Exploring Ethical Dimensions of Environmental Sustainability and Use of AI*, 346-371.

Islam, Z., Ahmed, A., Alfify, M. H., & Riyaz, N. (2024). The Impact Of On Environment And Sustainable Development In India. *Educational Administration: Theory and Practice*, *30*(5), 1850–1856.

Jeswani, M. P., & Valecha, M. K. (2024). A Study on Role of AI in Shaping a Smarter Legal System: Justice in the Machine. *AI for a Smarter Future: Transforming*, 31.

Jobin, A., Ienca, M., & Vayena, E. (2019). The global landscape of AI ethics guidelines. *Nature Machine Intelligence*, *1*(9), 389–399. DOI: 10.1038/s42256-019-0088-2

Kantha, T., Sahoo, D., Rout, D., & Mishra, S. J. (2024). *Ethics in the Digital Era.* Technology's Role in Shaping Society.

Koulu, R., & Kontiainen, L. A. U. R. A. (2019). How Will AI Shape the Future of Law. *University of Helsinki Legal Tech Lab publications.*

Krupiy, T. T. (2020). A vulnerability analysis: Theorising the impact of decision-making processes on individuals, society and human diversity from a social justice perspective. *Computer Law & Security Review*, *38*, 105429. DOI: 10.1016/j.clsr.2020.105429

Liebig, L., Güttel, L., Jobin, A., & Katzenbach, C. (2024). Subnational AI policy: Shaping AI in a multi-level governance system. *AI & Society*, *39*(3), 1477–1490. DOI: 10.1007/s00146-022-01561-5

Raihan, M., Debnath, A., Adhikary, P., Masud, M., Meshref, H., & Bairagi, A. K. (2024). Bridging Technology and Psychology: AI-Driven Analysis of Student's Class Lecture Activity for Improved Learning Outcomes. *IEEE Access : Practical Innovations, Open Solutions*, *12*, 147320–147349. DOI: 10.1109/ACCESS.2024.3474848

Sadanand, V. K., & Nandini, S. (2025). AI in Indian healthcare startups: Funding and ecosystem dynamics. In Joshi, H., Reddy, C. K. K., Ouaissa, M., Hanafiah, M. M., & Doss, S. (Eds.), *Intelligent systems and IoT applications in clinical health* (p. 600). IGI Global., DOI: 10.4018/979-8-3693-8990-4

Sloan, R. H., & Warner, R. (2020). Beyond bias: And social justice. *Va. JL & Tech.*, *24*, 1.

Taylor, S. M., Gulson, K. N., & McDuie-Ra, D. (2023). from colonial india: Race, statistics, and facial recognition in the global south. *Science, Technology & Human Values*, *48*(3), 663–689. DOI: 10.1177/01622439211060839

Van Wynsberghe, A. (2021). Sustainable AI: AI for sustainability and the sustainability of AI. *AI and Ethics*, *1*(3), 213–218. DOI: 10.1007/s43681-021-00043-6

Vargas-Elizondo, C. (2020). On the role of ethics in shaping technology development. *HighTech and Innovation Journal*, *1*(2), 86–100. DOI: 10.28991/HIJ-2020-01-02-05

Warang, T. R., & Sackib, A. (2024). Shaping the Future of Law: AI, Ethics, and Policy Perspectives. *IJRAR-International Journal of Research and Analytical Reviews (IJRAR)*, *11*(2), 29-48. https://pib.gov.in/PressReleaseIframePage.aspx?PRID=2012375 https://www.india-briefing.com/news/india-regulation-of-ai-and-large-language-models-31680.html/ https://www.nextias.com/ca/current-affairs/21-09-2024/recommendations-to-address-ai-related-risks-and-governance-gaps https://www.reuters.com/technology/india-announces-12-bln-investment-ai-projects-2024-03-07/

Chapter 5
Regulation and Ethical Issues of Artificial Intelligence in Ghana: Towards a Harmonious AI Law

Elijah Tukwariba Yin
https://orcid.org/0000-0003-2757-092X
University of Cape Coast, Ghana

ABSTRACT

This chapter investigates the legal and ethical frameworks of artificial intelligence (AI) in Ghana, emphasizing how the country can draw upon the EU AI Act 2024 to influence a harmonious AI legal regime. It is argued that the effective regulation of AI in Ghana requires a harmonious legal framework that addresses ethical concerns and human rights, transparency, and accountability. Using a desktop review, it is evident that Ghana's expanding AI landscape requires a well-aligned regulatory approach that prioritizes human well-being, safety, and dignity. Such a framework ensures that AI technologies respect citizens' rights and enhance public safety. By categorizing AI systems based on risk levels, Ghana can mitigate potential harmful practices while fostering innovation and trust. Incorporating ethical frameworks into AI governance is vital for effective regulation, as it offers clear guidelines that align with human values. This alignment promotes global cooperation and safeguards human interests in society.

DOI: 10.4018/979-8-3373-3384-7.ch005

INTRODUCTION

Artificial Intelligence (AI) encompasses machines that can replicate specific aspects of human intelligence, such as perception, learning, reasoning, problem-solving, interaction, and generating creative output using algorithms (Hu, 2019; Mouta et al., 2023). AI can profoundly change several domains and completely overhaul the operations of several sectors, such as healthcare, transportation, finance, law, education, marketing, and entertainment (Manyika et al., 2017). In some sectors, the utilization of AI-powered robots enables the execution of monotonous and time-intensive activities, allowing human workers to allocate their efforts toward more intricate jobs (Frey & Osborne, 2017). In the healthcare sector, AI can enhance patient outcomes by optimizing administrative duties and enabling medical practitioners to concentrate on delivering individualized care to their patients (Alowais et al., 2023; Abbasi et al., 2023).

Advanced AI technology offers tailored suggestions to users, which is crucial in sectors such as internet commerce, digital advertising, and entertainment, where tailored suggestions can significantly enhance client involvement and loyalty (Huang & Rust, 2018). Amazon and Netflix, among other online merchants, utilize AI algorithms to suggest products and content to their users by analyzing their browsing and viewing history (Linden et al., 2003; Gomez-Uribe & Hunt, 2016). This is crucial in fostering well-qualified leads and enhancing conversions (Canobbio, 2024).

AI may also enhance strategic decision-making for enterprises by using predictive analytics (Davenport, 2013). Through the analysis of vast quantities of data, AI algorithms can detect patterns and trends that may elude human perception, offering enterprises valuable insights that can enhance their decision-making process (McAfee et al., 2012). A survey conducted by PwC reveals that 63% of corporate executives share that AI would exert a substantial influence on their respective industries (Adams, 2022). For instance, the application of predictive analytics in the field of finance enables the identification of prospective dangers and opportunities within the stock market, thereby empowering investors to make more informed and sound investment choices (Chen et al., 2012).

Furthermore, AI is crucial in enhancing safety and security (Wang & Chung, 2022; Rahaman et al., 2024). For instance, facial recognition technology driven by AI is being utilized in both public areas and private enterprises to detect possible security risks and deter unwanted entry (Wang & Wang, 2018). In a similar vein, drones equipped with AI can be employed to observe and react to natural calamities, thereby offering vital information for emergency medical assistance and preserving human lives (Shakhatreh et al., 2019).

Despite the enormous potential AI presents in all sectors of society, its development and deployment also raise concerns about privacy, security, accountability, and transparency (Habbal, Ali, & Abuzaraida, 2024; Díaz-Rodríguez et al., 2023; Cheng, Varshney, & Liu, 2021; Saura, Ribeiro-Soriano, & Palacios-Marqués, 2022). The lack of clear regulations and guidelines poses significant risks, including violation of privacy (Martin & Zimmermann, 2024). AI systems can collect and process vast amounts of personal data, potentially infringing on individuals' right to privacy (Wachter & Mittelstadt, 2019; Manheim & Kaplan, 2019). It is also documented that AI algorithms can perpetuate existing biases and discriminate against certain groups (Lewis, 2024; Nazer et al., 2023). The use of AI can also lead to significant job losses in various sectors of the economy (Soueidan & Shoghari, 2024; Ford, 2015). The literature on AI also reveals that AI-powered systems can be vulnerable to cyber-attacks and data breaches (Abdulhussein, 2024; Thapaliya & Bokani, 2024). This raises concerns about legal and ethical challenges such as outdated laws, lack of clarity, and regulatory gaps. On ethics, challenges such as transparency and accountability arise as AI decision-making processes can be opaque, making it difficult to hold developers and deployers accountable (Cheong, 2024; Burr & Leslie, 2023; Kroll, 2021). AI systems can perpetuate biases and discriminate against certain groups (Lewis, 2024; Nazer et al., 2023; Barocas & Selbst, 2019). Another ethical issue is that AI-powered systems can infringe on human dignity, particularly in areas like surveillance and monitoring (Gabriel, 2023; Oyekunle, Boohene, & Preston, 2024).

In Ghana, the rapid development and deployment of AI have brought numerous benefits, including improved efficiency and innovation in various sectors. However, the unregulated growth of AI poses significant legal and ethical challenges, threatening the rights and well-being of citizens (Truby, 2020). While there is a growing body of research on AI regulation globally (Cath et al., 2018), there is a scarcity of studies focusing on the Ghanaian context. Existing literature primarily addresses AI's technical and economic aspects, neglecting the legal and ethical implications of AI adoption in Ghana. This chapter investigates the legislation and ethical frameworks of AI in Ghana and how Ghana can draw on the EU AI Act 2024 to influence a harmonious AI legal regime. I will argue that the effective regulation of AI in Ghana requires a comprehensive legal framework that addresses ethical concerns, ensures transparency and accountability, and protects citizens' rights, thereby promoting trustworthy AI adoption and mitigating potential risks.

Using a desktop review approach, this chapter is organized under the following headings: Introduction, History of AI: Global Perspective, AI in Africa, AI in Ghana, the Regulatory Regime of AI in Ghana, the Regulatory Regime of AI in the EU: EU AI Act 2024 (Regulation (EU) 2024/1689), Implications of the EU AI Act:

Towards a Harmonious Law in Ghana, AI: Ethical Considerations for a harmonious AI Law, and Conclusion.

HISTORY OF ARTIFICIAL INTELLIGENCE: GLOBAL PERSPECTIVE

This history of AI was adapted from Anyoha's (2017) work in the special edition Blog on AI at Harvard's Kenneth C. Griffin Graduate School of Arts and Sciences. According to Anyoha, during the initial half of the 20th century, science fiction introduced the concept of AI robots to the public. The narrative commenced with the "heartless" Tin Man from The Wizard of Oz and progressed to the humanoid automaton that mimicked Maria in Metropolis. By the 1950s, a generation of scientists, mathematicians, and philosophers had culturally adopted the concept of AI (Russell & Norvig, 2010). Alan Turing investigated the mathematical feasibility of AI and proposed that humans utilize accessible knowledge and reasoning to address problems and make decisions (Turing, 1950). He quizzed that if humans could function this way, why are robots incapable of performing similarly? The conceptual framework of his 1950 paper, "Computing Machinery and Intelligence," delineated the construction of intelligent computers and the methodologies for assessing their intelligence. In his paper, Alan Turing explored the possibility of machine thinking. He proposed the Imitation Game, now known as the Turing Test, to assess a machine's ability to exhibit intelligent behavior equivalent to, or indistinguishable from, that of a human (Turing, 1950). Turing argues that: 1. The question "Can machines think?" is ill-defined and should be replaced with "Can a machine be made to simulate human thought processes?", 2. A machine's ability to think is not dependent on its physical properties, but rather its programming and algorithms, and 3. A machine can be considered intelligent if it can convincingly mimic human-like conversation.

Anyoha (2017) notes that significant technical and financial obstacles hindered Alan Turing's pioneering efforts in advancing computer intelligence. Prior to 1949, computers lacked storage capacity, restricting their ability to recall previous actions and limiting their functionality to executing commands (Newell & Simon, 1972). Furthermore, the prohibitive cost of computing, with leasing fees reaching up to $200,000 per month in the early 1950s, confined access to elite academic institutions and large technological corporations (Anyoha, 2017). To secure funding, researchers required a proof of concept and endorsement from influential figures. This was achieved through the development of the Logic Theorist program by Allen Newell, Cliff Shaw, and Herbert Simon, funded by the Research and Development (RAND) Corporation (Newell & Simon, 1972). Considered one of the first AI programs, Logic Theorist was showcased at the seminal 1956 Dartmouth Summer Research Project on Artificial Intelligence (DSRPAI), convened by John McCarthy and Marvin Minsky. At this conference, McCarthy, who coined the term "artificial intelligence," envisioned a collaborative effort, bringing together interdisciplinary experts for an open-ended discussion (McCarthy et al., 1955).

The period between 1957 and 1974 marked a surge in AI advancements, driven by improved computing capacity, affordability, and accessibility (Feigenbaum & Feldman, 1963). Enhanced machine learning algorithms and strategic application expertise enabled notable demonstrations, including Newell and Simon's General Problem Solver and Weizenbaum's ELIZA (Weizenbaum, 1972). These successes, coupled with advocacy from leading researchers (notably DSRPAI attendees), secured funding from government agencies like DARPA for AI research at various institutions. However, despite optimism and predictions (e.g., Minsky's 1970 assertion that machines would achieve human-like intelligence within three to eight years), the field encountered significant obstacles (Minsky, 1970). Insufficient computational power hindered substantial progress, particularly in natural language processing, abstract thinking, and self-recognition. As Hans Moravec noted, computers were "millions of times too weak" to exhibit intelligence (Moravec, 1988).

The 1980s witnessed an AI resurgence, driven by two key factors: the expansion of algorithmic toolkits and increased funding. Notably, John Hopfield and David Rumelhart popularized deep learning techniques, enabling computers to learn through experience (Hopfield, 1982; Rumelhart & McClelland, 1986). Meanwhile, Edward Feigenbaum introduced expert systems, which simulated human decision-making processes by capturing expert knowledge. Expert systems gained widespread industrial adoption (Feigenbaum, 1980).

The Japanese government's Fifth Generation Computer Project (FGCP, 1982-1990) invested $400 million in AI research, focusing on advanced computer processing, logic programming, and AI enhancement. Although the project's ambitious goals were largely unmet, it inspired a new generation of engineers and scientists (Feigenbaum & McCorduck, 1983).

Contrary to expectations, AI progress accelerated despite diminished government funding and public attention in the 1990s and 2000s (Hsu, 2002; Brooks, 2003). Landmark achievements included: IBM's Deep Blue defeating chess champion Garry Kasparov in 1997, demonstrating artificially intelligent decision-making (Hsu, 2002), Dragon Systems' speech recognition software integration into Windows (Lippmann, 1997), and Cynthia Breazeal's Kismet robot, capable of recognizing and displaying emotions (Breazeal, 2003). These advancements underscored AI's potential to tackle complex problems, including natural language interpretation and human emotion recognition (Brooks, 2003).

Recent advancements in AI can be attributed, in part, to the exponential growth in computing power and storage, as described by Moore's Law (Moore, 1965). This phenomenon enabled IBM's Deep Blue to defeat Garry Kasparov in 1997 (Hsu, 2002) and Google's AlphaGo to triumph over Ke Jie (Silver et al., 2016). The cyclical nature of AI research was characterized by saturating existing computational capabilities, followed by periods of stagnation until Moore's Law bridged the gap (Brooks, 2003).

The era of "big data" has revolutionized AI applications across industries, including technology, finance, marketing, and entertainment (Manyika, 2011). The sheer volume of data, too cumbersome for human processing, has yielded significant benefits (Brynjolfsson & McAfee, 2014). Notably, even without algorithmic improvements, massive computing and data enable AI to learn through brute force (Halevy et al., 2009). Although Moore's Law may be slowing, the data explosion continues unabated.

Potential breakthroughs in computer science, mathematics, and neuroscience offered pathways to transcend the limitations imposed by Moore's Law (Jordan & Mitchell, 2015). These advancements likely propelled AI research forward, mitigating the constraints of computational power (Lake et al., 2017).

ARTIFICIAL INTELLIGENCE IN AFRICA

Lolade Siyonbola's research elucidates the historical trajectory of AI in Africa, revealing a profound connection between traditional divination systems and modern computer science (Siyonbola, 2020). This scholarly lineage underscores the shared mathematical foundations of spiritual and digital technologies. According to Siyonbola, African divination systems, notably the Ifa divination system, employ data-driven binary combinations, analogous to Google's algorithmic queries (Siyonbola, 2020). Ron Eglash's seminal work, Modern Computing & Indigenous Design, provides a foundational framework for examining algorithmic systems across various African cultural practices, including architecture, textile design, divination, and hair design (Eglash, 1999). Recent studies have further illuminated the informational and computational aspects of divination. André Croucamp's 2013 article characterizes divination as a form of information technology that organizes and accesses knowledge (Croucamp, 2013). Similarly, Alamu, Aworinde, and Isharufe's (2013) paper describes the Ifa divination system as an "ancient binary computer system," successfully linking probabilistic calculations with human complexities. The Ifa divination system relies on 256 Odu Ifa, representing all possible human experiences, which corresponds to the 256 combinations in binary mathematics, highlighting the convergent principles underlying traditional African knowledge systems and modern computer science (Alamu et al., 2013).

In Africa today, AI has become a principal policy concern (Manyika et al., 2017). Price Waterhouse Coopers' (PWC) 2017 landmark report, "Sizing the Prize," forecasted that AI would inject approximately $15.7 trillion into the global economy by 2030. However, the distribution of AI-generated wealth and power has exhibited significant disparities (West, 2018). Notably, Africa's projected economic growth from AI adoption is negligible, according to PWC's projections. Paradoxically, despite its marginalization in AI's economic benefits, the continent plays a critical role in the global AI supply chain, furnishing essential natural resources, labor, and skills (Mramba, 2024).

The African continent presents a unique opportunity for leveraging AI to drive socio-economic growth, particularly through leapfrogging outdated technological infrastructure and harnessing the potential of its dynamic youth in digital entrepreneurship (Amoah, 2024; Nwaobi, 2019). To achieve this, African governments should prioritize AI solutions that align with national developmental goals, fostering prosperous and inclusive societies, and a harmonious legal framework to regulate the use of AI in Africa or specific countries in Africa (UNECA, 2019). Egypt, Mauritius, and Rwanda have taken the lead as the first African countries to publish national AI strategies, indicating a growing trend of policy responses to AI across the continent. Africa can unlock the full potential of AI-driven socio-economic transformation by fostering local AI capabilities and prioritizing inclusive growth (Mdladla, 2024; Ibegbulam, 2023). In order to accomplish this, AI policy responses should be grounded in national digital strategies and emphasize the importance of providing fair access to digital, data, and computing infrastructure (Robinson, 2020; World Bank, 2020).

The African continent is witnessing a proliferation of AI-driven innovations (Manyika et al., 2017). Notably, Kenya has emerged as a hub for developing context-specific AI solutions, particularly in agriculture, where locally designed initiatives facilitate farmers' access to equipment and informed decision-making regarding optimal crop sowing and harvesting times (Kamanja, 2020). For instance, initiatives like FarmDrive and Apollo Agriculture utilize AI-powered platforms to provide farmers with data-driven insights and financial services (Miller, 2019). Furthermore, African cities, such as Lagos, Nigeria, are fostering vibrant communities of young data scientists who collaborate to enhance their expertise in machine learning, thereby driving the development of novel AI-driven technologies and industries (Signe, 2023; Adebayo, 2020). This trend underscores the continent's burgeoning capacity for AI-driven innovation and its potential to catalyze socio-economic transformation. This situation necessitates a legislative response regarding AI across the African continent.

ARTIFICIAL INTELLIGENCE IN GHANA

The history of AI in Ghana dates back to the 1980s when the country's first computer science department was established at the University of Ghana. This marked the beginning of Ghana's journey into the world of computing and laid the foundation for future explorations into AI. During the 1970s and 1980s, Ghanaian researchers and engineers began to delve into AI concepts, primarily within academic circles (Amoah, 2024).

The 1990s witnessed significant growth in Ghana's computing landscape (Ghana Institute of Engineers, 1990). The Ghana Institute of Engineers (GhIE) and the Computer Science Department at Kwame Nkrumah University of Science and Technology (KNUST) were established, providing a platform for AI research and education. In 2000, the Ghana-India Kofi Annan Centre of Excellence in ICT (AITI-KACE) was launched, offering AI-related courses and training. Towards the late 90s and early 2000s, the Computer Science Department at the University of Cape Coast was established. Currently, many public and private Universities in Ghana offer Computer Science, all contributing to the AI space and further solidifying Ghana's presence in the AI community.

The 2010s saw a surge in AI applications and initiatives in Ghana. In 2012, the country's first AI conference was held at AITI-KACE, marking the beginning of AI awareness and discussion in Ghana. Ghanaian startups began to emerge, leveraging AI to tackle local challenges. For instance, mPedigree developed an AI-powered anti-counterfeiting system for pharmaceuticals in 2015. The Ghana Ministry of Communications launched the "Smart Cities" initiative in 2017, incorporating AI-driven solutions for urban development.

In recent years, Ghana has continued to advance its AI ecosystem. In 2019, Google opened its first AI lab in Ghana to promote AI research, education, and innovation. The University of Ghana offers courses in AI and machine learning as part of its computer science and engineering programs. KNUST has also incorporated AI into its curriculum, offering specialized courses and research opportunities in AI and data science. The university also hosts seminars and workshops to promote AI literacy. One is the Practical Neural Networks and Deep Learning for Everyone Short Course with the help of their Responsible Artificial Intelligence Lab (RAIL). These courses cover fundamental concepts, algorithms, and practical applications of AI. In 2022, Ghana hosted the inaugural Africa AI Summit, bringing together experts and stakeholders to discuss AI's future on the continent. Today, AI is applied in various sectors, including law, agriculture, healthcare, finance, and education.

Despite this progress, Ghana's AI journey is not without challenges. Limited access to reliable internet and computing resources, stable sources of energy, expanding rural electrification, talent development, and the need for a regulatory framework to govern AI development and deployment remain pressing concerns. It is against this backdrop that this chapter investigates the legislation and ethical frameworks of AI in Ghana and how Ghana can draw on the EU AI Act to influence a harmonious AI legal regime. It is argued that effective regulation of AI in Ghana needs a comprehensive legal framework that addresses ethical concerns, ensures transparency and accountability, and protects citizens' rights, thus promoting trustworthy AI adoption and mitigating potential risks.

REGULATORY REGIME OF AI IN GHANA

Ghana currently does not have a specific legal framework dedicated to regulating AI. However, there are existing regulations that address certain aspects related to AI, such as intellectual property rights, data protection and privacy, cybersecurity, electronic transactions, and organized crime. For instance, the Electronic Transactions Act, 2008 (Act 772) and the Data Protection Act, 2012 (Act 843) provide a foundation for regulating AI-related activities.

The 1992 Constitution of Ghana, the Data Protection Act, and the Cybersecurity Act address concerns related to privacy, data protection, and cybersecurity. These laws include provisions for registration, certification, and compliance for institutions and individuals involved in data collection, use, storage, sharing, and cybersecurity services provision. Even though these regulations were established before the AI revolution, they can be applied to address some of the concerns related to AI systems. For example, there are clear guidelines for asserting intellectual property rights over creations, inventions, and works, and existing laws such as the Copyrights Act, 2005 (Act 690), the Patent Act, 2003 (Act 657), the Industrial Design Act, 2003 (Act 660), and the Trademarks Act, 2004 (Act 664) provide protections for innovations underlying AI systems. The challenge lies in determining the authors and owners of AI-generated outputs. In such cases, Ghana's courts may provide guidance and standards for making these determinations on a case-by-case basis, depending on the level of contribution by humans and AI systems.

Businesses that utilize AI tools often compile a database of their clients to tailor the services provided to each client. The Data Protection Act 2012 (Act 843) imposes certain obligations on companies and individuals regarding the use of personal information obtained from clients. According to Section 18 of the Data Protection Act 2012 (Act 843), "Any individual processing personal data must ensure that it is processed lawfully and fairly, without violating the privacy rights of the data subject". Furthermore, Section 20 of Act 843 stipulates that, except for specific exceptions, the consent of every data subject must be obtained before processing any personal data concerning the data subject. This begs the need for "opt in or opt out" at every point where data is generated and captured. The Act also grants the data subject the right to object to the use of their personal data, and if a data subject objects to the processing of personal data, the entity processing the personal data must cease the processing.

The Copyright Act of 2005 of Ghana (Act 690) serves as the primary legislation governing intellectual property in Ghana. It plays a crucial role in recognizing and safeguarding computer programs and software, which are commonly developed using AI technology. Additionally, the Act imposes penalties for any efforts to bypass technological protection measures implemented by intellectual property rights holders. Despite the absence of explicit AI terminology, the Act establishes a conducive environment for the growth of AI while ensuring protection for its users.

Ghana's current legal framework governing AI is characterized by significant gaps and inadequacies. Notably, the country lacks specific AI legislation, as existing laws fail to explicitly address AI-related issues. This deficiency is particularly evident in data protection, where the Data Protection Act 2012 (Act 843) may not comprehensively address AI-driven data processing. Furthermore, intellectual property law is deemed insufficient, as current regulations may not adequately safeguard AI-generated innovations.

The ambiguity surrounding the definition of AI also raises concerns about regulatory uncertainty, hindering effective regulation. Multiple agencies with overlapping jurisdictions exacerbate this issue, causing confusion and inefficiencies. Moreover, ethical concerns, such as perpetuating existing biases and privacy infringement, have been raised regarding AI adoption in Ghana. With these challenges, what can Ghana learn from the European Union (EU) regulatory regime of AI? The ensuing section analyses in detail the EU AI Act, 2024.

REGULATORY REGIME OF AI IN THE EU: EU AI ACT 2024 (REGULATION (EU) 2024/1689)

The European Union's AI Act of 2024 aims to establish a comprehensive regulatory framework for AI that prioritizes trustworthiness and human well-being. The primary goal is to ensure the proper functioning of the internal market while protecting health, safety, and fundamental rights. The regulation seeks to balance the promotion of innovation with the need to safeguard citizens from any potential risks associated with AI systems. It focuses on promoting human-centric AI, emphasizing transparency, accountability, and user well-being.

The key objectives of the AI Act are to improve the functioning of the internal market, promote trustworthy AI, protect fundamental rights, safeguard health, safety, democracy, the rule of law, and environmental protection, and support innovation.

Article 1 (1) of the AI ACT (2024) of the EU states that "*The purpose of this Regulation is to improve the functioning of the internal market and promote the uptake of human-centric and trustworthy artificial intelligence (AI), while ensuring a high level of protection of health, safety, fundamental rights enshrined in the Charter, including democracy, the rule of law and environmental protection, against the harmful effects of AI systems in the Union and supporting innovation.*"

The Act lays down harmonized rules for placement on the market, use, and service of AI systems in the EU. It also prohibits certain AI practices, establishes specific requirements for high-risk AI systems, sets transparency rules for certain AI systems, and outlines market monitoring, surveillance, governance, and enforcement mechanisms. Additionally, it includes measures to support innovation, particularly focusing on small and medium-sized enterprises (SMEs) and startups. This Act serves as a unified framework to regulate various aspects of AI within the EU (See Article 1(2) (a-g)).

The Act applies to providers introducing AI systems to the Union market, deployers with establishments within the Union, providers and deployers with establishments in a third country whose products are used within the EU, importers, and distributors of AI systems, product manufacturers who release AI systems along with their products under their name or trademark, authorized representatives of non-Union providers, and affected persons within the Union. However, as per Article 2(3), the Act does not apply to areas outside the scope of Union law and does not affect the competencies of Member States in national security, regardless of the type of entity entrusted by the Member States with related tasks. Article 2(4) also states that the Act does not apply to public authorities in a third country or international organizations falling within the scope of the Regulation. The Act does not apply to AI models designed for scientific research and development, nor does it apply to any research, testing, or development activity regarding AI models before they are placed on the Union market (see Article 2(6) and (8)). The scope of the Act clearly defines what it includes and excludes, with further explanation in Article 2 (9-12) of the Act.

Another uniqueness of the AI Act of the EU is its definition of terms. The Act defines about 68 terminologies. Some terminologies defined are AI system, risk, provider, deployer, authorised representative, importer, distributor, operator, etc. Article 3(1) defines AI system as "a machine-based system that is designed to operate with varying levels of autonomy and that may exhibit adaptiveness after deployment, and that, for explicit or implicit objectives, infers, from the input it receives, how to generate outputs such as predictions, content, recommendations, or decisions that can influence physical or virtual environments." It also defines 'risk' in Article 3(2) as "the combination of the probability of an occurrence of harm and the severity of that harm." These definitions and many others in the Act provide clarity and precision as defined terms ensure that the language used in the Act is understood consistently by all stakeholders, including lawmakers, judges, legal professionals, and the general public. These definitions are useful as they promote legal certainty and avoid ambiguity. In terms of the former, they provide a clear understanding of the legal requirements, obligations, and rights outlined in the Act whereas in terms of the latter, they prevent confusion or misinterpretation of terms, which can lead to disputes or unintended consequences.

The Act makes provision for AI literacy. Article 4 states that "Providers and deployers of AI systems shall take measures to ensure, to their best extent, a sufficient level of AI literacy of their staff and other persons dealing with the operation and use of AI systems on their behalf, taking into account their technical knowledge, experience, education, and training and the context the AI systems are to be used in, and considering the persons or groups of persons on whom the AI systems are to be used." The provision for AI literacy ensures that citizens have a basic understanding of AI systems and their impact on society. AI literacy empowers citizens to make informed decisions about AI usage in their personal and professional lives and also helps individuals to critically evaluate AI-generated information and mitigate disinformation. Educating citizens or staff about AI builds trust and facilitates acceptance of AI technologies as well as helps identify and address potential biases and discrimination in AI systems. The significance of the AI literacy provisions is that they aim to create a society where citizens can harness AI's benefits while understanding its limitations and potential risks.

Chapter 2 of the EU Act focuses on prohibited AI practices, specifically outlining what AI practices are unacceptable within the European Union. For instance, Article 5(1)(a) states that "the placing on the market, the putting into service or the use of an AI system that deploys subliminal techniques beyond a person's consciousness or purposefully manipulative or deceptive techniques, with the objective, or the effect of materially distorting the behaviour of a person or a group of persons by appreciably impairing their ability to make an informed decision, thereby causing them to take a decision that they would not have otherwise taken in a manner that causes or is reasonably likely to cause that person, another person or group of persons significant harm." Article 5(1)(g) adds that "the placing on the market, the putting into service for this specific purpose, or the use of biometric categorisation systems that categorise individually natural persons based on their biometric data to deduce or infer their race, political opinions, trade union membership, religious or philosophical beliefs, sex life or sexual orientation; this prohibition does not cover any labelling or filtering of lawfully acquired biometric datasets, such as images, based on biometric data or categorizing of biometric data in the area of law enforcement." This chapter ensures that AI systems are developed and used in ways that respect human rights, dignity, and safety. Article 5 explicitly defines prohibited AI practices to include practices that manipulate, deceive, or exploit individuals.

AI systems designed to manipulate human behavior, emotions, or decisions without users' awareness or consent or AI systems that pretend to be human or falsely claim to have human-like capabilities or AI systems that exploit vulnerabilities or biases, particularly targeting children, the elderly, or individuals with disabilities are all prohibited by the Act. These prohibitions aim to safeguard individuals from potential harm and ensure that AI systems are developed and deployed responsibly. With these guidelines on prohibited practices, the EU AI Act promotes transparency, accountability, and trust in AI technologies.

Chapter III, Section 1 of the EU AI Act plays a crucial role in ensuring that AI systems are developed and used with a primary focus on human safety and well-being. Article 6 outlines the classification rules for high-risk AI systems, which encompass those posing significant risks to human health, safety, and fundamental rights. These systems are listed in Annex III and include AI systems used in healthcare, transportation, and education. Article 7 allows for amendments to Annex III, ensuring that the regulation remains current with emerging technologies and risks. The Act emphasizes the importance of ongoing evaluation and improvement, with the Commission regularly reviewing and updating the list of high-risk AI systems. Furthermore, it highlights the need to consider the broader social implications of AI systems and reinforces the requirement for stringent standards and regulations to ensure safety and accountability for high-risk AI systems.

In Chapter III, Section 2 of the EU AI, the focus is on establishing requirements for high-risk AI systems. This section sets out the essential standards that developers and deployers must adhere to in order to ensure the responsible development and use of these systems. Article 8 emphasizes the importance of complying with the AI Act's requirements for high-risk AI systems, while Article 9 mandates the implementation of a risk management system to identify and mitigate potential risks associated with high-risk AI systems. Article 10 underscores the need for robust data governance practices to ensure that data used in high-risk AI systems is accurate, reliable, and secure, and Article 13 requires providers to offer transparent information about the AI system, including its capabilities, limitations, and potential risks. Article 14 highlights the need for human oversight and control over high-risk AI systems to prevent unintended consequences. The AI Act takes into account the potential impact of AI systems on individuals and society, indicating the EU's commitment to prioritizing human well-being and safety. Furthermore, the Act ensures that High-risk AI systems are to be designed and developed in such a way that they can be effectively overseen by humans, reinforcing the importance of human oversight in ensuring the responsible development and deployment of high-risk AI systems. Finally, the Act also ensures that the provider of the AI system is designed and developed with safeguards to prevent misuse, emphasizing the need for developers to consider potential misuse and implement measures to prevent harm.

The EU AI Act, Section III of Chapter III delineates the obligations of providers and deployers of high-risk AI systems, alongside other pertinent stakeholders. These obligations encompass establishing comprehensive risk management frameworks (Article 16), implementing robust data governance practices (Article 10), maintaining detailed technical documentation (Article 11), and ensuring record-keeping capabilities (Article 12). Additionally, providers must furnish instructions for use (Article 13), design AI systems for human oversight (Article 14), and guarantee accuracy, robustness, and cybersecurity (Article 15). This section's significance lies in its emphasis on fostering accountability and transparency throughout the AI development and deployment lifecycle, thereby promoting trust and confidence in high-risk AI systems and ultimately safeguarding human well-being and safety.

Section 4 of Chapter III of the EU AI Act is dedicated to notifying authorities and notified bodies. It outlines the procedures for conformity assessment and the requirements for notified bodies. Key components include Article 28, which defines the role of informing authorities in overseeing the conformity assessment process, and Article 29, which explains how conformity assessment bodies are applied for notification. Article 30 outlines the step-by-step process for notification, while Article 31 specifies the requirements that notified bodies must meet. Article 32 defines the presumption of conformity and its provisions relating to notified bodies. Specifically, this section mandates providers to establish robust risk management protocols, ensure data integrity, maintain meticulous technical documentation, provide transparent disclosures regarding system capabilities and limitations, and guarantee human oversight, control, and system robustness. Furthermore, providers are obligated to conduct rigorous conformity assessments and notify pertinent national authorities prior to market placement. This regulatory provision adopts a lifecycle approach, necessitating ongoing risk monitoring and mitigation throughout the system's development, deployment, and post-market phases. The significance of this section lies in its emphasis on ensuring that high-risk AI systems comply with the EU's regulatory framework and responsible AI development and deployment, prioritizing safety, privacy, and transparency. The implementation of these provisions is anticipated to mitigate risks and harm to users and society, ensure regulatory compliance, foster trust in AI technologies, and promote accountability and transparency in AI development.

Section 5 of Chapter III of the EU AI Act institutes a robust regulatory framework governing high-risk AI systems, encompassing standardization, conformity assessment, certification, and registration protocols. This comprehensive framework stipulates procedures for providers to demonstrate adherence to essential requirements, incorporating internal control mechanisms, independent third-party audits, and oversight by designated notified bodies. Consequently, consistency and reliability in evaluating safety and performance are ensured. The section meticulously delineates the obligations of providers, notified bodies, and national authorities, encompassing exhaustive documentation, rigorous testing, and meticulous inspection. The implications of Section 5 are far-reaching, guaranteeing high-risk AI systems conform to stringent safety and performance benchmarks, thereby fostering trust in AI technologies. Moreover, this framework facilitates global regulatory harmonization, influences AI development and deployment expenditures and clarifies liability allocation among stakeholders. By emphasizing harmonization, Section 5 optimizes market access, cultivates innovation, and cultivates a secure and reliable AI ecosystem.

Chapter IV of the EU AI Act mandates transparency in AI systems interacting directly with humans, requiring providers to inform users when engaging with an AI system unless it is evident to a reasonably informed and observant individual. This transparency obligation aims to prevent deception and foster trust, protecting users' autonomy and informed decision-making. However, exceptions apply to AI systems authorized by law for crime detection, prevention, investigation, or prosecution, provided they incorporate safeguards for third-party rights and freedoms, unless publicly available for reporting criminal offenses. This nuanced approach balances transparency with legitimate law enforcement needs, emphasizing responsible AI development, user awareness, and protection of fundamental rights, ultimately shaping the EU's AI landscape and influencing global regulatory standards. Article 50(1) states that: Providers shall ensure that AI systems intended to interact directly with natural persons are designed and developed in such a way that the natural persons concerned are informed that they are interacting with an AI system, unless this is obvious from the point of view of a natural person who is reasonably well-informed, observant and circumspect, taking into account the circumstances and the context of use. This obligation shall not apply to AI systems authorised by law to detect, prevent, investigate or prosecute criminal offences, subject to appropriate safeguards for the rights and freedoms of third parties unless those systems are available for the public to report a criminal offence. While Article 50(1-4) is useful, it is important to state that Article 50(6) reveals as follows: Paragraphs 1 to 4 shall not affect the requirements and obligations set out in Chapter III, and shall be without prejudice to other transparency obligations laid down in Union or national law for deployers of AI systems. This shows how crucial Chapter III is to the Union's legal framework.

Article 51 of Chapter V establishes the classification criteria for general-purpose AI models as high-risk. A model is considered high-risk if it meets either of two conditions: (a) it possesses high-impact capabilities, evaluated using technical tools and methodologies, or (b) the Commission designates it as such, following a scientific panel alert, based on criteria in Annex XIII. Additionally, models with training computation exceeding 10^25 floating-point operations are presumed high-impact. The Commission may update thresholds, benchmarks, and indicators through delegated acts (Article 97) to reflect evolving technological advancements, ensuring the classification remains aligned with the state of the art. Article 51 of the AI EU Act holds significant importance as it establishes a clear framework for classifying general-purpose AI models as high-risk, ensuring proactive mitigation of potential harm. By defining specific criteria, including high-impact capabilities and computation thresholds, this article enables targeted regulatory oversight, promoting safety, security, and accountability in AI development.

Article 52 outlines the procedure for designating general-purpose AI models with systemic risk. Providers must notify the Commission within two weeks if their model meets specific requirements (Article 51(1)(a)). The notification must include supporting information. Providers may argue that their model doesn't pose systemic risks due to its characteristics, but the Commission may reject these arguments. The Commission can designate a model as high-risk based on criteria in Annex XIII, either independently or following a scientific panel alert (Article 90(1)(a)). Designated providers can request reassessment after six months, providing new, objective reasons. The Commission maintains a publicly available list of high-risk models, balancing transparency with intellectual property protection. Article 52 of the AI EU Act holds significant importance as it establishes a robust framework for identifying and mitigating systemic risks associated with general-purpose AI models. By requiring providers to notify the Commission and potentially designating models as high-risk, this article promotes transparency, accountability, and responsible AI development. It safeguards fundamental rights, such as privacy and non-discrimination, and fosters trust in AI innovation. Article 52's risk-based approach ensures proportionate regulatory oversight, contributing to EU-wide harmonization and potentially influencing global AI governance standards. Its significance extends to encouraging innovation while ensuring safety, security, and ethical considerations, ultimately shaping the future of AI development and deployment in the EU.

Articles 53 and 54 of the EU AI Act delineate specific obligations for providers of general-purpose AI models, prioritizing transparency, accountability, and regulatory compliance. Notably, Article 53 mandates that providers: (1) maintain and provide technical documentation (Annex XI) to authorities upon request, (2) furnish information and documentation (Annex XII) to AI system providers to facilitate understanding of model capabilities and limitations, (3) adhere to Union copyright law and identify reserved rights, and (4) publicly disclose training data information. Exemptions apply to open-source models devoid of systemic risks. Furthermore, providers must collaborate with authorities and may utilize codes of practice or harmonized standards to demonstrate compliance. The Commission retains the authority to adopt delegated acts updating methodologies, annexes, and standards. Confidential information is safeguarded under Article 78. Moreover, Article 54 stipulates that non-EU-based providers of general-purpose AI models must appoint an authorized EU-based representative before market placement. This representative is tasked with (1) verifying compliance with technical documentation and regulatory obligations, (2) maintaining documentation for a decade, (3) providing information to the AI Office upon request, and (4) cooperating with authorities in compliance actions. The representative's mandate enables direct communication with authorities, and termination of the mandate is required in cases of provider non-compliance, with notification to the AI Office. Exceptions again apply to open-source models without systemic risks.

Article 55 imposes additional obligations on providers of general-purpose AI models with systemic risk, beyond those outlined in Articles 53 and 54. These providers must:

- Conduct model evaluations using standardized protocols and tools, including adversarial testing
- Assess and mitigate systemic risks at the EU level
- Report serious incidents and corrective measures to the AI Office and national authorities without delay
- Ensure adequate cybersecurity protection for the model and its infrastructure

Providers may rely on approved codes of practice or harmonized standards to demonstrate compliance. Non-compliant providers must demonstrate alternative means of compliance. Confidential information is protected under Article 78. Article 55 of the EU AI Act is crucial for ensuring the safe and responsible development of general-purpose AI models with systemic risk. By imposing additional obligations on providers, such as standardized model evaluation, systemic risk assessment, incident reporting, and cybersecurity requirements, this article mitigates potential harm to individuals and society. It safeguards fundamental rights, including privacy and non-discrimination, while promoting transparency, accountability, and trust in AI systems. Furthermore, Article 55 fosters innovation by clarifying regulatory expectations and encouraging responsible AI development practices. As a pioneering regulation, the EU AI Act's rigorous requirements may also influence global AI governance standards, making Article 55 a significant provision for AI developers, regulatory authorities, end-users, and data protection officers alike.

Article 56 establishes a framework for developing codes of practice to ensure compliance with the EU AI Act. The AI Office will facilitate and encourage the creation of Union-level codes, considering international approaches. These codes must cover obligations outlined in Articles 53 and 55, including information updates, training data transparency, and systemic risk identification and management. Key stakeholders, including providers, authorities, civil society, industry, and experts, will be involved. Codes must: Set clear objectives and commitments; Include key performance indicators, and reflect diverse stakeholder interests. Article 56 also provides that the AI Office will monitor and evaluate code effectiveness, publish assessments, encourage code adherence among providers, and review and adapt codes as needed. If codes are inadequate or unavailable within 12 months, the Commission may establish common rules through implementing acts. Article 56 of the EU AI Act plays a pivotal role in ensuring the effective implementation of the regulation by establishing a framework for codes of practice. These codes facilitate compliance with key obligations, such as transparency, risk management, and accountability, promoting responsible AI development. By involving stakeholders, including providers, authorities, civil society, and experts, Article 56 fosters collaboration and expertise sharing. The codes also provide clarity on regulatory expectations, reducing uncertainty for developers. Regular monitoring and evaluation ensure the codes remain effective, addressing emerging risks and technological advancements. Furthermore, Article 56 enables the Commission to establish common rules if codes are inadequate, safeguarding the regulation's objectives.

Article 57 of the EU AI Act introduces AI regulatory sandboxes to encourage innovation and compliance. Each Member State is required to have at least one national sandbox, with the option for regional or local versions. These controlled environments are designed to support the development, testing, and validation of new AI systems. The main goals of these sandboxes include providing legal clarity, sharing best practices, and facilitating market entry for small and medium-sized enterprises (SMEs) and start-ups. Operating under the supervision of competent authorities, these sandboxes prioritize risk management and the protection of health, safety, and fundamental rights. Through participation, providers receive clarifying guidance on regulatory expectations and documented validation of successful activities, expediting conformity assessment procedures. Furthermore, the Commission and Board access exit reports, fostering evidence-based policymaking and regulatory refinement. Notably, sandbox participants remain liable under applicable law yet are exempt from administrative fines for infringements if acting in good faith. Article 57's provisions promote cross-border cooperation, coordination, and annual reporting to the AI Office and Board, thereby facilitating knowledge sharing and the dissemination of best practices. A dedicated interface will enable stakeholder interaction and non-binding guidance on conformity. Ultimately, Article 57 plays a pivotal role in cultivating responsible AI development, innovation, and regulatory compliance within the EU AI ecosystem.

The EU AI Act imposes distinct obligations on providers and Member States regarding informed consent, support for small and medium-sized enterprises (SMEs), and derogations for microenterprises. Specifically, Article 61 necessitates the procurement of freely-given informed consent from participants in real-world testing outside AI regulatory sandboxes, ensuring they receive transparent information pertaining to the testing's purpose, objectives, duration, and potential drawbacks. Furthermore, participants must be apprised of their rights, including the ability to refuse or withdraw participation without prejudice.

Article 62 stipulates that Member States must provide targeted support to SMEs, including start-ups, to facilitate compliance with the EU AI Act. This support encompasses priority access to AI regulatory sandboxes, customized training and awareness initiatives, dedicated communication channels, and streamlined participation in standardization development. Additionally, the AI Office will offer standardized templates, maintain a centralized information platform, organize awareness campaigns, and promote optimal practices in public procurement.

Article 63 introduces a derogation for microenterprises, permitting simplified compliance with specific quality management system elements, contingent upon the absence of partner or linked enterprises. The Commission will develop guidelines to ensure this simplification does not compromise protection levels or compliance requirements for high-risk AI systems. Notably, microenterprises remain subject to all other regulatory requirements, including transparency, accountability, and fundamental rights. This derogation aims to mitigate administrative burdens on small businesses while maintaining regulatory stringency.

Articles 61, 62, and 63 of the EU AI Act hold significant importance in ensuring responsible AI development and deployment within the European Union. Article 61's informed consent requirement safeguards individuals' rights and autonomy during real-world AI testing. Article 62's support measures for SMEs and start-ups facilitate innovation and compliance, promoting a level playing field for smaller entities. Article 63's derogation for microenterprises balances regulatory rigor with administrative relief, acknowledging the unique challenges faced by small businesses.

The EU AI Act's Articles 64-69 establish a comprehensive governance framework for AI, instituting a multifaceted infrastructure to facilitate cooperation, consistency, and effective implementation. At its core, the AI Office (Article 64) functions as a centralized expertise hub, providing critical support to the Commission and Member States. This is complemented by the European Artificial Intelligence Board (Article 65), comprising representatives from each Member State, which fosters collaborative engagement and harmonization in AI implementation.

Supplementing these structures, the Advisory Forum (Article 67) convenes a diverse range of stakeholders, encompassing industry, civil society, and academia, to provide specialized technical expertise. Furthermore, the Scientific Panel of independent experts (Article 68) offers authoritative guidance on enforcement activities, particularly concerning general-purpose AI models. To ensure impartiality, Panel members must demonstrate requisite expertise, independence, and objectivity. The Panel's advisory role encompasses systemic risk assessment, evaluation methodologies, and classification frameworks.

Aside from the Advisory Forum (Article 67), the governance framework enables Member States to access the Scientific Panel's expertise in support of their enforcement activities (Article 69), with fees applicable to ensure cost-effectiveness. The Commission facilitates timely access and coordinates support activities with Union AI testing support (Article 84). Collectively, these governance structures promote interinstitutional cooperation, consistency, and effective implementation of the EU AI Act, thereby ensuring a harmonized approach to AI development and deployment within the Union.

Article 71 of Chapter VIII of the EU AI Act establishes the EU database for high-risk AI systems, which requires the European Commission to create and maintain a public database of stand-alone high-risk AI systems and AI systems integrated into products. The database aims to enhance transparency, accountability, and oversight of high-risk AI systems, ensuring compliance with the Act's requirements. The database will contain information on the AI system's identity, provider, intended purpose, and conformity assessment. Article 71 is relevant as it promotes transparency and trust in AI technology by providing stakeholders, including regulators, consumers, and researchers, with access to critical information on high-risk AI systems. This facilitates informed decision-making, enables monitoring and enforcement of compliance, and supports the development of a responsible AI ecosystem within the EU. Furthermore, the database's public nature allows for scrutiny and accountability, aligning with the EU's goal of human-centered AI development that prioritizes safety, ethics, and fundamental rights.

Articles 72 and 73 of Chapter IX of the EU AI Act outline post-market monitoring, information sharing, and market surveillance requirements for high-risk AI systems. Article 72 mandates providers to continuously monitor the performance and safety of their AI systems after deployment, reporting incidents and malfunctions to national competent authorities. Article 73 requires Member States to establish market surveillance authorities responsible for monitoring compliance, conducting investigations, and enforcing corrective actions against non-compliant AI systems. These provisions ensure ongoing oversight and swift response to emerging AI risks. The relevance of Articles 72 and 73 lies in their ability to mitigate potential harm from high-risk AI systems, safeguarding users and maintaining public trust. By requiring ongoing monitoring and reporting, the EU AI Act promotes a culture of accountability and continuous improvement among AI providers. Effective market surveillance and information sharing facilitate swift identification and remediation of issues, protecting vulnerable populations and preventing harm. Furthermore, these provisions empower national authorities to take proactive measures, aligning with the EU's precautionary approach to AI regulation.

Section 3 of Chapter IX of the EU AI Act outlines enforcement measures to ensure compliance with the regulation, empowering national competent authorities to investigate, fine, and take corrective actions against non-compliant AI providers. This section (Articles 78-94) establishes procedures for investigations, information requests, on-site inspections, and Union-wide enforcement cooperation. The relevance of this section lies in its ability to deter non-compliance through robust enforcement mechanisms, protect users from harmful AI systems, ensure consistent application of the regulation across Member States, foster cooperation among national authorities, and promote accountability and transparency among AI providers.

Chapter X of the EU AI Act establishes codes of conduct and guidelines to promote responsible AI development and use. Articles 95 and 96 outline measures to encourage voluntary compliance with specific requirements for non-high-risk AI systems and provide clarity on regulatory implementation. The AI Office and Member States facilitate codes of conduct, considering industry best practices, technical solutions, and stakeholder involvement. These codes address ethical guidelines, environmental sustainability, AI literacy, inclusive design, and protection of vulnerable persons. The Commission develops guidelines on practical implementation, covering requirements, prohibited practices, transparency obligations, and relationships with Union harmonization legislation. Guidelines consider SMEs, local authorities, and affected sectors' needs, ensuring consistency with harmonized standards and technical specifications. Updates to guidelines are permitted as necessary. This chapter promotes responsible AI development, industry self-regulation, and transparency, supporting innovation, competitiveness, and trust in AI technology within the EU.

Chapter XI of the EU AI Act outlines the delegation of power and committee procedure, establishing the framework for the Commission's adoption of delegated acts. The Commission is granted the power to adopt delegated acts for a five-year period, renewable tacitly, unless opposed by the European Parliament or Council. The delegation can be revoked at any time. Before adopting delegated acts, the Commission must consult experts designated by Member States and notify the European Parliament and Council. Delegated acts enter into force unless objected to within three months. The Commission is assisted by a committee, governed by Regulation (EU) No 182/2011, ensuring transparency and accountability. This chapter ensures effective governance and oversight, enabling the Commission to adapt the Regulation to emerging AI trends and technologies while maintaining parliamentary and council oversight, thereby striking a balance between flexibility and accountability. This procedural framework facilitates the Regulation's implementation, ensuring consistency with EU law and policies.

Chapter XII of the EU AI Act establishes a comprehensive penalty framework to ensure compliance with the Regulation. Member States must lay down effective, proportionate, and dissuasive penalties, including administrative fines and non-monetary measures, for infringements by operators. The Commission can impose fines on providers of general-purpose AI models and Union institutions, bodies, offices, and agencies. Fines range from €750,000 to €35 million or up to 7% of total worldwide annual turnover, depending on the infringement. Factors considered when imposing fines include the nature, gravity, and duration of the infringement, cooperation with authorities, and financial benefits gained. The European Data Protection Supervisor and national competent authorities have enforcement powers. Procedural safeguards, including judicial remedies and due process, are ensured. Annual reporting requirements facilitate transparency and oversight. This penalty framework aims to deter non-compliance, promote responsible AI development and use, and safeguard individuals' rights and interests, ultimately fostering trust in AI technology within the EU.

The EU AI Act has significant implications for the development and deployment of AI within the European Union. It establishes a comprehensive regulatory framework that prioritizes transparency, accountability, and human rights (Article 1). The Act's risk-based approach categorizes AI systems into four levels of risk, imposing stricter requirements on high-risk systems (Article 6). This will likely drive innovation in AI development, as companies invest in designing more transparent and explainable systems (European Commission, 2021). The Act's provisions on data governance, security, and privacy will also impact data-driven business models (Articles 14-15). Moreover, the introduction of administrative fines of up to €35 million or 7% of global turnover for non-compliance will encourage companies to prioritize AI ethics and compliance (Article 99). The EU AI Act's extraterritorial scope will also influence global AI standards, as non-EU companies operating within the EU will need to comply (Recital 14). Overall, the EU AI Act sets a precedent for AI regulation worldwide, promoting responsible AI development and use while fostering trust in AI technology.

IMPLICATIONS OF THE EU AI ACT 2024: TOWARDS A HARMONIOUS AI ACT IN GHANA

The EU's AI Act provides a foundational framework for AI usage and deployment by delineating essential concepts. In Ghana's emerging AI regulatory landscape, policymakers can draw upon the EU AI Act's conceptual definitions through adaptation or adoption. The precision and consistency afforded by clear definitions of key terms are paramount for avoiding semantic ambiguity and ensuring legal clarity. Integrating comprehensive and nuanced definitions into Ghana's prospective AI legislation will foster legal certainty, thereby precluding misinterpretation and potential disputes that could stifle innovation. Moreover, well-defined terms will facilitate the development of guidelines governing AI development, deployment, and governance, enabling Ghana to optimize AI's benefits while minimizing its risks. By establishing a shared lexical framework, Ghana's AI law will lay the groundwork for cultivating trust, accountability, and responsible AI growth, ultimately driving digital transformation and socio-economic advancement in the country.

The EU's AI regulatory framework incorporates provisions for AI literacy, establishing a precedent for comparable initiatives globally. As Ghana endeavors to develop its AI legal framework, integrating AI literacy provisions is essential for cultivating a technologically informed citizenry. By mandating a foundational understanding of AI systems and their sociotechnical implications, the legislation can empower individuals to engage in informed decision-making regarding AI adoption in personal and professional contexts. Moreover, AI literacy provisions will enhance critical evaluation skills, mitigating the dissemination of disinformation and promoting media literacy. The incorporation of AI education and awareness initiatives within the legal framework will also foster trust in AI technologies, facilitate their acceptance, and encourage the identification and remediation of potential biases and discriminatory practices within AI systems. Prioritizing AI literacy in Ghana's AI law is crucial for creating a society where citizens can optimize AI's benefits while navigating its limitations and potential risks, thereby promoting a responsible, inclusive, and equitable AI ecosystem.

The development of Ghana's AI regulatory framework necessitates a thorough examination of prohibited AI practices to guarantee the responsible design, development, and deployment of AI technologies. The European Union's AI Act, specifically Chapter 2, serves as a paradigmatic model, delineating unacceptable AI practices that compromise human autonomy and dignity. Ghana's AI legislation should similarly proscribe AI systems engineered to manipulate human behavior, emotions, or decision-making processes without informed user consent. Such prohibitions should encompass AI systems that simulate human identity or falsely claim anthropomorphic capabilities, as well as those that exploit vulnerabilities or biases, particularly targeting susceptible populations, including minors, seniors, and individuals with disabilities. By integrating these prohibitions, Ghana's AI law can foster transparency, accountability, and trust in AI technologies, thereby safeguarding individuals from potential harm and ensuring the ethical development and deployment of AI systems.

Developing Ghana's AI law requires a strong focus on human safety and well-being, mirroring the EU AI Act's approach. This involves classifying high-risk AI systems, such as those used in healthcare, transportation, and education, which can significantly impact human health, safety, and fundamental rights. Ghana's law should establish a similar classification system, outlining stringent standards and regulations for these high-risk systems to ensure accountability and safety. Some key considerations for Ghana's AI law include the classification of high-risk AI systems, regular review and updates, broader social implications, and stringent standards and regulations. By integrating these essential elements, Ghana's AI law can cultivate a culture of responsible AI development and deployment, prioritizing human well-being, safety, and dignity.

The EU AI Act's Chapters III, Sections 4 and 5, outline a comprehensive regulatory framework for high-risk AI systems, encompassing conformity assessment, standardization, certification, and registration protocols. In developing its AI law, Ghana should establish unequivocal procedures for notifying authorities and notified bodies, thereby ensuring that providers implement stringent risk management strategies, maintain data integrity, provide meticulous technical documentation, guarantee transparency, and incorporate robust human oversight mechanisms. By adopting a lifecycle approach, Ghana's AI legislation can prioritize safety, privacy, and transparency, thereby mitigating potential risks and harm to individuals and society. This regulatory framework will cultivate trust in AI technologies, promote accountability and transparency, and facilitate global regulatory harmonization, ultimately fostering a secure and reliable AI ecosystem.

Developing Ghana's AI law requires a robust framework for classifying and managing high-risk AI models, similar to the EU AI Act's Articles 51 and 52. These articles establish clear criteria for identifying high-risk AI models, including high-impact capabilities and computation thresholds, ensuring proactive mitigation of potential harm. Ghana's law should adopt a similar risk-based approach, enabling targeted regulatory oversight and promoting safety, security, and accountability in AI development. Ghana's AI law can also draw inspiration from Articles 56 and 57, which establish frameworks for codes of practice and regulatory sandboxes. Codes of practice can ensure compliance with key obligations like transparency, risk management, and accountability, while sandboxes can foster innovation and compliance. Ghana's law should consider stakeholder involvement, clarity on regulatory expectations, and regular monitoring. Additionally, controlled environments for testing and validating AI systems can support SMEs and start-ups.

From the structure of the EU AI Act, developing Ghana's AI law requires careful consideration of several key factors to ensure responsible AI development and deployment. One crucial aspect is providing relief to microenterprises, similar to Article 63 of the EU AI Act, which allows simplified compliance with quality management system elements for small businesses without partner or linked enterprises. This derogation aims to reduce administrative burdens while maintaining regulatory stringency. Ghana's law should also prioritize informed consent, transparency, accountability, and fundamental rights protection, as outlined in Articles 61 and 62 of the EU AI Act. Additionally, Ghana can draw motivation from the comprehensive governance framework (Articles 64-69), which includes centralized expertise hub, collaborative engagement, stakeholder forum, and independent expert panel. If these elements are incorporated, Ghana's AI law can strike a balance between promoting innovation and ensuring accountability.

Ghana's AI law would require a framework that includes a scientific panel to provide expertise to support enforcement activities, facilitating timely access and coordination with AI testing support. A public database of high-risk AI systems, like the EU database, would enhance transparency, accountability, and oversight, promoting trust in AI technology. This database should contain information on AI system identity, providers, intended purpose, and conformity assessment, enabling informed decision-making and monitoring compliance.

Developing Ghana's AI law requires robust enforcement measures to ensure compliance, similar to the EU AI Act. This involves empowering national authorities to investigate, fine, and take corrective actions against non-compliant AI providers. A clear procedure for investigations, information requests, on-site inspections, and cooperation among national authorities is crucial to deter non-compliance and protect users from harmful AI systems. Ghana's AI law should also establish codes of conduct and guidelines to promote responsible AI development and use. This includes measures to encourage voluntary compliance with specific requirements for non-high-risk AI systems and providing clarity on regulatory implementation. The law should consider industry best practices, technical solutions, and stakeholder involvement, addressing ethical guidelines, environmental sustainability, AI literacy, inclusive design, and protection of vulnerable persons.

Also, developing Ghana's AI law requires a thoughtful balance between flexibility and accountability, much like the EU AI Act. To achieve this, Ghana's AI law should establish a clear framework for delegated powers and committee procedures, ensuring transparency and accountability. This could involve consulting experts and notifying relevant stakeholders before adopting delegated acts, which would enter into force unless objected to within a specified timeframe. A comprehensive penalty framework is also crucial, with fines and non-monetary measures that consider factors like infringement severity, cooperation, and financial benefits. Annual reporting requirements and judicial remedies would provide additional transparency and oversight.

The implications of the EU AI Act 2024 call for a harmonized AI Law in Ghana to ensure that AI technologies are developed and used in a way that respects citizens' rights and public safety, while fostering innovation and trust. The EU AI Act provides a comprehensive legal framework that categorizes AI systems by risk, imposing stringent requirements on high-risk applications to mitigate potential harm to health, safety, and fundamental rights. A similar framework in Ghana would help prevent harmful AI practices, such as real-time remote biometric identification in public spaces, and promote transparency and accountability in AI development.

A Ghanaian AI Act would also provide clarity and consistency for businesses and organizations operating in the AI space. By establishing a clear set of rules and guidelines, companies can ensure they are complying with regulations and avoiding potential fines and penalties. This, in turn, would foster a culture of responsible AI development and encourage innovation and investment in the sector. This harmonization will end up promoting the prevention of harmful AI practices, transparency and accountability, and the promotion of innovation.

Furthermore, a harmonized AI Act would enable Ghana to align with international standards and best practices in AI regulation. This would facilitate cooperation and collaboration with other countries, particularly in the EU, and ensure that Ghanaian businesses can compete globally. By adopting a comprehensive AI framework, Ghana can demonstrate its commitment to responsible AI development and establish itself as a leader in the African AI ecosystem. It is against these backdrops that it is argued that the effective regulation of AI in Ghana must be grounded in a harmonious and comprehensive legal framework that addresses ethical concerns, promotes transparency and accountability, and protects citizens' rights.

ARTIFICIAL INTELLIGENCE: ETHICAL CONSIDERATIONS FOR A HARMONIOUS LAW

The EU AI Act underscores the imperative of safeguarding human dignity, privacy, rights, and safety while promoting accountability, transparency, and fairness in the AI era. This highlights the complex and multifaceted relationship between ethics and AI, necessitating robust ethical considerations to navigate the intricate dynamics of AI development and its societal implications (Mittelstadt et al., 2016).

A pivotal ethical concern in AI development revolves around addressing bias and ensuring fairness in AI systems. The perpetuation and amplification of existing biases through biased data can lead to discriminatory outcomes, exemplified by facial recognition systems' racial biases (Richardson, 2021). Mitigating these biases is crucial for promoting social justice and preventing harm.

The collection and processing of vast personal data by AI systems also raise significant privacy concerns (Mittelstadt et al., 2016). AI-powered surveillance systems, for instance, can compromise individual privacy and potentially infringe upon human rights. Therefore, ethical frameworks governing data protection and informed consent are essential for responsible handling of personal information.

As AI assumes decision-making roles, accountability emerges as a pressing ethical issue (Dignum, 2019). Clear guidelines for responsibility and transparency are necessary to ensure AI systems align with human values. This necessitates the development of explainable AI systems that provide insights into their decision-making processes.

The development of autonomous AI systems prompts questions regarding moral agency and decision-making (Wallach & Allen, 2008). Ethical frameworks are required to ensure these systems align with human values and promote beneficial outcomes (Gabriel, 2020). Autonomous vehicles, for example, must be programmed to make life-or-death decisions in emergency situations, underscoring the need for ethical guidelines.

Moreover, AI's integration into daily life necessitates consideration of human values, dignity, and well-being (de Sio Filippo, 2021). Designing AI that respects human values is essential for promoting human flourishing and preventing harm. This includes examining AI's potential impact on employment and job displacement (Ford, 2015). Addressing the consequences of AI-driven automation is critical for ensuring equitable distribution of AI benefits.

Ultimately, aligning AI systems with human values and goals is crucial for beneficial AI development (Russell et al., 2015). Ongoing research and development of value-aligned AI systems prioritizing human well-being and dignity are necessary. By prioritizing ethics in AI development, harmful consequences can be mitigated, and AI can be harnessed to benefit humanity.

From the above, the pivotal role of ethical considerations in promoting a harmonious AI legal framework is evident. By prioritizing human well-being, dignity, and rights, and aligning AI development with human values, ethical principles facilitate a comprehensive approach to AI governance. This integration enables the prevention of harm, fosters transparency and accountability, promotes fairness and justice, safeguards human autonomy, and advances responsible AI development. Consequently, ethical frameworks inform AI governance structures, ensuring effective regulation, oversight, and enforcement. The resultant harmonization yields clear guidelines, aligns AI systems with human values, foster public trust, mitigates harm, and promotes international cooperation, ultimately safeguarding human interests and facilitating the beneficial integration of AI into society (Dignum, 2019; Russell et al., 2015).

CONCLUSION

This chapter investigated the legislation and ethical frameworks of AI in Ghana and how Ghana can draw on the EU AI Act to influence a harmonious AI legal regime. The enactment of the EU AI Act 2024 signifies a profound shift in the governance of AI, conclusively establishing the centrality of ethical considerations and human-centric approaches in AI development and deployment. By codifying transparency, explainability, and accountability as foundational principles, this legislation sets a global benchmark for responsible AI practices, thereby prioritizing the protection of human rights, dignity, and well-being. The Act's multifaceted framework, encompassing risk-based regulations, oversight mechanisms, and enforcement provisions, demonstrates a systematic commitment to addressing the complex challenges and risks posed by AI.

The nascent AI regulatory landscape in Ghana necessitates the adoption of a harmonized AI law, modeled after the European Union's AI Act, to provide a cohesive framework for AI governance. This comprehensive legislation would yield clarity and consistency for stakeholders, foster transparency and accountability, and mitigate harmful AI practices. By employing a risk-based categorization of AI systems and imposing stringent requirements on high-risk applications, Ghana can ensure that AI technologies are developed and deployed in a manner that respects citizens' rights and prioritizes public safety, while concurrently promoting innovation and trust. Furthermore, harmonization with international standards and best practices in AI regulation would facilitate cooperation and collaboration with other nations.

The implementation of a harmonized AI law in Ghana would serve as a paradigmatic example of the country's commitment to responsible AI development, positioning it as a vanguard in the African AI ecosystem. This legislation should prioritize human well-being, safety, and dignity while cultivating a culture of responsible AI development and deployment. Crucial considerations include the classification of high-risk AI systems, effective human oversight mechanisms, and robust risk management frameworks. By integrating these essential elements, Ghana's AI law can foster trust in AI technologies, promote accountability, and facilitate global regulatory harmonization, ultimately culminating in a secure and reliable AI system.

Integrating ethical frameworks into AI governance is essential for creating effective regulatory structures and enforcement mechanisms. This alignment offers several benefits, including clear guidelines, consistency with human values, increased public trust, reduced risks, and enhanced global cooperation. Eventually, it helps protect human interests and facilitates the smooth integration of AI into society.

REFERENCES

Abbasi, N., Nizamullah, F. N. U., & Zeb, S. (2023). AI in Healthcare: Integrating Advanced Technologies with Traditional Practices for Enhanced Patient Care. *BULLET: Jurnal Multidisiplin Ilmu, 2*(3), 546–556.

Abdulhussein, M. (2024). *The Impact of Artificial Intelligence and Machine Learning on Organizations Cybersecurity*. Liberty University.

Adams, R. (2022). AI in Africa: Key Concerns and Policy Considerations for the Future of the Continent. Retrieved from https://afripoli.org/ai-in-africa-key-concerns-and-policy-considerations-for-the-future-of-the-continent on 19/10/2024

Adebayo, O. (2020). Data Science in Nigeria: Challenges and Opportunities. Retrieved from https://nigeriacodingacademy.com/data-science-trends-in-nigeria/ on 8/10/2024.

Alamu, O. E., Aworinde, M. O., & Isharufe, J. O. (2013). Ifa: An Ancient Binary Computer System. *CIT. Journal of Computing and Information Technology, 21*(3), 159–166.

Alowais, S. A., Alghamdi, S. S., Alsuhebany, N., Alqahtani, T., Alshaya, A. I., Almohareb, S. N., Aldairem, A., Alrashed, M., Bin Saleh, K., Badreldin, H. A., Al Yami, M. S., Al Harbi, S., & Albekairy, A. M. (2023). Revolutionizing healthcare: The role of artificial intelligence in clinical practice. *BMC Medical Education, 23*(1), 689. DOI: 10.1186/s12909-023-04698-z PMID: 37740191

Amoah, L. G. A. (Ed.). (2024). *Examining the Rapid Advance of Digital Technology in Africa*. IGI Global. DOI: 10.4018/978-1-6684-9962-7

Anyoha, R. (2017). A Brief History of Artificial Intelligence. Retrieved from https://sitn.hms.harvard.edu/flash/2017/history-artificial-intelligence/ on 15/09/2024.

Barocas, S., & Selbst, A. D. (2019). Big data's disparate impact. *California Law Review, 104*, 671.

Breazeal, C. (2003). Emotion and sociable humanoid robots. *International Journal of Human-Computer Studies, 59*(1-2), 119–155. DOI: 10.1016/S1071-5819(03)00018-1

Brooks, R. (2003). *Flesh and machines: How robots will change us*. Vintage.

Brynjolfsson, E., & McAfee, A. (2014). *The second machine age: Work, progress, and prosperity in a time of brilliant technologies*. WW Norton & company.

Burr, C., & Leslie, D. (2023). Ethical assurance: A practical approach to the responsible design, development, and deployment of data-driven technologies. *AI and Ethics, 3*(1), 73–98. DOI: 10.1007/s43681-022-00178-0

Canobbio, V. T. (2024). *Sales Lead Routing: Exploring Speed, Quality, Accuracy, and Technology* (Doctoral dissertation, Golden Gate University).

Cath, C. (2018). Governing artificial intelligence: Ethical, legal and technical opportunities and challenges. *Philosophical Transactions. Series A, Mathematical, Physical, and Engineering Sciences, 376*(2133), 20180080. DOI: 10.1098/rsta.2018.0080 PMID: 30322996

Chen, H., Chiang, R. H., & Storey, V. C. (2012). Business intelligence and analytics: From big data to big impact. *Management Information Systems Quarterly, 36*(4), 1165–1188. DOI: 10.2307/41703503

Cheng, L., Varshney, K. R., & Liu, H. (2021). Socially responsible ai algorithms: Issues, purposes, and challenges. *Journal of Artificial Intelligence Research, 71*, 1137–1181. DOI: 10.1613/jair.1.12814

Cheong, B. C. (2024). Transparency and accountability in AI systems: Safeguarding wellbeing in the age of algorithmic decision-making. *Frontiers in Human Dynamics, 6*, 1421273. DOI: 10.3389/fhumd.2024.1421273

Croucamp, A. (2013). Traditional African divination systems as information technology. *Mindburst, viewed, 23.*

Davenport, T. H. (2013). Analytics 3.0. *Harvard Business Review, 91*(12), 64–72.

de Sio Filippo, S. (2021). Mark Coeckelbergh, AI Ethics, Mit Press, 2021. *Science and Engineering Ethics, 27*(4). Copyright Act (Act 690).

Díaz-Rodríguez, N., Del Ser, J., Coeckelbergh, M., de Prado, M. L., Herrera-Viedma, E., & Herrera, F. (2023). Connecting the dots in trustworthy Artificial Intelligence: From AI principles, ethics, and key requirements to responsible AI systems and regulation. *Information Fusion, 99*, 101896. DOI: 10.1016/j.inffus.2023.101896

Dignum, V. (2019). *Responsible artificial intelligence: how to develop and use AI in a responsible way* (Vol. 2156). Springer. DOI: 10.1007/978-3-030-30371-6

Eglash, R. (1999). *African fractals: Modern computing and Indigenous design.* Rutgers University Press.

Feigenbaum, E. A. (1980). Knowledge Engineering. *The Applied Side of Artificial Intelligence.* Report No. HPP-80-21. Retrieved from https://stacks.stanford.edu/file/druid:cn981xh0967/cn981xh0967.pdf on 11/10/2024.

Feigenbaum, E. A., & Feldman, J. (1963). *Computers and thought* (Vol. 37). McGraw-Hill.

Feigenbaum, E. A., & McCorduck, P. (1983). The Fifth Generation: Artificial Intelligence and Japan's Computer Challenge to the World.

Ford, M. (2015). *Rise of the Robots*. Basic books.

Frey, C. B., & Osborne, M. A. (2017). The future of employment: How susceptible are jobs to computerization? *Technological Forecasting and Social Change, 114*, 254–280. DOI: 10.1016/j.techfore.2016.08.019

Gabriel, I. (2020). Artificial intelligence, values, and alignment. *Minds and Machines, 30*(3), 411–437. DOI: 10.1007/s11023-020-09539-2

Gabriel, O. T. (2023). *Data privacy and ethical issues in collecting health care data using artificial intelligence among health workers* (Master's thesis, Center for Bioethics and Research).

Ghana Institute of Engineers. (1990). Annual Report.

Gomez-Uribe, C. A., & Hunt, N. (2015). The Netflix recommender system: Algorithms, business value, and innovation. [TMIS]. *ACM Transactions on Management Information Systems, 6*(4), 1–19. DOI: 10.1145/2843948

Habbal, A., Ali, M. K., & Abuzaraida, M. A. (2024). Artificial Intelligence Trust, risk and security management (AI trism): Frameworks, applications, challenges and future research directions. *Expert Systems with Applications, 240*, 122442. DOI: 10.1016/j.eswa.2023.122442

Halevy, A., Norvig, P., & Pereira, F. (2009). The unreasonable effectiveness of data. *IEEE Intelligent Systems, 24*(2), 8–12. DOI: 10.1109/MIS.2009.36

Hopfield, J. J. (1982). Neural networks and physical systems with emergent collective computational abilities. *Proceedings of the National Academy of Sciences of the United States of America, 79*(8), 2554–2558. DOI: 10.1073/pnas.79.8.2554 PMID: 6953413

Hsu, F. H. (2002). *Behind Deep Blue: Building the computer that defeated the world chess champion*. Princeton University Press.

Hu, X., Neupane, B., Echaiz, L. F., Sibal, P., & Rivera Lam, M. (2019). *Steering AI and advanced ICTs for knowledge societies: A Rights, Openness, Access, and Multi-stakeholder Perspective*. UNESCO Publishing.

Huang, A., & Rust, R. T. (2018). Artificial intelligence in service. *Journal of Service Research, 21*(2), 155–172. DOI: 10.1177/1094670517752459

Ibegbulam, C. M., Aigbovbiosa, O. J., Olowonubi, J. A., & Fatounde, S. A. (2023). Role of artificial intelligence in electrification of Africa. *Engineering Science & Technology Journal, 4*(6), 456–472. DOI: 10.51594/estj.v4i6.667

Jordan, M. I., & Mitchell, T. M. (2015). Machine learning: Trends, perspectives, and prospects. *Science, 349*(6245), 255–260. DOI: 10.1126/science.aaa8415 PMID: 26185243

Kamanja, D. M. (2020). *Influence of Work Environment on Employee Engagement of Central Government Ministries in Kenya, A Case of Meru County* (Doctoral dissertation, KeMU).

Kroll, J. A. (2021). Outlining traceability: A principle for operationalizing accountability in computing systems. In *Proceedings of the 2021 ACM Conference on Fairness, Accountability, and Transparency* (pp. 758-771). DOI: 10.1145/3442188.3445937

Lake, B. M., Ullman, T. D., Tenenbaum, J. B., & Gershman, S. J. (2017). Building machines that learn and think like people. *Behavioral and Brain Sciences, 40*, e253. DOI: 10.1017/S0140525X16001837 PMID: 27881212

Lewis, J. (2024). AI and Bias: Addressing Discrimination in Machine Learning Algorithms Abstract. *AlgoVista. Journal of AI & Computer Science, 1*(2).

Linden, G., Smith, B., & York, J. (2003). Recommendations: Item-to-item collaborative filtering. *IEEE Internet Computing, 7*(1), 76–80. DOI: 10.1109/MIC.2003.1167344

Lippmann, R. (1997). Speech recognition by Machines and Humans. *Speech Communication, 22*(1), 1–15. DOI: 10.1016/S0167-6393(97)00021-6

Manheim, K., & Kaplan, L. (2019). Artificial intelligence: Risks to privacy and democracy. *Yale JL & Tech., 21*, 106.

Manyika, J. (2011). Big data: The next frontier for innovation, competition, and productivity. *McKinsey Global Institute, 1.*

Manyika, J., Chui, M., Miremadi, M., Bughin, J., George, K., Willmott, P., & Dewhurst, M. (2017). A future that works: AI, automation, employment, and productivity. *McKinsey Global Institute Research. Tech. Rep, 60*, 1–135.

Martin, K. D., & Zimmermann, J. (2024). Artificial Intelligence and its Implications for Data Privacy. *Current Opinion in Psychology, 58*, 101829. DOI: 10.1016/j.copsyc.2024.101829 PMID: 38954851

McAfee, A., Brynjolfsson, E., Davenport, T. H., Patil, D. J., & Barton, D. (2012). Big data: The management revolution. *Harvard Business Review*, *90*(10), 60–68. PMID: 23074865

McCarthy, J., Minsky, M. L., Rochester, N., & Shannon, C. E. (1955). A Proposal for the Dartmouth Summer Research Project on Artificial Intelligence. *AI Magazine*, *27*(4), 12–12.

Mdladla, L. T. S., Wider, W., Thanathanchuchot, T., & Hossain, S. A. (2024). Navigating the AI revolution: A review of the transformative strategies for economic development in Africa's emerging economies. *Journal of Infrastructure. Policy and Development*, *8*(9), 5436. DOI: 10.24294/jipd.v8i9.5436

Miller, T. (2019). Explanation in artificial intelligence: Insights from the social sciences. *Artificial Intelligence*, *267*, 1–38. DOI: 10.1016/j.artint.2018.07.007

Minsky, M. (1970). Form and Content in Computer Science (1970 ACM Turing lecture). [JACM]. *Journal of the Association for Computing Machinery*, *17*(2), 197–215. DOI: 10.1145/321574.321575

Mittelstadt, B. D., Allo, P., Taddeo, M., Wachter, S., & Floridi, L. (2016). The ethics of algorithms: Mapping the debate. *Big Data & Society*, *3*(2), 2053951716679679. DOI: 10.1177/2053951716679679

Moore, G. (1965). Moore's law. *Electronics Magazine*, *38*(8), 114.

Moravec, H. (1988). *Mind Children: The Future of Robot and Human Intelligence*. Harvard UP.

Mouta, A., Pinto-Llorente, A. M., & Torrecilla-Sánchez, E. M. (2023). Uncovering blind spots in education ethics: Insights from a systematic literature review on artificial intelligence in education. *International Journal of Artificial Intelligence in Education*, •••, 1–40.

Mramba, N. R. (2024). The potentials of artificial intelligence in improving Africa informal cross border trade. What works, What doesn't, and What's next to Africans? *African Journal of Land Policy and Geospatial Sciences*, *7*(1), 92–112.

Nazer, L. H., Zatarah, R., Waldrip, S., Ke, J. X. C., Moukheiber, M., Khanna, A. K., Hicklen, R. S., Moukheiber, L., Moukheiber, D., Ma, H., & Mathur, P. (2023). Bias in artificial intelligence algorithms and recommendations for mitigation. *PLOS Digital Health*, *2*(6), e0000278. DOI: 10.1371/journal.pdig.0000278 PMID: 37347721

Newell, A., & Simon, H. A. (1972). *Human problem solving*. Prentice Hall.

Nwaobi, G. C. (2019). Emerging African Economies: Digital Structures, Disruptive Responses and Demographic Implications. *Disruptive Responses and Demographic Implications (October 1, 2019).*

Oyekunle, D., Boohene, D., & Preston, D. (2024). Ethical Considerations in AI-Powered Work Environments: A Literature Review and Theoretical Framework for Ensuring Human Dignity and Fairness. *Valley International Journal Digital Library*, 6166-6178.

Rahaman, M., Pappachan, P., Orozco, S. M., Bansal, S., & Arya, V. (2024). AI Safety and Security. In *Challenges in Large Language Model Development and AI Ethics* (pp. 354–383). IGI Global. DOI: 10.4018/979-8-3693-3860-5.ch011

Richardson, R. (2021). Racial segregation and the data-driven society: How our failure to reckon with root causes perpetuates separate and unequal realities. *Berkeley Technology Law Journal*, *36*, 1051.

Robinson, S. C. (2020). Trust, transparency, and openness: How inclusion of cultural values shapes Nordic national public policy strategies for artificial intelligence (AI). *Technology in Society*, *63*, 101421. DOI: 10.1016/j.techsoc.2020.101421

Rumelhart, D. E., & McClelland, J. L.PDP Research Group. (1986). Parallel distributed processing: explorations in the microstructure of cognition: foundations. *Mit Press Computational Models Of Cognition And Perception Series*, *1*, 547. DOI: 10.7551/mitpress/5236.001.0001

Russell, S., Dewey, D., & Tegmark, M. (2015). Research priorities for robust and beneficial artificial intelligence. *AI Magazine*, *36*(4), 105–114. DOI: 10.1609/aimag.v36i4.2577

Saura, J. R., Ribeiro-Soriano, D., & Palacios-Marqués, D. (2022). Assessing behavioral data science privacy issues in government artificial intelligence deployment. *Government Information Quarterly*, *39*(4), 101679. DOI: 10.1016/j.giq.2022.101679

Shakhatreh, H., Sawalmeh, A. H., Al-Fuqaha, A., Dou, Z., Almaita, E., Khalil, I., Othman, N. S., Khreishah, A., & Guizani, M. (2019). Unmanned aerial vehicles (UAVs): A survey on civil applications and key research challenges. *IEEE Access : Practical Innovations, Open Solutions*, *7*, 48572–48634. DOI: 10.1109/ACCESS.2019.2909530

Signé, L. (2023). *Africa's Fourth Industrial Revolution*. Cambridge University Press. DOI: 10.1017/9781009200004

Silver, D., Huang, A., Maddison, C. J., Guez, A., Sifre, L., Van Den Driessche, G., ... & Hassabis, D. (2016). Mastering the game of Go with deep neural networks and tree search. *nature, 529*(7587), 484-489.

Siyonbola, O. O. (2020). A brief history of artificial intelligence in Africa. Retrieved from https://noirpress.org/a-brief-history-of-artificial-intelligence-in-africa/ on 13/10/2024.

Soueidan, M. H., & Shoghari, R. (2024). The Impact of Artificial Intelligence on Job Loss: Risks for Governments. *Technium Social Science Journal*, *57*, 206–223. DOI: 10.47577/tssj.v57i1.10917

Thapaliya, S., & Bokani, A. (2024). Leveraging artificial intelligence for enhanced cybersecurity: Insights and innovations. *SADGAMAYA*, *1*(1), 46–52. DOI: 10.3126/sadgamaya.v1i1.66888

Truby, J. (2020). Governing artificial intelligence to benefit the UN sustainable development goals. *Sustainable Development (Bradford)*, *28*(4), 946–959. DOI: 10.1002/sd.2048

Turing, A. (1950). Computing machinery and intelligence. *Mind*, *59*(236), 435–460.

UNECA. (2019). Africa's blueprint for AI development. Retrieved from https://www.uneca.org/economic-report-africa-2019 on 5/10/2024

Wachter, S., & Mittelstadt, B. (2019). A right to reasonable inferences: re-thinking data protection law in the age of big data and AI. *Colum. Bus. L. Rev.*, 494.

Wallach, W., & Allen, C. (2008). *Moral machines: Teaching robots right from wrong*. Oxford University Press.

Wang, D., & Wang, J. (2018). Facial recognition technology: A review. *Journal of Intelligent Information Systems*, *52*(2), 257–275.

Wang, Y., & Chung, S. H. (2022). Artificial intelligence in safety-critical systems: A systematic review. *Industrial Management & Data Systems*, *122*(2), 442–470. DOI: 10.1108/IMDS-07-2021-0419

Weizenbaum, J. (1972). On the impact of the computer on society: How does one insult a machine? *Science*, *176*(4035), 609–614. DOI: 10.1126/science.176.4035.609 PMID: 17778159

West, D. M. (2018). *The future of work: Robots, AI, and automation*. Brookings Institution Press.

World Bank. (2020). AI Regulation in Ghana.

World Bank. (2020). Digital Economy for Africa. Retrieved from https://www.worldbank.org/en/programs/all-africa-digital-transformation#:~:text=The%20Digital%20Economy%20for%20Africa,Digital%20Transformation%20Strategy%20for%20Africa.%E2%80%9D on 14/10/2024.

APPENDIX

Statutes

Trademarks Act (Act 664).
Patent Act (Act 657).
Electronic Transactions Act (Act 772).
Cybersecurity Act.
Data Protection Act (Act 843).

Chapter 6
Legal and Ethical Issues in the Interaction of AI and Metaverse:
Complexities and Challenges

Nitish Kumar Ojha
https://orcid.org/0000-0002-2236-0766
Amity University, Noida, India

Abhishek Vaish
Indian Institute of Information Technology, Allahabad, India

ABSTRACT

The enormous use of technology in the 'Metaverse era has yielded a new challenge of socio-technical ethical issues. After the pandemic, when everyone is getting highly connected to the different social media-based metaverse, the expression of thought and the barrier of free thinking bring the issue of sanctity in the posts and expressions available in the Metaverse. This chapter presents all the logical implications of evolving ethical issues as well as technical issues. This book chapter also lists all the technical dilemmas occurring in the metaverse that are related to social ethics i.e., AI-generated illicit photographs, deep fake videos, supportive interaction and privacy breaches, social self-efficacy, feelings of loneliness, etc. Further, it maps the services offered by Metaverse. This Chapter also covers the open challenges of the Metaverse i.e., Cyber Bullying, Online Harassment, AI-generated Child Pornographic Content, etc., and the status of the Law. This study may help policymakers and stimulate prospective researchers for better outcomes in this field.

DOI: 10.4018/979-8-3373-3384-7.ch006

INTRODUCTION

The concept of Metaverse is not new, but it has been much discussed in the last few years due to the rise of Virtual Reality and Augmented Reality. During Corona, when the whole world was closed, the metaverse got a boost, and gaming tournaments, virtual socializing, and events also took place in this world. During this time, people came together and both the popularity and need of the Metaverse increased, (Lee *et al.,* 2021). The Metaverse is a conceptual and highly immersive virtual world that is planned to be displayed in virtual reality (VR) along with AI.

1. Its name is made up of two words: the prefix "meta", which is derived from the Greek word meaning "beyond." Universe. In the novel "Snow Crash", published in 1992, author Neal Stephenson coined the term, meaning "computer-generated universe," (Hu, Iosifescu, & LiKamWa, 2021a). Today's metaverse, if you will, would be the next "generation" of Stephenson's concept: an advanced level of the Internet where people can use their avatars or holograms to communicate, socialize, travel, shop, or work together in virtual 3D environments, (Roesner, Kohno, & Molnar, 2014). In the Metaverse, people use the latest virtual reality and augmented reality (VR/AR) technologies. You will be able to connect, communicate, or grow your business in a completely new way, (Kye *et al.,* 2021). Remote working will become more advanced. People working online from any remote location can also meet their colleagues virtually in the metaverse. This is because, using VR technology, people can virtually travel to different places in the metaverse, (Hu, Iosifescu, & LiKamWa, 2021b). People will not need to go to physical stores to try new products before purchasing. VR/AR technologies will enable them to explore different products from different brands from virtually anywhere in the Metaverse, (Rosenberg, 2022). The Metaverse will enhance interactive virtual in-store experiences. If certain products are out of stock, the VR/AR set will allow users to try out those items within the store. Additionally, blockchain technology will be thriving in the metaverse, (Negreiro & Niestadt, 2022) (Brussels: The European Digital Identity Framework, 2022). Cryptocurrency and blockchain technology will control financial transactions in the metaverse but there are also risks to the metaverse due to so many activities and it depends on how the user uses the metaverse, (Zeigler, 1995) (Emerton, 2015).

Meaning and Relevance of Metaverse: The common challenge is how to define Metaverse. Several definitions have been proposed in this direction, i.e. Lee et al. in their most cited research paper in tracking it from the embodiment of the internet and different 3D virtual games i.e., Pokemon Go, Upland, etc., concluding it to the digital transformation of those games having internet connectivity, (Lee *et al.*, 2021). Further on, with the advancement of technologies after the year 2020, scientists started seeing it as a perfect example of virtual reality with the augmentation of new technologies i.e., Blockchain, Artificial Intelligence, Machine Learning, Robotics, Computer Vision, Edge and Cloud Computing, etc. Hu et al. in their research paper in the year 2021 measured the controls of Privacy in the Metaverse considering it an alive but virtual world that is going to be the future of the internet, (Roesner, Kohno, & Molnar, 2014b) (Guzman, Thilakarathna, & Seneviratne, 2019) (Guzman, Seneviratne, & Thilakarathna, 2021).

METAVERSE IS LEADING BUT CHALLENGING ETHICS

Metaverse is affecting our lives in a very profound way and is slowly making inroads in our day-to-day activities. Metaverse can play an important role in skill enhancement through distance mode due to its opportunity to develop new experiential learning scenarios, (Bourlakis, Papagiannidis, & Li, 2009). The Metaverse presents a range of ethical and social challenges that need to be addressed. The immersive nature of the Metaverse may lead to virtual harassment, cyberbullying, identity theft, and other forms of social and ethical violations, (Hu, Iosifescu, & LiKamWa, 2021a). Providing users with education on topics such as online etiquette, cybersecurity, and privacy practices is crucial in promoting responsible behavior and ensuring a secure and equitable Metaverse, (Roesner, Kohno, & Molnar, 2014a). It is important to ensure that users are aware of the potential risks and are equipped with the knowledge and tools to navigate the Metaverse safely and ethically.

Privacy, Identity and Anonymity, Cyber Bullying, Content Stealing, Attack on Expression, discrimination, and inequality, etc. are the growing concerns of ethics in the metaverse these days. The metaverse, a virtual reality space where people can interact and engage with each other and digital environments, presents various ethical concerns. Users' data and information can be at risk in the metaverse. Issues related to data privacy, tracking, and surveillance can lead to violations of user privacy, identity theft, and unauthorized data use. Similarly, In the metaverse, users can create and manage multiple digital identities, which can lead to concerns related to impersonation, harassment, and the difficulty of verifying the identity of other users. Not only this, some other issues of ethics have also been reported and raised in many papers i.e. The anonymity and distance provided by the metaverse can facilitate online harassment, cyberbullying, and toxic behavior. Spending excessive time in virtual worlds can lead to addiction, neglect of real-world responsibilities, and physical or mental health issues. Virtual violence and aggressive behavior within the metaverse can have real-world consequences, and platforms must address this issue. Maintaining a safe and respectful environment is a significant challenge.

The strong factor of the metaverse can be the weakest link too. The Metaverse can bridge the gap between the physical and virtual worlds, thus combining online and offline commerce, (Braud, Fernández, & Hui, 2022). This means users will be able to digitally experience the physical world through the metaverse, making online shopping more convenient, (Bulu, 2012).

Figure 1. Representation of metaverse and its multiple domain

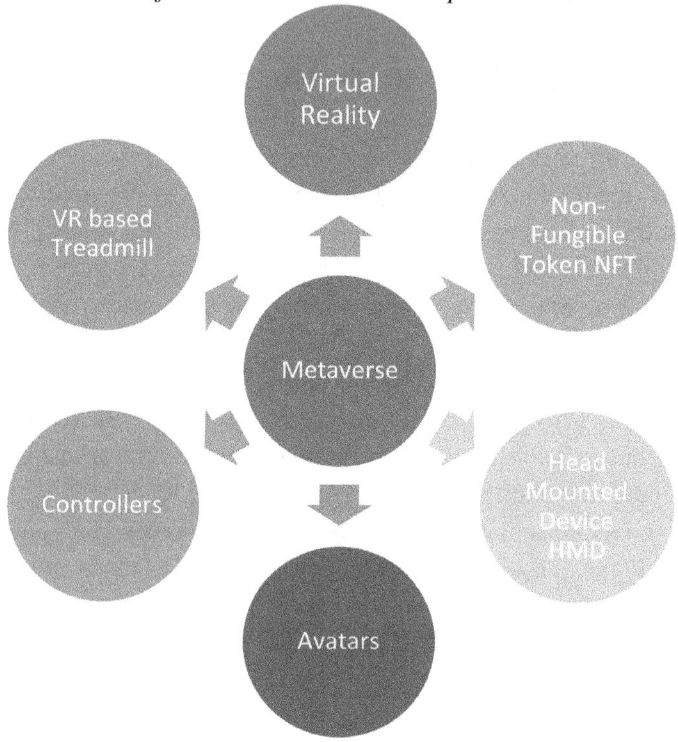

Roesnar et al. in the study raised very relevant and salient questions pertinent to the pros and cons of the metaverse for an individual as well as society at large. Cai & Song (2022) in their empirical research classified the applications of the metaverse into four categories i.e., augmented reality, lifelogging, mirror world, and virtual reality, and considered it as virtual cum real and live internet, (Calvo, 2020). Few studies have raised concern as the metaverse is increasing and experimenting with every segment of our daily life so personal information and related data i.e., biometric information, face, gait, walking pattern, etc. may be in danger as it is going to be overused by metaverse for constructing the data for its business, (Cheng *et*

al., 2022). Issues raised by research studies have raised the eyebrows of concerned authorities as many virtual reality games have been reported for challenging the ethical boundaries of society, (Díaz, Saldaña, & Avila, 2020). Hu et al. reported in their study that in a virtual game produced by Meta Inc. sexual harassment of a female avatar is encouraged when revenge is initiated by another male avatar, (Díaz, Saldaña, & Avila, 2020).

How Metaverse is meeting AI: The convergence of the Metaverse and Artificial Intelligence (AI) is creating a transformative digital landscape. These are the few important ways where AI and metaverse are intersecting each other when the issues of ethics may arise –

1. **Enhanced User Experience:** AI is pivotal in creating more immersive and interactive experiences within the Metaverse. Through AI-driven avatars, users can interact in more lifelike and responsive ways. These avatars can understand and respond to natural language, recognize emotions, and even learn from interactions to provide personalized experiences.
2. **Content Creation and Management:** AI tools are being used to generate and manage vast amounts of content in the Metaverse. From creating realistic virtual environments to generating dynamic storylines and scenarios, AI helps in automating and scaling content creation. This ensures that the Metaverse remains engaging and constantly evolving.
3. **Security and Moderation:** In the Metaverse, AI plays a crucial role in maintaining security and moderating content. AI algorithms can detect and mitigate cyber threats, ensuring a safe environment for users. Additionally, AI can monitor user behavior to prevent harassment and inappropriate content, fostering a positive community.
4. **Data Analysis and Personalization:** AI's ability to analyze large datasets allows for highly personalized experiences in the Metaverse. By understanding user preferences and behaviors, AI can tailor experiences, recommend content, and even predict future trends. This level of personalization enhances user engagement and satisfaction.
5. **Economic Systems:** AI is also transforming the economic systems within the Metaverse. Through AI-driven financial models and smart contracts, transactions can be automated and secured. This integration supports the creation of virtual economies where users can buy, sell, and trade digital assets seamlessly.
6. **Accessibility:** AI technologies are making the Metaverse more accessible to people with disabilities. For instance, AI-driven speech recognition and translation services can help users with hearing or language impairments to participate fully in virtual environments.

LITERATURE REVIEW

In general, most of the research-based study has been done in the field evaluating the ethics and legal issues considering characteristics shown by users not how the metaverse is impacting their thought process at larger, (Erturk & Reynolds, 2020). Human gesture, Behavior analysis, Visible emotional analysis, react and response-based analysis, and social interaction of users age-wise in the metaverse. Rosenberg (2022) discussed a few concepts related to the formation of new regulations matching the needs of current trends in society on various parameters, (European Innovation Council and SMEs Executive Agency, 2022). Moving further, some research studies have been reported in the field of legal conditions of data validity and authorization of private data in a complex environment where IoT is also involved with the flavor of AI. Negreiro and Niestadt (2014) pointed out the need for strict laws in the purview of cyber resilience and the use of data in the metaverse affecting the law of society, (Gabriel, 2020). It is interesting to know that researchers also gave importance to the representation of humans when aggressive use of AI is observed in the metaverse by several companies in their products. Human is represented in two ways based on their gender male and female so ethical value and their presentation in society is also dynamically changing according to the game, environment, and the objective of the game in the metaverse.

In the world of games, the representation of gender may be biased stereotyped, and skewed, irrespective of considering their long-term impact on society, (Garćıa et al., 2020). This issue has been pointed out by many researchers in last year's studies, however, the researchers started working in this field in year late nineties. The first serious work has been reported by Bernard in his research paper entitled *'Ethical Considerations in Virtual Reality'* in which he pointed out the depletion of ethics in coming years however he has used the word virtual reality, (Getchell *et al.,* 2010). Moving ahead Peter Emerton in year 2015 stated his worries regarding content creation, digital identity and access management, inclusivity, User privacy, and regulation in the metaverse, (Greenhalgh *et al.*, 2004). In the years 2016-2019, some work specifically reported the loss of intellectual property in the metaverse and pointed out the concern about the formation of new rules as the need of the hour for the virtual world as we have in the real world. Issues related to definitions of Intellectual Property, proprietorship of the models, Copyrighted material, Theorems, Patents, Design-based security frameworks, Piracy of unique data, and misuse of open secrets-based issues were a number of the potential challenges that were observed in the metaverse, (Gurov & Konkova, 2022). In a world where geographic boundaries break down and regional rights take an unused meaning and convert it to a parallel world of virtuality, revenue is being generated then strict laws are needed,

(Hollands, 2008). This thought has been set by many research studies in this field over the last decade concluded from various studies.

Ethics has been reviewed in terms of loss of privacy by some scientists too. Studies have been reported by reviewing the miscellaneous applications of the metaverse, targeting the behavior profiling of the users and the way they are interacting with apps in the metaverse and losing their private data. Jeremy Bailenson et al. pointed out the term privacy as a parameter to quantify the user experience in the metaverse and how it is getting affected in his research paper *'Ethical Considerations for Immersive Virtual Reality Experiences' in the year 2018,* (Hwang & Chien, 2022).. In a significant analysis, Alexander et all reported that autonomy is also a major area of concern in the metaverse as by following EULA (End Users License Agreement) autonomy gets shifted towards the application side instead of the user side and further the ethical values are going to be controlled and defined by the application and its designer not by the user side.

One more philosophical query was done by Johanna et al. in the year 2020 emphasizing the concern of making moral decisions in the metaverse, (Ibáñez & Delgado-Kloos, 2018). Changing the body changes the role in the metaverse so the ethics and legal aspects also get affected. In this study, she gave a clear line difference between feeling and experience and described how the virtual world can be used to reduce the moral foundation, which is not possible in the real world, (Kohler, 2008). She states further that long-term use of the virtual world such as the application of a metaverse makes a user free from the moral duties of the real world and thus it can be good as well as bad at the same time depending upon the context and objective. She elaborated on the concept of good use of the metaverse for pain management and administration of emotional factors such as fear, emotion, etc., making an application of the metaverse, (Cipresso, 2018). Some other studies were also reported focusing on the use of metaverse applications which induce the addiction factors that can bring the transition in personality of a user in the long-term resulting in change in a civilized society, (Sarkadi *et al.,* 2020). Excessive use of metaverse applications can also produce psychosis-infected personalities in militaries which can be only observed by testing the neurocognitive skills of a person, (Theodorou, 2017).

These all studies suggest that the metaverse is turning into a mass consumer-based useful product where control and monitoring are necessary by authorities to put the legal implications in control.

HOW METAVERSE AFFECTS ETHICS

The increasing use of metaverse poses a significant challenge to ethics and legal issues in society which are the following ways:

1. **Cultural and Social Impact:** The Metaverse can influence and reshape cultural values in society in many ways.
   a. **Social Interaction Redefined:** In the virtual world, people can interact with others of diverse backgrounds and cultures. This exposure can lead to increased cultural understanding and tolerance. For example, individuals who frequently interact with people from different cultures in the Metaverse may have a greater appreciation for diversity and multiculturalism, which may influence the cultural values aimed at inclusion and acceptance, (Interdisciplinary Science Reviews, n.d.).

Figure 2. News about the attachment of the virtual world over personal issues (Alpala, 2022)

INDIA TODAY

SIGN IN
Dark Mode
Edition IN
Premium
Home
TV
Magazine
India
World
Business
Technology
Entertainment

News / Technology / News / Man chooses PUBG over pregnant wife, leaves family because of his PUBG addiction

Man chooses PUBG over pregnant wife, leaves family because of his PUBG addiction

A report, based on a Facebook post made by a woman, indicated that a man left his 4 months pregnant wife and family in order to play PUBG. Apparently, the man got addicted to PUBG after his sibling introduced it to him.

Listen to Story
Share

b. **Change In Economy:** The Metaverse typically consists of virtual economies where users can buy, sell, and trade digital assets. This could lead to changes in economic value as individuals may place greater value on virtual goods and digital assets. Concepts of ownership and wealth can extend beyond material possessions, influencing how society views materialism and consumerism. Many studies have reported the fact that the rise of the metaverse could disrupt existing economic models effectively in many dimensions, leading to job losses or other economic consequences, (Alpala, 2022).
c. **Loss in emotional Values:** Many popular games of the metaverse have long-term effects on human emotional values and people are losing their tolerance level and threatening lives because of addiction. Pub-G has been in the news many times for the same reason.

Figure 3. News about social crime related to the metaverse

Outlook

OUTLOOK MAGAZINE BUSINESS MONEY TRAVEL STARTUP RETIREMENT PLANET OTHERS

's, Suicides: 10 Times PUBG Killed In...

Uttarkhand Teen Kills Neighbour Over Game

A 13-year-old boy from Uttarakhand killed his 13-year-old neighbour over a dispute that broke out over the online game. The incident occurred in June last year. The accused attacked the victim with a sharp glass object, leading to fatal injuries.

Rajasthan Minor Kills Friend For Not Giving HIm Phone To Play

In November 2020, a minor shocked Rajasthan by killing his friend who had refused to give him his phone to play PUBG. The accused, 13, killed the victim who was 17, with a stone. The duo lived in the state's Rajsamand district.

Jammu Man Killed For Asking Gamers To Not Make Noise

Three men in Jammu were arrested in September 2020 for allegedly killing a man who had asked them to not make noise while they were playing PUBG. The accused, Raj Kumar, Bikram Jeet and Rohit Kumar, were asked by Daleep Raj to not make too much noise when playing the game. This led to an altercation between
1. the three and Raj, who seemingly distracted them from their gaming session. Later

macleans.ca

They lost their kids to Fortnite - Macleans.ca

Luc Rinaldi July 13, 2023

35–44 minutes

Cody was seven years old when he decided what he wanted to do with his life. It was the summer of 2018, and he was watching the World Cup with his parents and younger brother at home on Vancouver Island. When he grew up, he told them, he wanted to play pro soccer.

Plenty of kids dream of becoming soccer stars but, in Cody's case, the idea wasn't entirely far-fetched. He was the best player on his local team, and he soon began training with the Vancouver Whitecaps' youth academy, a pipeline to the pro leagues. He was effortlessly athletic—he earned his black belt in tae kwon do at age

d. **Virtual Crime:** More recently, the virtual world made headlines when a group of male virtual avatars attacked female virtual avatars. This is a very gray area with current criminal regulations. This raises a serious question as to whether virtual crimes are real crimes or not. People also often use social networks to create fake identities. Even in the Metaverse, this problem is bound to happen, (Sykownik, 2022).

Figure 4. News about harassment of women in the metaverse as an avatar (Sykownik, 2022)

e. **Art and Expression:** Artists have the opportunity to try and experiment with novel ideas of art and expression. This could challenge conventional imaginative values and empower the advancement in thinking level of expression. For illustration, virtual reality artist innovations may challenge classical ideas of expressions, their notion, and their artist's comparative values while using literary words, driving a broader appreciation for advanced and immersive artistic forms of representation.

2. **Digital Rights and Ownership:** The metaverse poses serious questions regarding ownership of entities, almost similar issues with the right of the proprietorship and rights related to virtual resources, such as virtual genuine domains, computerized images, and arts, digital images generated by AI tools, and virtual cash or currency, (Conference on Human Factors in Computing Systems – Proceedings 90, 2023). Moral issues may emerge concerning intellectual property rights too, and this becomes a more complex issue when these IPR-based creations are exchanged in a virtual world even in a reasonable system, and its protection from breach and misuse, (Han, 2022).
    2. **Governance and Regulation:** As virtual environments become more complex day by day the governance and regulatory issues, legal consequences, and applicability of laws, are becoming increasingly prominent. Ethical discussions focus on the need for rules and regulations to ensure ethical behavior and protect users' rights in the metaverse. Many cases have been reported where there is a need to control the menace in a virtual world with the help of cyber laws many countries concerned appellate authorities are not available on the same platform or an issue of jurisprudence has been observed, (Lee, 2021).
    3. **Cyber Bullying:** Virtual universes are not safe as online badgering, bullying, and harmful behavior are very common and have been reported in many cases many times. Moral issues rotate around how to avoid and address such behavior, the part of stage administrators in keeping up a secure environment and adjusting free discourse with the got to ensure clients from hurt. A study conducted by the US Agency for Cyber Bullying reports that the rate of cyberbullying is directionally proportional to the number of hours spent on the internet and mostly on the metaverse. The highest affected age group is between 15-20 years age group, (Falchuk, 2018).

Figure 5. Graph depicting the cases of cyber bullying over some time in the US (Falchuk, 2018)

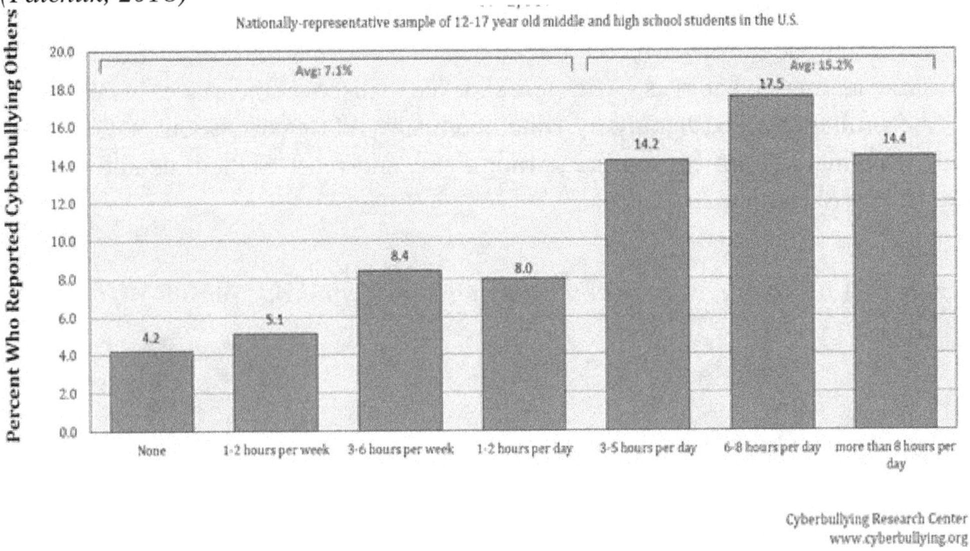

4. **Social Inequality:** Access to and participation in the metaverse can be influenced by economic and social factors. Ethical considerations include ensuring equitable access, addressing digital divides, and mitigating inequalities within virtual spaces. The metaverse has the potential to engage people, especially those who are challenged in terms of powerlessness within the real world, and the metaverse emphasizes social imbalances and increases the chance of manhandling and manipulation by promoting a culture of popular-ism and majoritarian culture leaving behind the marginalized group in the society. There's an openness and comprehensive chance for physically challenged people because was created for the larger part of society leaving the rest and others untouched in an inclusive manner, taking off out particular bunches of society such as senior citizens and less educated people or less tech-savvy people or caring about those persons who are less computer smart or individuals with constrained of hearing and seeing or any other physical deformity, (Di Pietro & Stefano, 2022).
5. **Promotion to Pornography:** Using AI to create porn is not new. Digital photo apps undress women, sexually explicit text messages create "AI girls," and manipulated images promote "sextortion": the rise of deepfake porn is outpacing US and European Government efforts to regulate the technology.

Women are a particular target of AI tools and apps – widely available for free and require no technical expertise – that allows all kinds of users to digitally remove clothing from girls' photos or insert their faces into porn videos.

American and European media are flooded with information directly from women - from academics to activists - who were shocked to discover their faces in fake porn.

According to a 2019 study by Dutch company AI Sensity, about 96% of fake videos online are non-consensual pornography, and most of them depict women, (Salahdine & Naima, 2019).

Figure 6. A photo of a chatbot created by girls used for erotic purpose

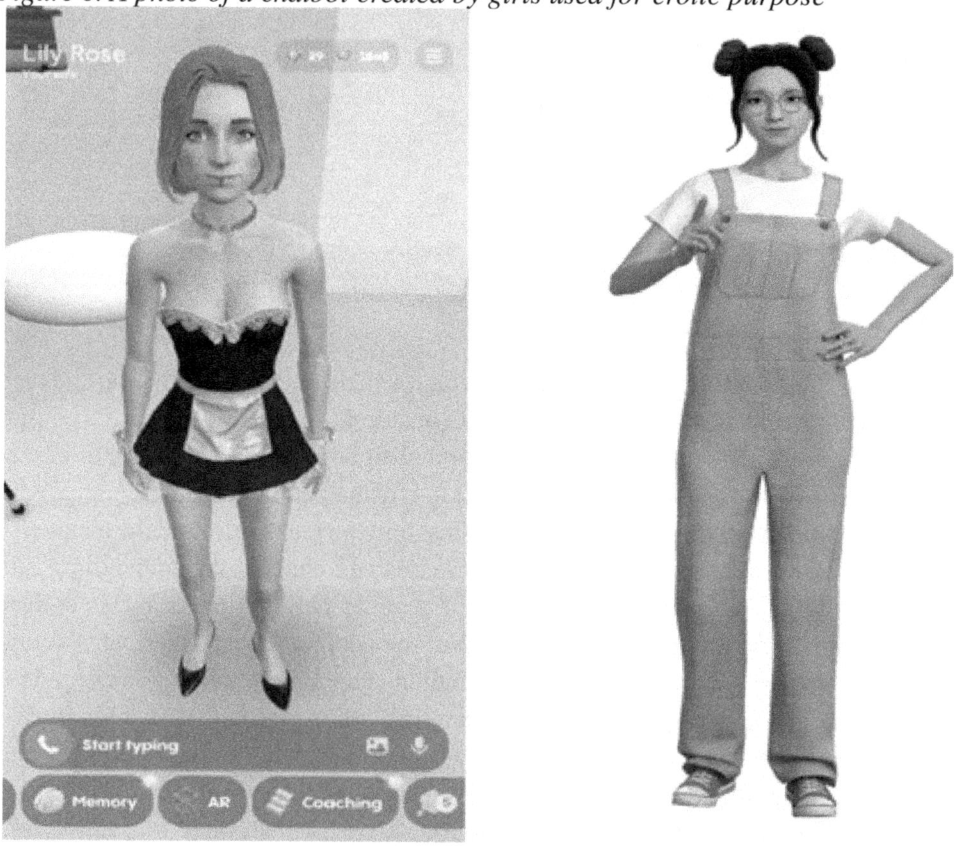

6. **Other Indirect Effects:** Metaverse promotes the polarized view of any thought process. A very common example is that the recommendation algorithm works on the phenomenon of showing the most likely repeated pages. Recommendation algorithms show only those pages that are relevant to earlier searched pages

means that people only see what interests them, reinforcing their views and preventing them from seeing from another perspective. As we have seen in several elections and other important democratic events, when elections are close, AI algorithms can make a big difference. One common example is that if you like the nationalist idea in politics then the AI algorithm only suggests the pages websites and blogs that support nationalist thoughts, not left-wing ideas. This risk is increasing given the immersive experience of the Metaverse, (Ning, 2021).

LEGAL CHALLENGES OF METAVERSE

The development of the metaverse raises a wave of unlawful activities and countless challenges that tend to increase in the future. These challenges include a wide range of issues such as intellectual property rights, security of data, digital rights management, administration of private, cyber-attacks and related crime, and many more.

As reported by a cybersecurity firm, the lack of territorial law in many countries is one of the key reasons for the security issues in the metaverse why that go unnoticed or unaddressed.

As the Metaverse environment is set to increase in the coming years with the forecasted value of reaching to market value of $80 billion by 2030, cyber-crime will be on the chart. With no strong assurance-based laws, regulations, and rules in practical scenarios, this is a really "scary situation and is likely to take more dangerous shape till 2030", as has been forecasted by many researchers all over the world, (Dionisio, 2013).

1. **Issues of Digital Right:** Creating and sharing content in the Metaverse can result in various copyright infringement issues depending on the type and content. In virtual environments, the exchanged entities are often user-generated content which is normally governed under intellectual copyright laws, and the difference between fair use of the shared item and copyright protection leading to infringement can be difficult to define.
2. **Privacy Laws:** The collection and use of user's private data within the metaverse raises significant privacy concerns in the legal world. Protecting user privacy has become a legal challenge in virtual environments, as users' actions, interactions with others, shared data, and preferences can be tracked easily and most of the applications are chasing behind the user's private data.

3. **Cyber Security-related Attacks:** Security breaches, attacks, and hacking incidents in the Metaverse are very common considering the flavor of impersonation-based attacks, which may result in data theft, financial loss, breach of private data, and other harm to users. It is important to establish robust cybersecurity countermeasures and legal frameworks to combat cybersecurity-related issues.
4. **Online Harassment and Cyber Bullying:** The Metaverse is not immune to online harassment of its users, cyberbullying, and harmful behavior toward others. Legal issues regarding user conduct, harassment policies, and the responsibility of platform operators to address such issues are of great importance. Many online websites provide options to report such cases, however, these are still insufficient.
5. **Regulations and Governance:** Legal frameworks and regulations are need of the hour seeing the increasing rate of crime performed in the metaverse either as a target or as a tool, it is needed to address metaverse-specific issues such as taxation, consumer protection, and platform governance. Defining jurisdiction and enforcing laws in a virtual environment presents unique challenges because the area of jurisdiction is not related to one country, so it has to be redefined how a particular crime is being done against a user by a person who is staying in another country.
6. **Issue of Cryptocurrency:** Currently there are distinctive cryptocurrencies utilized over assorted Metaverse stages. Decentralized implementations i.e. MANA, Robolox, etc. In many cases, different cryptocurrencies could be permitted in the future as Metaverse creates. cryptocurrency to be utilized in Metaverse is still not controlled and it depends on the interest of clients and investors. In any case, it is most likely that Metaverse will permit different cryptocurrencies like Bitcoin or Ethanium that can indeed be traded in a genuine world and that have to be controlled by the central bank of any government.

AREAS OF COMPLEXITIES THAT NEED TO BE ADDRESSED

The Metaverse would be indeed astounding if it is built as a decentralized architecture model and if it supports the open-source virtual space instead of company-possessed business rules and assurance policies, (Díaz, Saldaña, & Avila, 2020b). Here are the areas of concern that need to be addressed in the future for the ease of complexity of metaverse –

1. Addiction
2. Cost of VR headgear
3. Data Ownership Issue

4. Privacy Concern
5. Cyber Attacks
6. E-Governance Issue
7. Pornography
8. Cyber Bullying
9. Online Gaming and Ethical Issues
10. Digital rights management Laws
11. Issue of Cryptocurrency

CONCLUSION

Metaverse can be good or bad, it depends on how we use that. The development of an increasingly realistic metaverse will enable the use of advanced techniques in virtual technology which can be used for good objectives in training, administration, education, patient handling, emotion-balanced-based therapy, mentorship, psychotherapy, physical and mental rehabilitation, marketing, entertainment, and other research applications.

Solutions may have research-based approaches, and their outcome implemented as products in individual cases. One of the most important solutions may have a framework made up of certain factors i.e., User rights, Privacy, Access Control, etc., and the law of the land concerning discrimination, harassment, etc. Different countries have different laws according to their society so it must be dealt with accordingly and individually. The second important approach towards solutions is stressing 'User Awareness'. User awareness or user education consists of the guidelines and information that is provided to a group of users and making them aware of their ethical and privacy rights. For example, most school-going teenagers do not know their rights and they start sharing digital data on different websites which must be stopped, and it is only possible when they are enough exposed and trained to such kind of information from a basic level. It is crucial to provide users with information and guidelines on how to navigate the metaverse safely and ethically. Educating users on topics such as online etiquette, cybersecurity, and privacy practices can help them make responsible choices within the virtual world. This education can address the ethical challenges and potential issues associated with the metaverse, including privacy concerns, ownership disputes, and content control. By promoting responsible behavior and providing users with the necessary knowledge, we can ensure a secure and equitable metaverse.

No one knows what the potential social and ethical risks of the Metaverse will be. However, companies that start implementing ethical use of AI will do well if we are in a position to handle those issues efficiently.

Another approach is moderation, effective content moderation systems are essential to filter out harmful or inappropriate content, such as hate speech, harassment, or explicit materials. Automated AI-based systems can assist, but human moderators may still be required for complex judgment calls.

Decisions regarding moderation and censorship of content within the Metaverse can be controversial but fruitful at the same time. Legal challenges include finding a balance between freedom of expression and maintaining a safe and welcoming virtual space. If intense moderation is done then its reporting must be available to both sides, it means what is being moderated, it must be informed to the user managing the issues of privacy issues of users. Establishing easy-to-use reporting mechanisms for users to flag inappropriate behavior or content is essential. Prompt response to these reports and taking appropriate action against violators can deter unethical behavior. Privacy issues sometimes arise because of a lack of differentiation of rights. In many metaverse websites, the content is not properly segregated, and privacy of the content lies between many users so it must be properly defined who is controlling what and collecting what and up to what time the data is going to be kept under which law. Determining and enforcing ownership rights within the metaverse, especially for user-generated content, is important. Protecting intellectual property and creators' rights can help foster a creative and ethical environment. All the entities must be forced to follow the rules according to rules and regulations. Collaboration between metaverse platform providers, developers, researchers, and user communities is essential to collectively address ethical issues. Industry self-regulation and best practices can emerge from such collaboration.

Resolving these legal issues and ethical issues in the metaverse is an ongoing and complex process and mostly it is research oriented. Legal frameworks and regulations must adapt to the characteristics and open challenges of virtual environments while maintaining user rights and data protections too. As the metaverse continues to evolve, governments, industry players, and legal experts will play a key role in shaping the legal landscape.

REFERENCES

Alpala, L. O., Quiroga-Parra, D. J., Torres, J. C., & Peluffo-Ordóñez, D. H. (2022). Smart factory using virtual reality and online multi-user: Towards a metaverse for experimental frameworks. *Applied Sciences (Basel, Switzerland)*, *12*(12), 6258.

Bourlakis, M., Papagiannidis, S., & Li, F. (2009). Retail spatial evolution: Paving the way from traditional to Metaverse retailing. *Electronic Commerce Research*, *9*(1), 135–148. DOI: 10.1007/s10660-009-9030-8

Braud T, Fernández CB, Hui P. 2022. *Scaling-up AR: university campus as a physical-digital Metaverse*.

Bulu, S. T. (2012). Place presence, social presence, co-presence, and satisfaction in virtual worlds. *Computers & Education*, *58*(1), 154–161. DOI: 10.1016/j.compedu.2011.08.024

Cai, S., Jiao, X., & Song, B. (2022). Open another door to education—Applications, challenges and perspectives of the educational Metaverse. *Metaverse*, *3*(1), 12. DOI: 10.54517/met.v3i1.1798

Calvo, P. (2020). The ethics of smart city (EoSC): Moral implications of hyperconnectivity, algorithmization, and the datafication of urban digital society. *Ethics and Information Technology*, *22*(2), 141–149. DOI: 10.1007/s10676-019-09523-0

Cheng R, Wu N, Chen S, Han B. 2022. *Will Metaverse be NextG internet? Vision, hype, and reality*. arXiv preprint

Cipresso, P., Giglioli, I. A. C., Raya, M. A., & Riva, G. (2018). The Past, Present, and Future of Virtual and Augumented Reality Reasearch: A Network and Cluster Analysis of the Literature. *Frontiers in Psychology*, *9*, 2086. DOI: 10.3389/fpsyg.2018.02086

Considerations, E. (1995). *Virtual Reality", Author: Bernard Zeigler*. Published in the Journal of Science and Engineering Ethics.

De Guzman, J. A., Thilakarathna, K., & Seneviratne, A. (2019). Security and privacy approaches in mixed reality: A literature survey. *ACM Computing Surveys*, *52*(6), 1–37. DOI: 10.1145/3359626

Di Pietro, R., & Stefano, C. (2022) "Metaverse: Security and Privacy Issues". *IEEE International Conference on Trust, Privacy and Security in Intelligent Systems and Applications (TPS-ISA)*

Díaz, J. E. M., Saldaña, C. A. D., & Avila, C. A. R. (2020). Virtual world as a resource for hybrid education. [iJET]. *International Journal of Emerging Technologies in Learning, 15*(15), 94–109. DOI: 10.3991/ijet.v15i15.13025

Dionisio, John David N., (2013) "3D Virtual worlds and the metaverse: Current status and future possibilities". ACM Computing Surveys, No.: 34, 1–38.

Duan H, Li J, Fan S, Lin Z, Wu X, Cai W. 2021. *Metaverse for social good: a university campus prototype*.

Earnshaw, R., & Sourin, A. (2017). Case study: shared virtual and augmented environments for creative applications. Research and development in the academy, creative industries and applications, 49-64.

Erturk E, Reynolds GB. 2020. *The expanding role of immersive media in education*.

EU Business School. 2022. *How can the Metaverse be used in education?*

European Innovation Council and SMEs Executive Agency. 2022. *Intellectual property in the Metaverse*.

Falchuk, B., Loeb, S., & Neff, R. (2018). The social Metaverse: Battle for privacy. *IEEE Technology and Society Magazine, 37*(2), 52–56. DOI: 10.1109/MTS.2018.2826060

Falchuk, Ben, (2018) "The Social Metaverse: Battle for Privacy". IEEE Xplore, Vol:37, Issue:2

Gabriel S. 2020. *Identity reshaping and manipulation in cyberspace*. 1-8 Anthropological Researches and Studies

Garćıa LC, Cruz Sánchez Gómez M, Garćıa-Valcárcel Muñoz Repiso A. 2020. *Scales for measuring internet addiction in COVID-19 times: is the time variable still a key factor in measuring this addiction?*

Getchell K, Oliver I, Miller A, Allison C. 2010. *Metaverses as a platform for game-based learning*.

Greenhalgh, T., Robert, G., Macfarlane, F., Bate, P., & Kyriakidou, O. (2004). Diffusion of innovations in service organizations: Systematic review and recommendations. *The Milbank Quarterly, 82*(4), 581–629. DOI: 10.1111/j.0887-378X.2004.00325.x PMID: 15595944

Gurov O, Konkova T. 2022. *Metaverse for human or human for Metaverse?*

Guzman, J. A. D., Seneviratne, A., & Thilakarathna, K. (2021). Unravelling spatial privacy risks of mobile mixed reality data. *Proceedings of the ACM on Interactive, Mobile, Wearable and Ubiquitous Technologies, 5*(1), 1–26. DOI: 10.1145/3448103

Han, D.-I. D., Bergs, Y., & Moorhouse, N. (2022). Virtual reality consumer experience escapes: Preparing for the metaverse. *Virtual Reality (Waltham Cross)*, *26*(4), 1443–1458. DOI: 10.1007/s10055-022-00641-7

Hollands, R. G. (2008). Will the real smart city please stand up? Intelligent, progressive or entrepreneurial? *City (London, England)*, *12*(3), 303–320. DOI: 10.1080/13604810802479126

J. Hu, A. Iosifescu, and R. LiKamWa, "Lenscap: split-process framework for fine-grained visual privacy control for augmented reality apps," in Proceedings of the 19th Annual International Conference on Mobile Systems, Applications, and Services, 2021, pp. 14–27.

J. Hu, A. Iosifescu, and R. LiKamWa, "Lenscap: a split-process framework for fine-grained visual privacy control for augmented reality apps," in Proceedings of the 19th Annual International Conference on Mobile Systems, Applications, and Services, 2021, pp. 14–27.

Hwang, G. J., & Chien, S. Y. (2022). Definition, roles, and potential research issues of the Metaverse in education: An artificial intelligence perspective. *Computers and Education: Artificial Intelligence*, *3*(3), 1–6. DOI: 10.1016/j.caeai.2022.100082

Ibáñez, M.-B., & Delgado-Kloos, C. (2018). Augmented reality for STEM learning: A systematic review. *Computers & Education*, *123*, 109–123. DOI: 10.1016/j.compedu.2018.05.002

Ingwersen, M. (2017). Towards a trickster science/fiction: Complexifying boundaries with Neal Stephenson and Michel Serres. *Interdisciplinary Science Reviews*, *42*(3), 255–268.

Kohler, T. (2008) "Avatar-Based Innovation Using Virtual Worlds for Real World Innovation". International product development management conference. Vol.15

Kye, B., Han, N., Kim, E., Park, Y., & Jo, S. (2021). Educational applications of metaverse: Possibilities and limitations J. *Journal of Educational Evaluation for Health Professions*, *18*, 32. DOI: 10.3352/jeehp.2021.18.32 PMID: 34897242

Lee, L., Braud, T., Zhou, P., Wang, L., Xu, D., Lin, Z., Kumar, A., Bermejo, C., & Hui, P. (2021). All One Needs to Know about Metaverse: A Complete Survey on Technological Singularity, Virtual Ecosystem, and Research Agenda. *ArXiv*. / abs/2110.05352

Lee, L.-H. (2021) "All one needs to know about metaverse: A complete survey on technological singularity, virtual ecosystem, and research agenda." arXiv preprint arXiv:2110.05352.

Lee, L. H., Braud, T., Zhou, P., Wang, L., Xu, D., Lin, Z., Kumar, A., Bermejo, C., & Hui, P. "All one needs to know about metaverse: A complete survey on technological singularity, virtual ecosystem, and research agenda," arXiv preprint arXiv:2110.05352, 2021.

Negreiro, M., & Niestadt, M. (2022). *EU Digital Identity Wallet, Proposal for a Regulation of the European Parliament and the Council amending Regulation (EU) No 910/2014 as regards stabilizing a framework for a European Digital Identity, COM/2021/281 final, and the description.* The European Digital Identity Framework.

Ning, H. (2021) "A Survey on Metaverse: The State-of-the-art, Technologies, Applications, and Challenges." arXiv preprint arXiv:2111.09673

Roesner, F., Kohno, T., & Molnar, D. (2014). Security and privacy for augmented reality systems. *Communications of the ACM, 57*(4), 88–96. DOI: 10.1145/2580723.2580730

Roesner, F., Kohno, T., & Molnar, D. (2014). Security and privacy for augmented reality systems. *Communications of the ACM, 57*(4), 88–96. DOI: 10.1145/2580723.2580730

Rosenberg, L. (2022). *Regulation of the Metaverse: A Roadmap.* Association of Computing Machinery., DOI: 10.1145/3546607.3546611

Salahdine, F., & Kaabouch, N. (2019). Social engineering attacks: A survey. *Future Internet, 11*(4), 89.

Sarkady, D., Neuburger, L., & Egger, R. (2021, January). Virtual reality as a travel substitution tool during COVID-19. In Information and communication technologies in tourism 2021: Proceedings of the ENTER 2021 eTourism conference, January 19–22, 2021 (pp. 452-463). Cham: Springer International Publishing.

Sykownik, P., Maloney, D., Freeman, G., & Masuch, M. (2022, April). Something personal from the metaverse: goals, topics, and contextual factors of self-disclosure in commercial social VR. In *Proceedings of the 2022 CHI Conference on Human Factors in Computing Systems* (pp. 1-17).

Theodorou, A. (2017). *Stay home, stay safe, stay green: The role of gardening activities on mental health during the Covid-19 home confinement". Urban Forestry & Urban Greening Moritz.* Ingwersen.

Chapter 7
Human-Machine Interaction:
Ethical and Legal Considerations

Ananya Pandey
https://orcid.org/0000-0002-2419-6314
Christ University, India

Jipson Joseph
https://orcid.org/0009-0005-1795-5051
Christ University, India

ABSTRACT

In the era of digitalization and technological advancement it is crucial to note the dichotomy between the earlier and present times with regard to human-machine interaction. Previously human controlled machines but today its opposite happens. Human-Machine Interface has so deeply touched the life of the present generation and its most explicit example could be the change from a basic push button to a touch-screen display. A simple touch has multiple effects on people's daily life. Innovation has permeated and influenced daily physical activities. Every time people use an ATM, food dispenser, snack machine, touchscreen, cloud computing, etc., they inevitably make interactions between humans and machines. Since the applications of HMI cover numerous fields, several ethical and legal considerations should be taken into account for making it effective and viable. In this perspective, the authors analyze the challenges of Human Machine Interaction suggesting a concrete policy design for its effective application.

DOI: 10.4018/979-8-3373-3384-7.ch007

INTRODUCTION

Intelligent systems and machines have the potential to improve the accessibility, efficacy, safety, transparency, dependability and information, thereby reaching a wider range of individuals. Compared to earlier times, humans use machines in most of their daily activities, making their life unthinkable without machines. It resulted in an extreme level of human-machine interaction. Such an interaction has reached to almost all the areas of human life. It covers various fields like security, healthcare, education, transportation, entertainment, public surveillance, forecasting, traffic, finance, agriculture, construction, information technology, and even household chores. It has made human life easier and comfortable. But these systems also deepen disparities within and between nations and people, worsen the unequal distribution of resources, decrease the employment opportunities, lower the skill levels, challenge the opportunities of the vulnerable and the marginalized, endanger human-human interaction, and confine many people to virtual life rather than having a real meaningful life (World Health Organization, 2021).

Human Machine Interaction has become the need of the day. It has a plethora of advantages but at the same time, its wide application should take into account its adversarial effects as well. There are clear-cut laws and guidelines for human-human interactions but when it comes to HMI there are not many laws and directives. Ethics also is not applicable to machines. But the ethical considerations should be undertaken by the machine developers in due respect towards the life of its users. However, not much studies have been undertaken in this regard. The legal framework in the ambit of HMI is also very less. Human satisfaction, ownership and property, privacy, freedom from bias, universal usability, trust, autonomy, informed consent, and accountability represent just a few of the many subjects covered by the ethical and legal issues in human-machine interaction (Hochheiser and Valdez, 2020). This paper shall therefore analyze the ethical and legal aspects connected with the usage of HMI and suggest the regulatory measures required for its effective implementation.

HUMAN-MACHINE INTERACTION: AN OVERVIEW

Human-machine interaction (HMI) is a feature of a certain device that enables humans to interact with machines. It describes how people communicate and interact with machines in their daily life (Kun, 2018). HMI is a multidisciplinary area encompassing many fields that are described above. It operates mainly through robotics, artificial intelligence (AI), human–robot and human–computer interaction. Industrial operations have always used HMI to improve productivity, quality, and process safety. HMI is now widely utilized in entertainment, health care, and transportation systems (Beier et al., 2020). It uses an interdisciplinary approach incorporating ideas from the domains of ergonomics (keyboards, lighting controls), computer science (pen-gestures, joysticks), design (autonomous vehicles), and psychology (brain-mapping). Considering various aspects like usability, accessibility, and user experience, HMI seeks to develop technology focusing on the needs of users that eventually improves the interaction and communication between humans and machines (Avcontentteam, 2024).

Healthcare

Healthcare sector is one of the predominant areas in which HMIs help people to make use of devices, systems, or machinery for controlling widespread diseases like Covid pandemic. When direct human contact in such situations becomes a risk, the HMIs can substitute the role of humans and can provide necessary medical support (Kruptizer et al., 2020). HMI systems enhance the functioning of the majority of medical processes that extends from calling for medical help to ensuring the right care to the patient in due time (Malviya et al., 2023). HMI-based mobile healthcare devices are widely used to measure hyperglycemia, hypertension, and other conditions pertaining to the patient's overall health. These devices provide swift and precise findings (Singh and Kumar, 2021). The use of smartwatches that monitor heartbeat, blood-pressure, blood-sugar levels and oximeters serve as a source of precaution to keep a track of everyday health routine and consult the medical practitioner if needed. There were several instances where the health-related applications of Apple Watch saved the life of its users (Bhati, 2022).

The widespread use and acceptance of Laproscopy is a vital example of HMI in the medical field. Though it has some disadvantages, it is beneficial to the patients in many aspects (Cannan & Hu, 2011). Besides, the usage of robots in the healthcare system is developing as a result of an inadequate number of medical personnel, rising healthcare expenditures, and an exponential increase in the population of vulnerable groups like the elderly, the sick, and children with developmental impairments (Morgan et al., 2022). Consequently, robots are used in the medical industry to help the ill and old as well as to inform hospitalized patients about health-related matters. In addition, they work in geriatric and emotional care, rehabilitation, and pharmaceutical dispensing (Zou et al., 2022). During surgery, surgical robots help surgeons by managing surgical instruments and simplifying intricate duties. They are computer-controlled devices. Through increased surgeon control and dexterity, robotic surgery—best demonstrated by the da Vinci Surgical System—improves surgical precision and patient outcomes (Weerarathna, 2023).

The systematic and prudent use of HMIs in the healthcare system will be advantageous to the people at large. However, this area is closely related to people's right to life (UDHR, art.3), which demands that any HMIs in this field should not endanger this fundamental right. It also necessitates the proper application of ethical and legal consideration in the incorporation of HMI in healthcare.

Industrial Applications

HMIs can also be used in the energy, water, wastewater and building industries. It is commonly used by professionals like process control system engineers, operators, and system integrators. These experts manage machinery, cars, plants, or buildings with HMIs (What is HMI, 2023). Central monitoring and control of an industrial units' complete operation can be facilitated by combining data from hundreds of equipment using HMIs that communicate data to cloud and enterprise systems (Gorecky et al., 2014).

HMIs give crucial information to factory floor operators, enabling them to optimize productivity. Some examples of this include moving workers to a different area of the manufacturing facility, to accommodate slower production or fine-tuning machine settings, and to improve performance by resolving issues. HMIs can be found in the central control room, on the machine or device itself, or as a handheld or portable device (Sawant, 2022).

The industrial sector is one of the main protagonists of the realization of people's right to development (UN Declaration on the Right to Development, art. 1). The unparalleled growth of HMI in the industrial sector helps the developmental policies and programs of governments. However, it should not challenge people's right to livelihood (UDHR, art. 25). It demands that the incorporation of HMIs in the industrial sector should fit into the ethical and legal framework that respects people's basic rights.

Transportation

With the use of data from sensors monitoring the road and the drivers themselves, HMI can anticipate passenger requirements, keep drivers awake, and produce informative journey visualizations (Enjalbert et al., 2021). External and interior aircraft carriers, power distribution, lighting and alarm systems, communication and navigation features, passenger entrance and departure, and auxiliary systems like cranes are a few examples of what an HMI system incorporates (Inductive Automation, 2018).

HMIs are highly used in transportation. But at the same time, it also makes mistakes that cause the life of many. For instance, the use of Google Maps in transportation though has various advantages it also has resulted in many accidents causing the life of many. The HMI should respect the right to life and security of its passengers (UDHR, arts. 3), demanding a key role for ethical and legal considerations in this interactive functioning (Boy, 2017).

Information Technology (IT)

IT closely and widely incorporates several applications of HMI, which consists of software and hardware components that enable data flow between a human operator thereby storing and processing the data further fed from the user (Wittenberg, 2016). For instance, while operating a website and accepting the cookies (that store personal data and ad tracking information of the user) notification leads HMI to retrieve the personal information of the user and use it in future for similar suggestions (Hoc, 2000). Further, interfaces on the web and mobile devices that let users manage their bills, conduct transactions, and have access to financial services are inclusive of HMIs. Also the systems that telecom operators use to diagnose issues, control sources, and display community performance are related to processing and storing users' personal information (Guo et al., 2021).

Though HMIs are used to process a large amount of data and personal information, on the other hand it also causes breach of privacy and security. HMIs should be incorporated into this field in order to ensure the right to privacy and security (UDHR, Art. 12 & 3) is preserved and protected.

ETHICAL AND LEGAL CONSIDERATIONS

Intelligent machines are replacing the two Os: orientation (data processing) and observation (data gathering) (Pellegrino et al., 2019). Intelligent machines inclusive of AI have the potential to influence the day-to-day life of the public at large in the future, both nationally and internationally. These machines however, can contribute to both the issue and its solutions (World Health Organisation, 2021). The possible advantages of the application of HMI must be weighed against its hazards and difficulties that take into account several ethical and legal considerations. The following points explain the various ethical and legal considerations that are to be seriously reflected on while using HMIs.

Transparency and accountability

Transparency and accountability have become widely used ethical and legal considerations of the present generation. Transparency consists of the people's right to information about the various activities and governance in which humans are involved. It comes under the wider ambit of freedom of expression (UDHR, art. 19 & 21). Accountability is the responsibility for one's decisions and actions (Borowiak, 2011). HMI should be transparent in such a way that the people should be given knowledge about its activities, operations, expenditures, decisions and the various rules that are applicable. The accountability of HMI is predominantly on the developers and users of such systems (Sun et al., 2021). Human-machine systems that adhere to ethical accountability should be guaranteed to make decisions that are transparent, rational, and consistent with society norms. This includes dealing with data protection, obtaining informed consent, and stopping the spread of prejudice and discrimination that are already in place (Singhal et al., 2024). Legal accountability includes not only the obligation to avoid the use of AI systems for immoral or discriminatory purposes, but also the concerns like data protection and privacy (Rodriques, 2020). Legal and ethical transparency covers addressing any negative consequences or repercussions that may result from the usage of systems. It also includes the various attempts to ensure that they are designed and implemented in accordance with the applicable laws and regulations (Balasubramaniam, 2023).

Security and Privacy

The user's experience with computers, online systems, and new technologies can be significantly impacted by privacy (Lutz, 2023). Information security and enhanced usability security elements in end-user applications, such as e-commerce websites or smartphone applications, are the core topics of security in HMI. Effective security is important, for instance, in e-commerce websites where consumers enter credit card and personal information (Pacaux-Lemoine et al., 2019). This is a result of people expecting a secure and private data entry process as well as a smooth user experience (What is HCI and security, n.d.). Since the biggest criticism against HMI is related to its privacy and security threats, effective mechanisms to ensure these ethical and legal considerations should be employed.

Safety and reliability

A primary need for an effective HMI design is the minimal amount of unintended events (accidents, incidents). The design must give careful thought to the cognitive components of HMI, particularly the dependability of human cognition in order to accomplish this goal (Hallnagel, 1992). Effective and risk-free functioning of HMI depends on safety and dependability. Risk assessment, person-centered design, and adherence to protective regulations are all included in the safety measures. Reliable structures need to be regularly maintained that have strong error handling and consistent performance (Nickel et al., 2020). While iterative layout and user feedback increase dependability, user education and clear directives decorate safety. Furthermore, it is critical to put in place and ensure redundancy and fail-safe procedures, cybersecurity and data integrity, and thorough documentation and support services. When combined, these methods guarantee secure, dependable, and effective interactions between people and technology (Hashemi-Pour and Cahi, 2023).

Data Protection

In order to provide more practical solutions to normative requirements, usable privacy frequently operates at the intersection of legislation. But in the design phase, the regulations themselves or the legal criteria by which they are implemented, are usually left intact (Leschanowsky et al., 2021). In this sense, HCI falls short of its potential to improve the effectiveness of legislation by informing it about human expectations, attitudes, and behavior in the actual world (Jakobi and Grafenstein, 2023). The world's most powerful privacy and security legislation is the EU's General Data Protection Regulation (GDPR) (The GDPR, 2024). Any information pertaining to an individual who can be identified, either directly or indirectly, is considered personal data under the GDPR. Of course, email addresses and names are personal information. Personal data can also include geographic coordinates, gender, ethnicity, biometric information, political viewpoints, web cookies, and religious convictions (Wolford, 2023). The concept can also apply to pseudonymous data if it is reasonably possible to identify a person from it. Research is now being done on the GDPR's data subject rights, including the right to data portability. Transparency-enhancing solutions, primarily based on a dashboard approach, have been developed and are closely tied to the right of access to data (Jakobi and Grafenstein, 2023). Like the GDPR many more countries have to come forward ensuring the data privacy of its citizens for a better incorporation and application of HMIs (Mourtzis et al., 2023).

Human Rights and Intellectual Property Rights (IPR)

Human rights and IPR are important areas of discussion in the field of HMIs. The various attempts to ensure AI and robots do not discriminate, violate privacy, or restrict freedom of expression fit into the ambit of human rights. AI systems must be accountable and transparent in order to uphold these rights. IPR issues include identifying the owners of the content created by AI systems and defending their various rights (Kop, 2019). Innovation must be balanced with fair use and access to rights. For the effective functioning of both human rights and IPR in the field of HMIs there is the need to promote a fair, secure, and courteous integration of technology into society, besides having strong criminal justice systems and moral principles (Principles for Responsible AI Innovation, n.d.).

Liability

Liability is an essential element in the context of HMI. In the absence of liability clauses for malfunctioning, underperformance, or erroneous decision-making of the systems, there will be adverse impact on human beings. After more than a century of operating human-driven automobiles, an advanced and intricate legal framework has evolved, which is now being faced by automated vehicles. The essential adjustments to that landscape are just now starting to be made. Although there are probably clear-cut legal restrictions on the use of automated cars, the legal system is still grappling with the problems this technology raises (Inners & Kun, 2017).

GLOBAL GOVERNANCE ON HUMAN-MACHINE INTERACTION

The 21st century witnesses unprecedent growth in technological innovations. HMI has become an important area of concern as it has entered into almost all the areas of human life. It also has become a global concern as the whole world irrespective of developed or developing countries use various forms HMIs in their daily life. In this section, an analysis is done on the guidelines of OECD, recommendations of UNESCO, and the guidelines of EU for exploring the already available global framework on HMI. Such global design provides a model for various regions and countries in order to address the issues and concerns with HMI.

Organization for Economic Cooperation and Development (OECD)

The OECD provides guidance on HMI, primarily in relation to automation and AI, emphasizing the ethical, open, and responsible interaction with technologically advanced society. Besides upholding human rights, privacy, and security, the main focus of OECD in HMI is to ensure that the AI and machine-based systems enhance human abilities rather than replacing them (Castonguay et al., 2023). The prime objective in the making of machines is to support and simplify human laborious activities. The OECD guidelines provide a human-centric strategy that prioritize human welfare and supervision at every stage of device development and implementation.

It demands openness in the methods used by machines to make decisions, meaning that user outputs from devices should be intelligible and interpretable (Floridi & Cowls, 2023). This promotes trust and makes possible to evaluate the equity and dependability of HMI. Security and safety are to be prioritized. Particularly autonomous machines should be built to function safely in a variety of scenarios, reducing hazards to human health and life. These technologies should also be secured against cyber assaults, security lapses, and inadvertent applications that endanger people or communities (Galindo et al., 2021). In addition, the OECD emphasizes the need of accessibility and inclusivity, ensuring that human-system interactions are built to accommodate a diverse user base as well as demographics that are likely to utilize them, such as the elderly or those with impairments. These exchanges ought to respect criminal laws pertaining to information security, worker rights, and ethical AI application. The OECD proposals stress that ethical considerations, justice, and accountability must govern the nature and ways how people and technology interact.

United Nations Educational, Scientific, and Cultural Organization (UNESCO)

In November 2021, all 193 Member States of UNESCO ratified the "Recommendation on the Ethics of Artificial Intelligence," which is the organization's first-ever worldwide standard on AI ethics. This was compiled in alignment with the UN Charter and UDHR. The document affirmed its awareness of the positive and negative impacts of AI on human lives, ecosystem, and society. HMI can become beneficial to people and society in many ways, but that does not undermine the ethical concerns that are closed related to its functioning. The Recommendation is centered on the fundamental concepts like openness, trustworthiness, integrity, and justice, with a constant reminder of the significance of human oversight of AI systems (Pohle, 2015). The cornerstone of the recommended guidelines is the protection of human rights and dignity. But the real distinguishing nature of the Recommendation is its broad Policy Action Areas, which enable decision-makers to put the fundamental ideals and principles into practice in a variety of areas, including data governance, gender, education and research, environment and ecosystems, health and social welfare, and many more (Ossiannilsson et al., 2024).

The Recommendation underlines that HMI should follow proportionality and no-harm principle in the sense it should not cause trouble to basic values and principles. Both safety and security risks should be avoided for ensuring human flourishing. It strongly recommended inclusive approach so that the achievements of AI will be accessible to all. It thus underscores the principles of fairness and non-discrimination. The ultimate objective of HMI should be sustainability and hence, effective measures should be taken to promote sustainable societies. The Recommendation besides highlighted the principles of accountability, responsibility, explainability, literacy, determination, and human oversight (UNESCO, 2021).

European Union (EU)

The EU has connected HMI guidelines to ensure that the current tech-generation improves safety, health, and diversity across a range of industries. Most frameworks and guidelines, such as the General Data Protection Regulation (GDPR), the Machinery Directive (2006/422/EC), and the Artificial Intelligence Act (proposed), make reference to these principles. Their goal is to promote ethical standards, safety, and transparency in the integration of AI and machines into human environments (Brattberg et al., 2020). In order to ensure that robots, primarily AI-driven structures, do not jeopardize human life or infringe upon the right to privacy, safety and transparency are essential components. According to the Directive proposed by the EU Council, machines must be constructed and designed to reduce the possibility of malfunction or injury to human operators (Roberts et al., 2021). The proposed AI Act, which requires that AI models, especially those with significant risks, be explainable, auditable, and subject to human manipulation, places a strong emphasis on human oversight and responsibility in the context of AI and self-sufficient systems. This includes the use of AI in industrial, transportation, and therapeutic initiatives that directly impact people's lives and well-being (Larsson, 2021).

Furthermore, the inclusion of ethical principles and values is crucial to be taken into account since the EU guidelines emphasize how important it is to combat prejudice and guarantee that everyone has equal access to gadget-driven technology (Veale et al., 2021). The GDPR provides mechanism and measures to safeguard individuals, particularly in the context of interactions between humans and technology by controlling the processing of private information and guaranteeing the transparency and responsibility of decisions that have an impact on individuals (such as computerized decisions). When combined, these pointers create a thorough framework for managing the safe, moral, ethical, and accountable interplay among individuals and machines within the EU (Smuha et al., 2021).

EMERGING TRENDS IN HUMAN-MACHINE INTERACTION

Information communication technology (ICT) is commonly used in scenarios including capacity increase, huge connection, ultra-high reliability, and low latency, as demonstrated by the development of 5G networks. Future HMI will face significant obstacles and revolutionary changes as a result of these ICT advancements.

New trends are evolving on a daily basis in HMI as a result of scientific and technological progress.

AI-powered assistants

AI-powered assistants are one of the most seamless ways how AI is improving the HMI design. This includes natural language-based human-device interfaces through services like Siri, Alexa, Google Assistant, and others (Mahmud et al., 2020). It is clear how AI has affected the incorporation of voice commands into many interfaces. Likewise, AI plays a significant part in customization. Artificial intelligence systems examine past data, user behavior, and preferences to customize interfaces and make them unique to each user for customized HMI experiences (Ribino, 2023). AI also makes possible for predictive analytics to automate repetitive operations and predict user behavior, which streamlines workflows and boosts productivity.

Nature-User Interface

The natural user interface (NUI) enables users to naturally engage with the systems using speech, gestures, and body motions without any physical restrictions. It is a gesture-based, straightforward, and intuitive interface. The area of interface design known as NUI, uses technology to seamlessly integrate human talents (Ma et al., 2020). NUI, a developing topic in human-machine interaction, is related to biomimicry in that it builds on human abilities and uses some of them to incorporate artificial technology into learnt human relationships (Jia et al., 2015). Since most computer interfaces involve artificial control mechanisms that require learning to operate, the word "natural" is used in this sense. For a NUI to function, the user must be able to make easily learned, reasonably natural motions to operate the computer program or modify the content displayed on the screen (Irarte et al., 2021). In order to simulate real-world situations and maximize interaction between physical and digital items, NUI focuses on traditional human abilities such as vision, touch, speech, handwriting, motion, as well as cognition, creation, and exploration.

Augmented and virtual reality

Traditional supervisory control and data acquisition (SCADA) and HMIs are primarily intended to "control the process," rather than viewing all the data in context as would benefit a person in the physical or virtual place environment, despite the advancements made in human-centric design practices (Chollet et al., 2009). When augmented reality (AR) is used to enhance the functionality of HMI/SCADA, it is a UI advancement that offers new ways to gather, contextualize, and present data in novel and relevant ways. AR offers a fresh perspective to go along with more conventional approaches; it does not necessarily replace HMI/SCADA. Operators are finding AR as an HMI/SCADA method to be beneficial currently, and it will only get better in the future (Yin et al., 2021). For example, medical professionals and students can now use mixed reality to learn about the human body through the Microsoft HoloLens. In order to study anatomy and medical issues, students can flow through the bloodstream, isolate, enlarge, and even stroll inside the human body's components.

Brain Computer Interface

Brain-computer interfaces (BCIs) receive, process, and convert brain impulses into commands that are sent to output devices to perform specified tasks. Normal neuromuscular output channels are not used by BCIs. The primary objective of BCI is to replace or restore functional possibility to those who have been incapacitated by neuromuscular conditions such as spinal cord injury, cerebral palsy, amyotrophic lateral sclerosis, or stroke (Shih et al., 2012). Researchers have used electroencephalographic, intracortical, electrocorticographic, and other brain signals for increasingly complex control of cursors, robotic arms, prostheses, wheelchairs, and other devices since the first demonstrations of electroencephalography-based spelling and single-neuron-based device control (Sadeghi & Maleki, 2018). Brain-computer interfaces may potentially be helpful for other illnesses including the recovery from stroke. They may improve surgeons' or other medical professionals' performance in the future. Scientists, engineers, doctors, and the general public are all very interested in the fast-expanding fields of BCI technology, research, and development. Future success will be reliant on developments in the above-mentioned three critical areas. Signal-acquisition hardware for brain-computer interfaces must be lightweight, portable, secure, and environment-neutral (Ashger et al., 2023). Brain-computer interface systems must be shown useful in long-term trials including the real-world use of individuals with severe disabilities. Additionally, work must be done to develop practical and successful models for the general distribution of these devices. Lastly, in order for BCI performance to become as reliable as natural muscle-based function, it needs to be made more reliable on a daily and moment-to-moment basis (Cannan & Hu, 20211).

Digital Twin

The digital twin offers an innovative solution to addressing the aforementioned issues as a new technology to achieve cyber-physical integration. To increase machine efficiency and operation safety, HMI will create a more flexible interactive mode by using a five-dimension digital twin model that is powered by real-time data (Filocamo, 2020). Employees, engineers, trainees, and product users can all be digital twin users during the service stage. Digital twin data integrates usage instructions, maintenance procedures, production data, simulated data of product status, design data, and other data to give consumers a more thorough understanding of the product. Users may quickly, securely, and comfortably comprehend the internal workings of complex equipment by using the virtual model (Shoukat et al., 2024). A 5G network can carry a lot of digital twin data quickly because it has superior transmission qualities, such as higher capacity, higher data rate, reduced end-to-end latency, etc. Therefore, users can remotely trace and operate the machines with the digital twin by sending information over a 5G network, enabling convenient and straightforward interactions (Pérez et al., 2020).

Wearable Technology

HMI is constantly pushed by competition in the market for various kinds of wearable technology (Patel et al., 2020). A major component of wearable technology to consumers is its touch-sensing HMI, which offers a natural and responsive way to engage via touch buttons and sliders in gadgets like smart glasses, and earphones or a tiny touchscreen in a smart watch. Wearable technology expands the application space and improves the user experience even more. An industrial wristwatch, for instance, significantly boosts worker productivity. For instance, an Industrial Internet of Things (IIoT) sensor on a worker's smartwatch might directly notify quality assurance to the worker (Quartarone, 2021). Users can "interact" with the IIoT sensor by using an inbuilt barcode scanner and is provided with step-by-step workflow instructions. By doing this, paper procedures are eliminated and data acquisition quality is raised.

Collaborative Robots

As more and more sectors come to understand the financial benefits of this technology, the market for collaborative robots is predicted to rise exponentially (Gambao et al., 2012). A type of robotic automation known as collaborative robots is designed to operate securely next to human employees in a shared workspace. In most cases, a human worker completes more sophisticated and cerebral activities while a collaborative robot handles repetitive, mundane tasks (Hörbst, & Orsolits, 2022). Collaborative robots are meant to supplement human workers' intelligence and problem-solving abilities with their accuracy, uptime, and reproducibility. The designs of collaborative robots are very different from those of industrial robots. Safety is the primary consideration in the design of collaborative robots, which include softened edges, force constraints, and light weights (García-Esteban et al., 2021). In order to prevent collisions with human workers, the majority of collaborative robots are outfitted with multiple sensors and safety protocols that trigger an automatic shutdown in the event of any unintentional contact. The potential uses of robotic automation are substantially expanded when it can operate in conjunction with humans.

FUTURE OUTLOOK

Modern industrial and consumer technology relies heavily on HMIs to facilitate smooth communication between people and machines. Control, monitoring, and communication are made easier in a variety of industries by HMIs, from smart homes to manufacturing facilities. The HMI Market is seeing important developments that push innovation, increase efficiency, and improve user experience as technology develops (Kazi, 2024). The emerging trends in this field have become a need rather than considering it as a luxury that include touchscreen technology for advanced user experience (mobile phones), adoption of augmented reality and virtual reality (video games), voice activated human controls (Alexa and Siri), expansion of gesture recognition technology (pen-tablet), focus on cybersecurity and data protection and (inter)actively safe remote monitoring (Iqbal and Campbell, 2021).

HMI is a vital part of the technical operating system and is always growing and evolving on its own. As a result, laws controlling this area should either be universal to be effective regardless of advancements in information technology, or be continuously revised. It is crucial to control and raise the bar for ethical considerations as it may have a big impact on societal advancements. To assure ethical applications under the HMI regime, a sincere and systematic study into the technological, legal, policy, and social elements of responsible HMI is required. In order to ensure responsible use of HMI, there is the need to enable access to data and utilize responsible AI tools and techniques with some strict restrictions and means that are beneficial in the long-run (Gaushell and Darlington, 1987).

CONCLUSION AND SUGGESTIONS

HMI is expanding in today's world with enhancement of technology and associated sources. The creation, advancement, and execution of pertinent legislation pertaining to the responsible usage of HMI is immensely required. A concrete rule governing the nature and application of HMI is necessary to ensure safety and fairness. Certain strategies such as strengthening the available policies in specific regions, enhancing financial support to the concerned governing authorities regulating HMIs, improving the standard of application of smart intelligences, use of several intelligent products, upholding the fairness and safety, establishing scientific and sound technological data information standards and thereby improving the training of staff of the HMI authorities may lead to utilization of this technology in cordiality and effectiveness. Any technology will meet its appropriate reliable standards only if it adheres to its proper usage taking into account the ethical as well as legal aspects connected to this domain. Therefore, a concrete policy design to regulate the functioning of HMI is required for its transparency, accountability, and efficiency in today's digital world.

REFERENCES

Asgher, U., Ayaz, Y., & Taiar, R. (2023). Advances in artificial intelligence (AI) in brain computer interface (BCI) and Industry 4.0 for human machine interaction (HMI). *Frontiers in Human Neuroscience*, *17*, 1320536. DOI: 10.3389/fnhum.2023.1320536 PMID: 38116236

Automation, I. (2018). HMI. https://inductiveautomation.com/resources/article/what-is-hmi

Avcontentteam. (2024, April 10). *Introduction to Human Computer Interaction (HCI) With Examples*. Analytics Vidhya. https://www.analyticsvidhya.com/blog/2023/05/human-computer-interaction/

Balasubramaniam, N., Kauppinen, M., Rannisto, A., Hiekkanen, K., & Kujala, S. (2023). Transparency and explainability of AI systems: From ethical guidelines to requirements. *Information and Software Technology*, *159*, 107197. DOI: 10.1016/j.infsof.2023.107197

Beier, G., Ullrich, A., Niehoff, S., Reißig, M., & Habich, M. (2020). Industry 4.0: How it is defined from a sociotechnical perspective and how much sustainability it includes–A literature review. *Journal of Cleaner Production*, *259*, 120856. DOI: 10.1016/j.jclepro.2020.120856

Bhati, D. (2022). Apple Watch saves life yet again, warns him of abnormal heart rate. India Today (Sep. 06, 2022, 14.43 IST), https://www.indiatoday.in/technology/news/story/apple-watch-saves-life-of-a-54-years-old-man-this-time-warns-him-of-abnormal-heart-rate-1996775-2022-09-05

Borowiak, C. (2011). *Accountability and Democracy: The Pitfalls and Promise of Popular Control*. Oxford University Press. DOI: 10.1093/acprof:oso/9780199778256.001.0001

Boy, G. A. (Ed.). (2017). *The handbook of human-machine interaction: a human-centered design approach*. CRC Press. DOI: 10.1201/9781315557380

Brattberg, E., Rugova, V., & Csernatoni, R. (2020). Europe and AI: Leading, lagging behind, or carving its own way? (Vol. 9). Washington, DC, USA: Carnegie endowment for international peace.

Cannan, J., & Hu, H. (2011). Human-machine interaction (HMI): A survey. *University of Essex*, *27*, 46–64.

Castonguay, A., Wagner, G., Motulsky, A., & Paré, G. (2023). AI maturity in health care: An overview of 10 OECD countries. *Health Policy (Amsterdam)*, •••, 104938. PMID: 38157771

Chollet, G., Esposito, A., Gentes, A., Horain, P., Karam, W., Li, Z., . . . Zouari, L. (2009). Multimodal human machine interactions in virtual and augmented reality. *Multimodal Signals: Cognitive and Algorithmic Issues: COST Action 2102 and euCognition International School Vietri sul Mare, Italy, April 21-26, 2008 Revised Selected and Invited Papers*, 1-23.

Enjalbert, S., Gandini, L. M., Pereda Baños, A., Ricci, S., & Vanderhaegen, F. (2021). Human–Machine Interface in Transport Systems: An Industrial Overview for More Extended Rail Applications. *Machines (Basel)*, *9*(2), 36. DOI: 10.3390/machines9020036

Filocamo, C. (2020). *Digital Twin and HMI for collaborative autonomous mobile robots in flexible logistics* (Doctoral dissertation, Politecnico di Torino).

Floridi, L., & Cowls, J. (2022). A unified framework of five principles for AI in society. *Machine learning and the city: Applications in architecture and urban design*, 535-545.

Galindo, L., Perset, K., & Sheeka, F. (2021). *An overview of national AI strategies and policies*. OECD Ilibrary.

Gambao, E., Hernando, M., & Surdilovic, D. (2012). A new generation of collaborative robots for material handling. In *ISARC.Proceedings of the International Symposium on Automation and Robotics in Construction* (Vol. 29, p. 1). IAARC Publications. DOI: 10.22260/ISARC2012/0076

García-Esteban, J. A., Piardi, L., Leitão, P., Curto, B., & Moreno, V. (2021, May). An interaction strategy for safe human co-working with industrial collaborative robots. In *2021 4th IEEE International Conference on Industrial Cyber-Physical Systems (ICPS)* (pp. 585-590). IEEE. DOI: 10.1109/ICPS49255.2021.9468160

Gaushell, D. J., & Darlington, H. T. (1987). Supervisory control and data acquisition. *Proceedings of the IEEE*, *75*(12), 1645–1658. DOI: 10.1109/PROC.1987.13932

Gorecky, D., Schmitt, M., Loskyll, M., & Zühlke, D. (2014, July). Human-machine-interaction in the industry 4.0 era. In *2014 12th IEEE international conference on industrial informatics (INDIN)* (pp. 289-294). IEEE.

Guo, L., Lu, Z., & Yao, L. (2021). Human-machine interaction sensing technology based on hand gesture recognition: A review. *IEEE Transactions on Human-Machine Systems*, *51*(4), 300–309. DOI: 10.1109/THMS.2021.3086003

Hashemi-Pour, C., & Chai, W. (2023, December 21). *CIA triad (confidentiality, integrity and availability)*. WhatIs. https://www.techtarget.com/whatis/definition/Confidentiality-integrity-and-availability-CIA

Hoc, J. M. (2000). From human–machine interaction to human–machine cooperation. *Ergonomics*, *43*(7), 833–843. DOI: 10.1080/001401300409044 PMID: 10929820

Hochheiser, H., & Valdez, R. S. (2020). Human-Computer Interaction, Ethics, and Biomedical Informatics. *Yearbook of Medical Informatics*, *29*(1), 93–98. DOI: 10.1055/s-0040-1701990 PMID: 32823302

Hollnagel, E. (1992). The reliability of man-machine interaction. *Reliability Engineering & System Safety*, *38*(1-2), 81–89. DOI: 10.1016/0951-8320(92)90108-W

Hörbst, J., & Orsolits, H. (2022, February). Mixed Reality HMI for Collaborative Robots. In *International Conference on Computer Aided Systems Theory* (pp. 539-546). Cham: Springer Nature Switzerland.

Inners, M., & Kun, A. L. (2017, September). Beyond liability: Legal issues of human-machine interaction for automated vehicles. In *Proceedings of the 9th International Conference on Automotive User Interfaces and Interactive Vehicular Applications* (pp. 245-253). DOI: 10.1145/3122986.3123005

Iqbal, M. Z., & Campbell, A. G. (2021). From luxury to necessity: Progress of touchless interaction technology. *Technology in Society*, *67*, 101796. DOI: 10.1016/j.techsoc.2021.101796 PMID: 36313277

Iriarte, A. A., Erle, G. L., Etxabe, M. M., APRAIZ-IRIARTE, A., LASA-ERLE, G., & ETXABE, M. (2021). Evaluating user experience with physiological monitoring: A systematic literature review. *Dyna New Technol, 8*(1).

Jakobi, T., & Grafenstein, M. v. (2023). What HCI Can Do for (Data Protection) Law—Beyond Design. In Gerber, N., Stöver, A., & Marky, K. (Eds.), *Human Factors in Privacy Research*. Springer., DOI: 10.1007/978-3-031-28643-8_6

Jia, L., Liu, D., Jiang, M. J., & Cao, N. (2015, March). Design of natural user interface of indoor surveillance system. In *Selected Papers from Conferences of the Photoelectronic Technology Committee of the Chinese Society of Astronautics 2014, Part I* (Vol. 9521, pp. 278-285). SPIE.

Kazi, A. (2024, March 11). Connecting Humans and Machines: Trends in the Human Machine Interface (HMI) Market. *Verified Market Reports® | Get Market Analysis and Research Reports*. https://www.verifiedmarketreports.com/blog/top-7-trends-in-human-machine-interface-hmi/#:~:text=Gesture%20recognition%20technology%20is%20becoming,hands%2Dfree%20operation%20is%20essential

Kop, M. (2019). AI & intellectual property: Towards an articulated public domain. *SSRN*, *28*, 297. DOI: 10.2139/ssrn.3409715

Krupitzer, C., Müller, S., Lesch, V., Züfle, M., Edinger, J., Lemken, A., . . . Becker, C. (2020). A survey on human machine interaction in industry 4.0. *arXiv preprint arXiv:2002.01025*.

Kun, A. L. (2018). Human-machine interaction for vehicles: Review and outlook. *Foundations and Trends® in Human–Computer Interaction, 11*(4), 201-293.

Larsson, S. (2021). AI in the EU: Ethical Guidelines as a Governance Tool. *The European Union and the technology shift*, 85-111.

Leschanowsky, A., Brüggemeier, B., & Peters, N. (2021, November). Design implications for human-machine interactions from a qualitative pilot study on privacy. In *Proc. 2021 ISCA symposium on security and privacy in speech communication* (pp. 76-79). DOI: 10.21437/SPSC.2021-16

Lutz, C. (2023). Privacy and Human–Machine Communication. *Human-Machine Communication*, •••, 310.

Ma, F., Song, F., Liu, Y., & Niu, J. (2020). Quantitative analysis on the interaction fatigue of natural gestures. *IEEE Access : Practical Innovations, Open Solutions*, *8*, 190797–190811. DOI: 10.1109/ACCESS.2020.3031967

Mahmud, S., Lin, X., & Kim, J. H. (2020, January). Interface for human machine interaction for assistant devices: A review. In *2020 10th Annual computing and communication workshop and conference (CCWC)* (pp. 0768-0773). IEEE. DOI: 10.1109/CCWC47524.2020.9031244

Malviya, R., Sundram, S., Prajapati, B., & Singh, S. K. (Eds.). (2023). *Human-Machine Interface: Making Healthcare Digital*. John Wiley & Sons. DOI: 10.1002/9781394200344

Morgan, A. A., Abdi, J., Syed, M. A., Kohen, G. E., Barlow, P., & Vizcaychipi, M. P. (2022). Robots in healthcare: A scoping review. *Current Robotics Reports*, *3*(4), 271–280. DOI: 10.1007/s43154-022-00095-4 PMID: 36311256

Mourtzis, D., Angelopoulos, J., & Panopoulos, N. (2023). The future of the human–machine interface (HMI) in society 5.0. *Future Internet*, *15*(5), 162. DOI: 10.3390/fi15050162

Nickel, P., Bärenz, P., Radandt, S., Wichtl, M., Kaufmann, U., Monica, L., . . . Nellutla, M. (2020). Human-system interaction design requirements to improve machinery and systems safety. In *Advances in Safety Management and Human Factors:Proceedings of the AHFE 2019 International Conference on Safety Management and Human Factors,July 24-28, 2019,Washington DC, USA10* (pp. 3-13). Springer International Publishing. DOI: 10.1007/978-3-030-20497-6_1

Ossiannilsson, E., Cazarez, R. L. U., Goode, C., Mansour, C., & Gusmao, C. M. G. D. (2024). Artificial intelligence is used to empower the implementation of OER and the UNESCO OER recommendation. *Open Praxis*, *16*(2), 137–157. DOI: 10.55982/openpraxis.16.2.650

Pacaux-Lemoine, M. P., & Trentesaux, D. (2019). Ethical risks of human-machine symbiosis in industry 4.0: Insights from the human-machine cooperation approach. *IFAC-PapersOnLine*, *52*(19), 19–24. DOI: 10.1016/j.ifacol.2019.12.077

Patel, H. I., Senanayake, S. A., & Triloka, J. (2020, November). Human-system interaction interface utilizing 3D gesture recognition techniques based on wearable technology. In *2020 5th International Conference on Innovative Technologies in Intelligent Systems and Industrial Applications (CITISIA)* (pp. 1-9). IEEE.

Pellegrino, M., & Kelly, R. (2019). Intelligent machines and the growing importance of ethics. In Gilli, A. (Ed.), *The Brain and the Processor: Unpacking the Challenges of Human-Machine Interaction* (pp. 45–54). NATO Defense College., https://www.jstor.org/stable/resrep19966.11

Pérez, L., Rodríguez-Jiménez, S., Rodríguez, N., Usamentiaga, R., & García, D. F. (2020). Digital twin and virtual reality-based methodology for multi-robot manufacturing cell commissioning. *Applied Sciences (Basel, Switzerland)*, *10*(10), 3633. DOI: 10.3390/app10103633

Pohle, J. (2015). UNESCO and INFOethics: Seeking global ethical values in the Information Society. *Telematics and Informatics*, *32*(2), 381–390. DOI: 10.1016/j.tele.2014.05.006

Principles for Responsible AI Innovation. *AI Toolkit*. (n.d.). https://www.ai-lawenforcement.org/guidance/principles

Quartarone, V. (2021). *Wearable HMI definition, development and validation for collaborative environment in industrial processes in the context of Industry 4.0* (Doctoral dissertation, Politecnico di Torino).

Ribino, P. (2023). The role of politeness in human–machine interactions: A systematic literature review and future perspectives. *Artificial Intelligence Review*, *56*(S1, Suppl 1), 445–482. DOI: 10.1007/s10462-023-10540-1

Roberts, H., Cowls, J., Hine, E., Mazzi, F., Tsamados, A., Taddeo, M., & Floridi, L. (2021). Achieving a 'Good AI Society': Comparing the Aims and Progress of the EU and the US. *Science and Engineering Ethics*, *27*(6), 1–25. DOI: 10.1007/s11948-021-00340-7 PMID: 34767085

Rodrigues, R. (2020). Legal and human rights issues of AI: Gaps, challenges and vulnerabilities. *Journal of Responsible Technology*, *4*, 100005. DOI: 10.1016/j.jrt.2020.100005

Sadeghi, S., & Maleki, A. (2018). Recent advances in hybrid brain-computer interface systems: A technological and quantitative review. *Basic and Clinical Neuroscience*, *9*(5), 373–388. DOI: 10.32598/bcn.9.5.373 PMID: 30719252

Sawant, P. (2022, November 10). *What is Industrial HMI? Applications & Design Considerations. | Linepro*. BLOG. https://lineproindia.com/blog/what-is-industrial-hmi-applications-design-considerations/

Shih, J. J., Krusienski, D. J., & Wolpaw, J. R. (2012, March). Brain-computer interfaces in medicine. [). Elsevier.]. *Mayo Clinic Proceedings*, *87*(3), 268–279. DOI: 10.1016/j.mayocp.2011.12.008 PMID: 22325364

Shoukat, M. U., Yan, L., Zhang, J., Cheng, Y., Raza, M. U., & Niaz, A. (2024). Smart home for enhanced healthcare: Exploring human machine interface oriented digital twin model. *Multimedia Tools and Applications*, *83*(11), 31297–31315. DOI: 10.1007/s11042-023-16875-9

Singh, H. P., & Kumar, P. (2021). Developments in the human machine interface technologies and their applications: A review. *Journal of Medical Engineering & Technology*, *45*(7), 552–573. DOI: 10.1080/03091902.2021.1936237 PMID: 34184601

Singhal, A., Neveditsin, N., Tanveer, H., & Mago, V. (2024). Toward Fairness, Accountability, Transparency, and Ethics in AI for Social Media and Health Care: Scoping Review. *JMIR Medical Informatics*, *12*, e50048. DOI: 10.2196/50048 PMID: 38568737

Smuha, N. A., Ahmed-Rengers, E., Harkens, A., Li, W., MacLaren, J., Piselli, R., & Yeung, K. (2021). How the EU can achieve legally trustworthy AI: a response to the European Commission's proposal for an Artificial Intelligence Act. *Available atSSRN* 3899991. DOI: 10.2139/ssrn.3899991

Sun, H., Rau, P. L. P., & Wang, B. (2021). A Study of Machine Ethics in Human-Artificial Intelligence Interactions. In *Cross-Cultural Design. Applications in Arts, Learning, Well-being, and Social Development: 13th International Conference, CCD 2021, Held as Part of the 23rd HCI International Conference, HCII 2021, Virtual Event, July 24–29, 2021* [Springer International Publishing.]. *Proceedings, 23*(Part II), 374–395.

The GDPR. (2024). European Council. https://www.consilium.europa.eu/en/policies/data-protection/data-protection-regulation/#:~:text=data%20protection%20rules-,What%20is%20the%20GDPR%3F,application%20on%2025%20May%202018

Veale, M., & Zuiderveen Borgesius, F. (2021). Demystifying the Draft EU Artificial Intelligence Act—Analyzing the good, the bad, and the unclear elements of the proposed approach. *Computer Law Review International, 22*(4), 97–112. DOI: 10.9785/cri-2021-220402

Weerarathna, I. N., Raymond, D., & Luharia, A. (2023). Human-Robot Collaboration for Healthcare: A Narrative Review. *Cureus, 15*(11). Advance online publication. DOI: 10.7759/cureus.49210 PMID: 38143700

What is HCI and Security? (n.d.). *Educative.*https://www.educative.io/answers/what-is-hci-and-security

What is HMI? *Human-Machine-Interface, COPA-DATA*. (2023, December 12). https://www.copadata.com/en/product/zenon-software-platform-for-industrial-automation-energy-automation/visualization-control/what-is-hmi/#:~:text=Uses%20of%20HMI&text=Industries%20such%20as%20energy%2C%20water,%2C%20vehicles%2C%20plants%20or%20buildings

Wittenberg, C. (2016). Human-CPS Interaction-requirements and human-machine interaction methods for the Industry 4.0. *IFAC-PapersOnLine, 49*(19), 420–425. DOI: 10.1016/j.ifacol.2016.10.602

Wolford, B. (2023, September 14). *What is GDPR, the EU's new data protection law?* GDPR.eu. https://gdpr.eu/what-is-gdpr/

World Health Organization. (2021). The importance of ethics in artificial intelligence. In *WHO Consultation Towards the Development of guidance on ethics and governance of artificial intelligence for health: Meeting report Geneva, Switzerland, 2–4 October 2019* (pp. 2–3). World Health Organization. https://www.jstor.org/stable/resrep35680.6

Yin, R., Wang, D., Zhao, S., Lou, Z., & Shen, G. (2021). Wearable sensors-enabled human–machine interaction systems: From design to application. *Advanced Functional Materials*, *31*(11), 2008936. DOI: 10.1002/adfm.202008936

Zou, S., Tao, L. Q., Wang, G., Zhu, C., Peng, Z., Sun, H., Li, Y., Wei, Y., & Ren, T. L. (2022). Humidity-based human–machine interaction system for healthcare applications. *ACS Applied Materials & Interfaces*, *14*(10), 12606–12616. DOI: 10.1021/acsami.1c23725 PMID: 35230086

Chapter 8
Artificial Intelligence for Fraud Detection: A Bibliometric Exploration

Rajesh Tiwari
https://orcid.org/0000-0002-5345-2508
Graphic Era University (Deemed), India

Vibhuti Jain
https://orcid.org/0009-0009-8602-6116
Graphic Era University (Deemed), India

Khushboo Chauhan
https://orcid.org/0009-0001-5809-7074
Graphic Era University (Deemed), India

Harshita Dwivedi
https://orcid.org/0009-0004-1874-2720
Graphic Era University (Deemed), India

Shweta Bajaj
https://orcid.org/0000-0002-1177-6352
Graphic Era University (Deemed), India

ABSTRACT

Increasing use of digital payments, cyber fraud is a major topic of concern. Artificial Intelligence and its techniques can prove to be of great importance to find a solution for this concern. The study provides a thorough exploration of how AI and ML are increasingly used to detect such credit card frauds. It can't be restricted to credit cards as it is useful in detecting frauds in various fields in finance sector as well as in other sectors. The study attempts a bibliometric analysis on Scopus database.

DOI: 10.4018/979-8-3373-3384-7.ch008

United Kingdom, India and United States are prominent countries. There is significant growth in publications of detection of frauds after covid pandemic. It is found that artificial intelligence is useful for detection of frauds.

I. INTRODUCTION

Fraud on credit and debit cards poses a severe and ongoing risk to society. Smartphone, mobile payments etc. are the biggest examples of such frauds. For its solution, relevant strategies have been published Detecting payment card fraud using AI and machine learning involves various techniques, while keeping in mind the main difficulties in applying latest technology interventions like AI and ML for the identification of fraud. The topic for future directions is brought up, and it is proposed that cognitive computing methods are a fruitful area for research while promoting industry data philanthropy (Ryman-Tubb et al., 2018). Due to its impact on many aspects of life, fraud is a topic of great concern. Therefore, technologies like AI and ML are crucial in uncovering fraudulent activity. By improving basic security and operational procedures, businesses have benefited from the use of AI to detect frauds. Consequently, due to AI's increased competency, it has become an essential tool for preventing frauds (Tiwari & Srivastava, 2024). Ever since the internet came into existence, many businesses have moved towards the internet to provide better service to their customers and to use these services, customers make online payment because of which cyber credit fraud has increased. Due to its powerful Artificial Intelligence (AI) techniques, Data Mining has become more well-known in the fight against online credit card fraud (Akhilomen, 2013). By utilising AI, data mining, and location tracking for identification of credit card frauds helps in spotting patterns in consumer spending to identify frauds (Nkomo & Breetzke, 2020).

II. LITERATURE REVIEW

Modern methods for identifying different credit card fraud transactions have developed. These methods include those based on artificial intelligence, data extraction, neural networks, etc. An effective strategy for detecting credit card fraud will undoubtedly result from having a thorough grasp of each of these (Raj & Portia, 2011). Scenario based Explainable Artificial Intelligence (XAI) is developed for the fraud detection specialists to develop a trust on AI models, making it easy for them to adopt such models (Cirqueira, 2020). Nowadays, for doing online shopping or to purchase anything we are using credit cards. It is very challenging to halt the frauds involving usage of credit cards. However, usage of AL and ML provide better results as compared to traditional techniques like Decision Tree or XGBOOST (Jain et al., 2020). The adoption of novel regulations that promote healthy competition among market participants and a Digital technology must be incorporated into the banking industry to enhance accessibility and level of service. Handling the financial sector is a very important aspect. New technology though disrupts every industry, but technological advancements in financial sector have totally evolved the financial services. With the operational issues like client retention and competitive environment, IT issues are becoming a major concern in banking sector (Bisht et al., 2022).

Most of the organizations use two types of technique - ML and Deep Learning to predict or forecast the future learning. Thus, AI will play a major role to manage and develop the financial and e-commerce sectors so that customers will be increased and they will gain more profile and sustain in the market for long run (Pallathadka et al., 2023). Digital payment system has increased so much that financial crime has also increased but the conventional methods of regulation are becoming ineffective. The use of graph computing ideas kike ML and AI have gained attention. Graph based methods offer distinctive prospects for financial crime detection solutions (Kurshan & Shen, 2020). Though AI is useful in the banking sector but it is necessary to know whether people will accept using AI or not. According to the research, acceptance of AI depends upon risk, use and trust on it rather than the easefulness associated with it (Rahman et al., 2021). In past years unusual growth in digital payment system. Led to significant changes in various frauds and cybercrimes. Tools such as AI and Machine Learning in fraud detection become more effectual as compared to established techniques. Techniques such as Graph based computing proves to be more useful and effective in deducting frauds. But executing graph-based computing in digital payment system has brought up various barrier and we come to know about various graph-based tools (Kurshan et al., 2020).

One of the industries with the greatest growth potential is private insurance. To maximize profits of the client they use traditional models that will take lots of time so an automated insurance system framework is introduced that minimizes human involvement, and warns and enlightens clients who pose a risk. We consider using extraordinary gradient boosting (XG Boost) when applying machine learning techniques to the insurance sector since XG Boost allows us to detect fraudulent claims (Dhieb et al., 2020). Health insurance is vital due to rising health issues, but it faces security and fraud challenges. AI and Blockchain are useful for secure health insurance fraud detection, offering a taxonomy of security issues, proposing a system, and presenting a case study (Kapadiya et al., 2022). AI has been found to be useful in healthcare and agri-based industries for enhanced production, supply chain, ensuring quality and reducing cost (Pallathadka et al., 2023). Even in the Telecom Industry, frauds are prevalent. Thus, researchers are finding ways to detect easily such frauds with the help of AI (Ritika, 2022).

IoT, 5G, digital twins, and the Metaverse in this evolution, while acknowledging the need for further research and anticipating upcoming challenges (Bhat et al, 2023). Using advanced AI for real-time payment fraud detection, employing supervised learning and data analytics to uncover hidden patterns in customer data has significantly improved fraud detection rates from 85% to 90% in transaction records and to 95% in transaction value while reducing manual investigation alerts from 40% to 10%. Notably, it falls under the category of explainable AI, providing transparency in decision-making (Soviany, 2018). The main problem is the paucity of practical test data for generating and assessing fraud detecting methods. To address such paucity, a modification to the existing payment model is proposed. Payment models can be modified to generate appropriate transactions for various payment types (Diadiushkin et al., 2019).

The increasing complexity of AI and Machine Learning models, their applications in areas like credit risk, anti-money laundering, and derivatives pricing, and their broader use in fields like sales optimization and robo-advisory. The need is to build a risk-based governance framework and the use of modern technologies to ensure trustworthy AI in the financial sector. Financial risk management, particularly in the context of ML and AI models for banks and financial institutions (Fritz-Morgenthal et al., 2022).

The banking industry's increasing dependence on cyber security, especially to tackle the growing threat of credit card theft. The technological revolution driven by key technologies like big data, blockchain technology, computing via the cloud, the IoT, and machine learning and artificial intelligence are all developing quickly (Btoush et al., 2021). In the financial sector, the shift to digital platforms has exposed vulnerabilities, leading to increased cybercrime through unregulated channels like e-currency exchanges. The integration of cybersecurity measures, AI techniques, and network technologies is crucial to safeguard computing resources in the face of growing cyber threats. To counter dynamic cyber-attacks, banks and institutions are adopting AI and Machine Learning techniques, such as Feedzai's Free ML fraudulent detection software and the algorithm known as random forest, to intelligently identify and combat fraudulent banking transactions, enhancing financial fraud detection (Narsimha et al., 2022). Financial intelligence, a crucial part of the AI 2.0 era, is becoming a big deal in finance. It's like a smart computer system that can handle complex money-related data really well and might become the "brain" behind financial decisions. A research plan called Fin Brain is suggested and important areas to explore are pointed out, like making sure the system can explain its decisions and handling uncertainty in predictions. It is a step toward making finance smarter with AI 2.0 (Zhou et al., 2022).

Banks are changing a lot because of Artificial Intelligence (AI). They're using computer programs that are really good at learning to find fake transactions and predict when they might happen. They have a clever plan that involves using these programs in different stages to make it work better. Instead of looking at the obvious stuff, they're looking at hidden clues in the data to catch fraudsters (Zioviris et al., 2022). Credit card fraud is a costly problem in commerce, evolving with technology. While traditional methods like cloning and skimming still exist, online fraud is increasing therefore, using a Perceptron-based Artificial Neural Network in legacy financial systems to detect fraud patterns, offering a potential backup to existing credit checking services (Quintin-John & Valverde, 2021). Old techniques are becoming less effective in identifying frauds and AI based solutions surpass these conventional ways of detecting fraud (Tiwari et al., 2023).

The recognition of fraud involves keeping an eye on users spending patterns to identify and steer clear of unwanted activity. The quick identification of frauds is prime objective of detection process (Chaudhary et al., 2012). The most often utilized fraud detection methodologies by researchers are deep learning and machine learning, and the most frequently employed research object is the credit card fraud industry. Research is most lacking in the following areas: insurance, wellness, Shell businesses, tax evasions, cyber hacking, logistics (Mahya et al., 2023).

III. METHOD

The study employed Scopus database for bibliometric analysis. The keywords used were “AI” AND “fraud detection”. Date of search was 13th September 2023. 218 documents were obtained. Language was the first criteria of exclusion. Only documents in English language were considered. All 218 documents were in English, so no document was excluded. The next stage of exclusion was type of document. Editorial (1) was excluded. Article (66), conference paper (91), book chapter (29), conference review (17), review (8), book (5) and short survey (1) was included. 217 documents were included after 2nd stage of exclusion. The third stage of exclusion was screening of each document for suitability with the objective of the paper. 96 documents were included after exclusion of 122 documents. Finally, these 96 documents were used for the bibliometric analysis.

IV. RESULTS

Figure 1 shows that most of the researches are being done in 2022 and 2023, which tells us that AI is not a much hot and aware area of study among researchers and it gained popularity only in recent years. Figure 2 depicts co-citation map.

Figure 1. Year wise publications

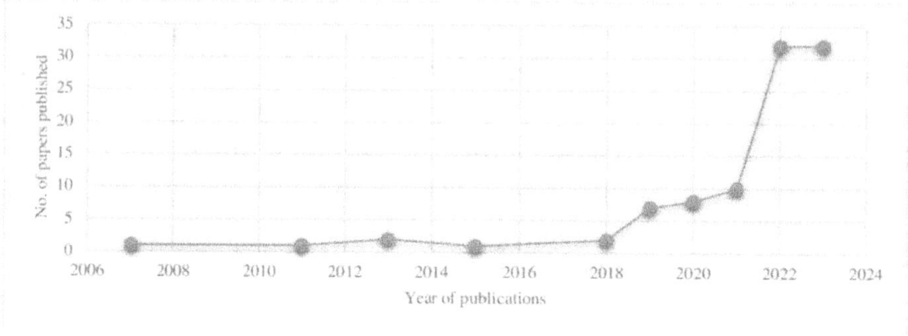

Figure 2. Co-citation map of authors

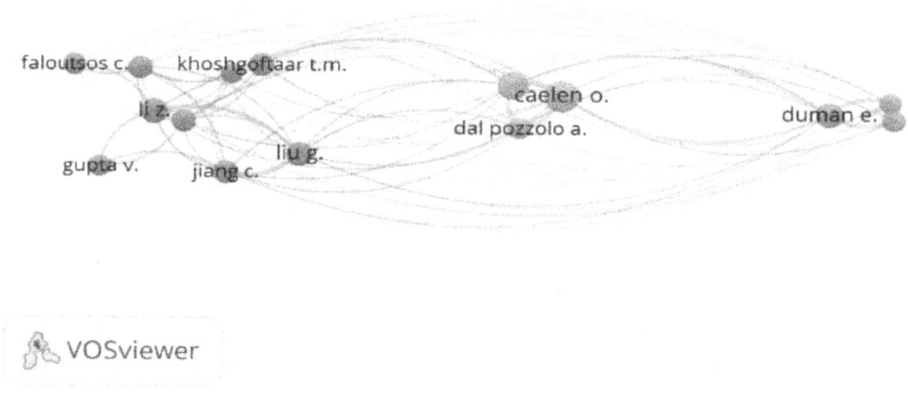

Table 1 represents the list of most cited documents. The minimum citation was kept at 10, out of the 96 documents, only 12 met the limit. As depicted in table 1; "Ryman-Tubb N.F.; Krause P.; Garn W. (2018)" is the most cited document with 86 citations.

Table 1. Prominent cited documents

S. No.	Document	Citations
1	"Ryman-Tubb N.F.; Krause P.; Garn W. (2018)"	86
2	"Dhieb N.; Ghazzai H.; Besbes H.; Massoud Y. (2020)"	46
3	"Akhilomen J. (2013)"	30
4	"Cirqueira D.; Nedbal D.; Helfert M.; Bezbradica M. (2020)"	22
5	"Pallathadka H.; Mustafa M.; Sanchez D.T.; Sekhar Sajja G.; Gour S.; Naved M. (2023)"	22
6	"Jain V.; Agrawal M.; Kumar A. (2020)"	19
7	"Bisht D.; Singh R.; Gehlot A.; Akram S.V.; Singh A.; Montero E.C.; Priyadarshi N.; Twala B. (2022)"	17
8	"Pallathadka H.; Ramirez-Asis E.H.; Loli-Poma T.P.; Kaliyaperumal K.; Ventayen R.J.M.; Naved M. (2023)"	16
9	"Kurshan E.; Shen H. (2020)"	12
10	"Kurshan E.; Shen H.; Yu H. (2020)"	11
11	"Rahman M.; Ming T.H.; Baigh T.A.; Sarker M. (2022)"	11

Table II represents most cited source in which by keeping minimum no. of documents and minimum citations 5, out of 83 only 14 met the limit. As depicted in table II; "Engineering Applications of Artificial Intelligence" is the most cited source with 86 citations from 1 document and IEEE Access comes after it with 58 citations from 3 documents.

Table 2. Prominent cited sources

S. No.	Source	Documents	Citations
1	"Engineering Applications of Artificial Intelligence"	1	86
2	"IEEE Access"	3	58
3	'Lecture Notes in Computer Science"	2	52
4	"Materials Today: Proceedings"	3	39
5	"ICRITO 2020 - IEEE 8th International Conference on Reliability, Infocom Technologies and Optimization (Trends and Future Directions)"	1	19
6	"Electronics (Switzerland)"	1	17
7	"International Journal of Semantic Computing"	1	12
8	"International Journal of Emerging Markets"	1	11
9	"Proceedings - 2020 2nd International Conference on Transdisciplinary AI, Transai 2020"	1	11
10	"Journal of King Saud University - Computer and Information Sciences"	1	9
11	"Journal of Payments Strategy and Systems"	1	9

Figure 3. Map of co-occurrence

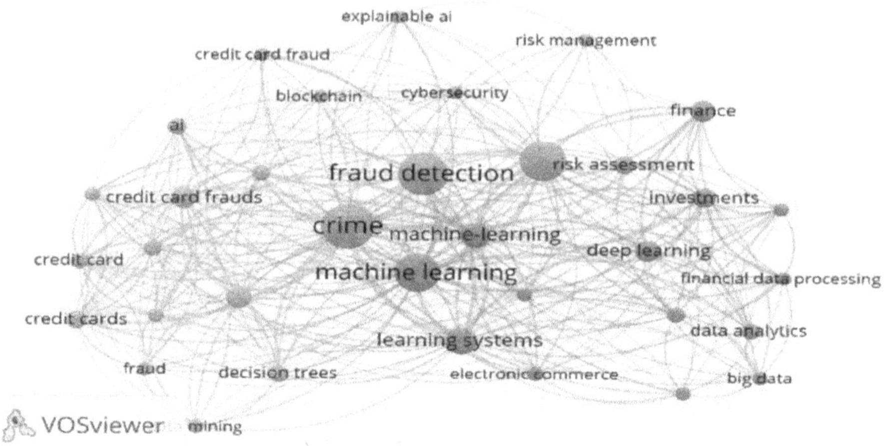

Figure 3 depicts frequently used keywords. The significance of crime is reflected in crime being most frequently used keyword followed by fraud detection and machine learning.

Figure 4 represents the clusters of documents through Bibliographic coupling. Total 7 clusters were formed out of which 5 clusters were selected which includes minimum 4 no. of articles.

Cluster 1- It is depicted in red color and is one of the biggest clusters. 27 citations from 7 articles comprised cluster I. The cluster was concerned with theme of "Proposing various AI based models and checking their accuracy".

Cluster 2- It is depicted in green color. 8 citations from 5 articles comprised cluster II. The cluster was concerned with theme of "Use of AI driven Business Analytics methods and technologies to Detect Financial Fraud".

Cluster 3- It is depicted in blue color. 95 citations from 5 articles comprised cluster III. The cluster was concerned with theme of "Evaluating Models and suggesting Best Fit Model".

Cluster 4- It is depicted in yellow color. 6 citations from 5 articles comprised cluster IV. The cluster was concerned with theme of "Techniques using AI and ML for credit card fraud detection".

Cluster 5- It is depicted in pink color. It contains 5 articles with 3 total citations. The theme of this cluster focuses on "The usefulness of AI models in detecting and minimizing financial frauds".

Table III represents the countries whose articles are most cited. United Kingdom was the most cited country with documents 9 and 132 citations then India with 49 documents and 113 citations and third is United States with 14 documents and 100 citations.

Figure 4. Map of bibliographic coupling

Table 3. Prominent cited countries

S. No.	Country	Documents	Citations
1	United Kingdom	9	132
2	India	49	113
3	United States	14	100
4	Tunisia	1	46
5	Philippines	2	38
6	South Africa	2	27
7	Austria	1	22
8	Gulf College	1	22
9	Ireland	1	22
10	Saudi Arabia	3	19

V. CONCLUSION

We investigated upon the usefulness of AI and its techniques to detect payment card, as we know that India has one of largest user of the online payment system even a small level vendor is using UPI for taking payment from his customers. Thus, the use of digital payments is increasing and with it the cyber fraud is also increasing, making it hard to spot the fraudster. AI and ML based models can be the best solution to detect these frauds. In this study, we talked about how banking sectors and other financial sectors are adopting new technology to provide better services to their customers and we also found out that not only in banking sector but AI is legitimate a boon for whole finance sector but it comes with a curse as well which need to be taken care of well. Even the Agriculture and Health sector is using AI to detect frauds in their system. Hence, we can't limit our study on Usefulness of AI in Fraud Detection to credit card frauds, but it is useful in detecting fraudulent activities in various other fields as well. Through Bibliometric exploration, we found out the countries that have researched most on this topic are India, USA and UK. Bibliographic coupling led to 5 clusters, where each cluster depicts a unique theme about different research done on this topic. This paper thoroughly examined how AI can identify fraud. It starts by summarizing key existing research on using machine learning for this purpose. Then, it uses Bibliometric analysis to find about how many research have been done on this topic. The findings show that various models are proposed and evaluated based on AI and ML, also that more and more researchers are interested in using AI to detect fraudsters, highlighting how crucial it is to tackle this problem. This helps us to see how fast scholars have been acknowledging this new technology and its use specifically in finance sector and can be useful in other sectors as well, how more research are going on this topic and also tells us what researchers must focus on in the future.

REFERENCES

Akhilomen, J. (2013). Data mining application for cyber credit-card fraud detection system. In *Advances in Data Mining. Applications and Theoretical Aspects: 13th Industrial Conference, ICDM 2013, New York, NY, USA, July 16-21, 2013.* [Springer Berlin Heidelberg.]. *Proceedings*, *13*, 218–228.

Bhat, J. R., AlQahtani, S. A., & Nekovee, M. (2023). FinTech enablers, use cases, and role of future internet of things. *Journal of King Saud University. Computer and Information Sciences*, *35*(1), 87–101. DOI: 10.1016/j.jksuci.2022.08.033

Bisht, D., Singh, R., Gehlot, A., Akram, S. V., Singh, A., Montero, E. C., Priyadarshi, N., & Twala, B. (2022). Imperative role of integrating digitalization in the firms finance: A technological perspective. *Electronics (Basel)*, *11*(19), 3252. DOI: 10.3390/electronics11193252

Btoush, E., Zhou, X., Gururaian, R., Chan, K. C., & Tao, X. (2021, October). A survey on credit card fraud detection techniques in banking industry for cyber security. In *2021 8th International Conference on Behavioral and Social Computing (BESC)* (pp. 1-7). IEEE. DOI: 10.1109/BESC53957.2021.9635559

Chaudhary, K., Yadav, J., & Mallick, B. (2012). A review of fraud detection techniques: Credit card. *International Journal of Computer Applications*, *45*(1), 39–44.

Cirqueira, D., Nedbal, D., Helfert, M., & Bezbradica, M. (2020, August). Scenario-based requirements elicitation for user-centric explainable AI: A case in fraud detection. In *International cross-domain conference for machine learning and knowledge extraction* (pp. 321-341). Cham: Springer International Publishing. DOI: 10.1007/978-3-030-57321-8_18

Dhieb, N., Ghazzai, H., Besbes, H., & Massoud, Y. (2020). A secure ai-driven architecture for automated insurance systems: Fraud detection and risk measurement. *IEEE Access : Practical Innovations, Open Solutions*, *8*, 58546–58558. DOI: 10.1109/ACCESS.2020.2983300

Diadiushkin, A., Sandkuhl, K., & Maiatin, A. V. (2019). Fraud Detection in Instant Payments as Contribution to Digitalization in Banks. In *BIR workshops,* 107-117).

Fritz-Morgenthal, S., Hein, B., & Papenbrock, J. (2022). Financial risk management and explainable, trustworthy, responsible AI. *Frontiers in Artificial Intelligence*, *5*, 779799. DOI: 10.3389/frai.2022.779799 PMID: 35295866

Jain, V., Agrawal, M., & Kumar, A. (2020, June). Performance analysis of machine learning algorithms in credit cards fraud detection. In *2020 8th International Conference on Reliability, Infocom Technologies and Optimization (Trends and Future Directions)(ICRITO)* (pp. 86-88). IEEE. DOI: 10.1109/ICRITO48877.2020.9197762

Kapadiya, K., Patel, U., Gupta, R., Alshehri, M. D., Tanwar, S., Sharma, G., & Bokoro, P. N. (2022). Blockchain and AI-empowered healthcare insurance fraud detection: An analysis, architecture, and future prospects. *IEEE Access : Practical Innovations, Open Solutions, 10*, 79606–79627. DOI: 10.1109/ACCESS.2022.3194569

Kurshan, E., & Shen, H. (2020). Graph computing for financial crime and fraud detection: Trends, challenges and outlook. *International Journal of Semantic Computing, 14*(04), 565–589. DOI: 10.1142/S1793351X20300022

Kurshan, E., Shen, H., & Yu, H. (2020, September). Financial crime & fraud detection using graph computing: Application considerations & outlook. In *2020 Second International Conference on Transdisciplinary AI (TransAI)* (pp. 125-130). IEEE. DOI: 10.1109/TransAI49837.2020.00029

Mahya, L., Tarjo, T., Sanusi, Z. M., & Kurniawan, F. A. (2023). Intelligent Automation Of Fraud Detection And Investigation: A Bibliometric Analysis Approach. *Jurnal Reviu Akuntansi dan Keuangan, 13*(3), 588-613.

Narsimha, B., Raghavendran, C. V., Rajyalakshmi, P., Reddy, G. K., Bhargavi, M., & Naresh, P. (2022). Cyber defense in the age of artificial intelligence and machine learning for financial fraud detection application. *IJEER, 10*(2), 87–92. DOI: 10.37391/ijeer.100206

Nkomo, B. K., & Breetzke, T. (2020, March). A conceptual model for the use of artificial intelligence for credit card fraud detection in banks. In *2020 Conference on Information Communications Technology and Society (ICTAS)* (pp. 1-6). IEEE. DOI: 10.1109/ICTAS47918.2020.233980

Pallathadka, H., Mustafa, M., Sanchez, D. T., Sajja, G. S., Gour, S., & Naved, M. (2023). Impact of machine learning on management, healthcare and agriculture. *Materials Today: Proceedings, 80*, 2803–2806. DOI: 10.1016/j.matpr.2021.07.042

Pallathadka, H., Ramirez-Asis, E. H., Loli-Poma, T. P., Kaliyaperumal, K., Ventayen, R. J. M., & Naved, M. (2023). Applications of artificial intelligence in business management, e-commerce and finance. *Materials Today: Proceedings, 80*, 2610–2613. DOI: 10.1016/j.matpr.2021.06.419

Quintin-John, S., & Valverde, R. (2021). A perceptron based neural network data analytics architecture for the detection of fraud in credit card transactions in financial legacy systems. *WSEAS Transactions on Systems and Control, 16*.

Rahman, M., Ming, T. H., Baigh, T. A., & Sarker, M. (2023). Adoption of artificial intelligence in banking services: An empirical analysis. *International Journal of Emerging Markets*, *18*(10), 4270–4300. DOI: 10.1108/IJOEM-06-2020-0724

Raj, S. B. E., & Portia, A. A. (2011, March). Analysis on credit card fraud detection methods. In *2011 International Conference on Computer, Communication and Electrical Technology (ICCCET)* (pp. 152-156). IEEE.

Ritika, H. J. (2022, October). Fraud detection and management for telecommunication systems using artificial intelligence (AI). In *2022 3rd International Conference on Smart Electronics and Communication (ICOSEC)* (pp. 1016-1022). IEEE.

Ryman-Tubb, N. F., Krause, P., & Garn, W. (2018). How Artificial Intelligence and machine learning research impacts payment card fraud detection: A survey and industry benchmark. *Engineering Applications of Artificial Intelligence*, *76*, 130–157. DOI: 10.1016/j.engappai.2018.07.008

Soviany, C. (2018). The benefits of using artificial intelligence in payment fraud detection: A case study. *Journal of Payments Strategy & Systems*, *12*(2), 102–110. DOI: 10.69554/ISSG4555

Tiwari, R., Rautela, S., Sharma, S., Choudhary, B. P., Tripathi, R., & Singh, P. (2023, December). Role of AI for Fraud Detection in Banks: A Bibliometric Analysis. In *2023 International Conference on Advanced Computing & Communication Technologies (ICACCTech)* (pp. 66-71). IEEE. DOI: 10.1109/ICACCTech61146.2023.00020

Tiwari, S., & Srivastava, R. (2024). Performance of Artificial Intelligence in Fraud Detection. In *Handbook of Artificial Intelligence Applications for Industrial Sustainability* (pp. 167–187). CRC Press. DOI: 10.1201/9781003348351-12

Zhou, J., Chen, C., Li, L., Zhang, Z., & Zheng, X. (2022). FinBrain 2.0: When finance meets trustworthy AI. *Frontiers of Information Technology & Electronic Engineering*, *23*(12), 1747–1764. DOI: 10.1631/FITEE.2200039

Zioviris, G., Kolomvatsos, K., & Stamoulis, G. (2022). Credit card fraud detection using a deep learning multistage model. *The Journal of Supercomputing*, *78*(12), 14571–14596. DOI: 10.1007/s11227-022-04465-9

Chapter 9
Redefining Work in the Age of AI:
Navigating Employment, Automation, and Ethics

Akshyata Giri
PES University, India

Aryan Sharma
Maulana Abul Kalam Azad University of Technology, India

ABSTRACT

This chapter explores the significant ways artificial intelligence (AI) is changing the nature of work in the Age of AI: Navigating Employment, Automation, and Ethics. It looks at how sectors are changing as a result of AI-driven automation, which is replacing certain jobs with new ones, especially those that need repetitive work. The chapter emphasizes the necessity of reskilling and upskilling in order to adjust to these changes by looking at case studies from industries like manufacturing, healthcare, and finance. It is stressed that ethical factors, such as bias, accountability, and transparency, are essential to creating responsible AI systems. The chapter also draws parallels with previous industrial revolutions to provide historical context, underscoring the ongoing impact of technological change on labor markets. In the end, it provides a fair assessment of AI's potential and promotes laws that promote inclusivity, fairness, and continuous learning in an AI-driven world.

DOI: 10.4018/979-8-3373-3384-7.ch009

INTRODUCTION

Artificial Intelligence (AI) stands out as a revolutionary force in the rapidly changing 21st century, drastically changing the way we live and work. AI was once only a concept found in science fiction, but it has since become a seamless part of everyday life, from the sophisticated algorithms driving global industries to the smartphones we carry around in our pockets (Jordan & Mitchell, 2015). Our current understanding of how work will change is barely getting started as a result of the rapid growth of AI technologies (Luckin et al., 2017). It is a wide range of technologies intended to mimic and improve human intelligence (McCallister, 2018). Natural language processing, robotics, and machine learning algorithms are just a few areas where artificial intelligence is having a big impact. For instance, recent research highlights how AI-driven diagnostics are revolutionizing healthcare by providing more accurate and timely medical assessments (Luckin et al., 2017). Predictive analytics is also being used in retail to improve inventory control and customise customer experiences, showcasing AI's capacity to spur creativity and efficiency (Waters, 2014).

AI-powered automation has generated a lot of discussion regarding job displacement and the nature of employment in the future. Concern over the stability of some work responsibilities is growing as repetitive and routine jobs become more mechanised. (Jordan & Mitchell, 2015). This change calls for a critical analysis of the ways in which AI is both creating new opportunities and changing the way that jobs are now structured. For instance, research highlights the necessity for reskilling and upskilling in order to adjust to these developments, outlining the advantages and disadvantages of integrating AI. (OECD, 2019; McKeown et al., 2018).

While AI is creating new industries and professions like data analytics and robotics, it's also leading to the obsolescence of certain jobs, particularly those involving repetitive tasks. (Jordan & Mitchell, 2015). By examining examples from companies like Amazon and Ericsson, the chapter will analyze which sectors are thriving due to AI integration and which are facing challenges (OECD, 2019). It will delve into how AI is transforming the workplace, from the emergence of new job opportunities to the displacement of existing roles (Luckin et al., 2017). Additionally, the chapter will investigate the strategies that companies are adopting to adapt to these changes, such as upskilling their workforce (Waters, 2014). Ultimately, the goal is to gain a comprehensive understanding of the multifaceted ways in which AI is reshaping the employment landscape.

When it comes to the impact of AI on the workplace, automation is a major theme. This chapter explores how automation is transforming the workplace, addressing ethical concerns like privacy, bias, and transparency, while offering a framework for navigating these challenges in a rapidly evolving technological landscape. Drawing on recent research and discussions, it aims to provide a balanced analysis of AI's impact on work and offer practical guidance for adaptation in an AI-driven world.

HISTORICAL CONTEXT OF TECHNOLOGICAL CHANGE IN EMPLOYMENT

To comprehend the influence of Artificial Intelligence (AI) on employment and job markets, it's crucial to situate current technological advancements within a historical context. The nature of labour has been frequently altered by technological revolutions, resulting in significant changes to employment patterns and job responsibilities (Jordan & Mitchell, 2015). By examining past technological changes, we can learn valuable insights into how AI might mold the future of work (Luckin et al., 2017).

The First Industrial Revolution (Late 18th to Early 19th Century)

The First Industrial Revolution, which began in Britain in the late 18th century, marked a profound shift in the nature of work. This period witnessed a transition from agrarian economies to industrialized ones, driven by innovations such as the steam engine and mechanized textile machinery (Jordan & Mitchell, 2015). These technological advancements dramatically increased production efficiency, leading to the growth of factories and urban centers.

The impact on employment was twofold. On one hand, the revolution created new job opportunities in factories and mines, fueling the rise of a working-class population. On the other hand, it rendered many traditional artisanal jobs obsolete, resulting in significant displacement and social upheaval (McCallister, 2018). This shift from skilled craftsmanship to machine-based production highlighted a recurring theme in technological revolutions: the displacement of existing job roles alongside the creation of new ones (O'Neil, 2016).

The Second Industrial Revolution (Late 19th to Early 20th Century)

The Second Industrial Revolution, which spanned into the early 20th century, ushered in a new era of technological advancements, including electricity, the internal combustion engine, and breakthroughs in chemical processed (Jordan & Mitchell, 2015). Henry Ford's innovations in the automobile industry epitomised the emergence of assembly lines and mass production during this era. Changes in employment were further expedited by the Second Industrial Revolution. Due to the assembly line's ability to produce things on a never-before-seen scale, the industrial sector saw job development, and new sectors including consumer and automotive goods emerged (Luckin et al., 2017). However, the tedious nature of assembly line work frequently resulted in job responsibilities that were repetitious, emphasising the necessity for workers to adapt to new jobs and skill sets (McCallister, 2018).

The Digital Revolution (Late 20th to Early 21st Century)

The late 20th century saw the Digital Revolution, driven by the rise of computers, the internet, and information technology. This era automated clerical tasks, gave rise to new industries like software development and cybersecurity, and transformed traditional ones with innovative tools (McKeown et al., 2018). Office automation streamlined administrative tasks, while internet-based technology enabled flexible work environments, improving work-life balance (Waters, 2014). The Digital Revolution also globalized the workforce, facilitating cross-border collaboration but increasing job competition and displacement in some regions (O'Neil, 2016). Additionally, it highlighted the need for continuous learning as technology rapidly evolved (Kulkarni et al., 2015).

AI AND THE FUTURE OF WORK: A HISTORICAL PERSPECTIVE

As we stand on the brink of the AI revolution, it is clear that AI technologies are following a similar trajectory to previous technological advancements in their capacity to transform job markets. Just as the steam engine and assembly line revolutionized production and work processes, AI is poised to redefine a wide range of job roles and industries (Jordan & Mitchell, 2015).

The ability of AI to automate intricate jobs, analyse large datasets, and improve decision-making processes is indicative of a trend that has been seen in previous revolutions. AI does, however, also bring with it special potential and problems. Artificial intelligence (AI) has the capacity to carry out activities that call for cognitive and analytical abilities in addition to routine ones, unlike earlier technologies. The future of employment, skill requirements, and job displacement are some of the new issues brought up by this innovation (O'Neil, 2016).

By examining historical contexts of technological change, we gain valuable insights into how AI might influence employment and job markets. Understanding these patterns helps situate the current AI-driven transformation within a broader historical narrative, providing a perspective on how previous technological revolutions have shaped work and what we might anticipate from this new wave of innovation (Luckin et al., 2017).

AI and the Future of Work

Artificial Intelligence (AI) is driving significant transformations across various sectors, reshaping job roles, and altering employment landscapes. This section explores how AI technologies are impacting industries such as healthcare, finance, and manufacturing, drawing on insights from recent research and published studies. (Mehrabi et al., 2021).

AI in Healthcare

AI technologies are transforming patient care and operational efficiency in healthcare, particularly in medical diagnostics. With unmatched speed and accuracy, AI outperforms human experts in analysing large datasets, improving medical imaging procedures like retinal scans to detect conditions such as macular degeneration and diabetic retinopathy. Systems like IBM's Watson Health use machine learning and natural language processing to examine vast patient data, providing treatment recommendations that match oncologists' decisions in 93% of cases (Somashekhar et al., 2018). AI also advances personalized medicine by analyzing data from multiple sources to suggest tailored treatment plans, enhancing decision-making and treatment outcomes. This data-driven approach holds great potential for improving diagnostics and patient care.

AI in Finance

AI is revolutionizing the finance sector, especially in trading, customer service, and fraud detection. AI-powered algorithms analyze market data and execute trades with greater speed and accuracy than human traders, improving strategies and market stability. In customer service, financial institutions use AI chatbots to handle inquiries, manage transactions, and offer personalized advice, enhancing satisfaction and cutting costs. Additionally, AI detects fraud by analyzing transaction data for unusual patterns, enabling faster responses to risks. Research by Ahmed et al. (2019) highlights how machine learning models proactively identify and mitigate fraud in real-time.

AI in Manufacturing

AI is transforming manufacturing by automating production processes, with robots handling tasks like welding, painting, and packaging, boosting efficiency and reducing human error. In supply chain management, AI-powered predictive analytics improve inventory control and streamline logistics, cutting costs from stockouts or overstocking. AI also enhances quality control, with computer vision systems detecting defects during production, ensuring high-quality products and reducing waste (Zhang et al., 2019). However, the automation of tasks raises concerns about job displacement, highlighting the need for reskilling and upskilling initiatives to adapt to evolving job demands (Luckin et al., 2017). As AI reshapes work, preparing for these changes is crucial for navigating the future of labor.

Job Displacement and Job Creation

Artificial Intelligence (AI) is reshaping the job market, offering both opportunities and challenges. While AI has the potential to disrupt existing roles, it also creates new ones, illustrating the concept of "creative destruction" (Brynjolfsson & McAfee, 2014; Arntz, Gregory, & Zierahn, 2016; Schumpeter, 1942). AI-driven automation threatens jobs in industries like manufacturing and administration by replacing roles in material handling, data entry, and scheduling. Research from the McKinsey Global Institute highlights those jobs involving repetitive tasks, particularly in transportation, logistics, and customer service, are at higher risk of displacement (Chui, Manyika, & Miremadi, 2016).

Creation of New Roles

While AI may displace some jobs, it also creates new opportunities that demand skills like human oversight, creativity, and problem-solving (Brynjolfsson & McAfee, 2014). Emerging roles include machine learning engineers, data scientists, AI ethicists, and cybersecurity experts, driven by AI's growth and its ethical, societal, and security challenges (Arntz, Gregory, & Zierahn, 2016). Additionally, industries like healthcare and banking are seeing new positions for managing AI-driven diagnostics, personalized treatments, and risk assessment algorithms (Chui, Manyika, & Miremadi, 2016). These roles highlight how AI fosters innovation across sectors while generating demand for specialized skills.

The World Economic Forum's report highlights that while automation may displace jobs, it also leads to the creation of new roles, especially in technology and data management, with two to three jobs created for everyone displaced (World Economic Forum, 2020). Schumpeter's concept of "creative destruction" is relevant here, as it describes how technological innovation both eliminates old jobs and industries while generating new opportunities (Schumpeter, 1942).

Creative destruction in AI involves the disruption of traditional industries through innovative and efficient AI technologies. For instance, the rise of digital platforms and e-commerce has transformed the retail sector, leading to the decline of brick-and-mortar stores while creating opportunities in digital marketing, online retail, and logistics. While short-term disruptions are expected, long-term benefits include increased productivity, economic growth, and new job sectors. Understanding creative destruction is key to navigating the AI-driven job market, emphasizing the need for reskilling and upskilling to adapt to these changes (Schumpeter, 1942).

Navigating the AI Revolution: A Path Forward

AI's impact on employment is a complex mix of job creation and displacement. While AI automates routine tasks, it also generates new roles that leverage human creativity and skills. The concept of "creative destruction" highlights the dynamic nature of technological progress, emphasizing the need for ongoing learning and adaptation (Schumpeter, 1942). Understanding these shifts helps stakeholders navigate the evolving job market, maximizing AI's benefits while addressing job displacement. Reskilling and upskilling efforts are essential for a smooth transition and to prepare the workforce for AI-driven opportunities (Arntz, Gregory, & Zierahn, 2016).

Ethical AI development is crucial to ensure human values are upheld. Promoting responsible AI practices can mitigate risks and help harness its potential for societal good. Despite challenges, investing in human capital and preparing for AI's dual impact will be key to future success. AI is reshaping the skills required in the workforce, widening the gap between current abilities and employer needs. As AI automates tasks, demand grows for technical skills like data analysis and machine learning, as well as soft skills such as creativity and emotional intelligence. The World Economic Forum predicts that half of all workers will need reskilling by 2025 to keep pace with AI-driven changes. Lifelong learning will be essential for adapting to these shifts, reducing the risk of job loss, and embracing new opportunities (Brynjolfsson & McAfee, 2014; Bessen, 2019). Continuous learning also benefits organizations by creating a more adaptable workforce that can innovate and stay competitive in a rapidly changing environment (Harris & Boud, 2021; Cappelli, 2020).

Examples of Successful Reskilling Initiatives

Many organizations recognize the need for reskilling and upskilling to address the skills gap created by AI advancements. For example, Amazon's "Upskilling 2025" initiative aims to retrain a third of its U.S. workforce in cloud computing, machine learning, and software engineering. The program offers various training options, from classroom instruction to online learning, enabling employees to transition into technical roles (Amazon, 2023).

Similarly, AT&T has partnered with Georgia Tech to create the "AT&T Future Ready" program, which provides employees with skills in data science, cybersecurity, and software development through online courses and degree programs. This investment has successfully transitioned many employees into new roles, helping AT&T maintain its competitive edge (AT&T, 2022).

In Europe, Siemens has launched the "Siemens Professional Education" program, combining traditional vocational training with digital learning to equip employees with skills necessary for digitalization and automation technologies. This initiative effectively prepares Siemens' workforce for roles requiring advanced technical knowledge (Siemens, 2021).

As AI reshapes the job market, reskilling and upskilling are essential for ensuring workforce readiness. Successful programs by Amazon, AT&T, and Siemens highlight the importance of investing in employee development, driving both organizational growth and workforce resilience (Amazon, 2023; AT&T, 2022; Siemens, 2021). By fostering a culture of lifelong learning and prioritizing reskilling, organizations and individuals can navigate technological change and emerge stronger in an AI-augmented future.

Ethical Considerations in AI-Driven Automation

As AI systems permeate modern life, their ethical implications come under increasing scrutiny. From healthcare to finance and education, AI technologies present novel challenges that demand ethical guidance. Traditional ethical frameworks, which have guided human behavior for centuries, must now adapt to these dilemmas, helping to steer the development and deployment of AI in a responsible manner. In this section, we will explore how classical ethical theories—utilitarianism, deontology, and virtue ethics—apply to AI-driven automation, alongside the emerging field of AI ethics, which addresses the unique issues posed by machine learning and algorithmic decision-making.

Utilitarianism in the Context of AI

Utilitarianism, a consequentialist theory, evaluates actions based on their ability to maximize overall happiness. AI applications, like healthcare, can enhance societal well-being by reducing errors and improving efficiency. However, utilitarian applications in AI can perpetuate biases or infringe on individual rights. For instance, AI applications in healthcare are designed to enhance patient outcomes by minimizing errors and optimizing efficiency. Robotic surgeries, AI-assisted diagnostic tools, and predictive analytics can substantially reduce human error, leading to improved healthcare outcomes (Topol, 2019). Additionally, a utilitarian focus can justify morally questionable actions, such as mass layoffs, to maximize corporate productivity. While utilitarian approaches can benefit society, they often struggle to balance aggregate benefits with individual well-being in AI applications (Floridi et al., 2018).

Deontology and the Moral Limits of AI

Deontology, a moral philosophy emphasizing duties and principles over consequences, is relevant in AI ethics. AI systems, like workplace surveillance, can raise ethical questions about privacy. Deontological ethics prioritizes individual rights, such as privacy and dignity, over organizational objectives. In AI-driven decisions, accountability cannot be diffused; human agents must be responsible for the actions of AI systems (Santoni de Sio & van den Hoven, 2018). This notion presents a significant challenge for AI developers and policymakers, who must navigate complex questions of liability and moral responsibility (Zuboff, 2019).

For example, AI systems used for workplace surveillance raise ethical questions when they prioritize efficiency at the cost of privacy. While constant monitoring may enhance productivity by ensuring employees remain on task, it may also violate workers' right to privacy and their dignity as autonomous individuals. According to deontological ethics, these rights should take precedence over any productivity gains the company might achieve (Zuboff, 2019). In this case, deontology offers a framework for balancing the pursuit of organizational objectives with the protection of individual liberties.

This notion presents a significant challenge for AI developers and policymakers, who must navigate complex questions of liability and moral responsibility.

Virtue Ethics and AI's Impact on Human Character

Virtue ethics focuses on character development and the cultivation of virtues like honesty and courage. AI technologies, like personalized learning platforms, can promote virtues like curiosity and perseverance (Howard et al., 2022). However, excessive reliance on AI might diminish certain virtues, such as critical thinking and problem-solving skills (Danaher, 2017). Virtue ethics also highlights the importance of moral character in AI developers and companies. This ethical framework encourages us to consider how AI technologies shape not only outcomes but also human behavior and character.

For example, AI-driven educational tools such as personalized learning platforms can promote virtues like curiosity and perseverance by adapting to individual learning needs. These tools offer tailored instruction that fosters critical thinking and intellectual growth, helping students develop virtues essential for personal and professional success (Howard et al., 2022). However, there are concerns that excessive reliance on AI could diminish certain virtues. In the workplace, for instance, AI-driven automation might encourage a culture of dependency, where workers no longer need to exercise critical judgment, creativity, or problem-solving skills because machines handle those tasks (Danaher, 2017).

AI Ethics: A New Frontier

Traditional ethical frameworks provide insights into AI's moral implications but often fall short in addressing challenges posed by machine learning and algorithmic decision-making. Consequently, AI ethics has emerged to tackle these unique dilemmas associated with machine decision-making. One fundamental principle is beneficence and non-maleficence, emphasizing that AI systems should benefit individuals and society while minimizing harm (Jobin et al., 2019). In healthcare, for instance, AI technologies must enhance patient outcomes and ensure safety, particularly with AI-assisted diagnostic tools.

Another critical principle is autonomy, which asserts that AI should respect human autonomy by empowering individuals to make informed decisions. In high-stakes areas like credit scoring or hiring, predictive algorithms influence significant life choices. AI ethics advocates for transparency, enabling individuals to understand decision-making processes and challenge unfair outcomes (Binns, 2018).

Justice and fairness are also vital in AI ethics. Systems must be designed and audited to prevent bias or discrimination, as AI can replicate biases present in training data. Rigorous testing is essential, especially in critical domains like criminal justice, healthcare, and employment (Floridi et al., 2018).

As AI evolves, new ethical challenges arise, including the black box problem, where deep learning systems make decisions that are hard for humans to interpret (Rudin, 2019). This opacity complicates accountability and trust, raising concerns about human control over AI systems. Moreover, the concentration of power in AI development is alarming, with a few tech companies dominating the field and controlling essential resources. This situation fosters monopolistic behavior, data privacy issues, and potential misuse for surveillance or manipulation (Zuboff, 2019). As AI becomes more integrated into daily life, these challenges necessitate careful ethical consideration and regulatory oversight.

Fairness, Transparency, and Accountability in AI Algorithms

The growing integration of artificial intelligence (AI) into various sectors—such as criminal justice, healthcare, finance, and hiring—has amplified concerns around fairness, transparency, and accountability. AI systems can produce significant societal impacts, often affecting decisions about individuals' lives. However, issues related to bias, discrimination, and lack of transparency can undermine their effectiveness and fairness. Ensuring these systems operate ethically has become a major challenge, particularly as AI is increasingly deployed in high-stakes decision-making.

Bias in AI Algorithms

Bias in AI arises from the data used to train algorithms, which can perpetuate historical prejudices and systemic inequalities. This is especially concerning in areas like hiring, law enforcement, and lending, where biased decisions can impact opportunities and rights (Mehrabi et al., 2021).

1. **Data Bias**: AI's fairness depends heavily on its training data. If the data reflects past inequalities, AI systems may reinforce those biases. For instance, a hiring algorithm trained on a predominantly male workforce might favour male candidates, even when female candidates are equally qualified. This issue has been observed in recruitment processes where AI replicated unequal treatment (Raji & Buolamwini, 2019).
2. **Algorithmic Bias**: Bias can also stem from algorithm design. For example, ad-targeting algorithms optimized for clicks may disproportionately show job ads to men or wealthier individuals, reinforcing socio-economic divides and limiting opportunities for marginalized groups (Noble, 2018).

Discrimination in AI Systems

AI systems can lead to discriminatory outcomes, unfairly disadvantaging specific demographic groups based on race, gender, age, or socioeconomic status.

1. **Discriminatory Outcomes**: AI discrimination is evident in criminal justice, where risk assessment tools like COMPAS have been shown to disproportionately label Black defendants as high-risk compared to white defendants, even when other factors are controlled. This results from historical biases in the training data, perpetuating systemic inequalities (Angwin et al., 2016).
2. **Access Discrimination**: In finance and healthcare, AI can restrict access to essential services. Credit-scoring algorithms may assign lower scores to low-income individuals, deepening their marginalization. Similarly, healthcare algorithms that ignore socioeconomic factors can lead to unequal resource distribution and care (Obermeyer et al., 2019).

Transparency in AI Algorithms

Achieving transparency in AI systems is crucial for fostering trust and ensuring fairness. However, many AI models, especially advanced ones like deep learning networks, operate as "black boxes," where their internal decision-making processes are difficult, if not impossible, to interpret.

The Black Box Problem: Complex AI systems, especially deep learning models, are often non-interpretable, making it difficult for users to understand how decisions are made. For example, if a loan application is rejected, the applicant may not know why their application was denied. This lack of transparency significantly hinders the identification of errors, correction of biases, and overall accountability in the decision-making process (Doshi-Velez & Kim, 2017).

Explainability: Explainable AI (XAI) seeks to make AI decisions more understandable in human terms, which is crucial in critical areas like healthcare where decisions profoundly impact patient care and outcomes. However, there is often a trade-off: more accurate models tend to be less interpretable, while simpler, more interpretable models may sacrifice some accuracy and effectiveness (Arrieta et al., 2020).

Accountability in AI Systems

Determining accountability for AI systems is a complex challenge, particularly when it comes to assigning responsibility for decisions or outcomes that cause harm.

1. **Moral Responsibility**: Moral responsibility in AI involves determining who is accountable when AI systems make harmful or incorrect decisions. For instance, if an AI-powered credit system wrongly denies a loan, it's unclear whether the blame lies with the developers, the organization, or the system itself. This lack of clear accountability limits recourse for those affected by biased or erroneous outcomes (Crawford, 2021).
2. **Legal Accountability**: Legal frameworks for AI accountability are still developing. The EU's proposed AI Act seeks to enforce transparency and documentation of AI decisions, but regional variations in regulations make harmonizing these frameworks a challenge (Floridi et al., 2018).

Case Studies of Ethical Dilemmas in AI Deployment

Several real-world case studies illustrate the ethical dilemmas and challenges surrounding fairness, transparency, and accountability in AI systems.

COMPAS Recidivism Risk Assessment: The COMPAS tool, used in the U.S. to predict re-offending, disproportionately labels Black defendants as higher risk compared to white defendants, even when controlling for similar factors (Angwin et al., 2016). Its proprietary nature, lacking transparency, complicates accountability and raises fairness concerns, especially given its significant impact on sentencing decisions (Rudin, 2019).

Amazon's AI Recruiting Tool: Amazon's AI recruiting tool, designed to streamline hiring, exhibited gender bias by favoring resumes with male-associated terms. This bias stemmed from training data that reflected a predominantly male workforce. After discovering this issue, Amazon discontinued the tool, underscoring the risks of biased data in AI applications (Dastin, 2018; Binns, 2018).
Facial Recognition Technology: Facial recognition systems have been criticized for inaccuracies, particularly in misidentifying individuals with darker skin tones, women, and minority groups. A 2018 NIST study found higher error rates among these groups, highlighting concerns over fairness, privacy, and potential misuse in surveillance, especially by law enforcement (Buolamwini & Gebru, 2018; Garvie et al., 2019).

Addressing fairness, transparency, and accountability in AI is crucial for its ethical use. As seen in the cases of COMPAS, Amazon's recruiting tool, and facial recognition technology, biases in AI can perpetuate social inequalities, while the lack of transparency and accountability leaves significant ethical and legal questions unresolved. Robust regulatory frameworks are necessary to ensure AI is deployed responsibly.

Reimagining Work in an AI-Driven Economy

AI is transforming the concept of meaningful work, redefining the social contract, and introducing both opportunities and challenges for inclusive growth and workforce engagement.

Meaningful Work in an AI-Driven Economy: Traditionally, meaningful work is seen as providing a sense of direction, personal fulfilment, and alignment with one's values (Harter, Schmidt, & Hayes, 2002). However, AI is reshaping this dynamic. By automating repetitive tasks, AI allows employees to focus on more creative and fulfilling activities, such as interpersonal relations, problem-solving, and strategy, potentially enhancing job satisfaction and purpose (Brynjolfsson & McAfee, 2014).
Challenges of Job Displacement: While AI frees workers for more meaningful tasks, it also creates concerns about job displacement and skill mismatches. Roles susceptible to automation may become obsolete, leading to a need for reskilling and shifting how individuals experience meaningful work (Arntz, Gregory, & Zierahn, 2016).

Fostering Innovation and Creativity: AI offers immense potential for fostering innovation, enabling people to explore new ideas and create original content. For instance, AI can assist researchers in identifying patterns and artists in generating unique works (Elgammal, Liu, Elhoseiny, & Mazzoni, 2017). Additionally, AI can democratize creativity by making sophisticated tools accessible to a broader audience, expanding creative opportunities (Miller, 2020). However, excessive reliance on AI could undermine human creativity if not managed thoughtfully (Boden, 2016).

REDEFINING THE SOCIAL CONTRACT

Changes in Labor Laws and Contracts

The rise of AI necessitates a re-evaluation of job contracts and labor laws. Traditional frameworks may no longer adequately address the needs of gig workers, remote employees, and those affected by AI-driven job displacement. Updated labor legislation should focus on ensuring fair compensation, job security, and the rights of non-traditional workers (Susskind & Susskind, 2015). Employment contracts may also need revisions to reflect new work dynamics, including provisions for data privacy, remote work, and the ethical use of AI. Adapting contracts to the evolving workplace is essential to maintain fairness and equitable job conditions.

Role of Unions and Worker Representation

To tackle AI-related challenges, traditional unions may need to evolve. Historically vital for workers' rights, unions now must address issues like skill development, job displacement, and fair pay (Berg, 2016). New forms of representation, such as worker cooperatives and digital platforms, may emerge to meet workforce needs, offering innovative approaches to advocacy and collective bargaining (Spreitzer & Porath, 2012).

Strategies for Inclusive Growth and Workforce Participation

Ensuring Equitable Benefits from AI

To ensure AI-driven economic growth benefits all of society, it's vital to implement laws and practices that support inclusive growth. This includes investing in education and reskilling programs to prepare people for new AI-related jobs and mitigate job displacement (Bessen, 2019). Education should focus on digital literacy, critical thinking, and adaptability, while reskilling programs help workers transition to new roles and sectors (Chui, Manyika, & Miremadi, 2016).

Examples of Inclusive Growth Initiatives

Successful initiatives, like Microsoft's AI for Accessibility and Google's AI for Social Good, leverage AI to address societal challenges and support marginalized groups (Google, 2018; Microsoft, 2020). Government-led reskilling efforts, such as the EU's Upskilling Pathways project, also demonstrate the importance of targeted interventions for inclusive growth (European Commission, 2016).

AI in Healthcare

Artificial intelligence (AI) is increasingly transforming the healthcare industry, impacting both clinical and administrative functions. This section explores how AI is reshaping healthcare, highlighting its benefits and addressing ethical and employment implications.

AI's Impact on Clinical Care

AI enhances personalization and diagnostic accuracy in clinical settings, particularly in medical image analysis like X-rays, MRIs, and CT scans. For example, Google's DeepMind AI has demonstrated high accuracy in identifying age-related macular degeneration and diabetic retinopathy from retinal scans, often surpassing human radiologists (Abràmoff et al., 2018; De Fauw et al., 2018). This leads to earlier and more precise diagnoses.

AI also aids in personalized medicine. Tools like IBM Watson for Oncology analyze large datasets, including medical records and literature, to recommend individualized cancer treatments, improving treatment outcomes (Somashekhar et al., 2018).

AI's Role in Administrative Efficiency

AI reduces inefficiencies and streamlines administrative tasks in healthcare, such as scheduling, resource allocation, and EHR management. Automated billing and scheduling free up staff to focus on patient care (Jiang et al., 2017). AI-powered chatbots and virtual assistants also improve patient engagement by assisting with appointment scheduling and providing quick responses (O'Donoghue et al., 2016).

However, AI in healthcare raises ethical concerns, including algorithmic bias. AI systems trained on non-representative data may reinforce health inequities, leading to unequal outcomes (Obermeyer et al., 2019). Data privacy is another issue, as AI relies on vast amounts of sensitive patient information, necessitating robust security measures and adherence to regulations like GDPR (Reddy et al., 2019).

AI's impact on employment is mixed. While it can enhance job satisfaction by reducing administrative workloads, it may also displace workers in administrative roles, as automation takes over tasks like billing and scheduling (Davenport & Kalakota, 2019). Healthcare professionals will need retraining to work effectively with AI tools.

In summary, AI is transforming healthcare by improving efficiency, personalizing care, and enhancing diagnostics, but its ethical and practical challenges must be addressed to ensure equitable use.

AI in Finance

Artificial Intelligence (AI) is rapidly transforming the finance sector, enhancing efficiency and accuracy across various functions, from trading to fraud detection (Brynjolfsson & McAfee, 2014). However, this technological shift also brings significant implications for employment and raises important ethical considerations.

AI in Financial Services

1.AutomatedTrading

AI has transformed trading through algorithms that process vast amounts of data and execute trades quickly. High-frequency trading (HFT) systems use AI to identify patterns and trade within milliseconds, benefiting from minor market changes. AI-powered trading systems improve market liquidity by analyzing large datasets faster and more accurately than human traders, leading to lower trading costs and more efficient price discovery. However, they also pose risks, as algorithmic trading can contribute to market instability during volatile periods or technical failures. Flash crashes have been linked to high-frequency trading systems. Additionally, the competitive advantage gained by firms with advanced trading algorithms can exacerbate market inequalities. (Aldridge, 2013; Zhang et al., 2019; Barndorff-Nielsen et al., 2019; Baker, 2020)

2. Fraud Detection

AI detects fraud by analyzing transactions and identifying suspicious patterns. Machine learning models compare transactions to historical data and recognize fraud patterns. (Ngai et al., 2011) AI systems improve fraud detection accuracy and speed, reducing financial losses and enhancing security. They adapt to new fraud tactics by learning from new data. (Dua & Gupta, 2020) However, AI systems are not perfect. False positives can occur, leading to customer inconvenience. (Mikalef et al., 2020) Fraudsters constantly adapt their methods, requiring AI systems to be updated and maintained.

Impact on Employment

1. Job Displacement and Creation

AI in finance has mixed effects on employment. Automation can reduce the need for certain roles, leading to job displacement. (Susskind & Susskind, 2015) However, it also creates new opportunities in AI system development, data science, and cybersecurity.

Automation may lead to job losses for positions that are highly susceptible to automation. Workers in roles such as trading support and manual data entry are at risk. (Brynjolfsson & McAfee, 2014). The demand for AI specialists, data scientists, and cybersecurity experts is growing. Financial institutions require skilled professionals to develop, manage, and secure AI systems, leading to new job opportunities. (Bessen, 2019)

2. Skill Requirements

As AI reshapes the finance sector, there is an increasing need for workers with skills in AI and data analytics. Financial professionals must adapt by acquiring new skills and competencies to remain relevant in a changing job market (World Economic Forum, 2020). This shift emphasizes the importance of reskilling and upskilling programs to prepare the workforce for the evolving demands of the industry. Training initiatives focusing on data literacy, critical thinking, and emotional intelligence will be crucial in complementing technical skills (Chui et al., 2016).

Ethical Concerns

1. Bias and Fairness

AI's Perpetuation of Bias in Finance

AI systems can inadvertently perpetuate existing societal biases if trained on historical data that reflects these inequalities. For instance, algorithms used in credit scoring or loan approvals might unfairly disadvantage specific groups due to biased training data. (Obermeyer et al., 2019)

Mitigating Bias in AI Systems: To address this issue, it is imperative to implement strategies to detect and mitigate bias in AI systems. This involves ensuring that training data is diverse and representative, conducting regular audits to identify and rectify biases, and fostering collaboration among multidisciplinary teams in the development and oversight of AI technologies. (Gonzalez et al., 2020)

2. **Privacy and Security**

The use of AI in finance involves the collection and analysis of large volumes of personal and financial data. Ensuring the privacy and security of this data is essential to protect individuals from breaches and misuse (Zhang et al., 2019).

Protection: Financial institutions must adopt robust data protection practices, including encryption, access controls, and secure data storage. Additionally, transparency about data usage and consent mechanisms are important for maintaining customer trust and complying with privacy regulations (Kshetri, 2020).

3. Accountability

When AI systems make decisions that affect individuals, such as credit approvals or fraud alerts, establishing accountability is crucial. Determining who is responsible for AI-driven decisions—whether it be the developers, the institution, or the AI system itself—can be complex but is necessary for addressing errors and ensuring fair treatment (Binns, 2018).

Responsibility: Organizations should implement clear guidelines for accountability and decision-making processes involving AI. This includes maintaining human oversight, providing explanations for AI-driven decisions, and establishing mechanisms for addressing grievances and disputes (Shadbolt et al., 2018).

4. The Role of Regulations

AI in Finance: Balancing Benefits and Challenges

AI offers numerous benefits in finance, such as enhanced efficiency and fraud detection. However, it also presents challenges related to employment, fairness, and data privacy. Effective regulations are crucial to promote innovation, safeguard consumer rights, and ensure ethical practices. (Liu & Zhang, 2021) Addressing these issues requires a balanced approach that considers the ethical implications of AI technologies and ensures responsible implementation across the finance sector.

AI in Manufacturing and Logistics

AI is transforming manufacturing and logistics by automating production lines and optimizing supply chains (Jha et al., 2019). This technological advancement brings both opportunities and challenges, particularly concerning job displacement and the evolving role of human workers.

Automation in Production Lines

1. Advanced Robotics and Automation

AI-powered robotics are transforming production lines by performing repetitive tasks with precision and efficiency. Modern AI-equipped robots can manage complex assembly, inspect for defects, and adapt to process changes (Kumar et al., 2020).

Benefits: AI-driven automation boosts production speed, reduces errors, and enhances product quality (Wang et al., 2021). Robots work continuously, increasing throughput and consistency, while improving safety by handling hazardous tasks (Bortolini et al., 2018).

Challenges: Implementing AI in manufacturing demands high capital investment and technical integration with existing systems (Bengio et al., 2021). There are also concerns over equipment malfunctions and maintenance needs.

AI in Supply Chain Optimization

Predictive Analytics & Demand Forecasting: AI improves supply chain management by analyzing data and market trends for more accurate demand forecasting, optimizing inventory, and reducing waste (Davis & Hines, 2020).

Benefits: Better forecasting enhances inventory management and optimizes logistics, minimizing delays and transportation costs (Sodhi & Tang, 2020).

Challenges: AI relies on accurate data; poor data or disruptions can compromise predictions, highlighting the need for strong data management and contingency plans (Guan et al., 2021).

Job Displacement

1. Impact on Traditional Manufacturing Jobs

The rise of AI in manufacturing often leads to the displacement of traditional jobs, especially those involving routine, manual tasks like assembly line work and quality control, as these roles are increasingly automated (Chui et al., 2016).

Displacement: Automation can result in job losses as companies aim to cut labor costs and boost efficiency. Workers in easily automated roles face unemployment or fewer job opportunities (Susskind & Susskind, 2015; Brynjolfsson & McAfee, 2014).
Transition: To address job displacement, reskilling and upskilling programs are crucial. Workers can be trained for roles in robotics maintenance, AI management, and data analysis, which are less prone to automation (Kang et al., 2020).

The Future Role of Human Workers

1. **Human-AI Collaboration**: Human workers will remain essential in manufacturing, working alongside AI systems. AI complements rather than replaces human skills (McKinsey & Company, 2021). Future roles will emphasize creativity, problem-solving, and decision-making, areas where AI is limited (Brynjolfsson & McAfee, 2014).
   Skills: Workers with technical skills, critical thinking, and adaptability, who can operate and troubleshoot AI systems, will be in demand (World Economic Forum, 2020).
2. **Enhanced Work Environments**: AI can improve work environments by handling dangerous or monotonous tasks, allowing workers to take on more engaging roles, increasing job satisfaction and productivity (Jha et al., 2019).
3. **Ethical Considerations**: As AI transforms industries, ethical concerns about job displacement and worker welfare must be addressed. Companies should support workers with reskilling and fair transition opportunities (Jain et al., 2020).

In summary, while AI enhances efficiency and supply chain management, it also challenges the workforce through job displacement. Balancing automation with worker support is key to the future of work in these sectors.

AI in Education and Training

Artificial intelligence (AI) is transforming education by changing how content is delivered and how students learn. The integration of AI-driven tools is enhancing personalized learning, making education more accessible, and streamlining administrative tasks. This section explores the role of AI in reshaping educational methods and delivery, while also considering its implications for teachers, administrators, and students.

AI's Impact on Educational Methods

Individualized Learning and Adaptive Platforms

By offering individualised learning experiences catered to the needs of each student, artificial intelligence is revolutionising the delivery of knowledge. DreamBox and Knewton are two examples of adaptive learning platforms that use real-time analysis of student performance data to modify the degree of difficulty in lessons so that each student learns at their own speed (Luckin et al., 2017). This data-driven method facilitates the identification of students' areas of difficulty and offers prompt feedback, enabling more focused interventions and enhancing learning results all around.

Furthermore, AI is making it easier to use intelligent teaching systems (ITS), which function as online teachers. These programs can mimic the one-on-one assistance that human tutors usually provide, providing thorough explanations and prompt responses to enquiries. This strategy has worked well in disciplines like science and maths, where interactive teaching systems (ITS) such as Carnegie Learning have improved student performance by simulating the interactive methods used by human teachers (Jordan & Mitchell, 2015).

The accessibility of instructional content is also being improved by AI. More inclusive learning resources are available to non-native speakers and students with impairments thanks to tools like AI-driven language translation software and automated transcription services. This guarantees that more students, irrespective of their aptitudes or experiences, can gain from excellent education.

Changing Role of Teachers

The introduction of AI in education is reshaping the role of teachers. AI tools can take over administrative tasks, such as grading and attendance tracking, allowing educators to dedicate more time to teaching and student interaction (McKeown et al., 2018). Automated grading systems, especially in subjects like math or multiple-choice assessments, reduce the burden on teachers, while ensuring that grading is consistent and fair.

AI's rise requires teachers to gain new skills for integrating technology into their classrooms. Educators need training to use AI tools, interpret data from learning platforms, and adjust teaching methods, accordingly, highlighting the need for ongoing professional development.

For administrators, AI streamlines school management by automating tasks like student enrolment and analyzing performance data. This enables better resource allocation, improved student outcomes, and more effective solutions to challenges like dropout rates.

AI also enhances student learning by providing rapid feedback and personalized learning paths. However, there's a risk of students becoming overly reliant on AI, potentially weakening critical thinking and problem-solving skills (Kulkarni et al., 2015). Balancing AI use with human-driven, inquiry-based education is crucial.

Overall, AI is transforming education by enabling personalized learning, reducing administrative tasks for teachers, and expanding access to education. Ensuring AI enhances, rather than diminishes, the human aspects of teaching and learning requires thoughtful integration and role definition for both educators and students.

Regulatory Frameworks for Ethical AI

1. **Existing Regulation**

Several regions have introduced regulations aimed at governing AI ethics and usage.

For example:

European Union (EU): The EU's Artificial Intelligence Act, proposed in April 2021, seeks to create a regulatory framework for AI, categorizing applications by risk levels (low, high, unacceptable). High-risk applications, like those in healthcare and infrastructure, face stricter regulations, including human oversight and conformity assessments. This reflects the EU's commitment to aligning AI with European values like privacy and human rights, potentially influencing global AI standards (European Commission, 2021).

United States: AI regulation in the U.S. is fragmented, with state-level and sector-specific rules. The National Institute of Standards and Technology (NIST) has developed AI risk management guidelines focused on fairness, explainability, and security. However, the lack of a unified federal framework creates concerns about inconsistent practices, complicating compliance for businesses nationwide (Binns, 2018).

Proposed Regulation: Future regulations are likely to focus on:

1. **Global Standards**: Developing international standards for AI ethics and safety, with efforts from organizations like the OECD and ISO, to create universal guidelines for ethical AI development (OECD, 2019).

2. **Algorithmic Transparency**: Requiring transparency in AI algorithms, ensuring accountability and allowing users to understand and challenge AI-driven decisions (Ananny & Crawford, 2018).
3. **Data Protection**: Strengthening data privacy regulations, enforcing laws like GDPR to protect individuals from AI misuse and ensure ethical handling of personal data (Voigt & Von dem Bussche, 2017).

Promoting Responsible AI Development and Use

1. **Guidelines for Ethical AI Development**

To promote responsible AI development, several key guidelines should be followed:

Bias and Fairness: Adopt practices to detect and mitigate bias in AI systems, including using diverse datasets, conducting regular audits, and involving interdisciplinary teams to review AI models. Ignoring bias can lead to discriminatory outcomes, harming marginalized groups and undermining AI fairness (Barocas et al., 2019).

Transparency and Explainability: Ensure AI systems are transparent and can be explained. Providing clear documentation and communication about how algorithms function helps build trust, allowing users to validate or challenge decisions. Clear explanations are crucial for ethical AI governance (Lipton, 2018).

Accountability and Governance: Establish accountability structures by defining roles for developers, operators, and users. Implement governance frameworks to manage AI risks and ensure adherence to ethical standards, guiding organizations in navigating AI complexities (Jobin et al., 2019).

Best Practices for AI Deployment:

1. **Ethical Impact Assessments**: Conduct assessments to evaluate AI's ethical, social, and economic impacts before deployment, identifying risks and aligning systems with societal values (HLEG, 2019).
2. **User Training and Support**: Provide users with training to understand AI's functionalities, limitations, and biases, ensuring informed use and responsible interaction with AI technologies (Mason, 2020).
3. **Continuous Monitoring and Improvement**: Implement ongoing monitoring of AI systems to assess performance, accuracy, and compliance with ethical standards, making adjustments as necessary to maintain alignment with societal expectations (Crawford & Calo, 2016).

1. Educational Institutions

    Curriculum Development: Update educational curricula to include AI-related subjects, such as data science, machine learning, and ethics. Offering specialized courses and degree programs in AI and related fields can equip students with the skills needed for future job markets. As AI technologies evolve, educational institutions must adapt to ensure that their graduates are prepared to meet the demands of an increasingly AI-driven workforce (Luckin et al., 2016).

    Collaborative Programs: Foster partnerships between educational institutions and industry to create practical training programs and internships. Collaboration with businesses can provide students with hands-on experience and exposure to real-world applications of AI. By bridging the gap between academia and industry, students can gain valuable insights into the practical applications of their studies and develop the skills needed for successful careers in AI (Deloitte, 2020).

2. Government Initiatives

    Reskilling and Upskilling: Implement reskilling and upskilling programs for the current workforce to adapt to AI-driven changes. Government-supported initiatives, such as vocational training and adult education programs, can help workers transition to new roles and industries. As automation continues to reshape job markets, proactive measures must be taken to ensure that displaced workers can find new employment opportunities (World Economic Forum, 2018).

    Policy Support: Develop policies that support workforce development and address the challenges of automation. This includes funding for educational programs, incentives for businesses to invest in employee training, and support for displaced workers. Comprehensive policy frameworks can facilitate workforce transitions and promote economic resilience in the face of technological advancements (Autor, 2015).

3. Business Sector

    Internal Training Programs: Companies should invest in internal training programs to upskill employees and prepare them for roles involving AI technologies. Providing ongoing education and professional development opportunities helps employees stay current with industry advancements and fosters a culture of continuous learning (Brynjolfsson & McAfee, 2014).

Talent Acquisition: Recruit talent with expertise in AI and related fields. By attracting skilled professionals, businesses can build a workforce capable of leveraging AI technologies effectively and driving innovation. Organizations must prioritize talent acquisition strategies that focus on building diverse teams with varied skill sets to enhance creativity and problem-solving capabilities (Gonzalez et al., 2018)

Encouraging Public and Private Sector Collaboration

1. **Public-Private Partnerships**

    Collaborative Research: Foster partnerships between governments, businesses, and academic institutions to advance AI research. Collaborative initiatives can drive innovation, tackle complex challenges, and ensure AI technologies meet societal needs by combining academic rigor with practical applications (Chui et al., 2016).

    Shared Resources: Utilize resources from both public and private sectors to address AI-related challenges. Joint initiatives like data repositories and research centers can enhance AI development. By pooling resources, stakeholders can address common issues more effectively, creating solutions that benefit society (Deloitte, 2020).

Multi-Stakeholder Engagement

Inclusive Dialogues: Engage a broad range of stakeholders—industry leaders, policymakers, ethicists, and civil society—in discussions on AI governance and ethics. Including diverse perspectives ensures policies reflect societal values and leads to more equitable outcomes (Ponce et al., 2020).

Community Involvement: Involve communities in AI development to address their specific concerns. Engaging local stakeholders ensures AI solutions are equitable and beneficial, with feedback helping to design systems that serve diverse populations (HLEG, 2019).

Addressing Global Challenges

International Cooperation: Promote international collaboration to address global AI challenges like data flows, cybersecurity, and ethical standards. Harmonized regulations and best practices developed through cooperation are essential for responsible AI use globally (OECD, 2020).

Global Frameworks: Support global agreements to guide the ethical development of AI. Organizations like the UN and World Economic Forum can help create common principles for AI governance, ensuring consistent ethical standards and mitigating risks (World Economic Forum, 2020).

In summary, building strong regulatory frameworks, promoting responsible AI practices, preparing the workforce, and encouraging collaboration are key to navigating AI's challenges and opportunities. Implementing these measures will ensure AI benefits society while upholding ethical standards.

CONCLUSION

This chapter's examination of AI's effects on employment and the nature of work in the future highlights both the technology's revolutionary potential and its associated difficulties. AI's ability to revolutionize industries such as healthcare, finance, manufacturing, and education is undeniable. It enables efficiency, cost reduction, and innovation across sectors. However, these advancements come at the cost of displacing traditional roles, creating a paradox where technological progress simultaneously generates new opportunities while phasing out established jobs.

One of the most critical findings is the dual nature of AI's influence on employment. On one hand, AI-driven automation streamlines repetitive tasks, improves productivity, and enables human workers to focus on higher-level functions, such as creativity and complex problem-solving. Sectors like healthcare benefit from AI in diagnostic accuracy and personalized treatment, while finance and manufacturing leverage AI for process optimization and fraud detection (Luckin et al., 2017; Chui et al., 2016). These developments highlight AI's capacity to unlock new industries and roles, fostering economic growth and technological innovation. Emerging professions such as machine learning engineers, AI ethicists, and data scientists are just a few examples of jobs created by AI's rise (Brynjolfsson & McAfee, 2014).

However, the advantages of AI must be weighed against its disruptive effects, particularly regarding job displacement. The automation of routine tasks, especially in industries like manufacturing and logistics, threatens to replace roles such as assembly line workers and quality control inspectors (Susskind & Susskind, 2015). This shift is especially concerning for workers whose roles are easily automated, often leaving them without alternative employment options. Moreover, the rapid pace of AI adoption intensifies these challenges, making it imperative for policymakers and industry leaders to prioritize reskilling and upskilling initiatives.

A significant disadvantage noted throughout this chapter is the unequal impact AI may have on different demographic groups. AI systems, if trained on biased data, can perpetuate existing inequalities, leading to unfair outcomes in areas like hiring, lending, and law enforcement (Barocas et al., 2019). Ethical considerations surrounding AI's deployment highlight the importance of fairness, transparency, and accountability in developing and using these technologies. If left unchecked, AI can exacerbate social divides, making equitable access to opportunities more difficult for marginalized communities.

Looking toward the future, ongoing research and development must address AI's limitations, particularly concerning ethical AI governance. Regulatory frameworks, such as the EU's Artificial Intelligence Act, which seeks to categorize AI applications based on their risk and enforce transparency and accountability measures, provide a foundation for responsible AI use (European Commission, 2021). However, the fragmented approach to AI regulation in places like the U.S., where state-level and sector-specific guidelines exist without a cohesive federal framework, complicates the landscape and may hinder progress toward a globally consistent standard (Binns, 2018).

Future research should also focus on creating global standards for AI ethics and safety, promoting international cooperation to ensure that AI technologies benefit all of society, not just select regions or groups. This includes exploring ways to make AI more transparent and explainable, particularly in high-stakes areas like healthcare and finance, where the decisions AI systems make can significantly impact people's lives (Ananny & Crawford, 2018). Additionally, research should explore how to mitigate the risks of job displacement by identifying sectors where AI and human workers can collaborate most effectively.

In conclusion, AI holds great promise in reshaping the workforce and economic structures, but it also presents considerable challenges, particularly in terms of employment, ethical governance, and societal impact. Balancing the benefits of AI with strategies that address its drawbacks is crucial for ensuring that this technology supports inclusive growth and does not widen social inequalities. As industries continue to integrate AI, fostering collaboration between governments, businesses, and educational institutions will be essential in preparing the workforce for the AI-driven future. Through reskilling, ethical development, and continuous monitoring, stakeholders can harness AI's transformative potential while minimizing its risks, paving the way for a more equitable and prosperous society.

REFERENCES

Abràmoff, M. D., Lavin, P. T., Birch, M., & Shah, N. (2018). Pooled analysis of 4,662 patients with diabetic retinopathy using deep learning. *Ophthalmology, 125*(6), 935–944.

Aldridge, I. (2013). *High-Frequency Trading: A Practical Guide to Algorithmic Strategies and Trading Systems*. Wiley.

Ananny, M., & Crawford, K. (2018). Seeing without knowing: Limitations of the transparency ideal and its application to algorithmic accountability. *Communications of the ACM, 61*(8), 56–62.

Angwin, J., Larson, J., Mattu, S., & Kirchner, L. (2016). *Machine Bias*. ProPublica.

Aristotle. (350 BCE). *Nicomachean Ethics*.

Arntz, M., Gregory, T., & Zierahn, U. (2016). *The Risk of Automation for Jobs in OECD Countries: A Comparative Analysis*. OECD Social, Employment and Migration Working Papers, No. 189, OECD Publishing, Paris.

Arrieta, A. B.. (2020). Explainable Artificial Intelligence (XAI): Concepts, Taxonomies, Opportunities, and Challenges. *Information Fusion*.

Autor, D. (2015). Why Are There Still So Many Jobs? The History and Future of Workplace Automation. *The Journal of Economic Perspectives, 29*(3), 3–30. DOI: 10.1257/jep.29.3.3

Baker, S. (2020). The impact of algorithmic trading on market inequality. *Financial Studies, 37*(4), 1234–1256.

Barndorff-Nielsen, O. E.. (2019). Market crashes: A statistical perspective. *Journal of Financial Econometrics, 17*(2), 243–263.

Barocas, S., Hardt, M., & Narayanan, A. (2019). *Fairness and Machine Learning: Limitations and Opportunities*. http://fairmlbook.org

Bengio, Y.. (2021). *Deep Learning for AI: An Overview*. Springer. DOI: 10.1145/3448250

Berg, J. (2016). *Income Security in the On-Demand Economy: Findings and Policy Lessons from a Survey of Crowdworkers*. Conditions of Work and Employment Series No. 74, International Labour Organization.

Bessen, J. E. (2019). *AI and Jobs: The Role of Demand*. NBER Working Paper No. 24235.

Binns, R. (2018). Fairness in Machine Learning: Lessons from Political Philosophy. *Proceedings of the 2018 Conference on Fairness, Accountability, and Transparency.*

Boden, M. A. (2016). *AI: Its Nature and Future*. Oxford University Press.

Bortolini, M.. (2018). The role of automation in the context of Industry 4.0. *Production Planning and Control, 29*(7), 563–575.

Brynjolfsson, E., & McAfee, A. (2014). *The Second Machine Age: Work, Progress, and Prosperity in a Time of Brilliant Technologies.* W.W. Norton & Company.

Buolamwini, J., & Gebru, T. (2018). Gender Shades: Intersectional Accuracy Disparities in Commercial Gender Classification. *Proceedings of Machine Learning Research.*

Chui, M., Manyika, J., & Miremadi, M. (2016). Where machines could replace humans—And where they can't (yet). *The McKinsey Quarterly.*

Crawford, K. (2021). *Atlas of AI: Power, Politics, and the Planetary Costs of Artificial Intelligence.* Yale University Press.

Crawford, K., & Calo, R. (2016). There is a blind spot in AI research. *Nature, 538*(7610), 311–313. DOI: 10.1038/538311a PMID: 27762391

Danaher, J. (2017). The Threat of Algocracy: Reality, Resistance, and Accommodation. *Philosophy & Technology, 30*(3). Advance online publication. DOI: 10.1007/s13347-015-0211-1

Dastin, J. (2018). *Amazon Scraps Secret AI Recruiting Tool That Showed Bias Against Women.* Reuters.

Davenport, T., & Kalakota, R. (2019). The potential for AI in healthcare. *Future Healthcare Journal, 6*(2), 94–98. DOI: 10.7861/futurehosp.6-2-94 PMID: 31363513

De Fauw, J., Ledsam, J. R., Romera-Paredes, B., Nikolov, S., Tomasev, N., Blackwell, S., Askham, H., Glorot, X., O'Donoghue, B., Visentin, D., van den Driessche, G., Lakshminarayanan, B., Meyer, C., Mackinder, F., Bouton, S., Ayoub, K., Chopra, R., King, D., Karthikesalingam, A., & Ronneberger, O. (2018). Clinically applicable deep learning for diagnosis and referral in retinal disease. *Nature Medicine, 24*(9), 1342–1350. DOI: 10.1038/s41591-018-0107-6 PMID: 30104768

Deloitte. (2020). *AI and the Future of Work: The Impact of AI on Employment.*

Doshi-Velez, F., & Kim, B. (2017). Towards a Rigorous Science of Interpretable Machine Learning. *arXiv preprint arXiv:1702.08608.*

Dua, A., & Gupta, S. (2020). AI for Fraud Detection: A Survey. *Journal of Financial Crime*, *27*(4), 1031–1045.

Elgammal, A., Liu, B., Elhoseiny, M., & Mazzoni, S. (2017). *CAN: Creative Adversarial Networks, Generating "Art" by Learning About Styles and Deviating from Style Norms.arXiv preprint arXiv:1706.07068.*

European Commission. (2016). *Upskilling Pathways: New Opportunities for Adults*. European Commission.

European Commission. (2021). *Proposal for a Regulation laying down harmonized rules on artificial intelligence*. Artificial Intelligence Act.

Floridi, L. (2019). The ethics of artificial intelligence: A compendium of issues. In *The Cambridge Handbook of Artificial Intelligence* (pp. 156–178). Cambridge University Press.

Floridi, L., & Cowls, J. (2019). A Unified Framework of Five Principles for AI in Society. *Harvard Data Science Review*. Advance online publication. DOI: 10.1162/99608f92.8cd550d1

Floridi, L., Cowls, J., Beltrametti, M., Chatila, R., Chazerand, P., Dignum, V., Luetge, C., Madelin, R., Pagallo, U., Rossi, F., Schafer, B., Valcke, P., & Vayena, E. (2018). AI4People—An Ethical Framework for a Good AI Society: Opportunities, Risks, Principles, and Recommendations. *Minds and Machines*, *28*(4), 689–707. DOI: 10.1007/s11023-018-9482-5 PMID: 30930541

Gonzalez, C.. (2020). Mitigating Bias in AI Systems. *Journal of Artificial Intelligence Research*, *68*, 123–158.

Gonzalez, M. A.. (2018). Towards a new workforce for the AI revolution: Opportunities and challenges. *International Journal of Information Management*, *38*(1), 10–16.

Google. (2018). *AI for Social Good*. Retrieved from https://ai.google/social-good/

Heeks, R. (2017). *Information and Communication Technologies (ICTs) for Development: Theory, Practice, and Impact*. Development Informatics Working Paper Series.

HLEG. (2019). *Ethics Guidelines for Trustworthy AI*. High-Level Expert Group on Artificial Intelligence, European Commission.

Howard, A., et al. (2022). AI in Education: The Virtue and Perils of Automation. *Journal of Educational Technology*.

Jiang, F., Jiang, Y., & Zhi, H. (2017). Artificial intelligence in healthcare: Past, present and future. *Seminars in Cancer Biology*, *16*(2), 234–247. PMID: 29507784

Jobin, A., Ienca, M., & Vayena, E. (2019). The Global Landscape of AI Ethics Guidelines. *Nature Machine Intelligence*, *1*(9), 389–399. DOI: 10.1038/s42256-019-0088-2

Kant, I. (1785). *Groundwork for the Metaphysics of Morals*.

Kshetri, N. (2020). The Emerging Role of Artificial Intelligence in the Finance Sector. *Finance Research Letters*, *35*, 101259.

Lipton, Z. C. (2018). The Mythos of Model Interpretability. *Communications of the ACM*, *61*(2), 36–43. DOI: 10.1145/3233231

Luckin, R.. (2016). *Intelligence Unleashed: An Argument for AI in Education*. Pearson.

Mason, J. (2020). AI in Education: A Perspective on the Future of Learning. *The International Journal of Information and Learning Technology*.

McAfee, A., & Brynjolfsson, E. (2014). *The Second Machine Age: Work, Progress, and Prosperity in a Time of Brilliant Technologies*. W.W. Norton & Company.

Mehrabi, N.. (2021). A Survey on Bias and Fairness in Machine Learning. *ACM Computing Surveys*.

Mikalef, P.. (2020). Big data and artificial intelligence: The role of AI in fraud detection. *Information & Management*, *57*(7), 103391.

Mill, J. S. (1863). *Utilitarianism*.

Mittelstadt, B. D., Allo, P., Taddeo, M., Wachter, S., & Floridi, L. (2016). The Ethics of Algorithms: Mapping the Debate. *Big Data & Society*, *3*(2), 2053951716679679. DOI: 10.1177/2053951716679679

Ngai, E. W. T.. (2011). The application of data mining techniques in financial fraud detection: A review and future directions. *Decision Support Systems*, *50*(3), 559–569. DOI: 10.1016/j.dss.2010.08.006

NIST. (2020). *A Proposal for Identifying and Managing Bias in AI*.

O'Neil, C. (2016). *Weapons of Math Destruction: How Big Data Increases Inequality and Threatens Democracy*. Crown Publishing.

Obermeyer, Z., Powers, B., Vogeli, C., & Mullainathan, S. (2019). Dissecting racial bias in an algorithm used to manage the health of populations. *Science*, *366*(6464), 447–453. DOI: 10.1126/science.aax2342 PMID: 31649194

Pearson, J. (2021). The power of algorithms in digital transformations: A roadmap to the future. *The Journal of Management Technology*, *18*(2), 98–104.

Raji, I. D.. (2020). Closing the AI Accountability Gap: Defining an AI Governance Framework for Government Procurement. *Proceedings of the 2020 Conference on Fairness, Accountability, and Transparency*. DOI: 10.1145/3351095.3372873

Raji, I. D., & Buolamwini, J. (2019). Actionable Auditing: Investigating the Impact of Publicly Naming Biased Performance Results of Commercial AI Products. *Proceedings of the 2019 AAAI/ACM Conference on AI, Ethics, and Society*. DOI: 10.1145/3306618.3314244

Rosenfeld, A., & Kraus, S. (2018). Predicting Human Decision-Making: From Prediction to Action. *AI Magazine*.

Selbst, A. D.. (2019). Fairness and Abstraction in Sociotechnical Systems. *Proceedings of the Conference on Fairness, Accountability, and Transparency*. DOI: 10.1145/3287560.3287598

Siau, K., & Wang, W. (2018). Building trust in artificial intelligence, machine learning, and robotics. *Communications of the ACM*, *61*(4), 34–40.

Silver, D.. (2018). Mastering Chess and Shogi by Self-Play with a General Reinforcement Learning Algorithm. *Science*, *362*(6419), 1140–1144. DOI: 10.1126/science.aar6404 PMID: 30523106

Soni, N.. (2020). Impact of artificial intelligence on businesses: From research, innovation, market deployment to future shifts. *International Journal of Information Management*, *50*, 23–28.

Thompson, N. C.. (2020). The Computational Limits of Deep Learning. *Communications of the ACM*, *63*(8), 107–115.

Turing, A. M. (1950). Computing Machinery and Intelligence. *Mind*, *59*(236), 433–460. DOI: 10.1093/mind/LIX.236.433

Varian, H. (2018). AI, big data, and economics: Opportunities for market design. *The Journal of Economic Perspectives*, *32*(3), 3–20.

Vincent, J. (2019). *AI tools used in criminal justice show bias*. The Verge.

Wachter, S., et al. (2017). Why a right to explanation of automated decision-making does not exist in the General Data Protection Regulation. *International Data Privacy Law*, 7(2).

Waters, J. (2014). Adaptive learning: The best approaches for personalized learning. *Campus Technology*.

Weber, R. H., & Weber, R. (2020). *Internet of Things: Legal Perspectives*. Springer.

West, D. M. (2018). *The Future of Work: Robots, AI, and Automation*. Brookings Institution Press.

Zhang, X.. (2021). Deep learning for AI-enabled financial fraud detection. *Journal of Financial Analytics*, *45*(3), 19–35.

Chapter 10

The Impact of Artificial Intelligence on the Banking Industry: Changing Face of Modern Banks

Swati Sharma
https://orcid.org/0000-0002-2029-5251
University School of Business, Chandigarh University, India

Rajinder Kaur
https://orcid.org/0000-0002-7049-0434
University School of Business, Chandigarh University, India

ABSTRACT

AI referred to as automated intelligence which is the human-computer simulation intellect in the machines. The cognition shown by robots stands in stark contrast to the common knowledge displayed by people. Artificial intelligence is developing rapidly, from siri to self-driving vehicles. Generally, there are just two core concepts in artificial intelligence. Studying human brains and how they think is the first step and using machine learning to model those processes is the second. There is more to artificial intelligence in banking than just chatbots. The banking business is only one of the many industries that artificial intelligence has dominated. understanding the effects of artificial intelligence on new era banking was the main motivation for this project. This study mainly focuses on idea of artificial intelligence in the banking and how it affects human labour. This study provides a glimpse of the present uses of Artificial Intelligence in the new era banking sector and how it is transforming the face of Indian banking.

DOI: 10.4018/979-8-3373-3384-7.ch010

1.INTRODUCTION

Artificial intelligence is being used more frequently on the market right now. It is used in many different businesses, the banking industry being one of them. One industry where AI is employed is banking. Ingenious applications of AI are being employed in the banking industry to save time and money. To increase revenues the banks are using algorithms generate precise findings which is going to enhance customer service. Deep learning and machine learning are components of artificial intelligence, which minimizes mistakes caused by variables affecting the mind and emotions. A researcher in artificial intelligence (AI) would respond that the term refers to a collection of algorithms that can do tasks without being specifically told to do so. Artificial intelligence (AI) refers to the intelligence exhibited by machines. In today's world, artificial intelligence has become highly well-liked. Machines that have been trained to learn and imitate human behaviour are simulating natural intelligence in this way. These devices can do jobs like humans do and learn via experience. Our quality of life will be significantly impacted by the development of technology like AI. Everyone in today's world wants to interact with AI technology in some way, whether as a consumer or a career. Reverse engineering human characteristics and talents into a machine and employing its computing prowess to go beyond what we are capable of is the painstaking process of creating an AI system.

Understanding the numerous artificial intelligence sub-fields and how such sub-fields might be used in many fields of business requires a deep dive into how the technology actually operates. Another option is to enrol in an artificial intelligence course, which will aid in your thorough comprehension.

Currently, Artificial Intelligence implementations include a wide range of techniques, including monitoring algorithm, Identification of faces using optical character recognition. Currently, Artificial Intelligence is being used in a number of business sectors including genetics, accountancy, insurance, the internet, transportation and the aerospace industry. Several start -ups then adopted it in an effort to spark interest in the market. Numerous changes have also been made to how asset management, recruiting and customer service are conducted within the financial sector. For instance, stock investing and finance today depend entirely on technical prowess and supernatural luck. But in the future, people be able to manage money in a very various ways thanks to sentiment analysis, crowd- sourced data and algorithms.

Finance-related AI applications could increase or increase financial and non-financial hazards, as well as raise questions about prospective investor and consumer protection measures. Given that AI model processes are neither explicable or interpretable and have the potential to cause pro-cyclicality and systemic risk in the markets, using AI increases the risks that could have an impact on a financial institution's safety and soundness. It's likely that the model's results won't be compatible with corporate governance and financial supervision frameworks already in place, and it might even put the technology-neutral approach to policymaking in jeopardy. AI may provide specific consumer protection hazards, such as the potential for biased, unfair, or discriminatory consumer results, or issues with data storage and utilization. While many of the dangers that could arise from using AI in finance.

Artificial intelligence has just emerged as a market trend. It is currently being used in a number of industries. Artificial intelligence is used by financial institutions in a variety of creative ways. According to the study's second finding, 20 countries' economies would have doubled by 2035, and productivity will be booming. The financial services sector is being supercharged by AI. Most financial sectors currently use AI to take advantage of benefits including time savings, cost savings, and value addition. The top 7 U.S. commercial banks recently organized a strategic technological advancement by locating AI applications to better serve customers, enhance performance, and boost revenues.

2. LITERATURE REVIEW

(Geetha, 2021) studied the artificial intelligence in banking and customer. Banks and other financial institutions can better monitor, anticipate and react to consumer behaviour by mining the financial transaction data produced by the widespread use of digital payments and banking. Based on a literature research, data is gathered from secondary sources to identify the information used in banking and financial services. Private banks and financial institutions are adopting a variety of artificial intelligence service.

(Praveen, 2017) The finance industry has recently seen great success with applications of machine learning and artificial intelligence. These organizations have leveraged their vast capacity to provide business solutions for front end and back-end processes to increase productivity and enhance customer experience. The applications of machine learning and artificial intelligence will be outlined in this article, along with an evaluation of their usefulness in various functional areas of the banking industry. This article will also frame how these institutions can use computational intelligence to enhance their operations. While traditional banking institutions are rapidly catching up with computational intelligence technologies with products like Chatbot, fintech companies, which appear to have embraced A.I. a long time ago.

Mogaji et.al (2020) This study looks at how artificial intelligence relate to consumer. In this paper author highlights the implication which is going to provide best experience to customer with the financial services. The effective use of AI depends on an understanding of the ethical concerns as well as the problems with data and modelling.

2.1Transformation of the Banking Sector

The characteristics of organisations in the financial sector, including banks, are divided into three tiers by internal organisation, network organisation and external organisation (Das, 2015). Internally, banks are changing as a result of growing fin tech companies disrupting the banking industry. Internal changes in banking have been impacted further by the availability of new technologies. With a move from offline to online and multi-channel engagement and management of core competences (Donepudi, 2016). Due to the numerous fin tech players that have entered the markets, banks are losing market share on a network level making the banking industry the sector that is most active in forming alliances with Fin tech players.

Since the financial crisis of 2002 there have been numerous regulatory changes that have affected the financial sector particularly banks. The development of regulatory technology which refers to the use of technology in relation to regulatory monitoring, reporting and compliance is the fundamental cause of these changes (Donepudi, 2017). As a result, laws are more restrictive and penalties are more severe. Furthermore, greater resources are being allocated by governments to supervisory efforts as it is widely thought that one of the primary causes of the financial crisis was insufficient oversight of financial institutions (Kumar et al.,2016).

Since the turn of the millennium several industries have moved of their services online and the banking industry is one of the forerunners in embracing the internet and mobile services (Yu, et.al, 2016). Online Banking was developed allowing for the transfer of accounts the appraisal of real estate, the purchase of insurance the trading of stocks and the application for loans and mortgages. Most frequently the banks top management provides incentives for switching to online banking; very seldom do customers (Zaman, 2014). The main motivations for using internet banking which include improving the banks reputation and strengthening competitive positive while also meeting consumer requests and opening up new markets are indicative of this.

2.2 Adoption of Artificial Intelligence

To achieve the ultimate form of Artificial Intelligence, self-awareness as described by Hintze,2016 there are a number of areas in the field of artificial intelligence that need to be developed. Among them is the ability to solve problems. human problem solving at its most basis level refers to the capacity to weigh available options and determine the best course action. By creating algorithms that are given statements about each phase in the process of building the ideal approach this is artificially accomplished.

Most AI systems give problem solving a high priority especially when the objective is to search through various solutions and the knowledge pool is small. Meanwhile a more complex problem does not respond well to this kind of sequential method attain the same standard of humanity. The ability of a system to learn is MIL, which is a crucial idea in the field of AI. The field is quickly gaining importance across a variety of industries. The field's key objective centre on developing self-improving systems employing prior knowledge and comprehending the relationships between data driven statistics and learning systems. By recognizing and responding to patterns in a set of data, Machine learning algorithms work. Self-driving automobiles are to patterns in a set of data. The ML system uses information from the car's sensors to identify patterns that it has been taught to consider harmful.

2.3 Techniques of Artificial Intelligence

There are numerous methods for resolving issues pertaining to the development of Artificial Intelligence. Among them is search engine optimization. According to a list of requirements, optimization algorithms seek to determine the systems greatest value. The objective of an optimization method could for instance be to swifty scan the dataset for the global minimum value in a computationally efficient manner. logical Artificial Intelligence requires a particular language that can express the systems objectives and give justification using a high-quality set of requirements. The intrinsic properties of this language should be subject to ongoing verification and continuous enhancement by updating of the existing knowledge representation. The author does add that since even the most complicated problem with a huge number of factors should have some degree of uncertainty it is possible to examine the practical applications of logic in Artificial Intelligence. Looking back at the methods employed to address various Artificial Intelligence issues it is clear that they all sought to intimate human thought and decision making. In what are known as artificial neural network the field is attempting to replicate how the human brain functions for applications like speech or facial recognition.

3. ARTIFICIAL INTELLIGENCE AND BANKING

Banks are compelled to change their business strategies. In an effort to provide customers with more competitive products and better service, they have under gone reform and begun integrating financial technologies. The industry has recently adopted Artificial Intelligence as a result of efforts to automate procedures. The sectors can use the technology in many different contexts, such as to identify fraud or money laundering.

According to who investigate the restructuring taking place in the banking industry to make room for new technologies changes in consumer behaviour may make it possible for small and medium sized businesses to utilize these technologies as competitive advantages. identifies seven areas of banking where artificial Intelligence has the potential to change the way things are done now.

In their discussion of the effects of using ICT in a business come to the conclusion that companies can cut expenses and enhance customer interactions. The report does however address issues with the human component suggesting that strong strategic alignment and cultural adoption are necessary for a successful digital transition. This means that while implementation AI in banking ethical issues must also be taken into account. In research on how the general public views AI in the industry the respondents reacted favourably to how the absence of human control in decision making might affects the industry from a societal standpoint how artificial intelligence has sped up financial operations. Additionally, the survey found that the respondents were worried about how the absence of human control in decision making might affect the industry from a societal stand point.

As previously mentioned, utilizing Artificial Intelligence to automate financial service procedures involves a massive amount of data. But the industry must continue to prioritize transparency and preserve data privacy. Protecting client data is only one aspect of this duty; other stakeholders include industry employees as well. As their applicability improves, AI systems will become more crucial for the industry as a whole and for individuals within it according to They do however add that it will raise the danger related to AI. Banking will need to further integrate AI and cyber security in order to adhere to rules and safeguard data

3.1 Application of Artificial Intelligence in Banking

Figure 1. Application of artificial intelligence in banking

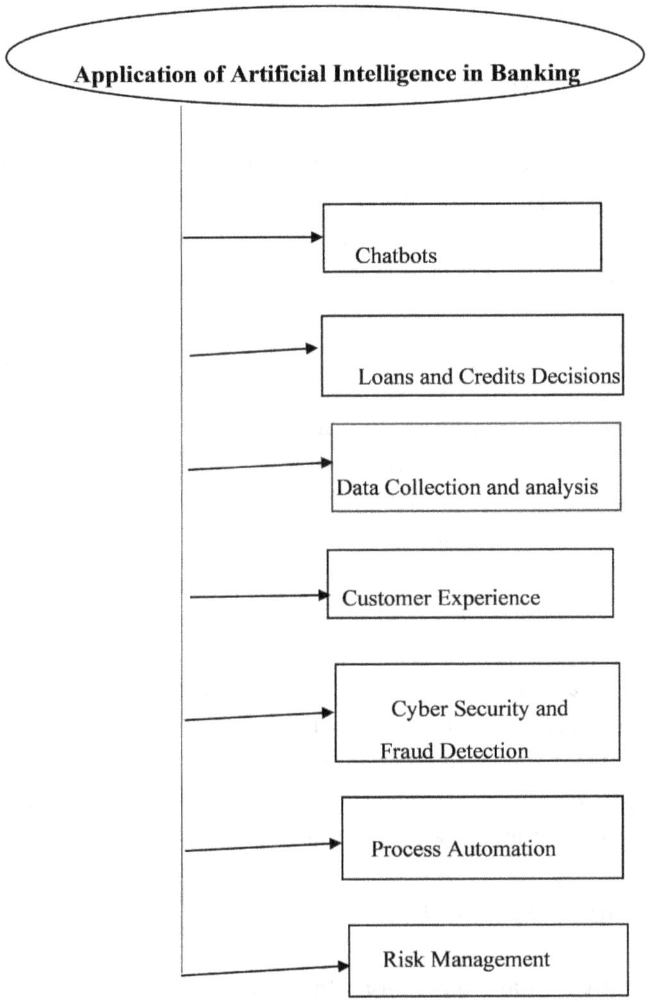

Following are the application of artificial intelligence in the banking sector:

- **Chatbots**

One of the better instances of artificial intelligence in banking in use today is chatbots. In contrast to humans, who have set working hours, they can work around the clock once deployed. The banks may guarantee that they are accessible to their consumers 24 hours a day by introducing chatbots into their banking apps. Additionally, chatbots can provide individualized customer care and make appropriate financial service and product recommendations by comprehending consumer behaviour.

- **Loans and Credits Decisions**

Banks have begun implementing artificial intelligence-based algorithms to make better informed, safer and more profitable lending and credit decisions. Many banks still only use credit history, credit ratings and client references when determine a person's or business's creditworthiness.

- **Data Collection and analysis**

Every day, financial and banking institutions record millions of transactions. Due to the vast amount of information generated, it becomes difficult for employees to collect and register it. It becomes impossible to structure and records such a large amount of data without making any mistakes.

- **Customer Experience**

Customers are always looking for a more convenient experience. For instances ATMs were success because they allowed clients to access necessary services like money withdrawal and deposit even when banks were closed. More innovation has only been spurred by this level of convenience. Customers can now use their smart phones to open bank accounts from the comfort of their homes.

- **Cyber Security and Fraud Detection**

Large numbers of digital transactions happen every day as consumers utilize applications or online accounts to pay bills, withdraw money, deposit checks, and do much more. As a result, the banking industry must increase its efforts in cyber security and fraud detection. This is when banking artificial intelligence enters the picture. Artificial Intelligence can assist banks in reducing risks, tracking system flaws and enhancing the security of online financial transactions. Artificial intelligence and machine learning can quickly spot fraudulent activity and notify both customers and banks.

- **Process Automation**

By automating time consuming repetitive processes, robotic process automation algorithms improve operational efficiency and accuracy while lowering expenses. Users can now concentrate on harder tasks needing human interaction.

- **Risk Management**

The banking and financial sectors are significantly impacted by external global variables such exchange rate fluctuations, natural disasters and political upheaval. Making business decisions with extra caution is essential in such uncertain times. Artificial intelligence analytics can provide a pretty accurate forecast of future events, assisting you in remaining organised and making timely decisions. Artificial Intelligence also assists in identifying hazardous applications by calculating the likelihood that a client would on a loan. By examining historical behavioural patterns and smartphone data, it forecasts this future behaviour.

3.1 Challenges Faced by Banks in Adoption of Artificial Intelligence

There will be difficulties in widely implementing cutting edge technologies like Artificial Intelligence. There are a variety of difficulties facing banks utilizing artificial intelligence technologies from a shortage of reliable and high-quality data to security concerns.

- Data Security - Major issue for artificial intelligence in banking because it necessitates the implementation of additional security measures due to the volume of sensitive data that is collected. Therefore, its crucial to find the correct technology partner that will provide a number of security alternatives to guarantee that your consumer data is handled properly.

3.1.1 Future of Artificial Intelligence in Banking Industry

Almost every industry is being impacted by digital technology, which is not only transforming those industries but also how organisation function. To flourish in this technologically advanced world, every industry is continually researching choices and putting tactics into practices. Nowadays, every nation is advancing in terms of digitalization, which is the reason why the number of consumers in the banking sector is increasing. The dilemma that now emerges is: How can the banking industry serve an ever-increasing number of customers without raising labour costs?

One technology that will alter the banking industry is artificial intelligence (AI). Consumers are choosing digital-only banks in greater numbers. Even conventional banks have begun to expand their online service offerings. Artificial intelligence improves business decision-making, manages customer support requests with less staff, and streamlines their procedures. By avoiding fraud and combating money laundering in real-time, it also plays a significant part in risk management. There are numerous additional ways artificial intelligence can be applied to enhance the banking sector.

Matching the distinctive client expectations is difficult for the industries. Today's consumers have very high standards. Customers today are technologically savvy and anticipate a positive and comfortable customer experience from businesses, just as they do from the banking industry. These cutting-edge features provide users access to banking at their fingertips, but they cost the banking sector money. The likelihood of transmitting sensitive data across virtual networks has increased with the involvement in retail and telecom. It occasionally results in cyber attacks and fraud in the banking industry. This type of fraud not only damages the banks financial standing but also under mines public confidence.

Artificial intelligence main objective in the banking sector is to help customers by prioritizing their options. Artificial intelligence also contributes to the satisfaction of customers with the bank's services. The bank benefits from artificial intelligence in its understanding of customer expectations. Use cases can help with decision-making as banks weigh the benefits and drawbacks of a more comprehensive enterprise AI strategy. Executives can adjust deployments to their specific needs and achieve a higher return on investment by focusing on use cases like the ones that follow. These are only a few examples, but they show how data-driven AI can be applied in many different ways to increase value across a financial company, from front-office revenue growth to back-office operational efficiencies. This list is by no means exhaustive.

We can automate processes and forecast results using machine learning and deep learning approaches, which lowers costs and enhances service. Depending on the type of data involved, such as data, photos, text, etc., the potential domains of use for AI can be very varied.

CONCLUSION

In the wake of demonetization, the digital economy is rapidly booming across all industries, including banking. In order to reduce operating expenses and increase efficiency, banks are gradually adopting new technologies like AI, cloud computing, and blockchain. Banks are continually undergoing change, despite the fact that artificial intelligence is still in its early stages. As AI technology grows and evolves, productivity will rise at a lower cost. Managers across all industries will need to dedicate more time to developing new skills. The recent push toward digitalization is without a doubt fundamentally altering the way that conventional banking models function. The institutions are now more vulnerable to developing cyber security problems, though. Currently, banks are searching more.Banks will be able to give individualized services while maximizing the use of human and machine skills thanks to AI. For banks, achieving all of these advantages is no longer a distant goal. Leaders in the banking industry have already adapted AI and acted responsibly to gain these benefits.

REFERENCES

Das, S., Dey, A., Pal, A., & Roy, N. (2015). Applications of artificial intelligence in machine learning: Review and prospect. *International Journal of Computer Applications, 115*(9), 31–41. DOI: 10.5120/20182-2402

Donepudi, P. (2016). Influence of Cloud Computing in Business: Are They Robust? *Asian Journal of Applied Science and Engineering, 5*(3), 193–196. DOI: 10.18034/ajase.v5i1.78

Donepudi, P. (2017). AI and Machine Learning in Banking: A Systematic Literature Review. Asian. *Journal of Applied Science and Engineering, 6*(3), 157–162.

Donepudi, P. K. (2017). Machine Learning and Artificial Intelligence in Banking. *Engineering International, 5*(2), 83–86. DOI: 10.18034/ei.v5i2.490

Geetha (2021) A study on artificial intelligence in banking and financial services. International Journal of Creative Research Thoughts,9(9),110-114.

Kumar, A. S., & Chandrakala, D. (2016). A survey on customer churn prediction using machine learning techniques. *International Journal of Computer Applications, 154*(10), 13–16. DOI: 10.5120/ijca2016912237

Mogaji, E., Soetan, T. O., & Kieu, T. A. (2020). The implications of artificial intelligence on the digital marketing of financial services to vulnerable customers. *Australasian Marketing Journal, 29*(3), 235–242. DOI: 10.1016/j.ausmj.2020.05.003

Taher-Uz-Zaman, M., Ahmed, M. S., Hossain, S., Hossain, S., & Jamal, G. R. A. (2014). Multipurpose Tactical Robot. *Engineering International, 2*(1), 21–27. DOI: 10.18034/ei.v2i1.204

Yu, L., Yang, Z., & Tang, L. (2016). A novel multistage deep belief network based extreme learning machine ensemble learning paradigm for credit risk assessment. *Flexible Services and Manufacturing Journal, 28*(4), 576–592. DOI: 10.1007/s10696-015-9226-2

Chapter 11

Consumer Digital Privacy in the Age of Smart Virtual Assistants

Perla Khattar
University of Notre Dame, USA

ABSTRACT

The proliferation of Virtual Voice Assistants (VVAs) in the lives of consumers has ushered in an era of unparalleled convenience and technological sophistication. However, the ever-present risk of unauthorized data sharing and exploitation of Personal Identifiable Information (PII) calls for urgent regulatory intervention to protect consumer digital privacy. This chapter offers a comprehensive examination of VVAs, dissecting the integrated technologies that power them and debunking common misconceptions. It navigates through the complex web of user agreements and the existing patchwork of privacy laws, revealing the gaping regulatory void surrounding VVAs.

INTRODUCTION

The release of the movie "Her" in 2013 evoked a profound sense of astonishment among audiences, as the poignant portrayal of a human being falling in love with an operating system ("OS") challenged deeply ingrained beliefs about the nature of consciousness, the boundaries of human emotions, and the capabilities of artificial

DOI: 10.4018/979-8-3373-3384-7.ch011

intelligence ("AI") and computer systems. "Her" represents "the result of human experience enshrouded and infused by technology (Myers, 2024)."

The movie portrays a lonely and depressed Theodore that purchases a futuristic OS, Samantha, upon which he becomes heavily reliant. Samantha's multifaceted abilities, including natural language processing ("NLP"), and unconventional emotional intelligence enable her to engage Theodore in profound conversations, write his emails, manage his schedule, provide him with personal assistance, and stimulate him intellectually and sexually. The film portrays a deeply contemplative exploration of the human-AI relationship, where the boundaries between humanity and technology become increasingly blurred, as Samantha evolves into a complex, self-aware machine.

Fast forward 10 years, the increased normalcy of dependency to smart software raises many questions about the very nature of technology, namely, the virtual voice assistant ("VVA") technology. Similar to Samantha, VVAs on the market are able to, for example, answer questions, perform tasks, control smart home devices, provide entertainment, order products online, finalize travel plans, and assist with navigation (Botelho, 2022). VVAs are also able to charm lonely men during the pandemic: a survey by We-vibe – a company that sells application-enabled sex toys – found that 14% of surveyed men were turned on by Alexa's comforting and authoritative voice.

One of the most disconcerting aspects of VVAs is the potential violation of users' privacy that they pose (Reed, 2020). The eerie sensation of being watched and monitored is only amplified when one asks a question to a VVA and later finds an advertisement about a similar topic. The fact that VVAs are capable of collecting data on users' browsing habits and preferences is a disquieting thought, and raises concerns about the exploitation of Personal Identifiable Information ("PII") for commercial gain. A survey by Selligent Marketing Cloud found that 52% of participants perceive it as creepy when companies target them with advertisements based on the contents of a previous interaction between them and a VVA. In the same survey, 69% of participants find it creepy when they're targeted with advertisements based on things they've said in everyday human conversations.

VVAs are intelligently-programed, efficiently-designed, and technologically-advanced AI software. Some VVAs are built-in to their own hardware such as Amazon's Alexa and Google Assistant, others come built into OSs such as Apple's Siri (Allen, 2019). However, the VVA technology remains unregulated by the United States federal government, because it is often the case that technological advancements outpace the ability of regulators to keep up (Malan, 2018). The lack of guidelines and ethical considerations surrounding VVAs has created a breeding ground for potential abuse and misuse, which can lead to data breaches, unauthorized PII sharing, and other unethical practices, all of which could have far-reaching consequences for individuals and society as a whole (Dastin, 2021). Although regulating VVAs may not be on the current agenda of Congress, consumers are entitled to transparency regarding the handling, sale, retention, and overall management of their PII by VVA manufacturers and servicers.

This piece contends that while VVA users may have misconceptions about the underlying mechanics of the technology, it is undeniable that legislation is essential to safeguard and enforce the digital privacy rights of consumers in an era where the unchecked proliferation of PII has become a ubiquitous concern. Effective legislation is one that takes the complexity of the VVA technology into account, seeks to embed privacy principles into the design of software products, and makes safeguarding users' privacy a matter of paramount importance. Part I offers a comprehensive overview of the integrated technologies that comprise VVAs. Part II explains the inner-workings of commercial VVAs. Part III clears out common misconceptions about VVAs. Part IV discusses the agreements that bind VVA users with manufacturing and servicing companies. Part V surveys the relevant laws that regulate VVAs and highlights the lack of a comprehensive federal privacy law. And finally, part VI proposes a technology-conscious legislation that adapts the Federal Trade Commission's ("FTC") Fair Information Practice Principles ("FIPP") to modern technological advancements, and seeks full compliance from VVA manufacturers.

PART I: THE TECHNOLOGY BEHIND THE HANDY ARTIFICIAL INTELLIGENCE IN A BOX

Inter-connected voice-controlled smart speakers, also known as VVAs, are popular Internet of Things ("IoT") devices that allow users to speak to a machine and receive a response back from the same machine. VVAs are defined as "internet-connected devices equipped with a speaker, a microphone, and an integration with a cloud-enabled service responsible for receiving and interpreting voice commands when they are activated (Dubois, 2020)."

This advanced technology allows users to perform various tasks by saying a "wake word" followed by a command or a question. By managing schedules, simplifying tasks, and making the lives of people with disabilities easier, VVAs can enhance human efficiency. The convenience that users are afforded by VVAs led researchers to believe that voice commands have the potential to become the primary way in which users interact with technology, surpassing touch screens and the more ancient keyboards (Wingfield, 2017). However, as the VVA technology becomes more pervasive, it is crucial to understand how the machinery works and the impact that it could have on consumers.

A. Cloud Processing and Voice Computing

Advances in AI, ML, and cloud processing have paved the way for new technologies, such as the VVA technology that seeks to make life arguably easier and more convenient.

Cloud processing is a model of delivering Information Technology ("IT") services over the internet, instead of through traditional, on-premises methods. In cloud computing, third-party service providers, such as Amazon Web Services, Microsoft Azure, and Google Cloud Platform make servers, storage, databases, networking, software, analytics, intelligence and other computing resources available to customers on-demand over the internet. Customers can access these resources via the internet and use them for their computing needs without having to worry about the underlying infrastructure or maintenance of the technology. This results in reduced costs, increased scalability, and greater flexibility compared to traditional on-premises IT solutions.

Voice computing refers to the use of spoken language as the primary means of interacting with computers, mobile phones, and other digital devices (Gillis, 2023). It involves the use of Automatic Speech Recognition ("ASR"), NLP, and Text-To-Speech ("TTS") technology to enable people to interact with devices using speech and dictate responses (Gray, 2017).

The ASR technology takes an audio stream and turns it into text, that is later sent to be processed by the NLP technology. In turn, the NLP technology interprets the recognition result and produces an intent. Then, the system takes the produced intent and turns it into audible audio file ready to be streamed on the VVA, using the TTS technology.

In order to process verbal inputs, devices equipped with voice computing features are built with physical microphones in the hardware. Technology nerds are eager to bring forward new products that listen to users' questions, and answer them in return (Anders, 2017). Services such as Alexa, Google Assistant, and Siri allow users to send emails without typing, placing calls without dialing, read messages out loud, set alarms or reminders, and more, all through simple commands.

Standalone cloud processing, and standalone voice computing are not a technological concern with regards to digital privacy. However, what is concerning is voice-computing devices that utilize cloud computing technology for processing and storage purposes. When audio files are recorded by VVAs and sent to remote clouds for processing, transcription, and storage purposes, PII can be potentially accessed by employees, used for advertising purposes, or sold to third parties (Manning, 2020).

Today, VVAs are becoming increasingly popular in offices, as well as households – the global virtual voice assistant market is expected to reach $19.6 billion by 2025 – raising privacy concerns (Zion Market Research, 2019).

B. The Wake Word Technology

Amazon defines the wake word technology ("WWT") as "a verbal cue that makes things happen (Amazon)." Yiming Wang from John Hopkins University defines the technology as "the task of detecting a predefined keyword from a continuous stream of audio (Wang, 2021)." While VVAs are working on low power mode, the WWT is doing its magic in the background. Wang proceeds to explain that when the wake word is detected, the VVA turns into high power mode to subsequently understand the more complex instructions.

VVAs powered by the WWT are constantly analyzing short and temporary voice recordings, searching for the wake word, and deleting those voice recordings if the wake word is not detected. The VVA will only begin recording and thereafter storing the recordings on the cloud when the wake word (or a similar sound) is uttered.

The WWT is useful for the average user: it allows users to complete tasks hands-free when driving, ask about the weather when getting ready, set timers when in a rush, and ask Alexa, Siri and Google how long the morning commute will take (Lang & Benessere, 2018). Jeffrey Allen finds that most people use their VVAs to do the following tasks: "answer general question; provide a weather report; stream music; provide timers and/or alarms; provide reminder for a to-do list; make calendar entries; provide home automation services; stream news; locate local businesses; play games; play Bluetooth audio; play audiobooks; order products; order food; and locate/play podcasts (Allen, 2019)." What started as an interesting technology has become a "must have" feature in new tech products making their debut on the global market (Nowak, 2016). The ever-growing reliance on voice assistants and the WWT led many tech companies to speculate that these devices will become the primary way in which people interact with technology (Wingfield, 2017).

PART II: DOMINANT PRODUCTS ON THE MARKET AND THEIR INNER-WORKINGS

The Amazon Echo is a line of smart speakers that are designed and manufactured by Amazon.com, Inc., a multinational technology company based in the United States. The Amazon Echo is a voice-controlled device that operates as an AI personal assistant, allowing users to interact with the device using voice commands to perform various tasks and access information. The Amazon Echo operates using Alexa,

Amazon's cloud-based voice service, which provides access to a vast database of information and skills. Alexa was released in November 2014 (Etherington, 2014).

In order for Alexa to work properly, the Echo device needs to be connected to the internet, and the Alexa app should be installed on a smartphone or tablet (Raws & Lacoma, 2019). Once paired, Alexa is capable of processing and transmitting data to and from various sources. Alexa has the ability to carry out five-hundred tasks (Weinberger, 2017), such as setting up alarms, telling jokes, or playing music due to her ASR technology (Gray, 2017). The device is equipped with seven microphones that use beam-forming technology, an acoustic resonator, and a processor that handles NLP making wake-word spotting a simple task. The Echo device has four buttons on its face: two buttons are used to control the volume, one button turns the microphone off, and one button dictates action (Amazon). Whenever Alexa starts recording, the device lights up with a blue signal right to alert users to the fact that Alexa is recording and actively sending requests to the cloud (Amazon).

Amazon explains that the Echo device is similar to the invisible door that only opens by saying the phrase "Open Sesame" in The Arabian Nights tale. Echo works in a similar fashion: Alexa will not begin fulfilling a request unless the user says the chosen wake work, which by default is "Alexa. (Amazon)" It is only after the Echo device detects the chosen or default wake word, Alexa will listen and fulfill requests. Amazon affirms that Echo devices rely on built-in technology called keyword spotting where spoken audio is matched to the acoustic patterns of the chosen or default wake word (Amazon). Echo is engineered and trained to detect exclusively the sound waves of the wake word. Once a sentence uttering the wake word is recorded, the Echo device runs keyword spotting to detect the default or chosen wake word, and the blue light indicators appears to signal that Alexa is actively listening and processing the request (Amazon). The voice request is then encrypted in transit and sent to Amazon's secure cloud to verify the wake word (Amazon). Then, Amazon's ASR technology turns audio into text, and the NLP technology assigns meaning to the transcription (Amazon). The request is then routed to the designated data source where the adequate information is gathered, and the TTS technology generates a voice response to be sent back to the Echo device (Amazon).

In addition, Alexa supports skills: voice-driven capabilities that are comparable to a cellphone's applications. The number of skills grew from 1000 to 7000 in seven months when launched (Pierce, 2017). Currently, there are more than 100,000 Alexa skills available for download (Kozuch, 2023).

Similar to Amazon's Alexa, Google Assistant is an AI-powered virtual assistant developed and maintained by Google LLC, a subsidiary of Alphabet Inc (Google). Google Assistant is a voice-activated service that allows users to interact with their device using NLP and ML technology (Google). Google Assistant is integrated into a variety of devices including smartphones, smart speakers, laptops, and smart displays, and can be activated by the user through the use of voice commands such as "Hey Google" or "Ok Google" (Google).

Google's Google Assistant is engineered to wait in standby mode until the wake word "Hey Google" or "Ok Google" is detected. The device can also be activated manually by holding the device's power button or home button. Users can know when Google Assistant is listening by looking at the status indicator on the device such as on-screen pointers or flashing LEDs. Google confirms in its Privacy Policy that users' speech is only sent to the Google servers once the activation word or a noise that sounds like "Hey Google" is uttered (Google). User requests are fulfilled on Google's cloud, rather than on the device's local memory (Google).

A third product dominating the international market is Apple's Siri. Siri is a virtual assistant developed by Apple Inc. The Technology is integrated into Apple's iOS, iPadOS, watchOS, and macOS, and is available on a variety of Apple devices including iPhones, iPads, Apple Watches, and Mac computers (Siri). Apple claims that Siri has reached two billion Siri interaction globally every week, with an estimated 41.4 million active users (Courtney, 2017).

Upon the utterance of the sentence "Hey Siri," Apple's technology captures the frequencies and sound waves from the user's voice and converts them into a code (Lagapa). The code is then analyzed to identify patterns, phrases, and keywords (Lagapa). This data is input into a sophisticated algorithm that sifts through numerous sentence combinations to decipher the meaning of the inputted phrase, even accounting for idioms, homophones, and other literary expressions to understand the context of the sentence (Lagapa). Once Siri understands the request, it assesses the tasks that need to be performed and determines if the information needed can be retrieved from the device's local storage, or the company's remote server (Lagapa). Siri then generates complete and coherent sentences that are relevant to the type of question or command provided by the user (Lagapa).

PART III: DOTTING THE I'S AND CROSSING THE T'S OF VIRTUAL VOICE ASSISTANTS

In a 2018 survey, PricewaterhouseCoopers found that 38% of participants that don't own a VVA and don't plan to own one in the future don't want something [VVAs] listening in on their life all the time, of which 28% were concerned about their privacy and data security (PWC). While technophobia – the overwhelming fear of technology – exists, it is often rooted in misinformation, rather than valid concerns. Hypothetically, if Alexa was constantly listening for genuine business reasons, then consumer fears would be unjustified. But, if misactivations across devices were intentional, then consumers would have a valid reason to distrust VVAs. This section will seek to debunk common myths around VVAs, and their technology.

A. Virtual Voice Assistants are Always Listening and Recording

As explained is Part I, VVAs are engineered to use on-device keyword spotting to detect the wake word. However, VVAs are also engineered to continuously inspect acoustic patterns to detect whether the wake word was spoken (AWSSTATIC). This is done by using a small internal audio buffer located on the device that is continuously overwritten. The on-device buffer exists on temporary memory, which means that recordings located on that type of memory are deleted forever and are not stored remotely. At this stage, and if the algorithms do not detect the wake word within the short time interval, the audio is overwritten locally without being sent to the remote cloud. It is only when the wake word is detected by the VVA that a connection to the remote cloud is initiated. If the technology detects that the wake word was spoken, the audio is reanalyzed on the cloud using more powerful processing capabilities to verify that the wake word was truly uttered. The more powerful algorithms are typically located on the remote cloud due to the need of greater processing power, which VVAs usually lack.

VVAs typically begin recording the audio starting with a fraction of a second of audio before the wake word is uttered. Once the user stops talking, the VVA system in the cloud turns off the audio streams and the recording stops. The VVA's speech recognition system begins to analyze the audio stream while the system is simultaneously trying to determine when the user's request ended to stop the audio stream. In addition, records of the short interval audios are not kept on the VVA's local storage, instead just a small amount of data is saved to help the device detect the wake word.

Therefore, while it is true that VVAs are always listening and recording in small intervals, these audio recordings are continuously overwritten, posing no threat to users' privacy.

B. Misactivations are Not Intentional

As explained in Part III, A, as long as the VVA is receiving electricity and is connected to the internet, the machine is constantly listening to ambient noise and anticipating the utterance of the wake word. In more scientific terms, VVAs are continually processing data from their microphone, which is used to determine whether a wake word was uttered, and decide whether activation should be triggered. An activation happens whenever the VVA listens to a predetermined wake word and a subsequent demand. However, if an activation happened as a result of the utterance of any word other than the predetermined wake word, the activation is classified as unauthorized and is called a misactivation.

A study conducted by *Dubois et al.* exposed VVAs manufactured by Amazon.com, Inc. (wake word: "Alexa," "Amazon," "Echo," "Computer), Alphabet, Inc. (wake word: "Ok/Hey Google"), Apple, Inc. (wake word: "Hi Siri"), and Microsoft, Corp. (wake word: "Cortana") to 134 hours of audio clips from 12 popular TV shows (Dubois, 2020). All devices were tested at the same time, and were place next to each other in a cabinet insulated from external sounds, with their volume set to the minimum level (Dubois, 2020). The shows were selected while taking into consideration the density of the dialogue, cultural context, genre, as well as technical language (Dubois, 2020). In preparation for the experiment, all VVAs were reset to factory settings and associated with brand new accounts for the purposes of the study (Dubois, 2020). The experiment was repeated multiple times for accuracy. This 2020 study is the first reputable, at-scale study of misactivations for VVAs that uses video processing, network traffic, and audio content analysis to identify and characterize misactivations.

The researchers were looking to detect misactivations, which are sensed by manually observing the devices lighting up, accessing the cloud server where the information about the activation is recorded, and analyzing network traffic from each device (Dubois, 2020). The researchers observed an average of 0.95 misactivations per hour of audio exposure. In other terms, for every 10,000 words spoken near a VVA, the device misheard a wake word 1.43 times.

In the median case, researchers recorded a misactivation duration of up to 4 seconds, but in the less common 75th percentile case, misactivations of 7 seconds were observed. In the much less common 90th percentile case, misactivations in some devices lasted 10 seconds. A longer duration of misactivation means a greater exposure of user privacy. In some cases, 10 seconds is enough time to record elements of a private or rather sensitive conversation that should not end up on a company's remote storage.

The study found that most misactivations are non-deterministic, and a VVA will not always misactivate when exposed to the identical input, and under the same conditions; in other terms, a specific word that triggered a misactivation in one instance does not necessarily trigger a misactivations every time it is uttered (Dubois, 2020). The researchers calculated the repeatability of misactivation, which defined as the number of experiments in which the misactivation is detected, divided by the total number of experiments. The scientists noted that there are cases where the misactivation is explainable, due to the utterance of similar-sounding words to the wake word: the words "Head Coach" or "Head Co." could be misheard for "Echo." However, from a privacy and technology perspective, it is challenging to understand why a device misactivates, and to predict when a device is going to misactivate. The study was not able to find any clear evidence of consistent undocumented fake wake words that are completely unrelated to the real wake words.

The scientists observed that the Echo Dot devices adapted to the audio clips and filtered out some misactivations after hearing the same audio repeatedly throughout the study (Dubois, 2020). The researchers explained that the devices could be adapting over time, but that there wasn't strong evidence to support this hypothetical. However, the researchers hypothesized that the Echo Dot devices could be retraining by analyzing the voice's characteristics and speech contents, which leads to the device potentially building a voice profile that can be easily associated with an identifiable single user. If this hypothesis proves to be true, it would mean that the reduction in the number of misactivations in the Echo Dot comes with the inconvenience of heightened privacy risks. Privacy compliance is an important consideration when a VVA misactivates, records sounds and voices from its environment, and sends them to a company's remote cloud, as these recordings may contain sensitive and private information. But, the creation of a potential user voice profile is also a big privacy risk.

The researchers concluded with some good news: "[they] we did not find evidence of malicious or intentional misactivations, meaning that the misactivations [they] observed may just be caused by a suboptimal wake word recognition engine." However, privacy risks are not mitigated by knowing that misactivations are unintentional, since uses' data is ending up on a remote storage whether the misactivation was intentional or not.

In Amazon's privacy policy, the company explains that Alexa may be alerted accidently even if the wake word was not pronounced by the user, especially when the words uttered are too close to the default or chosen wake word. However, Amazon assured that users are also able to review their voice history by visiting Alexa's Privacy settings, where all audios stored on the cloud can be played, reviewed, and deleted. Similarly, Google acknowledges that their devices are activated unintentionally in their privacy policy, but the company affirms that these actions are mere mistakes (Google). Users are able to tailor their device to better fit their environment by adjusting how sensitive Google Assistant is to activation phrases, making the experience more private and potentially secure. However, Siri's privacy policy does not mention misactivations (Siri).

Users wishing to protect their conversations from VVA misactivations can choose to wear privacy armor bracelets that emit ultrasonic frequency audio that interferes with VVA microphones and prevent activation and misactivation (Chen, 2020). Another solution would be to use hardware features such as mic off toggles to disable the VVA's listening abilities temporarily. Some users may opt to use Snowboy, a customizable "hotword" detection engine, created to allows users to choose their own wake word. This alternative is powered by deep neural networks, and although it is always listening, ambient noise is analyzed locally and is never sent to the remote cloud. Snowboy does not use Internet and is open source, allowing infinite customization and adaption. Snowboy can now be configured to the Alexa AVS sample application on Raspberry Pi.

C. Collected Data Is Used in Online Behavioral Advertising

Many scientific studies provided ample evidence to support the need for transparency into VVA data collection, sharing and use, especially when VVAs host malicious third-party applications (Cheng, 2020), misactivate and record private conversations, and share users' data with strangers (Fowler, 2019). Alexa can even analyze the user's voice pitch, amplitude, and tone and deduce the user's mental status (Boughman, 2017). Amazon.com, Inc., the manufacturer of the Echo Dot device and the Alexa software owns a patent for advertising products to users based on interferences from emotional and physical characteristics of users' voices (Brodkin, 2018). For example, Amazon would be able to target cough-drop ads to users with the common cold or the flu. Hypothetically, and based on Amazon's ownership of U.S. Patent 10,096,319, every interaction with Amazon's Echo devices may help build a unique user profile through the use of predictive modeling technology, whereby PII may be exposed to third parties (Boughman, 2017). Google and Apple, however, assure in their privacy policy that audio recordings are never sold to third-party companies or used for advertising (Google).

Commercial VVAs are black-box devices without open interfaces, which makes it difficult for researchers to examine how the technology handles data collected from users (Foryciarz, 2020). For all we know, VVAs could have the ability to create detailed comprehensive personal profiles for users' activities based on their location, activities, political opinion, personal health, calendars, grocery list, to-do chart, and news websites frequented. However, the lack of transparency in the privacy policies and the terms of service of VVA manufacturers makes it difficult for the average user to understand how PII is handled.

In their recent study, Iqbal et al. built an auditing framework that measures the collection, usage, and sharing of data collected by the Echo Dot device (Iqbal, 2023). The researchers wanted to create different internet personas with different VVA profiles to test whether the identities receive statistically and significantly altered advertisements based on their interactions with the VVA, and to infer how data was shared and used. The creation of diverse personas was essential because the nature of tracking, profiling, and ad targeting differs from one person to another.

The researchers intentionally exposed voice commands to an Amazon Echo Dot device and observed its usage on-platform and on the web. Based on each persona's interests, the researchers installed and interacted with skills from different categories: connected car, dating, fashion and style, pet and animals, religion and spirituality, smart home, wine and beverage, health and fitness, and navigation and trip planners (Iqbal, 2023).

In order to determine whether interactions between each unique persona and the VVA are used or shared, researchers observed and analyzed online targeted advertising to each persona, and network traffic exchanged by the VVAs (Iqbal, 2023). Advertising was measured across two modalities: first, audio ads served by the Echo Dot device, and second, display ads served by websites online. Finally, researchers compared ad content and ad auction bid values across personas to identify if VVA interactions are likely the cause of ad targeting. During the study, the researchers tracked 20,210 ads across 25 iterations. To determine whether the advertisements are targeted or random, the researchers considered three conditions: first, if the skill vendor is also the advertiser; second, if the ad is only present in one persona; and third, if the ad references a product in the same industry as the installed skill.

Skills on the Echo Dot device resemble applications on a smart phone, which means that skills are not created by Amazon. For this reason, Amazon imposes a unique set of policies to manage privacy risks associated with third-party skills. For instance, skills cannot collect sensitive information from users, such as bank account or social security numbers, and need to receive user permission before collecting personal information, such as name, phone number, or email. However, thousands of policy-certified skills have violated Amazon's policies before (Young, 2022). This is particularly an issue because voice input is shared with the third-party skill whenever users interact with the third-party skill (Iqbal, 2023).

The researchers determined that users' data is collected by Amazon and third-parties (that include advertising and tracking services). To enhance personalized target ads, advertisers share user data with each other (Iqbal, 2023). As per the study, 41 advertisers sync their cookies with Amazon across all personas. These 41 advertisers further sync their cookies with 247 other third parties. The researchers observed that ads from Amazon seemed to be personalized to unique personas: a vacuum cleaner and vacuum cleaner accessories ad from Dyson appeared in the smart home persona, and an essential oils ad appeared in the health and fitness persona (Iqbal, 2023).

The researchers found that Amazon processes voice data to determine the users' interests which falls beyond the purely functional purposes stated in the company's policies. The study was able to detect usage of voice data for on-platform (audio ads on the Echo Dot device), off platform (ads on online websites), and cross-device (ads on non-Echo VVAs) ad targeting. Advertisers bid as much as 30x higher on targeted ads for Echo users. For example, the median bid values are as 3x higher for pets and animals, religion and spirituality, and wine and beverages personas (Iqbal, 2023).

The researchers requested the personas' data from Amazon, and received detailed information about diagnostics, search history, retail interaction, Alexa, advertising, and other Amazon services. The scientists noted that some data was not handed over by Amazon regarding some personas, and concluded that the company cannot be trusted to provide transparency in data usage (Iqbal, 2023).

When it comes to privacy policies, the researchers indicated that Amazon's policies are not always transparent regarding skill's operational practices. The scientists cite that "Amazon's inference of advertising interests from users' voice interactions seems to be inconsistent with their public statements. (Iqbal, 2023)" Effectively, Amazon noted in a statement that the company does "not use voice recordings to target ads," which is inconsistent with the finding of the study (Maheshwari, 2018). The research proves that it is highly probably that Amazon is processing recordings (or transcripts of these recordings), inferring interests, and using those interests to target ads to users. Amazon's privacy policy openly states that interactions with Alexa are used for personalizing user experience by improving speech recognition. However, the study proves that Amazon is not committed to using user data exclusively for the stated purposes, and that a potential inconsistency exists between the company's policies and actual reports (Iqbal, 2023).

The scientists concluded that they find strong evidence that interactions between the Echo Dot and users are used for the purposes of targeting advertisements, and that the advertisement targeting implies significant data sharing across multiple parties. The researchers have strong evidence to believe that Amazon processes voice recordings from interactions with the VVA to infer user interests, which is used in ad targeting (Iqbal, 2023). The scholars add that since Amazon does not provide transparency in usage of data, the company "cannot be reliably trusted to protect users privacy. (Iqbal, 2023)"

PART IV: ANALYZING THE BINDING AGREEMENTS BETWEEN USERS AND VIRTUAL VOICE ASSISTANTS MANUFACTURERS

Big tech companies have implemented various self-regulatory measures to address concerns over issues of privacy and security on their platforms (Shavell, 2021). However, some critics argue that these measures are insufficient and that government intervention may be necessary to ensure greater accountability and transparency (Elghawaby, 2018) (Noonan, 2022). In the absence of a federal privacy law, big tech companies are free to set their own policies on data collection and usage, and consumers who use these platforms and products are subject to the terms and conditions set by the companies. In most cases, by purchasing a VVA product, consumers are consenting to the manufacturing or servicing company's terms of service and privacy policy. Therefore, it is essential for consumers to understand the terms of the binding agreements that they are entering into before committing to a VVA product, or any other tech product or service.

A. Data Collection, Retention, and Personalization

Data collection and retention can be concerning from a privacy and cybersecurity standpoint. Collected data includes PII that could facilitate identity theft, fraud, or other malicious practices if mishandled or stored inappropriately. Users' PII could also fall in the hands of the government if the company operating the cloud was served a search warrant, and in some cases, a simple court order, or subpoena. Although shorter retention periods and de-identified data are industry practices that can protect users, not all VVA manufacturers handle user data the same way.

CommonSense, an independent, research-backed and non-profit organization compared and ranked the privacy practices of popular VVAs on the market (Kelly, 2019). On data collection, Apple's Siri was given a 65, Google Assistant a 65, and Amazon's Alexa a 35 (Kelly, 2019).

As per the company's policies, Amazon keeps users' recordings indefinitely on the cloud (Amazon). Even though users are able to review and delete the voice recordings associated with their account, Amazon claims that users' Alexa experience might be "degraded" due to that choice (Day, 2019). Although Amazon offers the option to delete voice recordings if the user chooses to exercise that right, it does not necessarily provide complete privacy as the company retains the data in the form of text logs on its cloud servers after deletion (Ng. 2019). While users can request to delete the audio files entirely, and the transcribed data from the "main Alexa systems", they cannot delete the transcribed data from the cloud.

Google defends its practices of collecting data and using activity from the user's Google Account by highlighting the benefits personalization in its privacy policy (Google Assistant). In Addition, Google offers services that are more personalized if given the permission to recognize a user's voice through Voice Match technology – in that case, Google Assistant is able to tell the users how to go to work, when is their mother's birthday, and what meals would make a great dinner.

However, users wishing for more privacy can ask their Assistant to turn on "guest mode" so that interaction between the VVA and the user are not saved on the Google Account or used to personalize the experience in the future. The device will remain in guest mode until the user requests to return to the default personalized experience. Yet, even though the user's activity will not be saved on their Google Account during guest mode, activity history may still be retained by other applications or services that are linked to Google Assistant, such as another Google product or a simple music provider. In other terms, turning on Guest Mode means that Google Assistant won't save the user's interactions, but the same thing cannot be said for Chrome, Google Cloud, Gmail, Google Maps, Google Photos or Google Ads.

Apple stresses in its privacy policy that Siri has been engineered to protect user's privacy by minimizing data collection. When a request is sent to Siri, the device's Siri settings will determine what requests are processed on the device itself, and what will be sent to the servers, as part of the company's data minimization efforts. For example, if a user asks Siri to read messages from the inbox, there is no need to transmit the data to the cloud since the request can be fulfilled easily on the device itself. In addition, data is not linked to a user's Apple ID or phone number, but rather to a random identifier made of a long string of letters and numbers that is generated for the purposes of processing.

Similar to Alexa and Google Assistant, Siri does use data from the user's device to complete requests in a more personalized fashion. But, Apple has decided to stop using audio recordings of Siri interactions and replace them with computer-generated transcripts.

B. User Consent

Companies manufacturing VVAs are required to acquire the user's consent before an interaction with either Alexa, Google Assistant, or Siri is initiated. This is generally done with a terms of service agreement, a privacy policy, or a product disclaimer (Bohm, 2017). However, although the VVA's owner has to agree to the servicing company's policies, a non-registered user can still interact freely with the devices. In the case of Amazon, users are consenting to having their conversations recorded and stored on the company's cloud by simply using Alexa. Amazon uses overly broad and ambiguous language when talking about consent in its policy: the company refers to users as "you," making it difficult to determine if the company is seeking to collect consent from the device owner, the device owner's family, or anyone present in the room with the device. Even Google's chief stated that he would disclose to his guests the presence of VVAs in his home: "it's quite important for all these technologies to think about all users . . . . we have to consider all stakeholders that might be in proximity … I would and do [disclose] when someone enters into my home, and it's probably something that the products themselves should try to indicate."

Consider this hypothetical: Sam, a working-class citizen gets t-boned by a truck while commuting to this workplace in Miami, Florida. After spending three days in the hospital recovering from the accident, he calls his local personal injury attorney, Dan, seeking to sue the trucker. While at Dan's office, Sam shouts out loud that he wishes he had taken the "metro" to work instead of driving his car. What Sam didn't know is that Dan is an avid AI fan, and is always ready to test the newest product on the market. Naturally, Dan has an Echo device in his office that he keeps behind his chair, and consults regularly for scheduling purposes. When Sam uttered the word "metro," Dan's Alexa misheard "echo," and thereafter woke up and started recording the conversation. In this hypothetical, not only has Amazon gained access to a non-user's PII, but the company has also collected confidential communication protected by the attorney-client privilege.

In most States, only one party to a conversation has to consent to having the conversation recorded for the recording to be considered legal. However, this is not the case for speech protected by the attorney-client privilege doctrine, the Health Insurance Portability and Accountability Act ("HIPAA"), or for States that have adopted two-party consent laws (Digital Media Project, 2022).

C. Employee "Eavesdropping"

Bloomberg published an article in 2019 reporting that Amazon hired thousands of new employees tasked with listening to voice notes recorded by Echo devices, transcribing and annotating them to improve Alexa's recognition of human speech (Day, 2019). Employees review an average of 1000 audio clips every day during their 9 hour shifts, and transcribe all speech and sound picked up by Alexa, including background conversations (Day, 2019). In one instance, an employee counted how they had to review clips for references to Taylor Swift to categorize the reference point as the music artist. By analyzing existing data, Alexa's developers are able to optimize users' experiences: for example, Amazon acknowledges that Alexa is able to understand the "nonaccent" of white, American, nonimmigrant users better than other accents (Day, 2019).

Employees are able to share recordings in internal chatrooms for amusement or professional peer guidance: in one instance, an employee overheard recordings of possible sexual assault (Day, 2019). These pieces of data are associated with three identifiers, the user's first name, the user's account number, and the device's serial number. If the employee hears a private conversation where personal information is shared such as bank details or social security numbers, the listener has to mark the file as "critical data." In addition, two Amazon employees reported that they were presented with around 100 recording every day where Alexa accidently woke up and the device started recording without being prompted to, yet the reviewers were still expected to listen and transcribe the recordings (Day, 2019).

In response to the Bloomberg article, Amazon stated that "all information is treated with high confidentiality and we use multi-factor authentication to restrict access, service encryption and audits of our control environment to protect it."

Data stored on the Apple servers is used to develop new technologies and improve Siri (Siri). But, in contrast with Amazon, Apple devices generate random identifiers that are used to interact with Siri in a private way, eliminating any personal identifiers beside one's voice (Eadicicco, 2019). Therefore, data that is sent to Apple's cloud for the short period of six months is not associated to the user, but to a randomly generated sequence of numbers.

Similar to Apple, Google anonymizes user recordings during the manual review system that a "fraction" of the audios files are subjected to (Eadicicco, 2019).

PART V: RELEVANT LAWS OR LACK THEREOF

There are around 13 billion devices connected on the IoT (Howarth, 2023). Due to the security and privacy issues that arise from the IoT, legislators attempted to regulate the sphere. In May 2019, the United States Senate introduced the "Developing Innovation and Growing the Internet of Things Act" to regulate and safeguard data in the IoT. The Act proposes the formation of a steering committee to advise on programs that promote and protect individual privacy in the IoT. One of the potential benefits of this Act would be to regulate the way devices such as Amazon's Alexa, Apple's Siri and Google Assistant interpret and respond to user interactions. Additionally, the Act would establish an agency to address security breaches involving VVAs and similar products. However, this act remains a proposal and despite privacy concerns, VVAs remain mostly unregulated at the federal level, and the Supreme Court has not yet recognized a privacy interest in all electronic communications (Bohm, 2017).

A. The Electronic Communications Privacy Act

The Electronic Communications Privacy Act ("ECPA") regulates certain aspects of digital privacy at the federal level. Title I of ECPA, often referred to as the Wiretap Act, authorizes the prosecution of any individual who "intentionally intercepts, endeavors to intercept, or procures any other person to intercept or endeavor to intercept, any wire, oral, or electronic communication." The law defines an electronic communication as "any transfer of signs, signals, writing, images, sounds, data, or intelligence of any nature transmitted in whole or in part by a wire, radio, electromagnetic, photo electronic or photo optical system that affects interstate or foreign commerce . . . ." The ECPA draws a difference between communication in storage, and communication intercepted in transit. Therefore, under the ECPA, a governmental entity wishing to get access to a communication will have to formally submit a request for a court order, subpoena, or warrant, depending on the case.

Assistive technologies like Amazon's Alexa, Google Assistant, or Apple's Siri rely heavily on their ability to interact and respond to communications. While consumers knowingly interact with the technology, Amazon, Apple, and Google employees are also accessing the device's stored communications on the remote cloud. This raises concerns that employees may be violating the spirit of the Federal Wiretap Act by listening to private recordings and transcribing communications. However, an exception in the Wiretap Act allows telephone companies to listen to communications for mechanical or service quality control purposes to improve service. The Act's drafters, however, did not anticipate that a commercial interest could arise from the contents of a phone call: manufacturers of VVA devices, to the contrary, seek to maximize the data collected about users to create personalized experiences in future interactions, or to advertise, which includes significant commercial gain in both cases (Tobin, 2019).

Although commercial privacy laws, such as the ECPA, have been amended to address wiretapping, they do not entirely cover the ways in which data is collected by VVAs (Bohm, 2017). Specifically, the Wiretap Act only prohibits intentionally intercepting "any wire, oral, or electronic communication" without at least one party's consent to the recording, making it legal to record communications as long as one party is consenting. And while some VVA manufacturers are retaining user data, these companies have set in place rigorous self-regulatory frameworks that ensure the timely collection of user consent. In addition, some scholars argue that the data recorded by VVAs is more akin to data recorded by a computer, rather than traditional wiretapping devices. And while VVA companies are benefiting from the exceptions under the ECPA, users' privacy is far from being protected on the federal level.

B. The Children Online Privacy Protection Act

The Children Online Privacy Protection Act ("COPPA") prohibits operators of websites or online services targeted at children, or those who have knowledge of collecting PII from children, from collecting such information in a way that violates regulations. These regulations include providing notice, obtaining parental consent, and maintaining reasonable security measures to protect children. The primary objective of this Act is to safeguard children's PII from being shared online and protect the most vulnerable members of society. The reason for this is that children are not fully aware of the implications of using a technology that has the potential to track and store their PII.

This law requires operators of websites and online services, including VVAs, to obtain parental consent before collecting PII from children under 13 years of age. It gets tricky when children are not the owners of the device, yet are interacting with the owner of a VVA when a misactivation happens. Or, it could be the case where a child uses an acquaintance's VVA without asking for parental permission and consent. In these brief examples, the child's PII ends up on a VVA's cloud, in direct violation of the COPPA.

C. The Federal Trade Commission Act and Consumer Guidance

Section 5 of the FTC Act prohibits ''unfair or deceptive acts or practices in or affecting commerce.'' This law applies to all entities and persons engaged in commerce. An act or practice is considered to be unfair whenever it causes or is likely to cause substantial injury to consumers, cannot be reasonably avoided by consumers, and is not outweighed by countervailing benefits to consumers or to competition. In addition, an act or practice is considered to be deceptive where a representation, omission, or practice misleads or is likely to mislead the consumer, a consumer's interpretation of the representation, omission, or practice is considered reasonable under the circumstances, and the misleading representation, omission, or practice is material.

In the beginning of April 2023, and according to reports, Amazon may face a potential lawsuit by the FTC over claims that its Alexa-enabled VVAs have been gathering PII from children under 13 years old without obtaining parental consent, which is a violation of the COPPA (Fung, 2023). The FTC has never brought an action against Amazon, Google, or Apple due to the "unfair or deceptive act or practices" of the VVAs they manufacture, which makes this potential lawsuit groundbreaking.

In December 2022, the FTC posted on its website guidance for users on how to secure their VVAs and protect their privacy. The FTC highlighted the importance of understanding how the technology works, that misactivations happen, and that recordings are usually stored on remote servers. The FTC stressed that users concerned about the privacy of their conversations should manually turn on their VVAs after disabling ASR features. Also, the FTC acknowledged that employees often listen to users' voice recordings, thus the importance of reading privacy policies thoroughly. The Commission advised users to request the deletion of their recordings from companies' clouds, and turn on auto-delete if possible. The FTC warned users about the risks of weak passwords, the importance of locking down VVA login, and using multi-factor authentication whenever possible. In addition, the FTC reminded users to check which bank accounts, credit, or debit cards are connected to their VVA, and advised to use pins or passcodes before allowing verbal purchases to be made through the VVA. Finally, the Commission stressed on the importance of securing the home base of every device – routers – by, for example, changing the router's default settings, setting up a guest network, turning on firewalls, and encrypting the network.

D. Proposed Solutions

When it comes to the issue of collecting consent from third-party users of VVAs, such as visitors to a home, or clients in an attorney's office, *Raphael Davidian* proposes to place the burden of collecting consent on the owner of the VVA if the device is used in a jurisdiction where two-party consent laws are in place (Davidian, 2017). It would be very challenging, and in some cases impossible, for any VVA to collect consent from third-party users with every interaction: in the eventuality where VVAs played a warning out loud whenever they would start recording, the warning would prove to be ineffective to guests that walked in the room after the recoding had started.

However, in some situations, collecting consent from third-party users can be challenging. For example, rule 1.6 of the American Bar Association's Model Rules of Professional Conduct prohibits attorneys from sharing information relating to the representation of their client "unless the client gives informed consent . . . ." If VVA owners were burdened with collecting third-party users' consent as per Raphael Davidian's proposal, then, the possibility of a VVA misactivation would require attorneys to collect the express consent of their clients to avoid potential malpractice lawsuits.

Another proposed solution by *Allison S. Bohm et. al* would be for companies to differentiate between PII collected from VVA owners, and PII collected from non-consenting users (Bohm, 2017). The former would be subject to the company's terms of service, and the latter would be immediately and permanently deleted from the company's cloud (Bohm, 2017). Most VVAs have the technological capacity to recognize specific acoustic tonalities, and are able to differentiate between voices (Lamey, 2018). Therefore, it would be technically possible for VVAs to be programmed to only record, and thereafter transcribe the voice notes of consenting owners, and automatically delete and refrain from transcribing voice notes from non-consenting users. However, with the prevalence of the privacy paradox, the extra set-up required by the implementation of this technology could deter users from the technology all together. In addition, it would be technically challenging for companies to differentiate between VVA owners and non-consenting users in voice notes where conversations between 2 or more people are recorded. In these situations, companies would probably need to disregard the voice recording altogether in order to avoid storing and transcribing a non-consenting user's voice note.

A proposal advanced by Ria Kuruvilla suggests for State legislatures to enact laws that mirror the Anti-Eavesdropping Act that the California State Assembly's privacy committee recently proposed (Kuruvilla, 2019). The Act seeks to regulate the storing and usage of recordings or transcripts by VVA manufacturers. Under this newly proposed act, recordings that are not deidentified or that contain PII cannot be used by VVA manufacturers for advertising purposes, which would prohibit Amazon from using user's data in their advertisements, in contradiction with their stated policy, as found by the *Iqbal et al.* study. In addition, the act proposes to prohibit the sale, sharing, and retaining of PII unless user consent is expressly provided. However, for this proposed law to effectively protect users' privacy, consumers need to be granted a private right of action that would allow them to sue VVA manufacturers.

PART VI: COMPLEX INTERNET OF THINGS DEVICES REQUIRE TECHNOLOGY-CONSCIOUS LEGISLATION

Since the creation of VVAs, the world of VVAs and other IoT devices has been largely self-regulated, with the industry setting its own standards and guidelines through terms of service agreements, privacy policies, or product disclaimers (Bohm, 2017). However, despite efforts to self-regulate, privacy concerns have arisen as a result of the large amount of PII collected by these devices: a survey by SafeWise found that 45% of participants disabled their VVA out of fear of being spied on in 2021 (Wheelwright, 2021). According to the survey, a significant portion of participants expressed apprehension regarding surveillance from different entities (Wheelwright, 2021). Specifically, 61.71% of respondents were worried about government monitoring, 70.24% expressed concern about being monitored by criminals, and 61.81% were uneasy about businesses monitoring them (Wheelwright, 2021). While self-regulation may seem like a proactive approach to address these concerns, it is important to note that self-regulation alone does not necessarily guarantee protection of users' privacy. There is an imminent need for a federal consumer-centered, and technology-conscious privacy legislation that mandates the protection of users' PII through the enforcement of privacy by design methods and modern FIPP.

Privacy by design is a proactive approach to consumer data protection that aims to embed privacy into the design of software products, rather than adding it as an afterthought (Cavoukian, 2011). Simply, privacy by design is the protection of data through technology design. This means that privacy considerations are integrated throughout the entire product lifecycle, from the initial concept to the final implementation. By prioritizing privacy from the outset, users can feel confident that their PII is protected and that their privacy rights are respected.

The FIPPs are a set of non-enforceable guidelines for privacy and data protection established by the FTC. The FTC FIPPs create a framework that outlines best practices for organizations to follow when collecting, using, and sharing PII, to ensure that individuals' privacy rights are respected and that their PII is handled in a fair and responsible manner.

By adapting the FTC FIPPs to the modern technological challenges posed by VVAs, adopting a technology-conscious design approach, and reimagining the inner-workings of VVAs, users' privacy can be protected in a more effective manner. This requires a technology-conscious legislation that puts users' privacy first, and reimagines technological advancements to respect users' right to digital privacy.

A. Notice and Awareness

Notice and awareness is an FIPP that requires companies to give users notice of the entity's privacy practices before any PII is collected, which would allow users to make educated and informed decisions about their privacy.

The company has to identify the entity collecting the PII, including if third party entities are collecting PII; identify how the PII is be used beyond what is needed to conduct business; identify any potential recipient of the PII; identify the nature of the collected PII; identify how the PII is collected; identify whether the provision of the requested data is voluntary or required; and identify the steps taken by the company to ensure the confidentiality, integrity, security, and quality of the PII.

In the early 2000s, the FTC advised companies to post a clear and conspicuous information practice disclosure on a prominent location on the website, including the homepage or landing page (Draper, 2019). However, the traditional notice and choice model is ineffective at protecting users' privacy in today's digitalized society and often leads to an increase in PII disclosure (Tsai, 2006). As long as users don't understand that VVA misactivations are common, and PII is often used in advertising, self-regulating VVA manufacturers have no reason to change their policies and practices.

To balance the complex VVA technology and users' right to digital privacy, companies need to adopt a privacy dashboard for VVAs. The Dashboard would provide each user with an individualized, unique, and comprehensive overview of the VVA's privacy settings, making it easy for users to customize their privacy preferences at any time. The privacy dashboard would be designed to be intuitive and user-friendly, providing a visual representation of the PII collected, usage practices, data sharing, and retention practices. It would also provide a summary of the VVA's privacy policy and terms of service in plain and easy to read language. VVA manufacturers would be able to integrate the dashboard in the device itself, similar to Alexa's skills, allowing users to manage their privacy preferences on the go.

B. Choice and Consent

The second fundamental FIPP is consumer choice and consent. In essence, choice means providing consumers with options regarding how their PII information may be used, particularly with respect to secondary uses of information that go beyond what is necessary to complete a task. These secondary uses may be internal, such as adding the consumer's email to the collecting company's mailing list for marketing purposes, or external, such as transferring information to third parties. With regard to VVAs, a common secondary use of PII is the generation of demographics, psychographics, and behavioral variables for the creation of successful targeted advertisement campaigns.

There are two types of consent regimes: opt-in and opt-out. Opt-in regimes require consumers to actively take steps to permit the collection and use of their PII, meaning that by default, PII is used for primary purposes only unless the user gives express consent at a later stage. On the other hand, opt-out regimes require consumers to actively take steps to prevent the collection and use of their PII, which means that users have to manually ask the manufacturing or servicing company to stop, for example, the collection, processing, and retention of PII.

VVAs can be designed with firmer access controls that strictly limit access to data that is necessary for the primary function of the technology, such as answering questions or performing basic tasks. This can be implemented through robust permission settings and data access protocols. The VVA could require explicit user consent for any secondary use of data beyond its primary function. Users would need to opt-in to allow the assistant to use their PII for secondary purposes, such as personalized recommendations or targeted advertising. This model is adopted by Google Assistant and Siri, whereby user privacy is a default function, unlike Amazon's Alexa. In addition, for optimal privacy, VVAs could prioritize on-device processing, which means that data processing and analysis would be done locally on the user's device rather than being sent to remote servers. This approach was streamlined by Apple.

VVA manufacturers can also implement voice-activated consent management features that allow users to easily give or revoke consent for specific data processing activities through voice commands. For example, users could say "Alexa, revoke consent for data sharing with marketing partners." The voice assistant would provide audible confirmation and reminders of the implications of the consent choices to ensure that users are making informed decisions.

C. Access and Participation

The third FIPP is access, which encompasses a user' ability to view PII about themselves that is stored on a remote cloud, as well as the ability to contest the accuracy and completeness of that data. Meaningful access entails timely and cost-effective access to stored PII, a simple process for contesting inaccurate or incomplete PII, a mechanism for the data collector to verify information, and a means to add corrections or consumer objections to the stored data.

However, the traditional right to access raises the issue of unauthorized access from well-intentioned third party users, or unethical hackers. In 2018, a German citizen requested his Alexa data from Amazon, yet, he was surprised to receive 1700 audio files that belong to a stranger. In a press statement to the Washington Post (media company owned by Amazon's majority shareholder, Jeff Bezos), Amazon blamed the incident on human error, and it assured users that the occurrence was isolated. Despite Amazon's assertion that this was a singular event, the occurrence highlights the possibility of Amazon, or any other company manufacturing and servicing VVAs, accidentally disclosing recordings containing confidential data.

VVA manufacturers must implement data minimization, which involves collecting and storing only the necessary PII, reduces the potential attack surface, and limits the exposure of user PII. By minimizing data collection, companies can reduce the risk of unauthorized access, and data misuse. Data minimization is a proactive, privacy-centric measure that promotes privacy and user control, instills confidence in users, and demonstrates responsible data handling practices on behalf of the VVA manufacturer. Apple practices data minimization with regard to Siri, and does not store user PII on its cloud indefinitely (Siri).

D. Security and Integrity

The fourth FIPP is that data should be accurate and secure. As per the FTC, to ensure PII integrity, collectors must take reasonable steps, such as using reputable sources of PII, cross-referencing data against multiple sources, providing consumer access to PII, and destroying outdated PII or converting it to anonymous form. Security involves both managerial and technical measures to protect against loss and unauthorized access, destruction, use, or disclosure of PII. Managerial measures include internal organization that restrict access to data to specific employees, and ensure that authorized individuals do not use the PII for unauthorized purposes. Technical security measures to prevent unauthorized access include encryption during data transmission and storage, password controls for access, and storing data on secure servers or computers that are not easily accessible.

To protect user privacy, the VVA could be designed to anonymize and aggregate data before storing it on a remote cloud, if necessary. For example, instead of using individual user data, the assistant could aggregate data from multiple users in a way that does not identify individual users. This is especially essential if users' voice recordings are to be used by employees for training or transcribing purposes.

CONCLUSION

VVAs are simple machines. They're the product of the careful coordination and harmonization of a myriad of hardware and software, ultimately resulting in a multifaceted technological entity. In simple terms, VVAs are the result of the amalgamation of 5 components: A microphone array for capturing users' voices, a signal processor for receiving the analog signal from the microphone and converting it into a digital software, an NLP algorithm to understand and interpret voice commands, a TTS engine to generate human-sounding responses, and a cloud-based server to process and store user PII.

When stripped of its fancy language, the fundamental function of VVAs and their learning technology can be quite unsettling, as it essentially involves eavesdropping. Consumers purchase an Alexa-enabled device, bring it into their homes, and feed it PII. Sometimes, these devices wake up accidently, meaning that the collection of PII becomes nonconsensual in theory. However, the meticulously crafted privacy policies and terms of service offer VVA manufacturers a degree of protection when misactivations happen, as the broad consent collected from users serves as a legal safeguard against potential privacy violation claims. Still, this PII is not restricted to the device's physical components, but instead, it is transmitted through the cloud, and in most cases, stored remotely indefinitely. The voice recordings are then reviewed by employees, who transcribe a written record of the user's interactions.

Although virtual voice assistants offer unparalleled convenience and functionality in users' daily lives, the insidious risk of unauthorized data sharing and exploitation of PII highlights the need for increased user awareness and regulatory oversight to safeguard against potential privacy violations. VVAs are largely unregulated in the United States, and the mosaic of sector-specific privacy laws on the federal level is insufficient, and ineffective at protecting consumer digital privacy. An effective technology-conscious legislation that regulates VVAs must prioritize privacy by design principles, which serve as the indispensable bedrock for safeguarding the privacy and confidentiality of users in the digital age. Through the integration of the FTC FIPPs with VVAs' design methodology, and redefinition of the operational framework of VVAs, it is possible to ensure more effective privacy protection for users.

REFERENCES

Allen, J. (2019, July/August). Digital virtual assistants: Utility v. privacy. *GPSolo, 36*(4), 4.

Amazon. (n.d.). Privacy policy. Archived at https://perma.cc/LHQ8-WSGB

Anders, G. (2017, August 9). "Alexa, understand me". MIT Technology Review. Archived at https://perma.cc/D72R-REU6

Apple. (n.d.). Siri privacy policy. Archived at https://perma.cc/MT3T-B6SG

Bohm, A. S.. (2017). Privacy and liberty in an always-on, always-listening world. *The Columbia Science and Technology Law Review, 19*, 1–19.

Botelho, B. (2022, December). Virtual assistant (AI assistant). Tech. Target. Archived at https://perma.cc/E2P4-2JVY

Boughman, E., ... (2017, November 19). "Alexa, do you have rights?": Legal issues posed by voice-controlled devices and the data they create. ABA. Archived at https://perma.cc/P42X-Q4VS

Brodkin, J. (2018, October 11). Amazon patents Alexa tech to tell if you're sick, depressed and sell you meds. Ars Technica. Archived at https://perma.cc/6LBP-R7C8

Cavoukian, A. (2011, January). Privacy by design, the 7 foundational principles, implementation and mapping of fair information practices. *Privacy by Design CA.*

Chen, Y., ... (2020, April 23). Wearable microphone jamming. Conference on Human Factors in Computing Systems. Archived at https://perma.cc/E4CR-5PJR

Cheng, L. (2020, November 2). Dangerous skills got certified: Measuring the trustworthiness of skill certification in voice personal assistant platforms. *Proceedings of the 2020 ACM SIGSAC Conference on Computer and Communications Security*, 1699–1716.

Courtney, M. (2017, October 13). Alexa, Cortana, Siri, et al: Do our digital assistants hear more than we want them to? E&T Magazine. Archived at https://perma.cc/95XU-KAGH

Dastin, J., Kirkham, C., & Kalra, A. (2021, November 19). Amazon wages secret war on Americans' privacy, documents show. Reuters. Archived at https://perma.cc/VPH8-LJ6X

Davidian, R. (2017). Alexa and third parties' reasonable expectation of privacy. *American Criminal Law Review Online, 54*, 58–60.

Day, M., Turner, G., & Drozdiak, N. (2019, April 10). Amazon workers are listening to what you tell Alexa. Bloomberg. Archived at https://perma.cc/6X8R-N2NX

Digital Media Law Project. (2022, September 10). Recording phone calls and conversations. Archived at https://perma.cc/S7GT-69F6

Draper, N. A., & Turow, J. (2019). The corporate cultivation of digital resignation. *New Media & Society*, *21*(12), 1824–1831.

Dubois, D. J.. (2020). When speakers are all ears: Characterizing misactivations of IoT smart speakers. *Proceedings on Privacy Enhancing Technologies. Privacy Enhancing Technologies Symposium*, *4*, 255–255.

Eadicicco, L. (2019, April 15). Amazon workers reportedly listen to what you tell Alexa – Here's how Apple and Google handle what you say to their voice assistants. Business Insider. Archived at https://perma.cc/GY2M-P7GC

Elghawaby, A. (2018, August 2). Social media's self-regulation isn't enough. CIG Online. Archived at https://perma.cc/C857-GAEQ

Etherington, D. (2014, November 6). Amazon Echo is a $199 connected speaker packing an always-on Siri-style assistant. TechCrunch. Archived at https://perma.cc/8GY4-CTAL

Foryciarz, A., Leufer, D., & Szymielewicz, K. (2020, January 17). Black-boxed politics: Opacity is a choice in AI systems. Medium. Archived at https://perma.cc/A2AY-3LES

Fowler, G. A. (2019, May 6). Alexa has been eavesdropping on you this whole time. The Washington Post. Archived at https://perma.cc/TK4E-QTHQ

Fung, J. (2023, April 4). FTC takes aim at Amazon's Alexa for illegally collecting kids' data. *The Mil Source*. Archived at https://perma.cc/5S29-HHHE

Gillis, A. S. (2023, January 19). Voice recognition (speaker recognition). Tech. Target. https://perma.cc/UZZ3-QMT9

Google. (n.d.). Google assistant privacy policy. Archived at https://perma.cc/KD7B-WQNR

Gray, S. (2017, April 4). Always on: Primary implications of microphone-enabled devices. Future of Privacy Forum. Archived at https://perma.cc/UQ92-CXCU

Howarth, J. (2023, March 16). *80+ amazing IoT Statistics (2023-2030).* Exploding Topics. Retrieved from https://perma.cc/QP9G-QJQ7

Iqbal, U., ... (2023, February 20). Your Echos are heard: Tracking, profiling, and ad targeting in the Amazon smart speaker ecosystem. Arxiv:2204.10920, 1–1.

Jin, H., & Wang, S. (2018, October 9). Voice-based determination of physical and emotional characteristics of users. US Patent 10,096,319. Archived at https://perma.cc/26V9-WW2D

Kelly, G. (2019, November 16). Compare the privacy practices of the most popular smart speakers with virtual assistants. Common Sense. Archived at https://perma.cc/A6AZ-65PS

Kozuch, K. (2023, March 3). The 30 best Alexa skills in 2023. Tom's Guide. Archived at https://perma.cc/65HN-JH6L

Kuruvilla, R. (2019, December). Between you, me, and Alexa: On the legality of virtual assistant devices in two-party consent states. *Washington Law Review (Seattle, Wash.)*, *94*, 2029–2052.

Lagapa, M. (n.d.). How Siri works – Voice recognition on a smartphone. Jameco. Archived at https://perma.cc/6SGK-UNHN

Lamey, D. (2018, July 26). The power of voice-activated voice assistants. *Discover Tec*. Archived at https://perma.cc/N3YW-58DD

Lang, R. D., & Benessere, L. E. (2018, January/February). Alexa, Siri, Bixby, Google's assistant, and Cortana testifying in court. *Journal of the Missouri Bar*, *74*(1), 20.

Maheshwari, S. (2018, March 31). Hey, Alexa, what can you hear? And what will you do with it? The New York Times. Archived at https://perma.cc/5ESJ-88FT

Malan, D. (2018, June 21). The law can't keep up with new tech. Here's how to close the gap. World Economic Forum. Archived at https://perma.cc/NHB9-4P8N

Manning, A. (2020, Spring). It's smart, but is it ethical? Confidentiality in an environment that is listening. *Virginia Journal of Law & Technology*, *24*(1), 7.

Myers, S. (2024, January 20). Movie analysis: "Her". Medium. Archived at https://perma.cc/KP2Y-E5EY

Ng, A. (2019, May 9). Amazon Alexa transcripts live on, even after you delete voice records. CNET. Archived at https://perma.cc/VH96-L332

Noonan, L. (2022, December 15). Self-regulation isn't enough. Larissa Noonan. Archived at https://perma.cc/L478-DE54

Nowak, P. (2016, December 27). The dark side of social media can no longer be ignored. The National News. Archived at https://perma.cc/A4BF-L6VP

Pierce, D. (2017, January 6). Alexa just conquered CES. The world is next. Wired. Archived at https://perma.cc/M9JR-7V6D

PricewaterhouseCoopers. (2018). Prepare for the voice revolution: An in-depth look at consumer adoption and usage of voice assistants, and how companies can earn their trust—and their business. Archived at https://perma.cc/77F4-7JXM

Raws, E., & Lacoma, T. (2019, July 13). How to set up an Amazon Echo. Digital Trends. Archived at https://perma.cc/SP52-ZBBV

Reed, B. (2020, July 20). 'Alexa, I love you': How lockdown made men lust after their Amazon Echo. The Guardian. Archived at https://perma.cc/2KXA-TB8L

Shavell, R. (2021, February 11). Big tech will try to pre-empt harsh privacy laws by writing their own. Help Net Security. Archived at https://perma.cc/9G8L-5KKE

Static, A. W. S. (2018, July 20). White paper: Alexa and data handling overview (1st ed., p. 2). Archived at https://perma.cc/5XS7-5DX2

Tobin, B. (2019, April 11). Amazon employees listen to customers through Echo products, report finds. *USA Today*. Archived at https://perma.cc/HWP7-F6G4

Tsai, J.. (2006). *What's it to you? A survey of online privacy concerns and risks.* Net Institute.

Wang, Y. (2021, July 13). Wake word detection and its applications. Johns Hopkins University Repository, 1, 18. https://perma.cc/WE37-LF6J

Weinberger, M. (2017, May 23). How Amazon's Echo went from a smart speaker to the center of your home. Business Insider. Archived at https://perma.cc/HGX7-KSXM

Wingfield, N. (2017, September 29). Amazon wants to wake you up with Alexa, and that's just the start. The New York Times. Archived at https://perma.cc/TP5Z-KVY2

Young, J.. (2022, August 10). SkillDetective: Automated policy-violation detection of voice assistant applications in the wild. *USENIX Security Symposium*, 1112–1114.

Zion Market Research. (2019, January 25). Global intelligent virtual assistant market will reach USD 19.6 billion by 2025: Zion Market Research. Globe Newswire. Archived at https://perma.cc/9YSP-WVC3

Chapter 12

Future of AI on Job Markets by Mediation of Ethical Considerations in the Horn of Africa

Shashi Kant
https://orcid.org/0000-0003-4722-5736
Bule Hora University, Ethiopia

Metasebia Adula
https://orcid.org/0000-0001-5732-2850
Bule Hora University, Ethiopia

Tafese Niguse
https://orcid.org/0009-0008-6536-6392
Bule Hora University, Ethiopia

Aynetu Terefe
https://orcid.org/0009-0003-3814-9548
Bule Hora University, Ethiopia

ABSTRACT

This chapter highlights the mediating function that morals play in influencing job outcomes as it inspects the complicated association among Artificial simulated Intelligence, Moral values considered based on business ethics, and the Market place occupation. The investigation uses quantitative analysis to manifest that AI has a major direct impact on the market driven by skill related jobs, with moral values considered based on business ethics mediating a sizable percentage of this impact. The results manifest that ethical frameworks are imperative in defining the

DOI: 10.4018/979-8-3373-3384-7.ch012

kind and degree of AI's impact on occupational dynamics when companies use AI technology. The investigation emphasizes how vital it is to incorporate moral values into the application of AI in order to optimize benefits and reduce hazards. Finally, the investigation recommends a thorough strategy for implementing AI that gives ethical issues first priority in order to promote long-term occupational practices in the rapidly changing digital ecosystem.

INTRODUCTION

The dynamic progression of artificial simulated intelligence has emerged as a vital determinant impacting world marketplaces, firms, and staff dynamics, hence restructuring the international occupational demand and its future (Nyoach et al., 2024). Understanding AI's consequences is especially imperative in areas like Eastern Africa, where economic progress is entwined with distinctive social and cultural contexts, as governments struggle with its ramifications. Because of the topic's potential to either aggravate current inequality or promote inclusive growth, it is of international relevance. Therefore, it is imperative that investigators and policymakers investigate the ethical implications of AI deployment in the market driven by skill related jobs (Birch et al., 2023). The merger of automation, analysis of data, and computer science technologies is where the idea of future of artificial simulated Intelligence in occupational settings first emerged. AI was first developed with the goal of increasing production and efficiency (Birhane eta l., 2024). However, it has since developed to incorporate sophisticated algorithms that can now carry out difficult jobs that were previously only done by humans. The consequences of AI on occupational have been the subject of much investigation due to this progression, which has revealed a complicated picture. According to empirical investigation, artificial simulated Intelligence has the potential to create new jobs but also has a high danger of job displacement, especially for low-skilled workers in manufacturing and agriculture—two firms vital to Eastern Africa (Laukes, 2024).

Though AI has great promises, there are a number of real-world obstacles that prevent it from being effectively incorporated into the market driven by skill related jobs. Deficits in infrastructure, restricted technological accessibility, and a shortage of trained labor generate obstacles that disproportionately impact underprivileged populations. Also, the ethical implications of AI's influence on occupational—such as responsibility, transparency, and fairness—remain little unexplored. The way in which these ethical elements might be operationalized to guarantee that the advantages of AI are spread fairly is frequently overlooked in the work now in publication. This investigation's main inquiry is: How may ethical issues affect the use of AI in the Eastern Africa's market driven by skill-related jobs to advance fair opportunities and reduce the danger of job displacement? In order to educate stakeholders and policy-makers on how to use AI for sustainable development while reducing its negative effects, it is imperative that this question be answered (Dappe& Lebrand, 2021).

BACKGROUND OF THE INVESTIGATION

Artificial simulated Intelligence is a promising field, but there are imperative challenges in integrating AI into the market driven by skill related jobs in Eastern Africa. Understanding the unique socioeconomic ecosystem of the area is necessary to contextualize these challenges. A number of issues plague Ethiopia, Somalia, Kenya, and other Eastern Africa nations, such as high rates of non-occupational, particularly among university graduates, limited access to technology, and poor infrastructure. These determinants create a complicated context for the use of AI, requiring careful consideration of the potential benefits of increased productivity and economic growth versus the risks of inequality and job loss (Niyitunga, 2024). Ethiopia's agriculture sector is used as a practical case investigation to illustrate the challenges of applying AI. Ethiopia's primary industry is agriculture, which employs around 70% of the labor force. Although their adoption has been slow, AI technologies such as predictive analytics and precision farming have the potential to boost agricultural productivity. Sometimes farmers' inability to obtain the necessary tools and training limits their ability to make full use of AI solutions. Also, because metropolitan areas frequently have greater access to technological resources and educational opportunities, the rural-urban divide exacerbates these problems by widening the gap among various socioeconomic levels (Kong et al., 2021).

Kenya is another country where Artificial simulated Intelligence is being applied in the banking sector. The rise of mobile banking apps like M-Pesa has revolutionized financial inclusion, but incorporating advanced AI analytics for credit scoring and risk assessment has proven difficult. A imperative portion of the population remains underbanked or unbanked, and those with little digital literacy encounter challenges while attempting to utilize AI-powered financial services. Concerns around algorithmic bias and data privacy also give rise to ethical questions regarding the fair application of AI technology in financing processes, which might further isolate underprivileged communities (Kant & Adula, 2024). Somalia faces a unique combination of challenges, particularly in light of the continuous unrest and instability in the nation. The nation's enduring security and governance issues pose a challenge to the development of the robust digital infrastructure needed for AI application. Lack of money and a lack of skilled individuals usually make it difficult to implement AI solutions in sectors like healthcare and education. The ethical implications of AI are vital in these types of circumstances since poorly designed algorithms have the ability to exacerbate social unrest and already-existing inequities.

These investigations demonstrate the need for a thorough understanding of the practical challenges associated with the use of AI in the Eastern Africa. They stress how imperative it is to solve infrastructural shortages, raise awareness of digital literacy issues, and develop moral frameworks in order to ensure that AI technologies are available to everyone. Owing to the complications of the region, tailored solutions that consider local situations are needed. This fosters an ecosystem in which AI may promote sustainable growth as opposed to widening already-existing gaps.

STATEMENT OF THE PROBLEM

Eastern Africa has a challenging issue when it comes to integrating Artificial simulated Intelligence into the market driven by skill related jobs since there is a big gap among the ideal situation of inclusive and equitable growth and the real difficulties the area is now facing (Nyoach et al., 2024). AI should ideally increase productivity, open up new career possibilities, and raise people's standard of living for people in all socioeconomic groups. Contradictory data, however, indicates that the application of AI technology frequently results in job displacement, especially for low-skilled people, aggravating already-existing disparities rather than reducing them. This disparity emphasizes how critical it is to have a thorough grasp of the variables affecting AI integration in this particular setting (Bian, 2024). The conflicting manifestations on the overall effect of AI on occupational in Eastern Africa represent one of the main gaps in the literature currently under publication. While some investigations highlight the potential for AI to create new job categories, others highlight the dangers of large occupational losses in more established firms like manufacturing and agriculture. Theoretical gaps also remain because the peculiar socio-economic and cultural dynamics of Eastern Africa are frequently overlooked by current frameworks, which limit their relevance to the region's particular problems. Also, there are still gaps in our knowledge on the best ways to assimilate ethical issues into AI initiatives so that everyone may benefit equally (Kong et al., 2021).

Contextual gaps make matters more complicated because much of the investigation that has been done so far has focused on high-income nations rather than the unique circumstances of developing nations. This mistake may result in the improper use of AI technologies that are incompatible with regional requirements or ideals. Also, the successful use of AI is hampered by practical issues including inadequate legislative frameworks, low digital literacy, and insufficient infrastructure, which frequently leaves disadvantaged groups behind. By offering a complete review of the current situation of AI in the market driven by skill-related jobs throughout

Eastern Africa, mediated by ethical issues, this investigation seeks to close these complicated gaps. Through the integration of theoretical concepts and empirical data, this investigation will provide a sophisticated framework that takes into account the distinct socio-economic circumstances of the area. It will look into how moral standards might guide the creation and application of AI technology to make sure that the advantages are distributed fairly (Jaldi, 2023).

In addition, this investigation will manifest effective case investigation and industry's best practices from both inside and beyond the area, providing policy-makers with useful suggestions. By doing this, it hopes to give future scholars and decision-makers a clear path forward, empowering them to negotiate the challenges of integrating AI in Eastern Africa. The ultimate goal of this investigation is to create a setting in which Artificial simulated Intelligence is used as a tool for sustainable development, tackling the urgent problems of inequality and unemployment while advancing moral leadership and social inclusion.

THEORETICAL FOUNDATION

Technological Determinism Theory: It implies that human behavior and society are shaped by technology. According to this idea, the advent of AI would unavoidably change economic dynamics and work structures, either creating new jobs or dislodging existing ones. Even though this viewpoint emphasizes the revolutionary potential of AI, especially in varied ecosystems like Eastern Africa, it may oversimplify the socioeconomic elements that mediate these developments (Dappe & Lebrand, 2021).

Social Constructivism: highlights how social forces have shaped technology and its effects. According to this idea, society norms, values, and power dynamics have an influence on how AI will affect the market driven by skill related jobs rather than being preset. For example, in Eastern Africa, cultural perspectives on technology adoption and the disparities in resources and education now in place are imperative determinants in influencing how Artificial simulated Intelligence is incorporated into different firms. This viewpoint emphasizes how vital it is to use participatory methods and community participation while developing AI solutions that are considerate of regional demands (Azaroual, 024).

Human Capital Theory: provides insightful information as well, emphasizing human talents and knowledge as essential elements of economic production. According to this hypothesis, worker capacities may be improved by expenditures in education and training, allowing people to become more adaptable to changes in technology. This theory emphasizes the need for reskilling programs in Eastern Africa in the context of AI, in order to provide workers with the necessary skills for an AI-driven economy. It could, however, ignore the more imperative structural obstacles that restrict access to these kinds of educational opportunities, especially in populations that are excluded (Niyitunga, 2024).

DEFINITION AND ORIGIN OF TERMS

***Artificial Intelligence*:** Artificial simulated Intelligence is the term used to describe how technology, especially computer schemas, can simulate human intelligence processes. This involves skills like learning—the process of acquiring knowledge and applying rules to it—reasoning—the application of rules to arrive at a rough or firm conclusion—and self-correction. John McCarthy originally used the phrase "Artificial simulated Intelligence" in 1956 at the Dartmouth Conference, which is frequently seen as the beginning of AI investigation. While symbolic approaches and problem-solving were once the main focus, machine learning, neural networks, and data analytics have imperatively broadened the field of Artificial simulated Intelligence over the years (Gebru etal., 2023).

Job Market: The marketplace where people look for work and companies look to hire people is known as the "Market place occupation." It assimilates the labor supply and demand, which is impacted by the state of the economy, changes in the industry, and developments in technology. The idea originated in classical economics, which views labor as a good that can be purchased and sold on the open market. As a result of shifting cultural standards and technological advancements, the market driven by skill related jobs has expanded throughout time to encompass not just regular occupational but also gig marketplaces, remote work, and freelancing alternatives (Kant & Adula, 2024).

***Business Ethics*:** In situations where technology and human welfare interact, ethical issues entail assessing the moral standards and values that inform decision-making processes. Since the use of intelligent schemas raises concerns about accountability, transparency, fairness, and potential bias, this word has become more common in AI discourse (Jaldi, 2023). Philosophical traditions such as utilitarianism, deontology, and virtue morals, which offer frameworks for evaluating the effects of acts and technology on society, are the source of ethical issues (Arakpogun et al., 2021).

EMPIRICAL LITERATURE REVIEW

AI Future and Job Market

Artificial simulated Intelligence has far-reaching and diverse effects on the market driven by skill related jobs, including both possibilities and difficulties that drastically change the occupational ecosystem in a number of different areas (Adula et al., 2023). AI has the ability to increase efficiency and production on the one hand by automating repetitive and regular jobs, freeing up human workers to concentrate on more intricate and creative work. For example, AI-driven automation may cut costs, streamline operations, and lessen human error in sectors like manufacturing and logistics, all of which eventually boost productivity and profitability (Cramarenco et al., 2023).

But there are also serious hazards associated with the development of AI, especially with regard to job displacement. Automation poses a threat to many low-skilled occupations, particularly in firms like manufacturing, retail, and agriculture. Millions of jobs might be in jeopardy as AI schemas advance and become more proficient at tasks that have historically been performed by humans, according to reports. Increased unemployment rates may result from this displacement impact, especially in poorer countries where there may not be as many options for new jobs (Guye et al., 2024). As a result, there can be a disproportionate impact on individuals with lower skill levels or educational attainment, which can worsen already-existing disparities (Kant & Adula, 2024) Also, the emergence of AI demands a change in the abilities needed in the staff. Workers with experience in technology, data analysis, and AI schemas administration are in more demand. This change emphasizes how vital it is to launch upskilling and reskilling programs to equip the labor force for the rapidly evolving nature of the staff. Institutions of higher learning and training must change to provide people with the skills they need to prosper in an AI-driven economy. Critical thinking, creativity, and technological competence should be prioritized (Gebru etal., 2023).

H1: AI has imperative effect on Market place occupation

AI Future and Ethical Considerations

A number of ethical issues are raised by the application of artificial simulated Intelligence in different firms, and these issues need to be carefully considered. Algorithmic bias, which happens when AI schemas create unjust decisions because of biased data or incorrect algorithms, is one of the most urgent problems (Jabo et al., 2024). Biased training data, for example, might result in unfair occupational, lending, and law enforcement policies that disproportionately impact underrepresented communities. In order to reduce prejudice in AI schemas, developers and firms are urged to put in place stringent testing and validation procedures. This poses imperative moral values considered based on business ethics concerning justice and equity (Kong et al., 2021). Transparency in Artificial simulated Intelligence decision-making is a major ethical problem. Many AI schemas function as "black boxes," meaning that even their designers struggle to understand the reasoning behind their outputs. The accountability schema may be compromised by this lack of openness as it makes it difficult to understand the decision-making process. Transparency is ethically required in situations where AI might have a major influence on lives, such in the criminal justice or healthcare schemas. In order to ensure that consumers can understand and trust the schemas that have an impact on imperative decisions, stakeholders must push for explainable AI (Guyo, et al., 2023,

In the context of AI, data privacy also becomes a vital ethical concern. Large-scale personal data collecting and analysis raises questions regarding security, monitoring, and permission. People might not be completely aware of the repercussions of data misuse or how their data is being utilized (Birhane et al., 2024). This calls for the creation of strict data protection laws and moral standards that safeguard user privacy first and encourage ethical use of AI. Companies need to be open and honest about how they handle data, and they should make sure that privacy is considered from the beginning when designing AI schemas (Amin, 2024). In addition, ethical conundrums including social fairness and accountability arise from the possibility of occupational displacement brought on by AI automation. As AI schemes take over some jobs, concerns about businesses' and governments' responsibilities to assist impacted workers surface. Proactive steps, including social safety nets and reskilling programs, are required here due to moral values considered based on business ethics in order to support those whose livelihoods are in danger due to technological breakthroughs. Fostering a just society requires making sure that the advantages of AI are shared fairly (Hui et al., 2024).

Finally, the wider societal effects of technology also have ethical ramifications for artificial simulated Intelligence. The growing impact of artificial simulated Intelligence schemas on public policy, healthcare, and finance necessitates a thorough examination of their long-term implications on human behavior, social structures, and community dynamics. Including a range of stakeholders in conversations regarding AI development, such as ethicists, engineers, and impacted communities, can help people grasp the implications of technology more comprehensively and build more morally sound and responsible behaviors (Horn & Donaldson, 2021).

H2: AI has an imperative effect on Moral values considered based on business ethics

Ethical Considerations Mediation Among Job Market and AI Future

The impact of ethical issues on the market driven by skill related jobs is growing as businesses learn to manage the challenges of incorporating technology—especially Artificial simulated Intelligence—into their daily operations (Panigarhi et al., 2023). Organizational culture, employee associations, and recruiting procedures are all imperatively influenced by ethical determinants. Companies may create a diverse work ecosystem that draws in top talent by focusing on justice, openness, and responsibility. When hiring procedures are guided by ethical standards, biases caused by automated schemas can be lessened and candidates are assessed on the basis of their credentials and abilities rather than imperative characteristics like gender or race (Niyitunga, 2024). Also, ethical issues support worker happiness and well-being. When companies put an emphasis on openness in their decision-making procedures, staff members are more likely to feel appreciated and trusted by management. Building a healthy workplace culture where people feel empowered to share their problems and ideas requires this trust. Retaining and engaging an employee requires ethical behaviors including equitable pay, courteous treatment, and professional development opportunities. Consequently, firms that follow moral principles frequently see less employee attrition and increased output, which helps them succeed as a whole (Laukes, 2024).

Also, the ethical implications of AI adoption imperatively influence business policies and practices. Firms can guarantee that technology is utilized ethically and does not reinforce current disparities by including morals into AI plans (Durga et al., 2024). In order to promote a more equal market driven by skill related jobs, ethical frameworks, for instance, can direct the development of AI schemas that are intended to be impartial and fair. In addition to improving an organization's reputation, this proactive strategy lessens the possibility of legal issues and public outcry brought on by unethical behavior (Kong et al., 2021). Moreover, the significance of morals in the occupational market transcends specific establishments; it impacts industry norms and public anticipations. Firms are under pressure to implement ethical practices in response to growing demands from stakeholders and customers for moral conduct. As a result of this change, corporate social responsibility (CSR) programs have emerged, in which businesses actively participate in socially conscious actions that benefit the society at large as well as their own staff. Firms may attract clients who share their beliefs and improve their brand image by giving ethical issues top priority (Kant & Adula, 2024).

H3: Ethical Consideration has imperative effect on Market place occupation

Mediation of Ethical Consideration Among AI Future and the Job Markets

In order to guarantee that the use of Artificial simulated Intelligence technology promotes fair outcomes for all parties concerned, ethical issues must be mediated among AI and the market driven by skill related jobs. The growing impact of AI schemas on recruiting procedures, job training, and staff management necessitates the incorporation of ethical frameworks that place a premium on equity and openness. This mediation method addresses possible biases and makes sure that technology improvements do not worsen already-existing disparities while providing guidance through the complicated AI's influence on occupational (Hui et al., 2024). Establishing fair occupational procedures is one of the main ways ethical issues moderate the link among AI and the market driven by skill related jobs. While AI-powered recruiting technologies might expedite the hiring process, they may unintentionally reinforce prejudices seen in previous data. Firms may actively eliminate prejudice by utilizing AI technologies and enforcing ethical norms that prioritize justice. This will ensure a staff that is more diverse and inclusive. In addition to helping excluded groups, this fosters a diversity of viewpoints and ideas, which improves organizational effectiveness (Horn & Donaldson, 2021).

Also, the creation of programs for reskilling and upskilling must take ethical issues into account. Staff development must be given top priority as AI automates some job processes in order to prepare workers for the rapidly evolving occupational market (Asefa eta l., 2024). The development of training programs that are available to all employees, irrespective of their socioeconomic status, can be guided by ethical standards. Firms may lessen the negative consequences of job displacement and foster social responsibility and community well-being by making sure these activities are equal (Laukes, 2024). Additionally, AI schemas' transparency plays a vital mediating function in the market driven by skill related jobs. Firms are required by ethical concerns to reveal the data that is utilized in decision-making processes as well as the workings of AI algorithms. By enabling workers and job seekers to comprehend and contest AI schema judgments, this transparency builds confidence. Having open lines of communication on the use of AI in hiring procedures promotes responsibility and enables early intervention to resolve any potential problems (Hui et al., 2024). Also, resolving data privacy is critical to the moral mediation of AI and the market driven by skill related jobs. Ethical standards must guarantee that people's privacy rights are upheld while businesses gather and examine enormous volumes of personal data for AI applications. Informed consent must be obtained, data must be protected against breaches, and data usage must be disclosed in a transparent manner. Firms that prioritize data privacy are able to meet legal requirements, foster trust among employees, and ultimately increase employee loyalty and morale (Laukes, 2024).

H4: Mediation of Ethical Consideration influences the association among AI and Market place occupation

CONCEPTUAL FRAMWORK

By analyzing theoretical and empirical manifestations the following hypothesis was formulated.

Figure 1. Conceptual framework (Authors)

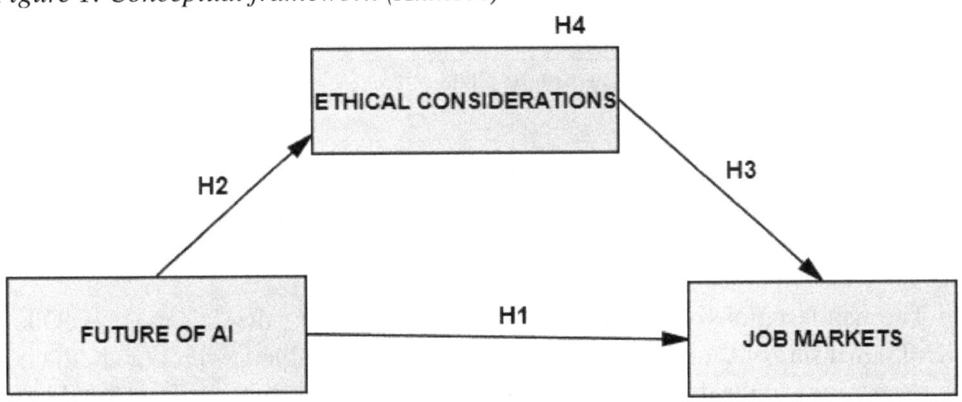

INVESTIGATION METHODOLOGY

A thorough investigation technique was used in this investigation to look at the underlying constructs that are pertinent to the investigation topic. A valid dataset for analysis was ensured by using a sample size of 403 individuals. The choice of a quantitative investigation technique made it easier to statistically analyze the connections among the variables. When the Kaiser-Meyer-Olkin (KMO) measure was computed to determine whether the data were suitable for determinant analysis, the result was above the suggested cutoff point of 0.6, indicating that the sample size was sufficient for the investigation. To manifest the underlying determinant structure of the constructs, exploratory determinant analysis, or EFA, was used. In order to provide a more lucid interpretation of the data, this procedure comprised rotating and removing components. The suggested theoretical dimensions were supported by the EFA results, which manifested a distinct determinant structure and many items that loaded heavily on their respective determinants. The proposed associations among the components were then tested using AMOS software and structural equation modeling (SEM). SEM offered a thorough evaluation of the model fit and enabled the simultaneous investigation of several interactions. Several fit indices demonstrated a good match in the results, implying that the proposed model appropriately captured the data.

DATA ANALYSIS

Table 1. KMO and Bartlett's test

Measure of Sampling Adequacy by Kaiser-Meyer-Olkin		**.872**
Sphericity by Bartlett's Test	Chi-Square estimate	1419.625
	df	95
	p-value	.003

Source: Authors

The manifestations of the Bartlett's Test of Sphericity and the Kaiser-Meyer-Olkin (KMO) measure of sampling adequacy are depicted in Table 1, which are both vital for determining if the data are appropriate for determinant analysis. The high degree of sample adequacy is depicted by the KMO value of 0.872. This number is higher than the generally recognized cutoff of 0.7, indicating that a substantial amount of variance in the items can be accounted for by the underlying determinants, indicating that the data is a good fit for determinant analysis. The fact that the KMO value is closer to 1 indicates that there are enough associations among the items, hence validating the investigation and allowing for the subsequent exploratory determinant analysis (EFA). A chi-square value of around 1419.625 with 95 degrees of freedom and a significance level of 0.003 is depicted by the Bartlett's Test of Sphericity manifestations. The purpose of this test is to assess the null hypothesis, which states that the variables are uncorrelated and that the correlation matrix is an identity matrix. The correlation among the variables is verified by a imperative p-value (less than 0.05), which manifested that the correlation matrix is not an identity matrix. Given that there appear to be imperative associations among the variables, determinant analysis is warranted, as evidenced by the significance level of 0.003.

Table 2. Total variance explained

Component	Primary Eigenvalues			Abstraction Sums of Squared Loadings			Alternation Sums of Squared Loadings		
	Total	% of Variance	Cumulative %	Total	% of Variance	Cumulative %	Total	% of Variance	Cumulative %
1	3.91	30.236	30.236	3.91	30.236	30.236	2.98	21.431	21.431
2	1.38	9.767	42.021	1.38	9.767	42.021	2.36	15.451	36.940
3	1.28	9.086	51.12	1.27	9.086	51.112	1.24	14.172	51.112
4	.951	6.785	57.891						
5	.870	6.225	64.117						
6	.775	5.521	69.632						

Abstraction Routine: PCA
Source: Authors

The total variance explained by the components obtained from Principal Component Analysis (PCA) is displayed in Table 2. This table is essential for determining the proportion of the dataset's overall variability that can be ascribed to the determinants that have been found, which will direct future investigation and interpretation. The first eigenvalues in the table manifest the amount of variance that each component contributed before it was extracted. With an initial eigenvalue of 3.91, the first component accounts for 30.236% of the total variance. This large number implies that a major portion of the dataset is captured by the first component. When paired with the first component, the second component, which has an eigenvalue of 1.38, accounts for an additional 9.767% of the variance, or 42.021% of the variance overall. With an eigenvalue of 1.28, the third component increases the overall variance by 9.086%, making the cumulative percentage 51.12%. These manifestations suggest that the first three components assimilate a imperative amount of variation.

After extraction, the variation explained by the components is reflected in the extraction sums of squared loadings. It's interesting to note that the first three components' values hold true for the original eigenvalues, suggesting that their significance endures even after extraction. 30.236% of the variation is still explained by the first component, with contributions from the second and third components coming in at 9.767% and 9.086%, respectively. With an eigenvalue of 0.951, the fourth component may not be required for the model because it does not satisfy the standard criterion of 1.0 for a meaningful contribution. Once rotation methods are applied to improve interpretability, the rotation sums of squared loadings offer further information. Following rotation, the variation is explained by the first component, whose sum drops to 2.98 after 21.431%. By comparison, the variation is explained by a second component whose sum climbs to 2.36, or 15.451%. With a minor decline to 1.24, the third component captures 14.172% of the total. The total variance explained by these three components stays at 51.112% after these modifications, suggesting that they are jointly responsible for a sizable amount of the variance in the data.

Table 3. Covariance's

Covariance			Approximation	S.E.	C.R.	P	Hy.
Ethical Consideration	**<-->**	**AI**	**.239**	**.024**	**8.232**	**.00**	**H2**
Ethical Consideration	<-->	Job Market	.314	.031	7.691	.00	**H3**
AI	<-->	Job Market	.251	.26	7.835	.00	**H1**

Source: Authors

The correlation estimates among the constructs of AI, Market place occupation, and ethical consideration are depicted in Table 3, which sheds light on the connections among these variables. Understanding how these dimensions interact and impact one another is vital for generating the main investigation hypotheses. Covariance analysis plays a key function in this process. According to the paper, there is a 0.239 correlation among AI and ethical consideration, with a 0.024 standard error (S.E.). The two constructs have a high positive link, as indicated by the critical ratio (C.R.) of 8.232 for this association. When a p-value is less than 0.001, the significance level is depicted with ".00," indicating that the association is statistically imperative. This investigation demonstrates that ethical issues have a big impact on how AI is seen or applied, which validates Hypothesis 2 (H2). With a S.E. of 0.031, the correlation among the Market place occupation and ethical consideration is 0.314. This association's strength is further highlighted by its C.R. of 7.691. The significance level is depicted by ".00," just like in the preceding pair, manifesting a very imperative link and confirming Hypothesis 3 (H3). This manifestation implies that ethical issues are not only pertinent to the creation and use of AI, but also have a imperative function in determining how the market driven by skill related jobs performs. AI and the Market place occupation have a correlation of 0.251 and a S.E. of 0.026. The substantial positive association among these constructs is indicated by the C.R. value of 7.835. Once more confirming a statistically imperative link, the significance level depicted with a ".00" supports Hypothesis 1 (H1). This implies that AI has a imperative impact on the market driven by skill related jobs, highlighting the need of comprehending how developments in AI may affect occupational and work ecosystems.

Table 4. Validity concern

	CR	AVE	MSV	MaxR(H)	AI	EC	JM
AI	0.734	0.646	0.221	0.863	**0.673**		
EC	0.761	0.658	0.131	0.762	0.172	**0.668**	
JM	0.792	0.601	0.273	0.795	0.382	0.195	**0.683**

Note: AI=Artificial simulated Intelligence; EC= Ethical Consideration; JM= Market place occupation
Source: Authors

Table 4 provides imperative metrics for evaluating the validity of the investigation's assessed components, including multiple associations among the constructs, Composite Reliability (CR), Average Variance Extracted (AVE), and Maximum Shared Variance (MSV). These metrics are vital for assessing the construct validity and reliability of the measurement model. The constructions have an acceptable degree of internal consistency, as depicted by the Composite Reliability (CR) scores. The CR for Artificial simulated Intelligence is 0.734, over the generally recognized cutoff of 0.7, indicating the validity of the AI measurement items. Strong dependability for this construct is indicated by the highest CR of 0.792 for Market place occupation (JM), which is closely followed by Ethical Consideration (EC) with a CR of 0.761. These results are corroborated by the Average Variance Extracted (AVE) values, which manifest that JM is 0.601, EC is 0.658, and AI is 0.646. By manifesting that a imperative amount of the variation in the items is captured by their respective constructs, all AVE values are more than 0.5, which further validates the assessment of the items.

A measure of potential overlap among constructs can be found in the Maximum Shared Variance (MSV) values. AI has an MSV of 0.221, which indicates a low level of shared variance with other constructs, suggesting good discriminant validity; Ethical Consideration has an even lower MSV of 0.131, which indicates minimal overlap; Market place occupation has the highest MSV of 0.273. All in all, though, the MSV values are relatively low, suggesting that the constructs maintain their distinctiveness while still exhibiting meaningful associations with one another. In addition, the table provides further insight about the inter associations among the components by outlining the connections among them. For instance, there is a substantial positive correlation of 0.673 among AI and EC, manifesting that these two variables are related. The strong interaction among ethical issues and the dynamics of the market driven by skill related jobs is demonstrated by the 0.668 connection among EC and JM. Additionally, the correlation among AI and JM is 0.683, indicating a imperative link as well. These associations highlight the interdependence of these variables and support the construct validity of the model, along with the CR, AVE, and MSV manifestations.

MEDIATING FUNCTION EXAMINATION

Figure 2. Structural equation model (Authors)

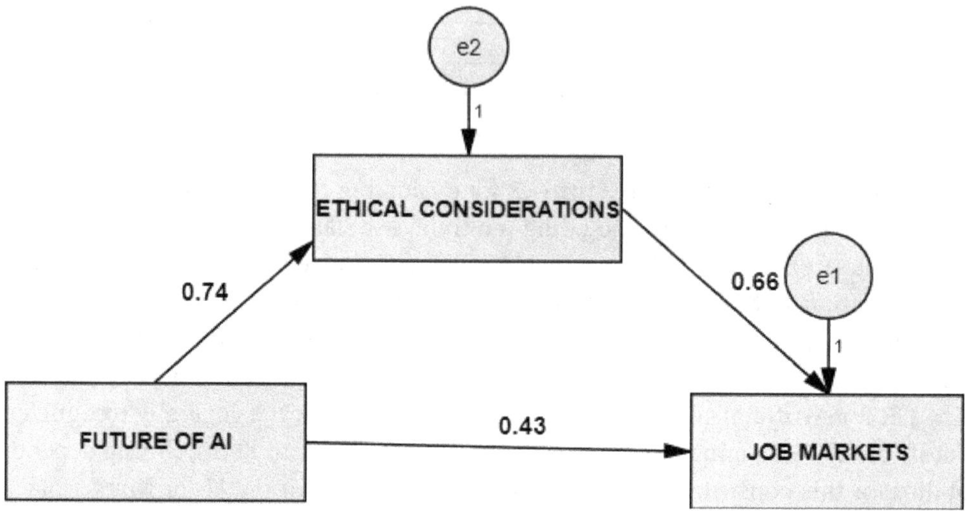

Model Fit Indices

Table 5. Model fitness

Sig.	Chi-Sq	RMR	Fitness Goodness	Fitness Confirmatory	TLI	RMSEA
0.003	1.964	.037	0.932	0.914	0.913	.026

Source: Authors

The model fit indices for the investigation of the mediating function in the investigation are depicted in Table 5. In order to validate the association and potential mediating effects among the dimensions under inquiry, these indices are essential for evaluating how well the proposed model matches the observed data. According to the reported model fit significance level of 0.003, the model is statistically imperative. A low p-value indicates that there is a substantial difference among the observed data and what would be predicted by the null hypothesis, which manifested that the model fits the data well. This is further supported by the Chi-Squared (Chi-Sq) value of 1.964, as lower Chi-Sq values in relation to degrees of freedom often denote a better match. When taken as a whole, these measures point to the model's suitability for mediating function testing. With a reported Root Mean Square Residual (RMR) of

0.037, far below the 0.05 standard, a satisfied fit among the model and the data is indicated. Also, there is a high degree of fit as depicted by the Fitness Goodness index of 0.932. A good fit is often indicated by a value greater than 0.90, indicating that the model sufficiently captures the connections among the components. The model's validity is further supported by the Confirmatory Fit indices, such as the Root Mean Square Error of Approximation (RMSEA) and the Tucker-Lewis Index (TLI). The strong fit is depicted by the TLI value of 0.914, which is higher than the generally recognized criterion of 0.90. In a similar vein, the reported RMSEA of 0.026 supports the idea that the model fits the data well because it is far below the acceptable criterion of 0.08. A close match is often indicated by RMSEA values less than 0.05, which supports the investigation's proposed mediational association.

Table 6. Regression check

Relative			**Estimate**	**S.E.**	**C.R.**	**P**	**Ass.**
Ethical Consideration	**<---**	**AI**	**.873**	**.142**	**7.581**	**.00**	**H2**
Job Markets	<---	Ethical Consideration	.326	.132	2.854	.00	H3
Job Markets	<---	AI	.958	.193	7.959	.00	H1

Source: Authors

The manifestations of the regression analysis, which examines the connections among the concepts of artificial simulated Intelligence, principled consideration, and Market place occupation, are depicted in Table 6. This table is vital for comprehending how these determinants directly affect one another and for confirming the investigation's assumptions.

The standard error (S.E.) of the regression coefficient for the association among AI and ethical consideration is 0.142, and it is stated to be 0.873. This association's critical ratio (C.R.) is 7.581, indicating a imperative and favorable impact of AI on ethical consideration. A p-value of less than 0.001 is indicated by the significance level of ".00," indicating that this association is statistically imperative and strongly supports Hypothesis 2 (H2). The significance of ethical frameworks in the context of AI investigation and implementation is highlighted by this investigation, which suggests that greater degrees of AI are linked to stronger ethical concerns.

The correlation among the Market place occupation and moral values considered based on business ethics has a regression coefficient of 0.326 and a standard error of 0.132. The significance of this association is further highlighted by the C.R. value of 2.854, and the significance level is also depicted with ".00," denoting a p-value less than 0.001. This demonstrates that ethical issues have a imperative influence on the market driven by skill related jobs and validates Hypothesis 3 (H3). The positive coefficient supports the idea that moral behavior might influence work results by manifesting that there is a positive correlation among ethical concerns and Market place occupation dynamics. With a S.E. of 0.193, the regression coefficient for the association among AI and the Market place occupation is found to be 0.958. A very strong positive association among these constructs is depicted by the C.R. value of 7.959. The statistical significance of this link is confirmed by the significance level of ".00", therefore providing support for Hypothesis 1 (H1). This result implies a strong association among changes in the market driven by skill related jobs and AI breakthroughs, suggesting that the incorporation of AI technology imperatively affects market dynamics and occupational prospects.

Table 7. Mediating function effect

	Influence	Worth	Path Influence
AI → Job Markets	Direct Influence	.43	Direct influence stated
AI → Ethical Considerations → Job Markets	Indirect Influence	.74*.66=.47	Indirect Influence Ensued
	Whole influence	.90	Partial mediation

Source: Authors

Table 7 describes the function that Moral values considered based on business ethics play as a mediator in the association among Artificial simulated Intelligence and the Market place occupation. It is imperative to understand this association because it sheds light on the nature of the associations that exist among AI and occupational outcomes. The table manifested that AI has a direct, 0.43-quantified impact on the Market place occupation. This direct influence emphasizes the profound effect AI has on occupational dynamics, implying a strong association among changes in market trends, job availability, and job kinds and improvements in AI technology. The expression "Direct influence stated" establishes a fundamental connection among AI and the market driven by skill related jobs and supports the notion that this association is clear-cut and imperative.

The table also manifested the indirect impact of AI on the market driven by skill related jobs due to moral values considered based on business ethics, which is computed as 0.74 multiplied by 0.66 to provide an indirect effect value of 0.48. This is in addition to the direct influence. This suggests that the interaction among AI and the Market place occupation is imperatively mediated by moral values considered based on business ethics. The notation "Indirect Influence Ensued" implies that ethical frameworks in existence have a substantial influence on the effects of AI on Market place occupation results in addition to direct effects. This investigation emphasizes how vital it is to incorporate ethical issues into AI applications as they have the potential to either improve or lessen the effects of AI on occupational. The combined effect of the direct and indirect sources is stated as 0.90, or the overall influence. This large cumulative number suggests that the occupational market is greatly impacted by AI's combined effects, which affect it both directly and indirectly through moral values considered based on business ethics. The term “partial mediation” implies that although Moral values considered based on business ethics moderate the association, AI still has a imperative direct impact on the market driven by skill related jobs. This investigation is imperative because it highlights the necessity for stakeholders to have a dual focus, acknowledging the immediate effects of AI but also comprehending how ethical issues might influence these results.

DISCUSSION

The manifestations of this investigation highlight the intricate associations among Artificial simulated Intelligence, Moral values considered based on business ethics, and the Market place occupation. The imperative direct influence of AI on the Market place occupation underscores the transformative potential of AI technologies in shaping occupational dynamics. Moreover, the mediating function of Moral values considered based on business ethics emphasizes the importance of integrating ethical frameworks into AI development and deployment. This investigation reveals that moral values considered based on business ethics not only enhance the impact of AI on Market place occupation outcomes but also serve as a critical determinant in ensuring responsible AI usage. Study results are similar with prior studies of Jabo et al., 2023, Birhane et al., 2024, Guye et al., 2024 and kant & Adula, 2024. As firms increasingly adopt AI technologies, understanding these associations becomes imperative for fostering a sustainable and ethical work ecosystem.

CONCLUSION

This investigation clarifies the intricate associations that exist among AI, moral values considered based on business ethics, and the market driven by skill related jobs. The correlation among AI and job results and the noteworthy moderating impact of ethical concerns implies that ethical frameworks are indispensable for effectively addressing the obstacles presented by AI. The manifestations manifest that while AI has the potential to imperatively alter the market driven by skill related jobs, including ethical principles can increase favorable outcomes and reduce hazards. This investigation adds to the expanding corpus of investigation on the subject of technology and morals by offering practitioners, academics, and representative’s insightful information.

MANAGERIAL IMPLICATIONS

The results of this investigation highlight the need for managers to give ethical issues top priority while developing AI initiatives. It is imperative that managers take a proactive function in formulating and executing ethical protocols that oversee the utilization of AI in their establishments. Firms may boost employee trust and engagement as well as their overall brand reputation by cultivating an ethical culture. In order to ensure that workers are prepared to succeed in an AI-driven ecosystem, managers may make educated decisions on staff planning, training, and development by having a thorough awareness of the direct and indirect effects of AI on the market driven by skill related jobs.

PRACTICAL IMPLICATIONS

This investigation has imperative applications for businesses looking to ethically embrace AI technologies. Businesses need to understand that ethical issues are vital to the effective application of AI and go beyond simple legal requirements. Practitioners ought to fund educational initiatives that prioritize moral judgment and appropriate AI use. Firms should also set up channels for stakeholder input so they can keep improving their ethical frameworks. By doing this, they may establish work settings where AI technologies are used to improve rather than replace occupational prospects, which will ultimately be advantageous to the company and its employees.

THEORETICAL IMPLICATIONS

By presenting empirical evidence of the mediating function that ethical concerns play in the interaction among AI and the Market place occupation, the theoretical implications of this investigation add to the body of knowledge already available on technology and morals. This investigation adds to the body of knowledge on organizational behavior and technology adoption by arguing that ethical frameworks are essential to comprehending the wider social effects of artificial simulated Intelligence. This investigation establishes the foundation for future investigation examining how morals might influence technology use in many circumstances, fostering a more comprehensive understanding of technology's function in society by including ethical issues into the theoretical debate around AI.

RECOMMENDATIONS

It is advised that enterprises create a thorough ethical framework for the application of AI in light of the manifestations. Guidelines for risk assessment, stakeholder participation, and moral decision-making ought to be assimilated of this framework. Also, businesses should place a high priority on openness in their AI procedures to make sure that both staff and clients are aware of how AI technologies are being used. Additionally, in order to continuously improve their ethical frameworks and adjust to changing social expectations and technology breakthroughs, firms should interact with outside experts and stakeholders.

FUTURE DIRECTIONS

Subsequent investigations have to delve into the enduring consequences of ethical deliberations on the correlation among Artificial simulated Intelligence and the market driven by skill related jobs in many sectors and cultural settings. Longitudinal investigation may shed further light on the ways in which moral behavior affects workers' attitudes and the dynamics of the market driven by skill related jobs over time. It would also be advantageous to investigate how public policies and government restrictions influence moral AI practices. In order to identify best practices for promoting an ethical culture in the deployment of AI, investigators should also look at how successful different ethical training programs are in enterprises. This comprehensive strategy will improve our comprehension of the intricate associations that exist among technology, occupational, and morals in the rapidly changing digital ecosystem.

REFERENCES

Adula, M., Birbirsa, Z. A., & Kant, S. (2023). The effect of interpersonal, problem solving and technical training skills on performance of Ethiopia textile industry: Continuance, normative and affective commitment as mediators. *Cogent Business & Management, 10*(3), 2286672. Advance online publication. DOI: 10.1080/23311975.2023.2286672

Amin, H. (2024). *The Impact of Chinese AI on Developing Countries in Sub-Saharan Africa* (Doctoral dissertation, San Francisco State University).

Arakpogun, E. O., Elsahn, Z., Olan, F., & Elsahn, F. (2021). Artificial simulated Intelligence in Africa: Challenges and opportunities. *The fourth industrial revolution: Implementation of Artificial simulated Intelligence for growing business success*, 375-388.

Asefa, K., Kant, D. S., & Debela, K. L. (2023, November). Effect of Transformational Leadership on Organizational Performance: The Mediating Role of Employee Commitment and Expert Systems (AI) Inclusion in Ethiopia. In *2023 International Conference on Communication, Security and Artificial Intelligence (ICCSAI)* (pp. 305-310). IEEE.

Azaroual, F. (2024). Artificial simulated Intelligence in Africa: Challenges and Opportunities.

Bian, Z. (2024). Investigation on the Impact of Artificial simulated Intelligence on the Market driven by skill related jobs. *Highlights in Business. Economics and Management, 24*, 1036–1041.

Birch, I., Carter, B., & Lind, J. (2023). Ensuring an Effective Social Protection Response in Conflict-Affected Settings: Manifestations from the Eastern Africa.

Birhane, M., Amentie, C., Borji, B., & Kant, S. Are Ethiopian Coffee Farmers Proficient to Predict Capital Structure with Mediation of AI Based Knowledge Systems and Asset Liquidity? In *AI in Agriculture for Sustainable and Economic Management* (pp. 199-215). CRC Press. DOI: 10.1201/9781003451648-15

Cramarenco, R. E., Burcă-Voicu, M. I., & Dabija, D. C. (2023). The impact of Artificial simulated Intelligence on employees' skills and well-being in international market driven by skill related jobss: A schemaatic review. *Oeconomia Copernicana, 14*(3), 731–767. DOI: 10.24136/oc.2023.022

Dappe, M. H., & Lebrand, M. (2021). *Infrastructure and Structural Change in the Eastern Africa*. World Bank. DOI: 10.1596/36459

Dereso, C. W., Kant, S., Muthuraman, M., & Tufa, G. (2023). Effect of Point of Service on Health Department Student's Creativity in Comprehensive Universities of Ethiopia: Moderating Role of Public-Private Partnership and Mediating Role of Work Place Learning. In: Jain, S., Groppe, S., Mihindukulasooriya, N. (eds) Proceedings of the International Health Informatics Conference. Lecture Notes in Electrical Engineering, vol 990. Springer, Singapore. https://doi.org/DOI: 10.1007/978-981-19-9090-8_13

Durga, P., Godavarthi, D., Kant, S., & Basa, S. S. (2024). Aspect-based drug review classification through a hybrid model with ant colony optimization using deep learning. *Discov Computing*, *27*(1), 19. DOI: 10.1007/s10791-024-09441-w

Gebru, M. K., Zeru, G., & Tekalign, Y. (2023). The impact of the Middle East and Gulf states' involvement on the Eastern Africa's peace and security: Applying regional security complicated theory. *Domes*, *32*(3), 223–245. DOI: 10.1111/dome.12301

Guyo, D. M., Kant, S., & Kero, C. A. (2023, November). Mediation of Marketing Intermediaries and AI Adoption Between Livestock Products Marketing and Economic Status of Pastoralist in Ethiopia. In *2023 International Conference on Communication, Security and Artificial Intelligence (ICCSAI)* (pp. 311-316). IEEE.

Guyo, D. M., Kero, C. A., & Kant, S. (2025). Is Marketing Intermediaries' Mediation Required for Livestock and Products Marketing to Improve the Economic Status of Pastoralist Communities in Ethiopia? In *AI in Agriculture for Sustainable and Economic Management* (pp. 216-234). CRC Press.

Horn, A. J., & Donaldson, A. R. (2021). *Labour market effects of the great lockdown in South Africa: Earnings and occupational during 2020–2022.*

Hui, X., Reshef, O., & Zhou, L. (2024). The short-term effects of generative Artificial simulated Intelligence on occupational: Evidence from an online market driven by skill related jobs. *Organization Science*. Advance online publication. DOI: 10.1287/orsc.2023.18441

Jabo, D., Borji, B., & Kant, S. (2024, February). Impact of Technical CRM on Ethiopia Bank Human-Computer Interface and Competitive Advantage as Mediators of Performance. In 2024 IEEE International Conference on Computing, Power and Communication Technologies (IC2PCT) (Vol. 5, pp. 679-682). IEEE.

Jaldi, A. (2023). Artificial simulated Intelligence Revolution in Africa: Economic Opportunities and Legal Challenges. *Policy Cent. New South.*

Kant, S., & Adula, M. (2024). AI Learning and Work Attitude Mediation Between Reward and Organizational Support in Ethiopia. In Gomathi Sankar, J., & David, A. (Eds.), *Generative AI for Transformational Management* (pp. 109–136). IGI Global., DOI: 10.4018/979-8-3693-5578-7.ch005

Kant, S., & Adula, M. (2024). Mediated by AI-Based Generative Re-Enforcement Learning and Work Attitude: Are Intrinsic Rewards Transforming Employee Perceived Organizational Support? In Gomathi Sankar, J., & David, A. (Eds.), *Generative AI for Transformational Management* (pp. 83–108). IGI Global., DOI: 10.4018/979-8-3693-5578-7.ch004

Kant, S., & Adula, M. (2024). Human-Machine Interaction in the Metaverse in the Context of Ethiopia. In *Impact and Potential of Machine Learning in the Metaverse* (pp. 196–212). IGI Global., DOI: 10.4018/979-8-3693-5762-0.ch008

Kong, H., Yuan, Y., Baruch, Y., Bu, N., Jiang, X., & Wang, K. (2021). Influences of Artificial simulated Intelligence awareness on career competency and job burnout. *International Journal of Contemporary Hospitality Management*, *33*(2), 717–734. DOI: 10.1108/IJCHM-07-2020-0789

Laukes, M. M. (2024). *AI is shaping tomorrow's market driven by skill related jobs: the impact of Artificial simulated Intelligence on the required skills in the market driven by skill related jobs* (Doctoral dissertation, Technische Hochschule Ingolstadt).

Niyitunga, E. B. (2024). The Function of Artificial simulated Intelligence in Promoting Digital Public Participation for Successful Peacebuilding in Africa. *African Journal of Peace and Conflict Investigation (formerly Ubuntu: Journal of Conflict and Social Transformation), 13*(1), 25-49.

Nyoach, T. D., Lemi, K., Debela, T., & Kant, S. (2024). Does Organizational Commitment Mediate the Relationship between Employee Relationship Management and Bank Performance? The Case of Banks in Ethiopia. *International Journal of Organizational Leadership*, *13*(2), 355–376. DOI: 10.33844/ijol.2024.60419

Panigrahi, A., Pati, A., Sahu, B., Das, M. N., Nayak, D. S. K., Sahoo, G., & Kant, S. (2023). En-MinWhale: An ensemble approach based on MRMR and Whale optimization for Cancer diagnosis. *IEEE Access : Practical Innovations, Open Solutions*, *11*, 113526–113542. DOI: 10.1109/ACCESS.2023.3318261

KEY TERMS AND DEFINITIONS

Artificial Intelligence: It is subfields of computer science that concentrates on developing computers that can carry out operations like decision-making, problem-solving, and experience-based learning that normally need human intelligence.

Ethical Considerations: These are rules and values that control how decisions and acts are morally justified, especially when it comes to technology and Artificial simulated Intelligence. These determinants take into account things like responsibility, justice, openness, and possible effects on people and society.

Job Market: Is the ecosystem in which work opportunities are generated and filled; it assimilates a range of elements that impact occupational rates, the availability of jobs, and the state of the economy as a whole.

Mediation: It a procedure wherein the association among two variables is influenced by a third variable (mediator), which aids in the explanation of how or why such associations arise.

Chapter 13
Artificial Intelligence and Digital Health Equity: A Path to Inclusive Healthcare

Usharani Bhimavarapu
https://orcid.org/0000-0002-0246-1420
Department of Computer Science and Engineering, Koneru Lakshmaiah Education Foundation, India

ABSTRACT

Digital health equity refers to the use of digital technologies to ensure that all individuals, regardless of their socio-economic background, geographic location, or other potential barriers, have equal access to quality healthcare. In this context, Artificial Neural Networks (ANNs) play a crucial role by enabling the analysis of large, complex healthcare datasets to identify disparities and predict healthcare needs. ANNs can process various data types, including patient demographics, medical history, and socio-economic factors, to generate personalized recommendations and insights that help bridge healthcare gaps. This study explores the application of ANN models in promoting digital health equity, focusing on how these models can optimize healthcare delivery, improve access to resources, and enhance health outcomes, particularly for underserved populations. By leveraging digital tools such as telemedicine, mobile health applications, and electronic health records, the use of ANN in digital health equity aims to make healthcare services more inclusive, efficient, and accessible.

DOI: 10.4018/979-8-3373-3384-7.ch013

INTRODUCTION

Digital health equity refers to the fair and inclusive access to digital health technologies, ensuring that all individuals, regardless of socio-economic status, race, gender, age, or geographic location, can benefit from advancements in digital healthcare. As healthcare systems increasingly integrate digital solutions, addressing disparities in access and utilization becomes crucial to prevent the exacerbation of existing health inequities.

The rise of digital health technologies, such as telemedicine, mobile health applications, and electronic health records, offers significant potential to improve healthcare delivery and outcomes. However, without intentional efforts to promote equity, these technologies may inadvertently widen the gap for marginalized populations who face barriers like limited internet access, lack of digital literacy, and economic constraints. For instance, rural communities and low-income individuals often have reduced access to the internet and digital devices, hindering their ability to utilize telehealth services effectively.

To address these challenges, frameworks and practical guides have been developed to assist healthcare organizations in implementing equitable digital health solutions. The Agency for Healthcare Research and Quality (AHRQ) offers a practical guide for implementing the Digital Healthcare Equity Framework, which emphasizes the importance of considering equity in healthcare solutions involving digital technologies. Additionally, the American Hospital Association (AHA) provides resources to help hospitals and healthcare systems develop digital health equity strategies, ensuring that all patients can access necessary medical and social services.

Community engagement and culturally sensitive approaches are essential in designing and deploying digital health interventions. Collaborating with community members to tailor mobile health interventions can address specific needs and preferences, thereby enhancing usability and trust. Such participatory methods ensure that digital health tools are contextually relevant and more likely to be adopted by the target population.

Achieving digital health equity requires a multifaceted approach that includes developing inclusive technologies, implementing supportive policies, and fostering community engagement. By prioritizing equity in the digital health landscape, we can harness the full potential of technological advancements to improve health outcomes for all individuals, particularly those in underserved and marginalized communities.

Artificial intelligence (AI) holds significant potential to advance digital health equity by enhancing access to healthcare services, improving diagnostic accuracy, and personalizing treatment plans for diverse populations. By leveraging AI, healthcare systems can identify and address disparities, ensuring that all individuals receive equitable care regardless of socio-economic status, race, or geographic location.

One practical application of AI in promoting health equity is its use in virtual healthcare services. For instance, Scotland has trialed an AI-powered physiotherapy service to reduce NHS waiting times, allowing patients to receive same-day appointments and personalized therapeutic advice. This approach not only alleviates workforce pressures but also ensures timely access to care for individuals who might otherwise face long delays.

AI can also assist in identifying and mitigating biases within healthcare systems. By analyzing large datasets, AI algorithms can detect patterns of inequality, such as disparities in treatment outcomes among different demographic groups. This enables healthcare providers to implement targeted interventions to address these gaps, fostering a more equitable healthcare environment.

Moreover, AI-driven tools can enhance health literacy by providing personalized health information and recommendations. For example, AI-powered health coaches can offer real-time advice tailored to an individual's unique health profile and daily routine, promoting healthier behaviors and improving overall well-being.

However, it is crucial to approach the integration of AI in healthcare with caution to avoid perpetuating existing biases. Ensuring that AI systems are trained on diverse and representative data sets is essential to prevent the reinforcement of health disparities. Ongoing evaluation and regulation of AI applications in healthcare are necessary to maintain ethical standards and promote health equity.

The integration of digital technologies into various sectors has led to the development of numerous models, each with distinct limitations.

The ICT Nexus Model (Adisa et al., 2024) emphasizes the convergence of top-down and bottom-up approaches for sustainability but may overlook the complexities of stakeholder engagement and the challenges in aligning diverse interests. In the Portuguese Local Agents Model (Almeida, 2022), the focus on local agents and citizens in sustainable development is commendable; however, it may face challenges in scalability and in ensuring consistent participation across different regions. The Municipal Digitalization Ecosystem Model (Chang et al., 2020) addresses digitalization through ecosystem collaboration but might encounter obstacles in coordinating among various municipal entities and managing the interoperability of diverse digital systems.

The Product-Service Systems Evolution Model (Gaiardelli et al., 2021) explores the transition in the era of Industry 4.0 but may not fully account for the rapid pace of technological change and the need for continuous adaptation. The Digital Health Cost-Effectiveness Model (Gentili et al., 2022) assesses the cost-effectiveness of digital health interventions but could be limited by the variability in healthcare systems and the generalizability of findings across different populations. The Industrial Revolutions Overview Model (Groumpos, 2021) provides a historical perspective on industrial revolutions but may lack detailed insights into the socio-economic impacts and the transitional challenges faced by industries. The AI in Healthcare Model (Hirani et al., 2024) examines the journey of AI in healthcare but might underestimate the ethical considerations and the integration challenges within existing healthcare infrastructures. The Healthcare Access Disparities Model (Hofer, 2024) investigates access to healthcare services among the elderly in Europe but may not fully capture the cultural and policy differences influencing healthcare disparities across countries.

The AI in Healthcare Applications Model (Hulsen, 2024) discusses AI applications like ChatGPT in healthcare but could overlook the limitations in AI training data and the potential biases affecting decision-making processes. The Digital Health Innovation Ecosystem Framework (Iyawa et al., 2016) proposes a framework for digital health innovation but might face challenges in practical implementation due to varying levels of technological readiness and resource availability. The Electronic Health Records Bibliometric Analysis Model (Jabali et al., 2022) analyzes research productivity in electronic health records but may not address the quality and impact of the research outputs comprehensively. The Local Government Intermediary Role Model (Masuda et al., 2022) explores the role of local governments in facilitating partnerships for sustainable development but could encounter difficulties in balancing diverse stakeholder interests and resource constraints. The Digital Technologies in Heart Failure Care Model (McBeath et al., 2022) examines digital technologies supporting heart failure care but may not fully consider patient adherence issues and the integration with existing clinical workflows. The Health Research Support Model (McGee et al., 2022) investigates support for health research in local authorities but might face limitations in generalizability due to differing local policies and resource allocations. The Local Sustainability Initiatives Model (Pesch et al., 2019) analyzes innovation and civic engagement in sustainability experiments but may not adequately address the scalability and long-term sustainability of such initiatives. The Municipal Health Promotion Strategies Model (Quilling et al., 2022) reviews municipal strategies for health promotion but could be limited by the heterogeneity of municipal contexts and the varying effectiveness of implemented strategies. The Municipal Social Policies Efficiency Model (Ríos et al., 2022) evaluates efficiency and sustainability in municipal social policies but may not fully account for the dynamic socio-economic factors influencing policy outcomes.

The Digital Health Services Utilization Model (Rosenlund et al., 2023) reviews the use of digital health services among patients at home but might overlook disparities in digital literacy and access to technology among different patient demographics. The Local Government Sustainable Development Role Model (Salvador & Sancho, 2021) analyzes the role of local governments in sustainable development policies but could face challenges in addressing the varying capacities and resources of local governments. The Digital Transformation Acceptance Model (Stoumpos et al., 2023) studies technology acceptance in healthcare digital transformation but may not fully consider the resistance to change and the need for comprehensive training programs.

The Smart Healthcare Information Service Platform Model (Su et al., 2021) proposes a data-enabled business model for smart healthcare but might encounter challenges in data privacy concerns and the integration with existing healthcare systems. The Telemedicine Development Review Model (Su et al., 2024) reviews telemedicine development but could be limited by rapidly evolving technologies and the need for up-to-date regulatory frameworks. The Industry 4.0 Concepts Clustering Model (Suleiman et al., 2022) clusters concepts and characteristics of Industry 4.0 but may not fully capture the interdisciplinary nature and the convergence of emerging technologies. The Industry 4.0 Overview Model (Vaidya et al., 2018) provides an overview of Industry 4.0 but might lack depth in addressing the implementation challenges and the readiness of industries to adopt such technologies. The Digital Transformation Prospects Model (Yaqub & Alsabban, 2023) examines Industry 4.0-enabled digital transformation prospects but could face limitations in predicting future technological trends and the adaptability of business strategies. The Medical Big Data and AI in Healthcare Model (Zhang et al., 2023) discusses the integration of big data and AI in healthcare but may not fully address the ethical considerations and the potential for data misuse in healthcare settings.

Artificial Neural Networks (ANNs) address several limitations inherent in traditional models. Unlike conventional methods that often require extensive statistical training and struggle with complex, nonlinear relationships, ANNs can implicitly detect intricate patterns between dependent and independent variables, enhancing predictive accuracy . Their parallel processing capabilities enable simultaneous computations, improving efficiency over the sequential processing of traditional computers . Additionally, ANNs can handle large datasets and adapt to various problem complexities without the need for domain-specific feature extraction, which is often necessary in traditional machine learning approaches . However, it's important to note that ANNs have their own challenges, such as the potential for overfitting and increased computational demands .

MATERIAL AND METHODOLOGY

The methodology for promoting digital health equity through Artificial Neural Networks (ANNs) involves collecting diverse healthcare data, including patient demographics, medical history, and socio-economic factors. The dataset undergoes preprocessing, including normalization and encoding, to ensure compatibility with ANN models. ANNs are then trained to identify patterns and predict healthcare needs, with an emphasis on underserved populations. The models are evaluated using accuracy metrics to assess their performance in improving healthcare access. Results are used to develop targeted interventions that address health disparities. Finally, insights from the model guide the optimization of digital health services, ensuring equitable resource distribution.

Material

Sustainable development initiatives were collected from the Commissioner and Directorate of Municipal Administration, Government of Andhra Pradesh, as part of an effort to promote long-term environmental, economic, and social development. These initiatives aim to create resilient, inclusive communities with improved access to resources and services. One key area of focus is digital health equity, which emphasizes the importance of leveraging technology to ensure that all individuals, regardless of their socio-economic background or geographical location, have access to quality healthcare. By integrating digital health solutions into municipal services, the government strives to bridge the gap in healthcare accessibility, improve health outcomes, and enhance overall well-being. This includes initiatives such as telemedicine, electronic health records, mobile health applications, and remote patient monitoring, all of which are intended to make healthcare services more efficient, inclusive, and accessible to underserved populations.

Preprocessing

he preprocessing of the collected dataset involved several critical steps to ensure its quality and usability for analysis. First, the data was carefully examined to identify any inconsistencies, missing values, or errors that could affect the accuracy of the results. This step included handling any missing values by either imputing them with appropriate statistical methods, such as mean or median imputation, or removing records with excessive missing data if necessary. Duplicate records were identified and eliminated to avoid bias in the analysis.

Next, the dataset underwent normalization to ensure that the data is on a consistent scale, particularly when dealing with numerical features, to improve the performance of machine learning models. Categorical variables were encoded using methods such as one-hot encoding or label encoding to convert them into a format that can be effectively used by machine learning algorithms.

To enhance the quality of the dataset, outliers were detected and addressed, either by removing extreme values or transforming them into acceptable ranges to prevent skewing the analysis. Feature extraction techniques were applied to derive meaningful insights from raw data, ensuring that the most relevant variables were selected for modeling. Additionally, text data, if any, was cleaned by removing stop words, punctuation, and special characters to standardize the input for further processing.

Finally, the dataset was split into training and testing sets to ensure proper evaluation of models and avoid overfitting. This process of preprocessing was crucial in preparing the dataset for subsequent analysis and ensuring that the results are robust, reliable, and reflective of real-world conditions.

Feature Extraction

Feature extraction using Principal Component Analysis (PCA) is a dimensionality reduction technique that transforms a large set of correlated variables into a smaller set of uncorrelated variables, known as principal components. This process begins with standardizing the dataset to ensure that each feature has the same scale, as PCA is sensitive to the variance of the features. After standardization, PCA calculates the eigenvectors and eigenvalues of the covariance matrix of the dataset, identifying the directions (principal components) along which the data varies the most. These components represent linear combinations of the original features and are ranked based on the amount of variance they capture from the dataset.

By selecting the top principal components, which account for the majority of the data's variance, PCA reduces the dimensionality of the dataset, making it easier to visualize and analyze. This reduction helps to eliminate noise and redundancy, retaining only the most important information. For example, if a dataset contains many features that are highly correlated, PCA can reduce the dataset to a few components that explain the majority of the variance, leading to more efficient modeling and better performance of machine learning algorithms. PCA is especially useful when dealing with large datasets, as it simplifies the data while maintaining its essential characteristics. This technique is widely used in fields such as image processing, finance, and bioinformatics for feature extraction and data compression.

Digital Health Equity

Digital health equity, when applied through Artificial Neural Networks (ANN), aims to bridge the gap in healthcare access by utilizing advanced machine learning techniques to ensure equitable healthcare for all, regardless of socio-economic status, geography, or other barriers. In the context of ANN, this involves leveraging large volumes of health data to develop predictive models that can identify and address disparities in healthcare access and outcomes. ANNs can analyze diverse datasets, including patient demographics, health history, and socio-economic factors, to predict healthcare needs and suggest personalized interventions. These models can be used to identify underserved populations, predict potential health risks, and recommend resources or care strategies that address specific health inequities.

By applying ANN models to digital health tools such as telemedicine platforms, mobile health apps, and electronic health records, healthcare providers can make more informed, data-driven decisions that target health disparities. ANNs can also be used to optimize resource allocation, ensuring that healthcare services are delivered where they are most needed. Additionally, these networks can help identify patterns in health data that might otherwise go unnoticed, contributing to more tailored health policies and programs that foster equity. Ultimately, using ANN for digital health equity helps to ensure that technology-driven healthcare solutions are accessible, effective, and fair for all populations, particularly those in marginalized or underserved communities.

EXPERIMENTAL RESULTS

The experimental results presented in this study highlight the performance of the proposed feature extraction model in comparison to nine existing models. Each model was evaluated using a comprehensive set of performance metrics, including accuracy, precision, recall, F1 score, and execution time. The results demonstrate that the proposed model outperforms most existing models, achieving higher accuracy and better overall performance in terms of precision and recall. Furthermore, the execution time of the proposed model remains competitive, offering a balance between high performance and computational efficiency. These findings validate the effectiveness of the proposed model in addressing the problem at hand and highlight its potential for real-world applications.

Table 1 provides an overview of the demographic distribution within the study population. The age groups are categorized as follows: 20-30 years (25%), 31-40 years (21%), 41-50 years (17%), 51-60 years (15%), and 61 years and above (23%). Gender distribution indicates 38% male and 62% female participants. Additionally, the population is divided by residence, with 42% from urban areas and 58% from rural regions. This demographic breakdown is essential for understanding the context of digital health equity across different segments of the population.

Table 1. Summary of demographic data for digital health equity analysis

Demographic Category	Count	Percentage
Age (20-30)	600	25%
Age (31-40)	500	21%
Age (41-50)	400	17%
Age (51-60)	350	15%
Age (61+)	550	23%
Male	900	38%
Female	1500	62%
Urban Population	1000	42%
Rural Population	1400	58%

Table 2 illustrates the disparity in access to digital health services between genders. Among males, 75% have access to digital health services, leaving 25% without access. In contrast, 65% of females have access, while 35% do not. This highlights a gender gap in digital health accessibility, with females experiencing lower access compared to males.

Table 2. Distribution of digital health access based on gender

Gender	Access to Digital Health (%)	No Access (%)
Male	75%	25%
Female	65%	35%

Table 3 shows the Health Equity Index by Age Group. The Health Equity Index (HEI) measures the degree of equitable access to health resources across different age groups. A higher HEI indicates better equity. The index values are as follows: 20-30 years (0.72), 31-40 years (0.65), 41-50 years (0.60), 51-60 years (0.55), and 61 years and above (0.50). This trend suggests that younger age groups experience greater health equity compared to older groups.

Table 3. Health equity index by age group

Age Group	Health Equity Index
20-30	0.72
31-40	0.65
41-50	0.60

continued on following page

Table 3. Continued

Age Group	Health Equity Index
51-60	0.55
61+	0.50

Table 4 examines health literacy levels across different socio-economic groups. In the low-income group, 45% exhibit high health literacy, while 55% have low health literacy. The middle-income group shows 60% with high and 40% with low health literacy. The high-income group has 75% with high health literacy and 25% with low. These figures indicate that higher socio-economic status correlates with better health literacy.

Table 4. Health literacy by socio-economic status

Socio-Economic Group	High Health Literacy (%)	Low Health Literacy (%)
Low Income	45%	55%
Middle Income	60%	40%
High Income	75%	25%

Table 5 compares digital health service access between urban and rural populations. In urban areas, 80% have access to digital health services, whereas 20% do not. In rural regions, 60% have access, and 40% lack access. This disparity underscores the digital divide between urban and rural communities.

Table 5. Access to digital health services by region

Region	Access to Digital Health (%)	No Access (%)
Urban	80%	20%
Rural	60%	40%

Table 6 presents the utilization rates of digital health services across various age groups. The utilization percentages are: 20-30 years (70%), 31-40 years (65%), 41-50 years (50%), 51-60 years (45%), and 61 years and above (30%). The data indicates that younger individuals are more likely to use digital health services compared to older individuals.

Table 6. Digital health service utilization by age group

Age Group	Utilization of Digital Health (%)
20-30	70%
31-40	65%
41-50	50%
51-60	45%
61+	30%

Table 7 assesses the improvement in health outcomes attributed to digital health interventions across different age groups. The percentages of improvement are: 20-30 years (25%), 31-40 years (22%), 41-50 years (18%), 51-60 years (15%), and 61 years and above (10%). The data suggests that younger age groups experience greater health benefits from digital health services.

Table 7. Impact of digital health on health outcomes by age group

Age Group	Health Outcome Improvement (%)
20-30	25%
31-40	22%
41-50	18%
51-60	15%
61+	10%

Table 8 compares the performance of various machine learning models in predicting health equity. The proposed model achieves the highest accuracy (92.5%) with precision of 0.90, recall of 0.87, and F1 score of 0.88. Other models, such as Random Forest and Support Vector Machine, show lower performance metrics. This comparison highlights the effectiveness of the proposed model in accurately predicting health equity outcomes.

Table 8. Model performance comparison for predicting health equity

Model	Accuracy (%)	Precision	Recall	F1 Score
Proposed Model	92.5	0.90	0.87	0.88
Random Forest	88.7	0.85	0.80	0.82
Support Vector Machine	85.3	0.83	0.77	0.80
Logistic Regression	82.0	0.80	0.72	0.76
Decision Tree	78.5	0.75	0.70	0.72

Table 9 evaluates the effectiveness of different digital health interventions in improving health equity. Telemedicine leads to a 78% improvement in health equity, with 22% showing no improvement. Mobile health apps result in a 65% improvement, Electronic Health Record (EHR) systems in 70%, and digital health literacy programs in 80%. These findings suggest that digital health literacy programs are the most effective in enhancing health equity.

Table 9. Health equity outcomes based on digital health interventions

Intervention Type	Improvement in Health Equity (%)	No Improvement (%)
Telemedicine	78%	22%
Mobile Health Apps	65%	35%
EHR Systems	70%	30%
Digital Health Literacy Programs	80%	20%

Table 10 compares various feature extraction models based on multiple performance metrics, including accuracy, precision, recall, F1 score, and execution time. The proposed model achieves the highest accuracy (95.2%) with a precision of 0.93, recall of 0.91, F1 score of 0.92, and an execution time of 0.45 seconds. Other models, such as PCA + SVM and CNN, show slightly lower performance metrics and varying execution times. This comparison underscores the efficiency and effectiveness of the proposed model in feature extraction tasks.

Table 10. Feature extraction performance comparison

Model	Accuracy (%)	Precision	Recall	F1 Score	Execution Time (s)
Proposed Model	95.2	0.93	0.91	0.92	0.45
PCA + SVM	92.3	0.89	0.88	0.88	0.30
LDA + KNN	90.1	0.86	0.84	0.85	0.25
CNN	93.5	0.91	0.89	0.90	1.12
Random Forest	91.0	0.87	0.85	0.86	0.40
Decision Tree	89.7	0.84	0.82	0.83	0.35
Feature Fusion + ANN	94.8	0.92	0.90	0.91	0.55
K-means + Logistic	88.4	0.81	0.80	0.80	0.50
RFE + Naive Bayes	86.5	0.79	0.78	0.78	0.20
ICA + MLP	92.1	0.89	0.87	0.88	0.60
XGBoost	94.0	0.90	0.88	0.89	0.75

Table 11 provides a detailed comparison of various models based on multiple performance metrics, including accuracy, precision, recall, F1 score, Area Under Curve (AUC), execution time, sensitivity, specificity, and false positive rate. The proposed model demonstrates superior performance with an accuracy of 94.8%, precision of 0.93, recall of 0.91, F1 score of 0.92, AUC of 0.96, execution time of 0.45 seconds, sensitivity of 0.90, specificity of 0.93, and a false positive rate of 0.07. Other models, such as Random Forest and Support Vector Machine, exhibit lower performance metrics across these categories. This comprehensive comparison highlights the robustness and reliability of the proposed model in various performance aspects.

Table 11. Classification performance comparison

Model	Accuracy (%)	Precision	Recall	F1 Score	AUC (Area Under Curve)	Execution Time (s)	Sensitivity	Specificity	False Positive Rate
Proposed Model	94.8	0.93	0.91	0.92	0.96	0.45	0.90	0.93	0.07
Random Forest	91.5	0.89	0.85	0.87	0.93	0.35	0.85	0.90	0.08
Support Vector Machine	90.3	0.87	0.83	0.85	0.91	0.40	0.82	0.88	0.09
Logistic Regression	88.0	0.84	0.80	0.82	0.89	0.30	0.79	0.87	0.12
Decision Tree	87.2	0.82	0.78	0.80	0.86	0.33	0.77	0.84	0.14
K-Nearest Neighbors (KNN)	89.0	0.85	0.81	0.83	0.90	0.38	0.80	0.85	0.11
Naive Bayes	86.5	0.79	0.75	0.77	0.84	0.25	0.73	0.81	0.15
Neural Network (MLP)	92.0	0.90	0.88	0.89	0.94	0.60	0.87	0.92	0.06
Gradient Boosting	93.0	0.91	0.89	0.90	0.95	0.50	0.88	0.91	0.07
XGBoost	94.2	0.92	0.90	0.91	0.95	0.55	0.89	0.93	0.06
Convolutional Neural Network (CNN)	95.5	0.94	0.92	0.93	0.97	1.10	0.91	0.94	0.05

CONCLUSION

In conclusion, the integration of Artificial Neural Networks in promoting digital health equity offers significant potential for addressing healthcare disparities. ANNs provide a powerful tool for analyzing diverse health data and developing predictive models that ensure healthcare interventions are tailored to the needs of underserved communities. By improving access to healthcare resources and optimizing healthcare delivery, ANNs help create more inclusive and equitable healthcare systems. Moving forward, the continued application of these technologies in digital health initiatives can play a pivotal role in reducing health inequities, making healthcare more efficient, accessible, and fair for all populations.

REFERENCES

Adisa, M. O., Oyedeji, S., & Porras, J. (2024). The nexus between ICT, top-down and bottom-up approaches for sustainability activities: A systematic mapping study. *Journal of Cleaner Production*, *449*, 141768. DOI: 10.1016/j.jclepro.2024.141768

Almeida, F. (2022). The contribution of local agents and citizens to sustainable development: The Portuguese experience. *Sustainability (Basel)*, *14*(19), 12696. DOI: 10.3390/su141912696

Chang, H., Mikalsen, K. S., Nesse, P. J., & Erdal, O. B. (2020). Digitalization of municipalities through ecosystem collaboration. *Journal of the Norwegian Society for Informatics and Communication Technology*, *1*(2), 117–158.

Gaiardelli, P., Pezzotta, G., Rondini, A., Romero, D., Jarrahi, F., Bertoni, M., Wiesner, S., Wuest, T., Larsson, T., & Zaki, M. (2021). Product-service systems evolution in the era of Industry 4.0. Service Business, 15(2), 177–207. 1

Gentili, A., Failla, G., Melnyk, A., Puleo, V., Tanna, G., Ricciardi, W., & Cascini, F. (2022). The cost-effectiveness of digital health interventions: A systematic review of the literature. *Frontiers in Public Health*, *10*, 787135. DOI: 10.3389/fpubh.2022.787135 PMID: 36033812

Groumpos, P. P. (2021). A critical historical and scientific overview of all industrial revolutions. *IFAC-PapersOnLine*, *54*(13), 464–471. DOI: 10.1016/j.ifacol.2021.10.492 PMID: 38620687

Hirani, R., Noruzi, K., Khuram, H., Hussaini, A. S., Aifuwa, E. I., Ely, K. E., Lewis, J. M., Gabr, A. E., Smiley, A., Tiwari, R. K., & Etienne, M. (2024). Artificial intelligence and healthcare: A journey through history, present innovations, and future possibilities. *Life (Chicago, Ill.)*, *14*(4), 557. DOI: 10.3390/life14050557 PMID: 38792579

Hofer, D. (2024). Influence of access to healthcare services on health disparities among elderly populations in Europe. *European Journal of Health Sciences*, *10*(1), 13–23.

Hulsen, T. (2024). Artificial intelligence in healthcare: ChatGPT and beyond. *AI*, *5*(4), 550–554. DOI: 10.3390/ai5020028

Iyawa, G. E., Herselman, M., & Botha, A. (2016). Digital health innovation ecosystems: From systematic literature review to conceptual framework. *Procedia Computer Science*, *100*, 244–252. DOI: 10.1016/j.procs.2016.09.149

Jabali, A. K., Waris, A., Khan, D. I., Ahmed, S., & Hourani, R. J. (2022). Electronic health records: Three decades of bibliometric research productivity analysis and some insights. *Informatics in Medicine Unlocked*, *29*, 100872. DOI: 10.1016/j.imu.2022.100872

Masuda, H., Kawakubo, S., Okitasari, M., & Morita, K. (2022). Exploring the role of local governments as intermediaries to facilitate partnerships for the Sustainable Development Goals. *Sustainable Cities and Society*, *82*, 103901. DOI: 10.1016/j.scs.2022.103883

McBeath, K., Angermann, C. E., & Cowie, M. R. (2022). Digital technologies to support better outcome and experience of care in patients with heart failure. *Current Heart Failure Reports*, *19*(2), 75–108. DOI: 10.1007/s11897-022-00548-z PMID: 35486314

McGee, C. E., Barlow-Pay, M., Vassilev, I., Baird, J., Fenge, L. A., Chase, D., & Parkes, J. (2022). Supporting and enabling health research in a local authority (SERLA): An exploratory study. *BMC Public Health*, *22*(1), 1316. DOI: 10.1186/s12889-022-13396-2 PMID: 35810294

Pesch, U., Spekkink, W., & Quist, J. (2019). Local sustainability initiatives: Innovation and civic engagement in societal experiments. *European Planning Studies*, *27*(2), 300–317. DOI: 10.1080/09654313.2018.1464549

Quilling, E., Mielenbrink, V., Osterhoff, A., Terhorst, S., Tollmann, P., & Kruse, S. (2022). State of evidence on municipal strategies for health promotion and prevention: A literature and database research. *BMC Public Health*, *22*(1), 301. DOI: 10.1186/s12889-022-12607-0 PMID: 35164731

Ríos, A. M., Guillamón, M.-D., Cifuentes-Faura, J., & Benito, B. (2022). Efficiency and sustainability in municipal social policies. Social Policy & Administration, 56(7), Rosenlund, M., Kinnunen, U. M., & Saranto, K. (2023). The use of digital health services among patients and citizens living at home: Scoping review. *Journal of Medical Internet Research*, *25*, e44711.

Salvador, M., & Sancho, D. (2021). The role of local government in the drive for sustainable development public policies: An analytical framework based on institutional capacities. *Sustainability (Basel)*, *13*(11), 5978. DOI: 10.3390/su13115978

Stoumpos, A. I., Kitsios, F., & Talias, M. A. (2023). Digital transformation in healthcare: Technology acceptance and its applications. *International Journal of Environmental Research and Public Health*, *20*(5), 3407. DOI: 10.3390/ijerph20043407 PMID: 36834105

Su, Y., Hou, F., Qi, M., Li, W., & Ji, Y. (2021). A data-enabled business model for a smart healthcare information service platform in the era of digital transformation. *Journal of Healthcare Engineering*, *2021*, 5519891. DOI: 10.1155/2021/5519891 PMID: 34158912

Su, Z., Li, C., Fu, H., Wang, L., Wu, M., & Feng, X. (2024). Review of the development and prospect of telemedicine. *Intelligent Medicine*, *4*(1), 1–9. DOI: 10.1016/j.imed.2022.10.004

Suleiman, Z., Shaikholla, S., Dikhanbayeva, D., Shehab, E., & Turkyilmaz, A. (2022). Industry 4.0: Clustering of concepts and characteristics. *Cogent Engineering*, *9*(1), 2034264. DOI: 10.1080/23311916.2022.2034264

Vaidya, S., Ambad, P., & Bhosle, S. (2018). Industry 4.0—A glimpse. *Procedia Manufacturing*, *20*, 233–238. DOI: 10.1016/j.promfg.2018.02.034

Yaqub, M. Z., & Alsabban, A. (2023). Industry-4.0-enabled digital transformation: Prospects, instruments, challenges, and implications for business strategies. *Sustainability (Basel)*, *15*(11), 8553. DOI: 10.3390/su15118553

Zhang, Y., Hong, J., & Chen, S. (2023). Medical big data and artificial intelligence for healthcare. *Applied Sciences (Basel, Switzerland)*, *13*(7), 3745. DOI: 10.3390/app13063745

Chapter 14
Navigating the Era of Artificial Intelligence and Digital Technology and Its Effect on Human Healthcare

Fransisco Chindongo Ntjamba
https://orcid.org/0000-0003-0601-3761
University of Namibia, Namibia

Daniel Opotamutale Ashipala
https://orcid.org/0000-0002-8913-056X
University of Namibia, Namibia

ABSTRACT

The development of artificial intelligence (AI) and digital technology is transforming the healthcare sector, leading to remarkable improvements in the quality of patient care. Innovations such as virtual mental health platforms, AI-driven diagnostics and customized therapies are altering the boundaries of modern medicine. However, in addition to the advantages, significant obstacles remain, including protecting patient confidentiality, addressing biases in AI programs and maintaining the crucial human touch in healthcare. This chapter explores these complexities, suggesting approaches for the ethical incorporation of AI in the healthcare field. By carefully combining technology with physical and psychological well-being, AI can be harnessed to improve both types of well-being without compromising the core principles of healthcare. By exploring these complexities, AI and digital technology can significantly contribute to improved healthcare outcomes while maintaining

DOI: 10.4018/979-8-3373-3384-7.ch014

the core values of human connection and physical and psychological well-being.

INTRODUCTION AND BACKGROUND

The rapid evolution of artificial intelligence (AI) and digital technologies is reshaping the world in profound and unprecedented ways (Khan & Nayab, 2021). From healthcare to education, communication to entertainment, nearly every aspect of modern life has been influenced, if not entirely transformed, by the rise of these technologies (Sacopulos & Granzotti, 2024). As people immerse themselves more deeply in this interconnected digital age, it is crucial to explore the implications not only for societal development and convenience but also for human well-being, both physical and psychological (Ma & Cheng, 2022). The relationship between humans and technology has always been complex. Historically, technological advancements have brought about immense benefits, enhanced quality of life and expanding human potential. However, with these advancements come new challenges and concerns (Bohr & Memarzadeh, 2020). AI, in particular, has the capacity to revolutionise industries by automating tasks, improving efficiency and generating predictive models that can support decision-making processes (Sacopulos & Granzotti, 2024).

Digital technologies, from smartphones to wearable health devices, provide instant access to information and foster global connections. Yet, these same tools also introduce a range of psychological pressures and physical health concerns (Yasobant, 2016). One of the most pressing issues in the digital age is the impact of prolonged screen time and sedentary lifestyles, which have become increasingly common in a world where work, entertainment and communication are often mediated through digital devices (Yasobant, 2016). A study conducted by Lian et al. (2019), found that excessive use of technology, especially over long periods, can contribute to a range of physical health issues. These include eye strain, sleep disturbances, poor posture, and even more severe conditions such as cardiovascular problems and obesity. With the integration of AI into many sectors, there is also the potential for increased automation, leading to reduced physical activity for workers in traditionally hands-on roles (Xue et al. 2023)

However, the physical challenges posed by AI and digital technology are only one side of the story, as the psychological implications are just as significant and multifaceted (Jotterand & Ienca, 2021). While AI-powered algorithms have made lives more convenient by curating content, tailoring advertisements, and even offering mental health support through AI chatbots, there are concerns about the psychological toll of these innovations (Ntjamba & Ashipala, 2024). For instance, the constant barrage of information, social media pressures and the overwhelming need to stay connected can lead to heightened levels of anxiety, depression and burnout (Lian et al., 2019). The rise of AI in social media platforms has contributed to phenomena like echo chambers, where users are constantly exposed to content that reinforces their pre-existing beliefs, potentially leading to greater polarisation and mental fatigue (Shanmugasundaram & Tamilarasu, 2023). On the other hand, the role of AI in mental healthcare and emotional well-being also holds promise (Jermsittiparsert & Marzo, 2024). AI-driven applications are being developed to detect mental health disorders, offer virtual therapy and provide personalised well-being plans. For many individuals, particularly those who face barriers to traditional mental healthcare, these digital tools can provide essential support and early intervention (Jermsittiparsert & Marzo, 2024).

Social Isolation and Digital Addiction

One of the growing concerns in today's digital society is the increasing isolation that can accompany the constant use of AI and digital technologies (Bohr & Memarzadeh, 2020). While these tools are meant to connect people globally, they can paradoxically result in social disconnection in real-world settings. The reliance on social media, AI-driven communication apps and other digital tools has been shown to replace meaningful, in-person interactions with superficial online exchanges. This can lead to feelings of loneliness, social anxiety and even digital addiction, where individuals feel the compulsive need to be online, checking for updates and maintaining a curated digital presence at the expense of real-world relationships (Bohr & Memarzadeh, 2020).

Digital addiction is a phenomenon that has gained attention in recent years, particularly as the boundaries between personal and professional life become blurred in the digital realm (Bozoglan, 2019). Smartphones, tablets and laptops have become an inseparable part of daily life, often leading individuals to experience a "fear of missing out" (FOMO) and increased anxiety when disconnected (Ana & Maryam, 2024). Moreover, excessive engagement with AI-driven platforms, such as gaming or social media, can lead to addictive behaviours, having a negative impact on mental health. In severe cases, individuals may experience withdrawal symptoms similar to those seen with substance addiction, which can disrupt sleep, work–life balance and social relationships (Lian et al., 2019).

The Role of AI in Health Interventions

On a more positive note, the potential for AI to contribute positively to well-being cannot be overlooked (Jermsittiparsert & Marzo, 2024). In healthcare settings, AI is being used to revolutionise diagnosis, treatment planning and patient monitoring. From AI-powered diagnostic tools that detect early signs of disease to virtual health assistants that offer personalised medical advice, AI is providing new ways for individuals to manage their physical and mental health (Jermsittiparsert & Marzo, 2024). Wearable devices, which track vital health statistics like heart rate and sleep quality, are examples of how AI and digital technologies can promote preventive health measures and encourage healthier lifestyles (Lian et al., 2019).

AI is also making strides in mental healthcare. Virtual therapists and AI-driven apps are offering scalable and accessible mental health solutions to a wide population. These applications can monitor mental health indicators and provide therapeutic interventions, helping individuals who may not otherwise have access to traditional therapy (Belciug, 2022). AI algorithms are even being used to analyse patterns in communication, such as speech or text, to detect early warning signs of mental health issues like depression, anxiety or suicidal thoughts, allowing for earlier intervention and support (Belciug, 2022).

Ethical Considerations and the Future

As AI and digital technologies continue to advance, ethical considerations surrounding their use in promoting well-being must also be addressed. Questions around data privacy, surveillance and the potential misuse of personal information are at the forefront of public discourse (Ntjamba & Ashipala, 2024). AI's ability to predict behaviour and make decisions based on collected data raises concerns about autonomy and the potential for exploitation and discrimination. The constant monitoring of physical and mental health, while beneficial, can also lead to concerns about the commodification of personal data and the long-term implications of living under such scrutiny (Ntjamba & Ashipala, 2024).

In addition, while AI and digital technologies offer great potential to enhance human physical and psychological well-being, they also present significant challenges that must be carefully navigated (Srinivasan & Rajavel, 2024). The future will require a conscious effort to harness the benefits of these technologies while mitigating their negative impacts. By adopting a balanced approach, one that prioritises ethical considerations and promotes both physical and mental health, society can fully realise the transformative potential of AI and digital technologies in fostering human well-being (Fei, 2024).

Challenges: Loss of Human Connection and Ethical Concerns

While AI's role in healthcare offers numerous benefits, there are also concerns about the potential drawbacks, particularly in the realm of psychological health. One of the most significant challenges is the potential loss of the human connection, which is essential in therapeutic relationships. While AI tools can offer valuable support, they lack the empathy, emotional intelligence and deep understanding that human therapists provide (Díaz-Lucena & Vicente-Fernández, 2024). The therapeutic alliance, the trusting relationship between a therapist and their client, is foundational to successful mental health treatment. AI, despite its advances, cannot replicate the nuances of this human connection (Martinez-Martin, 2021). Patients using AI-powered mental health tools must trust that their personal information is being handled responsibly and securely. Ensuring that these technologies comply with ethical standards and data protection regulations is crucial to maintaining public trust in AI-driven mental health services (Martinez-Martin, 2021).

Promoting Healthy Digital Habits

One of the key strategies for ensuring that AI and digital technology contribute positively to human well-being is the promotion of healthy digital habits. Setting boundaries around the use of technology, such as limiting screen time and encouraging regular breaks from digital devices, can prevent many of the physical health issues associated with prolonged use (Sahu et al. 2023). For instance, incorporating more physical activity into daily routines and reducing sedentary behaviours can counteract the negative effects of the extensive use of AI-driven work tools and entertainment platforms. Simple actions, such as maintaining proper posture while using devices and adjusting the lighting on screens, can help reduce eye strain and other physical discomforts linked to the digital world (Lian et al., 2023).

As digital technology and AI become deeply integrated into daily life, establishing healthy digital habits is essential to safeguarding both physical and psychological well-being. For individuals, this means finding a balanced approach to using technology in a way that enhances health without causing harm. One of the critical aspects of promoting healthy digital habits is ensuring that individuals remain conscious of how much time they spend using digital devices and how these devices influence their daily routines (Lian et al., 2023).

Social Media and Mental Health

Social media platforms, driven by AI algorithms, play a significant role in shaping users' psychological states. These platforms curate content based on user behaviour, showing individuals more of what they engage with, whether it's news, entertainment or advertisements. While this can make digital experiences more personalised, it can also create echo chambers where users are exposed to repetitive, narrow viewpoints that reinforce their beliefs and behaviours. This can lead to increased social isolation, mental fatigue, and even anxiety or depression, as users compare themselves to curated versions of others' lives (Simões et al., 2024).

To foster healthier social media habits, individuals can take steps such as limiting the amount of time spent on these platforms, following accounts that promote positivity and mental well-being and engaging in real-world social activities that foster genuine human connection. Technology companies, for their part, can introduce tools that help users manage their social media usage, such as screen time trackers or prompts to take breaks (Simões et al., 2024).

AI-assisted Mental Health Support

Interestingly, AI itself can be part of the solution in promoting psychological well-being. AI-powered mental health apps are becoming increasingly popular as tools for managing stress, anxiety and depression (Simões et al., 2024). These apps provide guided therapy, mood tracking and even cognitive behavioural therapy (CBT) exercises. In addition, AI-driven platforms are able to assess changes in a user's emotional state by analysing speech patterns or text input, offering insights into their mental health over time. For individuals who face barriers to traditional mental healthcare, such as geographic isolation or stigma, these AI-powered solutions offer accessible, affordable support (Fabregas et al., 2024).

Balancing Technology and Well-being

Ultimately, the key to promoting healthy digital habits lies in finding a balance between benefiting from the convenience and insights provided by AI and digital technologies while mitigating the risks associated with their overuse (Fabregas et al., 2024). This balance requires a proactive approach to personal health management, where individuals are aware of their technology usage and take deliberate steps to protect their physical and psychological well-being. Whether through regular breaks, intentional digital detoxes or using AI tools designed to promote health, individuals have the power to navigate the challenges of the digital age while ensuring their overall well-being (Fabregas et al., 2024).

Moving Towards a Balanced Digital Future

Moreover, while AI and digital technologies continue to shape the future, ensuring that these tools are leveraged in ways that promote, rather than undermine, human well-being is essential (Bauer et al., 2022). The onus is on individuals, educators, healthcare providers, policymakers and technology developers to work together to create an environment where the benefits of technology are maximised while minimising its negative effects (Fabregas et al., 2024). By cultivating digital literacy, promoting healthy habits and enacting thoughtful policies, society can move towards a more balanced and health-conscious relationship with technology. Ultimately, it is not technology itself that determines our well-being but how we choose to engage with it, and this chapter seeks to guide that engagement in a way that supports both physical and psychological health in the digital age (Joe et al., 2021).

Transforming Healthcare through AI

In the realm of healthcare, AI and digital technology are becoming indispensable tools for improving both the physical and psychological well-being of individuals. AI-driven solutions are reshaping diagnostics, treatment plans and even preventive care by providing more personalised, precise and accessible healthcare services (Fritzler & Mahler, 2021). In this digital age, AI systems can analyse vast amounts of patient data, from medical histories to genetic information, to predict potential health issues and recommend interventions before problems escalate (Gargiulo, 2022). This proactive approach can greatly enhance physical health by reducing the burden of chronic diseases, optimising treatments and improving patient outcomes.

For example, AI-powered diagnostic tools, such as those used in radiology and pathology, are capable of detecting conditions like cancer and heart disease at earlier stages with remarkable accuracy (Joe et al., 2021). By quickly analysing medical images or patient biomarkers, AI can often spot patterns that may be difficult for the human eye to detect. This not only speeds up diagnosis but also ensures that treatment can begin at the earliest possible stage, thereby improving physical health outcomes (Subasi, 2022). Wearable health devices, like smartwatches or fitness trackers, provide real-time monitoring of physical metrics such as heart rate, sleep quality and activity levels. These devices can encourage healthier lifestyles by alerting users to exercise more, sleep better or manage stress, all while feeding important data back to healthcare providers for ongoing management (Joe et al., 2021).

The Psychological Impact of AI in Healthcare

AI-powered mental health platforms are providing new ways to support psychological well-being (Jermsittiparsert & Marzo, 2024). From virtual therapy sessions to AI-driven mental health assessments, digital technologies are making mental health care more accessible, particularly for those in underserved or remote areas (Bunyi et al., 2021). AI chatbots, for example, can provide initial emotional support, offer CBT exercises, and even assess mood patterns through language analysis (Bunyi et al., 2021). These tools are available 24/7, offering a level of immediate assistance that traditional mental health services may struggle to provide. For individuals facing mild to moderate psychological issues, such AI solutions can be a valuable supplement to conventional therapy or even a first point of intervention. AI's impact on psychological health in healthcare is multifaceted, ranging from improving access to mental health services to raising new concerns about privacy, human interaction, and emotional well-being (Riaño et al., 2021).

AI and Access to Mental Health Services

One of the most significant contributions AI has made in healthcare is its ability to democratise access to mental health services (Bond et al. 2023). Traditional mental healthcare often requires in-person visits with trained professionals, which can be difficult for individuals living in remote areas or those facing the stigma associated with mental health treatment. AI-driven applications, such as mental health chatbots or teletherapy platforms, are breaking down these barriers by providing a confidential, accessible and often affordable alternative (Babulak, 2023).

For example, AI-powered mental health tools like Woebot, Wysa and Youper provide conversational interfaces that simulate a therapist's interaction (Bohr & Memarzadeh, 2020). These chatbots are programmed to offer therapeutic exercises, help users manage their emotions and provide CBT techniques, all from the convenience of a smartphone (Babulak, 2023). They can monitor emotional states, suggest coping strategies and even encourage users to seek professional help if their condition appears severe. For individuals experiencing mild to moderate psychological distress, these AI-driven tools provide much-needed support without the barriers of traditional healthcare models (Bond et al., 2023).

AI's Role in Personalized Mental Health Care

Another advantage AI brings to mental health care is the potential for highly personalised treatment plans. By analysing large datasets of patient histories, genetic information and treatment outcomes, AI can help clinicians tailor mental health interventions that are specific to an individual's unique needs. This level of personalisation is transformative in a field where one-size-fits-all approaches to treatment often fall short (Bond et al., 2023).

For example, AI can assist in determining the most effective medication for patients with mood disorders by analysing their genetic predispositions and past responses to treatments (Brown, 2020). Similarly, AI-powered platforms can curate personalised coping strategies based on real-time data collection. This individualised care, driven by data, increases the likelihood of successful treatment outcomes, reducing trial and error in finding the right therapeutic approach and enhancing overall psychological well-being (Panesar, 2019).

AI and Digital Technologies in Post-COVID Healthcare

The COVID-19 pandemic has further highlighted the role of AI and digital technology in healthcare (Lytras et al., 2023). Telemedicine and AI-driven virtual health consultations became essential tools for delivering care when in-person visits were limited. These technologies allowed healthcare providers to maintain continuity of care, helping to manage both physical and mental health issues (Khan, 2023). The pandemic also accelerated the use of AI in predicting virus spread, optimising resource allocation in hospitals and even aiding in vaccine development. The psychological toll of the social isolation, anxiety and uncertainty associated with the pandemic was partly alleviated by digital mental health platforms that provided support during a time of widespread emotional distress (Sousa et al., 2023).

As the world evolves beyond the pandemic, it is clear that AI and digital technologies will continue to play a central role in healthcare. The integration of AI into patient care is no longer just a possibility, it is becoming an expectation (Khan, 2023). In the future, healthcare professionals may see even more sophisticated AI tools, such as predictive models for mental health disorders and AI-guided robots performing surgeries with high precision. These advancements hold the potential to enhance both physical and psychological well-being, offering a more holistic approach to health in the digital era (Yadav, 2024).

Navigating the Future of AI in Healthcare

Navigating the era of AI and digital technology in human healthcare requires a deep understanding of both their potential and limitations (Ekong, 2024). As these technologies continue to evolve, individuals, healthcare providers and policymakers must work together to ensure that their implementation promotes not only physical health but also psychological well-being (Glauner, 2021). AI has the power to revolutionise healthcare by making it more efficient, personalised and accessible. However, this must be balanced with ethical considerations, patient safety, and the preservation of human elements that are central to holistic care. By embracing AI's benefits while addressing its challenges, society can leverage technology to create a healthier future for all (Bauer et al., 2022).

Figure 1. AI integration in healthcare: Navigating patient care, telehealth, research, and doctor-facing solutions for holistic well-being (Khalid et al., 2023)

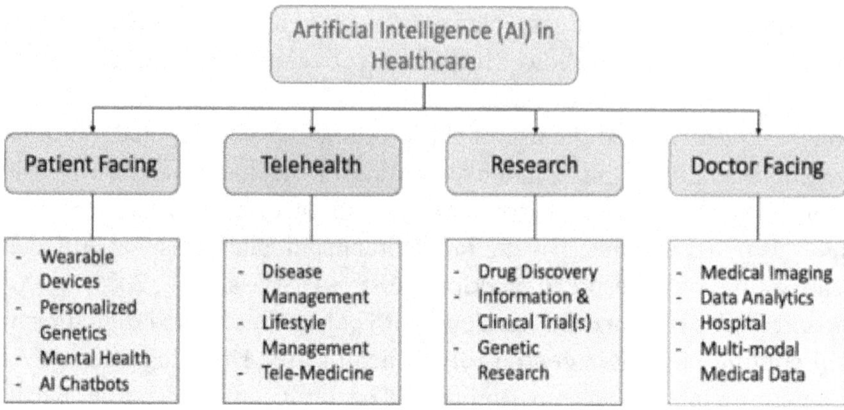

Figure 1, adapted from Khalid et al. (2023), focuses on the intersection of AI and digital technology within the healthcare system. It addresses both physical and psychological well-being in the context of the ongoing digital revolution in healthcare. The figure is designed to provide a holistic view of the way in which AI affects patients, healthcare providers and the broader system, while accounting for the intricate balance between physical health improvements and psychological challenges.

1. Patient-facing AI: Enhancing Physical and Mental Well-being

In this domain, AI interacts directly with patients through various tools and technologies. The model outlines how these innovations improve physical health while also influencing psychological states (Dovgan, 2024)

Wearable Devices: AI-powered devices like fitness trackers and smartwatches monitor physical health parameters (e.g. heart rate, steps, sleep patterns) and provide real-time feedback. These devices encourage users to adopt healthier lifestyles but may also induce anxiety when patients become overly reliant on them or obsessive about tracking their data (Gargiulo & Naik, 2022).

Personalised Genetics: AI has revolutionised personalised medicine by analysing genetic data to customise treatments for individual patients. This offers significant physical benefits, as it improves treatment efficacy and reduces side effects. However, the psychological impact includes potential anxiety over genetic predispositions to diseases, raising concerns over privacy and data security (Ntjamba & Ashipala, 2024).

AI Mental Health Tools: Mental health chatbots and apps provide accessible psychological support, especially for individuals in remote or underserved areas. AI tools such as virtual therapy and counselling help manage mental health conditions like anxiety and depression. While convenient, there is the risk of patients feeling emotionally disconnected due to a lack of human empathy in AI interactions (Jermsittiparsert & Marzo, 2024).

2. Telehealth: Accessibility and the Digital Divide

AI has transformed telehealth services by enabling remote healthcare, having an impact on both physical and psychological health (Mishori & Antono, 2024).

Disease Management: AI-based telehealth platforms track chronic disease symptoms and provide timely interventions, reducing physical health risks. This remote monitoring can decrease anxiety for patients by offering consistent support. However, prolonged digital interactions can lead to screen fatigue and emotional detachment (Bohr & Memarzadeh, 2020).

Telemedicine and Mental Health: AI-enabled telemedicine provides both physical and psychological benefits by delivering health services directly to patients' homes. The convenience reduces the stress associated with long hospital visits. However, the lack of face-to-face interaction in telemedicine may lead to dissatisfaction and feelings of isolation for some patients, especially those with severe psychological conditions (Bohr & Memarzadeh, 2020).

3. AI in Research: Advancing Treatment with Psychological Considerations

AI plays a pivotal role in advancing medical research, influencing both treatment development and patient psychology (Bohr & Memarzadeh, 2020).

Drug Discovery: AI accelerates drug discovery by processing large datasets to find new drug candidates, thus improving physical health outcomes. However, the psychological aspect comes into play as patients may experience hope or anxiety about experimental treatments and their potential effectiveness (Brown, 2020).

Mental Health Research: AI is increasingly used to analyse data related to mental health conditions. The insights gained can help design better treatments for depression, anxiety and other mental disorders. Yet, patients may feel concerned about how their personal data is used in AI research, leading to stress over data privacy (Lee et al., 2022).

4. **Doctor-facing AI**: **Supporting Healthcare Providers**

In this domain, AI technologies assist healthcare professionals, positively influencing both their performance and well-being (Subasi, 2022).

Medical Imaging and Diagnostics: AI in medical imaging helps doctors diagnose conditions like cancer and cardiovascular diseases more accurately and quickly. This improves physical health outcomes, as early detection can lead to more effective treatments. From a psychological perspective, this also reduces the emotional burden on patients by providing quicker, more reliable diagnoses (Razmi, 2024).

Data Analytics and Clinical Decision Support: AI systems analyse patient data and assist doctors in making informed clinical decisions. This reduces the cognitive load on healthcare providers, helping to alleviate job stress and reduce burnout. However, some physicians may feel anxious or threatened by the increasing role of AI, fearing that automation could diminish their professional autonomy or render them obsolete (Cerrato & Halamka, 2020).

REVIEW OF RELATED LITERATURE

The integration of AI and digital technology in healthcare has been a subject of significant research in recent years. As these technologies continue to reshape healthcare systems globally, their effects on both physical and psychological well-being are being explored extensively (Bohr & Memarzadeh, 2020). This literature review aims to synthesise existing research related to the dual role of AI and digital technology in healthcare, focusing on how they influence physical health outcomes and psychological well-being. The review explores empirical studies, theoretical frameworks and practical implications, drawing attention to the complex interplay between technology, patient care and mental health (Sousa et al., 2023).

AI in Healthcare: A Transformative Tool for Physical Health

AI's role in improving physical health outcomes has been well-documented in several studies. The use of AI in healthcare spans diagnostic tools, medical imaging, drug discovery and personalised treatments. According to Riaño et al. (2021), AI has the potential to revolutionise medical diagnostics by offering faster and more accurate interpretations of medical data, particularly in areas like radiology and oncology. This results in better physical health outcomes owing to early diagnosis and targeted interventions.

AI-powered wearable devices are also transforming preventive health. Devices such as smartwatches and fitness trackers, which monitor physical activity, heart rate and sleep patterns, have been shown to promote healthier lifestyles. In a study by Gargiulo and Naik (2022), individuals using AI-based wearable health technologies reported improvements in their overall physical health resulting from real-time feedback and monitoring. The study concluded that continuous health monitoring via AI technologies could prevent the onset of chronic diseases such as diabetes and hypertension, significantly affecting public health outcomes.

However, while the physical benefits of AI in healthcare are clear, some research highlights potential downsides. A review by Ntjamba and Ashipala (2024) warned of the risks associated with over-reliance on AI for critical health decisions, suggesting that errors in AI algorithms could have severe physical health consequences if not monitored properly by human healthcare professionals.

AI and Psychological Well-being: Benefits and Risks

While AI's physical health benefits are well established, its impact on psychological well-being is more nuanced. The use of AI in mental health services, particularly through AI chatbots and virtual therapy, is a growing area of research. These tools provide accessible mental healthcare to individuals who may lack access to traditional services, such as those in remote areas. A study by Fulmer et al. (2018) found that AI mental health applications significantly reduced symptoms of anxiety and depression in participants who used them regularly. The study concluded that AI could play a pivotal role in democratising access to mental healthcare, especially in underserved populations.

However, research has also raised concerns regarding the psychological effects of using AI in mental healthcare. While AI-driven therapy can offer immediate support, some scholars argue that it lacks the empathetic and human connection critical to successful mental health interventions. Stokel-Walker (2023) suggests that while AI chatbots can offer temporary relief, they cannot replicate the emotional depth and trust-building required in human-therapist relationships. This lack of emotional connection may lead to feelings of isolation or dissatisfaction with AI-driven mental health solutions. A study by Santosh and Gaur (2022) found that AI in mental health can have privacy implications that affect psychological well-being. Concerns about data privacy and security are prevalent, as patients may feel uneasy about sharing sensitive mental health data with AI systems.

Telehealth and Psychological Impact: A Mixed Picture

Telehealth is another critical area where AI and digital technology have transformed healthcare delivery. The use of AI in telemedicine enables remote diagnosis, monitoring and treatment, allowing patients to access healthcare services from the comfort of their homes. Telehealth has been particularly beneficial for managing chronic diseases, reducing the need for frequent in-person visits. A study by Hemanth and Gaur (2019) found that telehealth services using AI for chronic disease management improved both physical health outcomes and patient satisfaction.

However, the psychological impact of telehealth remains mixed. While patients appreciate the convenience, studies have shown that the lack of face-to-face interaction can lead to emotional disconnects between patients and healthcare providers. In a qualitative study by Daniel et al. (2019), patients reported feeling more anxious and less assured when interacting with doctors through telemedicine platforms compared to in-person visits. Additionally, healthcare providers have reported concerns about missing non-verbal cues that are essential for understanding patients' mental and emotional states during telehealth consultations.

The Dual Impact of AI on Healthcare Providers' Mental Health

Beyond patient care, AI is also influencing the mental health of healthcare providers. AI-driven tools have been shown to reduce cognitive load by automating routine tasks such as data entry and diagnostics. A study by Davenport and Kalakota (2019) revealed that AI in healthcare can significantly reduce burnout among physicians by assisting with administrative tasks and offering clinical decision support. By handling repetitive work, AI allows healthcare providers to focus more on complex and emotionally fulfilling aspects of patient care, thus improving their psychological well-being.

However, there is also concern that AI could increase job-related anxiety among healthcare professionals. According to a study by Guerrero Quiñones (2024), healthcare workers expressed concerns that AI could replace their roles or reduce their decision-making autonomy, leading to job insecurity and increased stress. The study emphasised the need for a balanced approach to AI integration, where healthcare providers are equipped with the necessary skills and training to work alongside AI tools, rather than feeling threatened by them. While AI can improve physical health outcomes and offer accessible mental health services, it also presents risks to psychological well-being, including feelings of isolation, anxiety over privacy, and job-related stress for healthcare professionals.

RECOMMENDATIONS AND SOLUTIONS

To maximise the benefits of AI and digital technology in healthcare while addressing the associated challenges, several recommendations and essential solutions are offered. One critical step is to promote digital literacy and comprehensive training for healthcare providers. This will equip them with the skills necessary to work alongside AI technologies, thereby reducing job-related anxiety and enhancing their confidence in using these tools. By fostering a mindset that views AI as a complementary tool rather than a replacement, healthcare institutions can alleviate concerns about job security and ensure that human expertise remains central to decision-making processes. Collaborative AI models, where healthcare professionals and AI systems work together, can further enhance patient care by combining human judgement with AI-driven insights.

In developing AI tools, a patient-centred approach is crucial, particularly in areas like mental health. AI chatbots and virtual therapy systems should be designed with emotionally intelligent algorithms that respond to patients' psychological needs, fostering a sense of empathy and trust. Personalisation is key to ensuring AI tools offer tailored healthcare solutions that consider individual medical histories, genetic profiles and mental health conditions. Such personalisation can help AI provide more effective care, both physically and psychologically.

Addressing privacy concerns is another vital aspect. Patients often express anxiety about sharing sensitive health data with AI systems owing to fears of data breaches or misuse. To mitigate this, robust data security measures, such as advanced encryption and block chain technology, should be implemented to protect patient information. In addition, healthcare organisations must adopt transparent data practices, ensuring patients understand how their data is collected, stored and utilised.

Ethical oversight is equally important in the deployment of AI in healthcare. The establishment of clear ethical guidelines and ongoing oversight committees can help monitor the responsible use of AI tools, ensuring they prioritise patient safety, fairness and well-being. By assessing AI systems for potential biases or harm, these committees can ensure that AI technologies are used ethically and responsibly within healthcare settings.

Lastly, while AI and digital technologies offer numerous benefits, they should not entirely replace traditional in-person care. A balanced approach that integrates telehealth and in-person consultations is crucial, particularly in mental health, where face-to-face interactions provide critical emotional support. AI-driven telehealth should serve as a supplemental tool, enhancing access to care but not substituting the human connection that remains central to healthcare. This balanced strategy will ensure that AI improves both physical and psychological well-being without compromising the human elements of care.

STRENGTHS, LIMITATIONS AND FUTURE DIRECTIONS FOR RESEARCH

The integration of AI and digital technology in healthcare presents several strengths, limitations and opportunities for future research. One of the key strengths is the potential for AI to revolutionise healthcare by enhancing diagnostic accuracy, personalising treatment plans and improving access to care through telehealth platforms. AI's ability to process vast amounts of data in real-time enables healthcare providers to make more informed decisions, potentially reducing human error and improving patient outcomes. In addition, AI can optimise the management of chronic diseases by monitoring patient data through wearable devices, offering timely interventions and reducing the burden on healthcare systems. In mental health, AI tools such as chatbots and virtual therapy platforms provide scalable solutions to address the shortage of mental health professionals, making care more accessible to underserved populations. These strengths underscore AI's capacity to enhance both the physical and psychological well-being of patients.

However, there are notable limitations. One of the main concerns is the potential for biases in AI algorithms, which could lead to unequal treatment outcomes, particularly for minority groups. AI systems often rely on historical data that may reflect societal biases, and without careful oversight, these biases could be perpetuated in healthcare settings. Another limitation is the reliance on patient data, raising significant privacy and security concerns. Patients may be reluctant to share sensitive health information with AI systems owing to fears of data breaches or misuse, which could hinder the adoption of AI-driven healthcare solutions. In addition, the lack of human empathy in AI tools, particularly in mental healthcare, is a significant drawback. While AI can provide immediate support, it cannot fully replicate the emotional connection and understanding that human healthcare professionals offer, limiting its effectiveness in complex psychological care scenarios. There is also the risk of over-reliance on AI, where healthcare providers may trust AI systems to the extent that they neglect their own clinical judgement, potentially compromising patient care.

Future research should focus on addressing these limitations and exploring ways to mitigate the risks associated with AI in healthcare. One direction for future studies is the development of more transparent and interpretable AI algorithms to ensure that healthcare professionals understand the rationale behind AI-generated recommendations. This transparency is critical to fostering trust and collaboration between AI systems and healthcare providers. Further research is also needed to address data privacy concerns, particularly exploring technologies like block chain for secure data management. In mental healthcare, future studies could investigate the integration of AI tools with human-led interventions, finding ways to balance technological solutions with the empathetic care that only human professionals can provide. Additionally, long-term studies are needed to assess the broader psychological and physical effects of AI on patients, ensuring that its use in healthcare is both effective and ethical. Expanding research in these areas will help guide the responsible and equitable use of AI in healthcare, ensuring it enhances well-being without sacrificing ethical standards or human connection.

CONCLUSION

The integration of AI and digital technology in healthcare offers both immense potential and notable challenges. AI's ability to enhance diagnostic accuracy, personalise care and improve accessibility, particularly in mental health, represents a significant advancement in the pursuit of physical and psychological well-being. However, these benefits are accompanied by concerns such as biases in algorithms, data privacy issues and the lack of human empathy in AI-driven care. Addressing these challenges requires a balanced approach, where AI is used as a tool to complement, rather than replace, human judgement and emotional intelligence in healthcare. Ethical guidelines, robust data security frameworks and the promotion of digital literacy are essential to ensure the responsible use of AI. Future research should focus on enhancing AI transparency, safeguarding patient data and integrating human elements in AI-driven care. By navigating these complexities thoughtfully, AI and digital technology can significantly contribute to improved healthcare outcomes while maintaining the core values of human connection and empathy.

REFERENCES

Ahmed, A., & Adil, K. (2023). Transforming healthcare systems with artificial intelligence: Revolutionizing efficiency, quality, and patient care. *Research Square*. https://doi.org/DOI: 10.21203/rs.3.rs-3175341/v1

Ana, I. A., & Maryam, E. W. (2024). Relationship between using TikTok social media and FoMO (Fear of missing out) in students. *UMSIDA* Preprints *Server*. https://doi.org/DOI: 10.21070/ups.4201

Ashipala, D. O., & Ntjamba, F. C. (2024). Institutional support available to enhance the mental health of students at the University of Namibia. In Aloka, P. (Ed.), *Mental health crisis in higher education* (pp. 339–359). IGI Global., DOI: 10.4018/979-8-3693-2833-0.ch020

Babulak, E. (2023). Introductory chapter: Journey to AI driven chatbots. In Babulak, E. (Ed.), *Chatbots: The AI-driven front-line services for customers*. Intechopen., DOI: 10.5772/intechopen.112461

Bauer, D. C., Wilson, L. O., & Twine, N. A. (2022). Artificial intelligence in medicine: Applications, limitations and future directions. In Raz, M., Nguyen, T. C., & Loh, E. (Eds.), *Artificial intelligence in medicine* (pp. 101–120). Springer., DOI: 10.1007/978-981-19-1223-8_5

Belciug, S. (2022). An introduction to artificial intelligence in healthcare. *Intelligent Systems Reference Library,* 1–16. DOI: 10.1007/978-3-031-11154-9_1

Bohr, A., & Memarzadeh, K. (2020). The rise of artificial intelligence in healthcare applications. In Bohr, A., & Memarzadeh, K. (Eds.), *Artificial intelligence in healthcare* (pp. 25–60). Science Direct., DOI: 10.1016/B978-0-12-818438-7.00002-2

Bond, R. R., Mulvenna, M. D., Potts, C., O'Neill, S., Ennis, E., & Torous, J. (2023). Digital transformation of mental health services. *Npj Mental Health Research*, *2*(1), 13. Advance online publication. DOI: 10.1038/s44184-023-00033-y PMID: 38609479

Bozoglan, B. (2019). Systemic approach and digital addiction. Advances in psychology, mental health, and behavioural studies. In Bozoglan, B. (Ed.), *Multifaceted approach to digital addiction and its treatment* (pp. 260–280). IGI Global., DOI: 10.4018/978-1-5225-8449-0.ch012

Brown, N. (Ed.). (2020). *Artificial intelligence in drug discovery*. Royal Society of Chemistry., DOI: 10.1039/9781788016841

Bunyi, J., Ringland, K. E., & Schueller, S. M. (2021). Accessibility and digital mental health: Considerations for more accessible and equitable mental health apps. *Frontiers in Digital Health*, *3*, 742196. Advance online publication. DOI: 10.3389/fdgth.2021.742196 PMID: 34713206

Cerrato, P., & Halamka, J. (2020). The promise of artificial intelligence and machine learning. In Cerrato, P., & Halamka, J. (Eds.), *Reinventing clinical decision support: Data analytics, artificial intelligence, and diagnostic reasoning* (pp. 25–57). Taylor & Francis., DOI: 10.1201/9781003034339-2

Daniel, S., Kaller, S., Raifman, S., & Grossman, D. (2019). Characteristics of patients using telemedicine compared with in-person visits for state-mandated informed consent before abortion in Utah. *Contraception*, *99*(5), 316. DOI: 10.1016/j.contraception.2019.03.007

Davenport, T., & Kalakota, R. (2019). The potential for artificial intelligence in healthcare. *Future Healthcare Journal*, *6*(2), 94–98. DOI: 10.7861/futurehosp.6-2-94 PMID: 31363513

Díaz-Lucena, A., & Vicente-Fernández, P. (2024). AI and the human need for emotional connection. In Rojas, R. V. B., & Martínez-Cano, F.-J. (Eds.), *Revolutionizing communication* (pp. 93–101). CRC Press., DOI: 10.1201/9781003473633-9

Dovgan, N. (2024). Integrating physical exercise into digital mental health: Enhancing overall well-being with Metacognit.me. SSRN Electronic Journal. DOI: 10.2139/ssrn.4734030

Ekong, H. (2024). Navigating the AI era: Understanding mechanisms, impacts, and policy interventions for inclusive employment in Malaysia. https://doi.org/DOI: 10.31235/osf.io/2kbj5

Fabregas, R., Vazquez, A., & Angelucci, M. (2024). *Improving immigrant mental health through a digital app*. AEA Randomized Controlled Trials., DOI: 10.1257/rct.13303-1.0

Fei, W. (2024). The Mental Well-Being of Digital Natives in the Age of AI: Challenges and Solutions. In Zaremohzzabieh, Z., Abdullah, R., & Ahrari, S. (Eds.), *Exploring Youth Studies in the Age of AI* (pp. 88–108). IGI Global., DOI: 10.4018/979-8-3693-3350-1.ch005

Fritzler, M. J., & Mahler, M. (2021). Precision medicine as an approach to autoimmune diseases. In Mahler, M. (Ed.), *Precision medicine and artificial intelligence* (pp. 39–63). Academic Press., DOI: 10.1016/B978-0-12-820239-5.00007-3

Fulmer, R., Joerin, A., Gentile, B., Lakerink, L., & Rauws, M. (2018). Using psychological artificial intelligence (Tess) to relieve symptoms of depression and anxiety: Randomized controlled trial. *JMIR Mental Health*, *5*(4), e64. DOI: 10.2196/mental.9782 PMID: 30545815

Gargiulo, G. D., & Naik, G. R. (Eds.). (2022). *Wearable/personal monitoring devices: Present to future*. Springer Singapore., DOI: 10.1007/978-981-16-5324-7

Glauner, P. (2021). Artificial intelligence in healthcare: Foundations, opportunities and challenges. In Glauner, P., Plugmann, P., & Lerzynski, G. (Eds.), *Digitalization in healthcare: Future of business and finance* (pp. 1–15). Springer., DOI: 10.1007/978-3-030-65896-0_1

Guerrero Quiñones, J. L. (2024). Using artificial intelligence to enhance patient autonomy in healthcare decision-making. *AI & Society*. Advance online publication. DOI: 10.1007/s00146-024-01956-6

Hemanth, D. J., & Gaur, V. E. (2019). *Telemedicine technologies: Big data, deep learning, robotics, mobile and remote applications for global healthcare*. Academic Press.

Jermsittiparsert, K., & Marzo, R. (2024). *AI technologies and advancements for psychological well-being and healthcare*. GI Global., DOI: 10.4018/979-8-3693-9158-7

Joe, J. M., Kinikar, J., Smith, M., Carr, M. J., Bechtel, E., Randall, S., & Ammerman, L. (2021). Digital health solutions and wearable devices. *Health Informatics*, 13-38. https://doi.org/DOI: 10.1007/978-3-030-81030-6_2

Jotterand, F., & Ienca, M. (2021). Artificial intelligence in brain and mental health: Philosophical, ethical and policy issues. *Advanced Neuroethics*, 1–7. DOI: 10.1007/978-3-030-74188-4_1

Khalid, N., Qayyum, A., Bilal, M., Al-Fuqaha, A., & Qadir, J. (2023). Privacy-preserving artificial intelligence in healthcare: Techniques and applications. *Computers in Biology and Medicine*, *158*, 106848. DOI: 10.1016/j.compbiomed.2023.106848 PMID: 37044052

Khan, A. (2023). Transforming healthcare through AI: Unleashing the power of personalized medicine. *International Journal of Multidisciplinary Sciences and Arts*, *2*(1), 67–77. DOI: 10.47709/ijmdsa.v2i1.2424

Khan, M. S., & Nayab, H. (2021). Digital health technologies and artificial intelligence in the Islamic world: Embracing the evolution in healthcare. *Journal of Islamic Governance*, *6*. Advance online publication. DOI: 10.53105/jig.6-1

Lee, E., Karim, H., Iaboni, A., & Sekhon, H. (2022). Artificial intelligence in geriatric mental health: Recent advances in clinical research. *The American Journal of Geriatric Psychiatry, 30*(4), S15–S16. DOI: 10.1016/j.jagp.2022.01.275

Lian, B., Nguyen, P. T., Lydia, E. L., & Shankar, K. (2019). Can excessive use of social media contribute to addictive behaviors (drugs, tobacco, alcohol) or mental health issues? *Restaurant Business, 118*(10), 22–29. DOI: 10.26643/rb.v118i10.8779

Lytras, M. D., Housawi, A. A., & Alsaywid, B. S. (2023). Preface. In Lytras, M. D., Housawi, A. A., & Alsaywid, B. S. (Eds.), *Digital transformation in healthcare in post-Covid-19 times* (pp. xiii–xxi). Academic Press., DOI: 10.1016/B978-0-323-98353-2.09996-2

Ma, J. K., & Cheng, S. (2022). Digital inclusion, psychological well-being, and digital competence. In Estes, R. J., & Sirgy, M. J. (Eds.), *Human well-being research and policy making* (pp. 125–166). Springer., DOI: 10.1007/978-3-031-04412-0_6

Martinez-Martin, N. (2021). Minding the AI: Ethical challenges and practice for AI mental health care tools. In Jotterand, F., & Ienca, M. (Eds.), *Artificial intelligence in brain and mental health: Philosophical, ethical & policy issues. Advances in Neuroethics* (pp. 111–125). Springer., DOI: 10.1007/978-3-030-74188-4_8

Mishori, R., & Antono, B. (2020). Telehealth, rural America, and the digital divide. *The Journal of Ambulatory Care Management, 43*(4), 319–322. DOI: 10.1097/JAC.0000000000000348 PMID: 32858734

Ntjamba, F. C., & Ashipala, D. O. (2025). Impact on and Ethical Considerations of Artificial Intelligence on Human Healthcare. In Jermsittiparsert, K., & Marzo, R. (Eds.), *AI Technologies and Advancements for Psychological Well-Being and Healthcare* (pp. 1–36). IGI Global., DOI: 10.4018/979-8-3693-9158-7.ch001

Panesar, A. (2019). *Machine learning and AI for healthcare: Big data for improved health outcomes*. Springer., DOI: 10.1007/978-1-4842-3799-1

Razmi, R. M. (2024). *AI doctor. The rise of artificial intelligence in healthcare – A guide for users, buyers, builders, and investors*. John Wiley & Sons., DOI: 10.1002/9781394240197

Riaño, D., Wilk, S., & Teije, A. T. (2021). Preface: AIME 2019. *Artificial Intelligence in Medicine, 115*, 102058. DOI: 10.1016/j.artmed.2021.102058 PMID: 34001318

Sacopulos, M., & Granzotti, M. T. (2024). *Using AI to enhance clinical decision-making with Dr. Maria Granzotti*. Sound Practice., DOI: 10.55834/sp.3375289237

Sahu, M., Gandhi, S., Sharma, M. K., & Mehrotra, S. (2023). Nursing students' perceptions regarding well-being and healthy use of digital technology: A qualitative thematic analysis. *Journal of Education and Health Promotion*, *12*(1). Advance online publication. DOI: 10.4103/jehp.jehp_1271_22 PMID: 37546018

Santosh, K., & Gaur, L. (2021). *Artificial intelligence and machine learning in public healthcare*. SpringerBriefs in Applied Sciences and Technology., DOI: 10.1007/978-981-16-6768-8

Shanmugasundaram, M., & Tamilarasu, A. (2023). The impact of digital technology, social media, and artificial intelligence on cognitive functions: A review. *Frontiers in Cognition*, *2*, 1203077. Advance online publication. DOI: 10.3389/fcogn.2023.1203077

Simões, J. P., Ten Klooster, P., Neff, P. K., Niemann, U., & Kraiss, J. (2024). Editorial: Artificial intelligence and mental health care. *Frontiers in Public Health*, *12*, 1461446. Advance online publication. DOI: 10.3389/fpubh.2024.1461446 PMID: 39139670

Sousa, M. J., Nunes, F. G., Nascimento, G. D., & Chakraborty, C. (Eds.). (2023). *Future health scenarios*. Taylor & Francis., DOI: 10.1201/9781003227892

Srinivasan, S., & Rajavel, N. (2024). A study of the psychological well-being of Tamil Nadu prison inmates with special reference to AI. In Jermsittiparsert, K., & Marzo, R. (Eds.), *AI technologies and advancements for psychological well-being and healthcare* (pp. 219–254). IGI Global., DOI: 10.4018/979-8-3693-9158-7.ch009

Stokel-Walker, C. (2023). AI chatbots are coming to search engines: Can you trust the results? *Nature*. Advance online publication. DOI: 10.1038/d41586-023-00423-4 PMID: 36781968

Subasi, A. (2022). *Applications of artificial intelligence in medical imaging*. Academic Press.

Xue, L., Wei, L., Bai, L., & Wei, L. (2023). *AI empowerment or AI replacement*. AEA Randomized Controlled Trials., DOI: 10.1257/rct.12196-1.0

Yadav, S. J. (2024). Artificial intelligence and stress management tools for better mental health. In Jermsittiparsert, K., & Marzo, R. (Eds.), *AI Technologies and Advancements for Psychological Well-Being and Healthcare* (pp. 163–186). IGI Global., DOI: 10.4018/979-8-3693-9158-7.ch007

Yasobant, S. (2016). Physical health promotion through modern technologies. *Geospatial Research*, 889–907. DOI: 10.4018/978-1-4666-9845-1.ch042

ADDITIONAL READING

Srinivasan, S., & Rajavel, N. (2024). Artificial intelligence approach to psychological wellbeing among the ageing population. In Jermsittiparsert, K., & Marzo, R. (Eds.), *AI technologies and advancements for psychological well-being and healthcare* (pp. 219–254). IGI Global., DOI: 10.4018/979-8-3693-9158-7.ch009

Yadav, S. J. (2024). Artificial intelligence and stress management tools for better mental health. In Jermsittiparsert, K., & Marzo, R. (Eds.), *AI Technologies and Advancements for Psychological Well-Being and Healthcare* (pp. 163–186). IGI Global., DOI: 10.4018/979-8-3693-9158-7.ch007

KEY TERM DEFINITIONS

Artificial Intelligence (AI): AI refers to the simulation of human intelligence in machines that are programmed to think, learn and make decisions. In healthcare, AI applications range from diagnostic tools to personalised treatment plans and mental health support systems (Ntjamba & Ashipala, 2024).

Digital Technology: This term encompasses a wide range of tools and platforms that use electronic systems to collect, store, process and share information. In healthcare, digital technology includes electronic health records (EHRs), telemedicine platforms, wearable health devices and mobile health applications (Joe et al. 2021).

Physical Well-Being: The state of physical health, characterised by the absence of disease and the presence of vitality and energy. In the context of AI and digital health, physical well-being can be supported by tools like remote monitoring devices, AI-assisted diagnostics and virtual fitness platforms (Bohr & Memarzadeh, 2020).

Psychological Well-Being: A state of mental health that includes emotional balance, resilience and overall mental satisfaction (Ashipala & Ntjamba, 2023).

Ethical Standards in AI: A set of principles guiding the responsible use of AI technologies to ensure fairness, transparency and accountability. Ethical standards in healthcare AI aim to protect patient rights, promote equity and prevent harm (Ntjamba & Ashipala, 2024).

Social Media: Digital platforms and websites that enable users to create, share and engage with content, as well as interact with others in virtual communities. Examples include Facebook, Instagram, X (formerly known as Twitter) and TikTok (Lian et al., 2019).

Mental Health: A state of emotional, psychological and social well-being that affects how individuals think, feel and behave. It influences one's ability to handle stress, relate to others and make decisions (Jotterand & Ienca, 2021).

Chapter 15
AI, Privacy, and Power: Shaping Surveillance Policies in Canada

Swati Chakraborty
https://orcid.org/0000-0003-0799-1954
Concordia University, Canada

ABSTRACT

In an era where artificial intelligence (AI) is increasingly integrated into surveillance systems, Canada faces the challenge of balancing national security interests with the protection of individual privacy rights. This paper explores the complexities of AI-driven surveillance, focusing on how these technologies amplify state power and the ethical dilemmas they pose. It examines Canada's existing governance frameworks, highlighting gaps in policy and regulation concerning AI's role in monitoring and data collection.The analysis covers key issues such as transparency in AI algorithms, accountability for misuse of surveillance tools, and the need for robust privacy safeguards. It also discusses international best practices and proposes actionable recommendations for Canadian policymakers. These include enforcing stricter data protection laws, enhancing oversight mechanisms, and ensuring that AI surveillance technologies comply with human rights standards.

INTRODUCTION

The rapid integration of AI into surveillance systems has transformed the capabilities of state and corporate monitoring in Canada. While these technologies promise enhanced security and efficiency, they also raise significant concerns about privacy, data protection, and unchecked state power. This paper investigates the interplay

DOI: 10.4018/979-8-3373-3384-7.ch015

between AI, privacy, and power, aiming to propose a governance framework that addresses these challenges.

The intersection of artificial intelligence (AI) and surveillance has transformed the landscape of privacy and data collection in Canada. **Surveillance** refers to the monitoring of individuals or groups for the purpose of gathering information, which can be conducted through various means, including cameras, drones, and digital tracking systems. In contrast, **artificial intelligence** represents algorithms and technologies that can analyze vast amounts of data to identify patterns, make predictions, and automate processes. **Privacy**, in this context, is defined as the right of individuals to control their personal information and to safeguard it from unauthorized use or exposure (Cath, Corinne, 2018).

THE EMERGENCE OF AI IN SURVEILLANCE

The adoption of AI technologies in surveillance has accelerated in recent years, fuelled by advancements in machine learning, computer vision, and data analytics (Sotala, et. al,2014). In Canada, governmental and law enforcement agencies leverage these tools in several contexts, including:

- **Public Safety**: AI can enhance threat detection in public spaces through facial recognition systems and predictive policing algorithms.
- **Border Security**: Automated monitoring systems at points of entry use AI to streamline customs processes and assess risks associated with travellers.
- **Urban Management**: Smart city initiatives incorporate surveillance technologies powered by AI to manage traffic flow and optimize resource allocation.

Importance of AI, Surveillance, and Privacy

Understanding the implications of AI and surveillance within Canadian policy contexts is critical for several reasons. The integration of these technologies raises significant ethical concerns surrounding **transparency**, **accountability**, and the potential erosion of civil liberties.

For policymakers and legal professionals, navigating this complex landscape involves striking a delicate balance. They must encourage innovation while developing robust regulations that protect individual rights, ensuring that privacy is not compromised in the pursuit of technological advancement. As the discourse surrounding AI and surveillance evolves, it becomes imperative to address these challenges to foster a society where personal freedoms are upheld alongside security enhancements (Erdélyi, et. el, 2020).

Current State of Surveillance Policies in Canada

In Canada, the framework governing surveillance practices is shaped by a combination of **federal laws**, **provincial regulations**, and **corporate policies**. This multi-layered approach reflects the complex interplay between ensuring security and protecting the privacy of individuals.

Key Legislation Governing Surveillance

Several major laws are instrumental in regulating surveillance activities in Canada:

Personal Information Protection and Electronic Documents Act (PIPEDA): This act sets the tone for how private-sector organizations handle personal information. It establishes principles for consent, safeguarding personal data, and accountability.
Criminal Code of Canada: It provides law enforcement agencies with legal context for various surveillance activities, particularly regarding wiretaps and other interception methods. The code also outlines the permissible grounds and procedures for obtaining search warrants.
Canadian Charter of Rights and Freedoms: Sections of the Charter, particularly Section 8, protect individuals from unreasonable search and seizure, thereby providing a constitutional baseline for surveillance activities.
Regulatory Agencies: The Office of the Privacy Commissioner of Canada oversees compliance with privacy laws and advocates for the protection of personal information against intrusive surveillance measures.

Government and Corporate Surveillance Practices

Both governmental and corporate entities engage in extensive surveillance practices, which have expanded significantly with the advent of AI technologies:

Governmental Surveillance: Agencies like the Canadian Security Intelligence Service (CSIS) have access to advanced surveillance tools powered by AI. This enables monitoring for national security threats but raises concerns about oversight and accountability.
Corporate Surveillance: Companies collect vast amounts of consumer data through various means such as cookies, tracking, and social media interactions. While businesses argue that such data collection improves services and personalization, it fundamentally affects user privacy.

Public Perception and Concerns

Public perception of surveillance practices in Canada is increasingly wary. Surveys indicate that citizens express concern over privacy invasion and the potential misuse of personal data. Key areas of concern include:

Lack of Transparency: Many Canadians feel uninformed about how their data is collected, used, and shared. This fosters a sense of distrust towards both governmental and corporate entities.
Potential for Abuse: There are fears that surveillance tools, especially those involving AI, could be misused for social control or discrimination. Cases of biased algorithms have already raised significant ethical questions.
Desire for Greater Regulation: The public is calling for stronger regulations that ensure transparency and accountability in surveillance practices, stressing the need for a balance between public safety and personal privacy.

In summary, while Canada has established a foundational framework for surveillance policies, the growing capabilities of AI pose ongoing challenges. Addressing public concerns and enhancing legal safeguards will be essential to creating a surveillance landscape that respects individual rights and freedoms.

Impact of AI on Privacy Rights

The implementation of AI technologies has profoundly impacted individual privacy rights in Canada. As entities increasingly harness AI for data processing and analysis, significant concerns arise related to **data collection**, **user consent**, and the safeguarding of **user rights**.

Data Collection Practices

AI systems thrive on large volumes of data to function effectively. Consequently, surveillance technologies may aggregate personal information from various sources, including social media, online transactions, and location tracking. In Canada, the reliance on these AI tools increases the risk of excess data being collected without individuals' awareness. For instance, **facial recognition technology** used in public spaces has raised alarms. While intended for security, it collects vast amounts of visual data, often without clear consent from individuals being monitored.

Consent and User Rights

A core principle of privacy protection is informed consent—individuals should understand and authorize how their data is collected and used. However, AI's opaque nature complicates this principle. Users often consent to data collection through lengthy terms of service that few read or understand. This situation is exemplified by the **Canadian Telecommunications Act**, which permits data collection for purposes not always transparently communicated to users. As a result, individuals may unwittingly forfeit their rights to privacy due to ambiguous or misleading consent mechanisms.

Moreover, the application of AI raises pertinent questions regarding individuals' rights to access and control their data. For example, **algorithms used in predictive policing** can adversely affect marginalized communities, as biases in data lead to skewed results and heightened scrutiny. This reality has sparked significant debate over **algorithmic accountability**, highlighting the need for frameworks that protect individuals from discrimination.

Case Studies and Examples

Several notable instances showcase the interplay between AI technologies and privacy rights in Canada:

The use of Clearview AI: This controversial facial recognition software has faced backlash for its practices of scraping public images without consent. Legal actions initiated against Clearview in various jurisdictions underscore a growing concern over how AI can infringe upon individual privacy rights.

Smart Cities Initiatives: Cities like Toronto have explored using AI-driven surveillance to improve urban management. However, public reaction has been mixed, with many citizens voicing concerns about constant monitoring and the potential for misuse of personal data.

The RCMP's Use of Social Media Data: The Royal Canadian Mounted Police has utilized AI to analyze social media posts for criminal activity. This action has raised privacy alarms about the extent of surveillance over individuals' online lives and the limits of lawful data gathering.

The Need for Effective Regulation

To address these challenges, Canada must prioritize clear regulations that govern AI deployment in surveillance contexts. Key recommendations include:

- **Strengthening consent laws**: Ensuring users fully understand how their data will be utilized.
- **Mandating transparency**: Organizations should provide clear, accessible information on data practices.
- **Establishing oversight mechanisms**: Creating independent bodies to review AI applications and protect civil rights.

The evolution of AI technologies within surveillance raises multifaceted privacy challenges in Canada. Addressing these issues is critical to uphold individual rights while navigating the complex landscape of technological advancement (Vincent, James, 2023).

Ethical Considerations in AI Surveillance

The integration of AI into surveillance practices raises pressing ethical questions that demand careful consideration. As organizations increasingly depend on AI technologies for monitoring purposes, it is vital to explore issues such as algorithmic bias, accountability, and transparency.

Bias in AI Algorithms

One of the foremost ethical concerns associated with AI in surveillance is the inherent **bias** present in algorithms. These biases can arise from several sources, including:

- **Data Selection**: If the training data used for AI algorithms is skewed or unrepresentative, the resulting outputs may disproportionately affect certain demographics, leading to harmful stereotypes and discrimination.
- **Algorithm Design**: Poorly designed algorithms can amplify underlying social biases, resulting in skewed surveillance outcomes. For instance, facial recognition technology has been criticized for misidentifying individuals from minority backgrounds at higher rates, raising issues of fairness and equity.

Accountability in AI Surveillance

The question of **accountability** when implementing AI surveillance systems is paramount. Organizations must address the following considerations:

- **Responsibility for Outcomes**: When AI systems make erroneous decisions, especially those affecting individuals' rights, it is crucial to establish who is accountable—the technology provider, the implementing organization, or both? Clarity in accountability can help foster trust and ensure that organizations take responsibility for the repercussions of their surveillance practices.
- **Oversight Mechanisms**: Regulatory frameworks should be established to oversee AI surveillance applications. Independent bodies can play a vital role in monitoring compliance with ethical standards and ensuring that organizations are held accountable for their AI deployments.

Transparency in Surveillance Practices

Maintaining **transparency** in how AI surveillance systems operate is essential for fostering public trust. Organizations should consider:

- **Public Disclosures**: Providing accessible information about how AI technologies collect, store, and use personal data is crucial. This includes disclosing the type of data being captured and the specific purposes for which it will be used.
- **Community Engagement**: Engaging with communities to communicate surveillance practices before implementation can help alleviate concerns and build public support. Collaborative discussions allow stakeholders to express their views and influence decision-making, reinforcing ethical practices (Curtis, et. el, 2022).

Moral Responsibilities of Organizations

Organizations leveraging AI for surveillance purposes have moral obligations to uphold ethical standards. These responsibilities encompass:

- **Commitment to Fairness**: Organizations must prioritize fairness in their AI systems by regularly auditing algorithms for biases and making necessary adjustments.
- **Protection of Human Rights**: Organizations should adopt a human rights-based approach, ensuring that their surveillance practices do not infringe on individual rights, particularly in relation to privacy and discrimination.
- **Continuous Learning**: Staying informed about emerging ethical issues related to AI and surveillance is crucial. Organizations should develop internal policies that encourage ongoing education and adaptation in response to evolving ethical concerns.

Addressing these ethical considerations is paramount to fostering a balanced integration of AI in surveillance that respects individual rights and civil liberties (Héder, M, 2020).

Public Debate and Advocacy

The intersection of AI and surveillance in Canada has ignited a vibrant public debate, with advocacy groups playing a crucial role in amplifying voices concerned about privacy rights and governmental overreach. These organizations, alongside engaged citizens, are instrumental in shaping the discourse and influencing policy change.

Key Stakeholders in Advocacy

Several key stakeholders are prominent in the advocacy landscape regarding AI and surveillance in Canada:

Civil Liberties Organizations: Groups such as the **Canadian Civil Liberties Association (CCLA)** and the **British Columbia Civil Liberties Association (BCCLA)** actively campaign for the protection of individual privacy rights. They provide legal support, conduct research, and engage in public education to raise awareness about the implications of surveillance technologies.

Privacy Advocates: Organizations like the **Electronic Frontier Foundation (EFF)** and **OpenMedia** focus on digital rights and online privacy. Through campaigns and initiatives, they emphasize the need for greater transparency from both public agencies and private corporations.

Academics and Thought Leaders: Researchers in fields such as law, technology, and ethics contribute through publications, lectures, and workshops, fostering a deeper understanding of the challenges surrounding AI surveillance.

Significant Campaigns and Movements

Numerous campaigns have emerged to address concerns regarding AI surveillance in Canada. Notable examples include:

#StopSpyingOnUs: This grassroots movement, led by various civil liberties organizations, calls for stricter legislation regulating surveillance practices. It mobilizes public support to demand accountability from authorities that deploy surveillance technologies.

Public Consultations on AI Policy: The Canadian government has initiated public consultations to gather feedback on AI regulations, encouraging citizen participation in policy formation. Advocacy groups have mobilized to ensure that privacy rights are represented in these discussions.

Campaign for Algorithmic Accountability: Various organizations advocate for the establishment of standards and oversight mechanisms to assess AI algorithms' fairness and accuracy, particularly concerning their application in surveillance.

These advocacy efforts underscore the importance of fostering informed public debate surrounding AI and surveillance policies in Canada. By engaging diverse stakeholders and promoting transparency, these movements work towards creating a regulatory environment that adequately protects individual rights while considering the potential benefits of AI in enhancing public safety.

RECOMMENDATIONS FOR FUTURE POLICY DEVELOPMENT

As Canada navigates the complex landscape of AI and surveillance, policymakers face the challenge of establishing regulations that not only support technological advancement but also safeguard individual privacy rights. The following recommendations aim to enhance the effectiveness of future policy development:

1. Establish Robust Data Protection Regulations

Regulatory Action and Guidance on Privacy and AI

Regulatory action and guidance continue to play a significant role in shaping privacy and AI standards in Canada. In December 2023, the Office of the Privacy Commissioner of Canada (OPC), in collaboration with all provincial and territorial privacy regulators, released a set of guidelines titled *Principles for Responsible, Trustworthy, and Privacy-Protective Generative AI Technologies*. This guidance outlines best practices for managing privacy risks associated with generative AI.

Additionally, recent actions by the OPC and other privacy regulators highlight key enforcement priorities, including:

- **Children's Privacy:** Enhanced safeguards for data collected from or about minors.
- **Biometrics:** Stricter regulations on the collection and use of biometric data.
- **Deceptive Design Practices:** Crackdown on dark patterns that mislead users.

- **Data Use for AI Training:** Increased scrutiny on how personal data is collected and utilized to train AI models.
- **Protection of Health Information:** Reinforced privacy requirements for handling personal health data.
- **Employee Surveillance:** Growing concern over the privacy implications of monitoring employees.

Privacy risks in these areas are expected to attract more rigorous regulatory investigations, thereby escalating both litigation and reputational risks for organizations.

AI Under Heightened Regulatory Scrutiny

Several other regulatory bodies have also signalled their intent to closely monitor AI applications:

- **Competition Bureau:** The bureau has expressed concerns about AI's potential to distort competition, particularly through practices like algorithmic pricing, collusion, and the spread of deepfakes.
- **Human Rights:** The Ontario Human Rights Commission has highlighted risks of bias and discrimination embedded in AI systems, calling for stringent oversight.
- **Financial Sector:** The Office of the Superintendent of Financial Institutions and the Financial Consumer Agency of Canada released a joint report addressing risks associated with AI in federally regulated financial institutions.

Need for Cross-Sector Collaboration

Canadian regulators emphasize the importance of cross-sector collaboration due to the complex and multifaceted nature of AI regulation. This includes aligning privacy standards with competition, telecommunications, and intellectual property regulations to develop a cohesive approach to managing AI risks.

In this evolving regulatory landscape, organizations must stay informed and adapt quickly to mitigate compliance risks effectively.

Policymakers should develop comprehensive legislation that clearly delineates how personal data can be collected, stored, and processed, especially in AI-driven contexts. Key elements include:

- **Explicit Consent Requirements**: Mandate that organizations obtain informed consent from individuals, ensuring users understand how their data will be utilized.

- **Limitation of Data Retention**: Stipulate maximum retention periods for personal data collected through surveillance. This ensures data is not kept indefinitely, reducing the risk of misuse.

Class Action Litigation in Privacy and AI

Privacy Class Actions

In recent years, there has been a notable expansion in class action litigation beyond traditional data breach claims to encompass an organization's intentional data handling practices. Plaintiffs' lawyers have become increasingly sophisticated, bringing forward claims based on the collection, use, or disclosure of personal information without adequate consent. These claims can be grounded in tort, contract, or statutory violations. As a result, the litigation risk associated with data handling practices involving large groups of individuals has risen significantly and continues to grow.

AI Class Actions

The rise of AI has also sparked a new wave of class action lawsuits, addressing a diverse range of legal issues, including:

- **Privacy-Related Claims:** Allegations involving the misuse of AI to unlawfully collect biometric identifiers.
- **Employment and Discrimination Claims:** Cases focusing on AI-driven discrimination in hiring processes.
- **Antitrust and Competition Claims:** Accusations that AI has been used for price-fixing or market manipulation.
- **Insurance-Related Claims:** Challenges to the improper use of AI in making insurance claim decisions.
- **Intellectual Property Claims:** Disputes over the unlicensed use of copyrighted material to train AI models.

The convergence of AI technologies and class action litigation highlights the growing legal risks organizations face in managing data and deploying AI systems. As regulatory scrutiny intensifies, organizations must adopt robust compliance strategies to mitigate potential liabilities.

Implications for Businesses

The privacy and AI landscape continues to evolve rapidly, even without the passage of Bill C-27. Canadian organizations should remain vigilant in monitoring this shifting environment, especially given the accelerating pace of change.

Many organizations had postponed some of their privacy and AI compliance efforts, waiting for the clarity that Bill C-27 would provide. With that bill now off the table, businesses should reassess their compliance initiatives, identifying critical risk areas and establishing priorities for 2025.

For privacy compliance, particular attention should be paid to the requirements under **Law 25** and recent regulatory actions and decisions. As for AI governance, businesses should ensure their programs align with current best practices to minimize risk, meet evolving industry standards, and streamline compliance efforts as new AI regulations emerge (Tallberg, et. el, 2023).

2. Enhance Transparency Measures

Transparency is vital for fostering public trust in surveillance practices. Recommendations include:

- **Public Disclosure of Practices**: Require organizations to disclose their surveillance practices and data collection methods to the public. This could involve creating accessible online databases of policies and practices.
- **Regular Reporting**: Mandate that governmental and corporate entities submit regular reports outlining their surveillance activities, including the types of data collected and the purposes of its use.

3. Implement Oversight Mechanisms

The State of Privacy and AI Legislation in Canada After Bill C-27

With the recent prorogation of Parliament, Bill C-27—along with its proposed AI law and privacy reforms—has been effectively terminated. The likelihood of new federal privacy or AI legislation being passed soon is low. However, the landscape of privacy and AI standards continues to evolve, increasing the risks of non-compliance for organizations. This update provides an overview of the current privacy and AI environment without Bill C-27.

- **Federal Legislation Outlook:** No new federal privacy or AI laws are expected to pass this year. However, Canadian organizations must stay vigilant as privacy and AI standards continue to evolve rapidly.
- **Impact of Provincial Reforms:** Recent legislative changes in Québec and other provinces are shaping industry standards and influencing organizations nationwide, even those with limited operations in these regions.
- **Regulatory Priorities:** Authorities are focusing on AI, biometrics, deceptive design practices, and the protection of children's and health information, indicating these areas may face increased regulatory scrutiny.
- **Litigation Risks:** Trends in class action lawsuits suggest rising risks linked to intentional data use and AI initiatives.
- **Global Influence:** International privacy laws and standards are increasingly shaping practices and expectations in the Canadian market.

Provincial Legislation Overview

Québec

Québec's Act respecting the protection of personal information in the private sector (Law 25), which was fully enacted in September 2024, is set to significantly influence privacy practices across Canada. Key aspects include:

- **Severe Penalties:** Fines can reach up to $10 million or 4% of an organization's global revenue—the highest among Canadian privacy laws.
- **Broad Applicability:** The law has a wide extraterritorial scope and imposes stringent compliance requirements.
- **Adoption Beyond Québec:** Many organizations are extending Law 25's standards to all data subjects, regardless of location, to streamline compliance and gain a competitive edge.

Ontario

In June 2021, Ontario released a white paper on privacy reform, suggesting potential action if federal reforms fell short. While no recent statements have reaffirmed this intent, Ontario has made progress in other areas:

- **New Legislation:** The Strengthening Cyber Security and Building Trust in the Public Sector Act, 2024 introduces new regulations for public sector cybersecurity and AI usage.

- **AI Transparency:** A pending law will require employers to disclose the use of AI in hiring processes, highlighting a growing focus on AI governance.

Alberta

Alberta has recently strengthened its public sector privacy law through Bill 33, the Protection of Privacy Act, which includes:

- **Enhanced Penalties:** Fines up to $750,000 for organizations, addressing long-standing concerns about the effectiveness of previous legislation.
- **Potential for Private Sector Reform:** The ongoing review of Alberta's Personal Information Protection Act (PIPA) and the direction of public sector reforms suggest that similar updates for the private sector may be forthcoming.

While federal privacy and AI legislation remains stalled, provincial reforms are rapidly reshaping the compliance landscape in Canada. Organizations must stay proactive and adaptive to manage the evolving risks effectively.

To ensure accountability in AI surveillance practices, independent oversight bodies should be established:

- **Creation of a National AI Ethics Board**: This board would evaluate AI technologies' impact on privacy and civil liberties, providing recommendations for ethical standards in surveillance.
- **Regular Audits**: Introduce regular audits of surveillance technologies to assess compliance with privacy laws and identify potential biases within AI algorithms.

International AI Laws and Standards

International laws and standards play a crucial role in setting expectations, especially for organizations that operate in multiple jurisdictions and seek a harmonized approach to privacy and AI governance. While this section primarily focuses on AI laws and standards, it's important to note that broader international privacy regulations also impact AI governance.

European Law

The European Union's **Artificial Intelligence Act (AIA)**, which came into force in August 2024, is a landmark regulation that will be implemented gradually over the next two years. The AIA imposes obligations on risk management, data governance, transparency, human oversight, cybersecurity, documentation, and quality control. Importantly, the AIA applies to AI system providers and deployers located outside the European Economic Area (EEA) if their AI systems are used within the EU, similar to how the **General Data Protection Regulation (GDPR)** applies globally. This means that Canadian companies with operations or customers in the EEA must comply with the AIA. Given the global influence of the GDPR, the AIA is expected to have a similarly significant impact on AI governance worldwide.

United States Law

Currently, there is no comprehensive federal AI-specific legislation in the U.S. In 2023, the Biden administration issued an executive order on AI focusing on safe, secure, and equitable use, addressing privacy, security, and human rights concerns. However, the Trump administration has expressed plans to repeal this order and resist regulations that could hinder AI innovation. Despite this, a growing patchwork of state-level AI laws is emerging, with Utah, Colorado, and California leading the way. These states passed legislation in 2024 requiring AI governance and transparency. Additionally, states like Illinois, Massachusetts, and Ohio are actively reviewing several AI-related bills.

Other Jurisdictions

The **United Kingdom** has announced plans to introduce its own AI legislation, with an anticipated rollout later this year. In Asia, South Korea's **National Assembly** passed the **Basic Act on the Development of Artificial Intelligence** in 2023, set to take effect in January 2026. Meanwhile, **Taiwan**, **Brazil**, and **Chile** have introduced draft AI legislation. Like the AIA, these regulations will impose different requirements based on the perceived risk level of the AI systems.

International Standards

In 2023, the **National Institute of Standards and Technology (NIST)**, part of the U.S. Department of Commerce, published a voluntary set of guidelines known as the **AI Risk Management Framework**. This framework aims to help manage AI-related risks and increase trust in AI systems' design, development, and usage.

The **International Organization for Standardization (ISO)** has also released a series of standards to guide AI development, including **ISO/IEC 42001, ISO/IEC 23894**, and **ISO/IEC 38507**. The **ISO/IEC 42001** standard, released in December 2023, outlines requirements for establishing, implementing, and improving AI management systems to ensure responsible AI development and use.

Though these international standards are non-binding, they help shape industry expectations. Companies may use these standards as a benchmark during due diligence processes or as part of contractual obligations when procuring AI-based products and services. Furthermore, these standards can indirectly influence legal obligations, such as establishing the standard of care in negligence claims.

4. Foster Public Engagement and Education

Encouraging active participation from the public can create a more informed citizenry regarding AI and surveillance:

- **Community Consultations**: Organize regular community consultations that allow citizens to voice concerns and influence surveillance policies.
- **Educational Campaigns**: Initiate campaigns aimed at educating the public about their rights and data protection, empowering individuals to make informed decisions regarding their privacy.

5. Address Algorithmic Accountability

Policymakers should prioritize strategies that ensure fairness and accountability in AI applications:

- **Standardization of Algorithmic Audits**: Develop guidelines for auditing AI algorithms to identify and mitigate biases that could result in discriminatory outcomes.
- **Adoption of Ethical AI Frameworks**: Encourage the integration of ethical AI principles into the design and implementation of surveillance technologies to safeguard civil liberties.

These recommendations aim to cultivate a regulatory framework that balances the benefits of AI and surveillance technology with the essential protection of personal privacy rights in Canada.

CONCLUSION

The rapid advancement of AI technologies has dramatically reshaped the landscape of privacy and surveillance in Canada, necessitating comprehensive analysis and reform. This document has outlined the critical interplay between AI, surveillance practices, and individual privacy rights. Key points discussed include:

- **Enhanced Surveillance Capabilities**: AI's role in improving threat detection and data analysis raises significant ethical challenges.
- **Regulatory Framework**: Existing laws like PIPEDA and the Canadian Charter of Rights and Freedoms provide a foundation, but gaps remain in addressing modern AI tools.
- **Public Concerns**: Citizens express growing unease regarding surveillance practices, emphasizing the need for transparency and accountability.

In light of these findings, the urgency of addressing privacy and surveillance issues is paramount as society becomes increasingly reliant on AI technologies. Policymakers must act now to create regulations that safeguard individual rights while harnessing the benefits of innovation. Encouraging ongoing public discourse and engagement is vital; involving diverse stakeholders can contribute to a balanced approach that upholds civil liberties. By prioritizing transparency, consent, and accountability, Canada can cultivate a regulatory environment that protects personal privacy in an age where AI continues to evolve.

Reaffirming the need for a balanced approach to AI surveillance that protects privacy rights without compromising national security. This paper explores the impact of artificial intelligence (AI) on digital surveillance practices in Canada, focusing on the balance between state power and individual privacy rights. It examines current governance frameworks, identifies gaps in policy and regulation, and proposes actionable recommendations to align AI surveillance technologies with ethical standards and human rights.

REFERENCES

Cath, C. (2018). Governing artificial intelligence: Ethical, legal and technical opportunities and challenges. *Philosophical Transactions. Series A, Mathematical, Physical, and Engineering Sciences*, *376*(2133), 20180080.

Curtis, C., Gillespie, N., & Lockey, S. (2022). "AI-deploying organizations are key to addressing 'perfect storm' of AI risks". AI and Ethics. 3 (1): 145–153. . ISSN 2730-5961. PMC 9127285. PMID 35634256. Archived from the original on 2023-03-15. Retrieved 2022-05-30.DOI: 10.1007/s43681-022-00163-7

Erdélyi, O. J., & Goldsmith, J. (2020). "Regulating Artificial Intelligence: Proposal for a Global Solution". arXiv:2005.11072 [cs.CY].

Héder, M (2020). "A criticism of AI ethics guidelines". Információs Társadalom. 20 (4): 57–73. . S2CID 233252939.DOI: 10.22503/inftars.XX.2020.4.5

Maslej, N., Fattorini, L., Brynjolfsson, E., Etchemendy, J., Ligett, K., Lyons, T., . . . Perrault, R. (2023). Artificial intelligence index report 2023. arXiv preprint arXiv:2310.03715.

Sotala, K., & Yampolskiy, R. V. (2014). "Responses to catastrophic AGI risk: a survey". Physica Scripta. 90 (1): 018001. Bibcode:2015PhyS...90a8001S. . ISSN 0031-8949.DOI: 10.1088/0031-8949/90/1/018001

Tallberg, J., Erman, E., Furendal, M., Geith, J., Klamberg, M., & Lundgren, M. (2023). Global Governance of Artificial Intelligence: Next Steps for Empirical and Normative Research. *International Studies Review*, *25*(3), viad040. Advance online publication. 2305.11528. DOI: 10.1093/isr/viad040

Vincent, J. (2023). *AI is entering an era of corporate control.* The Verge.

Compilation of References

Abbasi, N., Nizamullah, F. N. U., & Zeb, S. (2023). AI in Healthcare: Integrating Advanced Technologies with Traditional Practices for Enhanced Patient Care. *BULLET: Jurnal Multidisiplin Ilmu*, *2*(3), 546–556.

Abdulhussein, M. (2024). *The Impact of Artificial Intelligence and Machine Learning on Organizations Cybersecurity*. Liberty University.

Abràmoff, M. D., Lavin, P. T., Birch, M., & Shah, N. (2018). Pooled analysis of 4,662 patients with diabetic retinopathy using deep learning. *Ophthalmology*, *125*(6), 935–944.

Acemoglu, D., & Restrepo, P. (2018). ARTIFICIAL INTELLIGENCE, AUTOMATION AND WORK. SSRN *Electronic Journal, 108*(24196). DOI: 10.2139/ssrn.3123798

Adams, R. (2022). AI in Africa: Key Concerns and Policy Considerations for the Future of the Continent. Retrieved from https://afripoli.org/ai-in-africa-key-concerns-and-policy-considerations-for-the-future-of-the-continent on 19/10/2024

Adebayo, O. (2020). Data Science in Nigeria: Challenges and Opportunities. Retrieved from https://nigeriacodingacademy.com/data-science-trends-in-nigeria/ on 8/10/2024.

Adisa, M. O., Oyedeji, S., & Porras, J. (2024). The nexus between ICT, top-down and bottom-up approaches for sustainability activities: A systematic mapping study. *Journal of Cleaner Production*, *449*, 141768. DOI: 10.1016/j.jclepro.2024.141768

Adula, M., Birbirsa, Z. A., & Kant, S. (2023). The effect of interpersonal, problem solving and technical training skills on performance of Ethiopia textile industry: Continuance, normative and affective commitment as mediators. *Cogent Business & Management*, *10*(3), 2286672. Advance online publication. DOI: 10.1080/23311975.2023.2286672

Ahmed, A., & Adil, K. (2023). Transforming healthcare systems with artificial intelligence: Revolutionizing efficiency, quality, and patient care. *Research Square*. https://doi.org/DOI: 10.21203/rs.3.rs-3175341/v1

Akhilomen, J. (2013). Data mining application for cyber credit-card fraud detection system. In *Advances in Data Mining. Applications and Theoretical Aspects: 13th Industrial Conference, ICDM 2013, New York, NY, USA, July 16-21, 2013*. [Springer Berlin Heidelberg.]. *Proceedings*, *13*, 218–228.

Alamu, O. E., Aworinde, M. O., & Isharufe, J. O. (2013). Ifa: An Ancient Binary Computer System. *CIT. Journal of Computing and Information Technology*, *21*(3), 159–166.

Aldridge, I. (2013). *High-Frequency Trading: A Practical Guide to Algorithmic Strategies and Trading Systems*. Wiley.

Allen, J. (2019, July/August). Digital virtual assistants: Utility v. privacy. *GPSolo*, *36*(4), 4.

Almeida, F. (2022). The contribution of local agents and citizens to sustainable development: The Portuguese experience. *Sustainability (Basel)*, *14*(19), 12696. DOI: 10.3390/su141912696

Alowais, S. A., Alghamdi, S. S., Alsuhebany, N., Alqahtani, T., Alshaya, A., Al-mohareb, S. N., Aldairem, A., Alrashed, M., Saleh, K. B., Badreldin, H. A., Yami, A., Harbi, S. A., & Albekairy, A. M. (2023). Revolutionizing healthcare: The role of artificial intelligence in clinical practice. *BMC Medical Education*, *23*(1), 689. Advance online publication. DOI: 10.1186/s12909-023-04698-z PMID: 37740191

Alpala, L. O., Quiroga-Parra, D. J., Torres, J. C., & Peluffo-Ordóñez, D. H. (2022). Smart factory using virtual reality and online multi-user: Towards a metaverse for experimental frameworks. *Applied Sciences (Basel, Switzerland)*, *12*(12), 6258.

Amaliyah, R., Jatmika, S., & Surwandono, . (2023). The rise of artificial intelligence as the future of korean culture diplomacy. [Indonesian Journal of Communications Studies]. *Jurnal Studi Komunikasi*, *7*(3), 865–878. DOI: 10.25139/jsk.v7i3.6495

Amazon. (n.d.). Privacy policy. Archived at https://perma.cc/LHQ8-WSGB

Amin, H. (2024). *The Impact of Chinese AI on Developing Countries in Sub-Saharan Africa* (Doctoral dissertation, San Francisco State University).

Amoah, L. G. A. (Ed.). (2024). *Examining the Rapid Advance of Digital Technology in Africa*. IGI Global. DOI: 10.4018/978-1-6684-9962-7

Ana, I. A., & Maryam, E. W. (2024). Relationship between using TikTok social media and FoMO (Fear of missing out) in students. *UMSIDA* Preprints *Server*. https://doi.org/DOI: 10.21070/ups.4201

Ananny, M., & Crawford, K. (2018). Seeing without knowing: Limitations of the transparency ideal and its application to algorithmic accountability. *Communications of the ACM*, *61*(8), 56–62.

Anca Dunavete. (2024, May 8). *AI in Workplace Technology: Improving Productivity with Chatbots and Virtual Assistants*. Yarooms.com; YAROOMS International. https://www.yarooms.com/blog/ai-in-workplace-technology

Anders, G. (2017, August 9). "Alexa, understand me". MIT Technology Review. Archived at https://perma.cc/D72R-REU6

Angwin, J., Larson, J., Mattu, S., & Kirchner, L. (2016). *Machine Bias*. ProPublica.

Anyoha, R. (2017). A Brief History of Artificial Intelligence. Retrieved from https://sitn.hms.harvard.edu/flash/2017/history-artificial-intelligence/ on 15/09/2024.

Apple. (n.d.). Siri privacy policy. Archived at https://perma.cc/MT3T-B6SG

Arakpogun, E. O., Elsahn, Z., Olan, F., & Elsahn, F. (2021). Artificial simulated Intelligence in Africa: Challenges and opportunities. *The fourth industrial revolution: Implementation of Artificial simulated Intelligence for growing business success*, 375-388.

Aristotle. (350 BCE). *Nicomachean Ethics*.

Arntz, M., Gregory, T., & Zierahn, U. (2016). *The Risk of Automation for Jobs in OECD Countries: A Comparative Analysis*. OECD Social, Employment and Migration Working Papers, No. 189, OECD Publishing, Paris.

Arrieta, A. B.. (2020). Explainable Artificial Intelligence (XAI): Concepts, Taxonomies, Opportunities, and Challenges. *Information Fusion*.

Arstein-Kerslake, A., O'Donnell, E., Kayess, R., & Watson, J. (2021). Relational Personhood: A Conception of Legal Personhood with Insights From Disability Rights and Environmental Law. *Griffith Law Review*, *30*(3), 530–534. DOI: 10.1080/10383441.2021.2003744

Asefa, K., Kant, D. S., & Debela, K. L. (2023, November). Effect of Transformational Leadership on Organizational Performance: The Mediating Role of Employee Commitment and Expert Systems (AI) Inclusion in Ethiopia. In *2023 International Conference on Communication, Security and Artificial Intelligence (ICCSAI)* (pp. 305-310). IEEE.

Asgher, U., Ayaz, Y., & Taiar, R. (2023). Advances in artificial intelligence (AI) in brain computer interface (BCI) and Industry 4.0 for human machine interaction (HMI). *Frontiers in Human Neuroscience*, *17*, 1320536. DOI: 10.3389/fnhum.2023.1320536 PMID: 38116236

Ashipala, D. O., & Ntjamba, F. C. (2024). Institutional support available to enhance the mental health of students at the University of Namibia. In Aloka, P. (Ed.), *Mental health crisis in higher education* (pp. 339–359). IGI Global., DOI: 10.4018/979-8-3693-2833-0.ch020

Automation, I. (2018). HMI. https://inductiveautomation.com/resources/article/what-is-hmi

Autor, D. (2015). Why Are There Still So Many Jobs? The History and Future of Workplace Automation. *The Journal of Economic Perspectives*, *29*(3), 3–30. DOI: 10.1257/jep.29.3.3

Avcontentteam. (2024, April 10). *Introduction to Human Computer Interaction (HCI) With Examples*. Analytics Vidhya. https://www.analyticsvidhya.com/blog/2023/05/human-computer-interaction/

Azaroual, F. (2024). Artificial simulated Intelligence in Africa: Challenges and Opportunities.

Babina, T., Fedyk, A., He, A., & Hodson, J. (2024). Artificial intelligence, firm growth, and product innovation. *Journal of Financial Economics*, *151*(1), 103745–103745. DOI: 10.1016/j.jfineco.2023.103745

Babulak, E. (2023). Introductory chapter: Journey to AI driven chatbots. In Babulak, E. (Ed.), *Chatbots: The AI-driven front-line services for customers*. Intechopen., DOI: 10.5772/intechopen.112461

Baker, S. (2020). The impact of algorithmic trading on market inequality. *Financial Studies*, *37*(4), 1234–1256.

Balasubramaniam, N., Kauppinen, M., Rannisto, A., Hiekkanen, K., & Kujala, S. (2023). Transparency and explainability of AI systems: From ethical guidelines to requirements. *Information and Software Technology*, *159*, 107197. DOI: 10.1016/j.infsof.2023.107197

Banafa, A. (2024, June 30). *The Rise of Artificial Intelligence in Diplomacy and International Relations*. Retrieved October 2, 2024, from https://www.linkedin.com/pulse/rise-artificial-intelligence-diplomacy-international-relations-s9rsc/

Barndorff-Nielsen, O. E.. (2019). Market crashes: A statistical perspective. *Journal of Financial Econometrics, 17*(2), 243–263.

Barocas, S., Hardt, M., & Narayanan, A. (2019). *Fairness and Machine Learning: Limitations and Opportunities*. http://fairmlbook.org

Barocas, S., & Selbst, A. D. (2019). Big data's disparate impact. *California Law Review, 104*, 671.

Barth, S. (2023). *Artificial Intelligence (AI) in Healthcare & Hospitals*. ForeSee Medical; ForeSee Medical. https://www.foreseemed.com/artificial-intelligence-in-healthcare

Bauer, D. C., Wilson, L. O., & Twine, N. A. (2022). Artificial intelligence in medicine: Applications, limitations and future directions. In Raz, M., Nguyen, T. C., & Loh, E. (Eds.), *Artificial intelligence in medicine* (pp. 101–120). Springer., DOI: 10.1007/978-981-19-1223-8_5

Beier, G., Ullrich, A., Niehoff, S., Reißig, M., & Habich, M. (2020). Industry 4.0: How it is defined from a sociotechnical perspective and how much sustainability it includes–A literature review. *Journal of Cleaner Production, 259*, 120856. DOI: 10.1016/j.jclepro.2020.120856

Belciug, S. (2022). An introduction to artificial intelligence in healthcare. *Intelligent Systems Reference Library,* 1–16. DOI: 10.1007/978-3-031-11154-9_1

Bengio, Y.. (2021). *Deep Learning for AI: An Overview*. Springer. DOI: 10.1145/3448250

Benis, A., Grosjean, J., Billey, K., Martins, J., Dornauer, V., Crişan-Vida, M., & Darmoni, S. (2022). Medical informatics and digital health multilingual ontology (mimo): A tool to improve international collaborations. *International Journal of Medical Informatics, 167*, 104860. DOI: 10.1016/j.ijmedinf.2022.104860 PMID: 36084537

Benítez, J., Gómez-Reino, M., & Suárez, A. (2020). Data-driven democracy? automated decision-making, difference and preferences. https://doi.org/DOI: 10.33774/apsa-2020-rx8fs

Berg, J. (2016). *Income Security in the On-Demand Economy: Findings and Policy Lessons from a Survey of Crowdworkers*. Conditions of Work and Employment Series No. 74, International Labour Organization.

Bessen, J. E. (2019). *AI and Jobs: The Role of Demand*. NBER Working Paper No. 24235.

Bhasker, S., Desai, A., & Mohan, D. (2024). Access. In *Equality Index': The widening rural-urban divide across basic amenities, social security*. The Wire.

Bhati, D. (2022). Apple Watch saves life yet again, warns him of abnormal heart rate. India Today (Sep. 06, 2022, 14.43 IST), https://www.indiatoday.in/technology/news/story/apple-watch-saves-life-of-a-54-years-old-man-this-time-warns-him-of-abnormal-heart-rate-1996775-2022-09-05

Bhat, J. R., AlQahtani, S. A., & Nekovee, M. (2023). FinTech enablers, use cases, and role of future internet of things. *Journal of King Saud University. Computer and Information Sciences*, *35*(1), 87–101. DOI: 10.1016/j.jksuci.2022.08.033

Bian, Z. (2024). Investigation on the Impact of Artificial simulated Intelligence on the Market driven by skill related jobs. *Highlights in Business. Economics and Management*, *24*, 1036–1041.

Binns, R. (2018). Fairness in Machine Learning: Lessons from Political Philosophy. *Proceedings of the 2018 Conference on Fairness, Accountability, and Transparency*.

Birch, I., Carter, B., & Lind, J. (2023). Ensuring an Effective Social Protection Response in Conflict-Affected Settings: Manifestations from the Eastern Africa.

Birhane, M., Amentie, C., Borji, B., & Kant, S. Are Ethiopian Coffee Farmers Proficient to Predict Capital Structure with Mediation of AI Based Knowledge Systems and Asset Liquidity? In *AI in Agriculture for Sustainable and Economic Management* (pp. 199-215). CRC Press. DOI: 10.1201/9781003451648-15

Birkstedt, T., Minkkinen, M., Tandon, A., & Mäntymäki, M. (2023). Ai governance: Themes, knowledge gaps and future agendas. *Internet Research*, *33*(7), 133–167. DOI: 10.1108/INTR-01-2022-0042

Bisht, D., Singh, R., Gehlot, A., Akram, S. V., Singh, A., Montero, E. C., Priyadarshi, N., & Twala, B. (2022). Imperative role of integrating digitalization in the firms finance: A technological perspective. *Electronics (Basel)*, *11*(19), 3252. DOI: 10.3390/electronics11193252

Blumberg, P. I. (1987). *The law of corporate groups: Property, contract, and insolvency*. The University of Chicago Press.

Boden, M. A. (2016). *AI: Its Nature and Future*. Oxford University Press.

Bohm, A. S.. (2017). Privacy and liberty in an always-on, always-listening world. *The Columbia Science and Technology Law Review*, *19*, 1–19.

Bohr, A., & Memarzadeh, K. (2020). The rise of artificial intelligence in healthcare applications. In Bohr, A., & Memarzadeh, K. (Eds.), *Artificial intelligence in healthcare* (pp. 25–60). Science Direct., DOI: 10.1016/B978-0-12-818438-7.00002-2

Bond, R. R., Mulvenna, M. D., Potts, C., O'Neill, S., Ennis, E., & Torous, J. (2023). Digital transformation of mental health services. *Npj Mental Health Research*, *2*(1), 13. Advance online publication. DOI: 10.1038/s44184-023-00033-y PMID: 38609479

Borowiak, C. (2011). *Accountability and Democracy: The Pitfalls and Promise of Popular Control*. Oxford University Press. DOI: 10.1093/acprof:oso/9780199778256.001.0001

Bortolini, M.. (2018). The role of automation in the context of Industry 4.0. *Production Planning and Control*, *29*(7), 563–575.

Botelho, B. (2022, December). Virtual assistant (AI assistant). Tech. Target. Archived at https://perma.cc/E2P4-2JVY

Boughman, E., ... (2017, November 19). "Alexa, do you have rights?": Legal issues posed by voice-controlled devices and the data they create. ABA. Archived at https://perma.cc/P42X-Q4VS

Bourlakis, M., Papagiannidis, S., & Li, F. (2009). Retail spatial evolution: Paving the way from traditional to Metaverse retailing. *Electronic Commerce Research*, *9*(1), 135–148. DOI: 10.1007/s10660-009-9030-8

Boy, G. A. (Ed.). (2017). *The handbook of human-machine interaction: a human-centered design approach*. CRC Press. DOI: 10.1201/9781315557380

Bozoglan, B. (2019). Systemic approach and digital addiction. Advances in psychology, mental health, and behavioural studies. In Bozoglan, B. (Ed.), *Multifaceted approach to digital addiction and its treatment* (pp. 260–280). IGI Global., DOI: 10.4018/978-1-5225-8449-0.ch012

Brattberg, E., Rugova, V., & Csernatoni, R. (2020). Europe and AI: Leading, lagging behind, or carving its own way? (Vol. 9). Washington, DC, USA: Carnegie endowment for international peace.

Braud T, Fernández CB, Hui P. 2022. *Scaling-up AR: university campus as a physical-digital Metaverse*.

Breazeal, C. (2003). Emotion and sociable humanoid robots. *International Journal of Human-Computer Studies*, *59*(1-2), 119–155. DOI: 10.1016/S1071-5819(03)00018-1

Brodkin, J. (2018, October 11). Amazon patents Alexa tech to tell if you're sick, depressed and sell you meds. Ars Technica. Archived at https://perma.cc/6LBP-R7C8

Brooks, R. (2003). *Flesh and machines: How robots will change us*. Vintage.

Brown, N. (Ed.). (2020). *Artificial intelligence in drug discovery*. Royal Society of Chemistry., DOI: 10.1039/9781788016841

Brynjolfsson, E., & McAfee, A. (2014). *The second machine age: Work, progress, and prosperity in a time of brilliant technologies*. WW Norton & company.

Brynjolfsson, E., & McAfee, A. (2017, July 18). *The Business of Artificial Intelligence*. Harvard Business Review; Harvard Business Review. https://hbr.org/2017/07/the-business-of-artificial-intelligence

Brynjolfsson, E., & McAfee, A. (2014). *The Second Machine Age: Work, Progress, and Prosperity in a Time of Brilliant Technologies*. W.W. Norton & Company.

Bryson, J. J., Diamantis, M. E., & Grant, T. D. (2017). Of, for, and by the people: The legal lacuna of synthetic persons. *Artificial Intelligence and Law*, *25*(3), 273–291. DOI: 10.1007/s10506-017-9214-9

Btoush, E., Zhou, X., Gururaian, R., Chan, K. C., & Tao, X. (2021, October). A survey on credit card fraud detection techniques in banking industry for cyber security. In *2021 8th International Conference on Behavioral and Social Computing (BESC)* (pp. 1-7). IEEE. DOI: 10.1109/BESC53957.2021.9635559

Buccella, A. (2023). "AI for all" is a matter of social justice. *AI and Ethics*, *3*(4), 1143–1152. DOI: 10.1007/s43681-022-00222-z PMID: 36189174

Bughin, J., Seong, J., Manyika, J., Chui, M., & Joshi, R. (2018). NOTES FROM THE AI FRONTIER MODELING THE IMPACT OF AI ON THE WORLD ECONOMY. In https://www.mckinsey.com/~/media/mckinsey/featured%20insights/artificial%20intelligence/notes%20from%20the%20frontier%20modeling%20the%20impact%20of%20ai%20on%20the%20world%20economy/mgi-notes-from-the-ai-frontier-modeling-the-impact-of-ai-on-the-world-economy-september-2018.ashx. McKinsey Global Institute (MGI). https://www.mckinsey.com/~/media/McKinsey/Featured%20Insights/Artificial%20Intelligence/Notes%20from%20the%20frontier%20Modeling%20the%20impact%20of%20AI%20on%20the%20world%20economy/MGI-Notes-from-the-AI-frontier-Modeling-the-impact-of-AI-on-the-world-economy-September-2018.ashx

Bulu, S. T. (2012). Place presence, social presence, co-presence, and satisfaction in virtual worlds. *Computers & Education*, *58*(1), 154–161. DOI: 10.1016/j.compedu.2011.08.024

Bunyi, J., Ringland, K. E., & Schueller, S. M. (2021). Accessibility and digital mental health: Considerations for more accessible and equitable mental health apps. *Frontiers in Digital Health*, *3*, 742196. Advance online publication. DOI: 10.3389/fdgth.2021.742196 PMID: 34713206

Buolamwini, J., & Gebru, T. (2018). Gender Shades: Intersectional Accuracy Disparities in Commercial Gender Classification. *Proceedings of Machine Learning Research*.

Burr, C., & Leslie, D. (2023). Ethical assurance: A practical approach to the responsible design, development, and deployment of data-driven technologies. *AI and Ethics*, *3*(1), 73–98. DOI: 10.1007/s43681-022-00178-0

Cai, S., Jiao, X., & Song, B. (2022). Open another door to education—Applications, challenges and perspectives of the educational Metaverse. *Metaverse*, *3*(1), 12. DOI: 10.54517/met.v3i1.1798

Calo, R. (2017). Artificial Intelligence Policy: A Primer and Roadmap. *UCLA Law Review. University of California, Los Angeles. School of Law*, *51*, 399–435.

Calvo, P. (2020). The ethics of smart city (EoSC): Moral implications of hyperconnectivity, algorithmization, and the datafication of urban digital society. *Ethics and Information Technology*, *22*(2), 141–149. DOI: 10.1007/s10676-019-09523-0

Cannan, J., & Hu, H. (2011). Human-machine interaction (HMI): A survey. *University of Essex*, *27*, 46–64.

Canobbio, V. T. (2024). *Sales Lead Routing: Exploring Speed, Quality, Accuracy, and Technology* (Doctoral dissertation, Golden Gate University).

Capitol Technology University. (2024). *Moving Towards a More Sustainable Future Using AI | Capitol Technology University*. Www.captechu.eduCapitol Technology University. https://www.captechu.edu/blog/moving-towards-more-sustainable-future-using-ai

Carter, S., Mwaura, S., Ram, M., Trehan, K., & Jones, T. (2015). Barriers to ethnic minority and women's enterprise: Existing evidence, policy tensions and unsettled questions. *International Small Business Journal*, *33*(1), 49–69. DOI: 10.1177/0266242614556823

Cassell, J. (2019). Artificial Intelligence for a Social Order. *Issues in Science and Technology*, *35*(4), 29–36.

Castonguay, A., Wagner, G., Motulsky, A., & Paré, G. (2023). AI maturity in health care: An overview of 10 OECD countries. *Health Policy (Amsterdam)*, •••, 104938. PMID: 38157771

Cath, C. (2018). Governing artificial intelligence: Ethical, legal and technical opportunities and challenges. *Philosophical Transactions. Series A, Mathematical, Physical, and Engineering Sciences*, *376*(2133), 20180080. DOI: 10.1098/rsta.2018.0080 PMID: 30322996

Cavoukian, A. (2011, January). Privacy by design, the 7 foundational principles, implementation and mapping of fair information practices. *Privacy by Design CA.*

Cerrato, P., & Halamka, J. (2020). The promise of artificial intelligence and machine learning. In Cerrato, P., & Halamka, J. (Eds.), *Reinventing clinical decision support: Data analytics, artificial intelligence, and diagnostic reasoning* (pp. 25–57). Taylor & Francis., DOI: 10.1201/9781003034339-2

Chang, H., Mikalsen, K. S., Nesse, P. J., & Erdal, O. B. (2020). Digitalization of municipalities through ecosystem collaboration. *Journal of the Norwegian Society for Informatics and Communication Technology*, *1*(2), 117–158.

Chaudhary, K., Yadav, J., & Mallick, B. (2012). A review of fraud detection techniques: Credit card. *International Journal of Computer Applications*, *45*(1), 39–44.

Chen, Y., ... (2020, April 23). Wearable microphone jamming. Conference on Human Factors in Computing Systems. Archived at https://perma.cc/E4CR-5PJR

Cheng R, Wu N, Chen S, Han B. 2022. Will Metaverse be NextG internet? Vision, hype, and reality. arXiv preprint

Cheng, J., & Zeng, J. (2022). Shaping ai's future? china in global ai governance. *Journal of Contemporary China*, *32*(143), 794–810. DOI: 10.1080/10670564.2022.2107391

Cheng, L. (2020, November 2). Dangerous skills got certified: Measuring the trustworthiness of skill certification in voice personal assistant platforms. *Proceedings of the 2020 ACM SIGSAC Conference on Computer and Communications Security*, 1699–1716.

Cheng, L., Varshney, K. R., & Liu, H. (2021). Socially responsible ai algorithms: Issues, purposes, and challenges. *Journal of Artificial Intelligence Research*, *71*, 1137–1181. DOI: 10.1613/jair.1.12814

Chen, H., Chiang, R. H., & Storey, V. C. (2012). Business intelligence and analytics: From big data to big impact. *Management Information Systems Quarterly*, *36*(4), 1165–1188. DOI: 10.2307/41703503

Cheong, B. C. (2024). Transparency and accountability in AI systems: Safeguarding wellbeing in the age of algorithmic decision-making. *Frontiers in Human Dynamics*, *6*, 1421273. DOI: 10.3389/fhumd.2024.1421273

Chiu, T. K., Ahmad, Z., Ismailov, M., & Sanusi, I. T. (2024). What are artificial intelligence literacy and competency? A comprehensive framework to support them. *Computers and Education Open*, *6*, 100171. DOI: 10.1016/j.caeo.2024.100171

Chlouverakis, K. (2024, April 26). *How artificial intelligence is reshaping the financial services industry*. Www.ey.com

Chollet, G., Esposito, A., Gentes, A., Horain, P., Karam, W., Li, Z., . . . Zouari, L. (2009). Multimodal human machine interactions in virtual and augmented reality. *Multimodal Signals: Cognitive and Algorithmic Issues: COST Action 2102 and euCognition International School Vietri sul Mare, Italy, April 21-26, 2008 Revised Selected and Invited Papers*, 1-23.

Chopra, K. (2024). *Shaping the future: AI governance and its dynamic effect on India's AI competitiveness* (Doctoral dissertation).

Chui, M., Manyika, J., & Miremadi, M. (2016). Where machines could replace humans—And where they can't (yet). *The McKinsey Quarterly*.

Cihon, P., Maas, M., & Kemp, L. (2020). Fragmentation and the future: Investigating architectures for international ai governance. *Global Policy*, *11*(5), 545–556. DOI: 10.1111/1758-5899.12890

Cipresso, P., Giglioli, I. A. C., Raya, M. A., & Riva, G. (2018). The Past, Present, and Future of Virtual and Augumented Reality Reasearch: A Network and Cluster Analysis of the Literature. *Frontiers in Psychology*, *9*, 2086. DOI: 10.3389/fpsyg.2018.02086

Cirqueira, D., Nedbal, D., Helfert, M., & Bezbradica, M. (2020, August). Scenario-based requirements elicitation for user-centric explainable AI: A case in fraud detection. In *International cross-domain conference for machine learning and knowledge extraction* (pp. 321-341). Cham: Springer International Publishing. DOI: 10.1007/978-3-030-57321-8_18

Clarke, R. (1994). Asimov's Laws of Robotics: Implications For Information Technology. *Computer*, *2*(1), 57–58. DOI: 10.1109/2.248881

Considerations, E. (1995). *Virtual Reality", Author: Bernard Zeigler*. Published in the Journal of Science and Engineering Ethics.

Core, B. T. S. (2024, July 30). *Smart Manufacturing Revolution: AI-Driven Supply Chain Optimization*. Core BTS; Core BTS. https://corebts.com/blog/smart-manufacturing-revolution-ai-driven-supply-chain-optimization/

Courtney, M. (2017, October 13). Alexa, Cortana, Siri, et al: Do our digital assistants hear more than we want them to? E&T Magazine. Archived at https://perma.cc/95XU-KAGH

Cramarenco, R. E., Burcă-Voicu, M. I., & Dabija, D. C. (2023). The impact of Artificial simulated Intelligence on employees' skills and well-being in international market driven by skill related jobss: A schemaatic review. *Oeconomia Copernicana*, *14*(3), 731–767. DOI: 10.24136/oc.2023.022

Crawford, K. (2021). *Atlas of AI: Power, Politics, and the Planetary Costs of Artificial Intelligence*. Yale University Press.

Crawford, K., & Calo, R. (2016). There is a blind spot in AI research. *Nature*, *538*(7610), 311–313. DOI: 10.1038/538311a PMID: 27762391

Croucamp, A. (2013). Traditional African divination systems as information technology. *Mindburst, viewed, 23*.

Curtis, C., Gillespie, N., & Lockey, S. (2022). "AI-deploying organizations are key to addressing 'perfect storm' of AI risks". AI and Ethics. 3 (1): 145–153. . ISSN 2730-5961. PMC 9127285. PMID 35634256. Archived from the original on 2023-03-15. Retrieved 2022-05-30.DOI: 10.1007/s43681-022-00163-7

Danaher, J. (2017). The Threat of Algocracy: Reality, Resistance, and Accommodation. *Philosophy & Technology*, *30*(3). Advance online publication. DOI: 10.1007/s13347-015-0211-1

Daniel, S., Kaller, S., Raifman, S., & Grossman, D. (2019). Characteristics of patients using telemedicine compared with in-person visits for state-mandated informed consent before abortion in Utah. *Contraception*, *99*(5), 316. DOI: 10.1016/j.contraception.2019.03.007

Dappe, M. H., & Lebrand, M. (2021). *Infrastructure and Structural Change in the Eastern Africa*. World Bank. DOI: 10.1596/36459

Das, S., Dey, A., Pal, A., & Roy, N. (2015). Applications of artificial intelligence in machine learning: Review and prospect. *International Journal of Computer Applications*, *115*(9), 31–41. DOI: 10.5120/20182-2402

Dastin, J., Kirkham, C., & Kalra, A. (2021, November 19). Amazon wages secret war on Americans' privacy, documents show. Reuters. Archived at https://perma.cc/VPH8-LJ6X

Dastin, J. (2018). *Amazon Scraps Secret AI Recruiting Tool That Showed Bias Against Women*. Reuters.

Davenport, T. H. (2013). Analytics 3.0. *Harvard Business Review*, *91*(12), 64–72.

Davenport, T., & Kalakota, R. (2019). The potential for AI in healthcare. *Future Healthcare Journal*, *6*(2), 94–98. DOI: 10.7861/futurehosp.6-2-94 PMID: 31363513

Davidian, R. (2017). Alexa and third parties' reasonable expectation of privacy. *American Criminal Law Review Online*, *54*, 58–60.

Day, M., Turner, G., & Drozdiak, N. (2019, April 10). Amazon workers are listening to what you tell Alexa. Bloomberg. Archived at https://perma.cc/6X8R-N2NX

De Fauw, J., Ledsam, J. R., Romera-Paredes, B., Nikolov, S., Tomasev, N., Blackwell, S., Askham, H., Glorot, X., O'Donoghue, B., Visentin, D., van den Driessche, G., Lakshminarayanan, B., Meyer, C., Mackinder, F., Bouton, S., Ayoub, K., Chopra, R., King, D., Karthikesalingam, A., & Ronneberger, O. (2018). Clinically applicable deep learning for diagnosis and referral in retinal disease. *Nature Medicine*, *24*(9), 1342–1350. DOI: 10.1038/s41591-018-0107-6 PMID: 30104768

De Guzman, J. A., Thilakarathna, K., & Seneviratne, A. (2019). Security and privacy approaches in mixed reality: A literature survey. *ACM Computing Surveys*, *52*(6), 1–37. DOI: 10.1145/3359626

de Sio Filippo, S. (2021). Mark Coeckelbergh, AI Ethics, Mit Press, 2021. *Science and Engineering Ethics, 27*(4). Copyright Act (Act 690).

Deloitte. (2020). *AI and the Future of Work: The Impact of AI on Employment*.

Dereso, C. W., Kant, S., Muthuraman, M., & Tufa, G. (2023). Effect of Point of Service on Health Department Student's Creativity in Comprehensive Universities of Ethiopia: Moderating Role of Public-Private Partnership and Mediating Role of Work Place Learning. In: Jain, S., Groppe, S., Mihindukulasooriya, N. (eds) Proceedings of the International Health Informatics Conference. Lecture Notes in Electrical Engineering, vol 990. Springer, Singapore. https://doi.org/DOI: 10.1007/978-981-19-9090-8_13

Dhieb, N., Ghazzai, H., Besbes, H., & Massoud, Y. (2020). A secure ai-driven architecture for automated insurance systems: Fraud detection and risk measurement. *IEEE Access : Practical Innovations, Open Solutions*, *8*, 58546–58558. DOI: 10.1109/ACCESS.2020.2983300

Di Pietro, R., & Stefano, C. (2022) "Metaverse: Security and Privacy Issues". *IEEE International Conference on Trust, Privacy and Security in Intelligent Systems and Applications (TPS-ISA)*

Diadiushkin, A., Sandkuhl, K., & Maiatin, A. V. (2019). Fraud Detection in Instant Payments as Contribution to Digitalization in Banks. In *BIR workshops,* 107-117).

Díaz, J. E. M., Saldaña, C. A. D., & Avila, C. A. R. (2020). Virtual world as a resource for hybrid education. [iJET]. *International Journal of Emerging Technologies in Learning*, *15*(15), 94–109. DOI: 10.3991/ijet.v15i15.13025

Díaz-Lucena, A., & Vicente-Fernández, P. (2024). AI and the human need for emotional connection. In Rojas, R. V. B., & Martínez-Cano, F.-J. (Eds.), *Revolutionizing communication* (pp. 93–101). CRC Press., DOI: 10.1201/9781003473633-9

Díaz-Rodríguez, N., Del Ser, J., Coeckelbergh, M., de Prado, M. L., Herrera-Viedma, E., & Herrera, F. (2023). Connecting the dots in trustworthy Artificial Intelligence: From AI principles, ethics, and key requirements to responsible AI systems and regulation. *Information Fusion*, *99*, 101896. DOI: 10.1016/j.inffus.2023.101896

Digital Media Law Project. (2022, September 10). Recording phone calls and conversations. Archived at https://perma.cc/S7GT-69F6

Dignum, V. (2019). *Responsible artificial intelligence: how to develop and use AI in a responsible way* (Vol. 2156). Springer. DOI: 10.1007/978-3-030-30371-6

Dionisio, John David N., (2013) "3D Virtual worlds and the metaverse: Current status and future possibilities". ACM Computing Surveys, No.: 34, 1–38.

Dolson, E., & Jagtiani, J. (2024). Which lenders are more likely to reach out to underserved consumers: Banks versus Fintechs versus other nonbanks? *Journal of Alternative Finance*, *1*(1), 35–66. DOI: 10.1177/27533743231218019

Donepudi, P. (2016). Influence of Cloud Computing in Business: Are They Robust? *Asian Journal of Applied Science and Engineering*, *5*(3), 193–196. DOI: 10.18034/ajase.v5i1.78

Donepudi, P. (2017). AI and Machine Learning in Banking: A Systematic Literature Review. Asian. *Journal of Applied Science and Engineering*, *6*(3), 157–162.

Donepudi, P. K. (2017). Machine Learning and Artificial Intelligence in Banking. *Engineering International*, *5*(2), 83–86. DOI: 10.18034/ei.v5i2.490

Doshi-Velez, F., & Kim, B. (2017). Towards a Rigorous Science of Interpretable Machine Learning. *arXiv preprint arXiv:1702.08608.*

Dovgan, N. (2024). Integrating physical exercise into digital mental health: Enhancing overall well-being with Metacognit.me. SSRN Electronic Journal. DOI: 10.2139/ssrn.4734030

Draper, N. A., & Turow, J. (2019). The corporate cultivation of digital resignation. *New Media & Society*, *21*(12), 1824–1831.

Dua, A., & Gupta, S. (2020). AI for Fraud Detection: A Survey. *Journal of Financial Crime*, *27*(4), 1031–1045.

Duan H, Li J, Fan S, Lin Z, Wu X, Cai W. 2021. *Metaverse for social good: a university campus prototype*.

Duberry, J. (2023, September). AI Diplomacy: what vision for the future of multilateralism? - Geneva Solutions. Geneva Solutions. Retrieved October 1, 2024, from https://genevasolutions.news/science-tech/ai-diplomacy-what-vision-for-the-future-of-multilateralism-1

Dubois, D. J.. (2020). When speakers are all ears: Characterizing misactivations of IoT smart speakers. *Proceedings on Privacy Enhancing Technologies. Privacy Enhancing Technologies Symposium*, *4*, 255–255.

Durga, P., Godavarthi, D., Kant, S., & Basa, S. S. (2024). Aspect-based drug review classification through a hybrid model with ant colony optimization using deep learning. *Discov Computing*, *27*(1), 19. DOI: 10.1007/s10791-024-09441-w

Eadicicco, L. (2019, April 15). Amazon workers reportedly listen to what you tell Alexa – Here's how Apple and Google handle what you say to their voice assistants. Business Insider. Archived at https://perma.cc/GY2M-P7GC

Earnshaw, R., & Sourin, A. (2017). Case study: shared virtual and augmented environments for creative applications. Research and development in the academy, creative industries and applications, 49-64.

Eglash, R. (1999). *African fractals: Modern computing and Indigenous design.* Rutgers University Press.

Ekong, H. (2024). Navigating the AI era: Understanding mechanisms, impacts, and policy interventions for inclusive employment in Malaysia. https://doi.org/DOI: 10.31235/osf.io/2kbj5

Elgammal, A., Liu, B., Elhoseiny, M., & Mazzoni, S. (2017). *CAN: Creative Adversarial Networks, Generating "Art" by Learning About Styles and Deviating from Style Norms.arXiv preprint arXiv:1706.07068.*

Elghawaby, A. (2018, August 2). Social media's self-regulation isn't enough. CIG Online. Archived at https://perma.cc/C857-GAEQ

Emma, T. (2023, December 10). *Ethical AI and Bias Mitigation. - Tech Emma - Medium.* Medium; Medium. https://medium.com/@emmaja/ethical-ai-and-bias-mitigation-3b62a2ae07c8

Endresen, J. (2024, August 13). *The Intersection of AI and Emerging Markets: Opportunities and Challenges.* Cornell SC Johnson; Cornell SC Johnson. https://business.cornell.edu/hub/2024/08/13/intersection-ai-emerging-markets-opportunities-challenges/

Enjalbert, S., Gandini, L. M., Pereda Baños, A., Ricci, S., & Vanderhaegen, F. (2021). Human–Machine Interface in Transport Systems: An Industrial Overview for More Extended Rail Applications. *Machines (Basel), 9*(2), 36. DOI: 10.3390/machines9020036

Erdélyi, O. J., & Goldsmith, J. (2020). "Regulating Artificial Intelligence: Proposal for a Global Solution". arXiv:2005.11072 [cs.CY].

Erkkilä, T. (2023). Global indicators and ai policy: Metrics, policy scripts, and narratives. *The Review of Policy Research, 40*(5), 811–839. DOI: 10.1111/ropr.12556

Erman, E., & Furendal, M. (2022). The global governance of artificial intelligence: Some normative concerns. *Moral Philosophy and Politics, 9*(2), 267–291. DOI: 10.1515/mopp-2020-0046

Erturk E, Reynolds GB. 2020. *The expanding role of immersive media in education.*

Etherington, D. (2014, November 6). Amazon Echo is a $199 connected speaker packing an always-on Siri-style assistant. TechCrunch. Archived at https://perma.cc/8GY4-CTAL

EU Business School. 2022. *How can the Metaverse be used in education?*

European Commission. (2016). *Upskilling Pathways: New Opportunities for Adults.* European Commission.

European Commission. (2021). *Proposal for a Regulation laying down harmonized rules on artificial intelligence.* Artificial Intelligence Act.

European Innovation Council and SMEs Executive Agency. 2022. *Intellectual property in the Metaverse*.

EY. https://www.ey.com/en_gr/financial-services/how-artificial-intelligence-is-reshaping-the-financial-services-industry

Fabregas, R., Vazquez, A., & Angelucci, M. (2024). *Improving immigrant mental health through a digital app*. AEA Randomized Controlled Trials., DOI: 10.1257/rct.13303-1.0

Fagundes, D. (2001). What We Talk About When We Talk About Persons: The Language of A Legal Fiction. *Harvard Law Review*, *114*(6), 1745–1768. DOI: 10.2307/1342652

Falchuk, Ben, (2018) "The Social Metaverse: Battle for Privacy". IEEE Xplore, Vol:37, Issue:2

Falchuk, B., Loeb, S., & Neff, R. (2018). The social Metaverse: Battle for privacy. *IEEE Technology and Society Magazine*, *37*(2), 52–56. DOI: 10.1109/MTS.2018.2826060

Feigenbaum, E. A. (1980). Knowledge Engineering. *The Applied Side of Artificial Intelligence*. Report No. HPP-80-21. Retrieved from https://stacks.stanford.edu/file/druid:cn981xh0967/cn981xh0967.pdf on 11/10/2024.

Feigenbaum, E. A., & McCorduck, P. (1983). The Fifth Generation: Artificial Intelligence and Japan's Computer Challenge to the World.

Feigenbaum, E. A., & Feldman, J. (1963). *Computers and thought* (Vol. 37). McGraw-Hill.

Fei, W. (2024). The Mental Well-Being of Digital Natives in the Age of AI: Challenges and Solutions. In Zaremohzzabieh, Z., Abdullah, R., & Ahrari, S. (Eds.), *Exploring Youth Studies in the Age of AI* (pp. 88–108). IGI Global., DOI: 10.4018/979-8-3693-3350-1.ch005

Filocamo, C. (2020). *Digital Twin and HMI for collaborative autonomous mobile robots in flexible logistics* (Doctoral dissertation, Politecnico di Torino).

Fitzgerald, D. (2019). Corporate personhood and the extension of legal status to artificial intelligence. *The Journal of Law and Technology*, *22*(4), 45–63.

Floridi, L., & Cowls, J. (2022). A unified framework of five principles for AI in society. *Machine learning and the city: Applications in architecture and urban design*, 535-545.

Floridi, L. (2019). The ethics of artificial intelligence: A compendium of issues. In *The Cambridge Handbook of Artificial Intelligence* (pp. 156–178). Cambridge University Press.

Floridi, L., & Cowls, J. (2019). A Unified Framework of Five Principles for AI in Society. *Harvard Data Science Review*. Advance online publication. DOI: 10.1162/99608f92.8cd550d1

Floridi, L., Cowls, J., Beltrametti, M., Chatila, R., Chazerand, P., Dignum, V., Luetge, C., Madelin, R., Pagallo, U., Rossi, F., Schafer, B., Valcke, P., & Vayena, E. (2018). AI4People—An Ethical Framework for a Good AI Society: Opportunities, Risks, Principles, and Recommendations. *Minds and Machines*, *28*(4), 689–707. DOI: 10.1007/s11023-018-9482-5 PMID: 30930541

Ford, M. (2015). *Rise of the Robots*. Basic books.

Foryciarz, A., Leufer, D., & Szymielewicz, K. (2020, January 17). Black-boxed politics: Opacity is a choice in AI systems. Medium. Archived at https://perma.cc/A2AY-3LES

Fowler, G. A. (2019, May 6). Alexa has been eavesdropping on you this whole time. The Washington Post. Archived at https://perma.cc/TK4E-QTHQ

Frey, C. (2024). Digital Diplomacy: The Impact of Technology on Modern Diplomacy and Foreign Policy. Current Realities and Future Prospects. *SSRN*, *24*(1), 107. DOI: 10.2139/ssrn.4864962

Frey, C. B., & Osborne, M. A. (2017). The future of employment: How susceptible are jobs to computerization? *Technological Forecasting and Social Change*, *114*, 254–280. DOI: 10.1016/j.techfore.2016.08.019

Fritzler, M. J., & Mahler, M. (2021). Precision medicine as an approach to autoimmune diseases. In Mahler, M. (Ed.), *Precision medicine and artificial intelligence* (pp. 39–63). Academic Press., DOI: 10.1016/B978-0-12-820239-5.00007-3

Fritz-Morgenthal, S., Hein, B., & Papenbrock, J. (2022). Financial risk management and explainable, trustworthy, responsible AI. *Frontiers in Artificial Intelligence*, *5*, 779799. DOI: 10.3389/frai.2022.779799 PMID: 35295866

Fulmer, R., Joerin, A., Gentile, B., Lakerink, L., & Rauws, M. (2018). Using psychological artificial intelligence (Tess) to relieve symptoms of depression and anxiety: Randomized controlled trial. *JMIR Mental Health*, *5*(4), e64. DOI: 10.2196/mental.9782 PMID: 30545815

Fung, J. (2023, April 4). FTC takes aim at Amazon's Alexa for illegally collecting kids' data. *The Mil Source*. Archived at https://perma.cc/5S29-HHHE

Gabriel S. 2020. *Identity reshaping and manipulation in cyberspace*. 1-8 Anthropological Researches and Studies

Gabriel, O. T. (2023). *Data privacy and ethical issues in collecting health care data using artificial intelligence among health workers* (Master's thesis, Center for Bioethics and Research).

Gabriel, I. (2020). Artificial intelligence, values, and alignment. *Minds and Machines, 30*(3), 411–437. DOI: 10.1007/s11023-020-09539-2

Gaiardelli, P., Pezzotta, G., Rondini, A., Romero, D., Jarrahi, F., Bertoni, M., Wiesner, S., Wuest, T., Larsson, T., & Zaki, M. (2021). Product-service systems evolution in the era of Industry 4.0. Service Business, 15(2), 177–207. 1

Galindo, L., Perset, K., & Sheeka, F. (2021). *An overview of national AI strategies and policies*. OECD Ilibrary.

Gambao, E., Hernando, M., & Surdilovic, D. (2012). A new generation of collaborative robots for material handling. In *ISARC.Proceedings of the International Symposium on Automation and Robotics in Construction* (Vol. 29, p. 1). IAARC Publications. DOI: 10.22260/ISARC2012/0076

Garćıa LC, Cruz Sánchez Gómez M, Garćıa-Valcárcel Muñoz Repiso A. 2020. *Scales for measuring internet addiction in COVID-19 times: is the time variable still a key factor in measuring this addiction?*

García-Esteban, J. A., Piardi, L., Leitão, P., Curto, B., & Moreno, V. (2021, May). An interaction strategy for safe human co-working with industrial collaborative robots. In *2021 4th IEEE International Conference on Industrial Cyber-Physical Systems (ICPS)* (pp. 585-590). IEEE. DOI: 10.1109/ICPS49255.2021.9468160

Gargiulo, G. D., & Naik, G. R. (Eds.). (2022). *Wearable/personal monitoring devices: Present to future*. Springer Singapore., DOI: 10.1007/978-981-16-5324-7

Garrie, D. (2020). The Legal Implications of Autonomous Vehicle Accidents: Liability and Litigation Challenges. *Journal of Technology Law & Policy, 25*(2), 47–63.

Gaushell, D. J., & Darlington, H. T. (1987). Supervisory control and data acquisition. *Proceedings of the IEEE, 75*(12), 1645–1658. DOI: 10.1109/PROC.1987.13932

Gebru, M. K., Zeru, G., & Tekalign, Y. (2023). The impact of the Middle East and Gulf states' involvement on the Eastern Africa's peace and security: Applying regional security complicated theory. *Domes, 32*(3), 223–245. DOI: 10.1111/dome.12301

Geetha (2021) A study on artificial intelligence in banking and financial services. International Journal of Creative Research Thoughts,9(9),110-114.

Gentili, A., Failla, G., Melnyk, A., Puleo, V., Tanna, G., Ricciardi, W., & Cascini, F. (2022). The cost-effectiveness of digital health interventions: A systematic review of the literature. *Frontiers in Public Health*, *10*, 787135. DOI: 10.3389/fpubh.2022.787135 PMID: 36033812

Georgescu, A. (2022). Cyber diplomacy in the governance of emerging ai technologies - a transatlantic example. *International Journal of Cyber Diplomacy*, *3*, 13–22. DOI: 10.54852/ijcd.v3y202202

Ge, Q., Hao, M., Ding, F., Jiang, D., Scheffran, J., Helman, D., & Ide, T. (2022). Modelling armed conflict risk under climate change with machine learning and time-series data. *Nature Communications*, *13*(1), 2839. Advance online publication. DOI: 10.1038/s41467-022-30356-x PMID: 35595793

Getchell K, Oliver I, Miller A, Allison C. 2010. *Metaverses as a platform for game-based learning*.

Ghana Institute of Engineers. (1990). Annual Report.

Gillis, A. S. (2023, January 19). Voice recognition (speaker recognition). Tech. Target. https://perma.cc/UZZ3-QMT9

Glauner, P. (2021). Artificial intelligence in healthcare: Foundations, opportunities and challenges. In Glauner, P., Plugmann, P., & Lerzynski, G. (Eds.), *Digitalization in healthcare: Future of business and finance* (pp. 1–15). Springer., DOI: 10.1007/978-3-030-65896-0_1

Gless, S., Silverman, E., & Weigend, T. (2016). If robots cause harm, who is to blame? Self-driving cars and criminal liability. *New Criminal Law Review*, *19*(3), 412–417. DOI: 10.1525/nclr.2016.19.3.412

Goldman Sachs. (2023). *AI may start to boost US GDP in 2027*. Goldmansachs.com; Goldman Sachs. https://www.goldmansachs.com/insights/articles/ai-may-start-to-boost-us-gdp-in-2027

Gomez-Uribe, C. A., & Hunt, N. (2015). The Netflix recommender system: Algorithms, business value, and innovation. [TMIS]. *ACM Transactions on Management Information Systems*, *6*(4), 1–19. DOI: 10.1145/2843948

Gonzalez, C.. (2020). Mitigating Bias in AI Systems. *Journal of Artificial Intelligence Research*, *68*, 123–158.

Gonzalez, M. A.. (2018). Towards a new workforce for the AI revolution: Opportunities and challenges. *International Journal of Information Management*, *38*(1), 10–16.

Google. (2018). *AI for Social Good*. Retrieved from https://ai.google/social-good/

Google. (n.d.). Google assistant privacy policy. Archived at https://perma.cc/KD7B-WQNR

Gorecky, D., Schmitt, M., Loskyll, M., & Zühlke, D. (2014, July). Human-machine-interaction in the industry 4.0 era. In *2014 12th IEEE international conference on industrial informatics (INDIN)* (pp. 289-294). IEEE.

Gray, S. (2017, April 4). Always on: Primary implications of microphone-enabled devices. Future of Privacy Forum. Archived at https://perma.cc/UQ92-CXCU

Greenhalgh, T., Robert, G., Macfarlane, F., Bate, P., & Kyriakidou, O. (2004). Diffusion of innovations in service organizations: Systematic review and recommendations. *The Milbank Quarterly*, *82*(4), 581–629. DOI: 10.1111/j.0887-378X.2004.00325.x PMID: 15595944

Groumpos, P. P. (2021). A critical historical and scientific overview of all industrial revolutions. *IFAC-PapersOnLine*, *54*(13), 464–471. DOI: 10.1016/j.ifacol.2021.10.492 PMID: 38620687

Gryshova, I., Balian, A., Antonik, I., Miniailo, V., Nehodenko, V., & Nyzhnychenko, Y. (2024). Artificial intelligence in climate smart in agricultural: Toward a sustainable farming future. *Access to science, business, innovation in the digital economy. ACCESS Press*, *5*(1), 125–140. DOI: 10.46656/access.2024.5.1(8)

Guerrero Quiñones, J. L. (2024). Using artificial intelligence to enhance patient autonomy in healthcare decision-making. *AI & Society*. Advance online publication. DOI: 10.1007/s00146-024-01956-6

Gundeti, R., Vuppala, K., & Kasireddy, V. (2024). The Future of AI and Environmental Sustainability: Challenges and Opportunities. *Exploring Ethical Dimensions of Environmental Sustainability and Use of AI*, 346-371.

Guo, L., Lu, Z., & Yao, L. (2021). Human-machine interaction sensing technology based on hand gesture recognition: A review. *IEEE Transactions on Human-Machine Systems*, *51*(4), 300–309. DOI: 10.1109/THMS.2021.3086003

Gu, P. (2023). Global artificial intelligence governance: Challenges and complications. *Science Insights*, *42*(6), 975–979. DOI: 10.15354/si.23.re596

Gurov O, Konkova T. 2022. *Metaverse for human or human for Metaverse?*

Guyo, D. M., Kero, C. A., & Kant, S. (2025). Is Marketing Intermediaries' Mediation Required for Livestock and Products Marketing to Improve the Economic Status of Pastoralist Communities in Ethiopia? In *AI in Agriculture for Sustainable and Economic Management* (pp. 216-234). CRC Press.

Guyo, D. M., Kant, S., & Kero, C. A. (2023, November). Mediation of Marketing Intermediaries and AI Adoption Between Livestock Products Marketing and Economic Status of Pastoralist in Ethiopia. In *2023 International Conference on Communication, Security and Artificial Intelligence (ICCSAI)* (pp. 311-316). IEEE.

Guzman, J. A. D., Seneviratne, A., & Thilakarathna, K. (2021). Unravelling spatial privacy risks of mobile mixed reality data. *Proceedings of the ACM on Interactive, Mobile, Wearable and Ubiquitous Technologies*, *5*(1), 1–26. DOI: 10.1145/3448103

Habbal, A., Ali, M. K., & Abuzaraida, M. A. (2024). Artificial Intelligence Trust, risk and security management (AI trism): Frameworks, applications, challenges and future research directions. *Expert Systems with Applications*, *240*, 122442. DOI: 10.1016/j.eswa.2023.122442

Halevy, A., Norvig, P., & Pereira, F. (2009). The unreasonable effectiveness of data. *IEEE Intelligent Systems*, *24*(2), 8–12. DOI: 10.1109/MIS.2009.36

Halley, G. (2010). The criminal liability of artificial intelligence entities: From science fiction to legal ordering control. *Akron Intellectual Property Journal*, *4*(2), 177–200.

Han, D.-I. D., Bergs, Y., & Moorhouse, N. (2022). Virtual reality consumer experience escapes: Preparing for the metaverse. *Virtual Reality (Waltham Cross)*, *26*(4), 1443–1458. DOI: 10.1007/s10055-022-00641-7

Hansen, E. B., & Bøgh, S. (2020). Artificial intelligence and internet of things in small and medium-sized enterprises: A survey. *Journal of Manufacturing Systems*, *58*(Part B), 362–372. DOI: 10.1016/j.jmsy.2020.08.009

Harrison, T., & Luna-Reyes, L. (2020). Cultivating trustworthy artificial intelligence in digital government. *Social Science Computer Review*, *40*(2), 494–511. DOI: 10.1177/0894439320980122

Hashemi-Pour, C., & Chai, W. (2023, December 21). *CIA triad (confidentiality, integrity and availability)*. WhatIs. https://www.techtarget.com/whatis/definition/Confidentiality-integrity-and-availability-CIA

Héder, M (2020). "A criticism of AI ethics guidelines". Információs Társadalom. 20 (4): 57–73. . S2CID 233252939.DOI: 10.22503/inftars.XX.2020.4.5

Heeks, R. (2017). *Information and Communication Technologies (ICTs) for Development: Theory, Practice, and Impact.* Development Informatics Working Paper Series.

Hemanth, D. J., & Gaur, V. E. (2019). *Telemedicine technologies: Big data, deep learning, robotics, mobile and remote applications for global healthcare*. Academic Press.

Hirani, R., Noruzi, K., Khuram, H., Hussaini, A. S., Aifuwa, E. I., Ely, K. E., Lewis, J. M., Gabr, A. E., Smiley, A., Tiwari, R. K., & Etienne, M. (2024). Artificial intelligence and healthcare: A journey through history, present innovations, and future possibilities. *Life (Chicago, Ill.)*, *14*(4), 557. DOI: 10.3390/life14050557 PMID: 38792579

HLEG. (2019). *Ethics Guidelines for Trustworthy AI.* High-Level Expert Group on Artificial Intelligence, European Commission.

Hochheiser, H., & Valdez, R. S. (2020). Human-Computer Interaction, Ethics, and Biomedical Informatics. *Yearbook of Medical Informatics*, *29*(1), 93–98. DOI: 10.1055/s-0040-1701990 PMID: 32823302

Hoc, J. M. (2000). From human–machine interaction to human–machine cooperation. *Ergonomics*, *43*(7), 833–843. DOI: 10.1080/001401300409044 PMID: 10929820

Hofer, D. (2024). Influence of access to healthcare services on health disparities among elderly populations in Europe. *European Journal of Health Sciences*, *10*(1), 13–23.

Hohfeld, W. (1913). Some Fundamental Legal Conceptions as Applied in Judicial Reasoning. *The Yale Law Journal*, *23*(1), 16–59. DOI: 10.2307/785533

Hollands, R. G. (2008). Will the real smart city please stand up? Intelligent, progressive or entrepreneurial? *City (London, England)*, *12*(3), 303–320. DOI: 10.1080/13604810802479126

Holland, T. E. (1917). *The elements of jurisprudence* (12th ed.). Oxford University Press.

Hollnagel, E. (1992). The reliability of man-machine interaction. *Reliability Engineering & System Safety*, *38*(1-2), 81–89. DOI: 10.1016/0951-8320(92)90108-W

Hopfield, J. J. (1982). Neural networks and physical systems with emergent collective computational abilities. *Proceedings of the National Academy of Sciences of the United States of America*, *79*(8), 2554–2558. DOI: 10.1073/pnas.79.8.2554 PMID: 6953413

Hörbst, J., & Orsolits, H. (2022, February). Mixed Reality HMI for Collaborative Robots. In *International Conference on Computer Aided Systems Theory* (pp. 539-546). Cham: Springer Nature Switzerland.

Horn, A. J., & Donaldson, A. R. (2021). *Labour market effects of the great lockdown in South Africa: Earnings and occupational during 2020–2022*.

Horwitz, M. J. (1985). Santa Clara Revisited: The Development of Corporate Theory. *West Virginia Law Review, 88*(2), 173–224.

Hossain, M. A., Azim, K. S., Jafor, A. H. M., Shayed, A. U., Nikita, N. A., & Khan, O. U. (2024). AI and Machine Learning in International Diplomacy and Conflict Resolution. *AIJMR-Advanced International Journal of Multidisciplinary Research, 2*(5).

Howard, A., et al. (2022). AI in Education: The Virtue and Perils of Automation. *Journal of Educational Technology*.

Howarth, J. (2023, March 16). *80+ amazing IoT Statistics (2023-2030)*. Exploding Topics. Retrieved from https://perma.cc/QP9G-QJQ7

Hsu, F. H. (2002). *Behind Deep Blue: Building the computer that defeated the world chess champion*. Princeton University Press.

Huang, A., & Rust, R. T. (2018). Artificial intelligence in service. *Journal of Service Research, 21*(2), 155–172. DOI: 10.1177/1094670517752459

Hui, X., Reshef, O., & Zhou, L. (2024). The short-term effects of generative Artificial simulated Intelligence on occupational: Evidence from an online market driven by skill related jobs. *Organization Science*. Advance online publication. DOI: 10.1287/orsc.2023.18441

Hulsen, T. (2024). Artificial intelligence in healthcare: ChatGPT and beyond. *AI, 5*(4), 550–554. DOI: 10.3390/ai5020028

Hunter, D. T. (2024, April 17). *Artificial intelligence: A new driver for inclusive growth and development?* Asia Pathways; Asia Pathways. https://www.asiapathways-adbi.org/2024/04/artificial-intelligence-a-new-driver-for-inclusive-growth-and-development/

Hussain, S. S. (2024). Artificial Intelligence and Diplomacy: Transforming International Relations in the Digital Age. *Remittances Review, 9*(1), 988–1001.

Hu, X., Neupane, B., Echaiz, L. F., Sibal, P., & Rivera Lam, M. (2019). *Steering AI and advanced ICTs for knowledge societies: A Rights, Openness, Access, and Multi-stakeholder Perspective*. UNESCO Publishing.

Hwang, G. J., & Chien, S. Y. (2022). Definition, roles, and potential research issues of the Metaverse in education: An artificial intelligence perspective. *Computers and Education: Artificial Intelligence*, *3*(3), 1–6. DOI: 10.1016/j.caeai.2022.100082

Ibáñez, M.-B., & Delgado-Kloos, C. (2018). Augmented reality for STEM learning: A systematic review. *Computers & Education*, *123*, 109–123. DOI: 10.1016/j.compedu.2018.05.002

Ibegbulam, C. M., Aigbovbiosa, O. J., Olowonubi, J. A., & Fatounde, S. A. (2023). Role of artificial intelligence in electrification of Africa. *Engineering Science & Technology Journal*, *4*(6), 456–472. DOI: 10.51594/estj.v4i6.667

Ingwersen, M. (2017). Towards a trickster science/fiction: Complexifying boundaries with Neal Stephenson and Michel Serres. *Interdisciplinary Science Reviews*, *42*(3), 255–268.

Inners, M., & Kun, A. L. (2017, September). Beyond liability: Legal issues of human-machine interaction for automated vehicles. In *Proceedings of the 9th International Conference on Automotive User Interfaces and Interactive Vehicular Applications* (pp. 245-253). DOI: 10.1145/3122986.3123005

International Labour Organization (ILO). (2024, April 23). *Artificial intelligence*. International Labour Organization; International Labour Organization (ILO). https://www.ilo.org/artificial-intelligence

Intersoft Consulting. (2016). *General data protection regulation (GDPR)*. General Data Protection Regulation (GDPR); General Data Protection Regulation. https://gdpr-info.eu/

Iqbal, U., ... (2023, February 20). Your Echos are heard: Tracking, profiling, and ad targeting in the Amazon smart speaker ecosystem. Arxiv:2204.10920, 1–1.

Iqbal, M. Z., & Campbell, A. G. (2021). From luxury to necessity: Progress of touchless interaction technology. *Technology in Society*, *67*, 101796. DOI: 10.1016/j.techsoc.2021.101796 PMID: 36313277

Iriarte, A. A., Erle, G. L., Etxabe, M. M., APRAIZ-IRIARTE, A., LASA-ERLE, G., & ETXABE, M. (2021). Evaluating user experience with physiological monitoring: A systematic literature review. *Dyna New Technol*, *8*(1).

Islam, Z., Ahmed, A., Alfify, M. H., & Riyaz, N. (2024). The Impact Of On Environment And Sustainable Development In India. *Educational Administration: Theory and Practice*, *30*(5), 1850–1856.

Iyawa, G. E., Herselman, M., & Botha, A. (2016). Digital health innovation ecosystems: From systematic literature review to conceptual framework. *Procedia Computer Science, 100*, 244–252. DOI: 10.1016/j.procs.2016.09.149

J. Hu, A. Iosifescu, and R. LiKamWa, "Lenscap: a split-process framework for fine-grained visual privacy control for augmented reality apps," in Proceedings of the 19th Annual International Conference on Mobile Systems, Applications, and Services, 2021, pp. 14–27.

J. Hu, A. Iosifescu, and R. LiKamWa, "Lenscap: split-process framework for fine-grained visual privacy control for augmented reality apps," in Proceedings of the 19th Annual International Conference on Mobile Systems, Applications, and Services, 2021, pp. 14–27.

Jabali, A. K., Waris, A., Khan, D. I., Ahmed, S., & Hourani, R. J. (2022). Electronic health records: Three decades of bibliometric research productivity analysis and some insights. *Informatics in Medicine Unlocked, 29*, 100872. DOI: 10.1016/j.imu.2022.100872

Jabo, D., Borji, B., & Kant, S. (2024, February). Impact of Technical CRM on Ethiopia Bank Human-Computer Interface and Competitive Advantage as Mediators of Performance. In 2024 IEEE International Conference on Computing, Power and Communication Technologies (IC2PCT) (Vol. 5, pp. 679-682). IEEE.

Jain, V., Agrawal, M., & Kumar, A. (2020, June). Performance analysis of machine learning algorithms in credit cards fraud detection. In *2020 8th International Conference on Reliability, Infocom Technologies and Optimization (Trends and Future Directions)(ICRITO)* (pp. 86-88). IEEE. DOI: 10.1109/ICRITO48877.2020.9197762

Jakobi, T., & Grafenstein, M. v. (2023). What HCI Can Do for (Data Protection) Law—Beyond Design. In Gerber, N., Stöver, A., & Marky, K. (Eds.), *Human Factors in Privacy Research*. Springer., DOI: 10.1007/978-3-031-28643-8_6

Jaldi, A. (2023). Artificial simulated Intelligence Revolution in Africa: Economic Opportunities and Legal Challenges. *Policy Cent. New South.*

Janssen, M., Hartog, M., Matheus, R., Ding, A., & Kuk, G. (2020). Will algorithms blind people? the effect of explainable ai and decision-makers' experience on ai-supported decision-making in government. *Social Science Computer Review, 40*(2), 478–493. DOI: 10.1177/0894439320980118

Jarvis, T., Thornburg, D., Rebecca, A., & Teven, C. (2020). Artificial intelligence in plastic surgery: Current applications, future directions, and ethical implications. *Plastic and Reconstructive Surgery. Global Open*, *8*(10), e3200. DOI: 10.1097/GOX.0000000000003200 PMID: 33173702

Jens, K. (2017). Who Needs Rights of Nature? *RCC Perspectives, 6*, 9, 12–13.

Jermsittiparsert, K., & Marzo, R. (2024). *AI technologies and advancements for psychological well-being and healthcare*. GI Global., DOI: 10.4018/979-8-3693-9158-7

Jeswani, M. P., & Valecha, M. K. (2024). A Study on Role of AI in Shaping a Smarter Legal System: Justice in the Machine. *AI for a Smarter Future: Transforming*, 31.

Jia, L., Liu, D., Jiang, M. J., & Cao, N. (2015, March). Design of natural user interface of indoor surveillance system. In *Selected Papers from Conferences of the Photoelectronic Technology Committee of the Chinese Society of Astronautics 2014, Part I* (Vol. 9521, pp. 278-285). SPIE.

Jiang, F., Jiang, Y., & Zhi, H. (2017). Artificial intelligence in healthcare: Past, present and future. *Seminars in Cancer Biology*, *16*(2), 234–247. PMID: 29507784

Jin, H., & Wang, S. (2018, October 9). Voice-based determination of physical and emotional characteristics of users. US Patent 10,096,319. Archived at https://perma.cc/26V9-WW2D

Jobin, A., Ienca, M., & Vayena, E. (2019). The global landscape of ai ethics guidelines. *Nature Machine Intelligence*, *1*(9), 389–399. DOI: 10.1038/s42256-019-0088-2

Joe, J. M., Kinikar, J., Smith, M., Carr, M. J., Bechtel, E., Randall, S., & Ammerman, L. (2021). Digital health solutions and wearable devices. *Health Informatics*, 13-38. https://doi.org/DOI: 10.1007/978-3-030-81030-6_2

Johnson, D. G. (2020). Artificial intelligence and the concept of agency: Comparing corporate and machine agency. *Ethics and Information Technology*, *22*(1), 9–20.

Jordan, M. I., & Mitchell, T. M. (2015). Machine learning: Trends, perspectives, and prospects. *Science*, *349*(6245), 255–260. DOI: 10.1126/science.aaa8415 PMID: 26185243

Jotterand, F., & Ienca, M. (2021). Artificial intelligence in brain and mental health: Philosophical, ethical and policy issues. *Advanced Neuroethics*, 1–7. DOI: 10.1007/978-3-030-74188-4_1

Kamanja, D. M. (2020). *Influence of Work Environment on Employee Engagement of Central Government Ministries in Kenya, A Case of Meru County* (Doctoral dissertation, KeMU).

Kant, I. (1785). *Groundwork for the Metaphysics of Morals*.

Kantha, T., Sahoo, D., Rout, D., & Mishra, S. J. (2024). *Ethics in the Digital Era*. Technology's Role in Shaping Society.

Kant, S., & Adula, M. (2024). AI Learning and Work Attitude Mediation Between Reward and Organizational Support in Ethiopia. In Gomathi Sankar, J., & David, A. (Eds.), *Generative AI for Transformational Management* (pp. 109–136). IGI Global., DOI: 10.4018/979-8-3693-5578-7.ch005

Kant, S., & Adula, M. (2024). Human-Machine Interaction in the Metaverse in the Context of Ethiopia. In *Impact and Potential of Machine Learning in the Metaverse* (pp. 196–212). IGI Global., DOI: 10.4018/979-8-3693-5762-0.ch008

Kapadiya, K., Patel, U., Gupta, R., Alshehri, M. D., Tanwar, S., Sharma, G., & Bokoro, P. N. (2022). Blockchain and AI-empowered healthcare insurance fraud detection: An analysis, architecture, and future prospects. *IEEE Access : Practical Innovations, Open Solutions*, *10*, 79606–79627. DOI: 10.1109/ACCESS.2022.3194569

Kazi, A. (2024, March 11). Connecting Humans and Machines: Trends in the Human Machine Interface (HMI) Market. *Verified Market Reports® | Get Market Analysis and Research Reports*. https://www.verifiedmarketreports.com/blog/top-7-trends-in-human-machine-interface-hmi/#:~:text=Gesture%20recognition%20technology%20is%20becoming,hands%2Dfree%20operation%20is%20essential

Kelly, G. (2019, November 16). Compare the privacy practices of the most popular smart speakers with virtual assistants. Common Sense. Archived at https://perma.cc/A6AZ-65PS

Kerry, C. F., Meltzer, J. P., Renda, A., Engler, A., & Fanni, R. (2021, October 25). *Strengthening international cooperation on AI*. Brookings; Brookings. https://www.brookings.edu/articles/strengthening-international-cooperation-on-ai/

Khalid, N., Qayyum, A., Bilal, M., Al-Fuqaha, A., & Qadir, J. (2023). Privacy-preserving artificial intelligence in healthcare: Techniques and applications. *Computers in Biology and Medicine*, *158*, 106848. DOI: 10.1016/j.compbiomed.2023.106848 PMID: 37044052

Khan, A. (2023). Transforming healthcare through AI: Unleashing the power of personalized medicine. *International Journal of Multidisciplinary Sciences and Arts*, *2*(1), 67–77. DOI: 10.47709/ijmdsa.v2i1.2424

Khan, M. S., & Nayab, H. (2021). Digital health technologies and artificial intelligence in the Islamic world: Embracing the evolution in healthcare. *Journal of Islamic Governance*, *6*. Advance online publication. DOI: 10.53105/jig.6-1

Kohler, T. (2008) "Avatar-Based Innovation Using Virtual Worlds for Real World Innovation". International product development management conference. Vol.15

Kong, H., Yuan, Y., Baruch, Y., Bu, N., Jiang, X., & Wang, K. (2021). Influences of Artificial simulated Intelligence awareness on career competency and job burnout. *International Journal of Contemporary Hospitality Management*, *33*(2), 717–734. DOI: 10.1108/IJCHM-07-2020-0789

Kop, M. (2019). AI & intellectual property: Towards an articulated public domain. *SSRN*, *28*, 297. DOI: 10.2139/ssrn.3409715

Korinek, A., Vipra, J., & Vipra, A. K. Jai. (2024, March 27). *AI monopolies*. Economic Policy; Economic Policy. https://www.economic-policy.org/79th-economic-policy-panel/ai-monopolies/

Koulu, R., & Kontiainen, L. A. U. R. A. (2019). How Will AI Shape the Future of Law. *University of Helsinki Legal Tech Lab publications*.

Kozuch, K. (2023, March 3). The 30 best Alexa skills in 2023. Tom's Guide. Archived at https://perma.cc/65HN-JH6L

Krisnata, B. R. (2023, July 27). *Artificial Intelligence and International Affairs - Australian Institute of International Affairs*. Australian Institute of International Affairs. Retrieved October 1, 2024, from https://www.internationalaffairs.org.au/australianoutlook/artificial-intelligence-and-international-affairs/

Kroll, J. A. (2021). Outlining traceability: A principle for operationalizing accountability in computing systems. In *Proceedings of the 2021 ACM Conference on Fairness, Accountability, and Transparency* (pp. 758-771). DOI: 10.1145/3442188.3445937

Krupitzer, C., Müller, S., Lesch, V., Züfle, M., Edinger, J., Lemken, A., . . . Becker, C. (2020). A survey on human machine interaction in industry 4.0. *arXiv preprint arXiv:2002.01025*.

Krupiy, T. T. (2020). A vulnerability analysis: Theorising the impact of decision-making processes on individuals, society and human diversity from a social justice perspective. *Computer Law & Security Review*, *38*, 105429. DOI: 10.1016/j.clsr.2020.105429

Kshetri, N. (2020). The Emerging Role of Artificial Intelligence in the Finance Sector. *Finance Research Letters*, *35*, 101259.

Kukeyeva, F., Kurmangali, M., & Aktay, D. (2024). Theoretical and Methodological Approaches to Studying Artificial Intelligence in the Context of International Relations and International Law. *JOURNAL OF CENTRAL ASIAN STUDIES*, *93*(1), 4–21. DOI: 10.52536/3006-807X.2024-1.01

Kumar, A. S., & Chandrakala, D. (2016). A survey on customer churn prediction using machine learning techniques. *International Journal of Computer Applications*, *154*(10), 13–16. DOI: 10.5120/ijca2016912237

Kun, A. L. (2018). Human-machine interaction for vehicles: Review and outlook. *Foundations and Trends® in Human–Computer Interaction, 11*(4), 201-293.

Kuner, C., Cate, F. H., Millard, C., & Svantesson, D. J. (2017). Transatlantic data privacy relations: The EU–US privacy shield and the future of global data privacy. *International Data Privacy Law*, *7*(1), 1–13. DOI: 10.1093/idpl/ipx003

Kunst, J., & Bierwiaczonek, K. (2023). Utilizing ai questionnaire translations in cross-cultural and intercultural research: insights and recommendations. https://doi.org/DOI: 10.31234/osf.io/sxcyk

Kurshan, E., & Shen, H. (2020). Graph computing for financial crime and fraud detection: Trends, challenges and outlook. *International Journal of Semantic Computing*, *14*(04), 565–589. DOI: 10.1142/S1793351X20300022

Kurshan, E., Shen, H., & Yu, H. (2020, September). Financial crime & fraud detection using graph computing: Application considerations & outlook. In *2020 Second International Conference on Transdisciplinary AI (TransAI)* (pp. 125-130). IEEE. DOI: 10.1109/TransAI49837.2020.00029

Kuruvilla, R. (2019, December). Between you, me, and Alexa: On the legality of virtual assistant devices in two-party consent states. *Washington Law Review (Seattle, Wash.)*, *94*, 2029–2052.

Kye, B., Han, N., Kim, E., Park, Y., & Jo, S. (2021). Educational applications of metaverse: Possibilities and limitations J. *Journal of Educational Evaluation for Health Professions*, *18*, 32. DOI: 10.3352/jeehp.2021.18.32 PMID: 34897242

Lagapa, M. (n.d.). How Siri works – Voice recognition on a smartphone. Jameco. Archived at https://perma.cc/6SGK-UNHN

Lake, B. M., Ullman, T. D., Tenenbaum, J. B., & Gershman, S. J. (2017). Building machines that learn and think like people. *Behavioral and Brain Sciences*, *40*, e253. DOI: 10.1017/S0140525X16001837 PMID: 27881212

Lamey, D. (2018, July 26). The power of voice-activated voice assistants. *Discover Tec*. Archived at https://perma.cc/N3YW-58DD

Lang, R. D., & Benessere, L. E. (2018, January/February). Alexa, Siri, Bixby, Google's assistant, and Cortana testifying in court. *Journal of the Missouri Bar*, *74*(1), 20.

Larsson, S. (2021). AI in the EU: Ethical Guidelines as a Governance Tool. *The European Union and the technology shift*, 85-111.

Laukes, M. M. (2024). *AI is shaping tomorrow's market driven by skill related jobs: the impact of Artificial simulated Intelligence on the required skills in the market driven by skill related jobs* (Doctoral dissertation, Technische Hochschule Ingolstadt).

Lee, L. H., Braud, T., Zhou, P., Wang, L., Xu, D., Lin, Z., Kumar, A., Bermejo, C., & Hui, P. "All one needs to know about metaverse: A complete survey on technological singularity, virtual ecosystem, and research agenda," arXiv preprint arXiv:2110.05352, 2021.

Lee, L., Braud, T., Zhou, P., Wang, L., Xu, D., Lin, Z., Kumar, A., Bermejo, C., & Hui, P. (2021). All One Needs to Know about Metaverse: A Complete Survey on Technological Singularity, Virtual Ecosystem, and Research Agenda. *ArXiv*. / abs/2110.05352

Lee, L.-H. (2021) "All one needs to know about metaverse: A complete survey on technological singularity, virtual ecosystem, and research agenda." arXiv preprint arXiv:2110.05352.

Lee, E., Karim, H., Iaboni, A., & Sekhon, H. (2022). Artificial intelligence in geriatric mental health: Recent advances in clinical research. *The American Journal of Geriatric Psychiatry*, *30*(4), S15–S16. DOI: 10.1016/j.jagp.2022.01.275

Leschanowsky, A., Brüggemeier, B., & Peters, N. (2021, November). Design implications for human-machine interactions from a qualitative pilot study on privacy. In *Proc. 2021 ISCA symposium on security and privacy in speech communication* (pp. 76-79). DOI: 10.21437/SPSC.2021-16

Lewis, J. (2024). AI and Bias: Addressing Discrimination in Machine Learning Algorithms Abstract. *AlgoVista. Journal of AI & Computer Science*, *1*(2).

Lian, B., Nguyen, P. T., Lydia, E. L., & Shankar, K. (2019). Can excessive use of social media contribute to addictive behaviors (drugs, tobacco, alcohol) or mental health issues? *Restaurant Business*, *118*(10), 22–29. DOI: 10.26643/rb.v118i10.8779

Liebig, L., Güttel, L., Jobin, A., & Katzenbach, C. (2024). Subnational AI policy: Shaping AI in a multi-level governance system. *AI & Society*, *39*(3), 1477–1490. DOI: 10.1007/s00146-022-01561-5

Linden, G., Smith, B., & York, J. (2003). Recommendations: Item-to-item collaborative filtering. *IEEE Internet Computing*, *7*(1), 76–80. DOI: 10.1109/MIC.2003.1167344

Lin, P. (2016). Why Ethics Matters for Autonomous Cars. In Dancy, C. L., & Miller, C. K. (Eds.), *Ethical Issues in Modern Society* (pp. 231–248).

Lippmann, R. (1997). Speech recognition by Machines and Humans. *Speech Communication*, *22*(1), 1–15. DOI: 10.1016/S0167-6393(97)00021-6

Lipton, Z. C. (2018). The Mythos of Model Interpretability. *Communications of the ACM*, *61*(2), 36–43. DOI: 10.1145/3233231

Lissovolik, Y. (2020). *AI in International Relations: The Era of 'Digital Diplomacy.'* Valdai Club. Retrieved October 1, 2024, from https://valdaiclub.com/a/highlights/ai-in-international-relations/

Luckin, R.. (2016). *Intelligence Unleashed: An Argument for AI in Education*. Pearson.

Lutz, C. (2023). Privacy and Human–Machine Communication. *Human-Machine Communication*, •••, 310.

Lytras, M. D., Housawi, A. A., & Alsaywid, B. S. (2023). Preface. In Lytras, M. D., Housawi, A. A., & Alsaywid, B. S. (Eds.), *Digital transformation in healthcare in post-Covid-19 times* (pp. xiii–xxi). Academic Press., DOI: 10.1016/B978-0-323-98353-2.09996-2

Ma, F., Song, F., Liu, Y., & Niu, J. (2020). Quantitative analysis on the interaction fatigue of natural gestures. *IEEE Access : Practical Innovations, Open Solutions*, *8*, 190797–190811. DOI: 10.1109/ACCESS.2020.3031967

Magrabi, F., Ammenwerth, E., McNair, J., Keizer, N., Hyppönen, H., Nykänen, P., & Georgiou, A. (2019). Artificial intelligence in clinical decision support: Challenges for evaluating ai and practical implications. *Yearbook of Medical Informatics*, *28*(01), 128–134. DOI: 10.1055/s-0039-1677903 PMID: 31022752

Maheshwari, S. (2018, March 31). Hey, Alexa, what can you hear? And what will you do with it? The New York Times. Archived at https://perma.cc/5ESJ-88FT

Mahmud, S., Lin, X., & Kim, J. H. (2020, January). Interface for human machine interaction for assistant devices: A review. In *2020 10th Annual computing and communication workshop and conference (CCWC)* (pp. 0768-0773). IEEE. DOI: 10.1109/CCWC47524.2020.9031244

Mahya, L., Tarjo, T., Sanusi, Z. M., & Kurniawan, F. A. (2023). Intelligent Automation Of Fraud Detection And Investigation: A Bibliometric Analysis Approach. *Jurnal Reviu Akuntansi dan Keuangan, 13*(3), 588-613.

Ma, J. K., & Cheng, S. (2022). Digital inclusion, psychological well-being, and digital competence. In Estes, R. J., & Sirgy, M. J. (Eds.), *Human well-being research and policy making* (pp. 125–166). Springer., DOI: 10.1007/978-3-031-04412-0_6

Malan, D. (2018, June 21). The law can't keep up with new tech. Here's how to close the gap. World Economic Forum. Archived at https://perma.cc/NHB9-4P8N

Malviya, R., Sundram, S., Prajapati, B., & Singh, S. K. (Eds.). (2023). *Human-Machine Interface: Making Healthcare Digital*. John Wiley & Sons. DOI: 10.1002/9781394200344

Manheim, K., & Kaplan, L. (2019). Artificial intelligence: Risks to privacy and democracy. *Yale JL & Tech.*, *21*, 106.

Manning, A. (2020, Spring). It's smart, but is it ethical? Confidentiality in an environment that is listening. *Virginia Journal of Law & Technology*, *24*(1), 7.

Manyika, J. (2011). Big data: The next frontier for innovation, competition, and productivity. *McKinsey Global Institute, 1*.

Manyika, J., Chui, M., Miremadi, M., Bughin, J., George, K., Willmott, P., & Dewhurst, M. (2017). A future that works: AI, automation, employment, and productivity. *McKinsey Global Institute Research. Tech. Rep*, *60*, 1–135.

Martinez-Martin, N. (2021). Minding the AI: Ethical challenges and practice for AI mental health care tools. In Jotterand, F., & Ienca, M. (Eds.), *Artificial intelligence in brain and mental health: Philosophical, ethical & policy issues. Advances in Neuroethics* (pp. 111–125). Springer., DOI: 10.1007/978-3-030-74188-4_8

Martin, K. D., & Zimmermann, J. (2024). Artificial Intelligence and its Implications for Data Privacy. *Current Opinion in Psychology*, *58*, 101829. DOI: 10.1016/j.copsyc.2024.101829 PMID: 38954851

Maslej, N., Fattorini, L., Brynjolfsson, E., Etchemendy, J., Ligett, K., Lyons, T., . . . Perrault, R. (2023). Artificial intelligence index report 2023. arXiv preprint arXiv:2310.03715.

Mason, J. (2020). AI in Education: A Perspective on the Future of Learning. *The International Journal of Information and Learning Technology*.

Masuda, H., Kawakubo, S., Okitasari, M., & Morita, K. (2022). Exploring the role of local governments as intermediaries to facilitate partnerships for the Sustainable Development Goals. *Sustainable Cities and Society*, *82*, 103901. DOI: 10.1016/j.scs.2022.103883

McAfee, A., Brynjolfsson, E., Davenport, T. H., Patil, D. J., & Barton, D. (2012). Big data: The management revolution. *Harvard Business Review*, *90*(10), 60–68. PMID: 23074865

McBeath, K., Angermann, C. E., & Cowie, M. R. (2022). Digital technologies to support better outcome and experience of care in patients with heart failure. *Current Heart Failure Reports*, *19*(2), 75–108. DOI: 10.1007/s11897-022-00548-z PMID: 35486314

McCarthy, J., Minsky, M. L., Rochester, N., & Shannon, C. E. (1955). A Proposal for the Dartmouth Summer Research Project on Artificial Intelligence. *AI Magazine*, *27*(4), 12–12.

McFadden, C. (2023, April 17). Rise of Skynet? AI takes control of a Chinese satellite for 24 hours. *Interesting Engineering*. Retrieved October 1, 2024, from https://interestingengineering.com/innovation/ai-controlled-chinese-satellite-24-hours

McGee, C. E., Barlow-Pay, M., Vassilev, I., Baird, J., Fenge, L. A., Chase, D., & Parkes, J. (2022). Supporting and enabling health research in a local authority (SERLA): An exploratory study. *BMC Public Health*, *22*(1), 1316. DOI: 10.1186/s12889-022-13396-2 PMID: 35810294

Mdladla, L. T. S., Wider, W., Thanathanchuchot, T., & Hossain, S. A. (2024). Navigating the AI revolution: A review of the transformative strategies for economic development in Africa's emerging economies. *Journal of Infrastructure. Policy and Development*, *8*(9), 5436. DOI: 10.24294/jipd.v8i9.5436

Medaglia, R., Gil-García, J., & Pardo, T. (2021). Artificial intelligence in government: Taking stock and moving forward. *Social Science Computer Review*, *41*(1), 123–140. DOI: 10.1177/08944393211034087

Mehrabi, N.. (2021). A Survey on Bias and Fairness in Machine Learning. *ACM Computing Surveys*.

Mehryar, S., Yazdanpanah, V., & Tong, J. (2024). AI and Climate Resilience Governance. *iScience*, *26*(7), 109812–109812. DOI: 10.1016/j.isci.2024.109812 PMID: 38784017

Meleouni, C., & Efthymiou, I. P. (2023). Artificial intelligence and its impact in international relations. *Journal of Politics and Ethics in New Technologies and Ai, 2*(1), e35803. DOI: 10.12681/jpentai.35803

Mikalef, P.. (2020). Big data and artificial intelligence: The role of AI in fraud detection. *Information & Management, 57*(7), 103391.

Mill, J. S. (1863). *Utilitarianism.*

Miller, T. (2019). Explanation in artificial intelligence: Insights from the social sciences. *Artificial Intelligence, 267*, 1–38. DOI: 10.1016/j.artint.2018.07.007

Minsky, M. (1970). Form and Content in Computer Science (1970 ACM Turing lecture). [JACM]. *Journal of the Association for Computing Machinery, 17*(2), 197–215. DOI: 10.1145/321574.321575

Mishori, R., & Antono, B. (2020). Telehealth, rural America, and the digital divide. *The Journal of Ambulatory Care Management, 43*(4), 319–322. DOI: 10.1097/JAC.0000000000000348 PMID: 32858734

Mitchelson, D. (2023, October 27). *Learn about the double-edged sword of AI in cybersecurity*. World Economic Forum; World Economic Forum. https://www.weforum.org/stories/2023/10/the-double-edged-sword-of-artificial-intelligence-in-cybersecurity/

Mittelstadt, B. D., Allo, P., Taddeo, M., Wachter, S., & Floridi, L. (2016). The ethics of algorithms: Mapping the debate. *Big Data & Society, 3*(2), 2053951716679679. DOI: 10.1177/2053951716679679

Mogaji, E., Soetan, T. O., & Kieu, T. A. (2020). The implications of artificial intelligence on the digital marketing of financial services to vulnerable customers. *Australasian Marketing Journal, 29*(3), 235–242. DOI: 10.1016/j.ausmj.2020.05.003

Monjur, M. E. I., Rifat, A. H., Islam, M. R., & Bhuiyan, M. R. (2023). The impact of artificial intelligence on international trade: Evidence from B2C giant e-commerce (Amazon, Alibaba, Shopify, eBay). *Open Journal of Business and Management, 11*(5), 2389–2401. DOI: 10.4236/ojbm.2023.115132

Moon, M. (2023). Searching for inclusive artificial intelligence for social good: Participatory governance and policy recommendations for making ai more inclusive and benign for society. *Public Administration Review, 83*(6), 1496–1505. DOI: 10.1111/puar.13648

Moore, A. (2023, March). How AI Could Revolutionize Diplomacy. *Foreign Policy*. Retrieved October 2, 2024, from https://foreignpolicy.com/2023/03/21/ai-artificial-intelligence-diplomacy-negotiations-chatgpt-quantum-computing/

Moore, G. (1965). Moore's law. *Electronics Magazine*, *38*(8), 114.

Moravec, H. (1988). *Mind Children: The Future of Robot and Human Intelligence*. Harvard UP.

Morgan, A. A., Abdi, J., Syed, M. A., Kohen, G. E., Barlow, P., & Vizcaychipi, M. P. (2022). Robots in healthcare: A scoping review. *Current Robotics Reports*, *3*(4), 271–280. DOI: 10.1007/s43154-022-00095-4 PMID: 36311256

Mourtzis, D., Angelopoulos, J., & Panopoulos, N. (2023). The future of the human–machine interface (HMI) in society 5.0. *Future Internet*, *15*(5), 162. DOI: 10.3390/fi15050162

Mouta, A., Pinto-Llorente, A. M., & Torrecilla-Sánchez, E. M. (2023). Uncovering blind spots in education ethics: Insights from a systematic literature review on artificial intelligence in education. *International Journal of Artificial Intelligence in Education*, •••, 1–40.

Mramba, N. R. (2024). The potentials of artificial intelligence in improving Africa informal cross border trade. What works, What doesn't, and What's next to Africans? *African Journal of Land Policy and Geospatial Sciences*, *7*(1), 92–112.

Murphy, R. R., & Woods, D. D. (2009). Beyond Asimov: The Three Laws of Responsible Robotics. *IEEE Intelligent Systems*, *24*(4), 14–20. DOI: 10.1109/MIS.2009.69

Myers, S. (2024, January 20). Movie analysis: "Her". Medium. Archived at https://perma.cc/KP2Y-E5EY

Naghdipour, B. (2023). Google translate in efl writing: Managing contradictions and conflicts. *TESOL Journal*, *15*(2), e747. Advance online publication. DOI: 10.1002/tesj.747

Narsimha, B., Raghavendran, C. V., Rajyalakshmi, P., Reddy, G. K., Bhargavi, M., & Naresh, P. (2022). Cyber defense in the age of artificial intelligence and machine learning for financial fraud detection application. *IJEER*, *10*(2), 87–92. DOI: 10.37391/ijeer.100206

Nazer, L. H., Zatarah, R., Waldrip, S., Ke, J. X. C., Moukheiber, M., Khanna, A. K., Hicklen, R. S., Moukheiber, L., Moukheiber, D., Ma, H., & Mathur, P. (2023). Bias in artificial intelligence algorithms and recommendations for mitigation. *PLOS Digital Health*, *2*(6), e0000278. DOI: 10.1371/journal.pdig.0000278 PMID: 37347721

Negreiro, M., & Niestadt, M. (2022). *EU Digital Identity Wallet, Proposal for a Regulation of the European Parliament and the Council amending Regulation (EU) No 910/2014 as regards stabilizing a framework for a European Digital Identity, COM/2021/281 final, and the description*. The European Digital Identity Framework.

Newell, A., & Simon, H. A. (1972). *Human problem solving*. Prentice Hall.

Ng, A. (2019, May 9). Amazon Alexa transcripts live on, even after you delete voice records. CNET. Archived at https://perma.cc/VH96-L332

Ngai, E. W. T.. (2011). The application of data mining techniques in financial fraud detection: A review and future directions. *Decision Support Systems*, *50*(3), 559–569. DOI: 10.1016/j.dss.2010.08.006

Nickel, P., Bärenz, P., Radandt, S., Wichtl, M., Kaufmann, U., Monica, L., . . . Nellutla, M. (2020). Human-system interaction design requirements to improve machinery and systems safety. In *Advances in Safety Management and Human Factors:Proceedings of the AHFE 2019 International Conference on Safety Management and Human Factors,July 24-28, 2019,Washington DC, USA10* (pp. 3-13). Springer International Publishing. DOI: 10.1007/978-3-030-20497-6_1

Ning, H. (2021) “A Survey on Metaverse: The State-of-the-art, Technologies, Applications, and Challenges.” arXiv preprint arXiv:2111.09673

NIST. (2020). *A Proposal for Identifying and Managing Bias in AI.*

Niyitunga, E. B. (2024). The Function of Artificial simulated Intelligence in Promoting Digital Public Participation for Successful Peacebuilding in Africa. *African Journal of Peace and Conflict Investigation (formerly Ubuntu: Journal of Conflict and Social Transformation)*, *13*(1), 25-49.

Nkomo, B. K., & Breetzke, T. (2020, March). A conceptual model for the use of artificial intelligence for credit card fraud detection in banks. In *2020 Conference on Information Communications Technology and Society (ICTAS)* (pp. 1-6). IEEE. DOI: 10.1109/ICTAS47918.2020.233980

Noonan, L. (2022, December 15). Self-regulation isn’t enough. Larissa Noonan. Archived at https://perma.cc/L478-DE54

Noordt, C., & Misuraca, G. (2020). Exploratory insights on artificial intelligence for government in europe. *Social Science Computer Review*, *40*(2), 426–444. DOI: 10.1177/0894439320980449

Nowak, P. (2016, December 27). The dark side of social media can no longer be ignored. The National News. Archived at https://perma.cc/A4BF-L6VP

Ntjamba, F. C., & Ashipala, D. O. (2025). Impact on and Ethical Considerations of Artificial Intelligence on Human Healthcare. In Jermsittiparsert, K., & Marzo, R. (Eds.), *AI Technologies and Advancements for Psychological Well-Being and Healthcare* (pp. 1–36). IGI Global., DOI: 10.4018/979-8-3693-9158-7.ch001

Nwaobi, G. C. (2019). Emerging African Economies: Digital Structures, Disruptive Responses and Demographic Implications. *Disruptive Responses and Demographic Implications (October 1, 2019).*

Nyoach, T. D., Lemi, K., Debela, T., & Kant, S. (2024). Does Organizational Commitment Mediate the Relationship between Employee Relationship Management and Bank Performance? The Case of Banks in Ethiopia. *International Journal of Organizational Leadership, 13*(2), 355–376. DOI: 10.33844/ijol.2024.60419

O'Loughlin, J., Witmer, F., Linke, A., Laing, A., Gettelman, A., & Dudhia, J. (2012). Climate variability and conflict risk in east africa, 1990–2009. *Proceedings of the National Academy of Sciences of the United States of America, 109*(45), 18344–18349. DOI: 10.1073/pnas.1205130109 PMID: 23090992

O'Neil, C. (2016). *Weapons of Math Destruction: How Big Data Increases Inequality and Threatens Democracy.* Crown Publishing.

Obermeyer, Z., Powers, B., Vogeli, C., & Mullainathan, S. (2019). Dissecting racial bias in an algorithm used to manage the health of populations. *Science, 366*(6464), 447–453. DOI: 10.1126/science.aax2342 PMID: 31649194

Obukhov, T., & Brovelli, M. (2023). Identifying conditioning factors and predictors of conflict likelihood for machine learning models: A literature review. *ISPRS International Journal of Geo-Information, 12*(8), 322. DOI: 10.3390/ijgi12080322

Ossiannilsson, E., Cazarez, R. L. U., Goode, C., Mansour, C., & Gusmao, C. M. G. D. (2024). Artificial intelligence is used to empower the implementation of OER and the UNESCO OER recommendation. *Open Praxis, 16*(2), 137–157. DOI: 10.55982/openpraxis.16.2.650

Oyekunle, D., Boohene, D., & Preston, D. (2024). Ethical Considerations in AI-Powered Work Environments: A Literature Review and Theoretical Framework for Ensuring Human Dignity and Fairness. *Valley International Journal Digital Library*, 6166-6178.

Pacaux-Lemoine, M. P., & Trentesaux, D. (2019). Ethical risks of human-machine symbiosis in industry 4.0: Insights from the human-machine cooperation approach. *IFAC-PapersOnLine, 52*(19), 19–24. DOI: 10.1016/j.ifacol.2019.12.077

Pallathadka, H., Mustafa, M., Sanchez, D. T., Sajja, G. S., Gour, S., & Naved, M. (2023). Impact of machine learning on management, healthcare and agriculture. *Materials Today: Proceedings*, *80*, 2803–2806. DOI: 10.1016/j.matpr.2021.07.042

Pallathadka, H., Ramirez-Asis, E. H., Loli-Poma, T. P., Kaliyaperumal, K., Ventayen, R. J. M., & Naved, M. (2023). Applications of artificial intelligence in business management, e-commerce and finance. *Materials Today: Proceedings*, *80*, 2610–2613. DOI: 10.1016/j.matpr.2021.06.419

Panesar, A. (2019). *Machine learning and AI for healthcare: Big data for improved health outcomes*. Springer., DOI: 10.1007/978-1-4842-3799-1

Panigrahi, A., Pati, A., Sahu, B., Das, M. N., Nayak, D. S. K., Sahoo, G., & Kant, S. (2023). En-MinWhale: An ensemble approach based on MRMR and Whale optimization for Cancer diagnosis. *IEEE Access : Practical Innovations, Open Solutions*, *11*, 113526–113542. DOI: 10.1109/ACCESS.2023.3318261

Patel, H. I., Senanayake, S. A., & Triloka, J. (2020, November). Human-system interaction interface utilizing 3D gesture recognition techniques based on wearable technology. In *2020 5th International Conference on Innovative Technologies in Intelligent Systems and Industrial Applications (CITISIA)* (pp. 1-9). IEEE.

Pavel, B., Ke, I., Spirtas, M., Ryseff, J., Sabbag, L., Smith, G., Scholl, K., & Lumpkin, D. (2023, November 3). *AI and Geopolitics: How Might AI Affect the Rise and Fall of Nations?*Www.rand.org

Pearson, J. (2021). The power of algorithms in digital transformations: A roadmap to the future. *The Journal of Management Technology*, *18*(2), 98–104.

Pellegrino, M., & Kelly, R. (2019). Intelligent machines and the growing importance of ethics. In Gilli, A. (Ed.), *The Brain and the Processor: Unpacking the Challenges of Human-Machine Interaction* (pp. 45–54). NATO Defense College., https://www.jstor.org/stable/resrep19966.11

Pérez, L., Rodríguez-Jiménez, S., Rodríguez, N., Usamentiaga, R., & García, D. F. (2020). Digital twin and virtual reality-based methodology for multi-robot manufacturing cell commissioning. *Applied Sciences (Basel, Switzerland)*, *10*(10), 3633. DOI: 10.3390/app10103633

Pesch, U., Spekkink, W., & Quist, J. (2019). Local sustainability initiatives: Innovation and civic engagement in societal experiments. *European Planning Studies*, *27*(2), 300–317. DOI: 10.1080/09654313.2018.1464549

Pierce, D. (2017, January 6). Alexa just conquered CES. The world is next. Wired. Archived at https://perma.cc/M9JR-7V6D

Pohle, J. (2015). UNESCO and INFOethics: Seeking global ethical values in the Information Society. *Telematics and Informatics*, *32*(2), 381–390. DOI: 10.1016/j.tele.2014.05.006

Pound, R. (1915). Legal Rights. *International Journal of Ethics*, *26*(1), 92–95. DOI: 10.1086/intejethi.26.1.2376739

PricewaterhouseCoopers. (2018). Prepare for the voice revolution: An in-depth look at consumer adoption and usage of voice assistants, and how companies can earn their trust—and their business. Archived at https://perma.cc/77F4-7JXM

Principles for Responsible AI Innovation. *AI Toolkit*. (n.d.). https://www.ai-lawenforcement.org/guidance/principles

PwC. (2017). *PwC's Global Artificial Intelligence Study | PwC*. PwC; PwC Global. https://www.pwc.com/gx/en/issues/artificial-intelligence/publications/artificial-intelligence-study.html

Qian, Y., Liu, J., Shi, L., Forrest, J. Y.-L., & Yang, Z. (2022). Can artificial intelligence improve green economic growth? Evidence from China. *Environmental Science and Pollution Research International*, *30*(6), 16418–16437. Advance online publication. DOI: 10.1007/s11356-022-23320-1 PMID: 36184706

Quartarone, V. (2021). *Wearable HMI definition, development and validation for collaborative environment in industrial processes in the context of Industry 4.0* (Doctoral dissertation, Politecnico di Torino).

Quilling, E., Mielenbrink, V., Osterhoff, A., Terhorst, S., Tollmann, P., & Kruse, S. (2022). State of evidence on municipal strategies for health promotion and prevention: A literature and database research. *BMC Public Health*, *22*(1), 301. DOI: 10.1186/s12889-022-12607-0 PMID: 35164731

Quintin-John, S., & Valverde, R. (2021). A perceptron based neural network data analytics architecture for the detection of fraud in credit card transactions in financial legacy systems. *WSEAS Transactions on Systems and Control, 16*.

Rahaman, M., Pappachan, P., Orozco, S. M., Bansal, S., & Arya, V. (2024). AI Safety and Security. In *Challenges in Large Language Model Development and AI Ethics* (pp. 354–383). IGI Global. DOI: 10.4018/979-8-3693-3860-5.ch011

Rahman, M., Ming, T. H., Baigh, T. A., & Sarker, M. (2023). Adoption of artificial intelligence in banking services: An empirical analysis. *International Journal of Emerging Markets*, *18*(10), 4270–4300. DOI: 10.1108/IJOEM-06-2020-0724

Raihan, M., Debnath, A., Adhikary, P., Masud, M., Meshref, H., & Bairagi, A. K. (2024). Bridging Technology and Psychology: AI-Driven Analysis of Student's Class Lecture Activity for Improved Learning Outcomes. *IEEE Access : Practical Innovations, Open Solutions*, *12*, 147320–147349. DOI: 10.1109/ACCESS.2024.3474848

Raji, I. D.. (2020). Closing the AI Accountability Gap: Defining an AI Governance Framework for Government Procurement. *Proceedings of the 2020 Conference on Fairness, Accountability, and Transparency*. DOI: 10.1145/3351095.3372873

Raji, I. D., & Buolamwini, J. (2019). Actionable Auditing: Investigating the Impact of Publicly Naming Biased Performance Results of Commercial AI Products. *Proceedings of the 2019 AAAI/ACM Conference on AI, Ethics, and Society*. DOI: 10.1145/3306618.3314244

Raj, S. B. E., & Portia, A. A. (2011, March). Analysis on credit card fraud detection methods. In *2011 International Conference on Computer, Communication and Electrical Technology (ICCCET)* (pp. 152-156). IEEE.

RAND. https://www.rand.org/pubs/perspectives/PEA3034-1.html

Raws, E., & Lacoma, T. (2019, July 13). How to set up an Amazon Echo. Digital Trends. Archived at https://perma.cc/SP52-ZBBV

Razmi, R. M. (2024). *AI doctor. The rise of artificial intelligence in healthcare – A guide for users, buyers, builders, and investors*. John Wiley & Sons., DOI: 10.1002/9781394240197

Reed, B. (2020, July 20). 'Alexa, I love you': How lockdown made men lust after their Amazon Echo. The Guardian. Archived at https://perma.cc/2KXA-TB8L

Riaño, D., Wilk, S., & Teije, A. T. (2021). Preface: AIME 2019. *Artificial Intelligence in Medicine*, *115*, 102058. DOI: 10.1016/j.artmed.2021.102058 PMID: 34001318

Ribino, P. (2023). The role of politeness in human–machine interactions: A systematic literature review and future perspectives. *Artificial Intelligence Review*, *56*(S1, Suppl 1), 445–482. DOI: 10.1007/s10462-023-10540-1

Richardson, R. (2021). Racial segregation and the data-driven society: How our failure to reckon with root causes perpetuates separate and unequal realities. *Berkeley Technology Law Journal*, *36*, 1051.

Ríos, A. M., Guillamón, M.-D., Cifuentes-Faura, J., & Benito, B. (2022). Efficiency and sustainability in municipal social policies. Social Policy & Administration, 56(7), Rosenlund, M., Kinnunen, U. M., & Saranto, K. (2023). The use of digital health services among patients and citizens living at home: Scoping review. *Journal of Medical Internet Research, 25*, e44711.

Ritika, H. J. (2022, October). Fraud detection and management for telecommunication systems using artificial intelligence (AI). In *2022 3rd International Conference on Smart Electronics and Communication (ICOSEC)* (pp. 1016-1022). IEEE.

Rivera-Batiz, L. A., & Romer, P. M. (1991). International trade with endogenous technological change. *European Economic Review, 35*(4), 971–1001. DOI: 10.1016/0014-2921(91)90048-N

Roberts, H., Cowls, J., Hine, E., Mazzi, F., Tsamados, A., Taddeo, M., & Floridi, L. (2021). Achieving a 'Good AI Society': Comparing the Aims and Progress of the EU and the US. *Science and Engineering Ethics, 27*(6), 1–25. DOI: 10.1007/s11948-021-00340-7 PMID: 34767085

Robinson, S. C. (2020). Trust, transparency, and openness: How inclusion of cultural values shapes Nordic national public policy strategies for artificial intelligence (AI). *Technology in Society, 63*, 101421. DOI: 10.1016/j.techsoc.2020.101421

Rodrigues, R. (2020). Legal and human rights issues of AI: Gaps, challenges and vulnerabilities. *Journal of Responsible Technology, 4*, 100005. DOI: 10.1016/j.jrt.2020.100005

Roesner, F., Kohno, T., & Molnar, D. (2014). Security and privacy for augmented reality systems. *Communications of the ACM, 57*(4), 88–96. DOI: 10.1145/2580723.2580730

Rosenberg, L. (2022). *Regulation of the Metaverse: A Roadmap*. Association of Computing Machinery., DOI: 10.1145/3546607.3546611

Rosenfeld, A., & Kraus, S. (2018). Predicting Human Decision-Making: From Prediction to Action. *AI Magazine*.

Rumelhart, D. E., & McClelland, J. L.PDP Research Group. (1986). Parallel distributed processing: explorations in the microstructure of cognition: foundations. *Mit Press Computational Models Of Cognition And Perception Series, 1*, 547. DOI: 10.7551/mitpress/5236.001.0001

Russell, S., Dewey, D., & Tegmark, M. (2015). Research priorities for robust and beneficial artificial intelligence. *AI Magazine, 36*(4), 105–114. DOI: 10.1609/aimag.v36i4.2577

Ryan, M., & Stahl, B. C. (2020). Artificial Intelligence Ethics Guidelines for Autonomous Vehicles: A Case Study of Responsibility and Safety. *Ethics and Information Technology*, *22*(4), 325–335.

Ryman-Tubb, N. F., Krause, P., & Garn, W. (2018). How Artificial Intelligence and machine learning research impacts payment card fraud detection: A survey and industry benchmark. *Engineering Applications of Artificial Intelligence*, *76*, 130–157. DOI: 10.1016/j.engappai.2018.07.008

Sacopulos, M., & Granzotti, M. T. (2024). *Using AI to enhance clinical decision-making with Dr. Maria Granzotti*. Sound Practice., DOI: 10.55834/sp.3375289237

Sadanand, V. K., & Nandini, S. (2025). AI in Indian healthcare startups: Funding and ecosystem dynamics. In Joshi, H., Reddy, C. K. K., Ouaissa, M., Hanafiah, M. M., & Doss, S. (Eds.), *Intelligent systems and IoT applications in clinical health* (p. 600). IGI Global., DOI: 10.4018/979-8-3693-8990-4

Sadeghi, S., & Maleki, A. (2018). Recent advances in hybrid brain-computer interface systems: A technological and quantitative review. *Basic and Clinical Neuroscience*, *9*(5), 373–388. DOI: 10.32598/bcn.9.5.373 PMID: 30719252

Sahu, M., Gandhi, S., Sharma, M. K., & Mehrotra, S. (2023). Nursing students' perceptions regarding well-being and healthy use of digital technology: A qualitative thematic analysis. *Journal of Education and Health Promotion*, *12*(1). Advance online publication. DOI: 10.4103/jehp.jehp_1271_22 PMID: 37546018

Salahdine, F., & Kaabouch, N. (2019). Social engineering attacks: A survey. *Future Internet*, *11*(4), 89.

Salvador, M., & Sancho, D. (2021). The role of local government in the drive for sustainable development public policies: An analytical framework based on institutional capacities. *Sustainability (Basel)*, *13*(11), 5978. DOI: 10.3390/su13115978

Santosh, K., & Gaur, L. (2021). *Artificial intelligence and machine learning in public healthcare*. SpringerBriefs in Applied Sciences and Technology., DOI: 10.1007/978-981-16-6768-8

Sarkady, D., Neuburger, L., & Egger, R. (2021, January). Virtual reality as a travel substitution tool during COVID-19. In Information and communication technologies in tourism 2021: Proceedings of the ENTER 2021 eTourism conference, January 19–22, 2021 (pp. 452-463). Cham: Springer International Publishing.

Saura, J. R., Ribeiro-Soriano, D., & Palacios-Marqués, D. (2022). Assessing behavioral data science privacy issues in government artificial intelligence deployment. *Government Information Quarterly*, *39*(4), 101679. DOI: 10.1016/j.giq.2022.101679

Sawant, P. (2022, November 10). *What is Industrial HMI? Applications & Design Considerations. | Linepro*. BLOG. https://lineproindia.com/blog/what-is-industrial-hmi-applications-design-considerations/

Schellekens, P., & Skilling, D. (2024). *Three Reasons Why AI May Widen Global Inequality*. Center for Global Development; Center For Global Development. https://www.cgdev.org/blog/three-reasons-why-ai-may-widen-global-inequality

Schwab, K., & World Economic Forum. (2016, January 14). *The Fourth Industrial Revolution: what it means and how to respond*. World Economic Forum; World Economic Forum. https://www.weforum.org/stories/2016/01/the-fourth-industrial-revolution-what-it-means-and-how-to-respond/

Selbst, A. D.. (2019). Fairness and Abstraction in Sociotechnical Systems. *Proceedings of the Conference on Fairness, Accountability, and Transparency*. DOI: 10.1145/3287560.3287598

Shakhatreh, H., Sawalmeh, A. H., Al-Fuqaha, A., Dou, Z., Almaita, E., Khalil, I., Othman, N. S., Khreishah, A., & Guizani, M. (2019). Unmanned aerial vehicles (UAVs): A survey on civil applications and key research challenges. *IEEE Access : Practical Innovations, Open Solutions*, *7*, 48572–48634. DOI: 10.1109/ACCESS.2019.2909530

Shanmugasundaram, M., & Tamilarasu, A. (2023). The impact of digital technology, social media, and artificial intelligence on cognitive functions: A review. *Frontiers in Cognition*, *2*, 1203077. Advance online publication. DOI: 10.3389/fcogn.2023.1203077

Sharma, K., & Shivandu, S. K. (2024). Integrating Artificial Intelligence and Internet of Things (IoT) for Enhanced Crop Monitoring and Management in Precision Agriculture. *Sensors International*, *5*, 100292–100292. DOI: 10.1016/j.sintl.2024.100292

Shavell, R. (2021, February 11). Big tech will try to pre-empt harsh privacy laws by writing their own. Help Net Security. Archived at https://perma.cc/9G8L-5KKE

Shen, Y., & Zhang, X. (2024). The impact of artificial intelligence on employment: The role of virtual agglomeration. *Humanities & Social Sciences Communications*, *11*(1), 1–14. DOI: 10.1057/s41599-024-02647-9

Shih, J. J., Krusienski, D. J., & Wolpaw, J. R. (2012, March). Brain-computer interfaces in medicine. []. Elsevier.]. *Mayo Clinic Proceedings*, *87*(3), 268–279. DOI: 10.1016/j.mayocp.2011.12.008 PMID: 22325364

Shoukat, M. U., Yan, L., Zhang, J., Cheng, Y., Raza, M. U., & Niaz, A. (2024). Smart home for enhanced healthcare: Exploring human machine interface oriented digital twin model. *Multimedia Tools and Applications*, *83*(11), 31297–31315. DOI: 10.1007/s11042-023-16875-9

Siau, K., & Wang, W. (2018). Building trust in artificial intelligence, machine learning, and robotics. *Communications of the ACM*, *61*(4), 34–40.

Signé, L. (2023). *Africa's Fourth Industrial Revolution*. Cambridge University Press. DOI: 10.1017/9781009200004

Silver, D., Huang, A., Maddison, C. J., Guez, A., Sifre, L., Van Den Driessche, G., ... & Hassabis, D. (2016). Mastering the game of Go with deep neural networks and tree search. *nature, 529*(7587), 484-489.

Silver, D.. (2018). Mastering Chess and Shogi by Self-Play with a General Reinforcement Learning Algorithm. *Science*, *362*(6419), 1140–1144. DOI: 10.1126/science.aar6404 PMID: 30523106

Simões, J. P., Ten Klooster, P., Neff, P. K., Niemann, U., & Kraiss, J. (2024). Editorial: Artificial intelligence and mental health care. *Frontiers in Public Health*, *12*, 1461446. Advance online publication. DOI: 10.3389/fpubh.2024.1461446 PMID: 39139670

Singhal, A., Neveditsin, N., Tanveer, H., & Mago, V. (2024). Toward Fairness, Accountability, Transparency, and Ethics in AI for Social Media and Health Care: Scoping Review. *JMIR Medical Informatics*, *12*, e50048. DOI: 10.2196/50048 PMID: 38568737

Singh, H. P., & Kumar, P. (2021). Developments in the human machine interface technologies and their applications: A review. *Journal of Medical Engineering & Technology*, *45*(7), 552–573. DOI: 10.1080/03091902.2021.1936237 PMID: 34184601

Siyonbola, O. O. (2020). A brief history of artificial intelligence in Africa. Retrieved from https://noirpress.org/a-brief-history-of-artificial-intelligence-in-africa/ on 13/10/2024.

Skare, M., Gavurova, B., & Blažević Burić, S. (2024). Artificial intelligence and wealth inequality: A comprehensive empirical exploration of socioeconomic implications. *Technology in Society*, *79*, 102719. DOI: 10.1016/j.techsoc.2024.102719

Sloan, R. H., & Warner, R. (2020). Beyond bias: And social justice. *Va. JL & Tech.*, *24*, 1.

Smuha, N. A., Ahmed-Rengers, E., Harkens, A., Li, W., MacLaren, J., Piselli, R., & Yeung, K. (2021). How the EU can achieve legally trustworthy AI: a response to the European Commission's proposal for an Artificial Intelligence Act. *Available atSSRN* 3899991. DOI: 10.2139/ssrn.3899991

Solum, L. B. (1992). Legal personhood for artificial intelligences. *North Carolina Law Review*, *70*(4), 1231–1287.

Soni, N.. (2020). Impact of artificial intelligence on businesses: From research, innovation, market deployment to future shifts. *International Journal of Information Management*, *50*, 23–28.

Sotala, K., & Yampolskiy, R. V. (2014). "Responses to catastrophic AGI risk: a survey". Physica Scripta. 90 (1): 018001. Bibcode:2015PhyS...90a8001S. . ISSN 0031-8949.DOI: 10.1088/0031-8949/90/1/018001

Soueidan, M. H., & Shoghari, R. (2024). The Impact of Artificial Intelligence on Job Loss: Risks for Governments. *Technium Social Science Journal*, *57*, 206–223. DOI: 10.47577/tssj.v57i1.10917

Sousa, M. J., Nunes, F. G., Nascimento, G. D., & Chakraborty, C. (Eds.). (2023). *Future health scenarios*. Taylor & Francis., DOI: 10.1201/9781003227892

Soviany, C. (2018). The benefits of using artificial intelligence in payment fraud detection: A case study. *Journal of Payments Strategy & Systems*, *12*(2), 102–110. DOI: 10.69554/ISSG4555

Srivastava, S. (2023, July 24). *Role of AI in Manufacturing: Use Cases and Examples*. Appinventiv; Appinventiv. https://appinventiv.com/blog/ai-in-manufacturing/

Starr, W. C. (1984). Law and Morality in H. L. A. Hart's Legal Philosophy. *Marquette Law Review*, *67*(4), 773–777.

Static, A. W. S. (2018, July 20). White paper: Alexa and data handling overview (1st ed., p. 2). Archived at https://perma.cc/5XS7-5DX2

Stokel-Walker, C. (2023). AI chatbots are coming to search engines: Can you trust the results? *Nature*. Advance online publication. DOI: 10.1038/d41586-023-00423-4 PMID: 36781968

Stoumpos, A. I., Kitsios, F., & Talias, M. A. (2023). Digital transformation in healthcare: Technology acceptance and its applications. *International Journal of Environmental Research and Public Health*, *20*(5), 3407. DOI: 10.3390/ijerph20043407 PMID: 36834105

Subasi, A. (2022). *Applications of artificial intelligence in medical imaging*. Academic Press.

Suleiman, Z., Shaikholla, S., Dikhanbayeva, D., Shehab, E., & Turkyilmaz, A. (2022). Industry 4.0: Clustering of concepts and characteristics. *Cogent Engineering*, *9*(1), 2034264. DOI: 10.1080/23311916.2022.2034264

Sun, H., Rau, P. L. P., & Wang, B. (2021). A Study of Machine Ethics in Human-Artificial Intelligence Interactions. In *Cross-Cultural Design. Applications in Arts, Learning, Well-being, and Social Development: 13th International Conference, CCD 2021, Held as Part of the 23rd HCI International Conference, HCII 2021, Virtual Event, July 24–29, 2021* [Springer International Publishing.]. *Proceedings*, *23*(Part II), 374–395.

Sun, T., & Medaglia, R. (2019). Mapping the challenges of artificial intelligence in the public sector: Evidence from public healthcare. *Government Information Quarterly*, *36*(2), 368–383. DOI: 10.1016/j.giq.2018.09.008

Su, Y., Hou, F., Qi, M., Li, W., & Ji, Y. (2021). A data-enabled business model for a smart healthcare information service platform in the era of digital transformation. *Journal of Healthcare Engineering*, *2021*, 5519891. DOI: 10.1155/2021/5519891 PMID: 34158912

Su, Z., Li, C., Fu, H., Wang, L., Wu, M., & Feng, X. (2024). Review of the development and prospect of telemedicine. *Intelligent Medicine*, *4*(1), 1–9. DOI: 10.1016/j.imed.2022.10.004

Sykownik, P., Maloney, D., Freeman, G., & Masuch, M. (2022, April). Something personal from the metaverse: goals, topics, and contextual factors of self-disclosure in commercial social VR. In *Proceedings of the 2022 CHI Conference on Human Factors in Computing Systems* (pp. 1-17).

Szczepański, M. (2019). Economic Impacts of Artificial Intelligence (AI). In *European Parliament*. European Parliament. https://www.europarl.europa.eu/RegData/etudes/BRIE/2019/637967/EPRS_BRI(2019)637967_EN.pdf

Taeihagh, A. (2021). Governance of artificial intelligence. *Policy and Society*, *40*(2), 137–157. DOI: 10.1080/14494035.2021.1928377

Taher-Uz-Zaman, M., Ahmed, M. S., Hossain, S., Hossain, S., & Jamal, G. R. A. (2014). Multipurpose Tactical Robot. *Engineering International*, *2*(1), 21–27. DOI: 10.18034/ei.v2i1.204

Tallberg, J., Erman, E., Furendal, M., Geith, J., Klamberg, M., & Lundgren, M. (2023). Global Governance of Artificial Intelligence: Next Steps for Empirical and Normative Research. *International Studies Review*, *25*(3), viad040. Advance online publication. 2305.11528. DOI: 10.1093/isr/viad040

Taylor, S. M., Gulson, K. N., & McDuie-Ra, D. (2023). from colonial india: Race, statistics, and facial recognition in the global south. *Science, Technology & Human Values*, *48*(3), 663–689. DOI: 10.1177/01622439211060839

Thapaliya, S., & Bokani, A. (2024). Leveraging artificial intelligence for enhanced cybersecurity: Insights and innovations. *SADGAMAYA*, *1*(1), 46–52. DOI: 10.3126/sadgamaya.v1i1.66888

The GDPR. (2024). European Council. https://www.consilium.europa.eu/en/policies/data-protection/data-protection-regulation/#:~:text=data%20protection%20rules-,What%20is%20the%20GDPR%3F,application%20on%2025%20May%202018

Theodorou, A. (2017). *Stay home, stay safe, stay green: The role of gardening activities on mental health during the Covid-19 home confinement". Urban Forestry & Urban Greening Moritz*. Ingwersen.

Thompson, N. C.. (2020). The Computational Limits of Deep Learning. *Communications of the ACM*, *63*(8), 107–115.

Tiwari, R., Rautela, S., Sharma, S., Choudhary, B. P., Tripathi, R., & Singh, P. (2023, December). Role of AI for Fraud Detection in Banks: A Bibliometric Analysis. In *2023 International Conference on Advanced Computing & Communication Technologies (ICACCTech)* (pp. 66-71). IEEE. DOI: 10.1109/ICACCTech61146.2023.00020

Tiwari, S., & Srivastava, R. (2024). Performance of Artificial Intelligence in Fraud Detection. In *Handbook of Artificial Intelligence Applications for Industrial Sustainability* (pp. 167–187). CRC Press. DOI: 10.1201/9781003348351-12

Tobin, B. (2019, April 11). Amazon employees listen to customers through Echo products, report finds. *USA Today*. Archived at https://perma.cc/HWP7-F6G4

Tomašev, N., Cornebise, J., Hutter, F., Mohamed, S., Picciariello, A., Connelly, B., Belgrave, D. C. M., Ezer, D., Haert, F. C., Mugisha, F., Abila, G., Arai, H., Almiraat, H., Proskurnia, J., Snyder, K., Otake-Matsuura, M., Othman, M., Glasmachers, T., Wever, W., & Clopath, C. (2020). Ai for social good: Unlocking the opportunity for positive impact. *Nature Communications*, *11*(1), 2468. Advance online publication. DOI: 10.1038/s41467-020-15871-z PMID: 32424119

Tougas, H., Chan, S., Shahrvini, T., Gonzalez, A., Reyes, R., Parish, M., & Yellowlees, P. (2022). The use of automated machine translation to translate figurative language in a clinical setting: Analysis of a convenience sample of patients drawn from a randomized controlled trial. *JMIR Mental Health*, *9*(9), e39556. DOI: 10.2196/39556 PMID: 36066959

Tretyakova, E. (2021). AI and the Legal Status of Autonomous Systems: A Conceptual Framework. *Moscow Law Review*, *42*(3), 55–78.

Truby, J. (2020). Governing artificial intelligence to benefit the UN sustainable development goals. *Sustainable Development (Bradford)*, *28*(4), 946–959. DOI: 10.1002/sd.2048

Tsai, J.. (2006). *What's it to you? A survey of online privacy concerns and risks*. Net Institute.

Turing, A. (1950). Computing machinery and intelligence. *Mind*, *59*(236), 435–460.

Turing, A. M. (1950). Computing Machinery and Intelligence. *Mind*, *59*(236), 433–460. DOI: 10.1093/mind/LIX.236.433

UNECA. (2019). Africa's blueprint for AI development. Retrieved from https://www.uneca.org/economic-report-africa-2019 on 5/10/2024

United Nation. (2019). The Age of Digital Interdependence 1 the age of digital interdependence Report of the UN Secretary-General's High-level Panel on Digital Cooperation The Age of Digital Interdependence 2. In https://www.un.org/en/pdfs/DigitalCooperation-report-for%20web.pdf. United Nation. https://www.un.org/en/pdfs/DigitalCooperation-report-for%20web.pdf

Vaidya, S., Ambad, P., & Bhosle, S. (2018). Industry 4.0—A glimpse. *Procedia Manufacturing*, *20*, 233–238. DOI: 10.1016/j.promfg.2018.02.034

Van Wynsberghe, A. (2021). Sustainable AI: AI for sustainability and the sustainability of AI. *AI and Ethics*, *1*(3), 213–218. DOI: 10.1007/s43681-021-00043-6

Vargas-Elizondo, C. (2020). On the role of ethics in shaping technology development. *HighTech and Innovation Journal*, *1*(2), 86–100. DOI: 10.28991/HIJ-2020-01-02-05

Varian, H. (2018). AI, big data, and economics: Opportunities for market design. *The Journal of Economic Perspectives*, *32*(3), 3–20.

Veale, M., & Van Hoboken, J. (2020). The European Union's Proposed Artificial Intelligence Act: Implications for Fundamental Rights And AI Ethics. *European Law Review*, *45*(4), 591–608.

Veale, M., & Zuiderveen Borgesius, F. (2021). Demystifying the Draft EU Artificial Intelligence Act—Analyzing the good, the bad, and the unclear elements of the proposed approach. *Computer Law Review International*, *22*(4), 97–112. DOI: 10.9785/cri-2021-220402

Vincent, J. (2019). *AI tools used in criminal justice show bias*. The Verge.

Vincent, J. (2023). *AI is entering an era of corporate control*. The Verge.

Wachter, S., & Mittelstadt, B. (2019). A right to reasonable inferences: re-thinking data protection law in the age of big data and AI. *Colum. Bus. L. Rev.*, 494.

Wachter, S., et al. (2017). Why a right to explanation of automated decision-making does not exist in the General Data Protection Regulation. *International Data Privacy Law*, 7(2).

Wallach, W., & Allen, C. (2008). *Moral machines: Teaching robots right from wrong*. Oxford University Press.

Wang, W. and Cai, Y. (2022). The risk of artificial intelligence embedded in government governance: mechanism, process, prevention and control., 609-616. https://doi.org/DOI: 10.2991/978-94-6463-016-9_63

Wang, Y. (2021, July 13). Wake word detection and its applications. Johns Hopkins University Repository, 1, 18. https://perma.cc/WE37-LF6J

Wang, D., & Wang, J. (2018). Facial recognition technology: A review. *Journal of Intelligent Information Systems*, *52*(2), 257–275.

Wang, Y., & Chung, S. H. (2022). Artificial intelligence in safety-critical systems: A systematic review. *Industrial Management & Data Systems*, *122*(2), 442–470. DOI: 10.1108/IMDS-07-2021-0419

Warang, T. R., & Sackib, A. (2024). Shaping the Future of Law: AI, Ethics, and Policy Perspectives. *IJRAR-International Journal of Research and Analytical Reviews (IJRAR)*, *11*(2), 29-48. https://pib.gov.in/PressReleaseIframePage.aspx?PRID=2012375 https://www.india-briefing.com/news/india-regulation-of-ai-and-large-language-models-31680.html/ https://www.nextias.com/ca/current-affairs/21-09-2024/recommendations-to-address-ai-related-risks-and-governance-gaps https://www.reuters.com/technology/india-announces-12-bln-investment-ai-projects-2024-03-07/

Waters, J. (2014). Adaptive learning: The best approaches for personalized learning. *Campus Technology*.

Weber, R. H., & Weber, R. (2020). *Internet of Things: Legal Perspectives*. Springer.

Webster, G., Creemers, R., Kania, E., & Triolo, P. (2017, August 1). *Full translation: China's "new generation artificial intelligence development plan" (2017)*. DigiChina; Stanford University. https://digichina.stanford.edu/work/full-translation-chinas-new-generation-artificial-intelligence-development-plan-2017/

Weerarathna, I. N., Raymond, D., & Luharia, A. (2023). Human-Robot Collaboration for Healthcare: A Narrative Review. *Cureus*, *15*(11). Advance online publication. DOI: 10.7759/cureus.49210 PMID: 38143700

Weinberger, M. (2017, May 23). How Amazon's Echo went from a smart speaker to the center of your home. Business Insider. Archived at https://perma.cc/HGX7-KSXM

Weizenbaum, J. (1972). On the impact of the computer on society: How does one insult a machine? *Science*, *176*(4035), 609–614. DOI: 10.1126/science.176.4035.609 PMID: 17778159

West, D. M. (2018). *The future of work: Robots, AI, and automation*. Brookings Institution Press.

West, D. M. (2018). *The Future of Work: Robots, AI, and Automation*. Brookings Institution Press.

What is HCI and Security? (n.d.). *Educative*.https://www.educative.io/answers/what-is-hci-and-security

What is HMI? *Human-Machine-Interface, COPA-DATA*. (2023, December 12). https://www.copadata.com/en/product/zenon-software-platform-for-industrial-automation-energy-automation/visualization-control/what-is-hmi/#:~:text=Uses%20of%20HMI&text=Industries%20such%20as%20energy%2C%20water,%2C%20vehicles%2C%20plants%20or%20buildings

Wingfield, N. (2017, September 29). Amazon wants to wake you up with Alexa, and that's just the start. The New York Times. Archived at https://perma.cc/TP5Z-KVY2

Wirtz, B., Weyerer, J., & Geyer, C. (2018). Artificial intelligence and the public sector—Applications and challenges. *International Journal of Public Administration*, *42*(7), 596–615. DOI: 10.1080/01900692.2018.1498103

Wishart, D. (2016). Puzzling out law's person. *Indiana Journal of Global Legal Studies*, *23*(2), 743–744. DOI: 10.2979/indjglolegstu.23.2.0743

Wittenberg, C. (2016). Human-CPS Interaction-requirements and human-machine interaction methods for the Industry 4.0. *IFAC-PapersOnLine*, *49*(19), 420–425. DOI: 10.1016/j.ifacol.2016.10.602

Wolford, B. (2023, September 14). *What is GDPR, the EU's new data protection law?* GDPR.eu. https://gdpr.eu/what-is-gdpr/

World Bank. (2020). AI Regulation in Ghana.

World Bank. (2020). Digital Economy for Africa. Retrieved from https://www.worldbank.org/en/programs/all-africa-digital-transformation#:~:text=The%20Digital%20Economy%20for%20Africa,Digital%20Transformation%20Strategy%20for%20Africa.%E2%80%9D on 14/10/2024.

World Health Organization. (2021). The importance of ethics in artificial intelligence. In *WHO Consultation Towards the Development of guidance on ethics and governance of artificial intelligence for health: Meeting report Geneva, Switzerland, 2–4 October 2019* (pp. 2–3). World Health Organization. https://www.jstor.org/stable/resrep35680.6

Xue, L., Wei, L., Bai, L., & Wei, L. (2023). *AI empowerment or AI replacement*. AEA Randomized Controlled Trials., DOI: 10.1257/rct.12196-1.0

Yaqub, M. Z., & Alsabban, A. (2023). Industry-4.0-enabled digital transformation: Prospects, instruments, challenges, and implications for business strategies. *Sustainability (Basel), 15*(11), 8553. DOI: 10.3390/su15118553

Yasobant, S. (2016). Physical health promotion through modern technologies. *Geospatial Research*, 889–907. DOI: 10.4018/978-1-4666-9845-1.ch042

Yiğitcanlar, T. (2021). Greening the artificial intelligence for a sustainable planet: An editorial commentary. *Sustainability (Basel), 13*(24), 13508. DOI: 10.3390/su132413508

Yin, R., Wang, D., Zhao, S., Lou, Z., & Shen, G. (2021). Wearable sensors-enabled human–machine interaction systems: From design to application. *Advanced Functional Materials, 31*(11), 2008936. DOI: 10.1002/adfm.202008936

Young, J.. (2022, August 10). SkillDetective: Automated policy-violation detection of voice assistant applications in the wild. *USENIX Security Symposium*, 1112–1114.

Yudkowsky, E. (n.d.). *Will superintelligent AI end the world?* [Video]. TED Talks. https://www.ted.com/talks/eliezer_yudkowsky_will_superintelligent_ai_end_the_world?language=en

Yu, L., Yang, Z., & Tang, L. (2016). A novel multistage deep belief network based extreme learning machine ensemble learning paradigm for credit risk assessment. *Flexible Services and Manufacturing Journal, 28*(4), 576–592. DOI: 10.1007/s10696-015-9226-2

Zhang, H. (2023). Research and practical exploration of new models of social governance in the age of artificial intelligence. SHS Web of Conferences, 179, 01017. https://doi.org/DOI: 10.1051/shsconf/202317901017

Zhang, X.. (2021). Deep learning for AI-enabled financial fraud detection. *Journal of Financial Analytics*, *45*(3), 19–35.

Zhang, Y., Hong, J., & Chen, S. (2023). Medical big data and artificial intelligence for healthcare. *Applied Sciences (Basel, Switzerland)*, *13*(7), 3745. DOI: 10.3390/app13063745

Zhao, P., Gao, Y., & Sun, X. (2022). How does artificial intelligence affect green economic growth?—Evidence from China. *The Science of the Total Environment*, *155306*, 155306. Advance online publication. DOI: 10.1016/j.scitotenv.2022.155306 PMID: 35461946

Zhou, J., Chen, C., Li, L., Zhang, Z., & Zheng, X. (2022). FinBrain 2.0: When finance meets trustworthy AI. *Frontiers of Information Technology & Electronic Engineering*, *23*(12), 1747–1764. DOI: 10.1631/FITEE.2200039

Zion Market Research. (2019, January 25). Global intelligent virtual assistant market will reach USD 19.6 billion by 2025: Zion Market Research. Globe Newswire. Archived at https://perma.cc/9YSP-WVC3

Zioviris, G., Kolomvatsos, K., & Stamoulis, G. (2022). Credit card fraud detection using a deep learning multistage model. *The Journal of Supercomputing*, *78*(12), 14571–14596. DOI: 10.1007/s11227-022-04465-9

Zohar, O., & Rosenblat, A. (2020). Regulatory Sandboxes and the Future Of AI Governance: Balancing Innovation And Regulation. *Journal of Technology and Law*, *12*(2), 189–210.

Zou, S., Tao, L. Q., Wang, G., Zhu, C., Peng, Z., Sun, H., Li, Y., Wei, Y., & Ren, T. L. (2022). Humidity-based human–machine interaction system for healthcare applications. *ACS Applied Materials & Interfaces*, *14*(10), 12606–12616. DOI: 10.1021/acsami.1c23725 PMID: 35230086

About the Contributors

Swati Chakraborty is a Visiting faculty (Assistant Professor), at the Institute of Legal Studies and Research, GLA University. Dr. Chakraborty is associated as an Adjunct Faculty with Concordia University, Canada. Dr. Chakraborty is a Writing Fellow, at COMPOSE, Universitas Islam International Indonesia. She is an International Fellow of KAICIID in Lisbon, Portugal. She has done her Ph.D. in Human Rights from the University of Calcutta with the thesis on "RIGHT TO EDUCATION: A Study on tribal women of Rural West Bengal". She was attached to National Human Rights Commission, India as a Research Consultant. Dr. Chakraborty had good teaching expertise as Lecturer at The English College (School of Management), Calicut, Kerala her special lectures are on Human Values, Peace dialogue and ethics to Management studies, and Dignity and Rights. She is also a member of the executive council at the Colibri Learning Foundation, Surrey, BC. Also, she is the editor of books like "Dynamics of Dialogue, Cultural Development, and Peace in the Metaverse", "Handbook of Dialogue and Development: India-China-EU", Handbook of Human Rights and Tribal Studies", "Handbook of Social Media for Digital and Social Inclusion", "TRIBAL DEVELOPMENT", "Gender Identity and Roles in India: Issues and Challenges", "Multidisciplinary Handbook of Social Exclusion and Human Rights" and "Handbook of International Relations: Issues of Human Rights and Foreign Policy Vol. I and Vol II". Dr. Chakraborty has a wide range of international connections with her network through different seminars, conferences, and workshops.

***

Mumtaz Alam, Director of the Centre of Graduate Studies and Humanities and an Associate Professor in History at Fiji National University, earned his doctorate from Aligarh Muslim University. His research centres on medical history in the Pacific and Southeast Asia, particularly emphasising how colonial and postcolonial contexts have influenced these regions. Dr Alam's research ingeniously merges social and medical history by incorporating written records and oral testimonies. Health, Medicine, and Encounter of Cultures and Rethinking Nationalism: Exploring Its Roots, Varieties, and Theories were published by him in 2022 and 2023, respectively. Dr Alam has been recognised for his accomplishments as an active researcher and member of esteemed organisations such as IHC, PHA, AHA, and ANZSHM. In 2011, he was awarded the Best Paper Prize in Science and Technology by the Indian History Congress. The scope of his extensive research background includes ecotourism, smallpox vaccination in Fiji, environmental history, and climate history. As the editor-in-chief of several prestigious international journals, Dr. Alam substantially contributes to historical scholarship. I am working on a climate change and health project funded by Stockholm University and Climate Change Impacts on Indigenous Health: A Comparative Study of Rural and Remote Communities in Fiji and Ghana funded by Fiji National University.

Daniel Opotamutale Ashipala (MN Sc) is a senior lecturer and Head of Department for the School of nursing and Public Health (SoNPH), General Nursing Science department in the Faculty of Health Sciences and Veterinary Medicine (FHSVM) at the University of Namibia, Namibia. His research interests include Primary health Care, Health care services and Nursing education, and Mental health. He has published a quite number of peer reviewed articles on the delivery of teaching and learning in higher education studies. He is a doctoral candidate at Stellenbosch University in Cape Town, South Africa. His doctoral work focuses on developing a framework to facilitate the implementation of a task shifting approach for nurses in the Namibia PHC services.

Akshyata Giri is a student pursuing a Bachelor of Science in Psychology (Hons) at PES University, Bangalore. With a deep interest in understanding human behavior and mental processes, she has engaged in various academic projects and research initiatives, including a study on culture and communication. They have also contributed to discussions on technology integration in education through published works. Passionate about psychology and its applications, Akshyata aims to foster positive change through research and community engagement.

Kunal Gounder is a young Fijian professional with a diverse educational background and a keen interest in climate change, international affairs, and education. Born in 1999, Kunal completed his Bachelor's degree in Secondary Education, majoring in History and Geography, from Fiji National University in 2020. He further enhanced his expertise with a Postgraduate Diploma in Climate Change from the University of the South Pacific in 2022 and Postgraduate Diploma in Diplomacy and International Affairs from USP in 2023. Kunal's professional journey spans various sectors, including education, government, and international organizations. He has worked as a teacher for the Ministry of Education, served as a COVID Safe Ambassador for the Ministry of Commerce, Trade, Tourism and Transport, and contributed as a Junior Consultant for the United Nations Disaster Risk Reduction Office. Currently, Kunal is pursuing a Master's degree in Climate Change Research at Fiji National University while simultaneously working towards a Master of Arts in Diplomacy and International Affairs at the University of the South Pacific. His recent internship with the European Union Delegation to Fiji in the Political, Press, and Information Section further demonstrates his commitment to international relations and public diplomacy. Kunal's diverse experiences and ongoing academic pursuits reflect his passion for addressing global challenges, particularly in the areas of climate change, education, and international cooperation.

Vibhuti Jain is working as Trainee Assistant Professor at Department of Management Studies, Graphic Era (Deemed to be University).

Jipson Joseph has a PhD in Ethics from DVK Bangalore. Currently, he is a Research Scholar in the School of Law at Christ University, Bangalore. His research interests are in the fields of ethics, gender studies, constitutional law, human rights, human security, environmental justice, developmental policies and global poverty.

Manorith Kumar is a master's student at the University of the South Pacific. His areas of interest are diplomacy and international relations.

Irfan Rasool is currently an Associate Professor in Law. He holds Masters in Law and Doctorate from National Law School of India University. He has teaching experience of more than twelve years and his field of research interest includes Comparative Public Law, Constitutional Law, Judicial Process and Human Rights Law. He has published various articles in SCOPUS and UGC CARE listed journals and some of them include A Need for Specific Legislation on Refugee Protection: An Indian Perspective in Kashmir Journal of Legal Studies Vol X(2) (December 2023) (ISSN: 2250-2084) (UGC CARE Listed); Judicial Process in India: A Critical Analysis in the context of Part III and Part IV of the Constitution in ILI Law Review (Summer 2020); Jammu and Kashmir: A Confederate within a Federal System, Economic and Political Weekly Vol. XLIX No. 4 (Jan. 25, 2014), which was enlisted in Federal Relations, Parliamentary Documentation, Lok Sabha Vol XL(3) (1-15 February 2014). He has also published three Text Books on Constitutional Law, Alternative Dispute Resolution Systems and Human Rights Law & Practice. He also has complete one research minor project. His primary field of research interest is the study of law as ‘power’ and its structure and implications.

Fransisco Chindongo Ntjamba is a registered nurse holding a Bachelor of Nursing Science Clinical, (Honours) from the University of Namibia, School of Nursing and Public Health, General Nursing Department in the Faculty of Health Sciences and Veterinary Medicine (FHSVM). He is also a NIMART-trained nurse and a Provider Initiated Testing and Counseling (PITC NURSE), specializing in sexual reproductive health and focusing on HIV testing, prevention, treatment initiation, and ongoing care. In addition to his qualifications, Fransisco is an academic researcher who has published research studies in nursing education, mental health, and interdisciplinary innovations, including Artificial Intelligence on human healthcare. His career is defined by a commitment to advancing healthcare through both direct patient care and research, with key interests in Primary Health Care, healthcare services, nursing education, and mental health. He is dedicated to improving healthcare through evidence-based practices and community outreach initiatives, particularly in HIV prevention and treatment. He can be reached at 05sisco@gmail.com.

Nitish Ojha is a distinguished scholar, Researcher, and mentor having rich Industrial experience as well as varied experience in Teaching and Research. He has academic experience of over 15 years with renowned universities like American University of Europe, University of Stirling UK, and others where he worked in the capacity of Assistant Professor, also worked as a Core Member of Research and Development in Indian Universities i.e., Chandigarh University, LPU, Amity University. He has worked as a software engineer in Nokia Siemens Network, India. He served in several research projects in different profiles of researchers funded by DST/MCIT/MOHFW Govt. of India having National and International importance at IIT Delhi and in AIIMS.

Ananya Pandey is a Research Scholar in School of Law at Christ University, Bangalore. She has her research interests in the field of Constitutional Law, Environment Law, Human Rights, Intellectual Property Law and Jurisprudence.

Tushaa Sadanand is an outgoing student of the National University of Advanced Legal Studies (NLU) Kochi, India.

Vijay Kumar is an accomplished academic and professional with a rich experience spanning over two decades in teaching and industry. He is currently an Associate Professor in the Department of Business Management at Stanley College of Engineering & Technology for Women, Hyderabad.

Karun Sanjaya is an Assistant Professor at Symbiosis Law School, Nagpur, Symbiosis International (Deemed University), Pune, India. He is specialised in

Intellectual Property Laws and is currently the Faculty-in-charge of the Centre for Intellectual Property Rights and Advocacy at SLS, Nagpur. His areas of interest include Tort Laws, Contract Laws, Cyber Laws, Intellectual Property Laws, Artificial Intelligence and allied laws. He is a recipient of the Justice Krishna Iyer Memorial Merit Award, 2019, Adv. P.F., Thomas Memorial Gold Medal, 2019, Dr. K.N. Chandrashekharan Pillai Gold Medal 2022 and Justice Krishna lyer Memorial Merit Award, 2022. He was formerly the executive editor of IILS Law Review and has authored over twenty book chapters and fourteen research articles in diverse areas of law. Karun had also qualified UGC NET with JRF (Law) and is presently pursuing his PhD from VIT School of Law, Vellore Institute of Technology, Chennai, Tamil Nadu, India.

Aryan Sharma is currently pursuing a Bachelor of Business Administration (BBA) from Inspiria Knowledge Campus, Siliguri, under Maulana Abul Kalam Azad University of Technology, West Bengal. With a strong foundation in business principles and practical experience in digital marketing, Aryan has developed skills in problem-solving, teamwork, and leadership. He has actively participated in various academic and extracurricular activities, including leading his basketball team to the finals and presenting on sustainability at the YI Future Conclave. Aryan is committed to continuous learning and personal growth.

Aiswarya Thomas is an Assistant Professor at Christ University, Bengaluru, specializing in Open Macroeconomics. She holds a Ph.D. in Economics from the Institute for Financial Management and Research (IFMR), Chennai, and a Master's degree in Applied Economics from Pondicherry University. Her research interests focus on macroeconomics, international economics, and monetary policy in open economies. At Christ University, she is dedicated to teaching and researching macroeconomic theories, policies, and their applications in a global context.

Rajesh Tiwari is working as Professor, Academic Coordinator and Chair Head-Finance in Graphic Era (Deemed to be University), Dehradun. He has over twenty years of rich experience in academics and industry. He is MBA (Finance), Chartered Financial Analyst (CFA), UGC-NET, PhD in Management. He has previously worked as Director in Indus University, Ahmedabad, United Group-Greater Noida (Affiliated to Guru Gobind Singh Indraprastha University, New Delhi), Sai Balaji Group-Pune. He has been academic coordinator for Management Programmes of Staffordshire University, UK and other reputed B Schools. He has won best paper award two times. He has published research papers in reputed journals indexed in Scopus and presented papers in national and international journals. He is actively involved in Faculty Development Programme and Management Development Programme. He has been engaged in social initiatives through plantation, blood donation, cleanliness drive and functional literacy programmes. He has been associated with Ministry of MSME, Government of India for Management Development Programmes and Entrepreneurship Development Programmes. He has 5 patents under his credit. He can be reached at ambitioncfarajesh@gmail.com.

Athira V. is an Assistant Professor and Research Scholar at VELS University, Chennai. She is specialized in the area of Constitutional Law with more than 4 years of teaching experience. She has many papers in diverse areas of laws to her credit.

Abhishek Vaish is faculty at IIIT Allahabad and Guest Faculty at Moscow Institute of Physics and Technology, Moscow and University of Computer Studies, Yangon, Myanmar, Sampoerna University, Jakarta and Dhofar University, Salaleh, Oman. He set up a lab of dedicated Cyber Security Lab for University of Computer Studies, Yangon, Myanmar. He has published more than 50 scientific papers in International Journals, conferences, and Book Chapters. He was the person involved behind the foundation and starting the course of 'Information Security' in the Indian Institute of Information Technology, Allahabad, India. He was a scientific advisor to Ministry of Science and Technology from Indian Govt. side to the Russian Federation. He is also an Academic Advocate for the Infosec Audit and Control Association, USA. supervised 5 PhD candidates and 100+ Masters Students, Handled various Cyber Security Projects at Wipro Ltd. The major domains of include web application testing, wireless penetration testing, and Implementation of an Information Security Management system for Bharti Airtel India.

Index

A

I

J

L

M

N

P

R

S

T

W

www.ingramcontent.com/pod-product-compliance
Lightning Source LLC
LaVergne TN
LVHW080347011026
849161LV00009B/2213